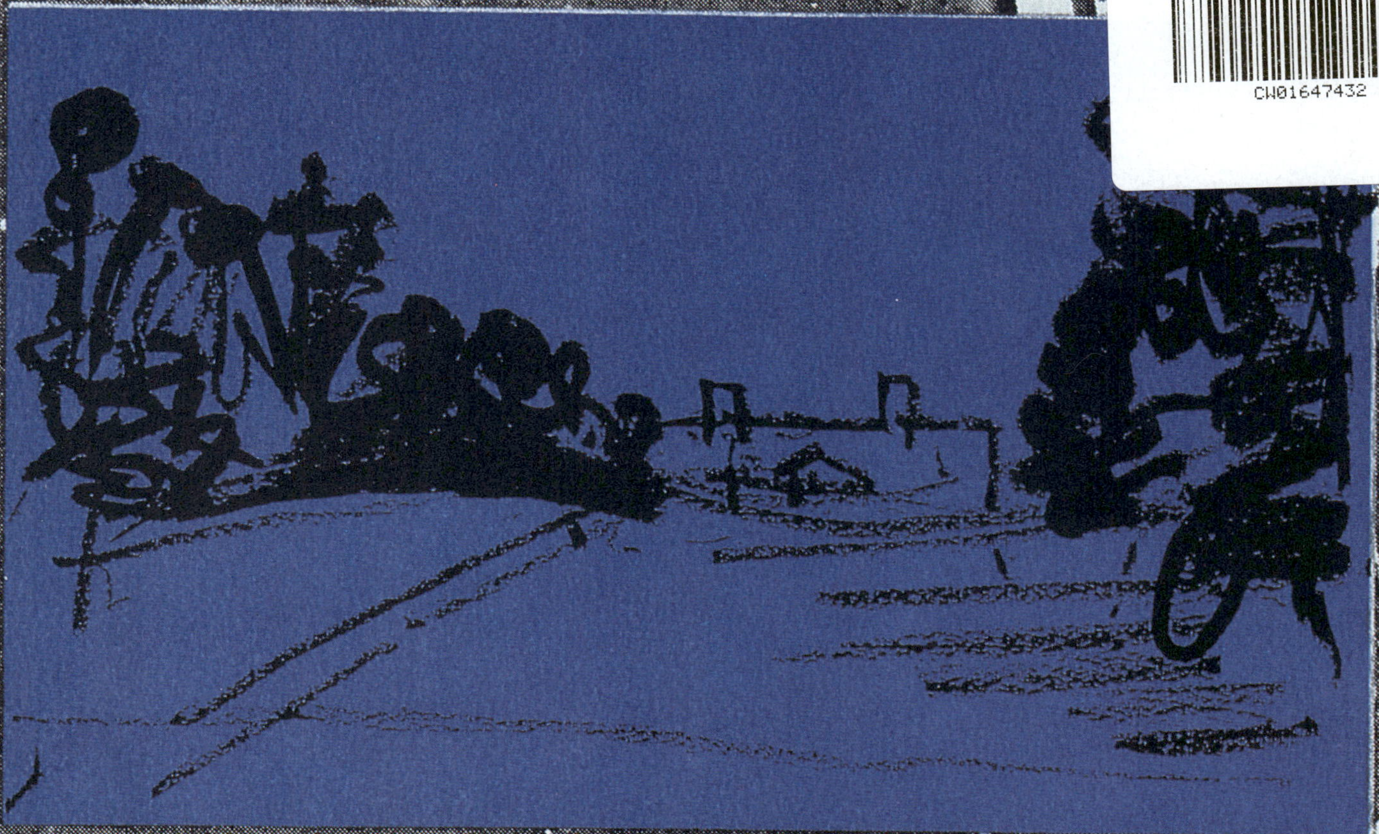

John Piper

JECP

A Catalogue Raisonné 1923–91

Orde Levinson

'Quality and Experiment': the Prints of John Piper

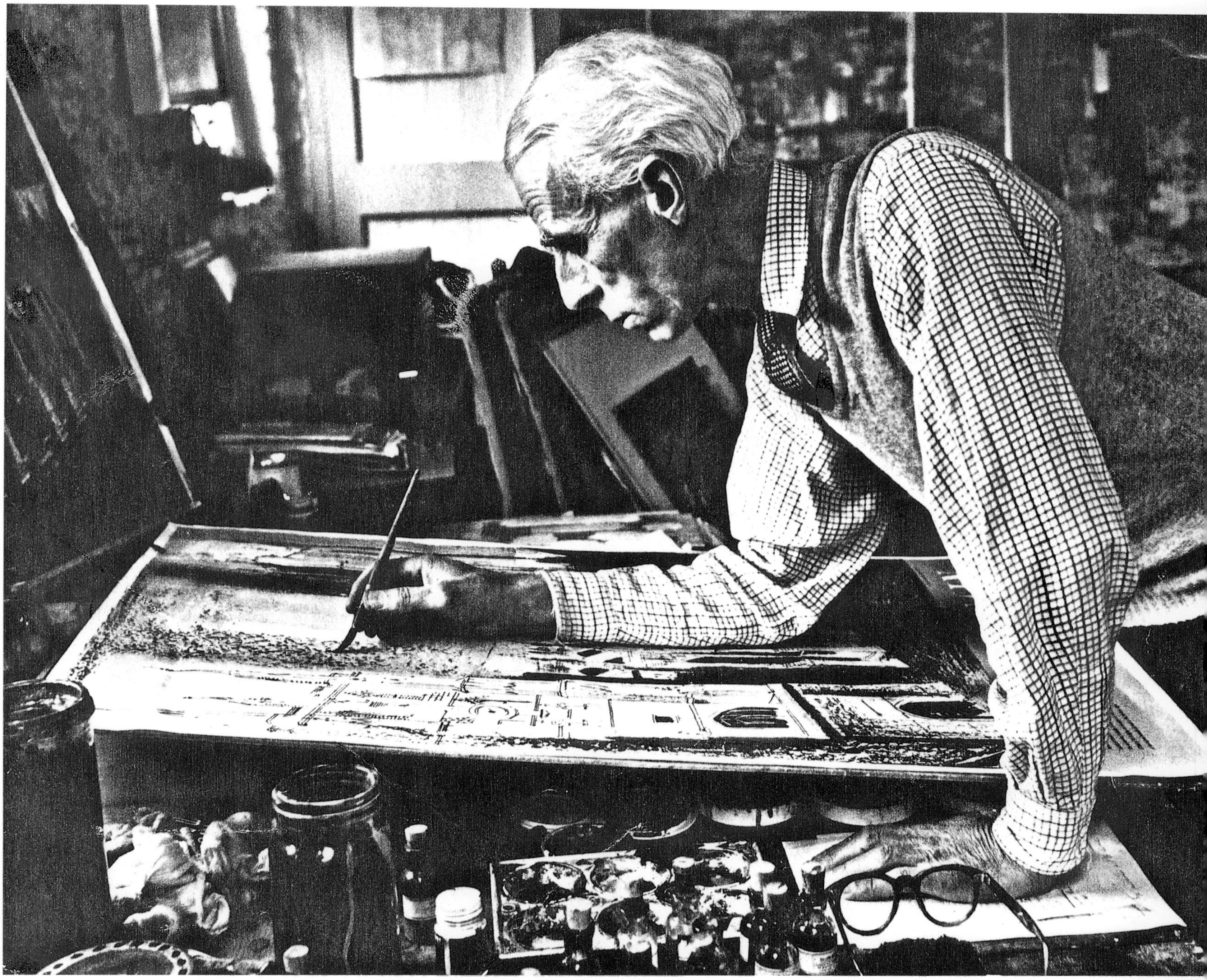

Lund Humphries Publishers London

'Quality and *Experiment': the Prints of John Piper*
A Catalogue Raisonné 1923–91
first published in 1996
by Lund Humphries Publishers Limited
Park House, 1 Russell Gardens
London NW11 9NN

British Library Cataloguing in Publication Data
A catalogue record of this book is available from the British Library

ISBN 0 85331 690 2

Designed by Alan Bartram
Copy-editor: Charlotte Burri
Colour photography by Miki Slingsby (Cats 1–368)
and Steve Green (Cats 369–433)
Black-and-white photographs by Orde Levinson
unless otherwise stated
Typeset in Monotype Ehrhardt
by Nene Phototypesetters, Northampton
Origination, printing and binding in Singapore
under the supervision of M.R.M. Graphics

Title-page illustration: Piper working on *Canterbury Cathedral* (Cat.102), 1956. Photograph: Piper Archives

The author is grateful to the following for supplying transparencies of works in their collections:

Berkeley Square Gallery (various)
Bodleian Library (Cat.6)
British Museum (Cat.26)
Marlborough Fine Art (various)
Tate Gallery, London (Cats 10, 121, 199)
Wakefield Art Gallery and Museum (Cat.71)

This book is based on material from *John Piper: The Complete Graphic Works. A Catalogue Raisonné 1923–1983* by Orde Levinson (Faber and Faber, London, 1987), which has been revised, updated and expanded for the present work. (The reader is referred to the Foreword for fuller details.)

Contents

Preface

This note is to welcome the new edition of Orde Levinson's catalogue raisonné of John Piper's prints, which brings it up to the end of his working life.

Orde's editing has been meticulous in execution and inexhaustible in research. It is, however, not only a work of scholarship but one of enthusiasm and love.

Thank you Orde.

MYFANWY

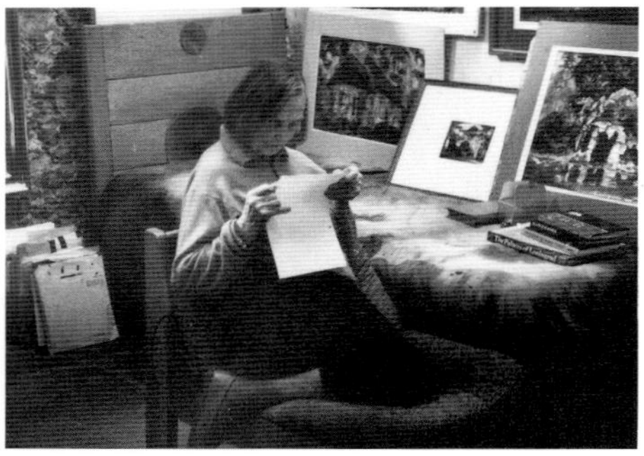

Myfanwy Piper, 1987

Acknowledgements

The names John and Myfanwy Piper are also magic words. They inspire so much affection that all I had to do is mention them to get as much advice and assistance as I needed to complete this book. My enquiries yielded an enthusiastic response and to all of you individuals, enthusiasts, collectors, curators, museum directors, art dealers, booksellers, printers and publishers, many thanks.

There are some whose contributions I wish to be singled out. Henry Garfit is a lover of Piper's work and brought his youthful enthusiasm to the early stages of the book. Kate Pierrepont laboured unstintingly to see it in print. Alexandra Wettstein spent years painstakingly collecting and gently passing on constructive information and suggestions. Neil Wells, a Piper enthusiast and expert on his illustrated books, made valuable observations, and signalled a number of publications and book illustrations which I might otherwise have missed.

My appreciation goes to Sarah Cannon, Mark Dicker, David Fraser Jenkins, Steve Green, Mark Harrell, Ben Hoggett, Michael Kay, Susan Kay, Stephen Laird, Duncan Large, Debbie Lauterpacht, Clarissa Lewis, Sebastian Piper, Jeremy Rowe, Marion Stone, Chorley Turner and Chris Wiltshire for their assistance and support. So, too, to Lucy Myers and especially for her patience and humour.

For checking of information I would like to thank Helen Bridle, Donal Cooper, Sue Evans, Edward Morgan-Jones and in particular Charlotte Burri and Mihai Cucos (with whom I enjoyed many pleasant and interesting conversations about Piper's work).

On issues of design it has been exciting working with Alan Bartram, the designer, who has done an excellent job, and with Lucy Myers.

And Myfanwy Myfanwy. Her life speaks for itself as she speaks – with eloquence, warmth and awareness, and utterly without pretension. Her home likewise. John and Myfanwy made a unique pair. Part of what they gave to others, others have given back to me. This book is therefore a present from all of us, offered with my respect, and love.

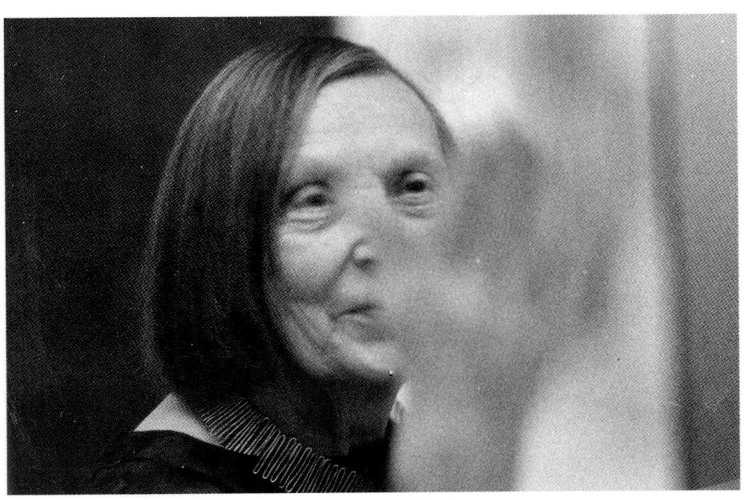

Myfanwy Piper, *c.*1987

Foreword

When my book *John Piper: The Complete Graphic Works. A Catalogue Raisonné 1923-1983* was published in 1987 it evaluated work up to 1983, and so it was inevitable that it could only draw a provisional balance. Indeed, by 1987 new prints had been created. In total, Piper created 65 new prints between 1983 and his death in 1992. For this reason alone an expanded new edition became necessary.

Furthermore, the book illustrations, comprising 106 of the 368 prints catalogued in the 1987 publication, were not in colour, and 10 new works (as well as 10 works referred to in that book, but not found) were discovered. All this amounted to a significant body of work – 191 items, in fact – which had not previously been catalogued or reproduced in colour. These have now been incorporated into this book.

Moreover, the reference material – including all the indices, the list of book illustrations and the list of exhibitions (substantially enlarged) – has been completely revised in line with the most accurate information currently available.

I have also included additional material of a different kind: new sections which situate Piper's prints in the context of his life and work as a whole. These include biographical details, a list of Piper's designs for stage sets, stained glass and tapestries, and a list of Piper's own writings – all closely related to his prints – as well as a short essay on the prints themselves. Finally, there is a list of writings about Piper. All this reference material is now certainly the most comprehensive ever compiled on Piper, and it allows one to gain a more general impression of his concerns within any one year, across the full spectrum of his production.

Finally, I have been especially pleased to be able not only to reproduce all colour works in colour – including the book illustrations – but also to include a section of large-format colour plates showing details of the prints. This is the first time that so many of the prints have been reproduced in colour, and they deserve it.

I hope that this book will allow those who already have my 1987 book to appreciate Piper anew, and enable all readers to recognise his stature as one of the most important printmakers this century.

ORDE LEVINSON
London, October 1995

Experiment and Quality
Orde Levinson

Frequently I am asked why I like Piper's work, and what he was like as a person. Neither question can be answered fully in a short introductory essay. What finally appears here is necessarily only an aspect of my personal response to Piper's prints: his experimentation and quality.[1]

I first encountered Piper's work in the early 1970s, in the home of a friend of my parents in Cape Town. Inspired and excited by the gouaches which I saw there, I wrote to John care of the Tate Gallery and received a warm handwritten reply, thanking me for my appreciation and interest, and letting me know that I would be welcome to visit him and Myfanwy at their home. That was the beginning of our friendship, and my respect for his work has never ceased to grow. Now that he is no longer with us, I see him as an artist who had the best possible understanding of the Modern Movement, its aims, techniques and freedoms, and at the same time created works of moving beauty. Piper absorbed the principles of Cubism, Surrealism, abstraction and Pop Art and combined them with his *personal* knowledge of stained glass and Romanesque carving.

His prints have a particular fascination, for taken in their entirety they reflect the course of Piper's life work and the breadth of his interests. They are among his earliest known works of art and cover almost every subject-matter of his creative life, displaying many of the shifts in his style: from the purely abstract prints (Cats 7, 10), to those showing an affinity with stained glass (Cat.113), set designs (Cats 224-33, 403-24), collages (Cat.117), or drawing notes (Cats 179, 180). Their subject-matter encompasses buildings (chapels, churches, mansions), ruins, gardens, flowers, foliate heads (his version of the Green Man), towns, mountains, the seaside, stones, and the human figure (in the *Eye and Camera* series).

But Piper never merely records. Just as the Impressionists showed us how to 'see' purple shadows, so Piper shows us objects that we have never noticed before: neglected masterpieces of architecture, monuments in churches by Gibbons, corbels at Kilpeck, Victorian 'Dream Palaces' before they became fashionable. Osbert Sitwell attributed a new description to a section of Piper's work, the so-called 'roofscapes': '... to coin a new word for a new kind of picture – the artist shows us the battlemented lines, so characteristic, where every church, even, and every wall, had to have its fortifications ...'[2]

What is as striking as the range of Piper's style and subject-matter is the precocity of his technique. His prints show how greatly advanced he was in terms of modern aesthetics and how well he mastered the print medium. Piper is arguably one of the most innovative twentieth-century print-makers, and was able to work across a range of different print media, producing aquatints (his *Brighton Aquatints* helped to revive the aquatint as a twentieth-century medium), stone-lithographs (the magnificent *A Retrospect of Churches*) and screenprints (especially the *Eye and Camera* themes). Piper experimented: 'booting the technique' was what he called it, well before the term 'to boot' was used for 'firing up' computers. He worked with knowledge *and* intuitive awareness. He had 'no fear of consequences' and as such '... [brought] forth images of magic awareness which we call art'.[3]

In order to convey the range of Piper's abilities as a print-maker, and to highlight the many different technical and stylistic innovations he made within the medium, I shall discuss his 'topographical' style and his romanticism, two key elements of Piper's work;[4] his 'Pop' experimentation with the human figure in the *Eye and Camera* series; his use of the aquatint and autolithograph in the book illustrations; and his portrayal of landscapes and buildings in the portfolios *Stones and Bones* and *A Retrospect of Churches.* Finally I shall look at the garden and flower series, the last prints created by Piper.

'... romantic and topographical'

Let us look at two early works, which are among Piper's first known 'finished'[5] artistic works: an early woodcut, *[Figures in a Landscape]* (Cat.2), and an autolithograph, *Nursery Frieze II* (Cat.9 and Plate 1).

All the early woodcuts and wood-engravings are in black-and-white. In *[Figures in a Landscape]* of *c.*1923, the white is used as thin line (the church, the horizon, the foreground below the figures and the head of the figure second from right) and as body texture (the backs and knees of the figures). The black serves as the backcloth.[6] The use of shading to create roundness also suggests forms in their own right: the white shading of the leg of the reclining female figure front left suggests the form of a tree.[7] There is a rhythm between the curved breasts, backs and buttocks of the figures, and the lines

1. Each of the sections in the book has been written as a part of the whole. Only with more space (the first draft of this essay ran to seventy-eight thousand words) can one fully contextualise Piper's works to evaluate his position in art history, past, present and future
2. Leicester Galley exh. cat., 1945
3. 'Introduction to His Paintings', *D. H. Lawrence Selected Essays*, Penguin Books, Harmondsworth, 1978, pp.307, 313. The quotations are from D.H. Lawrence's essay on Cézanne, but can equally well be applied to Piper. Lawrence was a major literary influence during Piper's teens and early twenties. As Piper wrote: 'Lawrence gave you a new way of life. You didn't talk about art any more. You behaved it.' Tate, p.13
4. For Piper 'Romantic art deals with the particular. The particularization of Bewick about a bird's wing, of Turner about a waterfall or a hill town ... is the result of a vision that can see in these things something significant beyond ordinary significance: something that for a moment seems to contain the whole world; and, when the moment is past, carries over some comment on life or experience besides the comment on appearance' (John Piper, *British Romantic Artists*, 1942, p.7). And on topography he writes: 'Topography at its best is the interpretation of the world as a vision of the place. The best topographical paintings have the spirit of the place in the time ... Giorgione's "La Tempesta" is the epitome of every virtue topographical art should have.' (John Piper note in exh. cat. John Piper, New Grafton Gallery, 1984)
5. I have excluded his sketch-books and church drawings of 1915 to 1923
6. In a similar way, Piper would use blocks of tone (sometimes white, sometimes black, sometimes coloured and in different shapes) in many of his later works. For example Cats 70, 87, 132, 134, 210, 318, 322, 385, 398, 418
7. This separation of the line and tone can be seen even more clearly in later prints (for example Cats 84, 102, 112 and 125), and it reaches the point where Piper experiments by eliminating line and creating an outline with pure colour blocks (see Cat.281)

beneath the seated figures echo the outline of the mountain range, and that of the two approaching figures.

[Figures in a Landscape] is also interesting for its multiple planes, and Piper's ability to incorporate into a single context images observed at different times and places. The figures are shown front-on, standing, sitting, crouching, lying. Their faces vary: some are silhouetted, others are detailed, and for the one second from the right there are just a few broken lines. To these varied figures Piper has brought his memory images of a tree and a church to create a sense of place.[8] It is not simply the Cubists' technique of separating line and tone for aesthetic reasons, or of the artist showing all that he knows about the reclining figure, front, back, side, but it is '… the spirit of the place in the time'.[9] Thus even in this early work we see Piper as both romantic and topographical artist.

Let us take these ideas further with a second work, *Nursery Frieze II*, 1936. The multiple memories are clearer here and are not yet amalgamated into a single symbol. The title indicates that this is a child's-eye view, and it is indeed an archetypal seaside scene, as it exists in our childhood memories or in our imagination: the curling bay with the jetty, the waves and multicoloured beach huts, the journey by train, the houses, beach parties with fires, the night-time and the images (sometimes frightening for the child) of the trees on the right.

The village is outlined by a couple of thick white lines on black indicating roof tops and a church (with a squirrel weather-vane perched on top), and by abstract red shapes. Then there are the train and the clouds of train-smoke, the smoke created by wiping away the black ink, whereas the smoke from the house immediately to the right is drawn into the black. In this print we see again the use of colour blocks as 'backcloth' and Piper's marvellous sense of colour. The blocks of colour - purple, pink, black and white (the paper) - are combined and interlinked, the purple water and sky on the left counterpointed on the right by the purple mountains. Piper's ability to combine colours is seen again in the purple house against a black background, and in the variously coloured and textured clouds: pink cross-hatched in black, grey (collage, brush) and white (the paper). The white of the paper is used extensively in this print to create form: for example, to represent the white jagged edges above the hill, or for the waves and the sections on the right.[10] From 1936 Piper was making new collages on the subject of the sea and the sea-shore. What is remarkable about his method is that these collages were created *en plein air* in front of the subject, with wads of paper brought along with him (many of them from printing studios) and occasionally with others found on the spot.[11]

In *Nursery Frieze II* we see many of the stylistic devices which Piper reworked in later prints: the use of white and black dots and marks (here in the roof of the more classical mansion house) and the distinctive detail of the station-house awnings.[12] We also see the anthropomorphising of nature (an aspect of many of his later prints): the fire is a happy fire, with the three flames of red reaching upwards like figures. A giant Catherine Wheel assumes the shapes of sea plants and flowers. Multiple associations arise from a single image. And as in the earlier woodcut there is the brilliant use of a single white line across the black to establish the horizon: the cliffs on the left and the mountain range on the right. The edge of the cliff with the lighthouse is a line of white paper, and the dots on the side of the hill suggest its texture, and the wall.

Both *[Figures in a Landscape]* and *Nursery Frieze II* contain figures used in different ways, in the former in classical poses, in the latter to give a sense of drama. In a different way, the *Eye and Camera* prints, which date from the late 1960s, also show a portrayal of the human figure.

'… *Eye and Camera* prints …'

The *Eye and Camera* prints are complex works, not yet appreciated for their approach to the figure and to modernism. The series is based on photographs of Piper's wife Myfanwy, and presents the female figure in semi-nude poses which at first glance are suggestive of advertising imagery. It shows Piper at the forefront of Pop Art, taking up Pop Art's concern with bright colours and images from popular culture.

Piper innovates, even ironically,[13] with modern technology. He also illustrates how the camera can distort our perception of the figure, so that its identity is concealed on the one hand, but the form is maintained. Piper's incorporation of camera images into his prints (predated only by a few years in *Llangloffan, Pembrokeshire: the Baptist chapel* (Cat.140))[14] was at a time when there was resistance in the art world to photography as an art form. His real innovation here, however, is not the use of photography, but his experimentation with the photo-image, with positive and negative counter-images, reworked in pen or with marbling, drawing, painterly strokes or gouache techniques.

Take a work such as *Eye and Camera: Claret and Blue* (Cat.235 and Plate 5). Two blocks of marvellous colour divide the work. The black of the left-hand side partly obscures the figure. This is counter-pointed by the red background of the right-hand side, with its clear shapes and wonderful use of marbling in the figure's face to create the eye and the mouth. The body has a sculptural feel, with the marble

8. I shall show how in later works Piper uses associated memory images, for example combining the history of a place with his personal experience
9. See note 4, above
10. For the use of the white of the paper see also Cats 69, 109, 130 (glass of lamp as white paper), 131, 133, 342 (the white is the paper on the figures outside left and right), 192, 193, 375, 423 (the central yellow sun in a sea of white, which is the paper)
11. See also Cat.117, which is created entirely from collage
12. The use of dots and other markings occurs very often in later works, see for example Cats 219, 333, 356, 363
13. 'Camera-eye' traditionally denotes realism in painting, exact pictorial representation
14. He used text in images as early as 1939, see Cat.21

foot on the right being cut into by strips of red. It is created as a collage, not with line.[15] Whereas Picasso in his linocuts cut away layer after layer of lino, Piper combined collage and his own personal love of books and marbling to build up layers of tone and imagery.

Other *Eye and Camera* works show different variations of this theme. In the masterly *Eye and Camera: Multifigure* (Cat.212 and Plate 3) a sense of depth is created by the central photographic image being reduced and placed as an inset in the print, flanked by two larger images on either side. This also gives the impression of three screens, like a medieval triptych. Negative versions of the same photograph are set as blocks of colour: as red cut-outs, blue shapes, scratchwork, variations (the two outer figures reverse the image with elbows facing inwards on either side, unifying the work, so that shapes are seen to metamorphose). In *Eye and Camera: Yellow and Green* (Cat.183) the figure is presented as a sculpture in a landscape, with the head a photographic negative and the body in black. The white paper is used as outline, to surround the figures. In *Eye and Camera: Red and Black* (Cat.211) the marbling on the left-hand side echoes the shapes of the twigs, leaves and branches. On the right-hand side an amazing silver light takes the form of a figure, whose shape suggests a bird-like form and is more clearly seen in the blood-red cut-out figure on the left. This unusual way of portraying the figure in a landscape is reminiscent of the *Foliate Head* series with its associations of fertility.[16]

In the two nudes (Cats 389 and 390), which contain no camera work but are informed by the *Eye and Camera* series, Piper has grasped the female figure as fetish, while making it seem ordinary and natural. The shading on the back of *Nude II* (Cat.390) is superb. Further rhythmical elements are revealed in the shading of the knees, with the arm forming a triangular shape directing the gaze towards the head and body. The high heels are in profile, so that the lace of the figure's left shoe, and the decoration around the right, echo her hair. One cannot see the detail of the shoe, nor that of the hair; the forms are simple, and even with a suggestion of a pornographic element, the prints have a lyrical, classical quality. As Piper wrote: 'The Classical Theory is based on an abstract idea of perfection, the romantic on a subjective use of particular details and moods of nature.'[17]

In *Nude I* (Cat.389), the quality of Piper's line is revealed in the nude's right hand, which is imbued with both wisdom and youth. The fused fingers next to the thumb could be a hand suffering and burnt after a fire; their nobility evokes also a stillness, a unity. If one's gaze moves up the arm, the feeling is of a vulnerable openness – the outstretched arm, palm upwards. The hand is very delicate. One notices how the hair flows down like foliage and contrasts with the feel of body, which is more solid.

The *Eye and Camera* series reduces the figure to its essential features, almost to an abstraction. Although the individual works are thematically similar, there is no repetition between them. The prints transform a photographic portrait of a nude into a more universal statement about love and the body. As Piper wrote in *British Romantic Artists* of Wordsworth, his urge was to record not places and things but life, in order 'to make a particular effect of sun or rain, calm or storm, light or shadow, gloom or gaiety, stand as a symbol for something universal'.[18]

'... aquatints or autolithographs ...'

Piper's book illustrations comprise 143[19] of his 458 prints. Many are aquatints or autolithographs, and show Piper's attempt to re-establish these printing methods as viable and interesting twentieth-century media. With larger-edition book illustrations, such as those for *English, Scottish and Welsh Landscape* (Cats 34-46), Piper tended to use autolithography, drawing directly onto the printer's plate.

The images of *English, Scottish and Welsh Landscape* show Piper as a complete master of autolithography, of colour combination and of the separation of line and colour. In *Pistyll Cain, North Wales* (Cat.35) the colour of the rocks on the right echoes the water and the trees alongside the stream (where the colour combination of yellow and grey produces a sombre mossy-green). The line is drawn in different weights: thin for the rock face, thick for the boulders, and broken, almost frivolous, for the churning fountain, echoed in the moss. As a composition, the work is also unified by the way the rocks on the right curl in and up, like the palm of a hand cupping beneath the water, creating a foreground within which the image can sit.

The rest of the book shows how the same colours can be used in very different ways. *Approach to Gordale Scar, Yorkshire* (Cat.42) conveys the sense of a place which is alive, swirling, as if some underlying currents have been made visible. The viewer is high up, and a sense of landing by plane is evoked by the swirl of the road which ends with tracery lines. The left-hand side is a mass of colour and no detail: moving to the right of the print one is given the dark centre of the mountain, overflowing with flecks of burnished yellow detail. In the left foreground are boulders, thickly drawn with the use of the white paper. It is a description of the landscape via the imagination, and shows an expert use of a limited colour palette and a masterful sense of line. In *Park Place, Berkshire* (Cat.44) we can see how Piper innovates with shapes and symbols: the halo around the crescent moon echoes the shape of the bridge joined with its reflection in the water; and the clouds pierce the moon just as the water divides the bridge from its reflection. This lyricism is seen not just in parallel shapes but in contrasting colours, with the yellow crescent moon echoing the black inside arch of the bridge and its reflection. The symbol is further enriched when we consider that the

15. I am reminded here of the paper cut-outs of Matisse
16. For example Cat.245, where the image of the face (male or female) is made up of natural forms and shapes: the eyes, leaves; the nose a stone. The shapes, both floating and changing, also all suggest growth
17. *British Romantic Artists*, p.29
18. *Ibid*, p.16
19. This includes the twenty-seven prints of *Stones and Bones* and the seven *Stowe* prints (Cats 238-44)

crescent moon's halo is a perfect circle in white, suggesting the sun. Symbolically the sun and moon are created in one sign.

Piper's illustrations for *Brighton Aquatints* (Cats 12-23) were successful attempts to revive the use of aquatint in three of its forms, coarse, fine and intermediate. In *Regency Square from the West Pier* (Cat.14) Piper uses the acid at several different stages to create a three-dimensional effect and to simulate the texture of the courtyard and the background. Stopping-out varnish is used in repeated applications to create the waves and the sky. Foul biting has been used deliberately for textural effect. This contrasts with the white paper of the building in the foreground to give depth. In *The Metropole Hotel from the West Pier* (Cat.23), Piper has bodly 'cancelled' the plate with striations along the building to create a mood of rain. He told me (in *c.*1983) that when he did this he had no idea if it would work. If it had not, he would have been unable to reuse the original image.[20]

One of Piper's frequently noted experiments with the aquatint process is *The Chapel of St George, Kemp Town* (Cat.21). It is the first time that text (from *The Spectator*) has been used in an aquatint, and Piper treats it as a collage to make up the bricks of the walls. Interestingly, in a later work (*Llangloffan, Pembrokeshire, the Baptist chapel*, Cat.140, which is part of *A Retrospect of Churches*), he continues this experimentation by using photography in the lithographic process.[21] In *Swansea Chapel* (Cat.175 and Plate 4) Piper uses letters in different typefaces for the bricks of the wall: these move outside the blue of the image and onto the 'border', giving a sense of movement, a blur, not usually associated with solid bricks and mortar, but apt for a sensation of place. The letters are also used marvellously to suggest railings. Piper's desire to create multiple associations is revealed in this print with the use of blue marbling for the sky. The clouds crashing together at the centre provoke an ambiguity between sky, rocks and sea.[22]

Brighton Aquatints is a gem not just for its technical innovations.[23] Its draughtsmanship, its humorous insights (in *The First Avenue Hotel, Hove*, Cat.12, the lamp-posts are like figures with hats) and the complexity of even the smallest detail (the face of the statue, its top-hat, profile, abstracted mouth) all contribute to create an interesting, idiosyncratic, 'Piperesque' view of Brighton.

'Landscape, stones and buildings ... a human sensitivity'

In *Stones and Bones* (Cats 288-314) Piper extends the concept *beau-livre* so that text and image are one. Its narrative theme is the relationship between stones and bones. Piper's interest in the subject began in the late 1940s, particularly with his experience of the rocks at Nant Ffrancon. He wrote: 'I felt then that I was seeing the mountains for the first time and seeing them as nobody had seen them before. This was partly due to the feeling of release after the confining of the war, partly to a "spurt" in my capacity to observe more clearly at a particular time. Each rock lying in the grass had a positive personality: for the first time I saw the bones and the structure and the "lie" of mountains, living with them and climbing them as I was, lying on them in the sun and getting soaked with rain in their cloud cover and enclosed in their improbable, private rock-world in fog.'[24]

Stones and Bones I (Cat.290) presents a key to looking at nature in terms of the human figure, and vice versa. With *Stones and Bones XVII* (Cat.306) there is an amalgamation of figure and stone, in that one can see in the left-hand side of the head a range of mountains, especially if one turns the image on its side (and many of the sections of the folio are printed so that one has to turn them sideways). The rich brown tones on the right-hand side suggest the velvetiness of skin. The print covers two pages, which gives it prominence and accentuates the fact that only a detail is in focus, with the remainder a hazy-soft background. In *Stones and Bones XIV* (Cat.303), which depicts Connemara, Piper has taken the line for a walk and has created his imagery from a completely separate colour background.[25] The lines lie at all angles, and the marks vary from dots and circles, to squares, scratches and furrows. We see these different types of marks used in many other works too, in buildings, in landscapes and with colours,[26] and this demonstrates not just a technical ability but a poetic mind. Piper combines many different visual elements in a single work without such dexterity appearing contrived.

Piper uses the depiction of landscapes, of stones and buildings, as a focus for his own emotions, thus giving the external world a human sensibility. As he wrote, quoting Constable: 'Painting is with me but another word for feeling' ... 'An art that is to *realise*, not to *feign*'.[27] Many of Piper's most vibrant landscape prints show him evolving the linear elements with a sure calligraphic stroke – creating them as painting in action, direct, forceful and beautiful – and the patterns and intensity of the colour are used to push an idea or a feeling. Myfanwy Piper pinpointed an element of this romantic vision of Piper when she wrote of the: '*genius loci*, that mysterious magic presence that collects the dreams of the past which, like wasp stings

20. The accompanying text to Piper's *Metropole Hotel* echoes the visual elements of the print with the description 'A heavy shower may just be over ...'
21. It is a print which is often commented on, being a composite of photographs from different periods, and views of the chapel. One can also note the uneven edges of the foliage suggesting the white sky
22. I am reminded of Rimbaud's words, as quoted in West (p.36) in relation to Piper's innovative use of imagery: 'We will free painting from its old habit of copying and give it supremacy. The material world will become only a means for evoking aesthetic expressions. Objects will no longer be reproduced, but feelings will be expressed through the medium of lines, colours, and designs, taken from the external world but simplified or controlled – sheer magic'
23. Even the plates are used differently on the paper, producing sometimes a black frame to the image with a rounded bevelled edge, sometimes an image bled to the edge, sometimes a rounded image
24. Piper/Ingrams, p.105
25. One is reminded of the lines in *Connemara* (Cat.328), which are also similar to the designs on the side of the figure in this print
26. For example *Gothic Folly, Stowe* (Cat.376), where there is no sky but a use of watercolour line and an extreme abstraction of colours on the left-hand side. The variations of colour suggest the continuation of the line of the arch
27. *British Romantic Artists*, p.20

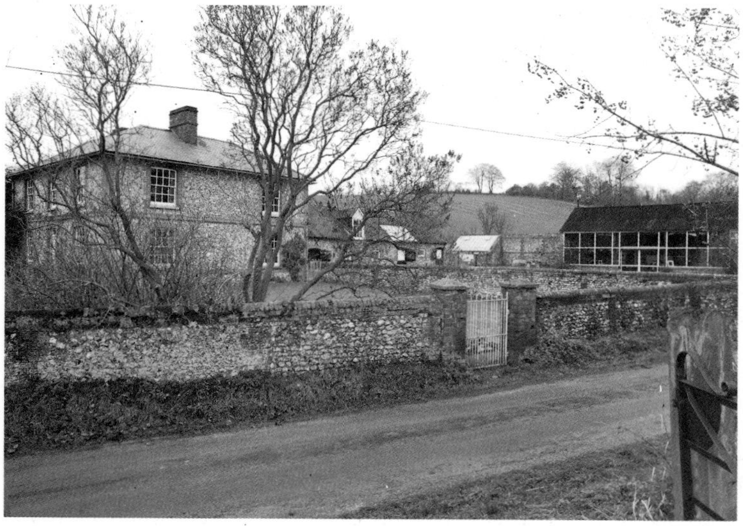

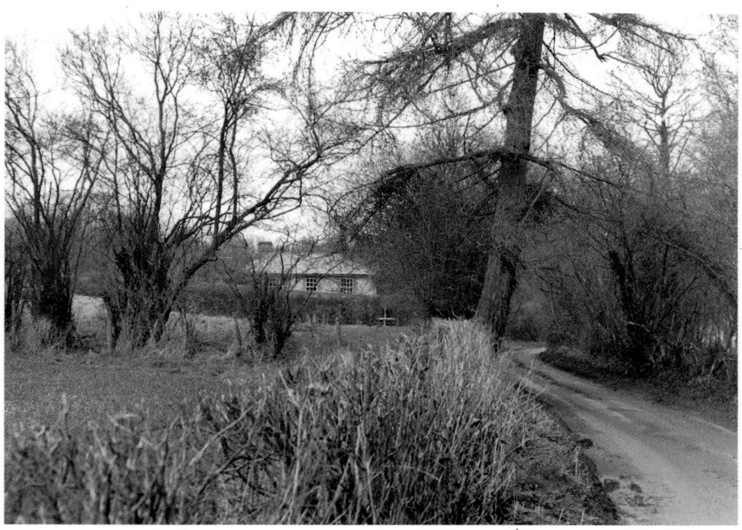

Two views of Fawley Bottom Farmhouse, 1986

accumulating in the blood, accumulate in the mind and the imagination'.[28]

The other works in the portfolio contain many elements central to Piper's interests: 'eye and camera'-type prints, landscapes, details from Romanesque stone sculpture, ink drawings and collages. But the subject-matter here is in a sense secondary to the craft, the manner of creating the marks and the links between landscapes and objects, between large and small, texture and detail, heritage and form.

A Retrospect of Churches (Cats 121A–45) is a magnificent series. Piper uses all known techniques of stone lithography: a quick wash, a solid line, scraped away to give a highlight, often against shadows created by dense inks. Stanley Jones, the master-printer of the lithographs, recalls Piper saying 'what if ...', 'what if we tried this' or 'what if we did that' – and then doing it.[29]

His chosen subject in this portfolio is his great love, church architecture. The prints portray details, exteriors and interiors, sites and combinations of these. The portfolio also works as a guide by achieving two cardinal aims of Piper: to indicate to the visitor items of interest, and to encourage the armchair traveller to go out and explore.

Each of the works in this portfolio is wonderful to look at, and each evokes completely the 'feel' of a place as well as Piper's own feelings for it. Contrast the different techniques and images used in *Leckhamstead, Berkshire: a Victorian church, by S. S. Teulon* (Cat.134) and *Easton, Portland, Dorset: St George Reforne, an 18th-century church among the quarries* (Cat.137). With *Easton, Portland, Dorset* he has conveyed the spirit of the place, cutting into the image to simulate the white cutting marks of the quarryman found in Portland stone. The atmosphere of the area is also given by the overpowering sense of rocks everywhere, and the formal link between the blocks in the foreground and the roofs and walls of the houses in the background. The skyline is pierced by the shape of the church, which almost takes the form of a chisel. Nothing is arbitrary with Piper.

Leckhamstead, Berkshire is a superb abstract collage, yet very different from the collage and drawing of *Inglesham, Wiltshire: a rustic medieval interior* (Cat.132). Abstraction for Piper was a means and not an end in itself. He saw Turner as '... a great abstract painter but never a pure and total one ...'[30] It was the process of abstraction that he found absorbing and the attempt to maintain a link to reality: as Piper put it, the 'double "read-over" of abstraction and reality'.[31] This is the function of *papiers collés* in his prints. Piper shows how poetry can be created from everyday objects, and, like Picasso, manages in his collages to generate intense poetry just by placing together two or three blocks of coloured paper, or by making ink marks seemingly at random. He talked of how a sheet of paper that has had some runs out of register can be used to create waves, stormy seas[32] or textured walls (as in Cat.134). As he said, his collages were his '... means of keeping in touch with natural appearances. The bits of paper were parallels for seen things – not representations of anything concrete.'[33]

Redenhall, Norfolk: the tower (Cat.124) is an evocative tower with its detail, soft colour and large white areas. The detail at the top of the tower resembles the spires of a miniature city. Another type of detail is used in *Extôn, Rutland: monument by Grinling Gibbons, 1686* (Cat.126). Here colour is created by overprinting, the powder-blue over black making a greenish-blue colour. Contrast this with *St Kew,*

28. Myfanwy Piper, 'Introductory letter, December 1993', *John Piper – A retrospective – Works from the Artist's Studio*, Waddington Galleries, 1994. Although referring to their home, I think these words are also applicable to many of Piper's paintings
29. Stanley Jones in conversation with the author, *c.*1977
30. *British Romantic Artists*, p.21
31. Ingrams/Piper, p.21
32. See also Cat.7
33. Ingrams/Piper, p.22

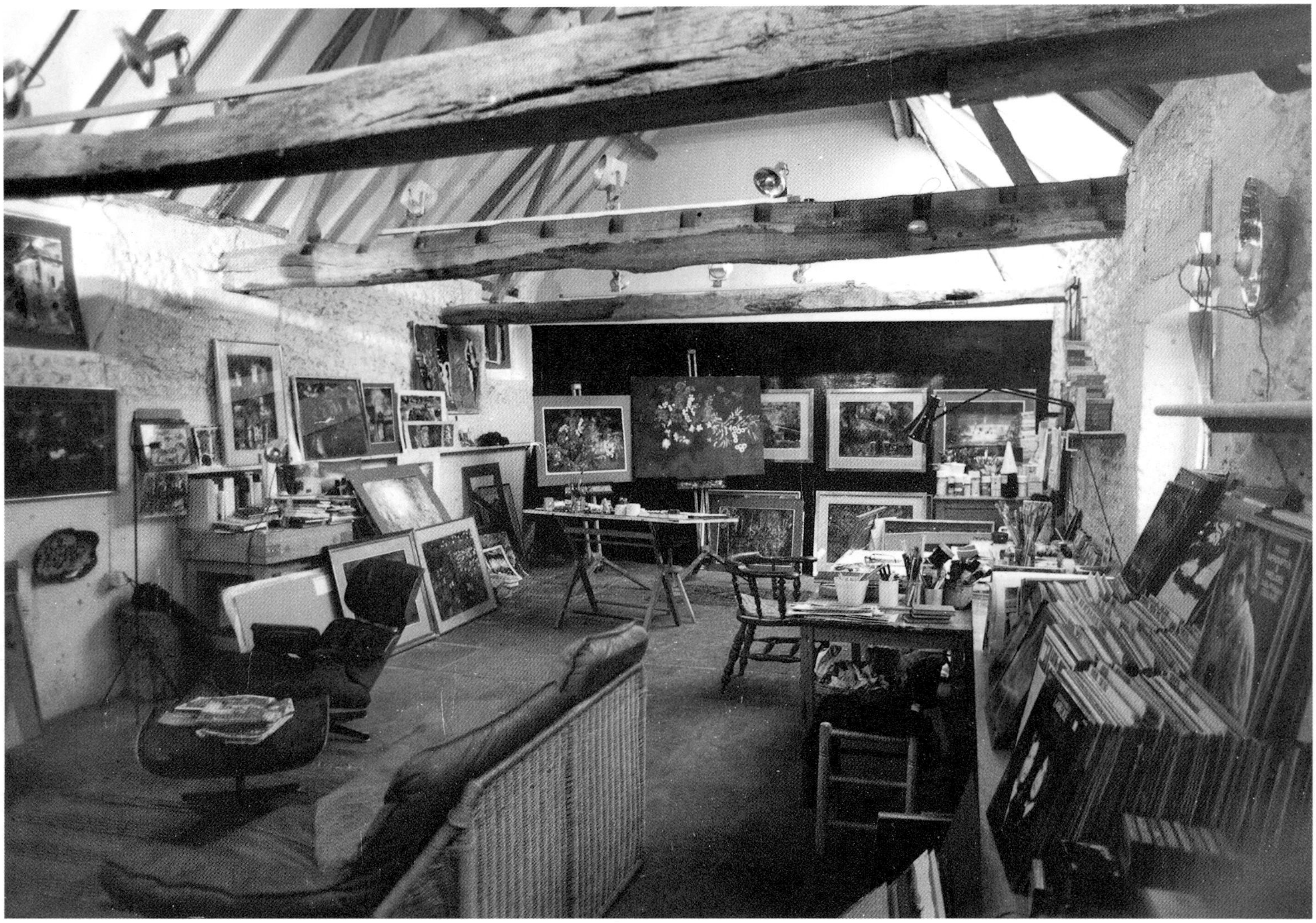

The cowshed studio, Fawley Bottom Farmhouse

Cornwall: church in a hilly landscape (Cat.127), where the church is barely glimpsed on the left in the shaft of the lancet-shaped light-brown block, and through the overgrown foreground shrubs. A larger 'window' on the right has the village houses outlined in white.

Tickencote, Rutland: The Norman chancel arch (Cat.130) shows a range of yellows and blacks with touches of red, but it is also an abstraction of a building, as Piper only represents the most significant features of this 800-year-old Norman arch: its five orders carved with different foliate designs. The patterns begin to form the shape of an arch rising out of the pillars (which are black and brush-flecked in yellow). The abstracted black shape on the right, another pillar or a lectern, has an almost human-like shape, hands in prayer, facing the now almost human forms of the pillars. The hanging lamp is delineated by the touches of red line, and the white is the paper. It is a study of particular features of Norman architecture. Piper quotes William Blake in *British Romantic Artists*: 'To Generalize is to be an Idiot. To particularise is the Alone Distinction of Merit.'[34]

The abstracting of shapes is seen in another work, *Rudbaxton, Pembrokeshire: 17th-century monument, 19th-century furnishings* (Cat.131), where the black silhouette figures are like cut-outs and are extremely modern. The shape of the left-hand figure's leg is echoed in the space between the legs of the two figures. And the clothes and positions of the sets of figures suggest different eras, modern and medieval (the left-hand figure is most modern in its slouching stance, hands in pocket). There is humour and philosophy: the figure facing us on the right holds a skull in one hand, and the finger of the other hand points to it. Yet if one follows the line from this pointing finger back to the shoulder one realises that the face of the figure is a

34. *British Romantic Artists*, p.29

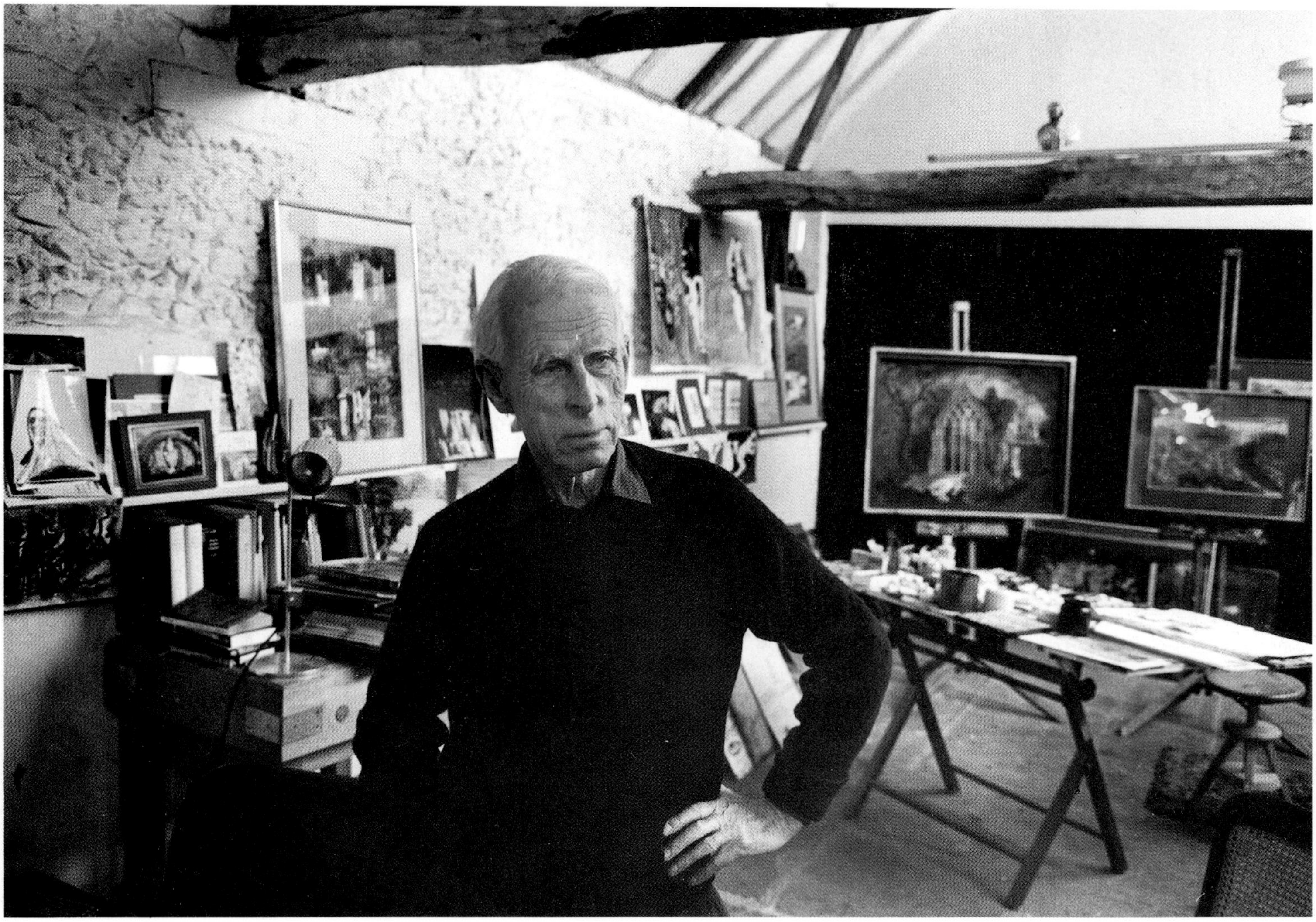

Piper in the cowshed studio, 1983. Photograph by Michael Ward

silhouette of an acorn or pod-like structure – a suggestion of the regeneration of seed, life and death, and especially so when one notices that the figure has no right shoulder.[35]

There are innovations in all the prints of this portfolio, as in many others. For example, in an earlier work, *Château de Taillebourg* (Cat.111), the most distant object, in this case the building on the right, is simply raised and placed at the top, with a few sketched abstract lines allowing us to read the three distances of the picture. Many different types of marks are used in this work to create texture, including scraping, fingerprints,[36] thick and thin wash.

In *Holkham Gate, Norfolk* (Cat.262) the entire gate is created with colour in a pointillism of white dots (which are often used and suggest the influence of stained glass). This creates not just the texture but gives a unity to the work. (The use of dots is also seen in *The Quest* (Cat.384), a set design.) Below the pink sky, the stars and the moon are abstract block-shapes. The castle is one of these shapes, with the detail created by an extra layer of thicker white and the use of an almost identical reflection to give it the 'appearance' of a real object (the other abstract blocks have no such reflection). Reflection is used differently in *Scotney Castle, Kent* (Cat.265): the tower and the tree on the left are not reflected in the water. However the walls seem to reflect the watery foliage, and at the same time Piper gives the feeling of the surface of the water, especially around the tower, with the speckles of black and shading, which are echoed in the wall. Another impressive work is *Stansfield* (Cat.385), where the sides are abstract echoes of the structure and all but the tower building itself is

35. The *Foliate Head* series is also about the Green Man, the symbol of regeneration of life

36. Also used in other works, for example Cat.184

eliminated. The texture of colours on both sides echoes the structure, and is built up with infinite care.

'... the garden and flower prints ...'

Piper's last works were the garden and flower prints, mostly created at Fawley Bottom Farmhouse. These prints show Piper's use of colour, shapes and forms, and they seem also to be infused with the philosophy of old age: reflections on life, regeneration and nature – themes which have occurred again and again in his work.[37] In *Flowers in a Black Pot* (Cat.410) the background is subdued and cohesive, as though the artist is resigned in his old age. There is a glow, a richness such as that found in a Rembrandt painting. It is a deep and complex work, not a mere flower painting. In *Blue Hydrangea* (Cat.429 and Plate 8) there is the remarkable shape of the hydrangeas, like a face in silhouette, which establish a relationship with the jug facing them. The look is delicate and loving; the shape of the jug is sensuous. The red at the bottom is equally evocative. The brown flower-pot merges with the others and one feels the rhythm of the wonderful china-white tone of the jug sprinkled throughout the work.

In the flower prints the shapes dissolve into one another. This gives us a sense of abstraction, but it is painterly abstraction at its best – not literary or mathematical. In the garden at Fawley Bottom nature does not have to battle against cultivation. As in so many of Piper's works, there is a transference of human emotion onto the landscape and nature.[38]

In the latter half of the twentieth century we have been led to believe that a genius ought to be different, eccentric, perhaps wild, and show an early or fiery talent, if not temperament. Piper's life was extraordinary in the true sense of real work and activity, real innovation, experiment and quality. He was also remarkable in being without arrogance, self-promotion or egotism. His home, too, was open to all, no doors were ever locked, no gates prevented entry, friends were welcome, one could come and look at the work and talk. Lunch, always tea (or coffee), biscuits, a drink, a bottle of wine, a walk in the garden to dig up vegetables and pick herbs.

The wonder of this is that it has left me to work out for myself the importance of Piper's work. Neither John nor Myfanwy would ever have dreamt of pushing anyone to see it. I remember once when we were digging up the potatoes – or rather Piper was with the spade, having refused my offer of help with the words that it was 'good for him' (he was around eighty years old then). I remember as he was digging, thinking about him, his work, watching him – it was twilight – and saying to him as I thought of the day, of the work I had seen, that I thought he was very under-rated. He turned to me, still getting another potato out of the ground, and said 'You know Orde, I think I am rather over-rated'.

37. Take an early work such as *Byland Abbey, Yorkshire* (Cat.25). The building is ruined, but there is the proud west front, and if one gazes at the broken window there is a sense of resurgence in the small turret and cross-like ornament. And the door – like a cloaked figure – is still there. The other doors then take on a more human presence, and the ruin is not dead in our imagination. The sweep of the clouds, the three shafts of light on the right, are like flying angels, ever present. It is this that makes Piper's work so remarkable. Not a mere recording – more than just a superb juxtaposition of shapes and forms – it is the emotion that he puts into the work which brings it alive

38. David Fraser Jenkins wrote: 'Kenneth Clark, in his study of the history of European landscape painting *Landscape into Art*, although he stopped short of mentioning contemporary artists directly, recommended then that such an approach [Piper's approach of transferring human emotion to the scenery] might serve for the future of art ...' David Fraser Jenkins, 'Introduction', *John Piper in Wales*, Oriel 3, 1990, p.13

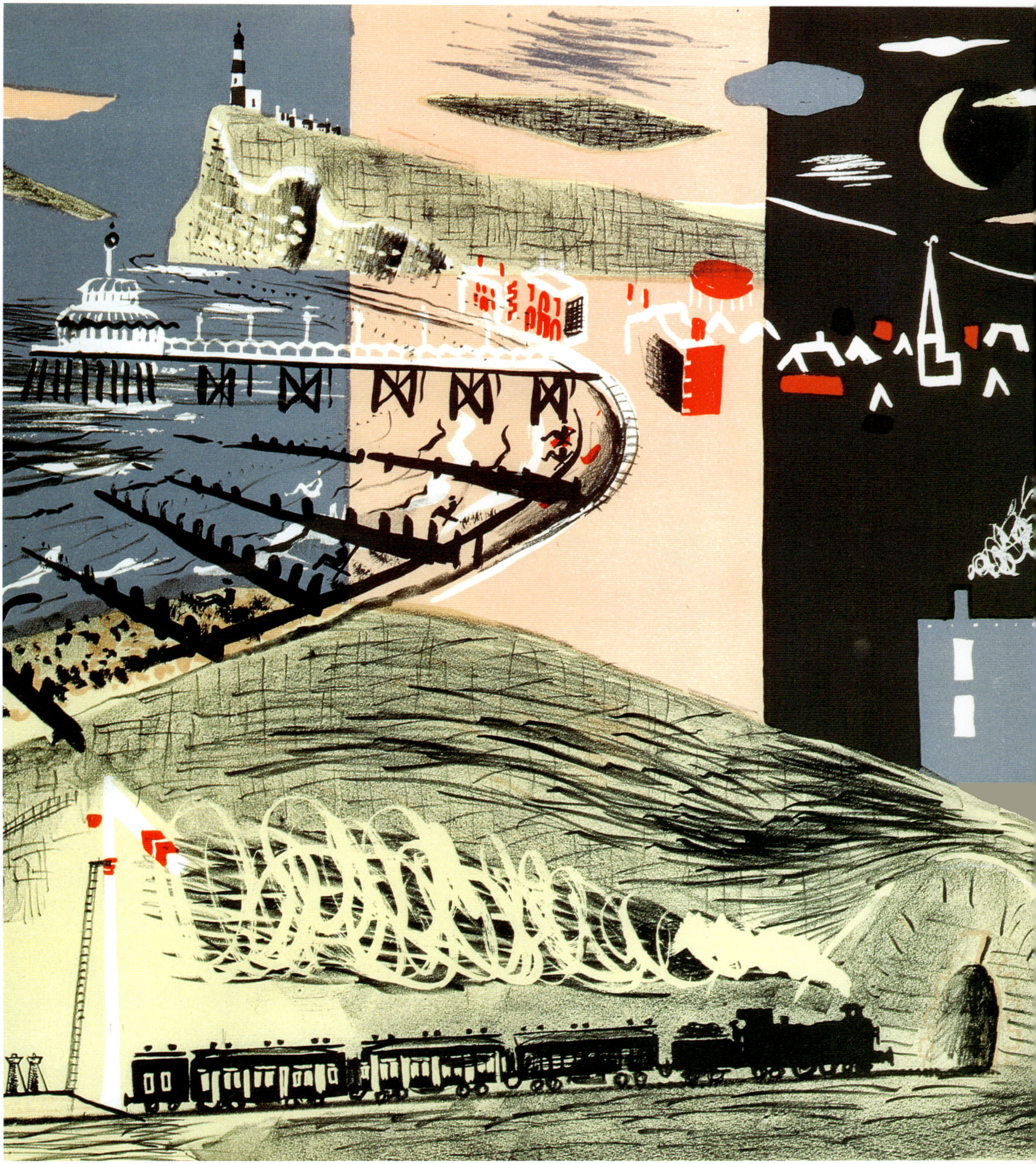

Plate 1
Detail from *Nursery Frieze II* 1936
autolithograph (Cat.9)

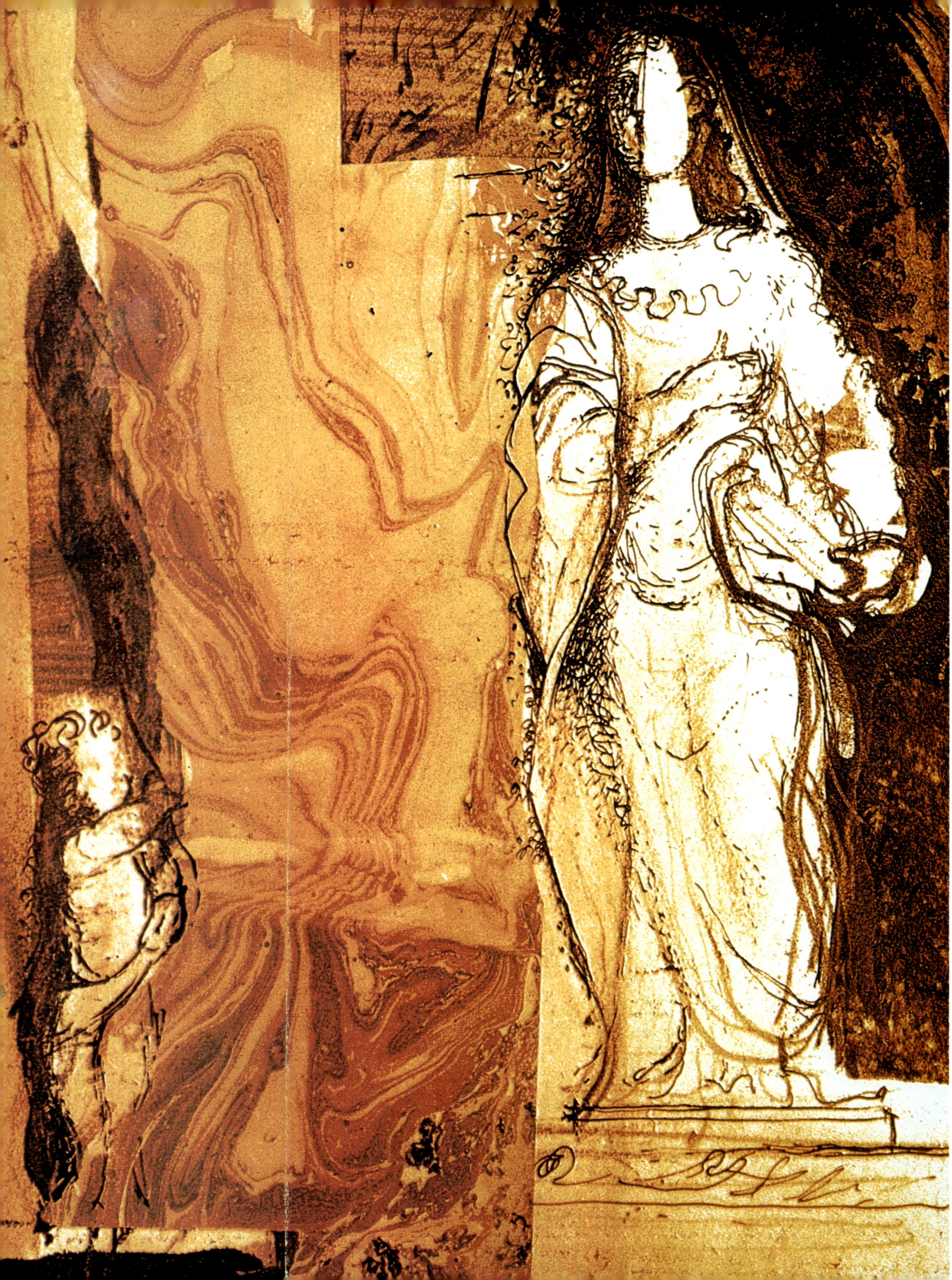

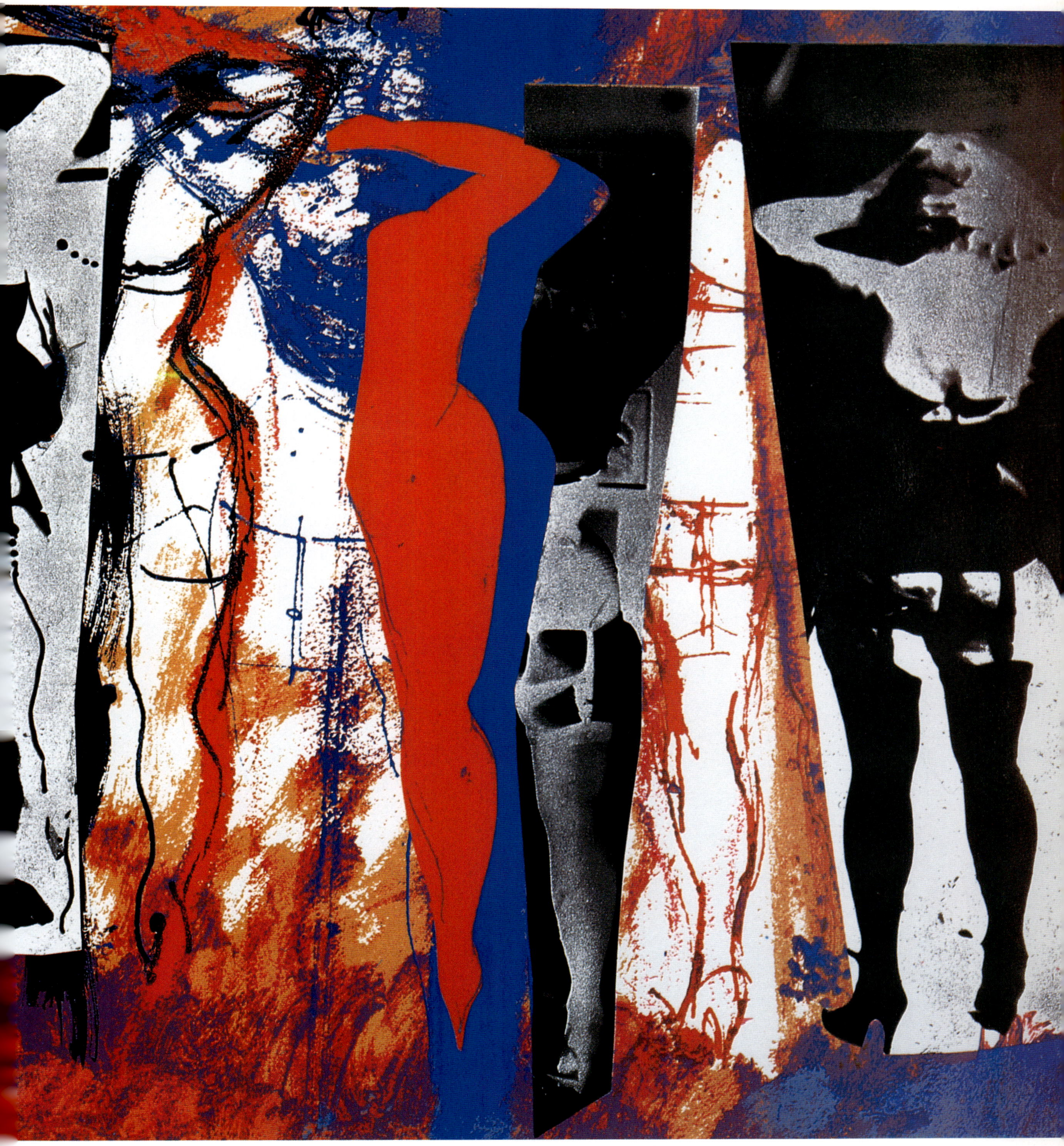

Plate 2 (left)
Detail from *Stones and Bones XX* 1978
screenprint (Cat.309)

Plate 3 (above)
Detail from *Eye and Camera: Multifigure* 1972
screenprint (Cat.212)

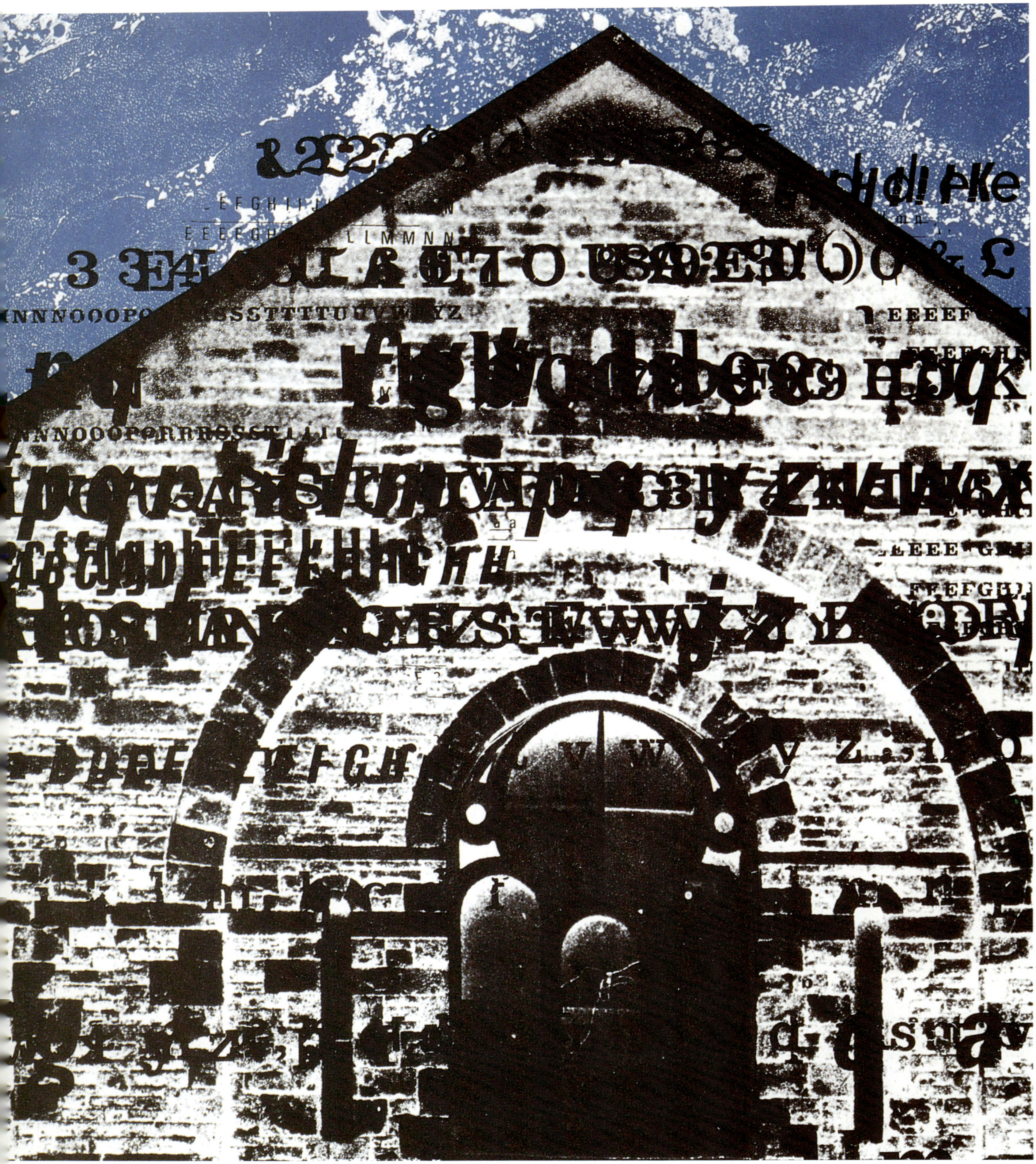

Plate 4 (above)
Detail from *Swansea Chapel* 1966
lithograph (Cat.175)

Plate 5 (right)
Detail from *Eye and Camera: Claret and Blue* 1973
screenprint (Cat.235)

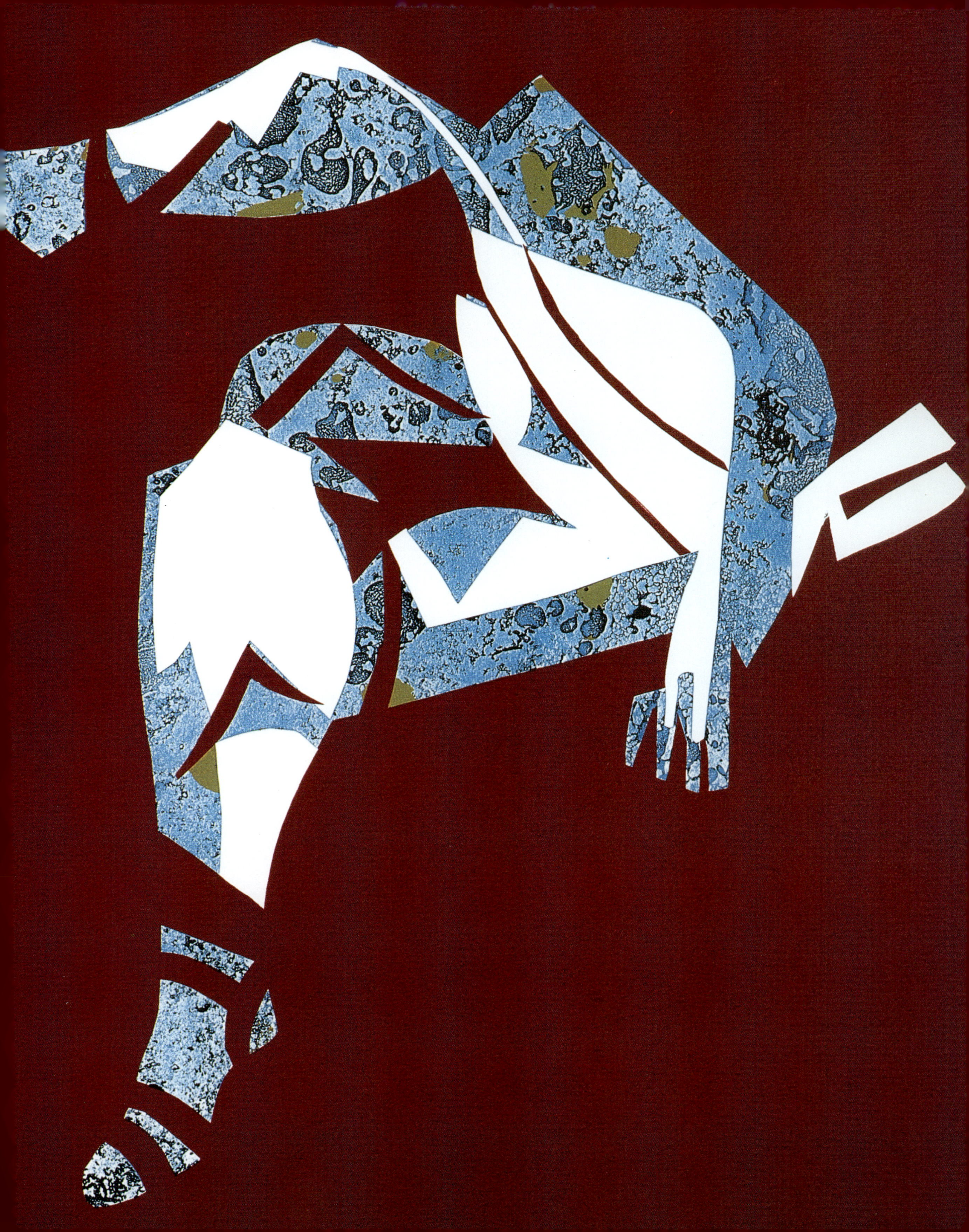

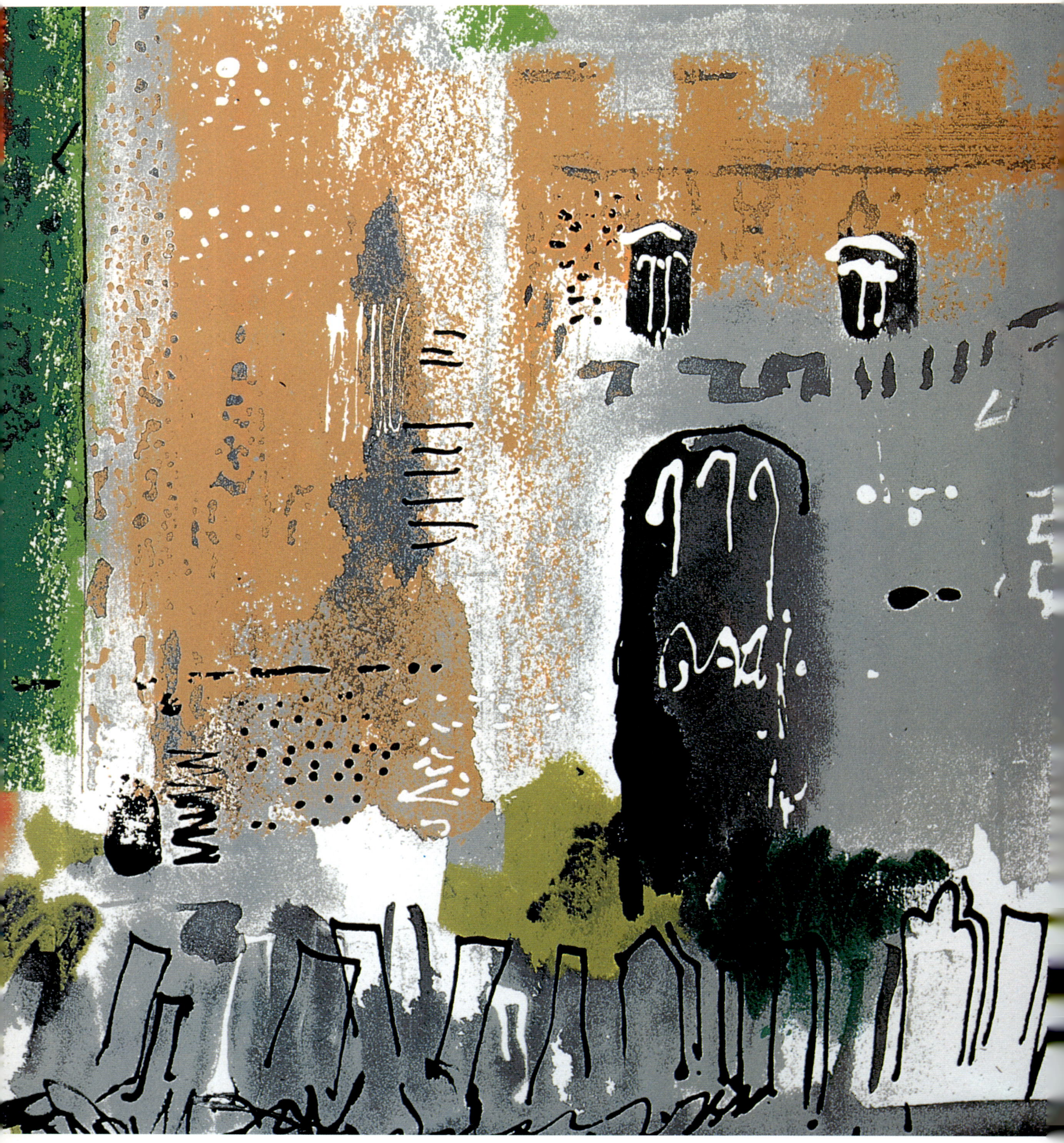

Plate 6
Detail from *Buckden in a Storm* 1977
screenprint (Cat.281)

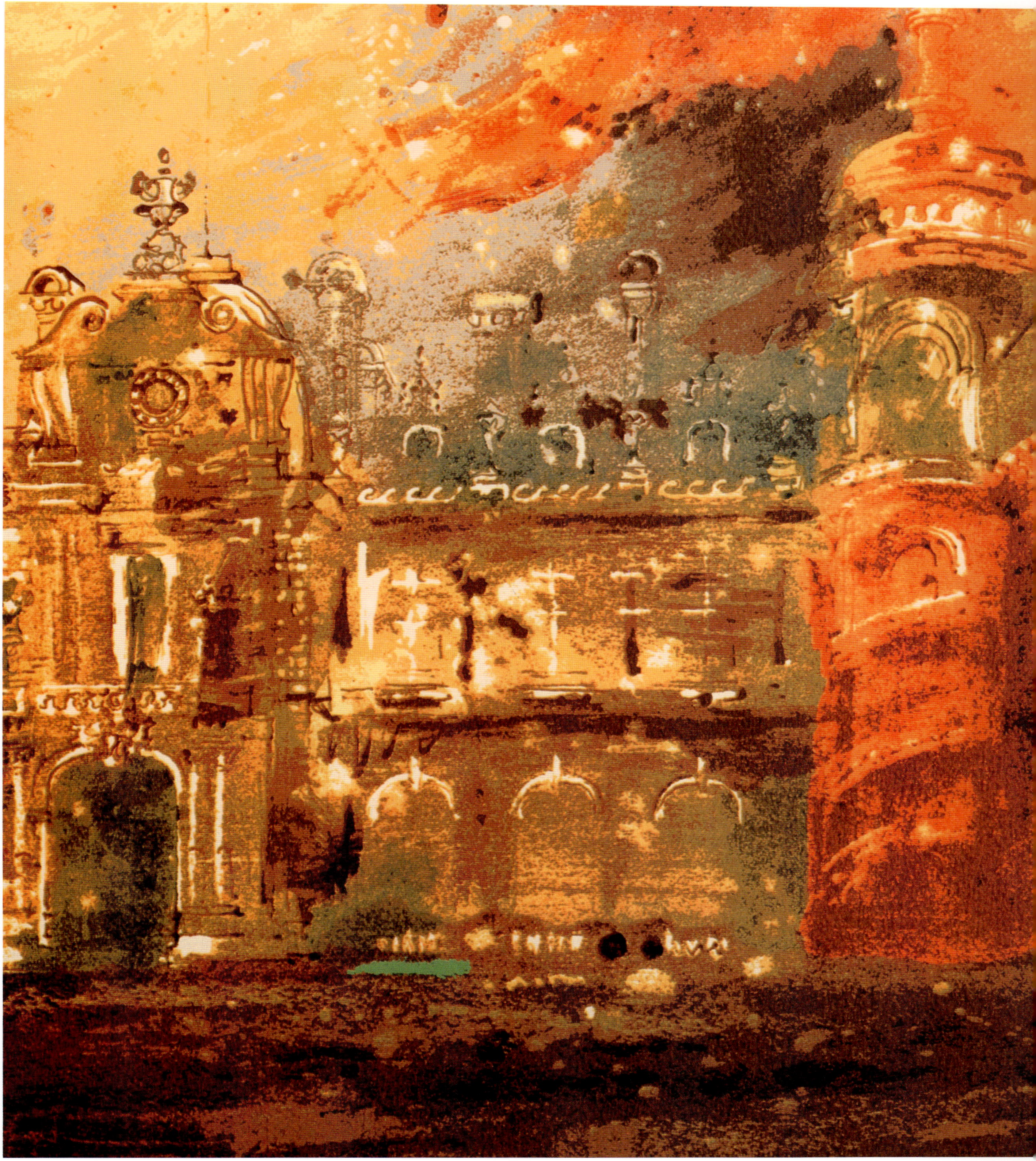

Plate 7
Detail (actual size) from *Waddesdon* 1989
screenprint (Cat.423)

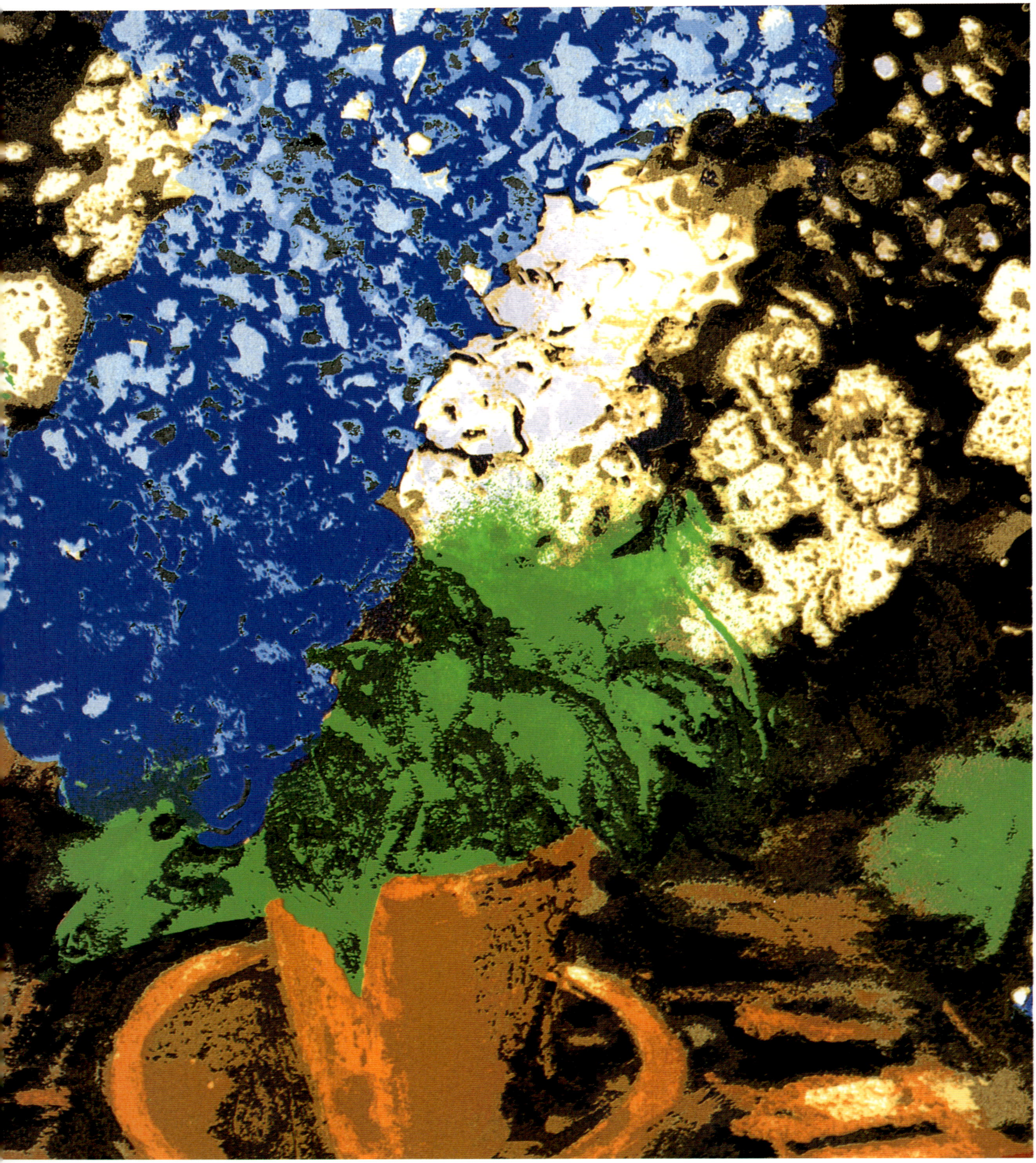

Plate 8
Detail (actual size) from *Blue Hydrangea* 1990
screenprint (Cat.429)

Biographical Notes

'New areas of responsibility, new problems, new materials, new human beings, which are open for co-operation – this is what John Piper is always looking for; what he hates are mired terms and habits'.[1]

This chronology is a catch-all – of places, friends, travels, parents, schooling, commissions and unusual facts, which I believe are all inter-related and have shaped Piper's subject-matter and development.

The early years are covered here in greater detail and reveal a most remarkable and unusual man. Piper's later life is more fully documented in the lists of designs, illustrations and exhibitions that appear at the back of this book. In this section I have therefore concentrated on some of his public honours and duties.

I have not incorporated Myfanwy Piper's activities, although she has been a major element in John's life, not only as his lifelong companion but also as a librettist, writer, travelling companion and critic.[2]

1903
John Egerton Christmas Piper born 13th December at Alresford House, Ashley Road, Epsom, Surrey. His father, Charles Piper, was the senior partner in the solicitors' firm Piper, Smith and Piper at 13 Vincent Square, London. His mother, Mary Matthews, was a working partner in a hat-shop in Stratton Street, Piccadilly, London. Two older brothers: the eldest, Charles, was killed at Ypres in 1915 and the second brother, Gordon, became a partner in his father's solicitors' firm.

Solid and comfortable middle-class family which employed a cook, gardener and housemaids. Victorian house, Alresford House, Epsom, set in about an acre of garden with greenhouse, a tennis court and full-sized billiard room (reproduced as the cover to the first edition of *The Castles on the Ground*, Cat.58).

Father visited churches and made drawings and notes of interesting features, and attended weekly art classes at St Mary's School in Vincent Square.

1910-19
Attended Dame School near Epsom. Drew minute copies of railroads, locomotives and rolling stock.

1913
Uncle Willie Harrison introduced him to Methuen's 'Little Guides' and Pre-Renaissance English architecture. Used his pocket-money to buy *Highways and Byways*, county guide-books published by Macmillan. Visited the Tate Gallery with his father and developed a love for the work of Turner. Read Hilaire Belloc's *The Stane Street*. (Acquired a No.2 Brownie camera.)

1915-17
Began to develop his own films, and as a game, wrote and illustrated his own guide-books. His comparison of his own photographic prints and drawings with those in guide-books led him to question the relationship in art between vision, experience and meaning.

Embarked on a pilgrimage to visit Surrey churches, looking particularly at the stained glass. Kept notes in the form of photographs, illustrations and written text. Began a novel '... full of people going to places in the Upper Thames Valley and descriptions of sunsets and thunderstorms'.[3] Continued copying stained glass until the outbreak of the Second World War and set a pattern of exploration to last until the 1970s of week-long expeditions to places, churches or whatever took his interest.

1919-22
Day-boy at Epsom College, a school also attended by Graham Sutherland. Took art classes.

Piper, his best friend Frank Milward and art master David Birch jointly subscribed to *The Studio* and *Colour* magazines.

John Hilton, one of the first well known broadcasters, took an interest in Piper and widened his horizons by introducing him to G.K. Chesterton and Jean Marchand and choosing books for him to read.

Father Victor Kenna, curate of the Epsom parish church of St Martin's, became a major influence, introducing Piper to contemporary painting, Celtic art, music, scholarship, writers and magazines such as *Wheels*, *Criterion*, *Coterie* and *Arts and Letters*. Became an avid reader of D.H. Lawrence. Rouault and Picasso his two great loves in contemporary art.

Piper played the piano for the Epsom amateur band and in a combo at private dances (3 guineas to hire) and on Saturday night at the Epsom Co-op with Frank Milward (drums) and Antony Curtis (tenor sax). He played music by ear and his preferences were Mozart and Beethoven.

Visited Romney Marsh for the first time with Frank Milward. First encounter with William Blake's work, which greatly impressed him.

1919
Became secretary of the Surrey Archaeological Society. Saw Diaghilev's Ballets Russes productions in London of *The Three-Cornered Hat* and *Parade* (designs by Picasso) and *La Boutique Fantastique* (designs by Derain).

Piper took piano lessons from James McKay Martin, church organist at Fetcham. His father acquired a 'player' piano with large library of Pianola rolls.

1920
Began to keep topographical notebooks of English architecture, with drawings, photographs and summaries of guide-books. Went to great lengths to obtain a book on Rouault, which was only available in French. Won Epsom College Drawing Prize. Designed sets for annual Epsom Congregational Hall musical shows.

c.1921
Admired and copied thirteenth-century stained-glass nave window in the church at Grateley, Hampshire.

1921
Kept a record of car and boat trips with his parents through Oxford and the Cotswolds, and then later in Cambridge and East Anglia. In September visited north and central Italy with his parents. (Progressed from his Brownie to his first sophisticated camera, a second-hand Ideal with a $2\frac{1}{4} \times 3\frac{1}{4}$ Zeiss lens.)

1923–7
Articled clerk in his father's office. During lunch breaks visited the Tate Gallery (which then had only a limited collection of international contemporary art). Admired James Ward's *Gordale Scar*, and works by J. M. W. Turner, John Constable and William Blake.

Established strong friendship with Eden and 'Socrates' Woodger, whom he visited often at Tanhurst House in Langley Bottom. Friendship continued to the early 1930s.

1925
Failed Law Society's examinations (apparently deliberately by publicly announcing he had no intention of continuing with the Law).

1927
Father died. Encouraged by his mother, Piper left Piper, Smith and Piper to study art: accepted by the painting school of the Royal College of Art providing he did a one-year foundation course at Richmond School of Art (a private Victorian house with about forty paying pupils concentrating on arts and crafts). Taught by Raymond Coxon ('by far the best teaching I ever had').[4]

1928
Jim Ede, then an assistant at the Tate Gallery, noticed Piper copying a loaned painting, by Cézanne, befriended him and introduced him to Braque at his house in Hampstead.[5] Piper attended the painting school at the Royal College of Art. Impressed by Francis Spear, who taught lithography and stained glass. Made and mixed his own colours.

Moved to 'Chalkpit Cottage', Betchworth, Surrey, which had been bought for him by his mother at the persuasion of Eden Woodger. To assist, the Woodgers established a building company and erected a studio for Piper on the land.

1929
Left Royal College of Art a year early to marry Eileen Holding, a fellow student from Richmond College of Art. Moved with Eileen to 22 St Peter's Square, Hammersmith, London, retaining the studio at Betchworth. Ceri Richards a neighbour. Financially supported by his mother. Supplemented income by writing art criticism in the *Athenaeum* and *The Nation,* for which he also reviewed books, concerts, plays and films.

Visited Isle of Portland, Dorset.
Made and painted a box as a homage to Braque.

1930s
Interest in jazz extended to his playing jazz tunes on the piano at home.
Preoccupations: churches, stained glass, chapels, beaches, the sea and rocks.

1932
Met Alexander Calder. Created first totally abstract works: mainly constructions with rods, few of which survive, and first collages.

1933–9
Wrote art and theatre criticism and articles in *The Listener*, *New Statesman and Nation*, *Apollo*, *Architectural Review*, *Signature*, *XXe Siècle* and other periodicals. First to champion the work of William Coldstream and the Euston Road School in an article in *The Listener*. Developed a passion for Romanesque church architecture and carving, expressed in articles such as 'England's Early Sculptors', which appeared in the *Architectural Review*. Continued writing after the war (articles rather than criticism).

1933
Friendship with Ivon Hitchens.

1934
January: elected member of the Seven and Five Society and became its Secretary. At the general meeting of the Seven and Five Society approved revised rules allowing only 'non-representational' work to be displayed.

Visited Paris with Eileen.

Summer: met Myfanwy Evans (later to become his wife) while holidaying with Ivon Hitchens at Sizewell, Suffolk. Experimented with collage as his 'way of keeping in touch with natural appearances';[6] first abstract watercolours using collage. Began making abstract relief constructions, and in 1935, totally abstract oil paintings.

Rented a room with Myfanwy in Abbotsbury, near Weymouth, Dorset. Piper began to assist with the layout for *Axis*, a magazine of abstract art edited by Myfanwy and published in eight issues between 1935 and 1937.

Autumn: Myfanwy met Hélion, Mondrian, Jean Arp and Sophie Taeuber-Arp, Brancusi, Giacometti and Kandinsky in Paris.

Separated by mutual agreement from his wife Eileen, who had since become involved with Ceri Richards.

1935–40
Piper felt that he had absorbed the '*classical* exercises' and the 'discipline' of abstraction which 'open a road to ones heart - but they are not the heart itself',[7] and wanted to return to figuration. Ben

Nicholson and Barbara Hepworth were unhappy about this change of direction, seeing it as a betrayal of abstraction.

1935
January: series of BBC radio broadcasts entitled: 'Talks to unemployed clubs'.

February: with Myfanwy rented Fawley Bottom Farmhouse, near Henley-on-Thames, Oxfordshire, their home ever since. (It was later purchased for them by Piper's mother.)

Much excited by an exhibition at the Galerie Pierre, Paris, of Picasso's *papiers collés*. '... deeply impressed by the intense poetry [of them] ...'. Kept a book of his copies of Picasso. Expressed great admiration for Matisse, especially the works of 1914–17.

Began to document, in photographs, lettering, statues, buildings, ironwork, marine architecture and Anglo-Saxon and Romanesque sculpture.

Contributor and chief layout artist to *Axis*. Used new method of colour reproduction, cutting paramat blocks for each colour illustration.

1936
With Robert Wellington and Oliver Simon set up Contemporary Lithographs, which published a series of autolithographs by contemporary artists (over twenty-six eventually produced) printed at Curwen and Baynard Presses.

J.M. Richards succeeded John Betjeman as assistant editior of the *Architectural Review*. Richards commissioned Piper to do work for the *Architectural Review* and introduced him to Betjeman. Betjeman, who had a nickname for everyone, settled on 'Goldilegs' for Myfanwy, and 'Mr Piper' (in a north-country accent) for John.

Formed the Group Theatre with Robert Medley, Stephen Spender, Benjamin Britten, Christopher Isherwood, Rupert Doone and W.H. Auden.

1937–8
Organised for BBC TV seven arts programmes involving artists and craftsmen in discussion: 'London Galleries I'; 'Art and Modern Architecture: Discussion between Piper and Serge Chermayeff'; 'London Galleries II: Pictures in the Modern Home'; 'Modern Art in Stage Design: Piper and Robert Medley'; 'London Galleries IV: Piper and W. Staite Murray on Modern Pottery'; 'London Galleries V: Piper and Others'; 'Artists and their Work, "A trip to the Seaside": Talk by John and Myfanwy Piper'.

1937
First painting trip to Wales.
Friendships with Paul Nash, Frances Hodgkins and Eric Ravilious.
Commissioned by John Betjeman to write Shell Guide to Oxfordshire.
Divorced from Eileen Holding and married Myfanwy Evans.
Visited Stowe in Buckinghamshire for the first time.
September: John and Myfanwy stayed at Varengeville, Normandy with the Calders.
November: Alexander and Louisa Calder and their daughter stayed with the Pipers at Fawley Bottom Farmhouse.

1938–41
Assembled extensive collection of eighteenth-century and early nineteenth-century guide-books. Returned to his interest in Turner.

1938
Abstract mural for the architect Francis Skinner's flat in Highgate, London (later destroyed).
John and Myfanwy toured Ireland with American critic James Johnson Sweeney, particularly looking at Romanesque sculpture.
Piper took lessons in etching and aquatint at Royal College of Art.
Birth of first child, Edward.

1939
Visited Shropshire with John Betjeman.
Considered joining the RAF and spent some time at the air photography centre at Medmenham, then was seconded as a War Artist for the War Artists' Advisory Committee programme initiated by Kenneth Clark.
Joined Church of England.

With Myfanwy devised the paper games the 'Church Game' (drawn) and the 'Guide Book Game' (written), which they played with their friends.

1940–1
Commissioned by Duckworth Press to do a sequel to *Brighton Aquatints* on Stowe (never published as a book, although Piper printed some individual images himself, see Cats 238–44).
Architectural watercolours commissioned by Pilgrim Trust for *Recording Britain*.
Commissioned by War Artists' Advisory Committee to paint bombed buildings, including the House of Commons (1941).

Visitors to Fawley Bottom during the war years included Osbert Lancaster, Geoffrey Grigson, John Betjeman.

1940
Met Sir Osbert Sitwell, who had admired and favourably reviewed Piper's *Brighton Aquatints* of 1939.

1941–2
Commissioned by Sir Osbert Sitwell to paint Renishaw Hall and by Queen Elizabeth (now the Queen Mother) to make twenty-four paintings of Windsor Castle.
Met Evelyn Waugh at Renishaw Hall, home of the Sitwells. Declined Waugh's proposal that Piper should illustrate *Brideshead Revisited* (still in manuscript form) with imaginary landscapes.[9]

1942
Birth of second child, Clarissa.

1943
Murals at British Restaurant, London.
Commissioned by Edward Sackville-West to paint Knole.
Considered a book of etchings and aquatints on 'farmyard chapels'. This was never realised, although Cats 29–33 would have formed part of it.
Met the art critic John Russell, a friend for life.
Visited the quarries in the Manod Mountains in Snowdonia where the National Gallery paintings were being stored. Commissioned by the War Artist's Advisory Committee to paint the interior cavern.
Painted in Devon and Cornwall.

1944
Appointed Official War Artist, attached to Ministry of War Transport. Made frequent visits to Wales.

1945
S. John Woods, Art Director of Ealing Studios, commissioned Piper to design film posters.

1946
Appointed Trustee of the Tate Gallery (served May 1946 – May 1953, November 1954 – November 1961 and January 1968 – October 1974 (as National Gallery Liaison Trustee).
Visited Snape Maltings. Returned almost yearly. Visited Snowdonia.
As Fawley Bottom Farmhouse was still without electricity, used an upstairs room at Stonor Park for the following years as a dark-room for developing photographs.

1947
Painted at Montegufoni, near Florence, for Sir Osbert Sitwell, and at Romney Marsh.
Birth of third child, Suzannah.
Established with Eric Crozier and Benjamin Britten the English Opera Group. Britten and Piper first Artistic Directors.
Frances Hodgkins died aged seventy-eight. The Pipers were executors of her estate.

1948
Painted in Portland, Snowdonia.
Employed on a year's 'retainer' basis to do cover designs for Chapman and Hall Ltd.
Invited by Clifford and Rosemary Ellis to become a governing member of Bath Academy of Art, which then occupied premises at Corsham Court, outside Bath.

1949
Murals for British Embassy, Rio de Janeiro.
Met Reynolds Stone and proposed a guide-book of Snowdonia to be illustrated with wood engravings by Stone after drawings by Piper. Project never realised.
Moved studio from front room of Fawley Bottom Farmhouse to adjacent converted cowshed.
In the winter, rented rooms in 'Bodesi', a farmhouse above Llyn Ogwen in Snowdonia and continued to visit throughout the 1950s.
Met the choreographer John Cranko, with whom he was to collaborate throughout the rest of Cranko's life.
Declined an invitation by the Prime Minister to become a CBE.

1950–4
Painted a number of studies of Old Masters including Poussin's *Massacre of the Innocents* and Giorgione's *The Tempest*.

1950
Commissioned to design mural for exterior of 'Houses and Gardens Pavilion' at the Festival of Britain and, with Osbert Lancaster, decoration of 'Main Vista'.
Member of Oxford Diocesan Advisory Committee (until his death).
Birth of fourth child, Sebastian.

1951
Mural *The Englishman's Castle* for the *Observer* exhibition at the National Gallery.
Appointed to Ballet Advisory Panel, Royal Opera House (reappointed until 1957).
First designs for stained glass to be interpreted by Patrick Reyntiens.

1952
With Myfanwy and a group of friends restored the Kenton Theatre, Henley-on-Thames. Piper designed the proscenium arch.
Appointed member of the Arts Council Art Panel (to 1957).

1953–63
Painted in France (first paintings of foreign landscapes).
Drawings and photographs of medieval roof bosses: transformed into the 'Foliate Heads' which appeared frequently in his work from then on.

1954
Visited Venice and on way back studied stained glass at Bourges and Chartres.

1955–7
Trips to France including to Charente, Toulouse, Moissac, Dordogne.

1955
Mural *Man's Relation with Nature* for Mayo Clinic, Rochester, Minnesota.

1957
Elected Honorary Associate of the Royal Institute of British Architects.
Saw Léger's stained glass at Audincourt and Le Corbusier's at Ronchamp.
Mother died aged ninety-three.

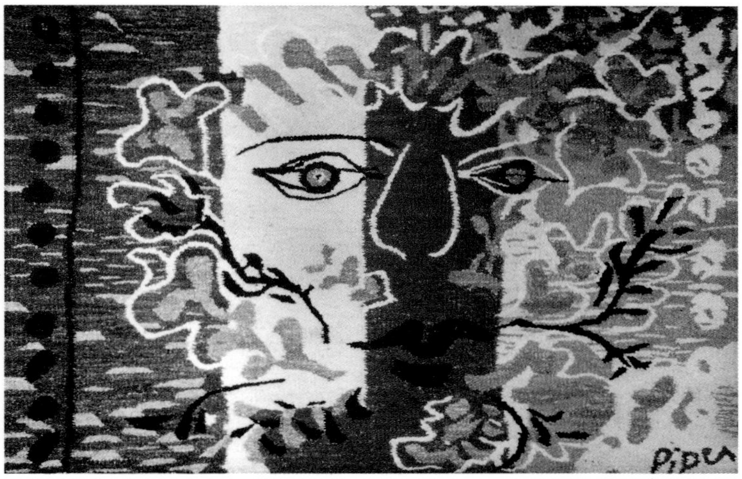

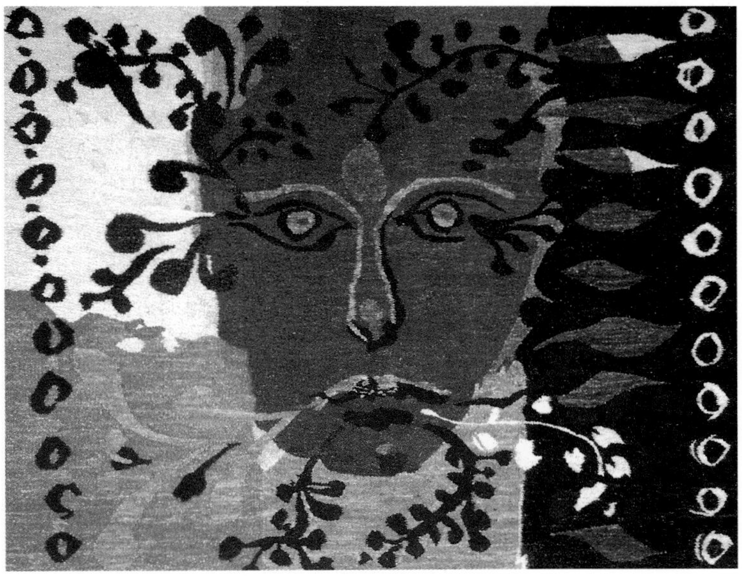

Top: *Foliate Head: blue to yellow* 1976 tapestry
Bottom: *Foliate Head: blue to brown* 1983 tapestry. Photograph: Miki Slingsby

Appointed Visitor to the Department of Engraving, Royal College of Art.
Awarded third prize (painting section) in the Hallmark Art Award, New York.
Declined offer of Visiting Professorship at Washington University.
Converted large barn at Fawley Bottom Farmhouse to enable him to work on full-size stained-glass cartoons.

1958
Murals for Morley College, London.
Abstract mural for west wall of the main entrance hall, BBC Television Centre, London.
Painted in Venice and Roussillon.
Elected Associate Member and Fellow of the British Society of Master Glass-painters (resigned 1963).

1959
Member of Royal Fine Art Commission (retired 1977).
Fabric design for Arthur Sanderson & Sons Ltd, London.
Designs for mosaic for St Paul's Church, Harlow and for a series of mosaic tables executed by Dennis Williams.
Painted in Venice, Burgundy and Aix-en-Provence.
Elected Honorary Fellow of the Royal College of Art.

1960–5
Art politics dominated the British contemporary art scene during this period and a division emerged, centering around John Rothenstein, then Director of the Tate Gallery, and Douglas Cooper. Piper, as a Trustee of the Tate, refused to become involved. This made him 'the target of a sustained campaign of derision and denigration'.[10] Furthermore, at this time there was a resurgence in abstraction (which Piper had rejected in the 1930s) and a lack of interest in works on paper (Piper's most prolific medium), all of which may have contributed to the misunderstanding of his art.

1960
Abstract murals for SS *Oriana*.
Mosaic for Chamber of Commerce, Edgbaston, Birmingham.
Co-selector with John Commander of exhibition *Modern Stained Glass* for Arts Council.
Awarded Honorary Doctorate of Letters, University of Leicester.

1961
Visited stained-glass factory at Darmstadt, Germany.
Designed the conversion of loft to chapel at Nuffield College, including the altar, glass and furnishings.
Visited Brittany, Rome and Switzerland.

1962
Designed murals for North Thames Gas Board and vestments for Coventry Cathedral.
Acquired cottage 'Garn Fawr', at Trefasser near Strumble Head, Pembrokeshire, with about fourteen acres of small, stony fields and remains of an Iron Age camp.

1963
Awarded prize for lithography by Vietnamese Government.
Worked in Italy and Wales. (Acquired a Hasselblad camera.)

1964
Theale Green School, near Reading, named a House after Piper.

1965
Member of management committee for the opening of the Museum of Modern Art, Oxford. Associate member of MOMA council until his death.

1966
Made Honorary Doctor of Letters, University of Oxford.

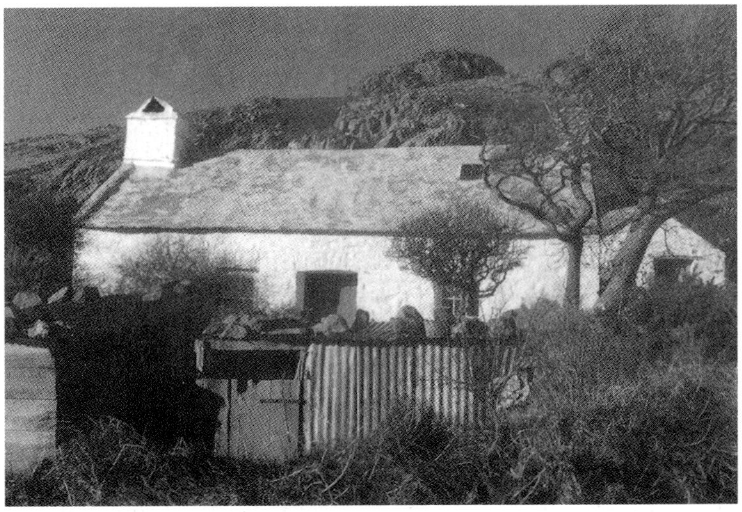

'Garn Fawr', Pembrokeshire. Photograph: Tate Gallery Archive

1967
Appointed Trustee of the National Gallery (reappointed until 1977).

1968
12th August: first-day cover in second series of 'British Paintings' stamps illustrated an oil painting by Piper.
Created pottery studio at Fawley Bottom and with assistance of Geoffrey Eastop began to work in ceramics.

1971
Elected Honorary Fellow of the Royal Institute of British Architects.

1972
Made Companion of Honour.
Awarded the Gold Medal of the Commune of Lucca.
Mrs Heinemann, wife of the President of West Germany, paid a courtesy call on the Pipers during State visit to Britain.

1974
Made Honorary Doctor of Letters, University of Sussex.

1981
Made Honorary Doctor of Literature, University of Wales.

1983-4
Tate Gallery organised a one-man exhibition of Piper's work on the occasion of his eightieth birthday.

1984-5
Donated all of his photographic negatives (about 5000) to Tate Gallery Archives.

1984
Given the Freedom of the City of Reading.

1985
Made Honorary Doctor of Letters, University of Oxford (second award), and made Honorary Doctor of Letters, University of Leeds.
Elected Honorary Fellow of Robinson College, Cambridge.

1986
Fawley Bottom Farmhouse listed as a Grade II building.

1987
Elected Honorary Fellow of St Cross College, Oxford.

1990
Piper's son Edward died.

1992
28th June: John Piper died at Fawley Bottom Farmhouse.
Buried, Fawley Churchyard; funeral service, Fawley Bottom Farmhouse.

1. Myfanwy Piper, John Piper, *John Piper*, exh. cat. Baukunst, Cologne, 1965, translated by Dierk Rosenberg, London, 1996. ['Neue Aufgabengebiete, neue Probleme, neue Materialien, neue Menschen, die zur Zusammenarbeit bereit sind - danach ist John Piper immer auf der Suche; was er haßt, sind festgefahrene Begriffe und Gewohnheiten'.]
2. In 1937, aged twenty-six, Myfanwy Evans, an Oxford graduate in English and a blue in swimming, had already published, among other things, her *The Painter's Object*, an important document which included articles by Léger, Moore, Hélion, Nash, Ozenfant, Kandinsky, Calder, Piper, Ernst, Picasso, Sutherland, de Chirico, Moholy-Nagy and Trevelyan
3. Tate, p.16
4. Ingrams/Piper, p.15
5. His later home was Kettle's Yard, Cambridge, which he acquired in 1957 and which still contains his art collection
6. Ingrams/Piper, p.22
7. John Piper, letter to Paul Nash, 12th January 1943, Tate, p.38
8. Ingrams/Piper, p.21
9. It is possible that the artist Charles Ryder in *Brideshead Revisited* was based at least in part on Piper
10. West, p.153

Working with Printers
John Piper

In 1926, before I finished my reluctant years in the law, I met Miles Marshall of the Marshall Press, an old-fashioned printing works in Milford Lane off the Strand. They printed and published *Foulsham's Almanack*, *The Bird Fancier's Gazette* and other mysteries. As I often had to go from my father's office in Victoria to the Law Courts, Miles and I would meet for lunch and then go back to the works and talk about type faces and type books, look at all the lovely paper and card samples, watch things coming off the machines and smell the pervasive printer's ink. There I probably realized for the first time what a lot there was to be learnt from perfectly ordinary non-art expertise. When, years later, Myfanwy told me that she intended to start a quarterly magazine of Abstract Art *Axis*, it was Miles who suggested we got in touch with the printers Hunt Barnard of Aylesbury. They had not at the time done much 'fine art' printing, nor were they familiar with any kind of modern art, let alone abstract. But the manager, Mr Johnson, puzzled and amazed as he was, took immense trouble to do what we wanted and to help us find ways of doing what we would like to do but could not afford. I like to think that it was partly his conscientious interest in the production of *Axis* that later made Hunt Barnard much sought after for the printing of 'fine art' books.

Half-tone blocks for *Axis* were made by The Elite Process Engraving Co (a name we much enjoyed) in Gray's Inn Road – another helpful, grimey London works. The Scotch manager succeeded in being obsequious, patronizing, cross and co-operative all at the same time and the blocks were good. But on the few occasions that we could run to colour we wanted something livelier as well as cheaper than the orthodox three-colour half-tones that they could have provided. I cribbed a method used in the advertising world: Paramat blocks. They consisted of a thin sheet of aluminium mounted by a thin sheet of rubber composition which could be cut away with a model maker's knife to leave the area required in relief which could then be inked and printed. One or two pictures, a Miró for example, could be done purely by this method but others, notably a small Picasso head, needed a half-tone as well. It needed a lot of juggling and getting the blocks in register was often a nightmare. It was a poor man's parallel to the French 'pochoir' process, all hand done, involving girls with stencils and which produced beautiful results in pricey art books in Paris. It was also at one time used by the Curwen Press.

This rather lengthy exposition is to explain how much I have relied on and enjoyed working with experts in their own job and have tried to adapt both their techniques and mine for my own ends. That is what, for me, prints have been about.

I first experienced the world of printing and lithography that was both posh *and* ingenious, that is to say quality *and* experiment, through friendship with Oliver Simon of the Curwen Press. He kept the press nourished and in touch through his quadrimestrial publication *Signature* (a must for all members of the Double-Crown Club). He subscribed to *Axis* from the beginning and was much interested in the lengths we went to on our shoe-string, sometimes using my discoveries himself. He even encouraged me to reproduce a Miró which had been painted on glass paper, on *real glass paper*, and bound it into *Signature*. One of the things I most enjoyed in the old Curwen lithography studio at Plaistow in those early days was picking discarded sheets off the floor: once a whole lot of music sheets (Curwen had been much involved with lithographic printing of music) that had been used to clean the presses. The relentless lines with their musical notation had been smudged and criss-crossed, and looked very abstract and handsome. I put them in my own portfolio of paper for collages.

The first time I used letterpress print was in one of the images for *Brighton Aquatints*. The plates were printed by the two brothers Alexander in a basement workshop in Henrietta Street, Covent Garden. They were very old and highly skilled. In her Catalogue for the Arts Council Exhibition *The Mechanised Image, an Historical Perspective of Twentieth Century Prints*, the well-known print authority Pat Gilmour writes: 'There were even earlier attempts to knit process and autography together, John Piper in a book of aquatints of Brighton, begun just before World War II, suggested patterns of brickwork by photo-engraving typography onto his plate before beginning etching …'.

I was not much concerned with prints for a time, but quite suddenly three opportunities to produce lithographs presented themselves, which kept me busy for some time. First, there was Robert Erskine who was running an enterprising gallery in the early fifties in Central London and he was commissioning lithographs. He was in contact with Mourlot Frères in Paris, who were Picasso's favourite lithographic printers, and I went over there for two or three weeks and produced a number of sheets for him, and also for Curt Valentin in New York, at whose gallery I had already had two shows of paintings and drawings. So at Curt's request I did a few sheets for him. Two of the images (for Robert Erskine) were more complicated than all the others, requiring seven colours besides black, but the master printer made a plan of work dividing the surface into two areas with the two hand rollers charged with different colours on each side (Cats 83 and 84). The printer's name was Célestin, and I was most impressed with the dense and compelling colour he achieved in his printing.

At this time Robert Erskine was also in touch with Harley Brothers, an efficient though old-fashioned firm of litho printers in Edinburgh. The manager and chief operative was a man who appeared to enjoy his work enormously, and took it very seriously and had some fine results. But within a couple of years the firm had gone bankrupt, and this excellent fellow had disappeared without trace overnight. Meanwhile the firm did some very well-printed editions, all listed here.

This was my second opportunity. The third came when Marlborough Graphics suggested a series of lithographs all related to English churches or details of them, exploring the different techniques available in the whole gamut of the lithographic art, or as many as possible. This was a suggestion made by Harry Fischer, whose careful concern to find suitable and inspiring projects for his artists produced some ingenious ideas that were totally appropriate.

I was lucky enough to find that Stanley Jones of the Curwen Press was available and willing to put the whole plan into action. Together we explored, talked and explored some more – always in promising moments backed by his wide experience of possibilities and impossibilities – and began to tackle the first of twenty-four. I made quite a few boss shots, but we gradually built up a series of twelve (first) and then another twelve. Stones and plates were used according to the technique involved, sometimes with a 'minimal' effect, sometimes a crowded and varied one. With Stanley's constant encouragement I used many different kinds of texturing by rubbing, scratching and spotting, much resort to transfer paper, flooded in places with black and then hardly touched except by a few simple lines and a simple pattern of one colour. One or two had areas of photographic prints (my own) applied mechanically to the plate. Pat Gilmour also refers to this in the same catalogue: 'Since he was adept with a camera, it's not surprising that he was well to the fore in breaking down post-war prejudice against the use of photographic images in art, utilising their rather literal ability to suggest the starkly Non-Conformist chapels – such as Llangloffan.'

In the early sixties, Chris Prater made the first screenprints of my work. Those first prints from the Kelpra Studios were a new experience in my graphic life. He not only made beautiful prints of places but, by his enthusiasm for and brilliant realization of the *Eye and Camera* series, in which I had pursued my interest in combining drawing and photography, encouraged me to continue them in the face of a certain resigned silence from others.

It has often been said that the involvement of the artist in screenprints is not a true involvement because he doesn't always make them himself as he does a lithograph. True, but the chemistry is of a different kind. When Chris first made prints of my work, I realized that here was a matter of empathy – or rather a double empathy, mine for my picture and his for my picture. Over the years, when he has come to the studio, he will pick up a work and see something in it that I hadn't seen, and when he works on something he often brings out an aspect of it that was not emphasized, even not exactly understood. He recreates, but he doesn't invent things that are not there. His patience is infinite. If a colour is not right (for both of us), or the relationship is wrong he will change it, if still wrong will add an extra colour, or colours. He is an artist in personal relations as well as in colour or tone relations. I never feel that I have finished with a work if I have given it to him to work on and I firmly believe that good screenprints are a double act.

I have always liked working with other people and in other media. I hate parties but I love working parties.

Fawley Bottom Farmhouse, February 1987

1 Piper discussing *Surgères* (Cat.112) with the printer at Harley Brothers, 1958. Photograph: Piper Archives
2 Chris Prater, 1986
3 Nigel Oxley at Kelpra Studio, 1986
4 Piper with Chris Prater, 1986. Photograph by Susan Kay
5 Stanley Jones, 1986

2

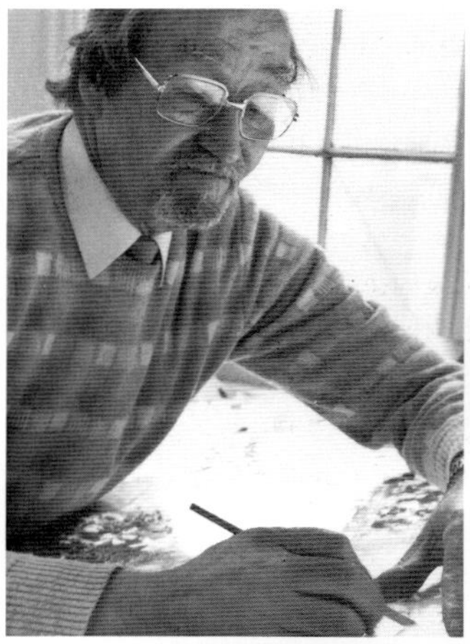

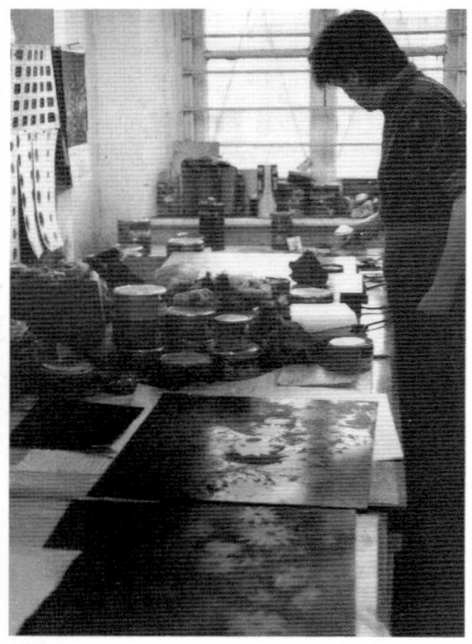

3

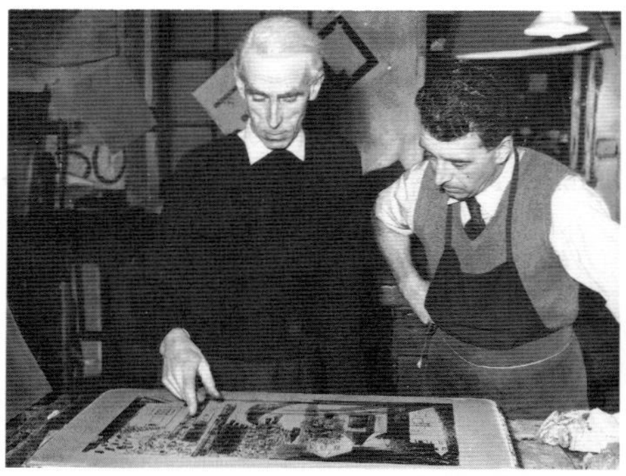

1

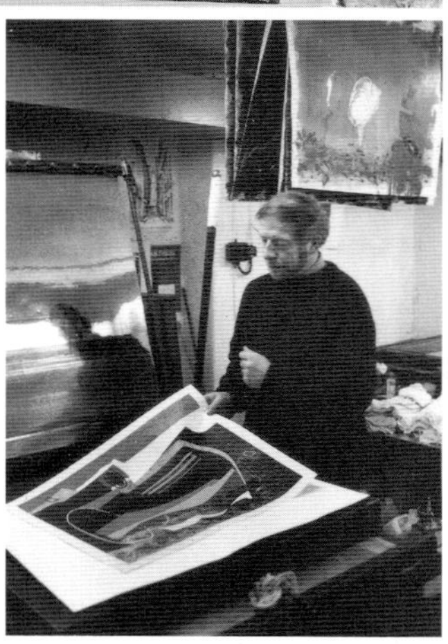

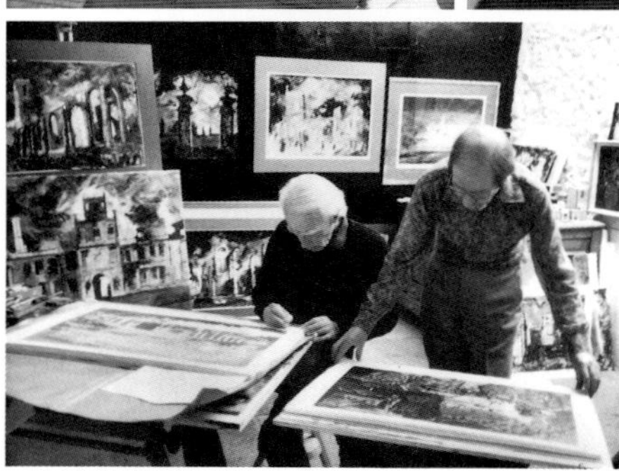

4

5

Extracts from Writings by John Piper

The tradition, once more, has to stretch. It always has to stretch – must be forced if necessary even to bursting point – to include anything and everything that has a pointed reference to life, however little it appears to agree, or to be able to shake down comfortably with what has gone before it, or what we feel has got to come after, in point of time. People think it dishonest to be chameleon-like in one's artistic allegiances. On the other hand, I think it dishonest to be anything else. Not only must one change one's spots or stripes or other outward markings according to the influences one truly experiences, within oneself, but surely one's whole nature, aesthetic-sensually, as it were, should be susceptible of change. André Breton's remarks at the opening of the Surrealist Exhibition in London last year – 'Changez la vue … Changez la vie!' have almost as much validity as Blake's 'Prudence is a rich, ugly old maid courted by Incapacity'.

'Aspects of Modern Drawing', 1937. See no.26 in 'Writings by John Piper' on p.177 of the present volume

I think this has been an age where particularly one has needed to change. People have had a great example, of course, in Picasso who changes all the time. But he merely reflects a need of our age. I think that the way he has developed and changed is a necessity of the first half of the twentieth century … I feel I have derived a great … [deal] … from doing lithography and etching and aquatint – and all the allied crafts; the things we do in the theatre – the rough and ready way of making fabrics for costumes. Or the techniques of silk-screen printing. And if I read backwards to my ordinary oil, water-colours or inks from these techniques, I sometimes find myself saying, 'How would I do this in lithography?' I know I would scratch it, or perhaps gum it out for printing – or something else. And this enriches one's own technique in oil and water-colour. It's safe to say that Picasso derived a great deal of change and benefit from all the pottery he made at Vallauris. Undoubtedly. Not a direct influence possibly, but something he got from using his hands and the colour, and the way he put the decorations on the pottery. He didn't do that simply for the fun of making pots. He did it to enrich his own technique and life.

Conversations with Painters, 1964. See no.157 on p.179

Things that came out in magazines. I copied them, spending an immense amount of winter evenings, copying Picassos, and I made a whole book of Picasso before there ever was a book on Picasso. Mostly drawings and things which I printed through on this contact paper from a book in the London Library. It was my form of learning the actual technique of drawing and painting. I did very elaborate copies of stained glass at that time, too, which still exist. The camera was awfully useful for that sort of thing. You could take a close-up with a wide-angle lens, for instance, and I'd take photographs of something I didn't have time to copy standing up on the window ledge and then add it to the copy that I'd done. But not colour, never colour! I never took a colour photograph at all, until well after the War. I don't suppose there was much colour film until after the War, anyway.

'The Arbitrary Eye', 1983. See no.223 on p.181

A lot of craft workers in my view make a great mistake in thinking their craft is self-sufficient, because it satisfies fairly permanent urges in them. I don't believe this is so at all. It can't be. They've only got a few ideas until they work out some new ideas – like living on the products of the garden for one year for ever. They don't re-sow the seeds next year at all; and if they don't do that, they turn over in the same spot and do the same thing over and over and over.

I don't think there are any secrets in art – I think everything should be shared and, if there are any secrets, it's high time to shout them from the rooftops. I'm referring, of course, to all methods of technique and new discoveries. If people say 'This is a secret of mine' and they won't share it, then it's not worth having. One can usually tell, you know.

Conversations with Painters, 1964. See no.157 on p.179

It is the business of the interpretative craftsman not just to interpret a design into the language of his craft, but to re-create it as a lively image. A designer may understand tapestry thoroughly, may be learned in its history and contemporary practice and possibilities, but design remains design until someone's imagination brings it to life in the new medium. I have had the pleasure – thrill is really a more appropriate word – of seeing this happen with my own designs for the stage, for colour reproduction, for stained glass and for tapestry.

Master Weavers: Tapestries from the Dovecot Studios, 1980. See no.209 on p.180

It is the interpretative illustrator that has always been the curse – and still is, as the present book proves again. The examples with a primarily embellishing intention – those by Picasso, Léger, Dufy, Braque, Alexander Calder, for instance – are so much happier in result than those … in any sort of didactic mood (aesthetic merit itself apart). Rockwell Kent's drawing for *Moby Dick* may be taken as a horrible warning. It interprets *Moby Dick* in a personal and, as it happens, an indecently sentimental-tough-guy manner. Charles Demuth's explanatory water-colour for *The Turn of the Screw* is another bad example. Not that it is bad drawing, but it is stultifying to any natural growth of feeling that a sensitive reader must experience in a novel by Henry James. It not only adds nothing to the text, but in effect it forces the text back on itself, so that its meaning is everywhere curbed and mortified by the special significance of Demuth's lines and washes. It would be better by far to use old half-tone blocks from the *Daily Mirror* to illustrate Henry James – and perhaps that is not an absurd suggestion, for they would have the actuality, the impersonality and the period flavour of the writing: about the only qualities that illustrators of it need.

So the best here, as in the early wall-painting, the painted-glass panel and the carved capital, are the least personal – whether it is the impersonality of greatness they possess (Picasso, *Le Chef-d'œuvre Inconnu*) or the impersonality of good craftsmanship (Despiau, *Poèmes de Baudelaire*, for want of a better example). For in these Picasso drawings there is an absence of sentiment, lewdness, prudery and every other single *chosen* virtue and vice that gives a picture a personal, distracting quality. If Picasso had shown nothing else by his work he would at least have demonstrated again that personality is a thing to be avoided rather than wooed in book illustration – as in any other form of art indeed, except, perhaps, interior decoration and popular acting.

Review of *Modern Painters and Sculptors as Illustrators*, 1937. See no.25 on p.177

You don't take the other things, you just take the things you are trying to see. When I was photographing 'golliwogs'[1] I didn't look at anything else much. Well, I didn't look at anything with the camera in mind. I'm perfectly capable of photographing cows, for instance. In fact, I think I shall do some cows because I've done one or two paintings with cows in, and I've suddenly seen cows as I wanted to see them, or think I can. And now that I've painted cows I think I might conceivably be able to photograph them. That's another way of pointing out that I photograph from paintings – that really is a literal description of it – it's the best description I've given you yet.

'The Arbitrary Eye', 1983. See no.223 on p.181

1 Author's note: This is the name that the distinguished art historian and archaeologist A.W. Clapham used when referring to the more primitive manifestions of Romanesque sculpture.

I know perfectly well that I would rather paint a ruined abbey half-covered with ivy and standing among long grass than I would paint it after it has been taken over by the Office of Works, when they have taken all the ivy off and mown all the grass with an Atco. And also I would rather paint a new house when it's twenty years old than when it's new. You can call it reaction, or prejudice, or anything you like – but sitting down to paint a new house would give me the same feeling as sitting down to paint a new-born baby. It's just one of those things I'd rather not do.

Wrought-iron lamps, gates and balustrades, station hotels in fading brick, expanses of promenade with a shelter or two – all the things that are usually referred to as the 'egregious architectural excesses of the Victorian era' – all these things have lately fallen into the lap of the painter of architecture. It is not a question of taste. It is not a vague searching-after-something-new-to-admire that makes me like them as subjects. It is the fact that time has presented them to us as splendid subjects, as things of beauty, as part of a valuable tradition.

'John Piper at the AA', 1941. See no.55 on p.177

I think the discipline of Cubism and the styles which followed Cubism have been a great help to me, as they were to other painters of my generation. They made me realise the absolute need, however romantic or sentimental one wanted to be, for extreme discipline in painting. Otherwise the goods simply would not be delivered. I hope this discipline is more obvious in my work to-day. I hope it has taken a lot of the unnecessary rhetoric away, and that I'm left with something more worth having. My painting is just as romantic, but I hope it's more unified, more united.

Conversations with Painters, 1964. See no.157 on p.179

The Classical Theory is based on an abstract idea of perfection, the romantic on a subjective use of particular details and moods of nature. The subjective artist who does not particularise and define makes no progress but loses himself in a miasma, and becomes a sham romantic. Blake, always intent on definition, in no sense a sham, and a madman only to fools, was a dangerous enemy of academies, schools and officials. And still is so.

British Romantic Artists, 1942. See no.59 on p.177

Montpellier-de-Didonne, Charente; St Raphael, Dordogne; Jazenne, Charente; Besse, Dordogne; St Amand-de-Coly, Dordogne; La Chapelle St Robert, Dordogne; Moutou; Creysse, Dordogne; Garn Fawr; Woodman's Cottage, Charente.
The titles are the names of places, meaning that there was an involvement *there*, at a special time: an experience affected by the weather, the season and the country, but above all concerned with the exact location and its spirit for me. The spread of moss on a wall, a pattern of vineyards or a perspective of hop-poles may be the peg, but it is not hop-poles or vineyards or church towers that these pictures are meant to be about, but the emotion generated by them at one

moment in one special place. They are about what Paul Nash liked to call the *genius loci*. Romantic painting is about the particular, not the general. I have enjoyed the fields and stone walls and smart hills of south-west Wales, and the darker, more insular-feeling West of Scotland landscape, and the poplars and water-meadows and the figs and mistletoe and walnuts of northern and central France.

European Topography, 1969. See no.173 on p.179

The wall is the Universal Exhibitor, and has been from the time when mammoths were scratched on the walls of prehistoric caves. If you consider the way people at any time have dealt with walls (in medieval times, for example), you see how everything that is embedded in them, or depends from them, is indicative of the period's art. The Romanesque arch, or wall-arcade, is the perfect geometrical wall object. At its most elaborate it could be no less fussy than a Victorian overmantel mirror. The medieval architect took every opportunity of objectifying his walls. Wall-tombs, wall-paintings, door-cases, window-frames, cornices, wall-arcades, sedilias, reredoses, corbels, gargoyles, niches with figures, flying buttresses – every wall, outside and in, was plastered with things.

'Notes on Wall Objects Old and New', 1938. See no.41 on p.177

The guide book writers encourage us all to look at churches as 'objects of interest' rather than as objects of beauty.

When Cotman did his hundreds of drawings of Norfolk churches for Dawson Turner, the banker-archaeologist of Yarmouth, he found rich beauties in every building he visited. He found against the weathered masonry of a chancel east wall a decaying wooden sexton's shed, with the old uneven glass of the east window rising above it. He drew round-towered churches with bulging walls and moss-grown roofs that stay precariously among scythed grass on treacherous ground in the East Anglian marshes. He found infinite beauty in a porch doorway made of palings, and the view beyond it through an unrestored Norman door of a font and the panelling of a high-backed pew. His drawings, and the engravings he did from them, are living records of pre-Victorian church beauty. Such beauty is still to be found, though not in every church, as it was in those days.

'Grey Tower and Panelled Pew', 1940. See no.49 on p.179

For just as a baker is a baker, so an artist is an artist, and if he is a Christian, it is likely that he will do his best work for the church. Among the best artists of the nineteenth century were the sculptors whose works are now so often hidden away behind organs, or are out of general sight behind the tower screen. In calling such monuments 'hideous' we are pitting our taste against the taste of believers of a previous age, whose thought and whose religious attitude we do not necessarily comprehend.

There is a feeling that art in a church must teach; but surely, if it is good art, it does teach, without laying down laws or doctrines, or telling stories that may be better told in words.

'The Artist and the Church', 1946. See no.91 on p.178

I am a painter and draughtsman of landscape and architecture. I am more fitted by birth and environment to enjoy painting such subjects than any others. And since painting is physically and mentally an arduous task it is necessary to have every encouragement – like this enjoyment of subject – if you are going to persist in it for long. Otherwise, as with any other full-time job that you think about most of the time, when you are not actually working, as well as when you are, you are likely to get bored and irritated, and to dissipate your energies, whenever the opportunity occurs, in relaxations. And you soon begin to make such opportunities.

... This does not mean that I paint landscapes and architecture all the time. Doing that, it would be easy to get into a rut. For doing exactly what you think you like all the time makes you feel in the end that nothing at all is worth doing.

For five years I painted nothing but abstract pictures, which I found a good discipline: especially then, ten years ago, when there were so many 'directions' and 'isms' that it was difficult for a student to know which way to turn. I found abstract painting helpful because it taught me something of the value of clear colours, one against another, when they have no goods to deliver except themselves. Some colours seem to advance in front of other colours, others seem to retire; some 'kill' others, while some seen to make others more vivid.

... But I think the best subject to return to (and a good painter always, in one sense, remains a student) is the nude. Because, in the human figure you can find simple forms and subtle forms combined better than in any other subject. Also, because you can easily recognise any positive mistakes you make when you draw and paint it. If you draw a tree and add a big branch that isn't there, or add two or three big branches, so long as they join onto the trunk properly, nobody is any the wiser. But if you make a head too big for a body, let alone adding an extra leg to the human trunk, you can see what you have done at once; and you have done it for one of three reasons – you tried, and failed, to get it 'right', you did it to be funny, or you did it for some symbolic purpose. The human form, to humans, is the best-known and most easily recognised form of all, which means that we notice more of the subtle variation in it than in any other form. One sunflower is much like another sunflower, except perhaps to a botanist; but we all recognise one human being from the next.

But, in general, for me, the subject is landscape and architecture. I believe it is necessary in these days, to like, and even if possible to love, your subject: 'in these days' because there is a great deal of hate about, and there are many temptations to paint 'hate' pictures. In the past 'hate' pictures have by no means always been bad pictures, but to-day the artist, in so far as he is a leader, has an urge to counterbalance, rather than to increase, hatred.

... I am not interested in 'copying' what is in front of me. I find copying *pictures* very useful and enjoyable up to a point, but copying *nature* is a different affair. It is, at the best, a dull occupation, though I much enjoy using a camera, and find taking photographs of people and places a good jog to the memory: and they can help you to see and record things in a fresh light, or an aspect that had not struck you before. Naturalistic painting can, probably, do the same thing; but it would seem to me a duller occupation than any of the crafts such as weaving, or basket-making or thatching or brick-laying. 'Good' painting has never been naturalistic painting. What is it, then? That is not so much a mystery as a thing it is impossible to describe in words, though a good critic – a rarity – will sometimes suggest what it is. Good paintings in the long run tell their own story – though not in words – to those who have intent eyes, an open mind, and much patience. There is no quick, and no other, road to being able to tell a good painter from a bad one.

The nearest I can get to describing what I try to do in painting is to say that I want to make a pictorial parallel for what I see, complete in itself and yet *derived* from nature – a lively symbol that seems to belong in a picture frame. I know when I have done it, up to my own limit, but it is never completely satisfactory to me; and I always go on trying to do better. After a time you get interested; it becomes an absorbing occupation, and you cannot stop.

... I draw in pencil, black and coloured inks, chalks (both pastel and greasy-crayon kind), water-colour, gouache [opaque water-colour rather like distemper] and oils. All except the last I *sometimes* combine in one work. I see no reason why gouache should not be combined with water-colour in the same work, though it is against traditional and conventional practice ...

As a rule, I use inks and water-colours out-of-doors, sometimes adding several pages of written notes, or sketched notes, about colours and tones, relative shapes and proportions of parts of a subject. All these I take home and, at leisure, with the aid of 'squaring up' (making relatively-sized squares of the same number on the original drawing and on the larger canvas), and with the aid, too, of all the paraphernalia of a home-studio (easel, brushes, turpentine and linseed oil, large palette of glass or metal, rags, constant and well-known light) paint in oils from them. The careful deliberation allowed by working later in the studio gives me time to reconsider, and make more careful and leisurely statements. One can lose 'freshness' doing this; but 'freshness' belongs to the out-of-doors sketch, probably; and sometimes this is complete enough in itself.

The trouble is to keep up a really *interested* feeling for your subject *and* painting, letting one play itself off against the other. Sometimes it seems to me that the ability to do this constitutes the whole of the art.

'The Practical Business of Painting', *The Artist and the Public*, 1945. See no.78 on p.178

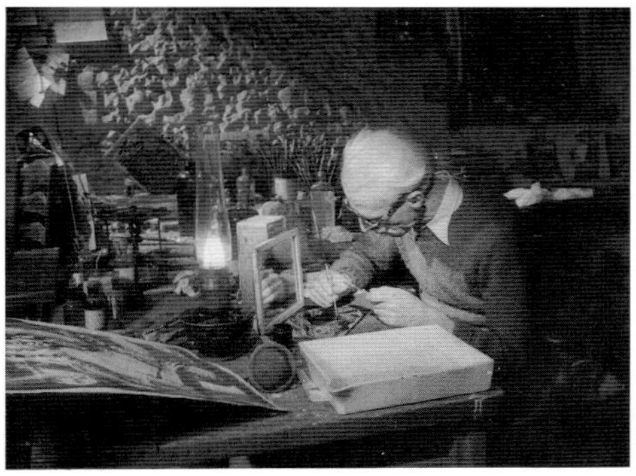

Piper at work in the cowshed studio, 1985.
Photograph: Piper Archives

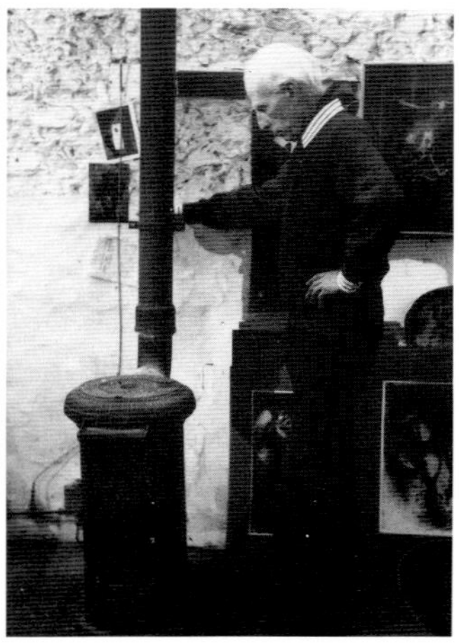

Piper in the cowshed studio, 1986

Catalogue of Works

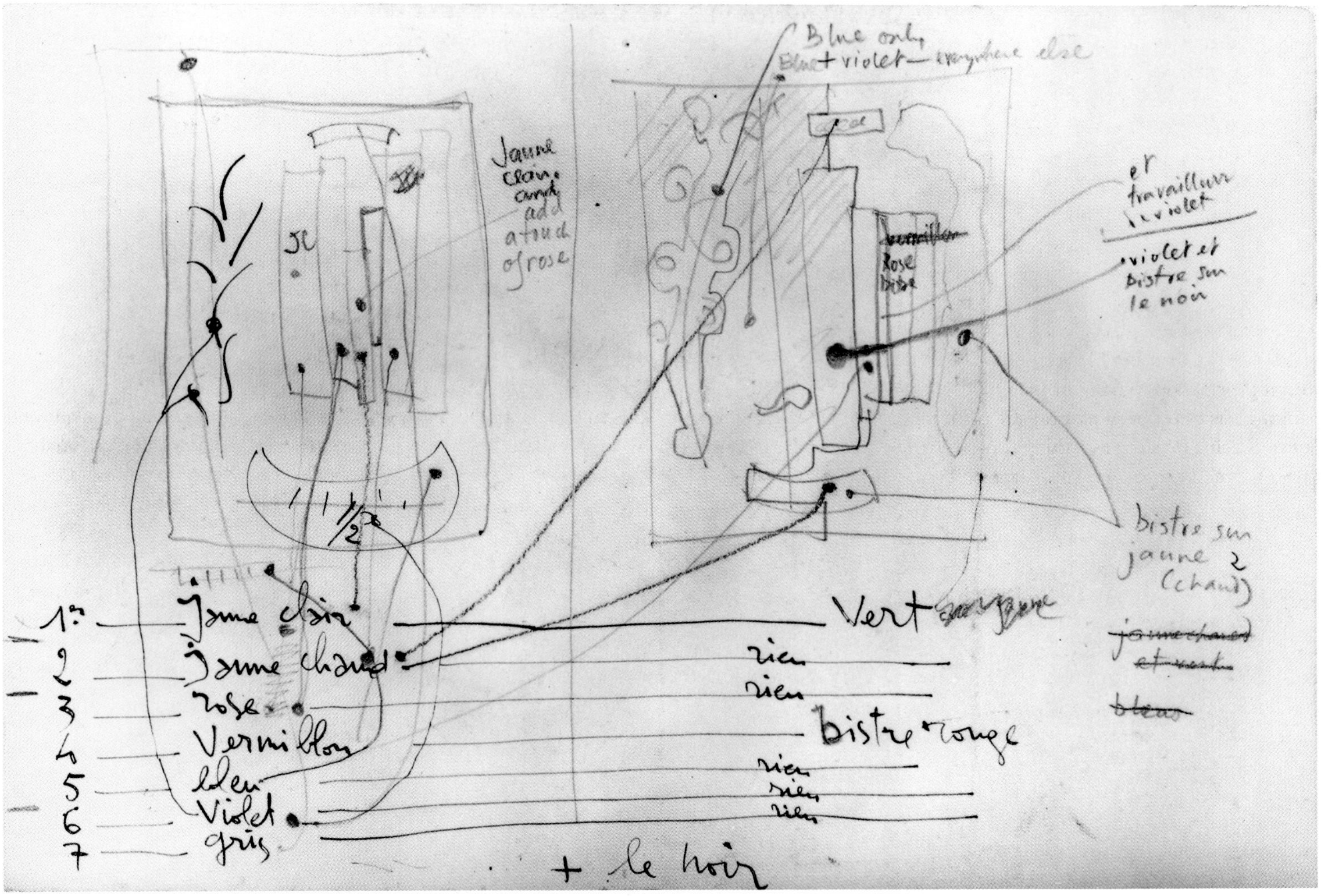

Master printer's plan of work for
Foliate Heads II, 1953 (Cat.84)

The Organisation of the Catalogue

The prints are catalogued chronologically according to the month and then year of printing.

Newly discovered and reallocated prints which would have appeared in the first edition (*ie* works printed prior to 1983) have been allocated a position as close as possible to their estimated year of printing. They have been given sequential alphabetical letters added onto the catalogue number of the work published immediately before. However, the extra prints found for the book illustrations have been placed before the edition of which they would have formed a part. For example, the reallocated book illustration *[Prometheus I]* is Cat.87A; the unpublished image *Brunswick Square*, Cat.11A. I felt it better not to renumber the prints of the first edition as then all lists and referenced works based on the first edition catalogue numbers would be erroneous. Unnecessary and impractical. These new prints are Cats 4A, 4B, 5A, 5B, 5C, 5D, 11A, 57A–C, 67A–B, 71A, 85A, 87A–C, 101A, 121A, 145A, 171D, 328A, 328B.

In the first edition all book illustrations appeared in black-and-white. For this publication all colour book illustrations are now in colour.

All the indices have been completely updated.

The term 'autolithograph' has been used for those lithographs where the artist himself has drawn on the plates or stones, distinguishing them from lithographs in general which may contain photographic images or be drawn/interpreted at the printing studio by a master printer. After consultation with the artist and others it was decided that only autolithographic book illustrations should be included in the main catalogue. Thus, for example, *John Piper's Stowe* 1983 (see 'Illustrations by John Piper' no.180, p.158 below) which has illustrations photomechanically reproduced from drawings, is not included in the main catalogue. Nevertheless, a comprehensive list of all the artist's book, pamphlet and article illustrations not considered original graphic work is given in 'Illustrations by John Piper: Books, Articles, Pamphlets, Almanacs, Film Posters, Records and Compact Discs' on pp.154–9. After viewing correspondence with the artist, his wife and Faber and Faber (as publishers) it was decided to reverse the earlier decision not to include as autolithographs the three illustrations appearing in *Prometheus*, and these have accordingly been listed as Cats 87A–C.

Incorrect titles for the prints, where known, are given throughout the catalogue in inverted commas and collected in the 'Incorrect Titles' on pp.148–9, to help avoid confusion in cases where the correct title is unknown. These alternatives, however, are incorrect and the title of the prints has been established in consultation with the artist. The 'Index of Prints' on pp.143–7 contains references to previous publications wrongly cataloguing 'prints' which in fact are works in some other medium or do not exist. With some prints editioned after 1983 Piper changed or revised the title, after the original publication, and while these titles at the time of publication were correct they now are considered to be incorrect and have been listed as such. To differentiate these originally correct publications from incorrect titles I have listed the former as 'Originally published as …' and the latter as 'Sometimes incorrectly known as …' Clearly the publishers should not be considered at fault as a result of this change.

Cats 171A–D are extra autolithographs included in the second edition of *Venice* (Cats 146–71), published in the same year (1965). I felt that they should be listed as extra to the first edition and not separately.

While all the prints and colour book illustrations are reproduced in colour, the hand-coloured deluxe edition of *Brighton Aquatints* (Cats 12–23) have not been reproduced as each print would vary.

The monotypes which the artist has produced were not included as no plates are known still to exist and no comprehensive details could be compiled – no information about them since the first edition having been received by me or others. However, I would welcome any information for the future.

With the indices my intention has been to allow the viewer as much information as possible – thus the list of 'Incorrect Titles' on pp.148–9 is not merely to correct but to allow one to see how early work (by means of titles given) was viewed by the public.

I have included comprehensive information on works by Piper – not only written works but also all his designs realised as sets, stained glass and tapestries. It is hoped that this section will not only show the versatility of Piper and the interrelationship of his prints and his other work, but also that this basic information will provide a framework for a full-scale book or books on Piper's various designs.

Where prints were published together in a collection (portfolio or book), the relevant information is given in a general introduction to the collection. Only when there is some variation between the individual prints, for example between image sizes, are separate details given. The location of printers and publishers is given in the relevant indices on pp.151–2 and not in the body of the catalogue.

For the indexing, the consecutive catalogue numbers of the book illustrations only have been elided. Where a deluxe edition (or second edition) of a book has been published containing extra prints (*eg* Cats 71A and 171D) separate catalogue numbers have been given for these publications in the lists of 'Printers' and 'Publishers' on pp.151–2.

O.L.
Oxford, 1995

Short Forms and Abbreviations Used

CURWEN

Artists at Curwen: a celebration of the gifts of artists' prints from the Curwen Studio, ed. by Pat Gilmour, Tate Gallery Publications, 1977 (catalogue for the exhibition of 23rd February – 11th April)

ELBORN

John Piper on his Eightieth Birthday, ed. by Geoffrey Elborn, Stourton Press, London, 1983

INGRAMS/PIPER

Piper's Places: John Piper in England and Wales, by Richard Ingrams and John Piper, Chatto and Windus, Hogarth Press, London, 1983

KELPRA PRINTS

Kelpra Prints, Arts Council, 1970 (catalogue for the exhibition held at the Hayward Gallery, 17th June – 7th July)

KELPRA STUDIO

Kelpra Studio: The Rose and Chris Prater Gift, Artists' Prints 1961–1980, Tate Gallery, 1980 (catalogue for the exhibition of 9th July – 25th August)

TATE

John Piper, Tate Gallery Publications, 1983 (catalogue for the exhibition of 30th November 1983 – 22nd January 1984)

WEST

John Piper, by Anthony West, Secker and Warburg, London, 1979 and 1983

WOODS

John Piper: Paintings, Drawings and Theatre Designs, 1932–1954 (arranged and with an introduction by S. John Woods), Faber and Faber, London, 1955

AP	artist's proofs
b.l./b.c./b.r.	bottom left/bottom centre/bottom right
c.	*circa*
Cat./Cats	catalogue number/s
ed./eds	editor/edited/editors
EU	Edition size unknown
exh./exh. cat.	exhibition/exhibition catalogue
gsm	grams per square metre of paper
HC	*hors de commerce*
IC	insurance copies
illus.	illustration/s; illustrated
incl.	include/d/s; including
lbs	pounds per ream of paper
no./nos	number/s
No.	number in publications
p./pp.	page/s
pl. no.	plate number
PP	printer's proofs
PuP	publisher's proofs
repr.	reproduced
sc.	*scilicet* (namely)
t.l./t.c./t.r.	top left/top centre/top right
UU	unsigned, unnumbered
Vol./Vols	volume/s
wmk	watermark

The information for each individual graphic is arranged as follows:

Catalogue number
Title[1]
Medium, Size of image: mm(in)[2]
Printer,[3] Date printed[4]
Publisher, Date of publication
Type of paper,[5] Size of paper: mm (in)[6]
Size of edition,[7] Signature,[8] Artist's proofs (AP), Other copies[9]

Incorrect titles
Other comments[10]
Reproductions[11]

Public Collections[12]

1 Square brackets are used in the titles to prints that were either not titled or their original titles are unknown or where a title could not be confirmed with the artist (as with Cat. 101A).

2 The sizes of etchings and woodcuts are those of the plate and block size respectively.

3 With unpublished prints, where the artist was the printer, all trial proofs were hand-pulled by the artist.

4 The printing order of works of 1990 could not be established and I have made my own deductions based on signature, which may not be accurate.

5 Weight of paper and ream quantity are given only where known. For unpublished prints on proofing paper these cannot be exactly specified since the artist, at the time, used whatever types of paper he found available and suitable. Details of any watermark (abbreviated 'wmk') are given where it is clearly visible. Where possible the weight in lbs has been converted to the current, more accurate usage of gms, and the editor wishes to acknowledge the assistance of Falkiner Fine Papers Ltd in this task, and also for identifying certain types of paper.

6 Where the size is that of the plate, this is indicated by '(plate)'.

7 'Unspecified' is used to indicate a large, unspecified print run usually in excess of 500 copies. EU is used to indicate edition size unknown.

8 The signature 'John Piper' is in pencil b.r. unless otherwise stated. When he became ill towards the end of 1989, John Piper began signing his prints with his initials 'JP' in pencil b.r. (Cats 427–9) and with the failing of his health in late 1990 he designed a single block-stamp with his name 'John Piper' and below this his initials 'JECP', which were stamped under his supervision in ink b.r. for the last four prints (Cats 430–3). Upon the death of the artist certain earlier prints were found in his estate, which had been unsigned and unnumbered. In error a few of these prints were signature stamped with the 'JECP' block, obviously without the artist's knowledge or supervision, but unfortunately no record was kept of which prints these were and they cannot be indicated in this volume. Examples of his signature appear on p. 142.

9 In describing other copies, the following abbreviations have been used: HC (*hors de commerce*); PP (printer's proofs); IC (insurance copies); PuP (publisher's proofs); UU (unsigned, unnumbered).

10 Other comments include details concerning the blind stamp of printers and publishers and any other particular features of the print. It should be noted that the editor has usually had access, during cataloguing, only to proof copies in his or the artist's possession, and since human error has led to blind stamps, where used, being omitted from certain prints, it is regretted that in some cases such impresses may have escaped attention. Moreover, the blind stamp of Christie's Contemporary Art and the combined blind stamp of Christie's Contemporary Art and The National Trust were impressed only when the prints were sold, so on artist's proofs they are lacking.

11 References are given to the most widely available publications in which prints have been reproduced (see opposite).

12 Cities are not included in the main catalogue but in the list of 'Prints in Public Collections' except where identical or similar names exist, *eg* Museum of Modern Art in New York, Oxford, Rio de Janeiro etc.

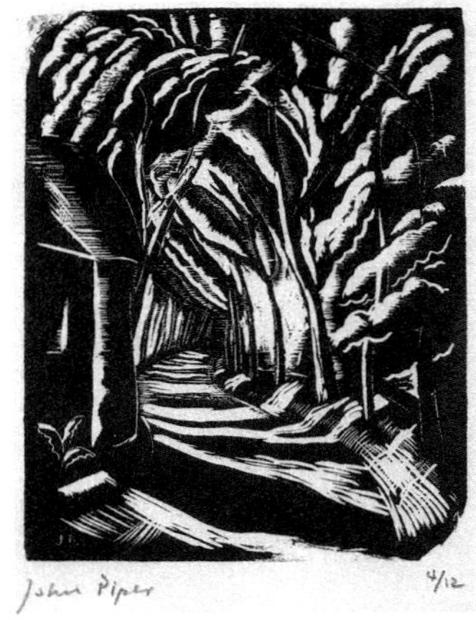

1

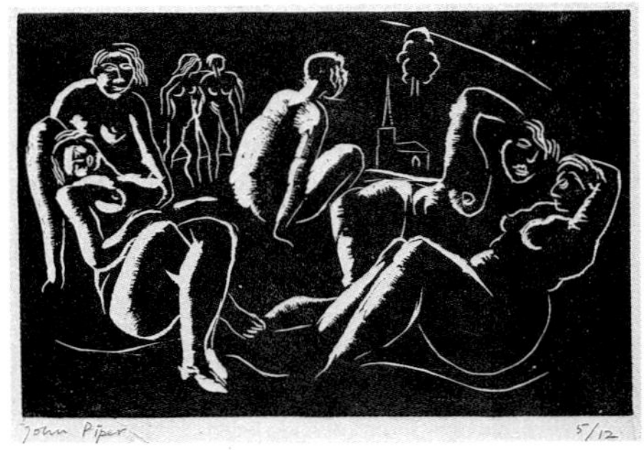

2

1
[Avenue]
Wood engraving 127×101 (5×4)
The artist *c.* 1923
The artist *c.* 1923
Cream laid 251×196 ($9\frac{7}{8}\times7\frac{3}{4}$)
12 'John Piper' in pencil b.l.

2
[Figures in a Landscape]
Wood engraving 152×229 (6×9)
The artist *c.* 1923
The artist *c.* 1923
Cream laid (ragged edges) 233×358 ($9\frac{1}{8}\times14\frac{1}{8}$)
12 'John Piper' in pencil b.l.

Sometimes incorrectly known as '*Figure Composition I*'

3
[Adam and Eve]
Wood engraving 150×115 ($5\frac{7}{8}\times4\frac{1}{2}$)
The artist *c.* 1923
The artist *c.* 1923
Cream laid (ragged edges) 249×185 ($9\frac{3}{4}\times7\frac{5}{16}$)
6 'John Piper' in pencil b.l.

4
The Pond
Wood engraving 203×151 ($8\times5\frac{15}{16}$)
The artist *c.* 1923
The artist *c.* 1923
Cream laid 245×198 ($9\frac{5}{8}\times7\frac{3}{4}$)
12 'John Piper' in pencil b.l.

The title and the name of the artist are printed on the paper, b.r. and b.l. respectively.
Repr. in *London Mercury,* Vol.XXI, No.125, January 1930

4A
[Farmhouse]
Wood engraving 128×102 ($5\frac{1}{8}\times4\frac{1}{8}$)
The artist *c.* 1923
The artist *c.* 1923
Cream laid 283×213 ($11\frac{3}{16}\times8\frac{3}{8}$)
EU 'John Piper'

The edition size was probably 12.

4B
[The Road]
Wood engraving 178×128 ($7\times5\frac{1}{8}$)
The artist *c.* 1923
The artist *c.* 1923
Cream laid 284×213 ($11\frac{1}{8}\times8\frac{3}{8}$)
EU 'John Piper'

The edition size was probably 12.

5
Coldkitchen Farm
Lithograph 280×356 (11×14)
The artist (using the presses of the Royal College of Art) 1929
Unpublished
Proofing paper 376×415 ($14\frac{13}{16}\times16\frac{5}{16}$)
25 'John Piper'

Certain proof copies have, in the artist's hand, 'Coldkitchen Farm' b.l. in pencil, and are signed 'John Piper 1929' b.r. in pencil.

5A
Marepond Farm
Wood engraving 213×278 ($8\frac{3}{8}\times10\frac{15}{16}$)
The Marshall Press *c.* July 1929
Magazine of the Students of the Royal College of Art
July 1929
Cream wove 146×184 ($5\frac{3}{4}\times7\frac{1}{4}$)
EU Unsigned

Appearing on p.25 of the student magazine *Leaves from Eden*, Royal College of Art, London, July 1929. 'Marepond Farm' and 'Piper' printed b.l. and b.r. respectively.

5B
[Farmyard Gate]
Woodcut 180×128 ($7\frac{1}{8}\times5\frac{1}{8}$)
The artist *c.* 1929
The artist *c.* 1929
Cream laid 279×200 ($11\times7\frac{7}{8}$)
25 'John Piper'

5C
[Landscape]
Woodcut 169×125 ($6\frac{5}{8}\times4\frac{7}{8}$)
The artist *c.* 1929
The artist *c.* 1929
Cream laid 282×216 ($11\frac{1}{8}\times8\frac{1}{2}$)
EU 'John Piper'

The edition size was probably 25.

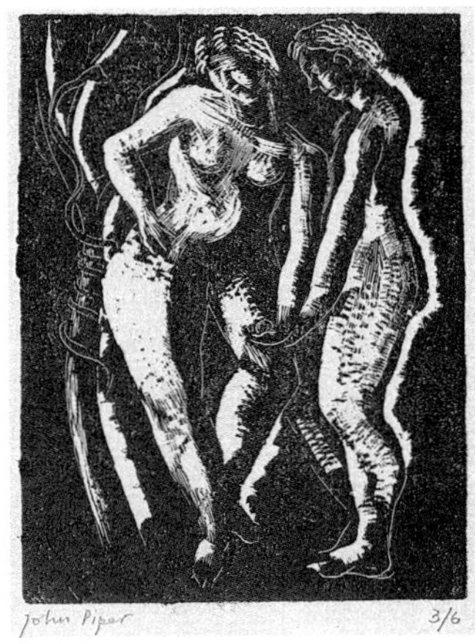

3

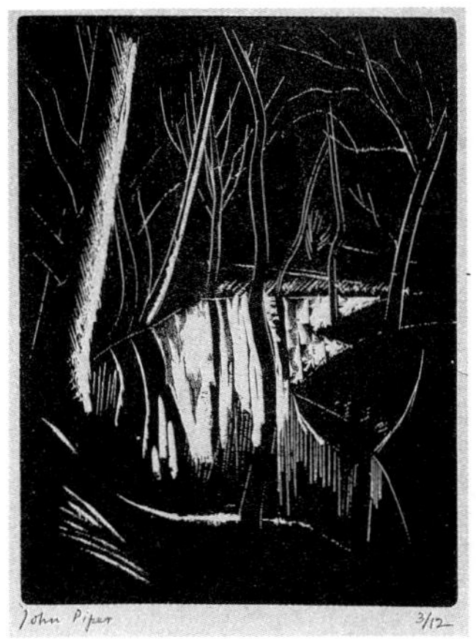

4

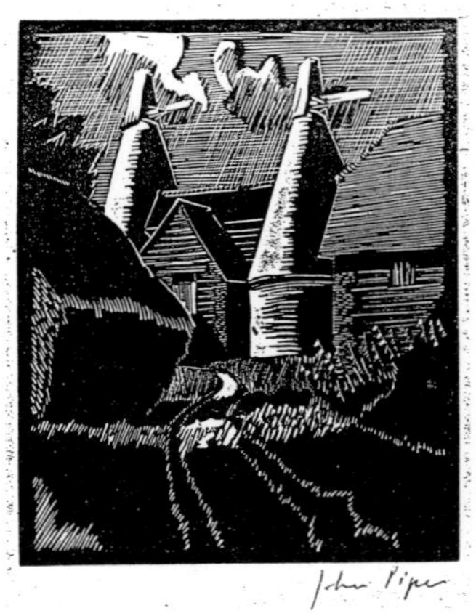

4A

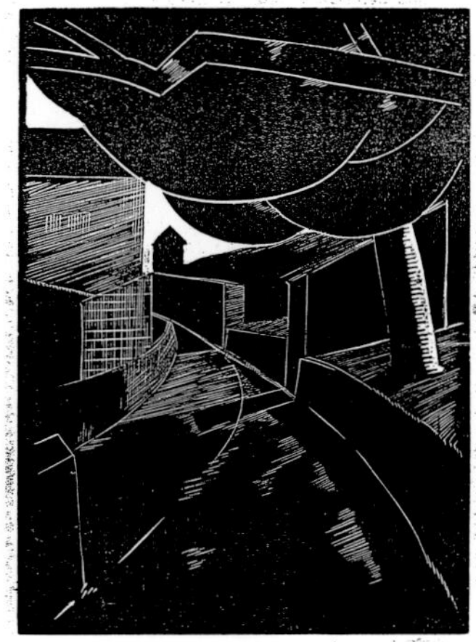

4B

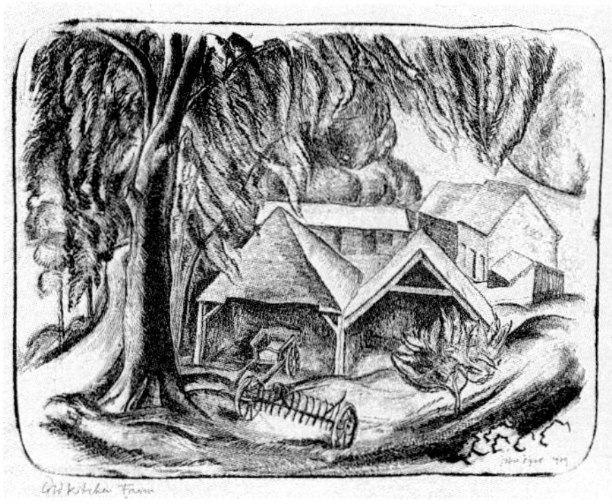

5

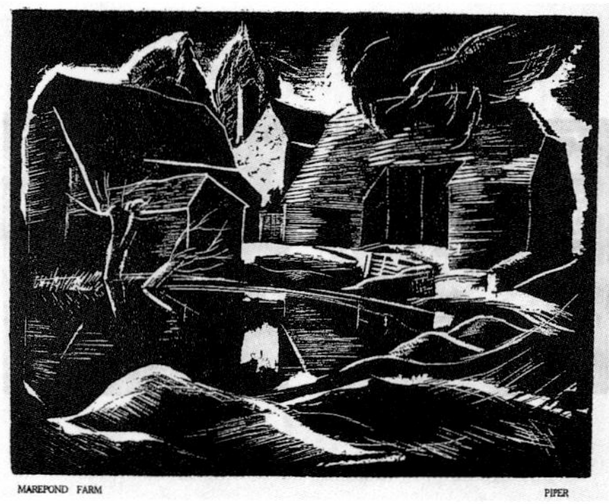

5A

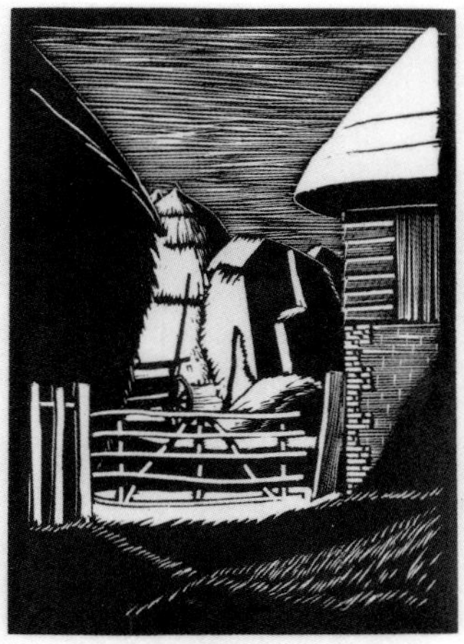

5B

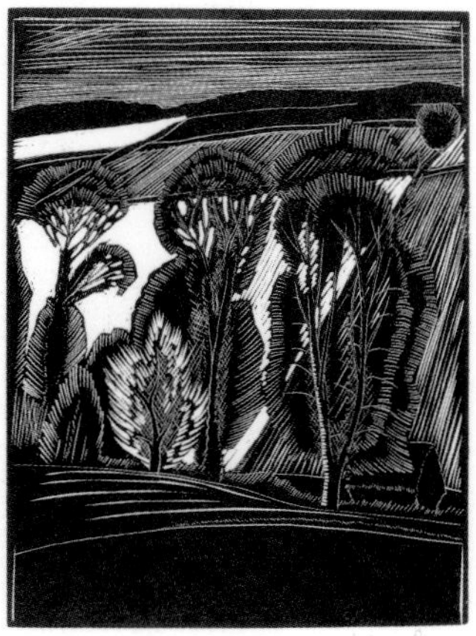

5C

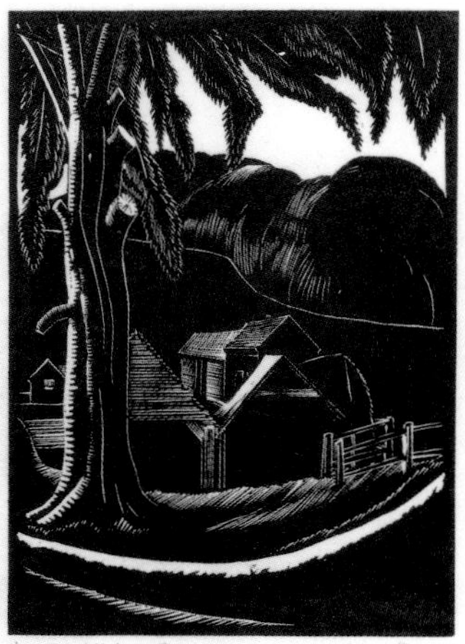

6

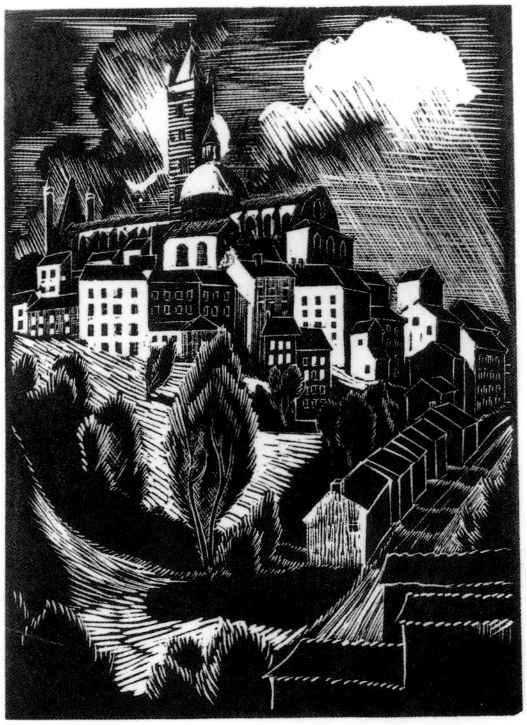

5D

5D
[Siena]
Woodcut 180×125 (7×5)
The artist *c.* 1929
The artist *c.* 1929
Cream laid 282×199 (11×7¾)
25 'John Piper'

6
Coldkitchen Farm
Woodcut 177×121 (7×4¾)
Mercury Press 1930
The London Mercury 1930
Cream laid 248×168 (9¾×6⅝)
25 'John Piper'

Inscribed b.l. in pencil 'Coldkitchen Farm'
Repr. in *London Mercury*, Vol.XXI, No.125, January 1930, with the page number, '209', printed t.c. and the words 'Coldkitchen Farm Woodcut by John Piper' b.c. It is possible that the woodcut was printed by the artist or somewhere other than at Mercury Press.

The lithographic repr. in the *London Mercury*: Bodleian Library; British Library; Cambridge University Library

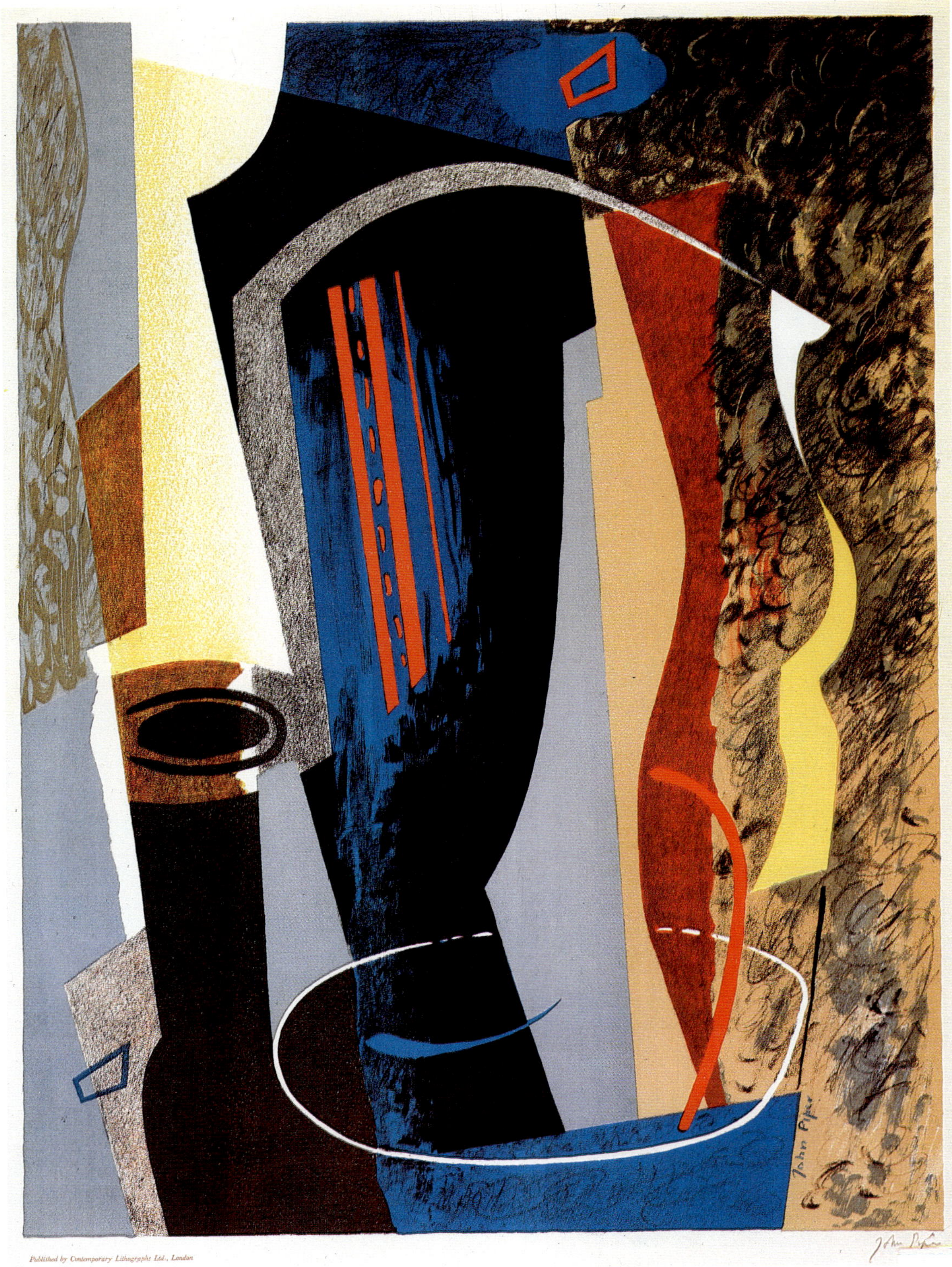

7

7
Abstract Composition
Autolithograph 610×458 (24×18)
Curwen Press 1936
Contemporary Lithographs 1936
Machine-made lithographic cartridge 670×508 (26⅜×20)
500–1000 Unsigned

Sometimes incorrectly known as '*Abstract Still Life*' or '*Abstract*'
This lithograph was printed in six workings and signed 'John Piper' in the plate b.r. (printed in blue). Some copies signed 'John Piper' in pencil b.r. and a few copies numbered out of 75 in pencil and dated '1937' b.l. are known to exist. The words 'Published by Contemporary Lithographs Ltd., London' are printed in red b.l.

British Museum; Scottish National Gallery of Modern Art; Victoria and Albert Museum

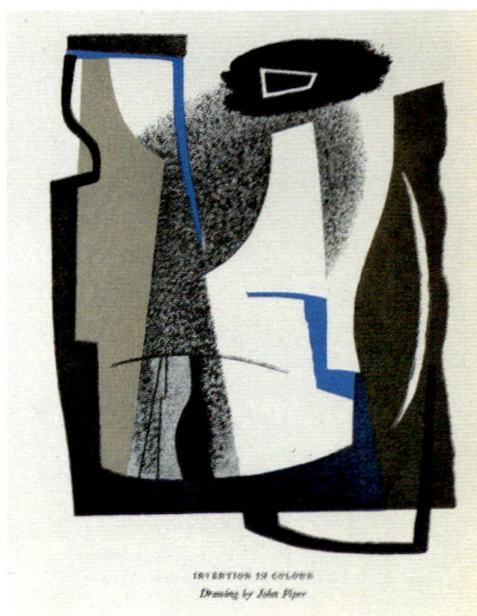

10

8
Nursery Frieze I
Autolithograph 460×1214 ($18\frac{1}{8}\times47\frac{3}{4}$)
Waterlow and Sons 1936
Contemporary Lithographs 1936
Machine-made lithographic cartridge 495×1252 ($19\frac{1}{2}\times49\frac{1}{4}$)
Unspecified Unsigned

Tate Gallery; Victoria and Albert Museum

9 (detail Plate 1)
Nursery Frieze II
Autolithograph 460×1214 ($18\frac{1}{8}\times47\frac{3}{4}$)
Waterlow and Sons 1936
Contemporary Lithographs 1936
Machine-made lithographic cartridge 495×1252 ($19\frac{1}{2}\times49\frac{1}{4}$)
Unspecified Unsigned

Tate Gallery; Victoria and Albert Museum

10
Invention in Colour
Autolithograph 173×130 ($6\frac{13}{16}\times5\frac{1}{8}$)
Curwen Press 1937
Signature 1937
Machine-made lithographic cartridge 245×185 ($9\frac{5}{8}\times7\frac{1}{4}$)
1000 Unsigned

Printed 'Invention in Colour Drawing by John Piper' b.c.
Printed from paramat blocks cut by the artist as the frontispiece to *Signature*, No.6, July 1937

Bodleian Library; British Library; Cambridge University Library; Tate Gallery

11
Brighton Street
Etching and aquatint 195×280 ($7\frac{11}{16}\times11$)
A. Alexander and Sons 1939
Unpublished Proofing paper 217×299 ($8\frac{9}{16}\times11\frac{3}{4}$) (plate)
Not issued as an edition Unsigned

Sometimes incorrectly known as *'Brighton Street, Sussex'*. A small number of trial proofs were hand-pulled by the artist. Part of the series *Brighton Aquatints* (Cats 12-23), but not included in the book. Repr. in Ingrams/Piper (plate 40)

11A
Brunswick Square
Etching and aquatint 256×160 ($10\frac{1}{8}\times6\frac{1}{4}$)
A. Alexander and Sons 1939
Unpublished
Proofing paper 292×191 ($11\frac{1}{2}\times7\frac{1}{2}$)
Not issued as an edition Unsigned

One known proof of this exists in a hand-coloured version. Part of the series *Brighton Aquatints* (Cats 12-23), but not included in the book

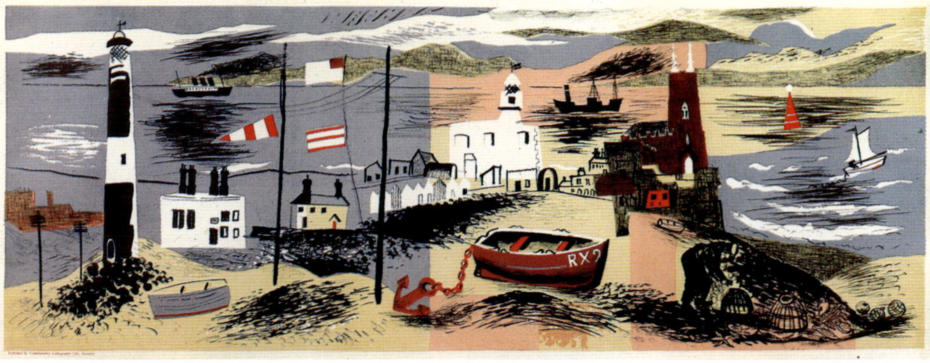
8

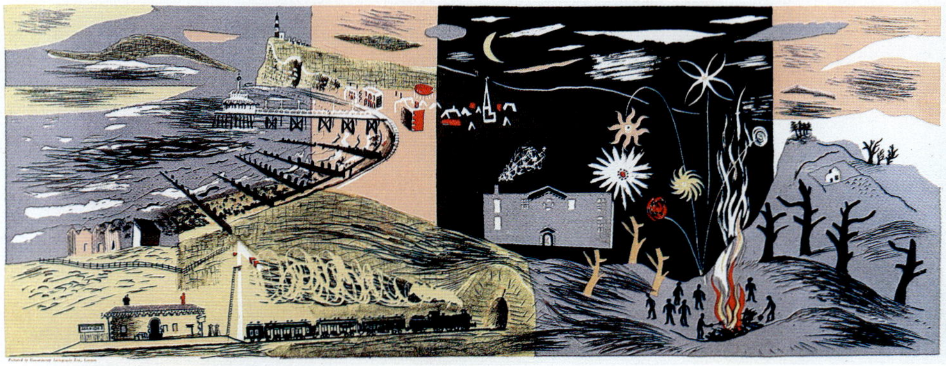
9

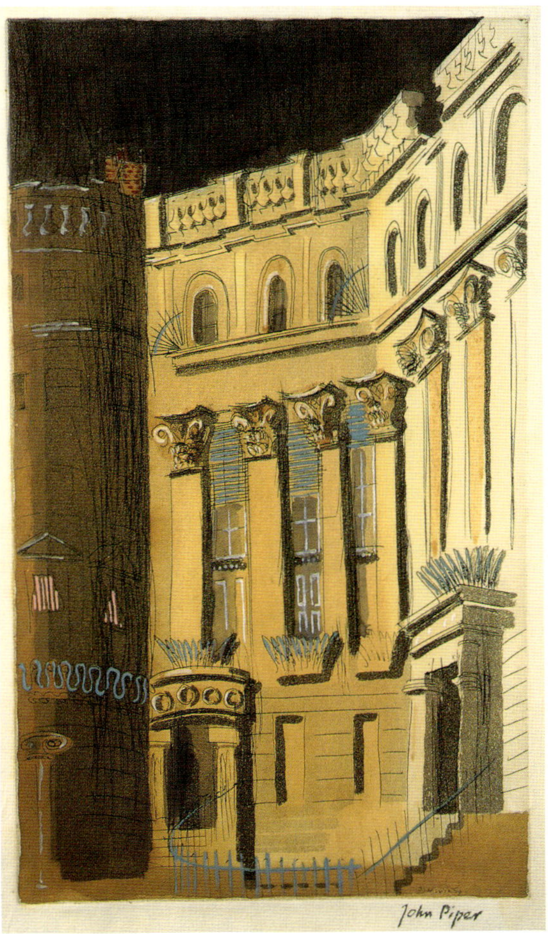

11A

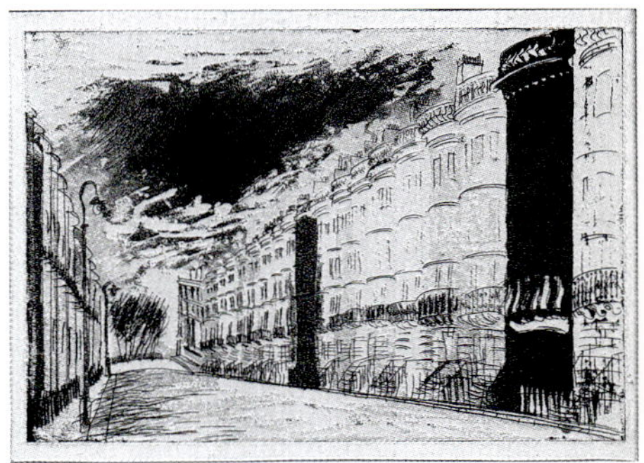
11

12-23

Brighton Aquatints, 1939

A book consisting of twelve etchings and aquatints of Brighton with short descriptions by the artist and an introduction by Lord Alfred Douglas. The etchings and aquatints were hand-printed by A. Alexander and Sons, the text printed by the Curwen Press and the whole published by Duckworth. All the etchings and aquatints are bound into the book with a title-page and a description page. Two hundred standard copies were printed and a further fifty-five copies were hand-coloured by the artist, some unbound. No prints are signed, although on occasion over the years the artist would personally dedicate and sign a copy of the book, and on occasion sign prints from books which had been split up.

The size of the book is 258×400 (10¼×15¾). The paper size of each aquatint is 253×385 (9¹⁵⁄₁₆×15⅛) and the image size given is always that of the plate. The paper is hand-made by F. J. Head with an original size probably of 394×516 (15½×20½) which was cut in half and had the deckle edges trimmed off, hence the three watermarks that appear will vary in position from image to image. The watermark of the hand with the cross represents that of the Pope raised in blessing; the head, that of Christ as transferred onto the Kerchief of St Berenice, and the date '1399' below the head is part of the head watermark. The weight of the paper was probably 25-30lbs.

Standard edition: Arts Council Collection; Bodleian Library; British Library; British Museum; Cambridge University Library; Museum of Modern Art, New York; National Library of Scotland; National Library of Wales; Trinity College Library, Dublin; Victoria and Albert Museum (except Cats 19, 22) and Victoria and Albert Museum (hand-coloured versions of Cats 12, 18, 21)

Introduction to *Brighton Aquatints* by Lord Alfred Douglas

Looking with admiration, not unmingled with emotion, at these charming aquatints of Mr Piper's it is surprisingly borne in on me that there is still a good deal left of old Brighton which I knew in my youth. I have lived in Brighton (or, to be strictly accurate, Hove) for the last ten years, but somehow it has never hitherto seemed to me to be the same place as it was when between the ages of twelve and sixteen I used to come for a week or two's stay with my father in lodgings kept by a retired butler and his wife in Oriental Place, between the Bedford and the Metropole. As a rule, children don't go for a week or two to 'stay' with their father, but in my case this was the process, simply because my father, equally famous as the author of the 'Queensberry Rules' and the vindicator of late Victorian morality, did not reside at home with his wife and children. In fact, we very seldom saw him, and although I was in my childhood devoted to him and regarded him as a marvellous and heroic figure who, according to the firm belief of my brothers and myself, was capable of wrestling single-handed with a bull or 'taking on' seven men in single combat (with or without boxing gloves), my devotion to him was largely, if not mainly, due to the very circumstances that I seldom saw him. Choosing between two expressions of proverbial wisdom, 'Les absents ont toujours tort' and 'Absence makes the heart grow fonder', I find myself constrained by the weight of evidence to come down heavily on the side of the English proverb in the case of my father.

The fantastic 'topsy-turviness' of the situation in relation to my father, regarded as an object of idolatry on the part of his ingenuous offspring and the stern guardian of public and private morals in the 'nineties, may be said to find some reflection in my consideration of Brighton as it was then and as it now is. Actually, nowadays, I believe, murders and other crimes are sometimes committed in Brighton; 'painful cases' and 'grave charges' are not infrequently associated with it in the reports in the papers; in the summer months it is invaded by a huge army of 'the unwashed of Ipswich' (that is to say, metaphorically speaking, for of course, they have no actual connection with Ipswich) and 'the front' becomes almost impassable and quite intolerable. Whereas at the time when my father used to sit nightly with me in the 'lounge' (horrible, but now firmly established word) of the newly-built Metropole Hotel, and when goat-carriages still abounded on the front, it was a place given over to the most profound decorum and placid respectability. It was also intensely 'fashionable'.

When I was staying with my father, generally also accompanied by my sister, four years younger than myself, I seemed (looking back at it all now from the distance of about fifty years, more or less) to spend a very large part of my time on the Pier, where there was a man described as a Professor who had performing fleas, and another man, or perhaps it was the same man, who had a performing dog called 'Spot' (as far as I remember, its only 'performance' was that it would, as its master wittily announced about forty times a day, 'die on this spot for the Queen'), and when I was not on the Pier I was generally to be found gazing at the fish or the seals in the Aquarium which also ran a perpetual and rather depressing 'Variety Show' in a theatre which has now ceased to exist. My father, though he was fond of his children, was not infrequently bored by them, and when in their company spent a great deal of time in silent meditation as to what he ought to do to amuse them, and, incidentally, to get them out of his way. And these meditations, when he was at Brighton, almost invariably ended by suggesting to his mind the Pier and the Aquarium as desirable resorts for the young. My sister and I were quite pleased about this. Evidently children in those days were more easily amused than they are now, and as the process of going on to the Pier (either the 'Chain' or the 'Western' variety) or visiting the Aquarium invariably involved being handed sums of money grossly in excess of what would have been sufficient for the purpose, we rather inclined to believe that we were having a very gay and dashing time. So we were, of course, simply because the enjoyment and amusement we obtained were largely created by our own imaginations instead of being supplied readymade by picture theatres, or wireless sets, or gramophones, none of which had been so much as thought of in those nineteenth-century days.

I had almost forgotten all this till I saw Mr Piper's aquatints and discovered that the Brighton of my youth is still in existence, and that nearly all the old landmarks remain exactly as they were. If only I were fourteen instead of nearly seventy, no doubt I could easily recapture that first fine careless rapture of the middle 'eighties and the early 'nineties. It is probably still there if one could only come by it. In any case, I notice that in the long run nearly everyone ends by coming to live (and die) in Brighton. When I say 'everyone' I mean, of course, just what the papers mean when they announce that 'everyone now agrees' that so-and-so is the case. I mean that I could give at least a hundred cases of people I know, among what the Paris newspapers used to call les High-lifers, turning up late in life and announcing that they now live in Brighton. Refreshing myself with another glance through Mr Piper's aquatints, and looking back with my mind's eye to Oriental Place, I arrive at the conclusion that they might easily do worse.

Notes to *Brighton Aquatints* by the artist

The First Avenue Hotel, Hove

The yellow-brick end of Hove has many charms. Going west from the West Pier one passes buildings that gradually become later in date, and on reaching first Avenue one is in an atmosphere of the late Victorian. Balconies and other decorative features have more importance, more flourish; porches are richly wreathed in wrought iron, and white-painted pinnacles stick up like the pins in a well-stocked pincushion. But the atmosphere is still gay. Victorian architects let themselves go in Brighton: the air and the clients were encouraging. Compared with the Regency calm, the static elegance of most of Brighton front, the buildings here are frantically 'busy', but they have none the less a vivid sense of seaside, and a magnificent swagger. Queen Victoria, imposing in dark bronze, looks out to sea from the pedestal.

The Royal Pavilion

Built for George IV when Prince Regent. first he enlarged a villa on the site, till it became a prepossessing Regency house. Then he commissioned

Porden to build stables (now the Dome) and a riding house in Indian style, and soon found that these overpowered his charming seaside villa. Then he saw Cockerell's wonderful new house at Sezincote, in Gloucestershire, and envied its Hindu fancifulness. Repton laid out the gardens there. The Regent commissioned Repton to design the new Pavilion, but money ran out. It was completed in 1823 by John Nash, who designed Regent Street, Regent's Park crescents and terraces, and a good many other London buildings. It has been called all kinds of rude names by generations of residents and visitors, but most people start by laughing and later develop a great affection for it. It has an extravagant beauty, and in some ways reflects exactly the effervescent spirit of the great holiday resort itself in its most hilarious and human moods. It is at once acutely vulgar and extremely sensitive. It now belongs to the Brighton Corporation, and is carefully preserved. (You can go into it for 6d.) Inside, there is a fine collection of early prints and pictures of Brighton, and it has not been shorn of all its internal beauties – such as the palm-leaf dome decorations and the Chinese wallpapers. A good deal of its original furniture is now in Buckingham Palace. During the War it was used as a hospital for wounded Indian troops, who must have found it only vaguely like home.

Regency Square from the West Pier
A dazzling white meringue, brittle and sweet, the pier has none of that delicate efficiency that the old chain pier possessed. The town was first in the English field with a pier, and its present ones are as florid and grand as any anywhere. They both look as if they are trying to project Brighton's swagger half across the Channel. Regency Square is laid out on the gentle slope immediately behind, and the busy part of Hove climbs the hill behind that.

Brighton from the Station Yard
This is the first view of Brighton which many visitors get. Perhaps after a stuffy train journey it is disappointing not to find oneself delivered right on the beach, but the view of Brighton's villas climbing the further hill by Kemp Town, beyond the gay, jumbled foreground is a compensation. There are other English towns to be seen from neighbouring hills spreading out in the same semi-ordered way, but in few others is the air so clear, the whole look of the place so sharp and clean. Quite absent is the Midland haze or the foliaged softness of the west. The only haze that Brighton knows is the early-morning mist, or the all-obscuring sea-fog. Even critical William Cobbett, when he got over his megrims about the Pavilion, was complimentary about the air and the houses, and said generously of the town that it 'certainly surpassed in beauty all other towns in the world'. In this picture, the street in the middledistance leads down towards the Pavilion. The white church (St Peter's) was built by Barry. (A later and bigger building of his was the London Houses of Parliament.)

Brunswick Terrace
Brunswick Terrace and Brunswick Square, Hove, were designed by an architect named Wild, who did other work at Brighton, including the Royal Chapel of St George. His work is representative of the combined ebullience and restraint that one associates with seaside terraces of stucco houses. But Decimus Burton, architect (1800-81), was probably more responsible than anyone else for the Regency architectural character of south coast watering places. He is associated with Hastings and St Leonard's, as Foulston is with Plymouth and Papworth with Cheltenham. Burton designed the screens at Hyde Park Corner and the Athenaeum Club in Pall Mall. He was less busy at Brighton than at Hastings, but his style (as Professor Richardson has written) 'collectively conveyed something of the manner of the Regency to the seaside, and there are reminiscences of it from Dover to Sidmouth'.

Bedford Square
A small square, opening onto the promenade at Hove, just east of Brunswick Terrace and the new Embassy Court building. The Regency houses are stuccoed, and some of them painted in pale yellows, greys and browns. Others are of unpainted stucco, and all their pale colours part and mingle like the counterpoint in the slow movement of a symphony. The verandahs and awnings provide the decorative motif, and the bowed house-fronts themselves have an ebullience that suits the seaside scene. They are, in feeling, as near as English architecture ever is to the spirit of a Rowlandson print – a rare English spirit that combines health and heartiness with sense and elegance. On a misty October morning the beauty of shapes and colours in Bedford Square takes the breath away. The yellow and grey houses appear through the faint yellow-grey mist; the sea begins to sparkle with prickly sunlight beyond the fanciful bandstand on the promenade – even the Brighton Corporation lamp-standard has a suitable gaiety.

Mixed Styles: Regency – Victorian – Modern
This view is drawn looking westwards along the promenade to Brunswick Terrace, at the point where Bedford Square opens out on to the front. The corner house is one of the Regency series that surround the square in pale grey-painted stucco, with characteristic pilasters, verandahs and bows. Beyond it is an imposing Victorian building, and beyond that again the recently-built block of flats known as Embassy Court, designed by Wells Coates. Each of these buildings, in design and materials, belongs very much to its own age, and each is excellent of its kind. The designs are, respectively, pseudo-classical, florid, and modern-severe. The materials are, respectively, stucco, brick and cast iron, steel and glass and concrete.

Kemp Town
The double curve of Regency buildings shown here forms part of the beautiful spacious layout of Kemp Town. Wide, elaborate curved blocks of houses here sweep away from the sea front, enclosing gardens between them. Balconies and windows are finely managed in the designs, so as to enhance the total effect of the curves. A panoramic view of the buildings on the front at Kemp Town, contemporary with these Regency development proposals, may be seen in the Royal Pavilion.

Regency Square
Regency Square is laid out on a gentle slope in the 'best part' of Hove. The West Pier runs straight out to sea in front of it. The terrace of houses at the top of the square, which this aquatint shows, is built in yellow brick, with delicate details. The bowed verandahs, with their generous curved caps, and the complicated balustrades, are a feature here.

The Chapel of St George, Kemp Town
This building stands in a small quiet square in Kemp Town, not far from the sea front. It was built in the 1820's by Wild and Busby, architects. (Busby was probably the architect who designed Euston Square, London.) Inside, it has been spoilt: that is to say, its original fittings have been removed, and it has been made more conventionally 'ecclesiastical' in appearance. But outside it is still one of the most charming of the Brighton churches, its stucco and yellow-brick walls having very much the colour and texture of faded newspaper. The building on the extreme right is a bath house, built in the would-be Hindu style of the Pavilion.

St Bartholomew's Church
This extraordinary red-brick pile dominates the busy Brighton streets in the region below the railway station and to the north of the Royal Pavilion. It was built in the '80's of the last century, and has a great deal of beauty. Its design is unusually simple and bold for the period. The site, needing a unifying element, called for something striking, and something striking was certainly achieved. The architect was Edmund Scott. The interior has been altered. Originally a complete scheme of decoration was prepared by H. Wilson, and the arched baldachino, the pulpit and the font are his. But the rest of his scheme was abandoned, and since that time a lot of semi-Byzantine mosaic work has been inserted.

The Metropole Hotel from the West Pier
The Metropole and the Grand are two enormous hotels that change the whole nature of the part of Brighton front between the two piers. But it is only a change from jollity to frivolity. Old prints hung in the Pavilion show the Regency houses that were swept away to make room for these giants. The Metropole (which occupies the centre place in this aquatint, with the Grand disappearing out of the picture on the right) is dark, lurid red, with fanciful porches, balconies, roofs and chimneys – with a good deal of cast iron in its construction. To see it best, go along the pier and look back across the strip of sea. From here on the right day big waves will be washing away from you towards the Metropole as if they intend to swamp it. A heavy shower may just be over, and dark clouds may hang behind, to provide a sombre backcloth for this extraordinary inanimate stage turn.

12
The First Avenue Hotel, Hove
Plate I
175×278 ($6\frac{7}{8} \times 10\frac{15}{16}$)

Victoria and Albert Museum (hand-coloured version)

13
The Royal Pavilion
Plate II
193×277 ($7\frac{5}{8} \times 10\frac{7}{8}$)

14
Regency Square from the West Pier
Plate III
212×292 ($8\frac{5}{16} \times 11\frac{9}{16}$)
Repr. in Tate (p.23) and West (illus.55)

15
Brighton from the Station Yard
Plate IV
212×292 ($8\frac{5}{16} \times 11\frac{9}{16}$)

Sometimes incorrectly known as *'Brighton from the Station Yard with St Peter's'*. Repr. in Curwen (plate 16), Ingrams/Piper (plate 41, hand-coloured version) and in West (illus.53)

16
Brunswick Terrace
Plate V
211×279 ($8\frac{5}{8} \times 11$)

17
Bedford Square
Plate VI
193×278 ($7\frac{5}{8} \times 10\frac{15}{16}$)

18
Mixed Styles: Regency – Victorian – Modern
Plate VII
193×278 ($7\frac{5}{8} \times 10\frac{15}{16}$)

19
Kemp Town
Plate VIII
187×277 ($7\frac{3}{8} \times 10\frac{7}{8}$)

Birmingham Museum and Art Gallery

20
Regency Square
Plate IX
276×211 ($10\frac{7}{8} \times 8\frac{5}{16}$)

British Council

21
The Chapel of St George, Kemp Town
Plate X
194×278 ($7\frac{5}{8} \times 10\frac{15}{16}$)

Sometimes incorrectly known as '*St George Kemptown, Brighton, Sussex*' or '*St George, Kemptown*'. Repr. in Elborn (p.19) and in Ingrams/Piper (plate 42, hand-coloured version)

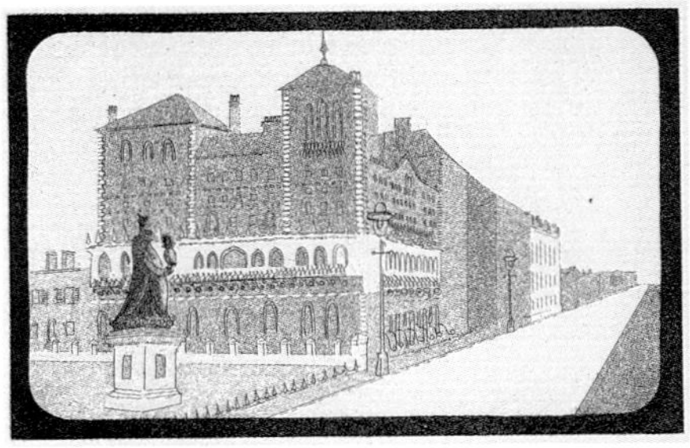

12

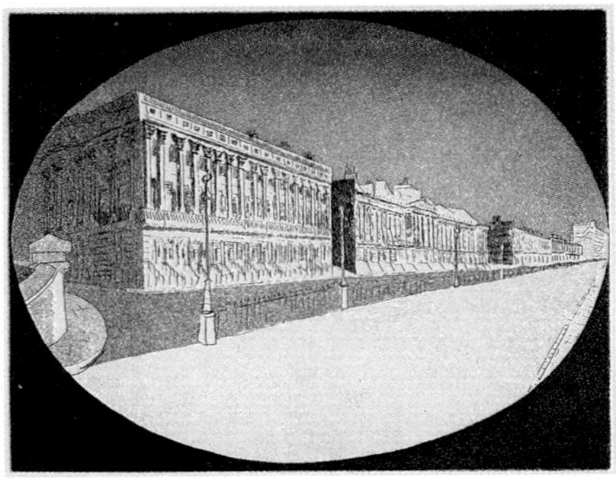

16

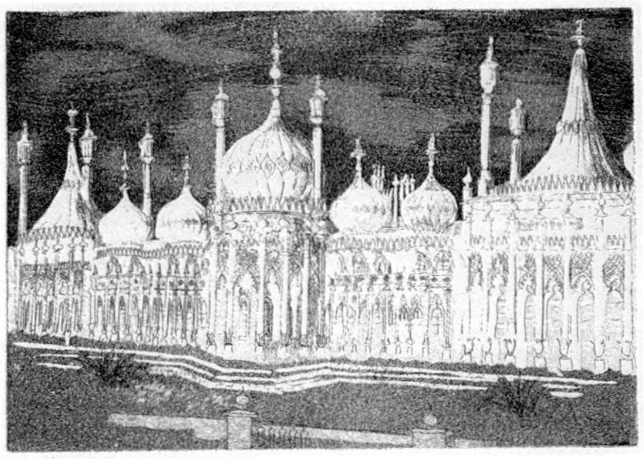

13

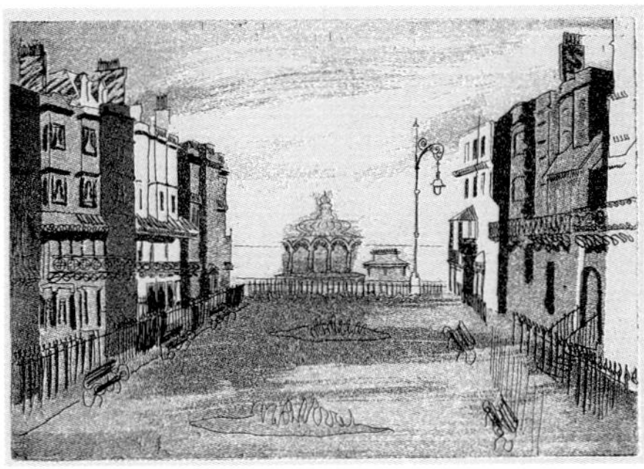

17

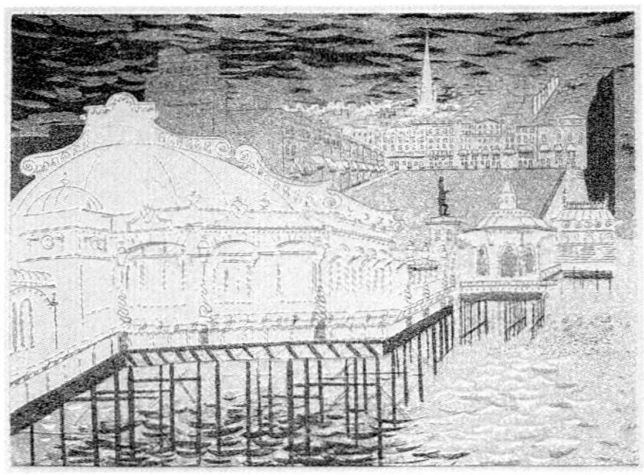

14

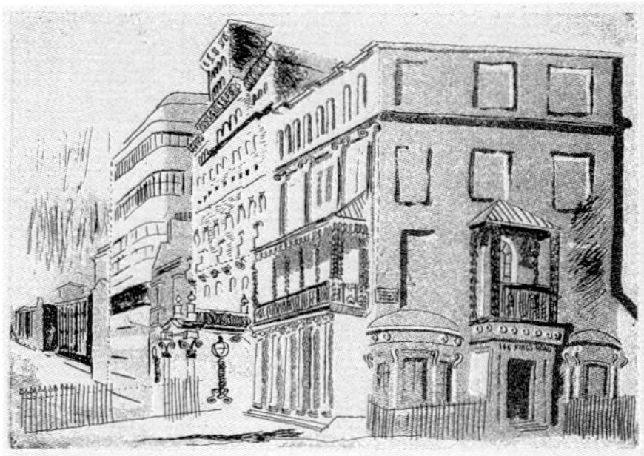

18

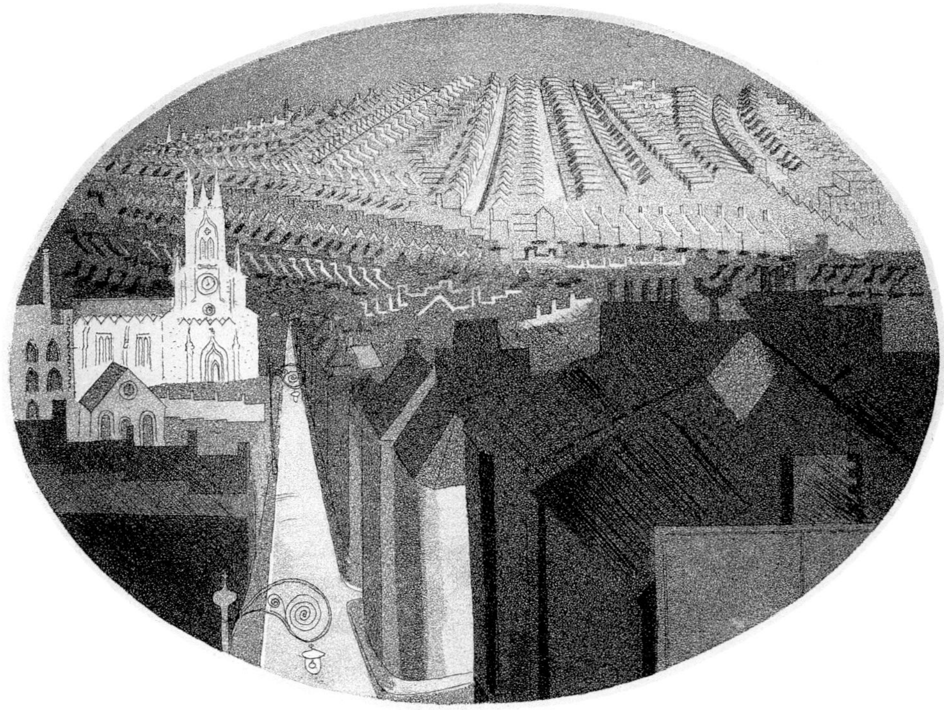

15

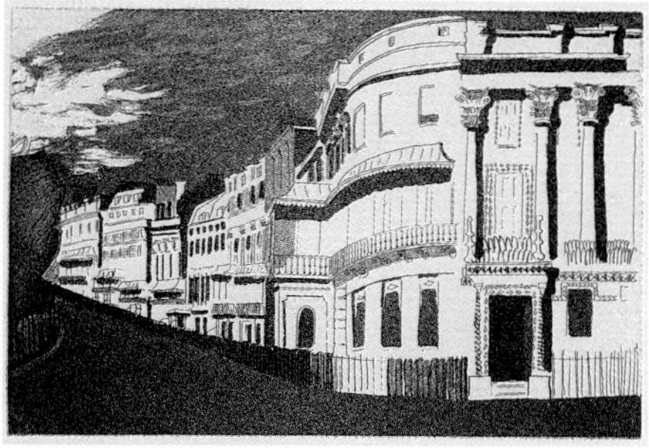

19

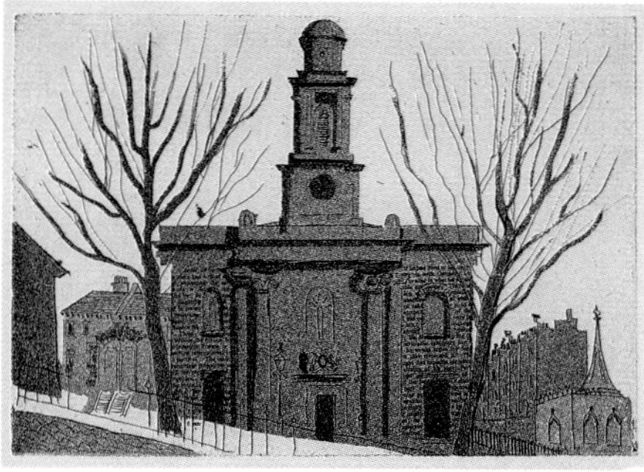

21

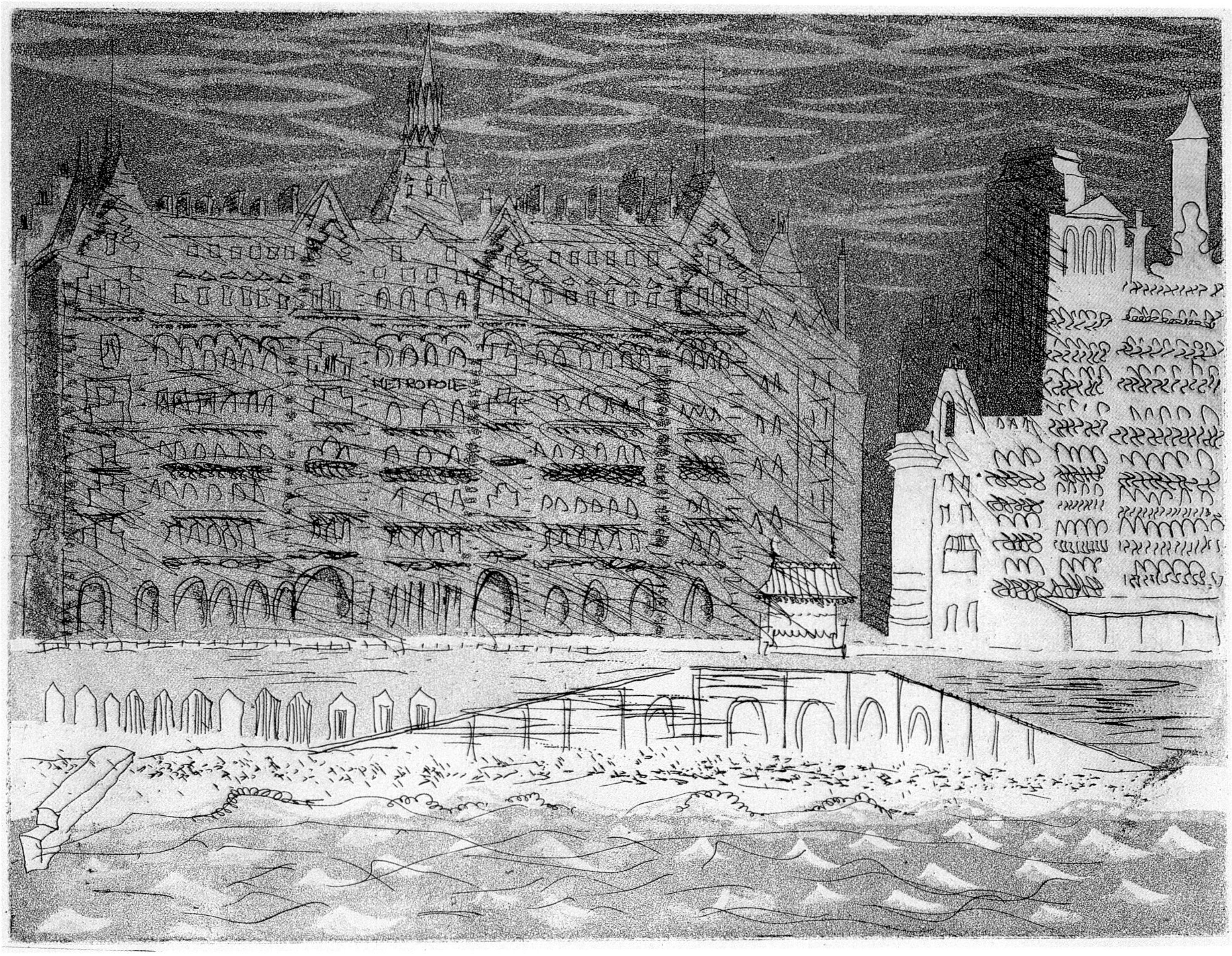

23

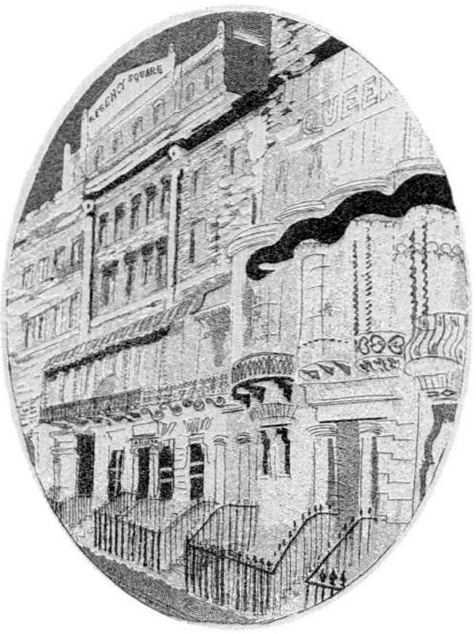

20

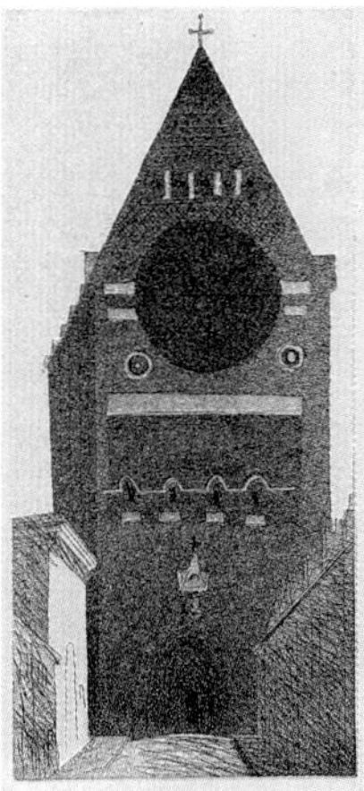

22

22
St Bartholomew's Church
Plate XI
277 × 124 ($10\frac{7}{8} \times 4\frac{7}{8}$)

Sometimes incorrectly known as '*St Bartholmew*'.
Repr. in West (illus.54)

23
The Metropole Hotel from the West Pier
Plate XII
212 × 276 ($8\frac{3}{4} \times 10\frac{7}{8}$)

24
Welsh Waterfall
Etching and aquatint 96×75 ($3\frac{13}{16} \times 3$) (plate)
The artist *c.* 1939
Unpublished
Proofing paper 239×149 ($9 \times 5\frac{7}{8}$)
Not issued as an edition Unsigned

A small number of trial proofs exist. The image was drawn directly on to the plate and was therefore reversed in the trial proofs.

25
Byland Abbey, Yorkshire
Etching and aquatint 178×276 ($7 \times 10\frac{7}{8}$) (plate)
The artist *c.* 1940
Unpublished
Proofing paper 280×330 (11×13)
Not issued as an edition Unsigned

A small number of trial proofs exist, some signed, some printed on blue-grey paper and some hand-coloured. The image was drawn directly on to the plate and was therefore reversed in the trial proof. Repr. in Ingrams/Piper (plate 68, hand-coloured version)

Victoria and Albert Museum

26
Ruined Cottage near Roman Wall
Etching and aquatint 76×100 ($3 \times 3\frac{15}{16}$) (plate)
The artist *c.* 1940
Comforts Fund for Women and Children of Soviet Russia *c.* 1942
Laid paper with deckle edges on two sides and wmk 'Hand Made' 227×162 ($8\frac{15}{16} \times 6\frac{3}{8}$)
100 'John Piper'

Various proofs exist – one is hand-tinted in yellow. The edition was given to raise funds for the publisher, and the print was included for sale in a booklet *Salvo for Russia* (typography by S. John Woods), a privately-produced publication of new poetry by Dylan Thomas, Nancy Cunard and Cecily Mackworth, containing etchings and engravings by John Banting, John Buckland-Wright, Ithell Colquhoun, Oskar Kokoschka, John Piper, Dolf Rieser, Charles Salisbury, Geza Szobel, Julian Trevelyan and Mary Wykeham. The booklet in the British Museum does not contain poetry by Dylan Thomas (as advertised), but two poems by James Law Forsyth and J. F. Henry.

British Museum

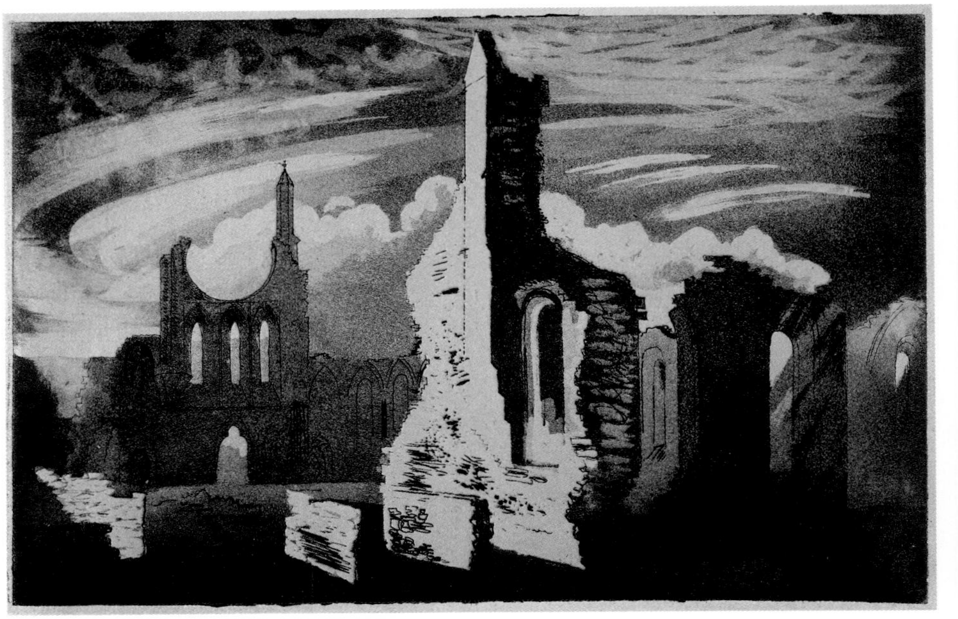

25

27
Cheltenham
Autolithograph 246×710 ($9\frac{11}{16} \times 27\frac{15}{16}$) (not allowing for binding)
Curwen Press 1940
Signature 1940
Machine-made lithographic cartridge 246×710 ($9\frac{11}{16} \times 27\frac{15}{16}$)
750 Unsigned

A fold-out lithographic panorama of Cheltenham with printed descriptions, appearing between pp. 36 and 37 of *Signature*, No. 13, January 1940, to accompany an article on Cheltenham by John Betjeman. See no. 15 on p. 154

Bodleian Library; British Library; Cambridge University Library; National Library of Scotland; National Library of Wales

28
Font and Tortoise Stove: Britwell Salome
Lithograph (offset) 308×207 ($12\frac{1}{8} \times 8\frac{1}{8}$)
Artists International Association (AIA) 1940
Artists International Association (AIA) 1940
Machine-made lithographic cartridge 350×229 ($13\frac{3}{4} \times 9$)
Unspecified Unsigned

Sometimes incorrectly known as '*The Font*'. The words 'The Font by John Piper' appear on some graphics in pencil b.l. The words 'A.I.A. Everyman Prints' are printed in red b.r. One of a series of 'Everyman Prints' (no. 52)

British Museum; Victoria and Albert Museum

29
Hall Place, Botallack, Fowey, Cornwall
Aquatint 200×277 ($7\frac{7}{8} \times 10\frac{7}{8}$)
The artist *c.* 1943
Unpublished
Proofing paper 234×292 ($9\frac{3}{16} \times 11\frac{1}{2}$) (plate)
Not issued as an edition Unsigned

Sometimes incorrectly known as '*Botallack Chapel, Near Fowey, Cornwall*'. Approximately six trial proofs exist. Repr. in Ingrams/Piper (plate 79)

Victoria and Albert Museum

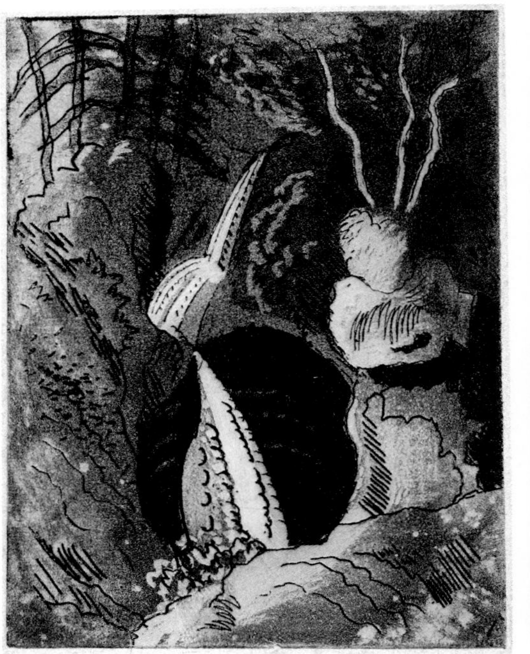

24

30
The Hall, Trecarrel, Cornwall
Etching 202×253 ($7\frac{15}{16} \times 9\frac{15}{16}$)
The artist *c.* 1943
Unpublished
Proofing paper 222×309 ($8\frac{3}{4} \times 12\frac{3}{16}$)
Not issued as an edition Unsigned

Sometimes incorrectly known as '*Launceston*' or '*Chapel near Launceston*'. A small number of trial proofs exist. The image was drawn directly on to the plate and was therefore reversed in the trial proof.

Victoria and Albert Museum

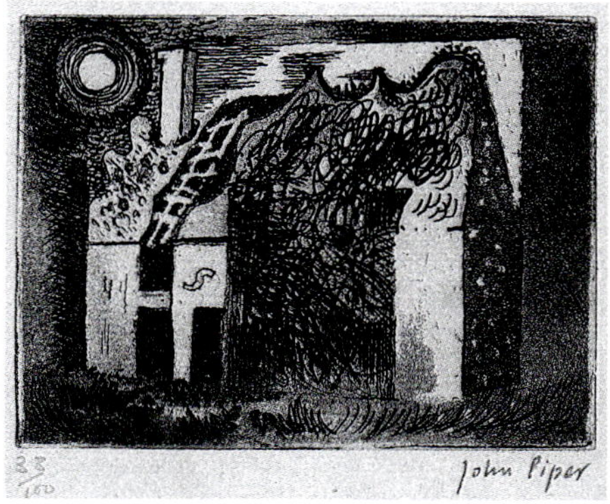

26

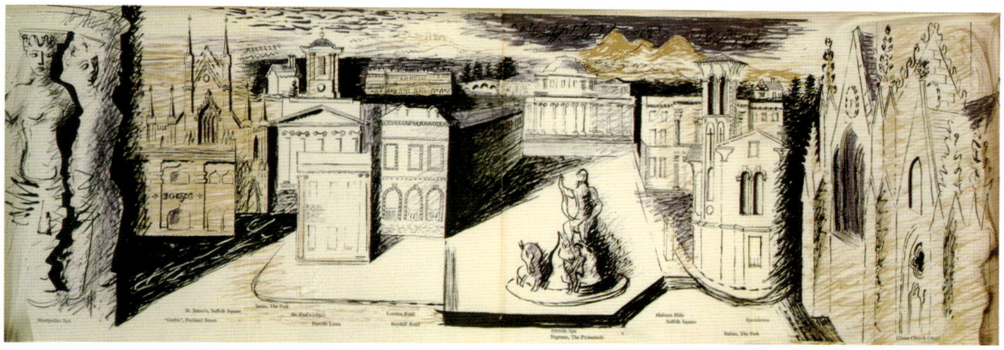

27

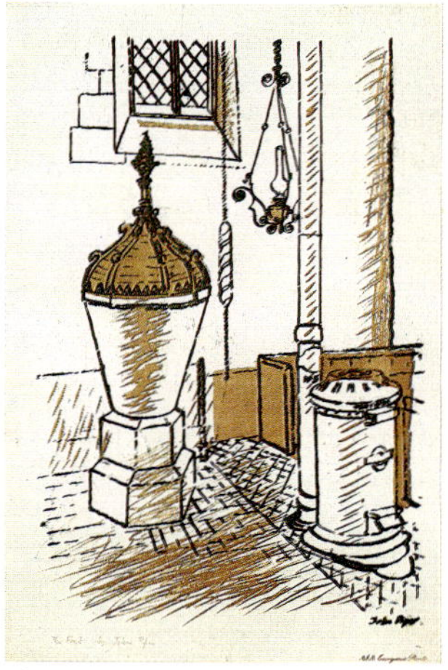

28

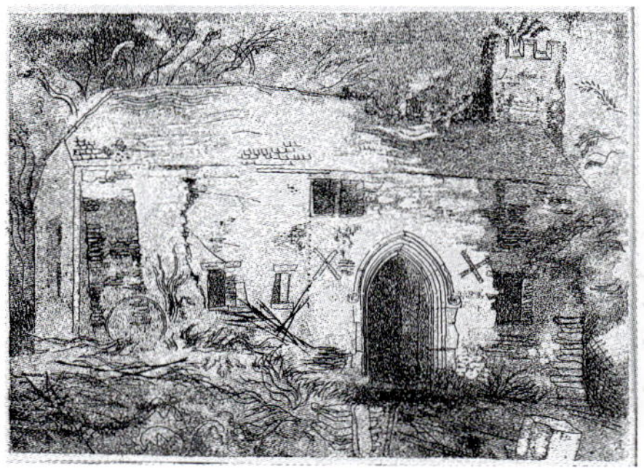

29

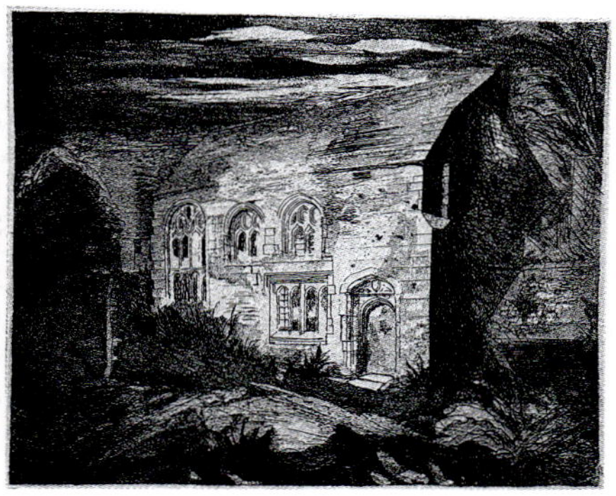

30

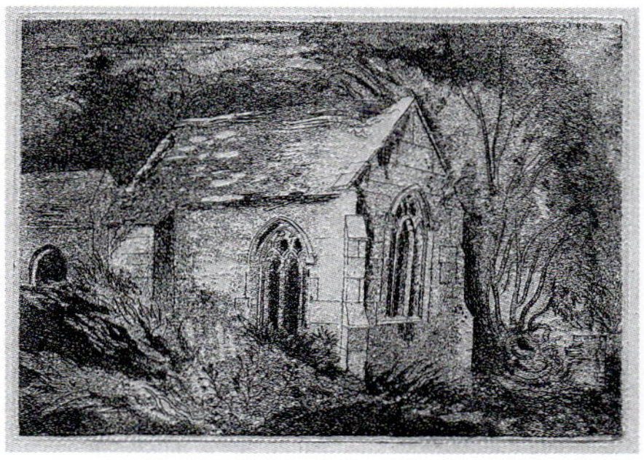

31

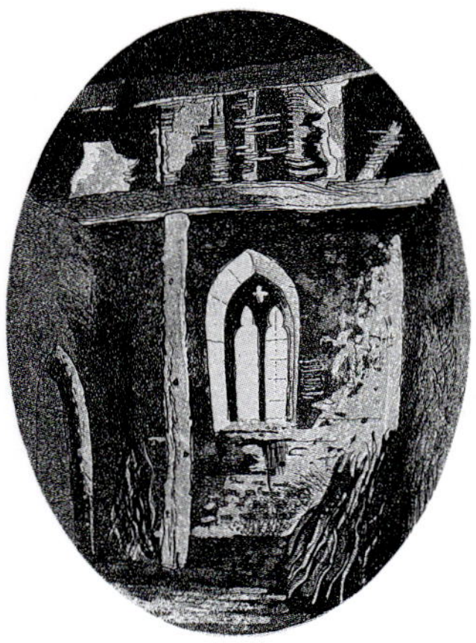

32

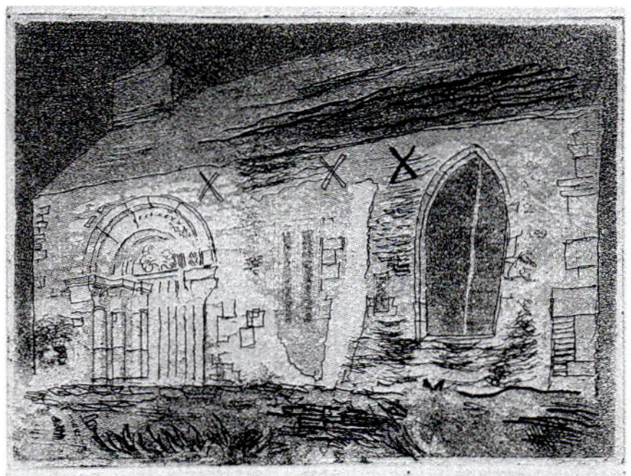

33

31
Trecarrel Chapel, Cornwall
Etching and aquatint 178 × 254 (7 × 10)
The artist *c.* 1943
Unpublished
Proofing paper 265 × 308 (10$\frac{7}{16}$ × 12$\frac{3}{16}$) (plate)
Not issued as an edition Unsigned

Sometimes incorrectly known as '*Farmyard Chapel, Trecarrel, Cornwall*' or '*Trecarrel Chapel, Lezant, Cornwall*'. A small number of trial proofs exist. Repr. in Ingrams/Piper (plate 78)

32
Yatton, Herefordshire (Interior)
Etching and aquatint 202 × 152 (7$\frac{15}{16}$ × 6)
The artist *c.* 1943
Unpublished
Proofing paper 254 × 193 (10 × 7$\frac{9}{16}$) (plate)
Not issued as an edition Unsigned

One known trial proof exists.

33
Yatton, Herefordshire
Etching and aquatint 140 × 190 (5½ × 7½)
The artist *c.* 1943
Unpublished
Proofing paper 195 × 249 (7$\frac{11}{16}$ × 9¾) (plate)
Not issued as an edition Unsigned

Sometimes incorrectly known as '*Chapel at Yatton, Herefordshire*' or '*Yatton Chapel, Herefordshire*'. A small number of trial proofs exist. Repr. in Ingrams/Piper (plate 80)

34-46
English, Scottish and Welsh Landscape, 1944
A book containing twelve autolithographs with a lithographic dust-jacket which formed part of New Excursions into English Poetry (edited by W.J. Turner and Sheila Shannon), a series which also included *The Poet's Eye*, *Sea Poems*, *Poems of Death*, *Soldier's Verse* and *Traveller's Verse*. Each book had the verse selected by different editors and was in turn illustrated by an artist who created original lithographs. The verse for *English Scottish and Welsh Landscape* was chosen by John Betjeman and Geoffrey Taylor. The lithographs are unconnected with individual poems.

The lithographs were printed by the Curwen Press and published by Frederick Muller. The book was produced by Adprint and was unsigned, unnumbered and in an unspecified large print run. The paper is standard quality machine-made lithographic cartridge paper with a weight of approximately 120gsm. The title of each lithograph is printed b.l. and its county b.r. They were all drawn directly on to the plates by the artist, but the design for the dust-jacket was printed first on to cloth for tinting. A few of the lithographs were sold in sheet form without the artist's knowledge. Subsequently some were signed by him on request.
Book size: 213×147 ($8\frac{3}{8} \times 5\frac{3}{4}$)

Bodleian Library; British Library; British Museum; Cambridge University Library; Museum of Modern Art, New York; National Library of Scotland; National Library of Wales; Tate Gallery; Trinity College Library, Dublin

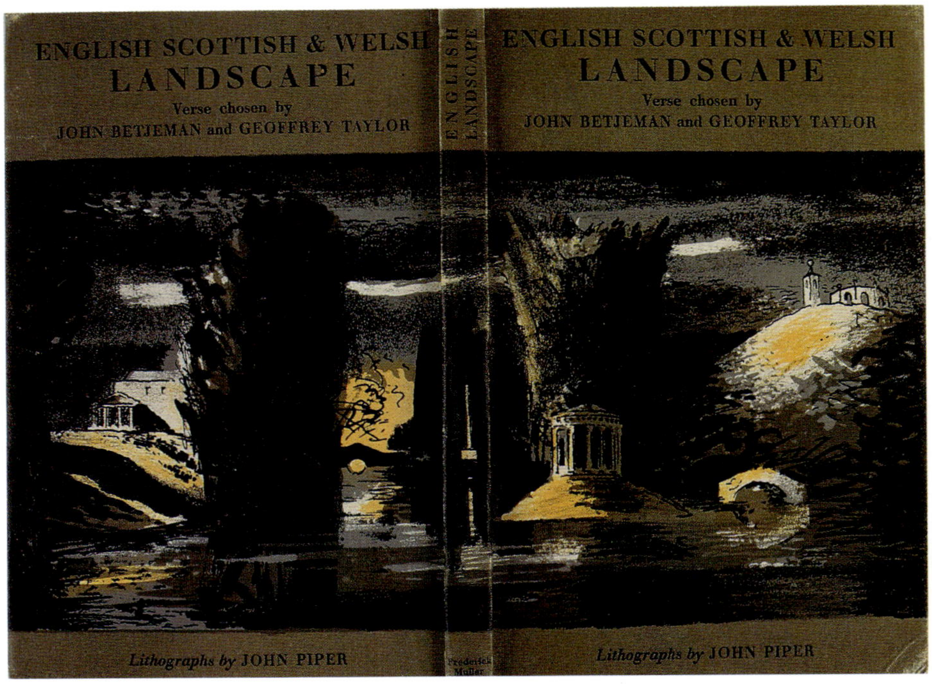

34

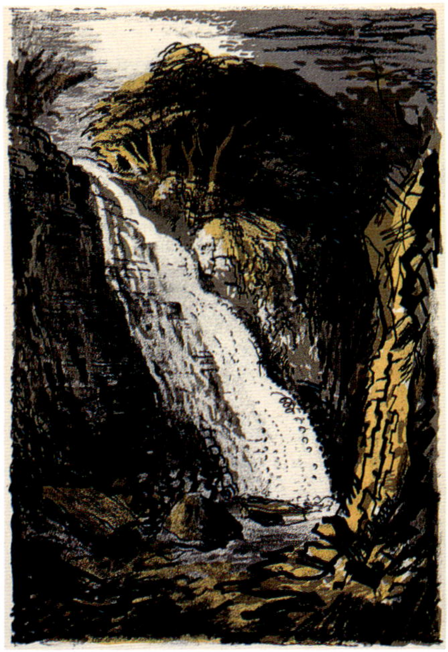

35

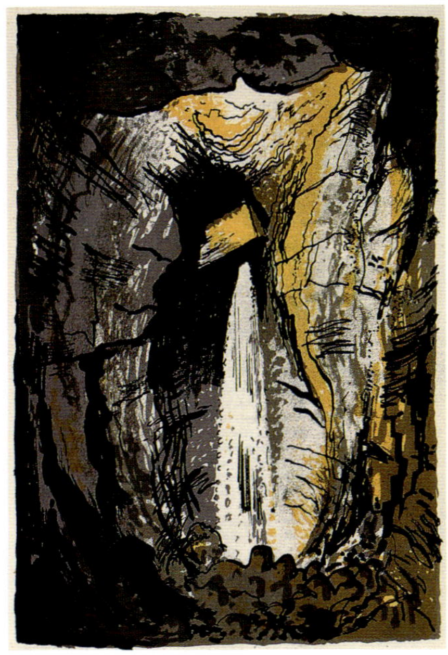

36

34
English, Scottish and Welsh Landscape (dust-jacket)
146×313 ($5\frac{3}{4} \times 12\frac{1}{4}$)
Repr. on the dust-jacket

35
Pistyll Cain, North Wales
Plate I (facing p.1)
180×120 ($7\frac{1}{16} \times 4\frac{3}{4}$)
Repr. in black-and-white in Tate (p.23)

36
Weathercote Cave, Yorkshire
Plate II (facing p.4)
181×118 ($7\frac{1}{8} \times 4\frac{5}{8}$)

37
Tomen-y-Mur and Roman Amphitheatre, North Wales
Plate III (facing p.11)
120×181 ($4\frac{3}{4} \times 7\frac{1}{8}$)

38
Grongar Hill, Carmarthenshire
Plate IV (facing p.26)
120×181 ($4\frac{3}{4} \times 7\frac{1}{8}$)

Repr. in Ingrams/Piper (plate 110)

39
At Lewknor, Oxfordshire
Plate V (facing p.43)
120×180 ($4\frac{3}{4} \times 7\frac{1}{16}$)

40
Rievaulx Abbey, Yorkshire
Plate VI (facing p.58)
120×180 ($4\frac{3}{4} \times 7\frac{1}{16}$)

41
Trawsfynnydd, Merioneth
Plate VII (facing p.63)
120×180 ($4\frac{3}{4} \times 7\frac{1}{16}$)

42
Approach to Gordale Scar, Yorkshire
Plate VIII (facing p.70)
120×181 ($4\frac{3}{4} \times 7\frac{1}{8}$)

43
Easegill, Lancashire
Plate IX (facing p.75)
181×120 ($7\frac{1}{8} \times 4\frac{3}{4}$)

44
Park Place, Berkshire
Plate X (facing p.90)
118×180 ($4\frac{5}{8} \times 7\frac{1}{16}$)

45
Talland Church, Cornwall
Plate XI (facing p.95)
120×181 ($4\frac{3}{4} \times 7\frac{1}{8}$)

46
Stonesfield, Oxfordshire
Plate XII (facing p.102)
120×181 ($4\frac{3}{4} \times 7\frac{1}{8}$)

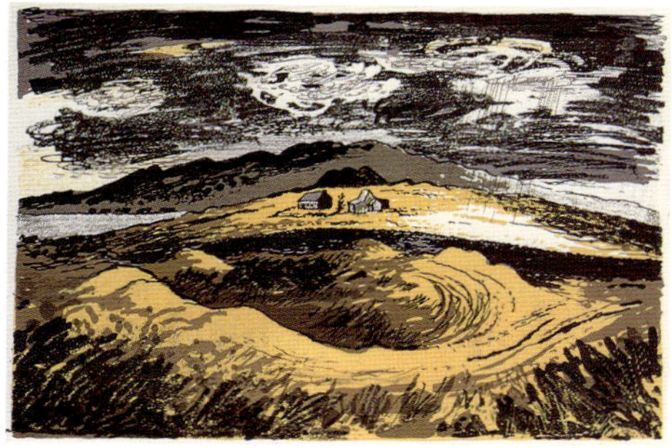
37

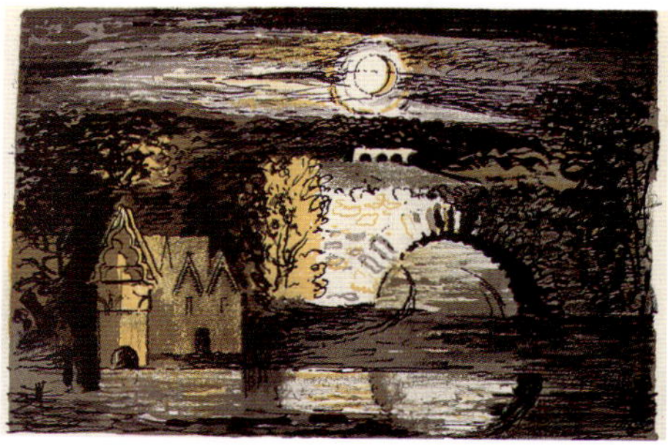
44

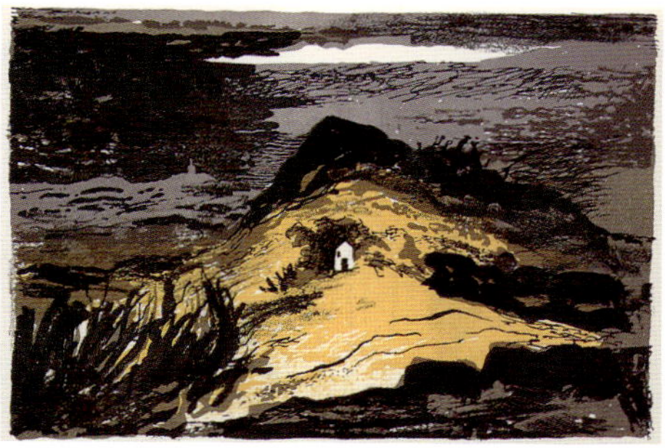
38

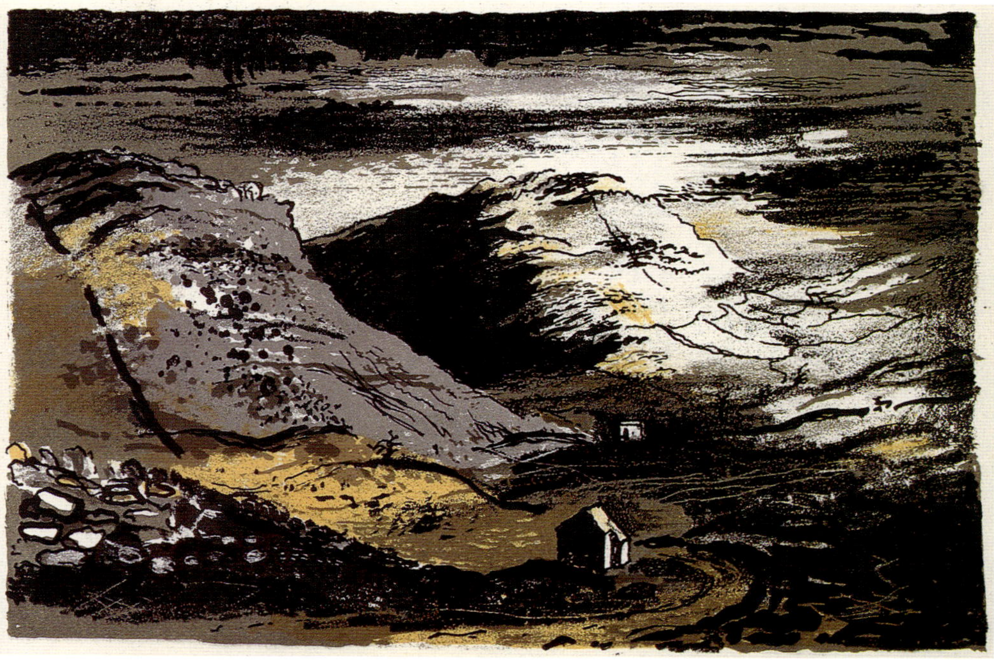
42

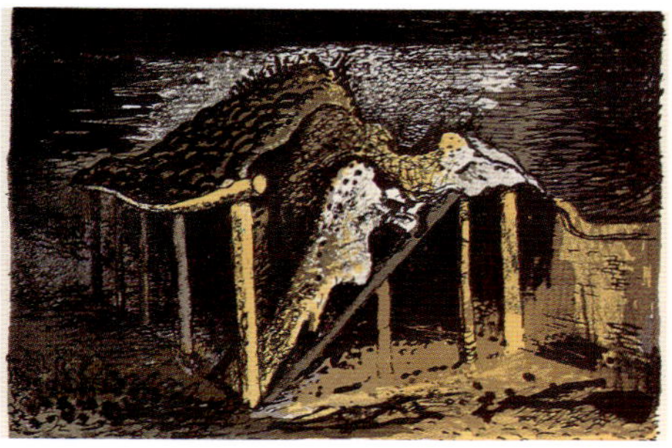
39

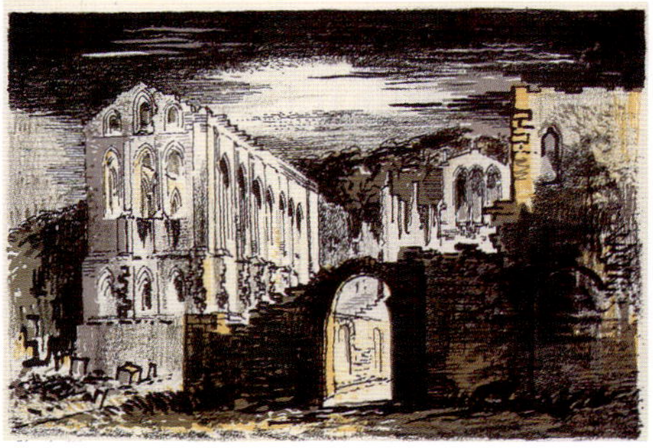
40

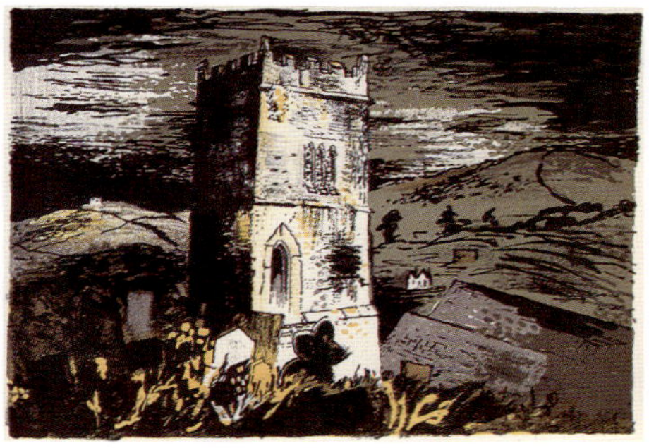
45

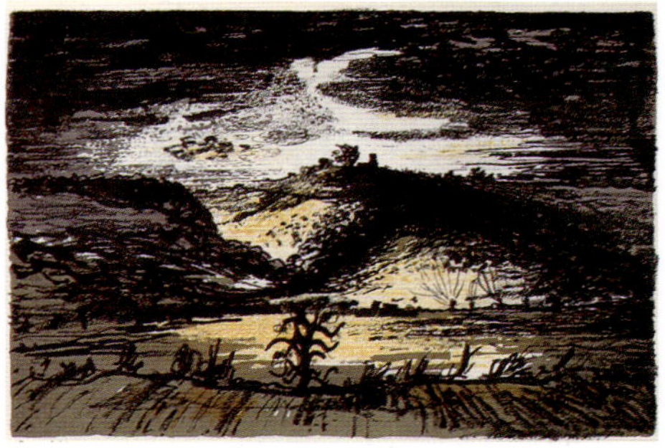
46

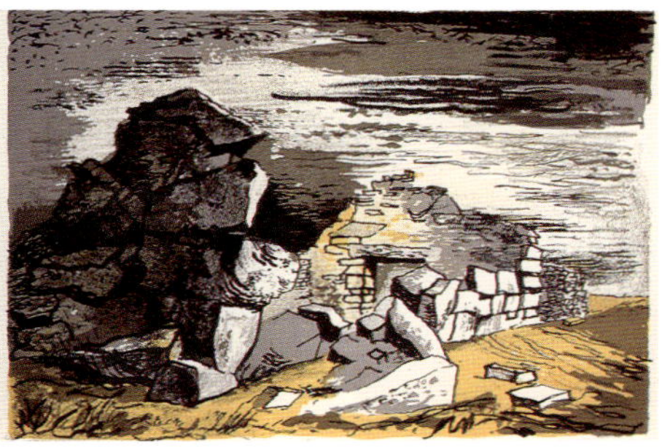
41

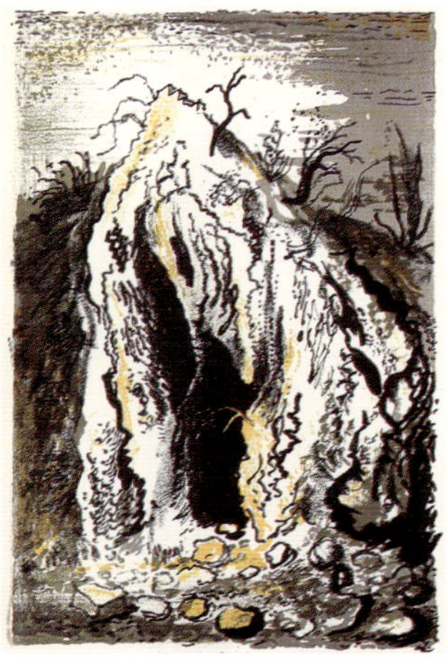
43

47–57
The Colour of English Country Houses, 1944
A collection of twelve autolithographs, unsigned, unnumbered and in an unspecified large print run, printed by the Curwen Press, as an 8-page pamphlet and published by *International Textiles*.

The paper is standard quality machine-made lithographic cartridge paper with a weight of approximately 110gsm. Page size: 349×248 ($13\frac{3}{4}\times9\frac{3}{4}$). The front page carries descriptions (not by the artist) of each house. Plates VI and IX have 'Sunset at Knole and at Hafod' as a double-page title. Plates X and XI have 'Classic and Romantic' as a page title.

British Library

Notes to *The Colour of English Country Houses* not by the artist

Chicheley Hall, Buckinghamshire
A house in brick with warm stone dressings, standing in the green and quiet landscape of North Buckinghamshire. It was built in the early part of the eighteenth century. Dark elm-trees, wind-stirred grass and water-meadows form its landscape setting.

Mereworth Castle, Kent
Another eighteenth-century classical design, by Colen Campbell, 1723–5. An almost exact copy of Palladio's Villa Almerico at Vicenza, 'quite unsuitable for the English climate and requirements'; and yet it has gained a charm and propriety in the Kentish countryside with the passage of two hundred years. Shockingly enough for present-day fashions, it is built of yellow brick.

Seaton Delaval, Northumberland
Built by Sir John Vanbrugh, dramatist-architect, for a rich and eccentric family. It now stands, gutted by fire, derelict and empty, in a colliery district near the North Sea coast, and is one of the most richly romantic of large English country houses. Its colour is umber, ochre and purple – the stone was stained by the fire – and this admirably suits the character of the bare, industrial landscape where it stands.

Sudbrooke Park, Richmond, Surrey
A Palladian design by James Gibbs, architect of St Martin's-in-the-fields Church, London. The contrast between the pale stucco and the darker brick, set off by the elaborate flights of stone steps, is a carefully studied feature.

Kirby Hall, Northamptonshire
A yellow stone house of the seventeenth century, in rolling green hunting-country. It gleams in the sun, forms a warm eye-catcher in dull weather and glimmers whitely in moonlight. It is another ruin, partly roofless, and has been recently taken over by the Office of Works to be preserved as a show-place.

Knole, Kent
The Palace of the Sackville family, near Sevenoaks. Of yellow-grey Kentish ragstone, mostly fifteenth century. From its beautiful park, and especially from the north east, with its ranges of long, red-tiled roofs, it looks like a beautifully-planned and weathered medieval town.

Bolsover Castle, Derbyshire
A hill-top castle of the seventeenth century, by an architect called Smythson. Eccentrically planned, with details that are at once heavy and exquisite, it dominates a landscape fretted with collieries and ironworks. One wing – the south – only is shown in the drawing.

Attingham, Shropshire
A grey stone house in a rich, low-lying landscape near Shrewsbury. Eighteenth century; of elegant proportions.

Hafod, Cardiganshire
Built of yellow stone in the early nineteenth century, with a later addition in granite, this romantic house occupies a remote and beautiful valley in central Wales. King Edward VII wondered if he would take it, but took Osborne in the Isle of Wight instead.

West Wycombe Park, Buckinghamshire
A yellow, Italianate, symmetrical mansion, in a romantic irregular park; as beautiful in the pale sunshine of an English spring as it would be in the glaring sun of an Italian summer.

Fonthill, Wiltshire
Gothic splendour conceived for William Beckford by James Wyatt. Now vanished, except for fragments. 'Fonthill Splendens' dominated a hilly, romantic country; a gigantic piece of scene-painting in three dimensions of greyish yellow stone.

47
Chicheley Hall, Buckinghamshire
Plate I (p.1)
130×203 ($5\frac{1}{8}\times8$)
Title printed b.r.

The words 'The Colour of English Country Houses' printed t.c.

48
Mereworth Castle, Kent
Plate II (p.2)
119×182 ($4\frac{11}{16}\times7\frac{1}{8}$)
Title printed centre below image

49
Seaton Delaval, Northumberland
Plate III (p.2)
119×182 ($4\frac{11}{16}\times7\frac{1}{8}$)
Title printed centre above image

50
Sudbrooke Park, Richmond, Surrey
Plate IV (p.3)
229×188 ($9\times7\frac{3}{8}$)
Title printed b.r.

51
Kirby Hall, Northamptonshire
Plate V (pp.4 and 5)
255×464 ($10\times18\frac{1}{4}$)
Title printed in bold above image

52
Knole, Kent
Plate VI (p.6)
146×203 ($5\frac{3}{4}\times8$)
Title printed below image b.l.

53
Bolsover Castle, Derbyshire
Plate VII (p.6)
83×113 ($3\frac{1}{4}\times4\frac{7}{16}$)
Title printed above image t.l.
Reproduction (or second edition) in S. John Woods' 'John Piper as a Topographical Illustrator', *Image: a quarterly of the visual arts*, 1949

The Phillips Collection

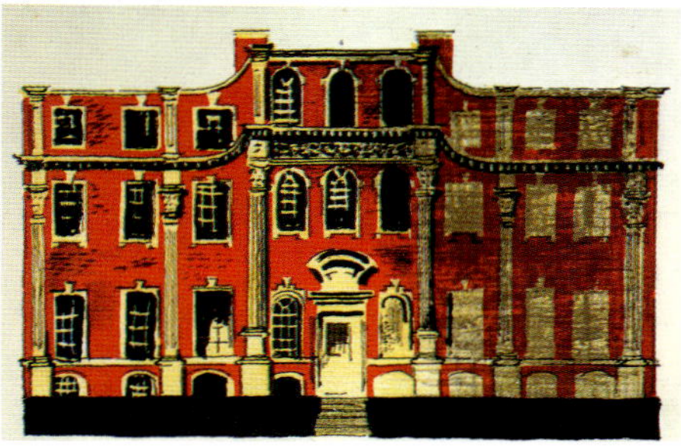

47

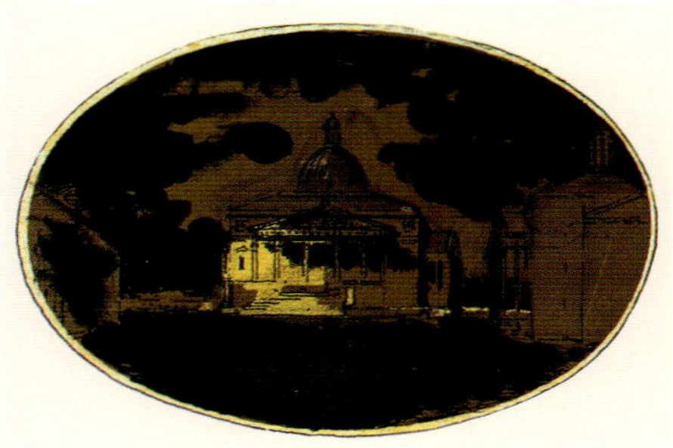

48

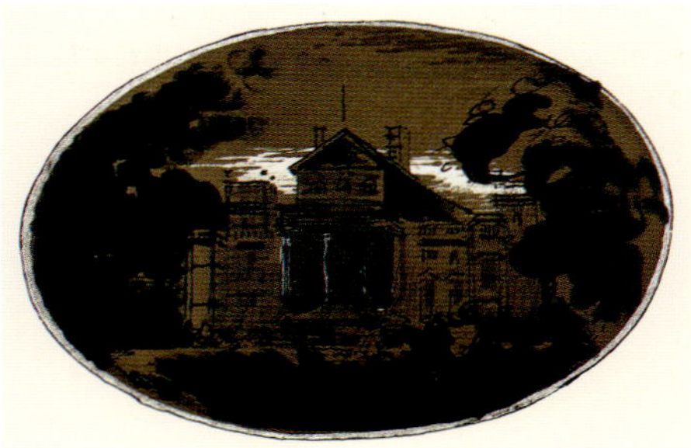

49

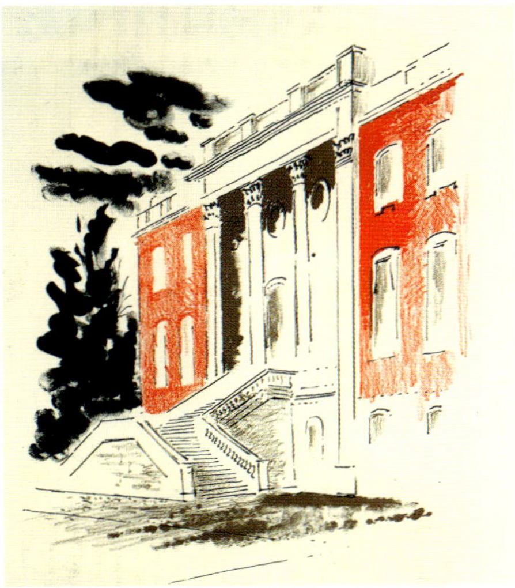

50

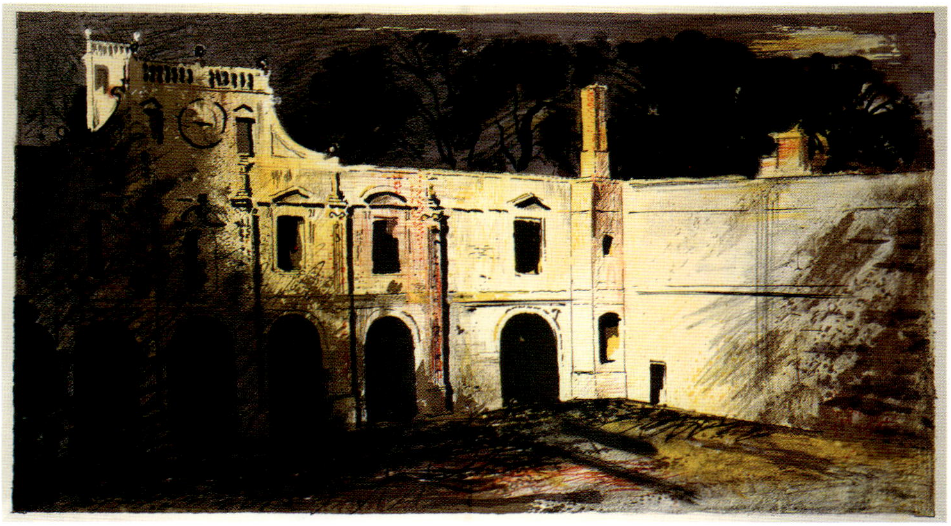

51

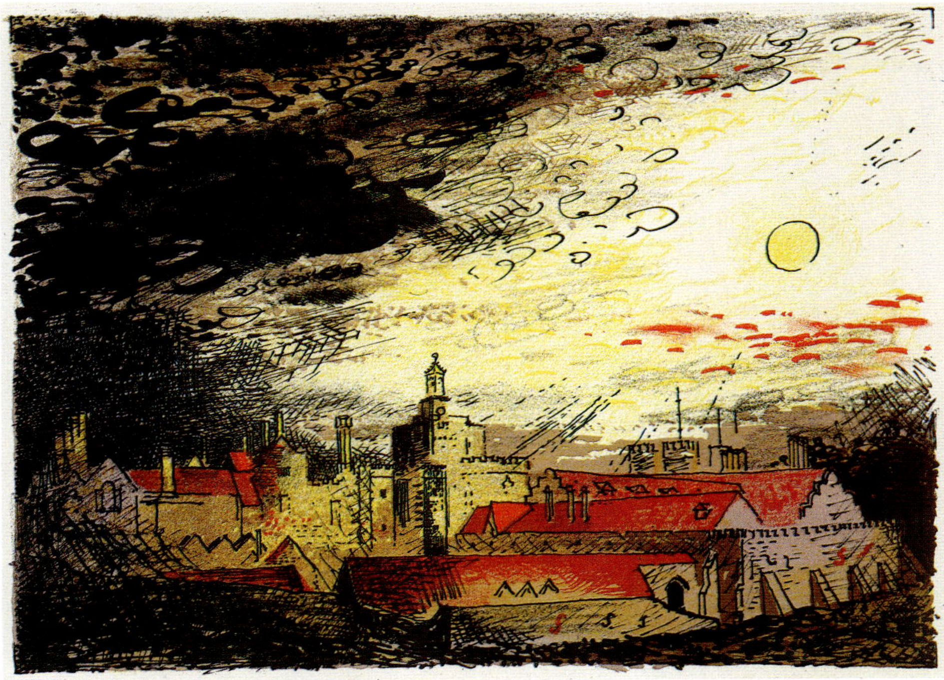

52

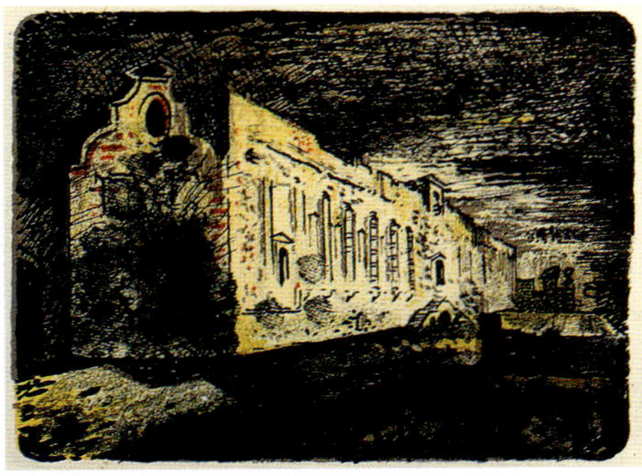

53

54
Attingham, Shropshire
Plate VIII (p.7)
83×113 ($3\frac{1}{4}\times4\frac{7}{16}$)
Title printed below image b.r.
Reproduction (or second edition) in S. John Woods' 'John Piper as a Topographical Illustrator', *Image: a quarterly of the visual arts*, 1949

55
Hafod, Cardiganshire
Plate IX (p.7)
151×205 ($5\frac{15}{16}\times8\frac{1}{16}$)
Title printed above image t.r.

56
West Wycombe Park, Buckinghamshire
Plate X (p.8)
136×204 ($5\frac{5}{16}\times8\frac{1}{16}$)
Title printed below image b.l.

57
Vanished Fonthill, Wiltshire
Plate XI (p.8)
157×203 ($6\frac{5}{8}\times8$)
Title printed below image b.l.

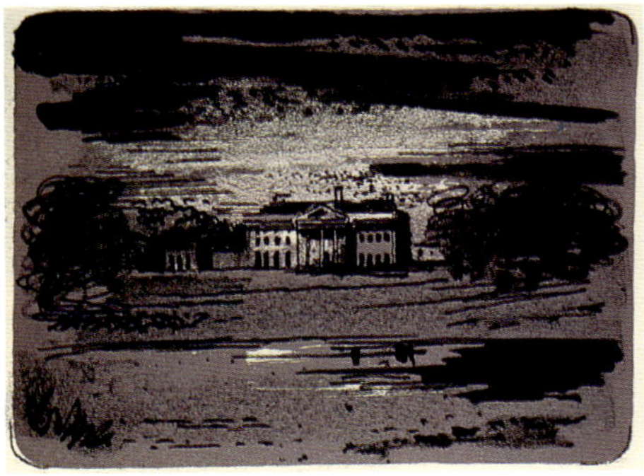
54

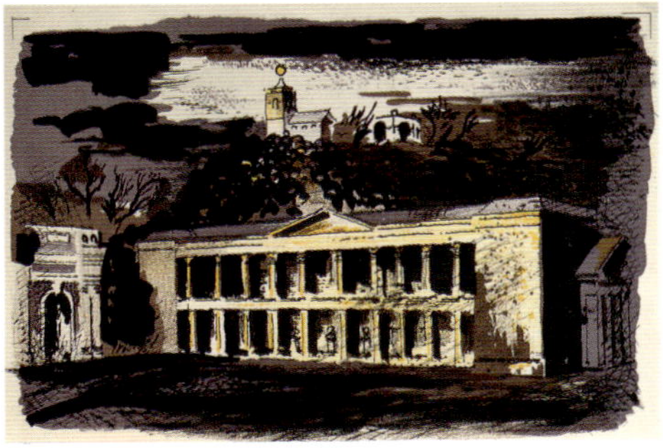
56

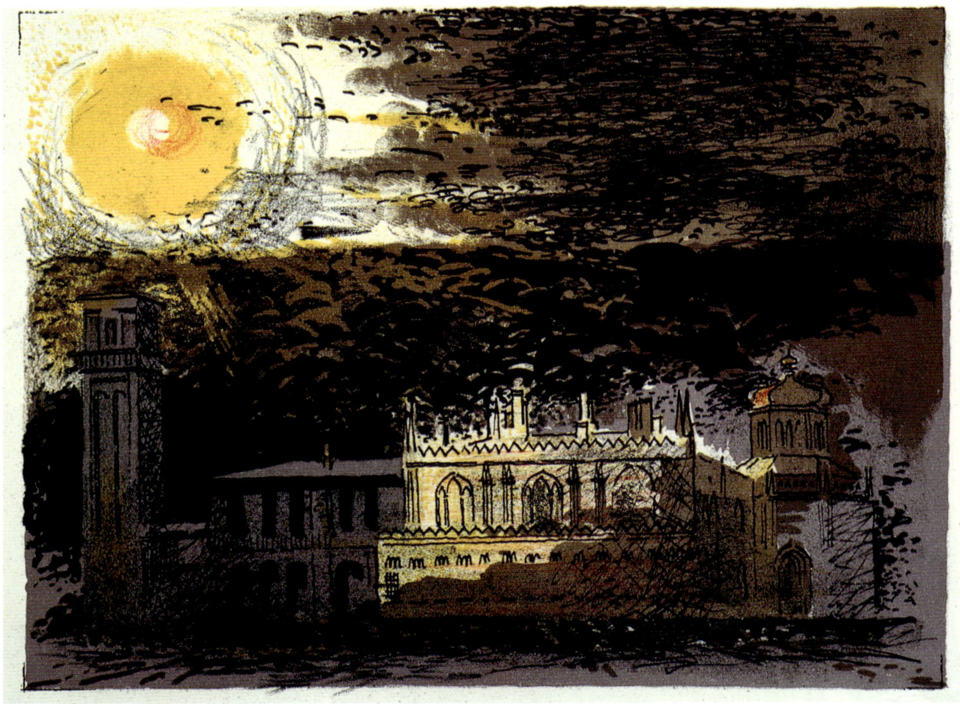
55

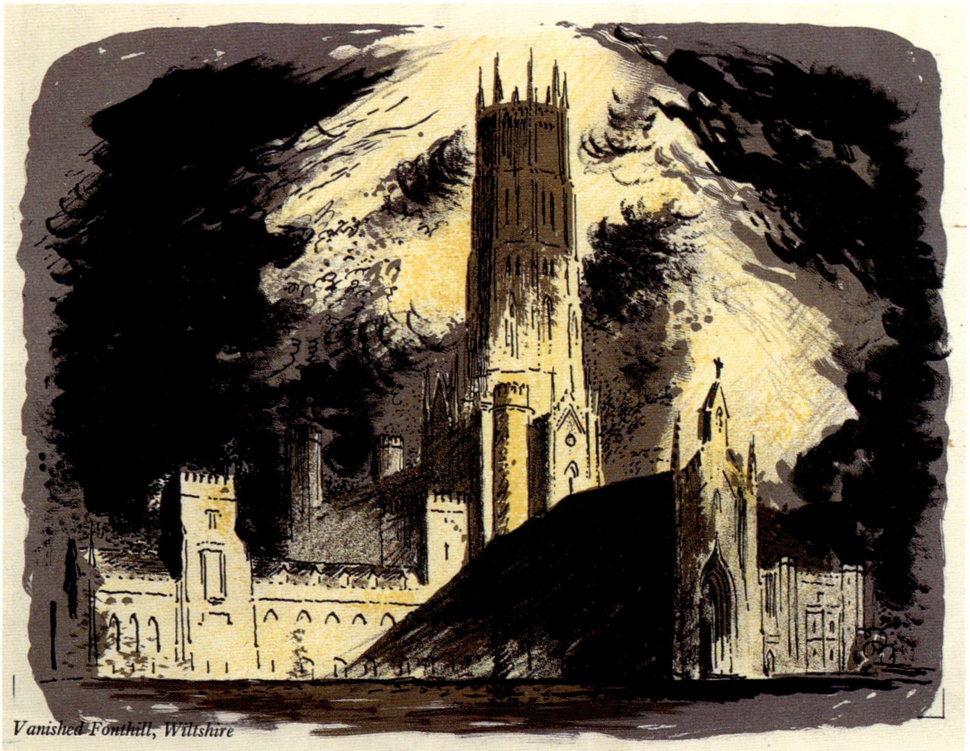

57

57A-C
Topographical Letter from Devizes,
November 1944
An article, written by John Piper, containing three autolithographs appearing in *Cornhill*, Vol.161, No.963, November, pp.190-5, published by John Murray. The lithographs were printed at Butler and Tanner.
Revised and republished in *Buildings and Prospects*, 1948 by John Piper
The paper is standard quality machine-made lithographic cartridge paper with a weight of approximately 100gsm and a size of 218×134 ($8\frac{1}{2} \times 5\frac{1}{4}$).

Bodleian Library; British Library; Cambridge University Library; National Library of Scotland; National Library of Wales; Trinity College Library, Dublin

57A
Devizes: In Long Street
(facing p.192)
Autolithograph 124×185 ($4\frac{7}{8} \times 7\frac{1}{4}$)

57B
Devizes: The Market Place
(between pp.192-3, double-spread)
Autolithograph 244×185 ($9\frac{5}{8} \times 7\frac{1}{4}$)

This image was adapted and hand-coloured for the autolithograph *The Market Place at Devizes* (Cat.68).

57C
Avebury Restored
(facing p.193)
Autolithograph 120×185 ($4\frac{3}{4} \times 7\frac{1}{4}$)

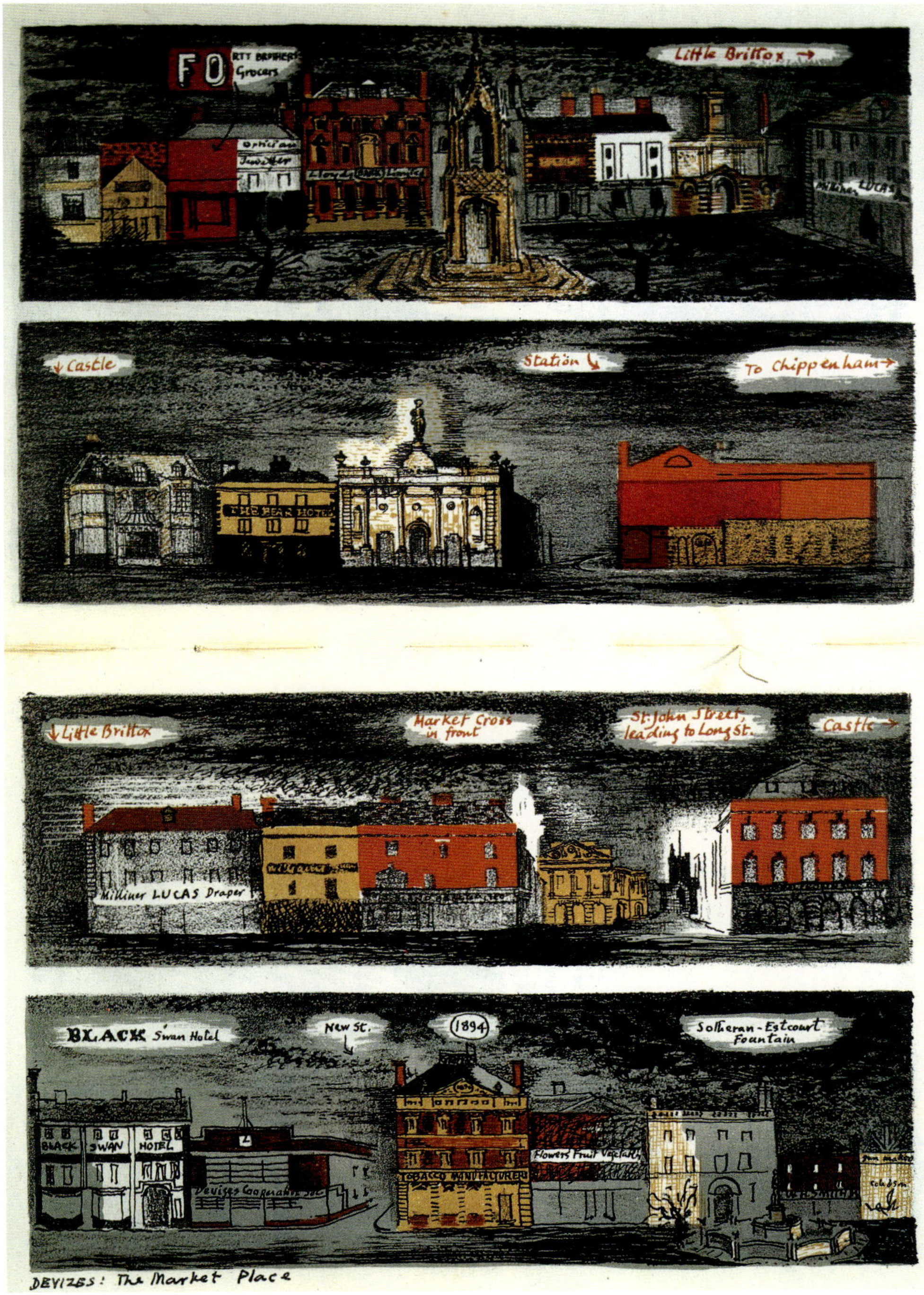

57B

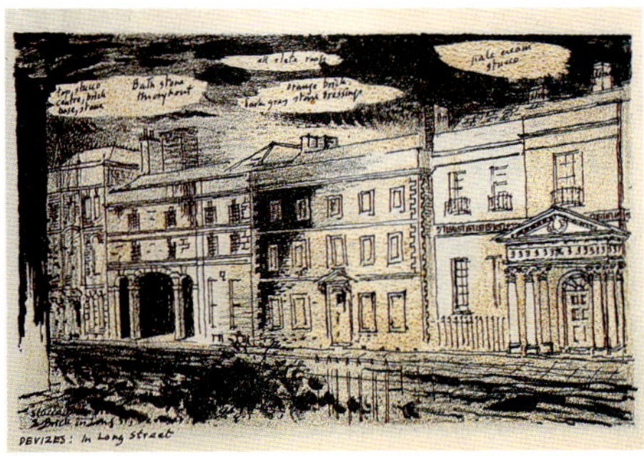

57A

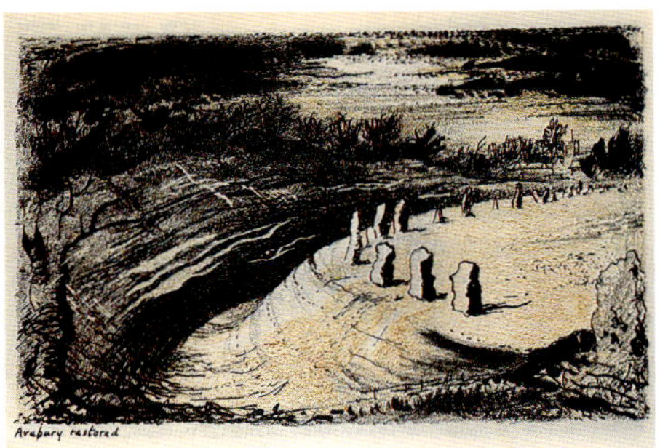

57C

58-66
The Castles on the Ground, December 1946
A book containing eight autolithographs and a lithographic dust-jacket, written by J. M. Richards, published by the Architectural Press and printed by Robert Maclehose and Co, University Press, Glasgow. The lithographs were printed at the Baynard Press, they were unsigned and unnumbered and the edition size is unknown. In 1973 a second edition was published with four new images and a new cover incorporating one new image. Though all these were photographically reproduced they are not reproductions from the first edition despite *prima facie* similarities.

Book size: 216 × 142 ($8\frac{1}{2} \times 5\frac{9}{16}$). Paper size (lithographs): 211 × 134 ($8\frac{5}{16} \times 5\frac{1}{4}$). The paper is standard quality machine-made lithographic cartridge paper with a weight of approximately 100gsm

Bodleian Library; British Library; Cambridge University Library; Museum of Modern Art, New York; National Library of Scotland; National Library of Wales; Trinity College, Dublin

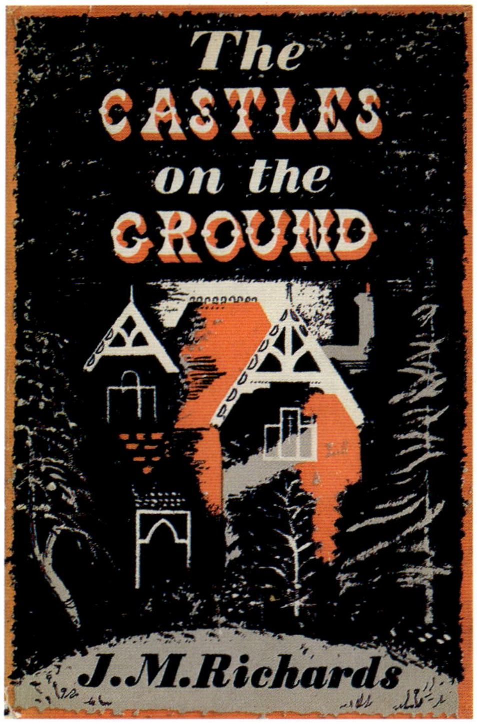

58

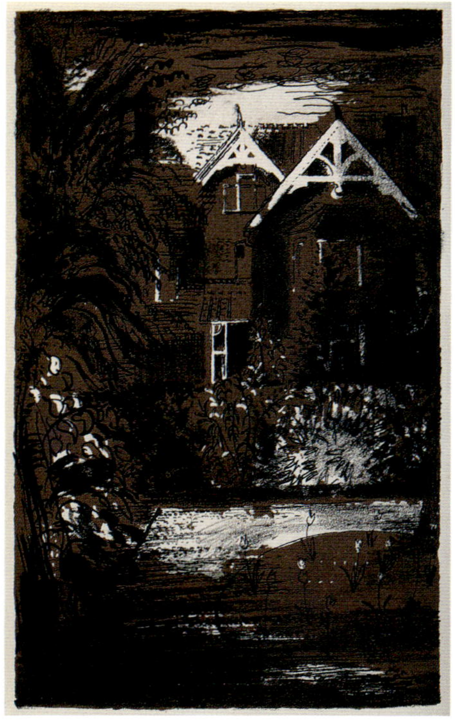
59

58
The Castles on the Ground (dust-jacket)
217 × 142 ($8\frac{1}{2} \times 5\frac{9}{16}$)
Repr. in Ingrams/Piper (plate 30)

59
The Castles on the Ground I
Frontispiece
189 × 116 ($7\frac{7}{16} \times 4\frac{9}{16}$)

60
The Castles on the Ground II
(facing p.22)
190 × 115 ($7\frac{1}{2} \times 4\frac{1}{2}$)
Repr. in S. John Woods' 'John Piper as a Topographical Illustrator', *Image: a quarterly of the visual arts*, 1949

61
The Castles on the Ground III
(facing p.29)
115 × 190 ($4\frac{1}{2} \times 7\frac{1}{2}$)

62
The Castles on the Ground IV
(facing p.39)
115 × 192 ($4\frac{1}{2} \times 7\frac{9}{16}$)

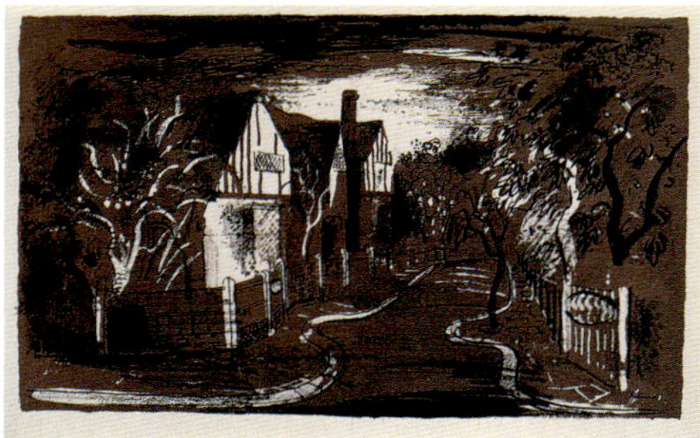
61

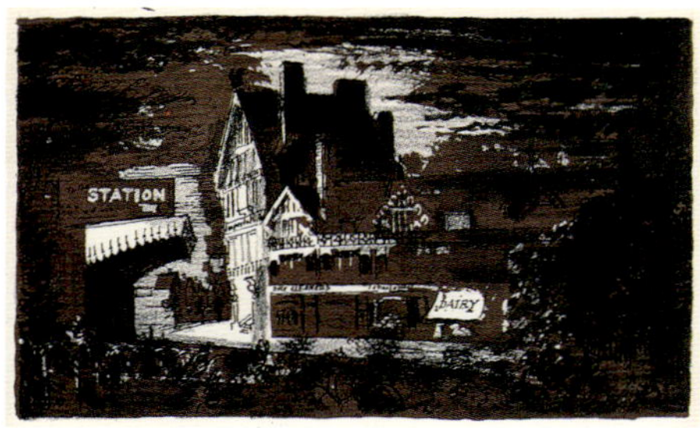

62

63
The Castles on the Ground V
(facing p.42)
115 × 190 ($4\frac{1}{2} \times 7\frac{1}{2}$)

64
The Castles on the Ground VI
(facing p.52)
190 × 113 ($7\frac{1}{2} \times 4\frac{7}{16}$)

Repr. in black-and-white in Tate (p.22)

65
The Castles on the Ground VII
(facing p.67)
115 × 189 ($4\frac{1}{2} \times 7\frac{7}{16}$)

66
The Castles on the Ground VIII
(facing p.78)
189 × 115 ($7\frac{7}{16} \times 4\frac{1}{2}$)
Repr. in S. John Woods' 'John Piper as a Topographical Illustrator', *Image: a quarterly of the visual arts*, 1949

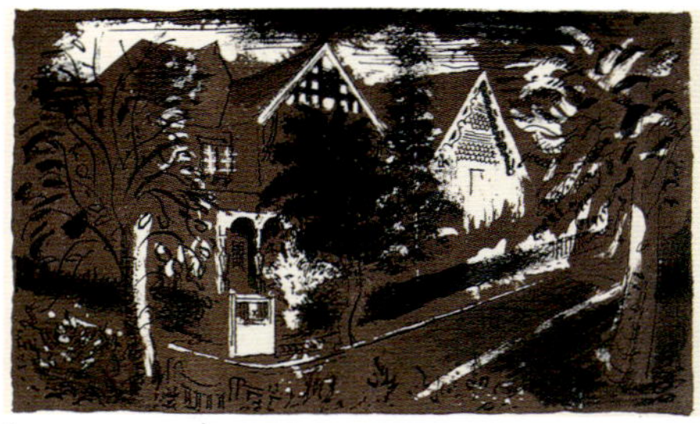
63

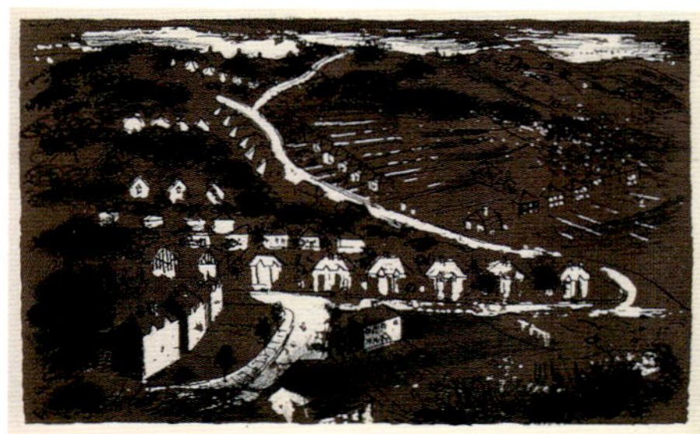
65

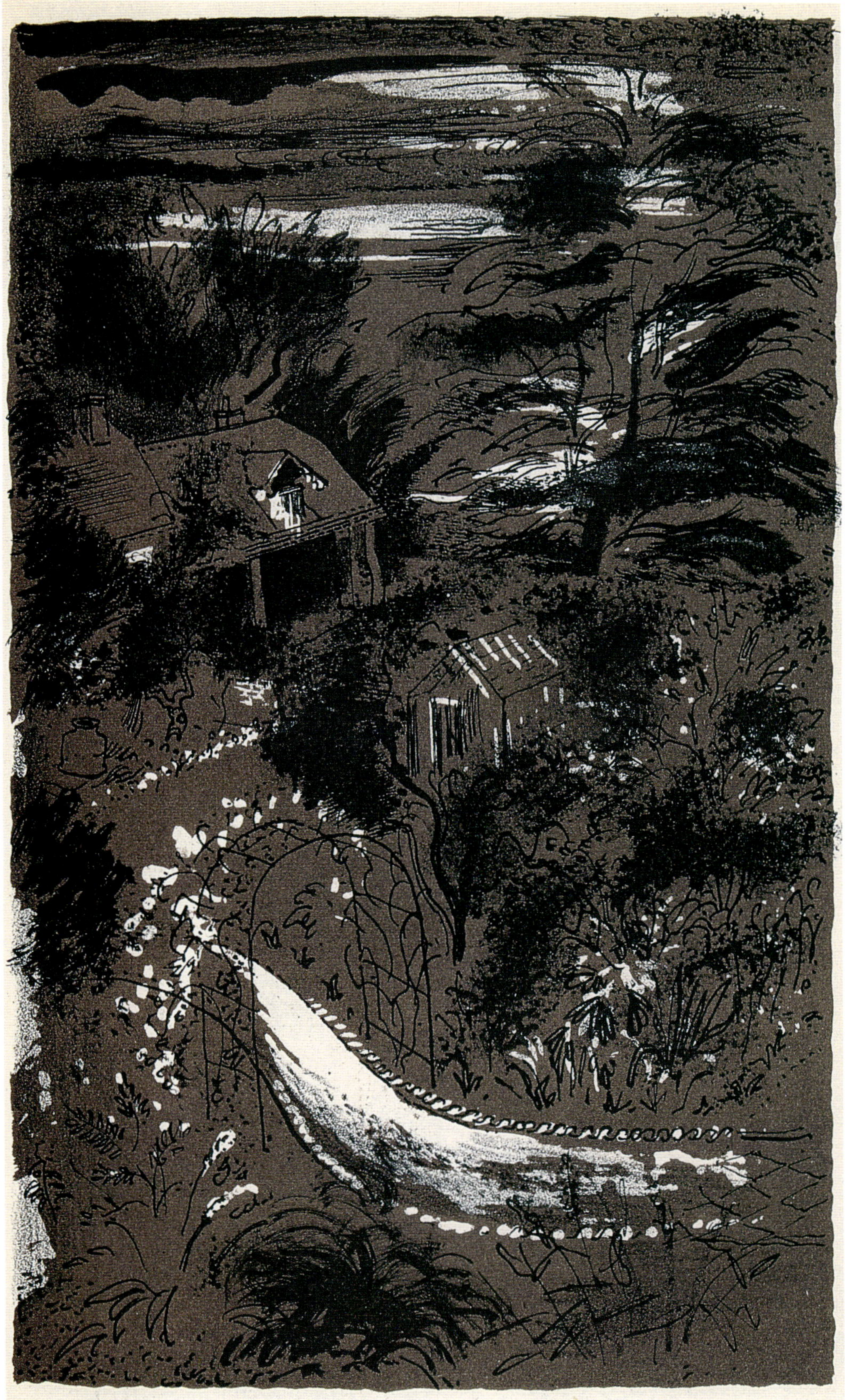

60

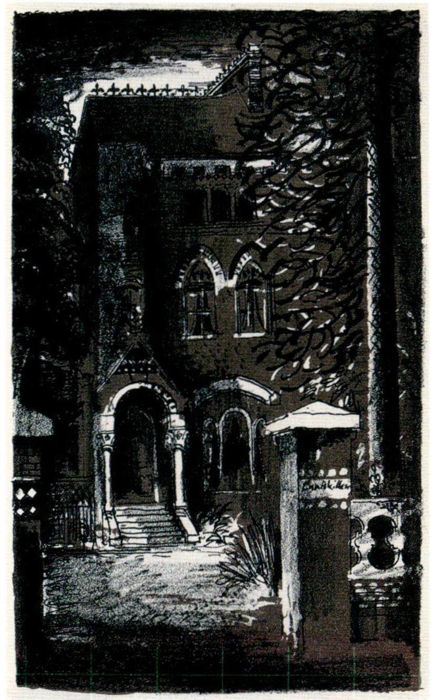

64

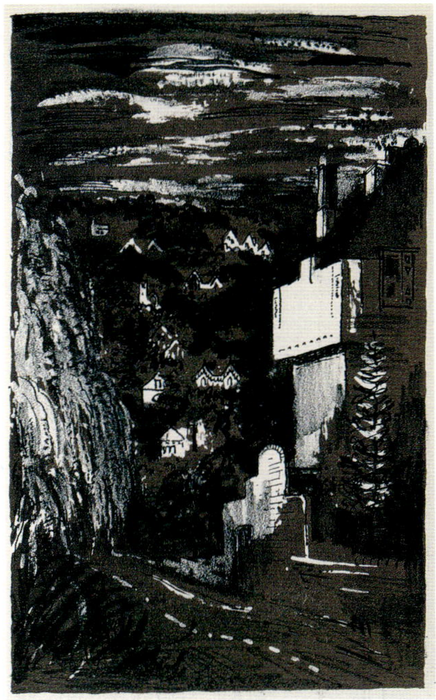

66

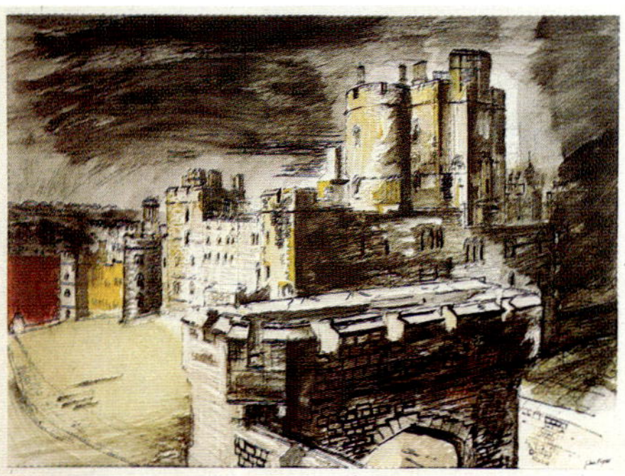

67

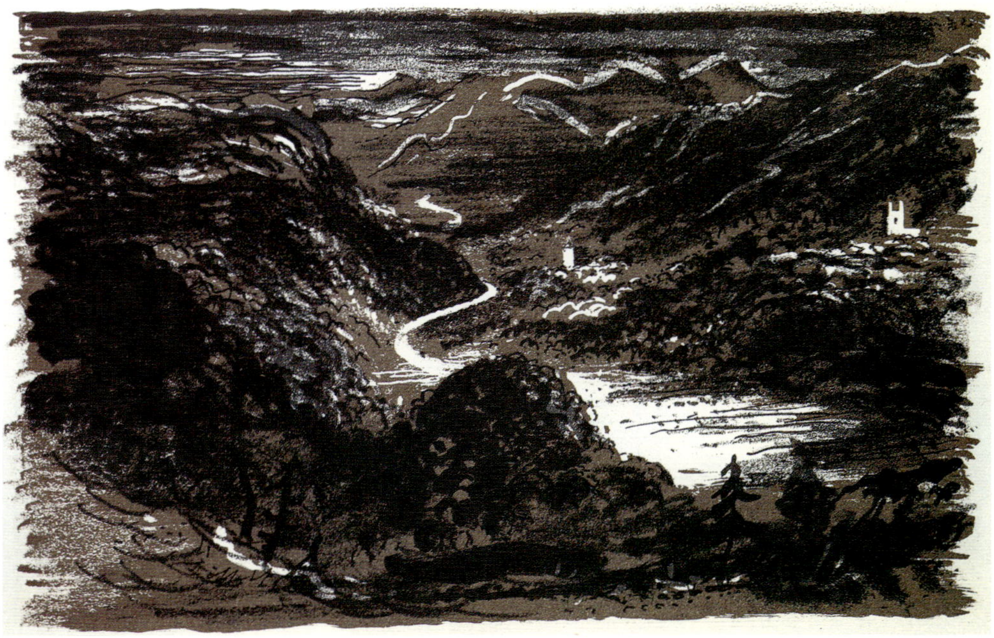

67B

67
Windsor Castle
Lithograph 267 × 369 (10½ × 14½)
Unknown *c.* 1948
Penguin Prints *c.* 1948
Machine-made lithographic cartridge 381 × 508 (15 × 20)
Unspecified Unsigned

The print was signed in the plate by the artist. The third print in the Penguin series

Victoria and Albert Museum

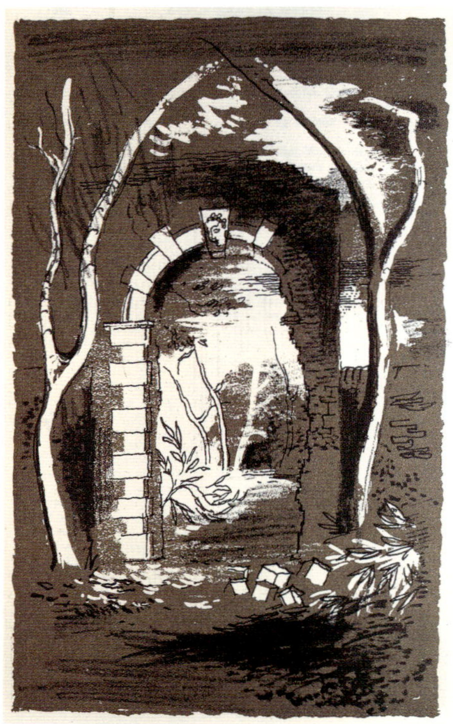

67A

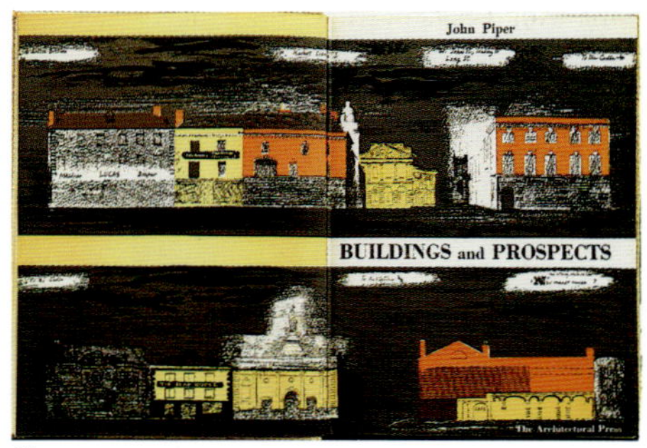

68

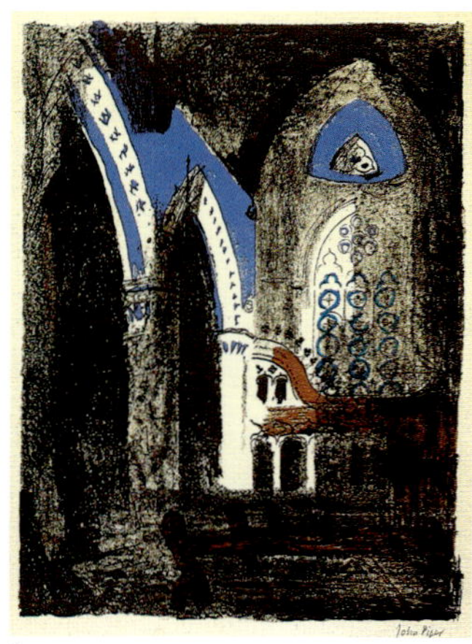

69

67A–B
Kubla Khan in Wales – Hafod and the Devil's Bridge, Spring 1947
An article, written by Geoffrey Grigson, containing two autolithographs, appearing in *Cornhill*, Vol.162, No.970, Spring 1947, pp.275–83, published by John Murray. The lithographs were printed at Butler and Tanner.

The paper is machine-made lithographic cartridge with a weight of approximately 100gsm and a size of 218 × 134 (8½ × 5¼).

Bodleian Library; British Library; Cambridge University Library; National Library of Scotland; National Library of Wales; Trinity College Library, Dublin

67A
[Adam and Eve's Garden]
(tipped in between pp.278–9)
Autolithograph 185 × 116 (7¼ × 4½)

67B
[Hafod]
(tipped in between pp.278–9)
Autolithograph 121 × 190 (4¾ × 7½)

68
The Market Place at Devizes
Autolithograph 248 × 368 ($9\frac{3}{4} \times 14\frac{1}{2}$)
Knapp, Drewett and Sons 1948
Architectural Press 1948
Machine-made lithographic cartridge 248 × 368 ($9\frac{3}{4} \times 14\frac{1}{2}$)
Unspecified Unsigned

Tipped in as the double-spread frontispiece and title-page to *Buildings and Prospects*, a book containing a number of articles written by Piper. The image is also reproduced on the dust-jacket with one minor colour change. The image *Devizes: The Market Place* (Cat. 57B) that appeared in 'Topographical Letter from Devizes' (Cats 57A–C) was adapted and hand-coloured for this autolithograph.

Bodleian Library; British Library; Cambridge University Library; National Library of Scotland; National Library of Wales; Trinity College Library, Dublin

69
Sutton Waldron
Lithograph 463 × 342 ($18\frac{1}{4} \times 13\frac{7}{16}$)
Central School of Arts and Crafts 1948
Redfern Gallery 1948
Lana 1590 150gsm, wmk b.r. 'Lana' 662 × 510 ($26\frac{1}{16} \times 20\frac{1}{16}$)
50 'John Piper'

British Council; City Art Gallery, Manchester; Detroit Institute of Arts; Museum of Modern Art, New York; National Gallery of Canada

70
Yarnton Monument, Oxon
Lithograph 390 × 517 ($15\frac{3}{8} \times 20\frac{3}{8}$)
Central School of Arts and Crafts 1948
Redfern Gallery 1948
Cream wove 150–200gsm 500 × 669 ($19\frac{11}{16} \times 26\frac{5}{16}$)
50 'John Piper'

Sometimes incorrectly known as '*Interior with Red Curtains*' or '*Yarnton Waldron*'. E. G. Devonish was the printer.

Albright-Knox Art Gallery; Arts Council Collection; British Council; Harrogate Museums and Art Gallery Service; Museum of Modern Art, New York; National Gallery of Canada; Victoria and Albert Museum

71
Stone Wall, Anglesey
Lithograph 390 × 520 ($15\frac{3}{8} \times 20\frac{1}{2}$)
Central School of Arts and Crafts *c.* 1949
Unknown *c.* 1949
Cartridge 506 × 636 ($19\frac{15}{16} \times 25\frac{1}{16}$)
50 'John Piper'

One known print numbered out of 50. Sometimes incorrectly known as '*A Wall in Anglesey*'

Museum of Modern Art, New York; Wakefield Museums, Galleries and Castles

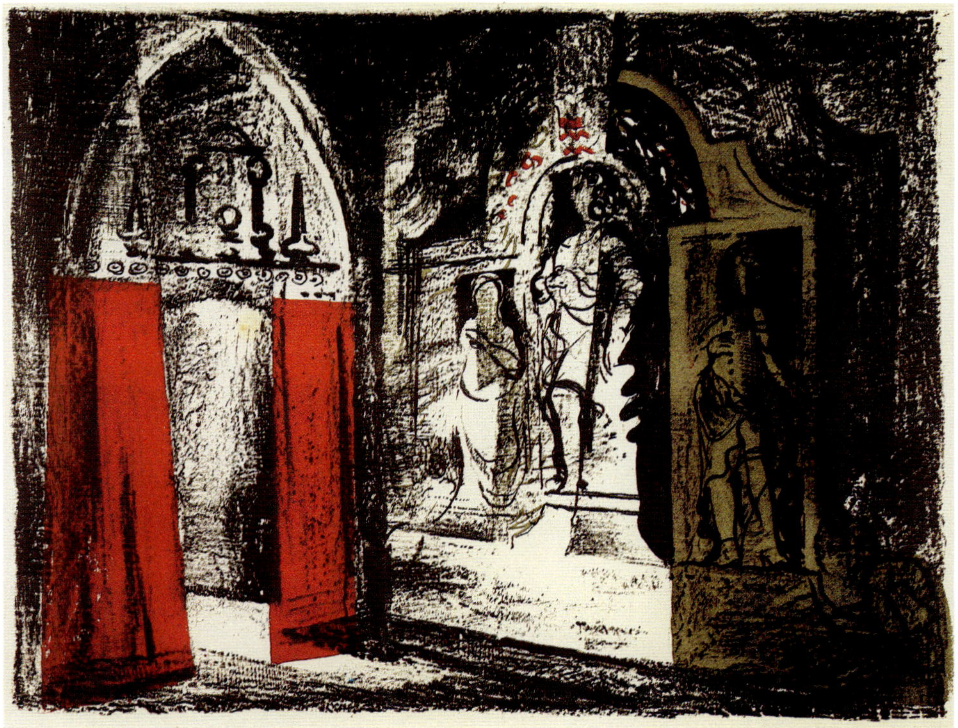

70

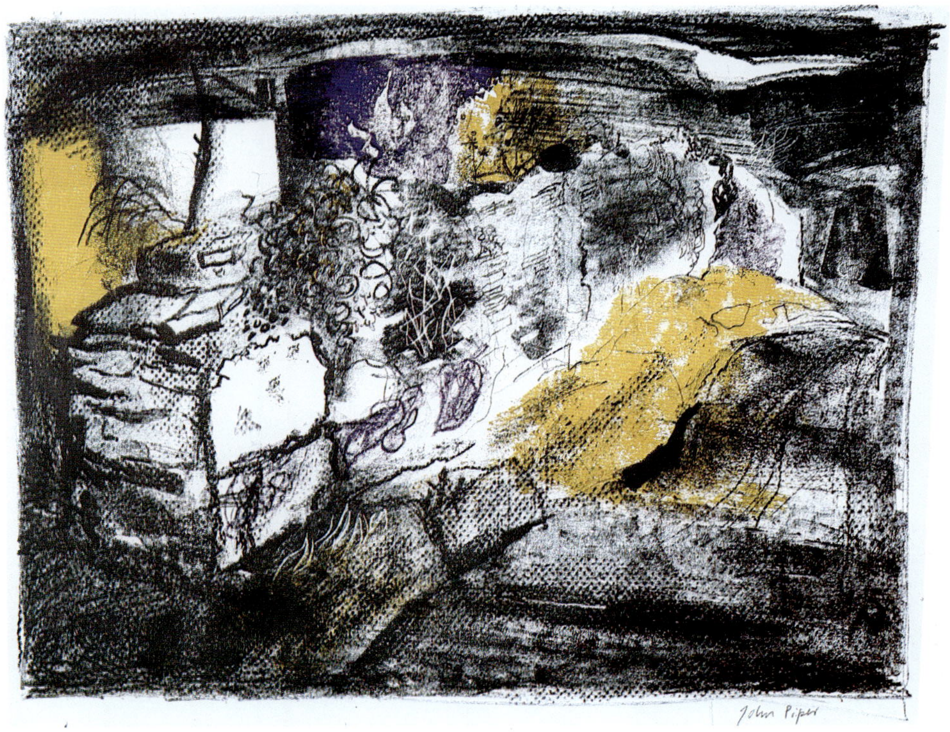

71

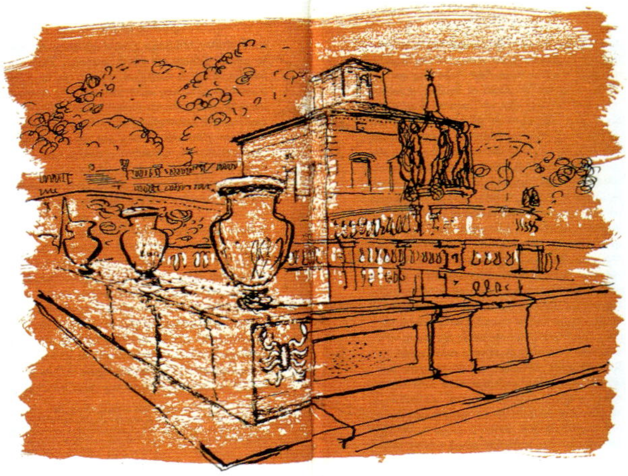

73

74

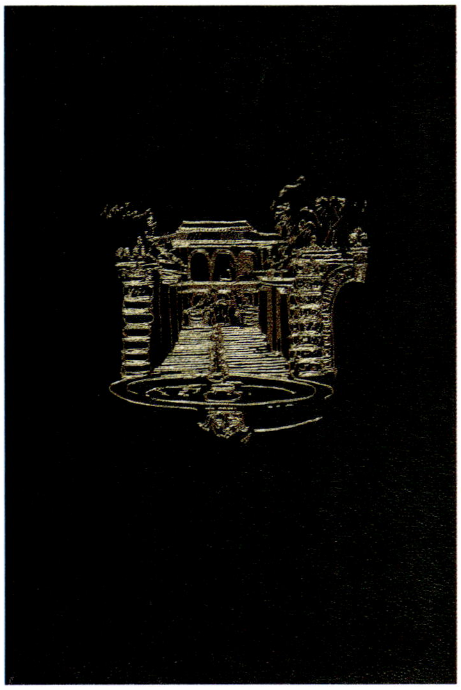

71A

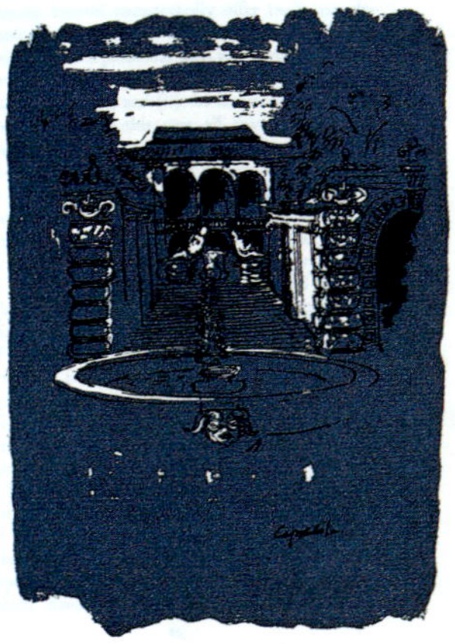

76

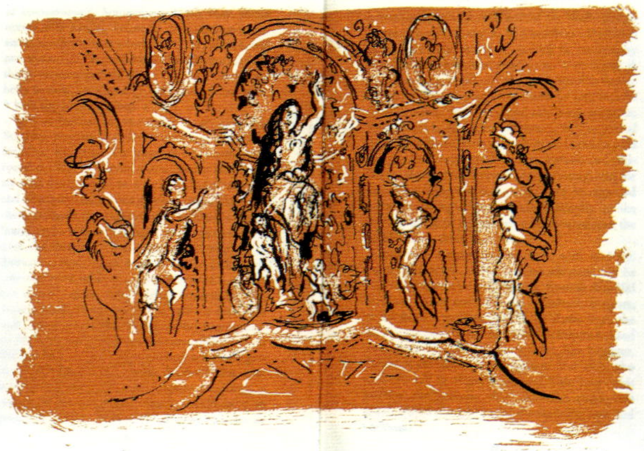

77

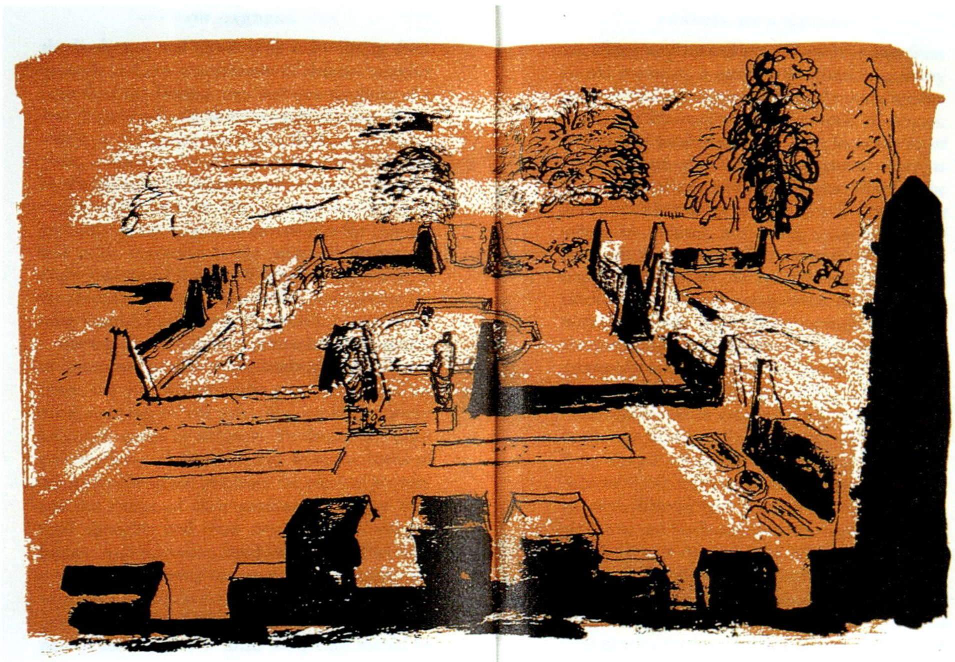

75

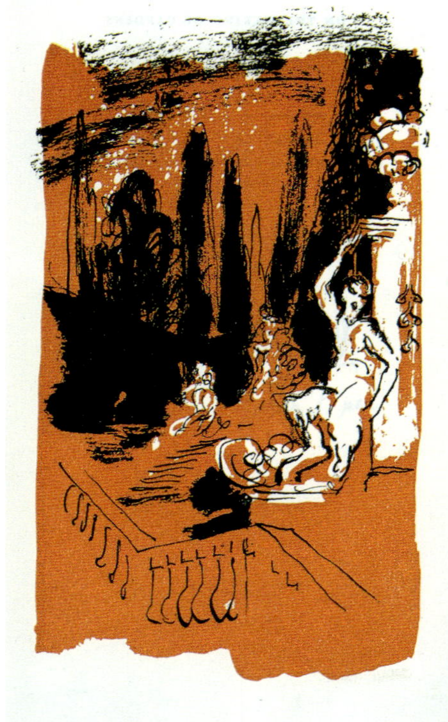

72

71A-77
On the Making of Gardens, September 1949
A book containing six line-block autolithographs written by Sir George Sitwell and with an introduction by Sir Osbert Sitwell. The deluxe edition containted an extra line-block autolithograph blocked onto the cover. Both editions were printed and published by the Dropmore Press.

1000 copies of the book were printed, of which numbers 1-100 were specially bound in green Niger morocco, numbered, and signed by Sir Osbert Sitwell and John Piper and containing the extra line-block on the cover in gold (Cat.71A). Numbers 101-1000 were bound in green buckram, and both editions were printed on cream-wove paper hand-made by Hodgkinson of Wells, Somerset.

Book size: 238×161 ($9\frac{3}{8}\times6\frac{5}{16}$) (edition 1-100). The size of the paper varies as it is hand-made and hand-cut, the average being 228×142 ($8\frac{15}{16}\times5\frac{9}{16}$).

Bodleian Library; British Library; Cambridge University Library; National Library of Scotland; National Library of Wales; Trinity College Library, Dublin

71A
On the Making of Gardens (cover)
(deluxe edition only)
87×90 ($3\frac{3}{4}\times3\frac{1}{2}$)

72
On the Making of Gardens I
Frontispiece
172×101 ($6\frac{3}{4}\times3\frac{15}{16}$)

73
On the Making of Gardens II
(following p.16, double-spread)
143×200 ($5\frac{5}{8}\times7\frac{7}{8}$)

74
On the Making of Gardens III
(facing p.32)
170×104 ($6\frac{11}{16}\times4\frac{1}{16}$)

75
On the Making of Gardens IV
(following p.48, double-spread)
138×214 ($5\frac{7}{16}\times8\frac{3}{8}$)

76
On the Making of Gardens V
(facing p.64)
142×100 ($5\frac{9}{16}\times3\frac{15}{16}$)

77
On the Making of Gardens VI
(following p.80, double-spread)
149×210 ($5\frac{7}{8}\times8\frac{1}{4}$)

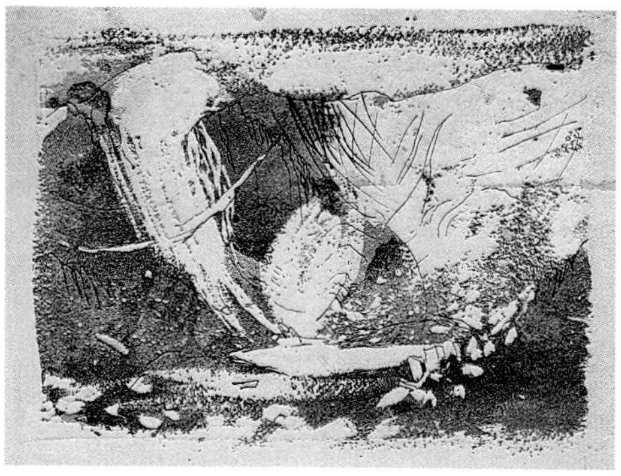
78

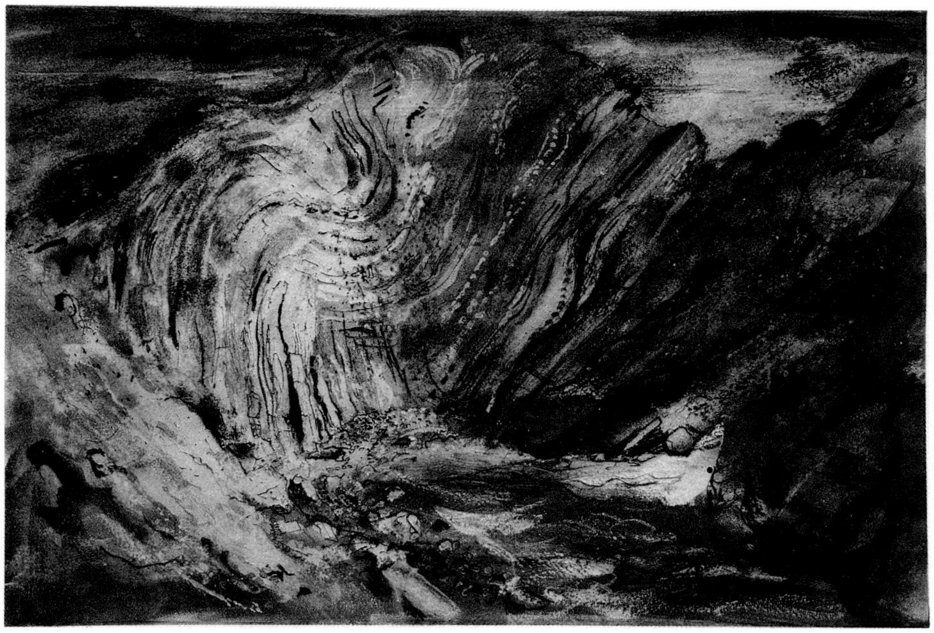
79

78
Ffynnon Loer
Aquatint 149×193 ($5\frac{7}{8}\times7\frac{5}{8}$)
The artist *c.*1950
Unpublished
Proofing paper 190×245 ($7\frac{1}{2}\times9\frac{5}{8}$) (plate)
Not issued as an edition Unsigned

One known trial proof is overworked by the artist in pen and ink.

79
Stair Hole, Lulworth
Aquatint 182×269 ($7\frac{1}{8}\times10\frac{9}{16}$)
The artist *c.*1950
Unpublished
Proofing paper 309×402 ($12\frac{3}{16}\times15\frac{13}{16}$) (plate)
Not issued as an edition Unsigned

A small number of trial proofs exist.

80
Stonehenge
Etching and aquatint 165×216 ($6\frac{1}{2} \times 8\frac{1}{2}$)
The artist 1950
Unpublished
Proofing paper 195×286 ($7\frac{13}{16} \times 11\frac{1}{4}$) (plate)
Not issued as an edition Unsigned

One known trial proof exists.

81
Clymping Beach
Lithograph 408×560 ($16\frac{1}{16} \times 22\frac{1}{16}$)
Mourlot Frères 1953
Curt Valentin Gallery 1953
Arches 504×665 ($19\frac{7}{8} \times 26\frac{3}{16}$)
70 'John Piper'

Sometimes incorrectly known as '*Clymping*'. Repr. in Elborn (p.82)

82
Dryslwyn Castle
Lithograph 377×532 ($14\frac{13}{16} \times 20\frac{15}{16}$)
Mourlot Frères 1953
Mourlot Frères 1953
Arches 250gsm, wmk 'Arches' 502×652 ($19\frac{3}{4} \times 25\frac{11}{16}$)
75 'John Piper'

Sometimes incorrectly known as '*The Golden Valley*'. Various proofs on 'Japon' and one black-and-white trial proof exist.

Tate Gallery

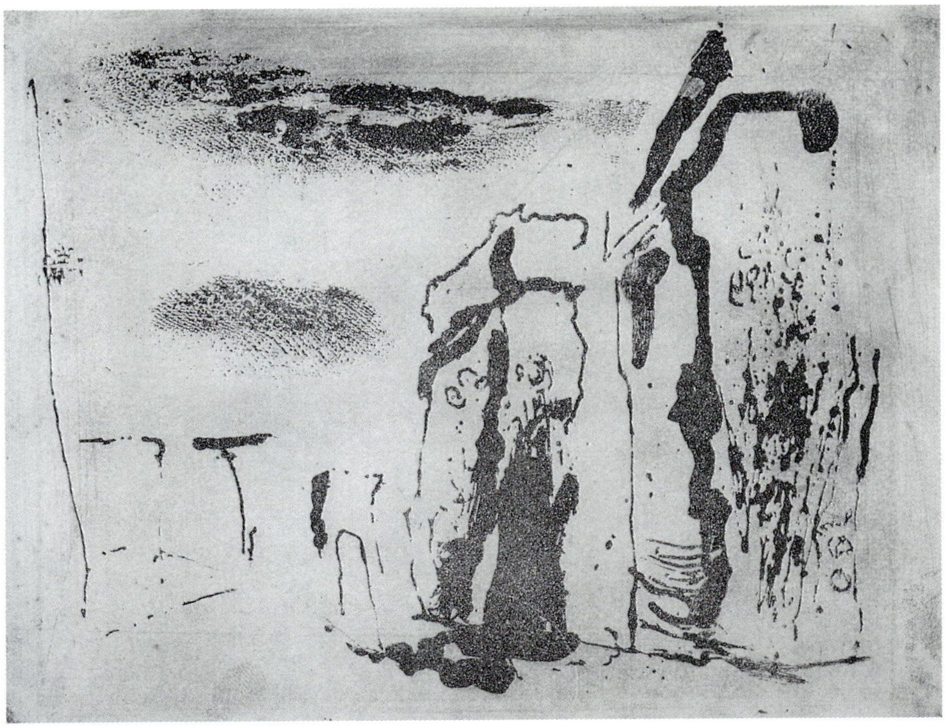
80

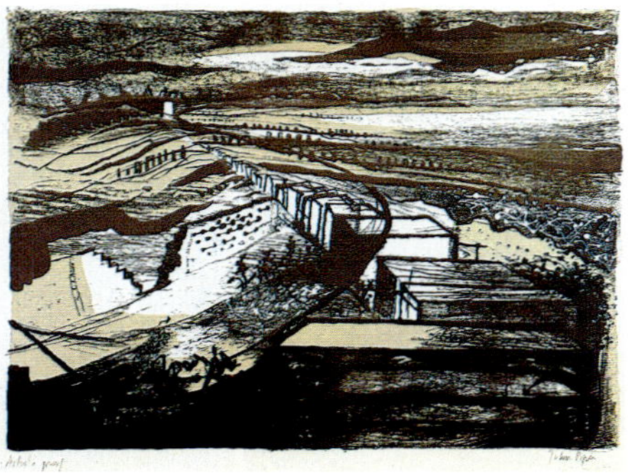
81

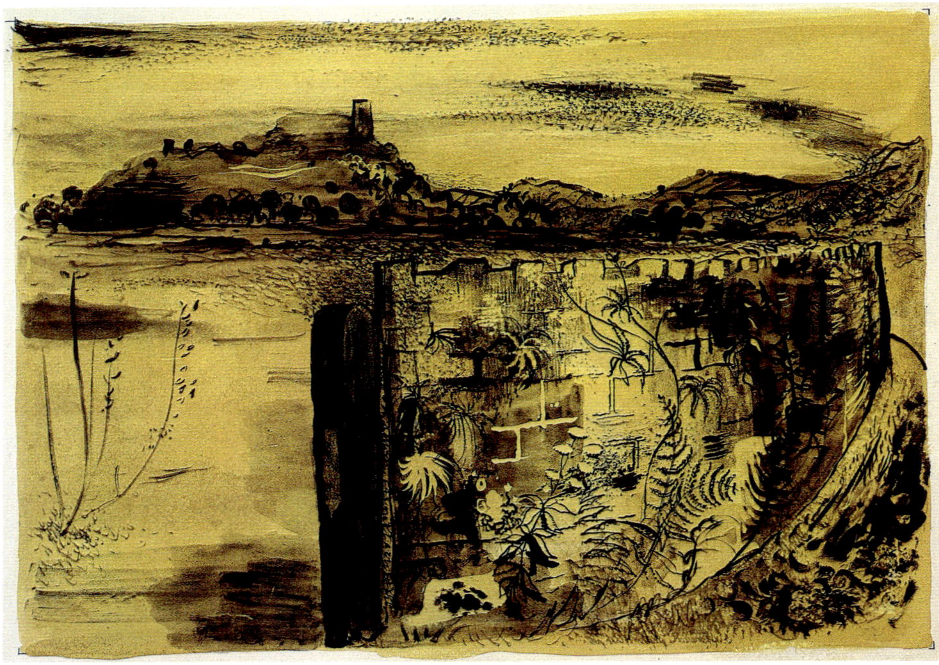
82

83
Foliate Heads I
Lithograph 475×635 ($18\frac{11}{16} \times 25$)
Mourlot Frères 1953
Robert Erskine 1953
Arches 533×680 ($21 \times 26\frac{3}{4}$)
70 'John Piper'

City Art Gallery, Manchester; Victoria and Albert Museum

84
Foliate Heads II
Lithograph 492×630 ($19\frac{3}{8} \times 24\frac{13}{16}$)
Mourlot Frères 1953
Robert Erskine 1953
Arches, wmk 'Arches' 565×767 ($22\frac{1}{4} \times 30\frac{3}{16}$)
70 'John Piper'

Lincolnshire Recreational Services: Usher Gallery

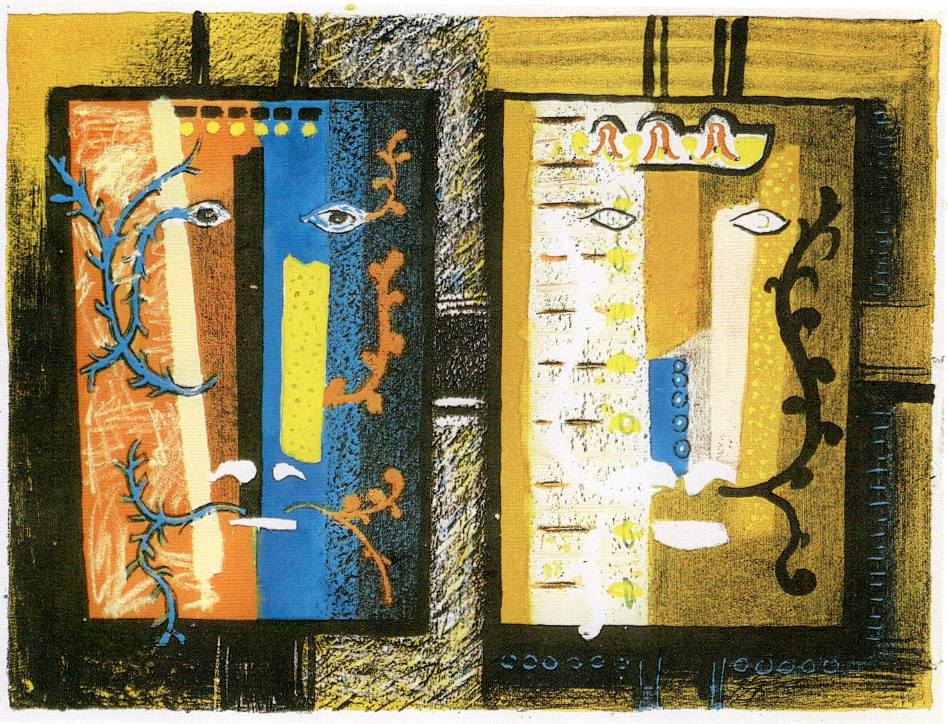

83

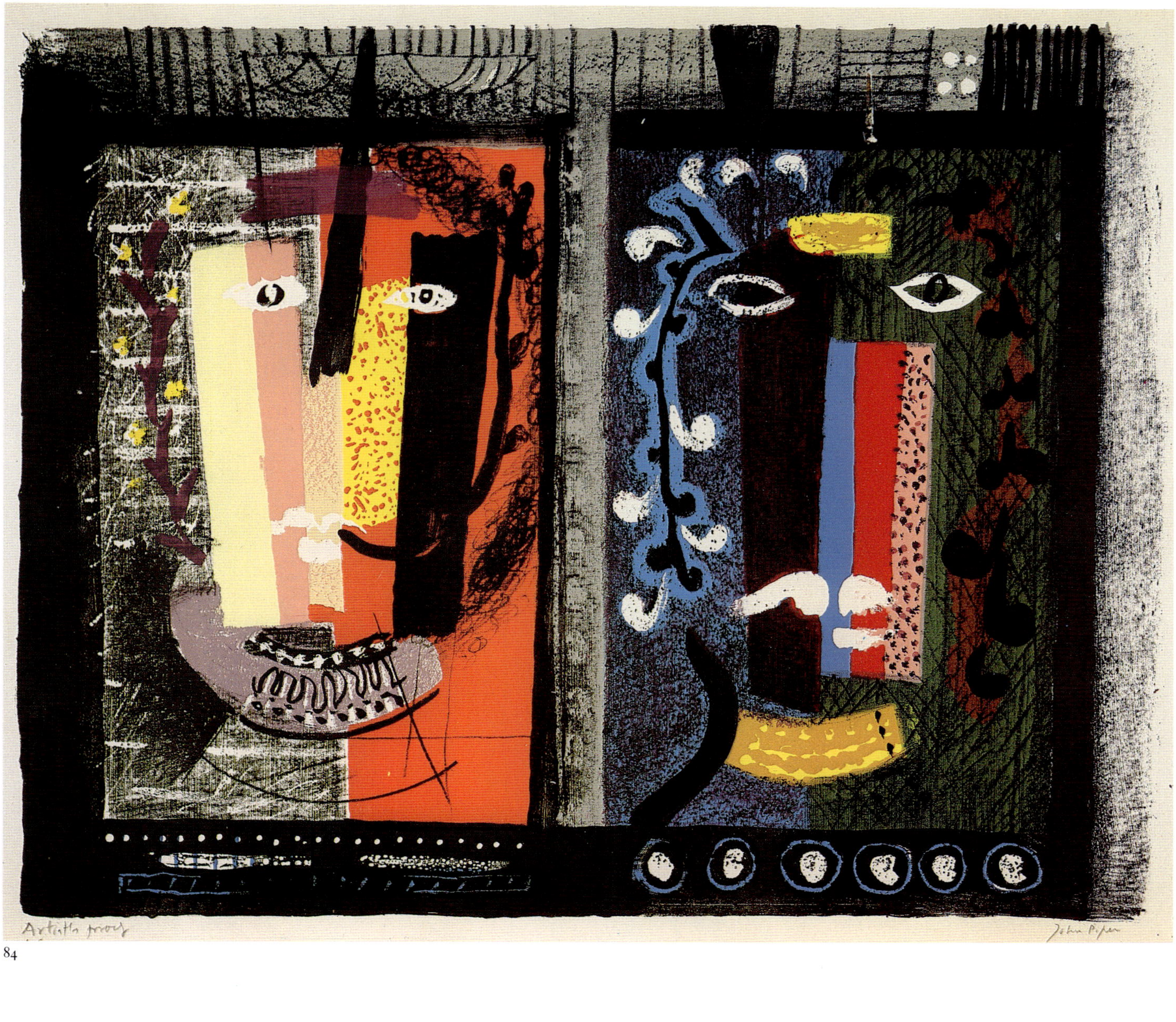

84

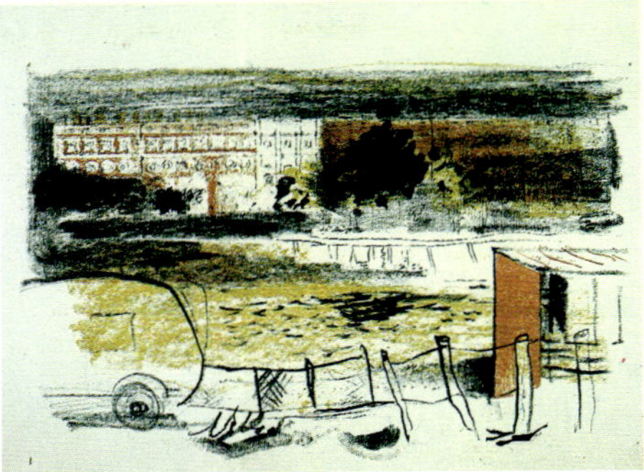

85

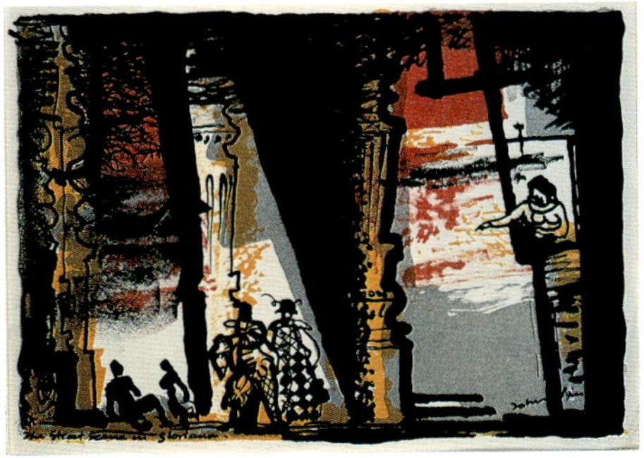

85A

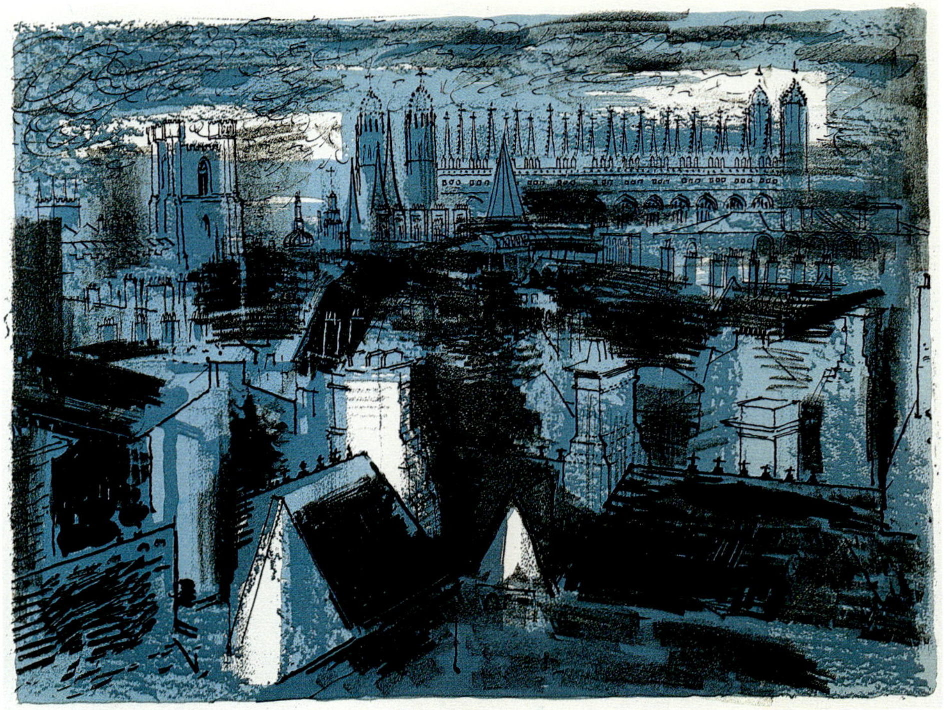

86

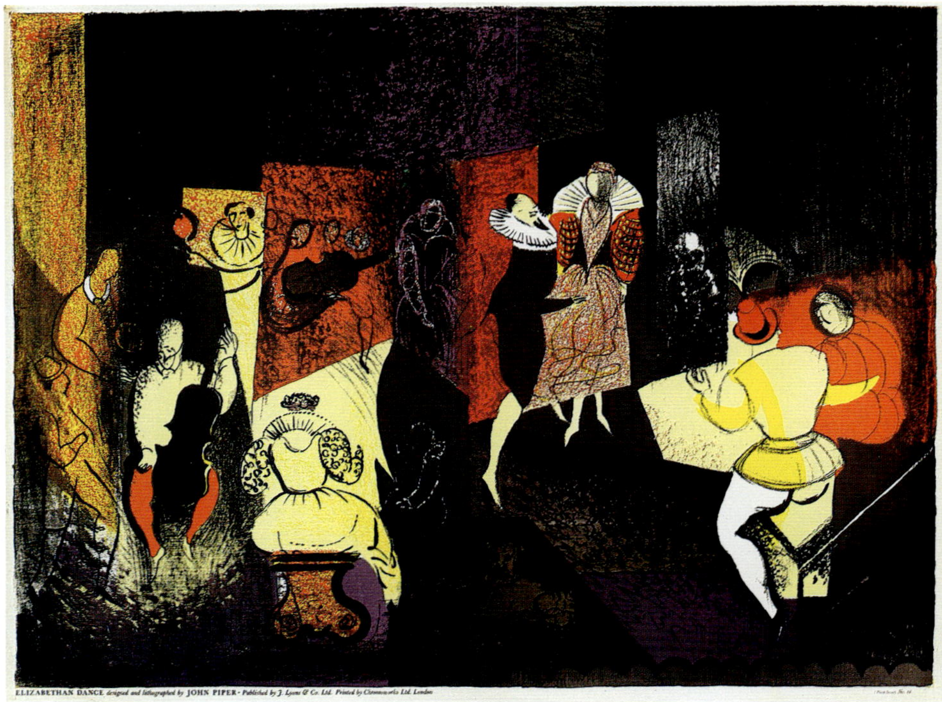

87

85
Hampton Court
Lithograph 286×439 (11¼×17$\frac{5}{16}$)
Royal College of Art 1953
Royal College of Art 1953
Engineering cartridge 384×562 (15⅛×22⅛)
70 'John Piper'

Sometimes incorrectly known as '*Royal Residence*'. Part of the RCA Coronation Series

Leicestershire Museums, Arts and Record Service

85A
Gloriana Street Scene
Lithograph 155×217 (6¼×8½)
Royal College of Art 1953
Royal College of Art 1953
Engineering cartridge 170×231 (6⅝×9$\frac{1}{16}$)
Unknown Unsigned

Originally referred to on p.123 of the 1987 publication of this book where it was alleged to have been printed in *Ark*. The author has not, at the time of going to press, seen the copy of *Ark* allegedly containing the image.

86
King's College, Cambridge, from Trinity
Lithograph 410×546 (16⅛×21½)
Harley Brothers 1953
Contemporary Arts Trust, Kings College JCR 1953
T.H. Saunders 250gsm, wmk 'Saunders England 1956' 518×683 (20⅜×26$\frac{15}{16}$)
75 'John Piper'

Sometimes incorrectly known as '*View of Cambridge*'
Various black-and-white proofs are known to exist. The print was organised by Martin Newell and Michael Jaff for the Contemporary Arts Trust.

Arts Council Collection

87
Elizabethan Dance
Lithograph 737×991 (29×39)
Chromoworks *c.*1954
J. Lyons and Co *c.*1954
Machine-made lithographic cartridge 762×1016 (30×40)
Unspecified Unsigned

Number 11 in the third of 3 series of 12 prints by various artists. The words 'Elizabethan Dance designed and lithographed by John Piper published by J. Lyons & Co. Ltd., Printed by Cromoworks Ltd., London' are printed b.l. All the prints were pulled off conventional offset lithographic presses. Half of the total of 36 prints, including *Elizabethan Dance* were lithographed by the artists who drew either on plates or transfer paper. Few of these prints survive as they were usually mounted unframed.

Victoria and Albert Museum

87A-C
Prometheus, 1954
A book by Edwin Muir published in 1954 by Faber and Faber ('Ariel Poem' series), containing three autolithographs, printed by Jesse Broad and Co Ltd, all on an unknown type of commercial printing paper. The print run size is not verifiable but approximately 500. None of the prints were signed by the artist, who, however, on occasion signed the front cover of the book. Each book was sold in a light pale-green envelope on which were printed the title, author, illustrator, publisher and price.

Book size: 212×146 ($8\frac{3}{8}\times5\frac{3}{4}$). Envelope size: 170×232 ($6\times9\frac{1}{4}$)

87A
[Prometheus I]
Autolithograph 150×140 ($6\times5\frac{1}{2}$)
214×140 ($8\frac{3}{8}\times5\frac{1}{2}$)

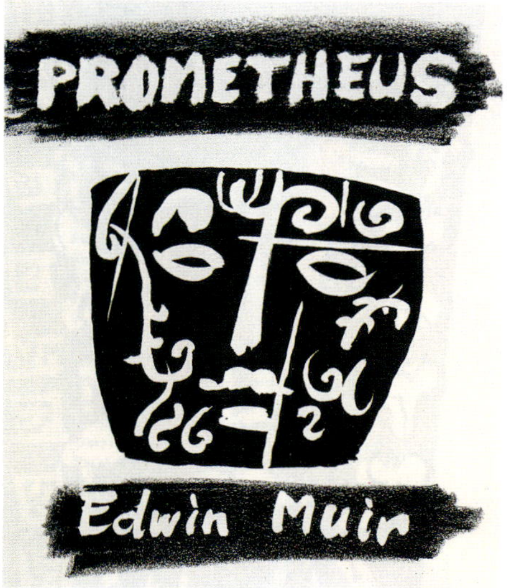

87A

87B
[Prometheus II]
Autolithograph 200×130 ($8\times5\frac{1}{4}$)
214×140 ($8\frac{3}{8}\times5\frac{1}{2}$)

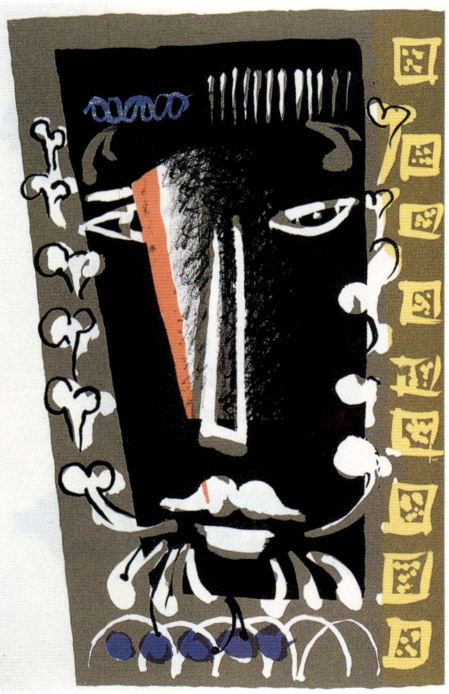
87B

87C
[Prometheus III]
Autolithograph 70×100 ($2\frac{3}{4}\times3\frac{15}{16}$)
214×140 ($8\frac{3}{8}\times5\frac{1}{2}$)

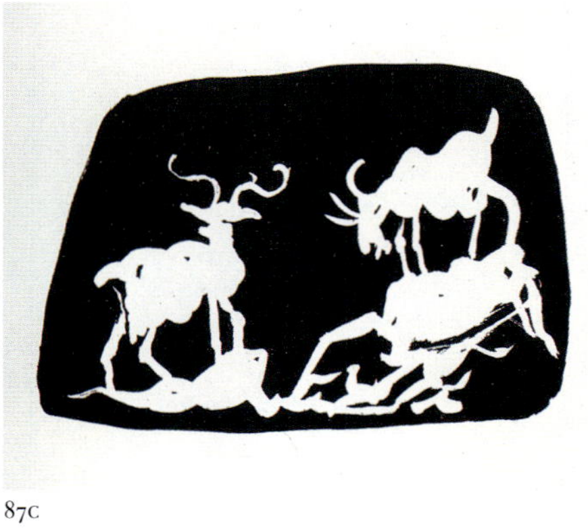
87C

88-92
John Piper: Paintings, Drawings and Theatre Designs, 1932-1954, 1954
A book arranged and with an introduction by S. John Woods published in 1955 by Faber and Faber, containing an aquatint printed in 1954 by A. Alexander and Sons and four autolithographs printed in 1954 by Mourlot Frères, all on machine-made lithographic cartridge paper. The edition size was 1900 with 50 copies signed in the front, by the artist as a limited edition. None of the prints were signed by the artist. Subsequently, on request Piper did sign many of the *Figures from a Seal* (Cat.88) prints as well as a few of the autolithographs. Woods in the book lists with the titles the date of the four autolithographs as 1953. It is possible that this is an error or that Piper began work on them in 1953 although they were only printed in 1954. Engraved on to the hardback cover is a foliate head drawing by Piper created especially for the book.

Book size: 322×260 ($12\frac{11}{16}\times10\frac{1}{4}$)

Bodleian Library; British Library; Cambridge University Library; National Library of Scotland; National Library of Wales; Trinity College Library; Dublin

88
Figures from a Seal
Frontispiece
Aquatint 210×155 ($8\frac{1}{4}\times6\frac{1}{16}$)
305×238 ($12\times9\frac{3}{8}$) (plate)

Sometimes incorrectly known as '*Cretan Seal*' or '*Figures from Ancient Seals*'. Some copies have been signed on request 'John Piper' b.r. A few hand-coloured versions are known to exist.

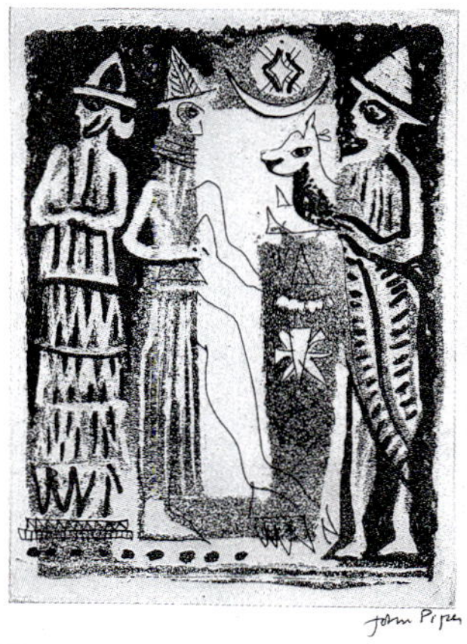
88

89
Bullslaughter Bay, Pembrokeshire I
Illus.101
Autolithograph 270×210 ($10\frac{5}{8}\times8\frac{1}{4}$)
313×250 ($12\frac{5}{16}\times9\frac{3}{16}$)

Sometimes incorrectly known as '*Bullslaughter Bay I*'

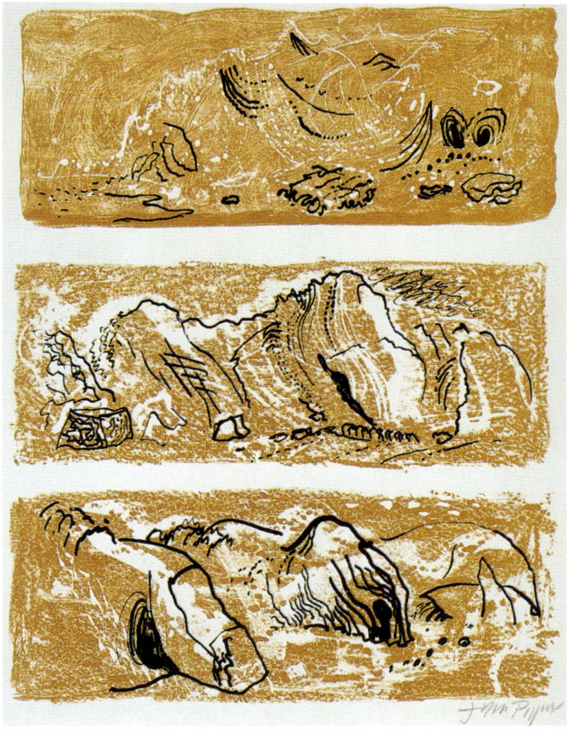
89

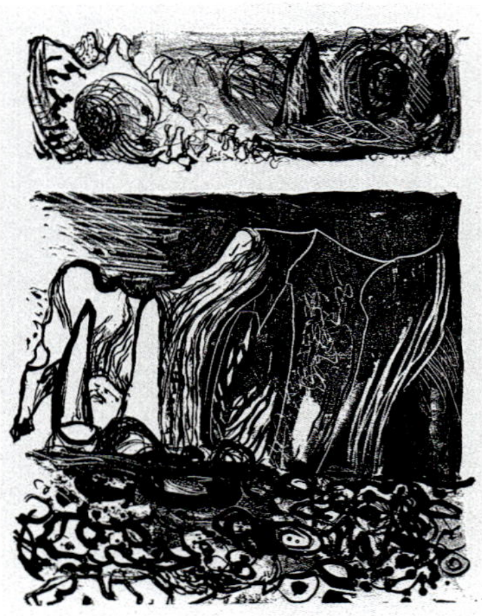

91

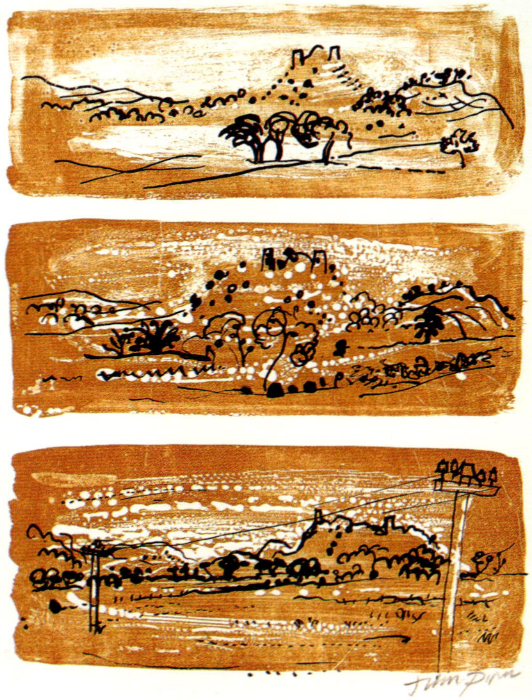

90

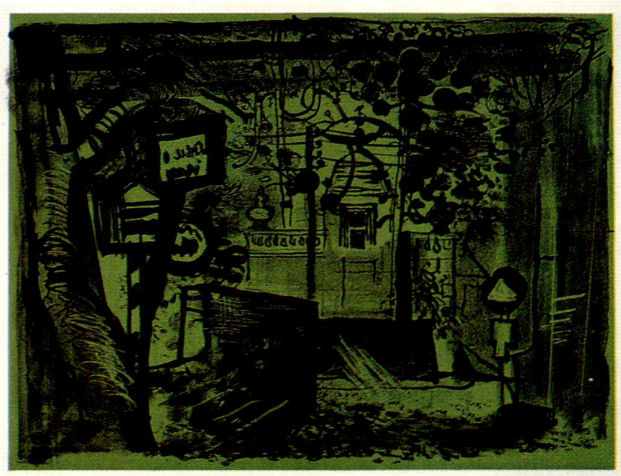

92

90
Dryslwyn Castle
Illus. 102
Autolithograph 275×210 ($10\frac{3}{16} \times 8\frac{1}{4}$)
313×250 ($12\frac{5}{16} \times 9\frac{13}{16}$)

91
Bullslaughter Bay, Pembrokeshire II
Illus. 152
Autolithograph 275×225 ($10\frac{3}{16} \times 8\frac{7}{8}$)
313×250 ($12\frac{5}{16} \times 9\frac{13}{16}$)

Sometimes incorrectly known as '*Bullslaughter Bay II*'

92
Niton, Isle of Wight
Illus. 153
Autolithograph 215×281 ($8\frac{1}{16} \times 11\frac{1}{16}$)
313×250 ($12\frac{5}{16} \times 9\frac{13}{16}$)

Sometimes incorrectly known as '*Niton*'

93-100
Elizabethan Love Songs, 1955
A book containing eight autolithographs edited by John Hadfield and published by Cupid Press in an edition of 660. The text were set and printed by W. S. Cowell. Each book was numbered and signed 'John Piper' in ink on a description page facing the title-page.

The paper for the book is antique laid mould made by T. H. Saunders and the paper boards were hand-marbled by Douglas Cockerell and Son. The decorative borders of the text are monotype versions of Elizabethan fleurons. All the lithographs were drawn by the artist directly on to plastocowell film (as opposed to zinc plates or solnhofen stone blocks).

Book size: 233×149 ($9\frac{3}{16} \times 5\frac{7}{8}$). Paper size (lithographs): 228×139 ($8\frac{15}{16} \times 5\frac{1}{2}$)

Bodleian Library; British Library; Cambridge University Library; National Library of Scotland; National Library of Wales; Trinity College Library, Dublin

93
Elizabethan Love Songs I
(facing the title-page)
'I am two fooles, I know', John Donne
165×111 ($6\frac{1}{2} \times 4\frac{3}{8}$)

94
Elizabethan Love Songs II
(facing p. 6)
'When I was fayre and younge and favour graced me', Queen Elizabeth the First
160×106 ($6\frac{5}{16} \times 4\frac{3}{16}$)

95
Elizabethan Love Songs III
(facing p. 31)
'Sweet birds, that sit and sing amid the shadie vallies', Nicholas Breton
188×125 ($7\frac{3}{8} \times 4\frac{15}{16}$)

96
Elizabethan Love Songs IV
(facing p. 38)
'I saw the object of my pining thought', Thomas Watson
171×116 ($6\frac{3}{4} \times 4\frac{9}{16}$)

97
Elizabethan Love Songs V
(facing p. 70)
To his Mistress going to bed, John Donne
167×115 ($6\frac{9}{16} \times 4\frac{1}{2}$)

98
Elizabethan Love Songs VI
(facing p. 79)
'Come away, come away, death', William Shakespeare
186×121 ($7\frac{5}{8} \times 4\frac{3}{4}$)

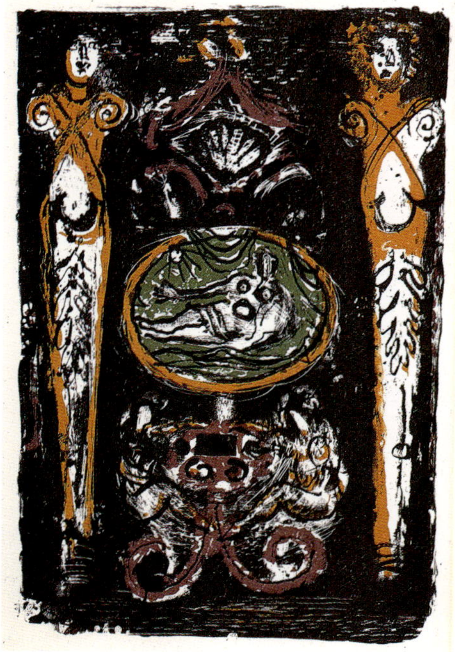

93

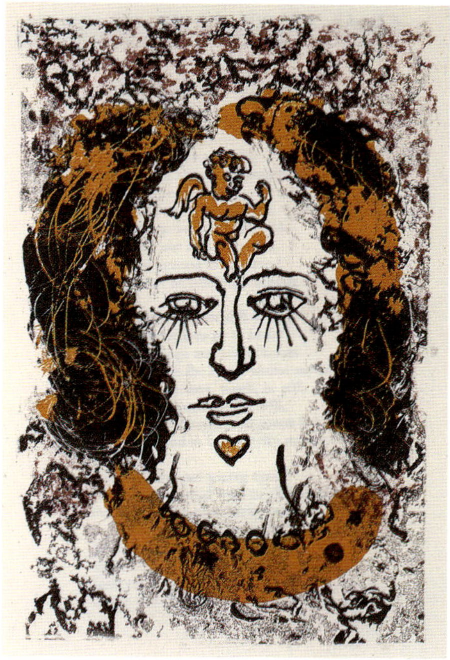

94

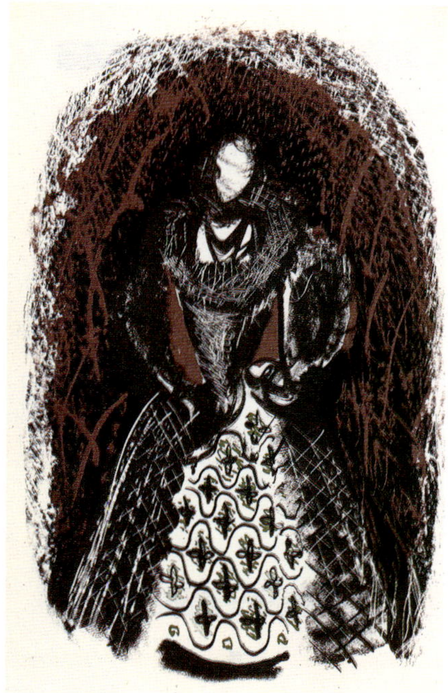

95

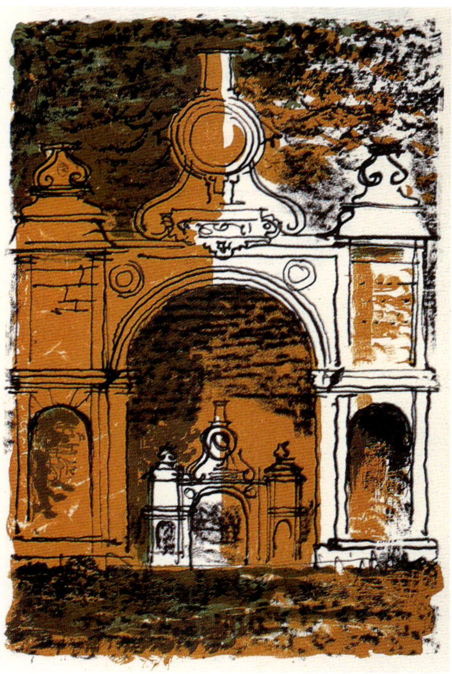

96

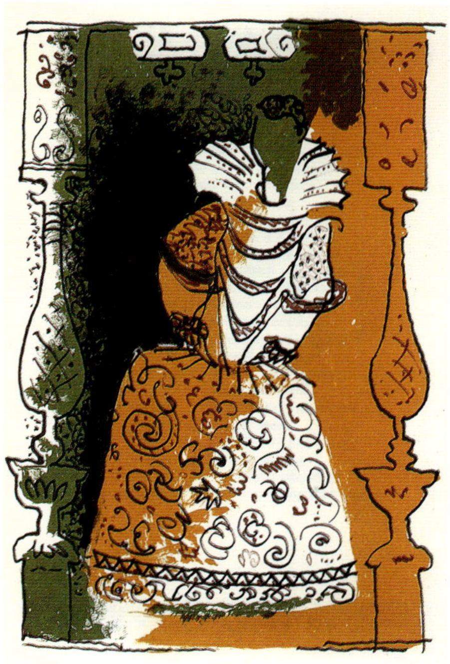

97

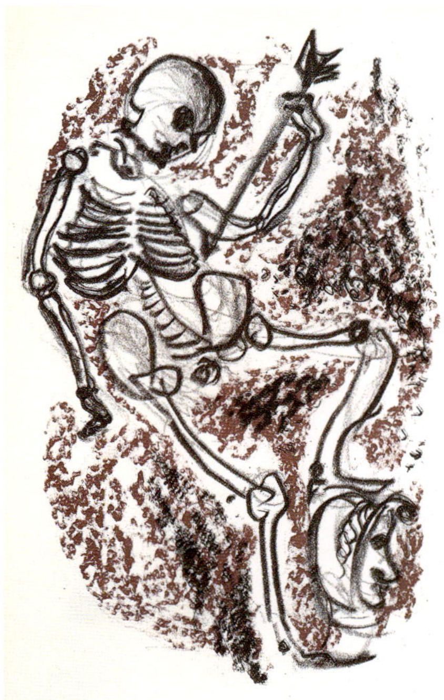

98

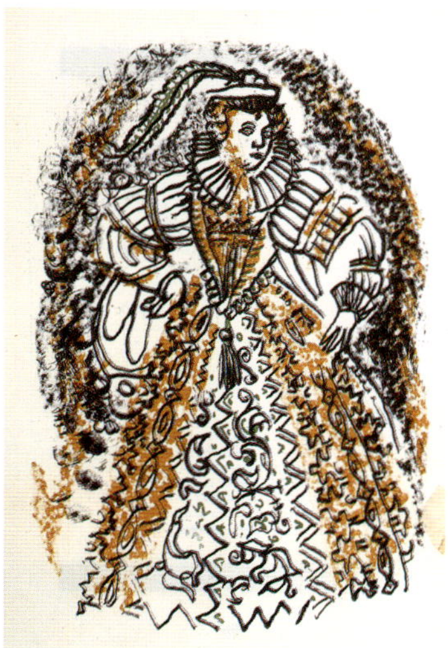

99

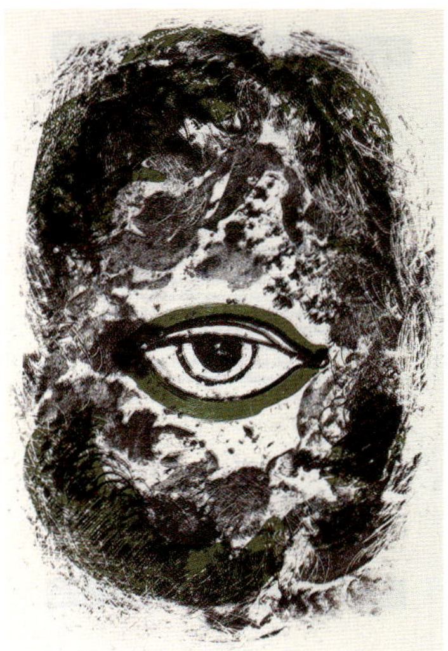

100

99
Elizabethan Love Songs VII
(facing p.103)
A Madrigal ('My love in her Attyre doth shew her witt', Anon.)
174 × 119 ($6\frac{7}{8} \times 4\frac{11}{16}$)

100
Elizabethan Love Songs VIII
(facing p.110)
To her Eyes, A.W.
177 × 125 ($6\frac{15}{16} \times 4\frac{15}{16}$)

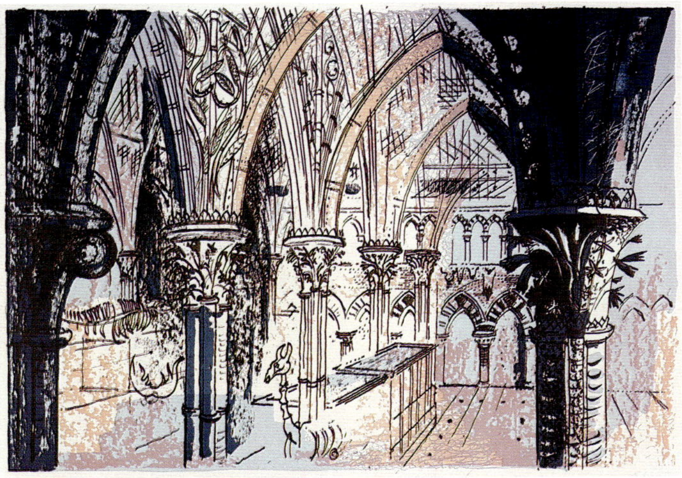

101

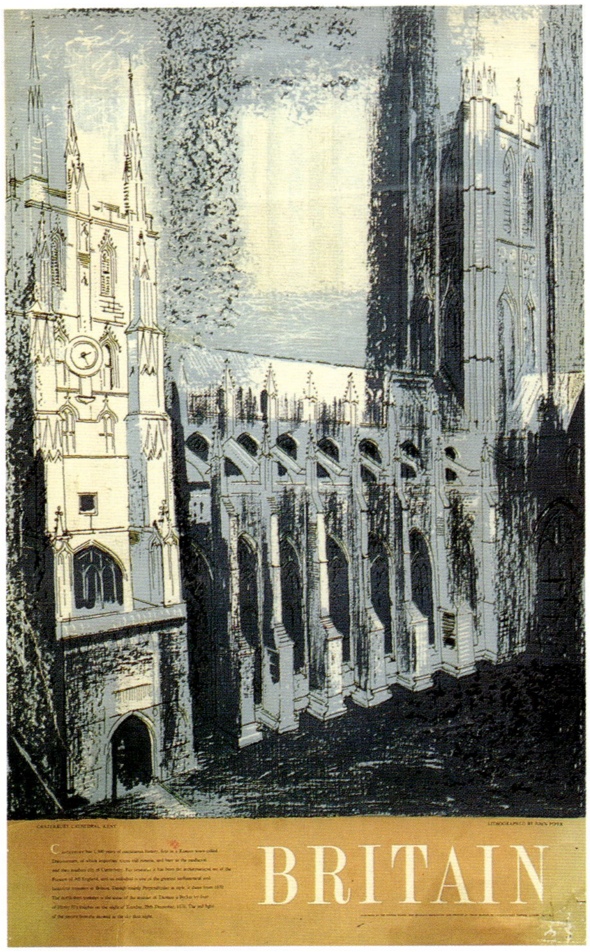

102

101
The University Museum (Founded 1855)
Offset lithograph 300×430 ($11\frac{13}{16} \times 16\frac{15}{16}$)
Oxford University Press (OUP, Printing Division) 1955
Oxford University Press (OUP) 1956
Mellotex 135gsm 761×559 (30×22)
2000 Unsigned

A print commissioned by *The Oxford Almanack*, the plates for the print being deposited by the Delegates of the Press in the Ashmolean Museum. Printed immediately below the image is the title b.c. and 'From a drawing by John Piper' b.r., which forms the upper half of the paper – 'The Oxford Almanack', with the names of the University Officers and of the Heads of Colleges and Halls, occupying the lower half. Several trial proofs in various colours exist, some printed over the words below the image.

Victoria and Albert Museum

101A
[Waterloo Bridge]
Autolithograph 242×195 (9½×7¾)
Curwen Press 1955
Directors of Penguin Books 1955
Machine-made lithographic cartridge 330×672 (13×26½)
Unspecified Signed 'JP' in the plate b.r.

Issued for the Directors and Staff of Penguin Books as their Christmas Card. Contains a brief history of John Rennie's Waterloo Bridge and a description of the bridge's remaining stones now at Harmondsworth, Middlesex, neither by the artist

102
Canterbury Cathedral
Autolithograph 839×610 (33×24)
Chromoworks 1956
British Travel and Holidays Association 1956
Machine-made lithographic cartridge 1016×635 (40×25)
Unknown Unsigned

Issued as a poster. Printed immediately below the image are the words 'Canterbury Cathedral, Kent', b.l., and 'lithographed by John Piper' b.r. A brief description of Canterbury, not by the artist, appears b.l. and 'Britain' appears in bold capitals b.r.

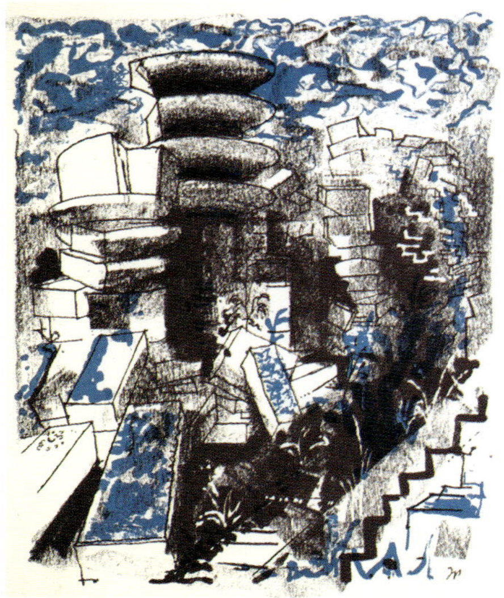

101A

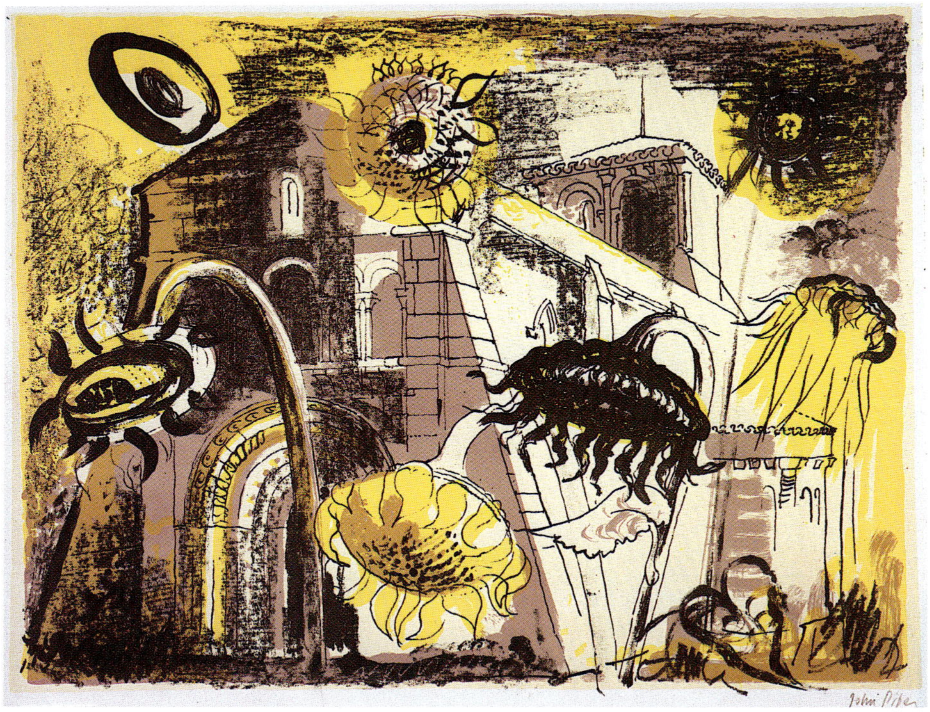

103

103
Sunflowers at Marignac
Lithograph 426×564 ($16\frac{3}{4} \times 22\frac{3}{16}$)
Mourlot Frères 1956
Curt Valentin Gallery 1956
Arches 250gsm, wmk 'Arches' 503×657 ($19\frac{13}{16} \times 25\frac{7}{8}$)
50 'John Piper'

Sometimes incorrectly known as '*Sunflowers*' or '*Church and Sunflowers*'
One black-and-white trial proof exists.

Aberdeen Art Gallery and Museums; Leicestershire Museums, Arts and Record Service; Victoria and Albert Museum

104
Sunflowers
Lithograph 432×530 ($17 \times 20\frac{7}{8}$)
Mourlot Frères *c.* 1957
Unpublished
Proofing paper 482×603 ($19 \times 23\frac{3}{4}$)
Not issued as an edition Unsigned

105
Petworth Park Gate
Lithograph 434×566 ($17\frac{1}{8} \times 22\frac{1}{4}$)
Harley Brothers *c.* 1958
Harley Brothers *c.* 1958
Arches 250gsm, wmk 'Arches' 507×660 ($19\frac{7}{8} \times 26$)
75 'John Piper'

Sometimes incorrectly known as '*Holland Park Gateway*', '*Park Gates*' or '*Petworth Park, Sussex, Entrance Gates*'

City Art Gallery, Manchester; Leicestershire Museums, Arts and Record Service

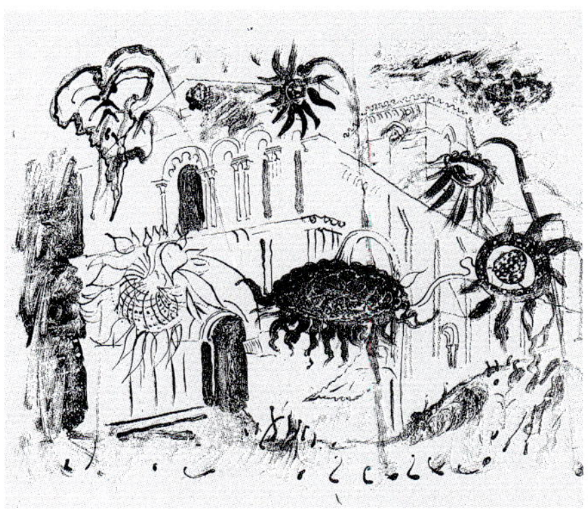

104

106
Three Somerset Towers I
Lithograph 539×756 ($21\frac{3}{16} \times 29\frac{3}{4}$)
Harley Brothers *c.* 1958
Harley Brothers *c.* 1958
Barcham Green 250gsm, wmk 'Crisbrook Shield' 578×810 ($22\frac{3}{4} \times 31\frac{7}{8}$)
5 'John Piper'

Sometimes incorrectly known as '*Three Somerset Towers (black version)*'. Printer's blind stamp b.r.

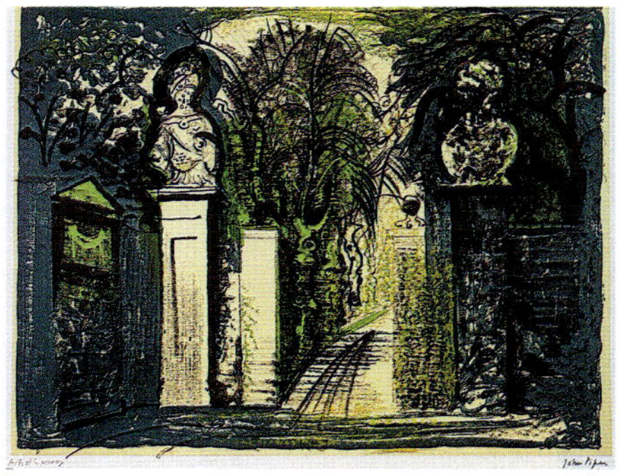

105

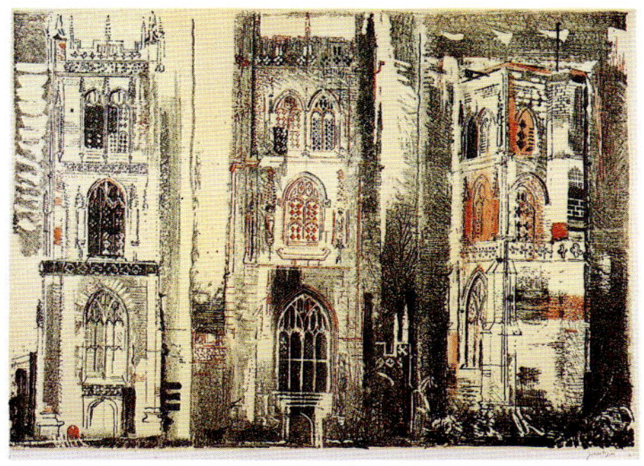

106

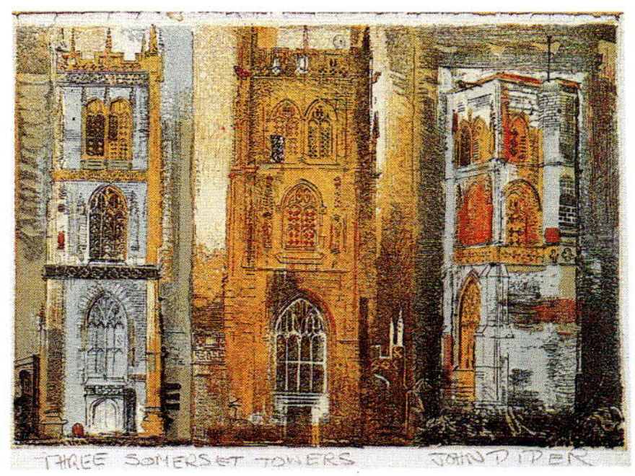

107

107
Three Somerset Towers II
Lithograph 537×758 ($21\frac{1}{8} \times 29\frac{13}{16}$)
Harley Brothers 1958
Harley Brothers 1958
Barcham Green 280gsm, wmk 'Crisbrook Shield' 578×806 ($22\frac{3}{4} \times 31\frac{3}{4}$)
70 'John Piper'

Printer's blind stamp b.r.

Aberdeen Art Gallery and Museums; Glasgow Art Gallery and Museum; Victoria and Albert Museum

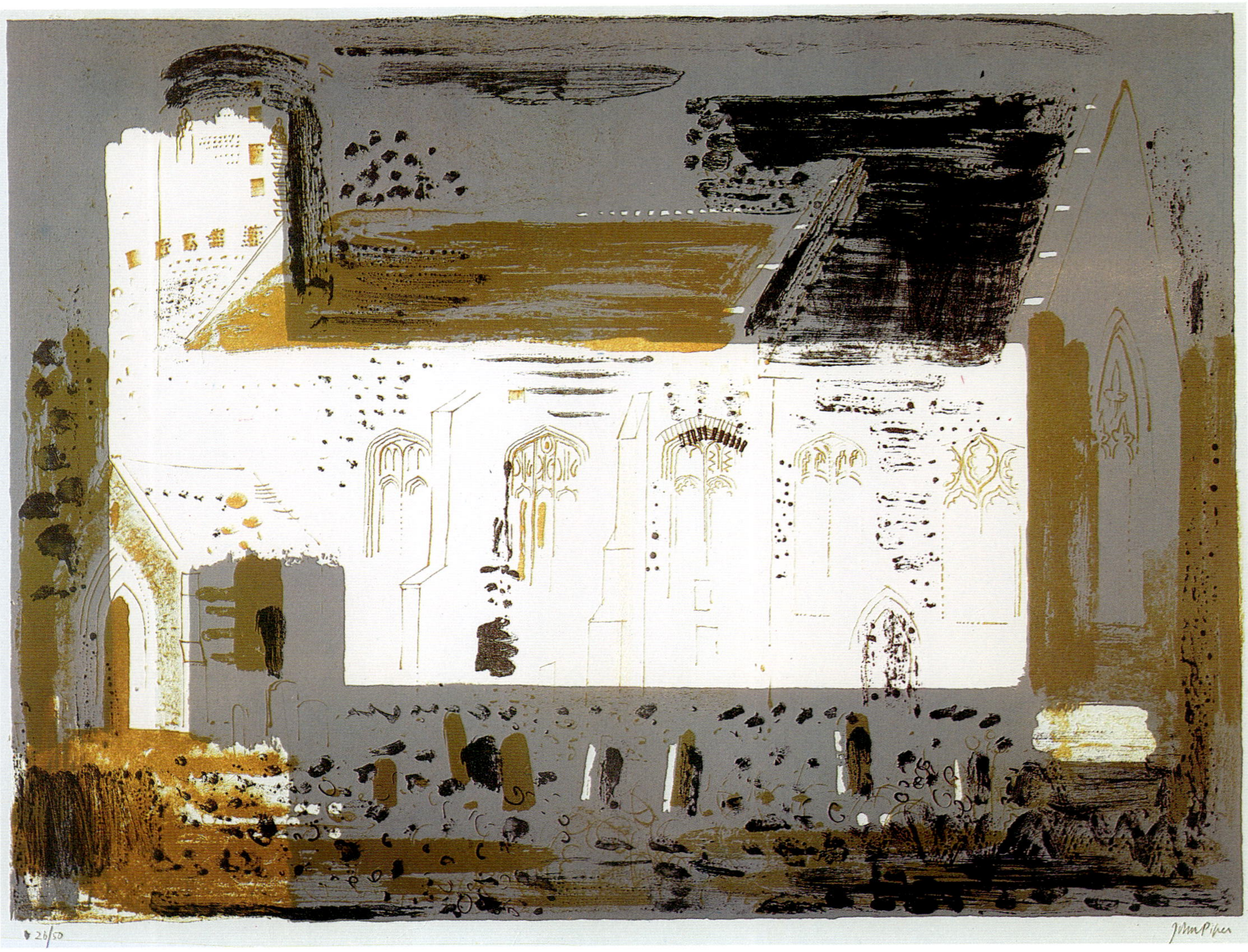

108

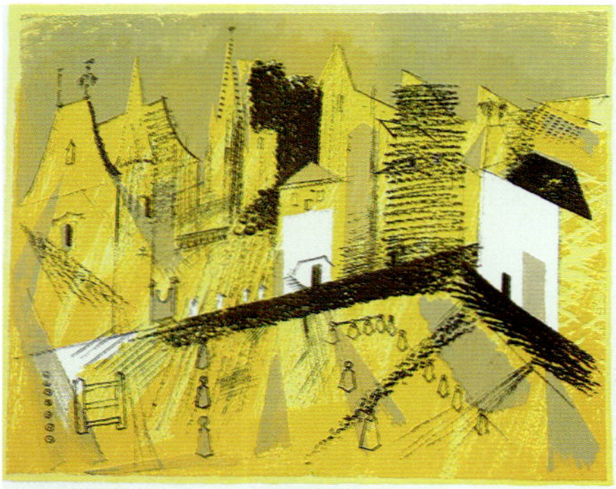

109

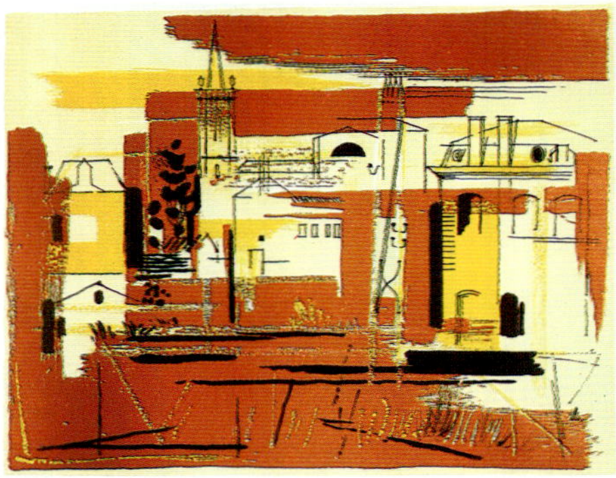

110

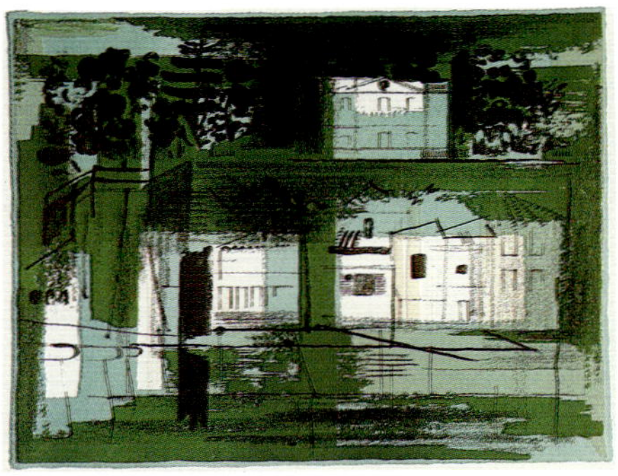

111

108
Syleham
Lithograph 477 × 648 $(18\tfrac{3}{4} \times 25\tfrac{1}{2})$
Harley Brothers 1958
Curt Valentin Gallery 1958
J.Whatman 250gsm, wmk 'J.Whatman 1959 England' 578 × 793 $(22\tfrac{3}{4} \times 31\tfrac{1}{4})$
50 'John Piper' 5AP

Sometimes incorrectly known as '*Syleham Church, Suffolk*'. Printer's blind stamp b.r.

Leeds City Art Galleries

109
Parthenay
Lithograph 460 × 570 $(18\tfrac{1}{8} \times 22\tfrac{7}{16})$
Harley Brothers 1958
Harley Brothers 1958
Barcham Green 250gsm, wmk 'Crisbrook Shield' 556 × 682 $(21\tfrac{7}{8} \times 26\tfrac{7}{8})$
70 'John Piper'

Leicestershire Museums, Arts and Record Service

110
Île-d'Elle
Lithograph 445 × 572 ($17\frac{1}{2} \times 22\frac{1}{2}$)
Harley Brothers 1958
Harley Brothers 1958
Barcham Green 250gsm, wmk 'Crisbrook Shield'
553 × 681 ($21\frac{3}{4} \times 26\frac{13}{16}$)
70 'John Piper' 5AP

Printer's blind stamp b.r.

111
Château de Taillebourg
Lithograph 441 × 576 ($17\frac{5}{16} \times 22\frac{11}{16}$)
Harley Brothers 1958
Harley Brothers 1958
Barcham Green 250gsm, wmk 'Crisbrook Shield'
530 × 677 ($20\frac{7}{8} \times 26\frac{5}{8}$)
70 'John Piper' 5AP

Printer's blind stamp b.r.

112
Surgères
Lithograph 412 × 646 ($16\frac{1}{4} \times 25\frac{7}{16}$)
Harley Brothers 1958
Harley Brothers 1958
J. Whatman 250gsm 533 × 750 ($21 \times 29\frac{1}{2}$)
70 'John Piper'

One known trial proof in black-and-white in existence.

Scottish National Gallery of Modern Art

113
French Village under a Cliff: St Véran
Lithograph 516 × 719 ($20\frac{5}{16} \times 28\frac{5}{16}$)
Harley Brothers *c.*1958
Unpublished
J. Whatman 250gsm 578 × 795 ($22\frac{3}{4} \times 31\frac{5}{16}$)
Not issued as an edition Unsigned

A few proof copies are known to exist.

114
Westminster School I
Lithograph 446 × 600 ($17\frac{9}{16} \times 23\frac{5}{8}$)
Curwen Studio 1961
Paul Cornwall-Jones 1961
Barcham Green 300gsm, wmk 'Handmade England' 577 × 806 ($22\frac{5}{8} \times 31\frac{11}{16}$)
100 'John Piper' 10AP

Sometimes incorrectly known as '*Westminster School (A)*'. Published by subscription for the school's 400th anniversary. One known pink and grey trial proof, signed 'John Piper' in ballpoint b.l. exists.

Tate Gallery

115
Westminster School II
Lithograph 423 × 583 ($16\frac{5}{8} \times 22\frac{15}{16}$)
Curwen Studio 1961
Paul Cornwall-Jones 1961
Barcham Green 300gsm, wmk 'Crisbrook Shield'
575 × 805 ($22\frac{5}{8} \times 31\frac{11}{16}$)
100 'John Piper' 10AP 2PP

Sometimes incorrectly known as '*Westminster School (B)*'. Published by subscription for the school's 400th anniversary. One known trial proof signed 'John Piper' in ballpoint b.r. exists.

Tate Gallery

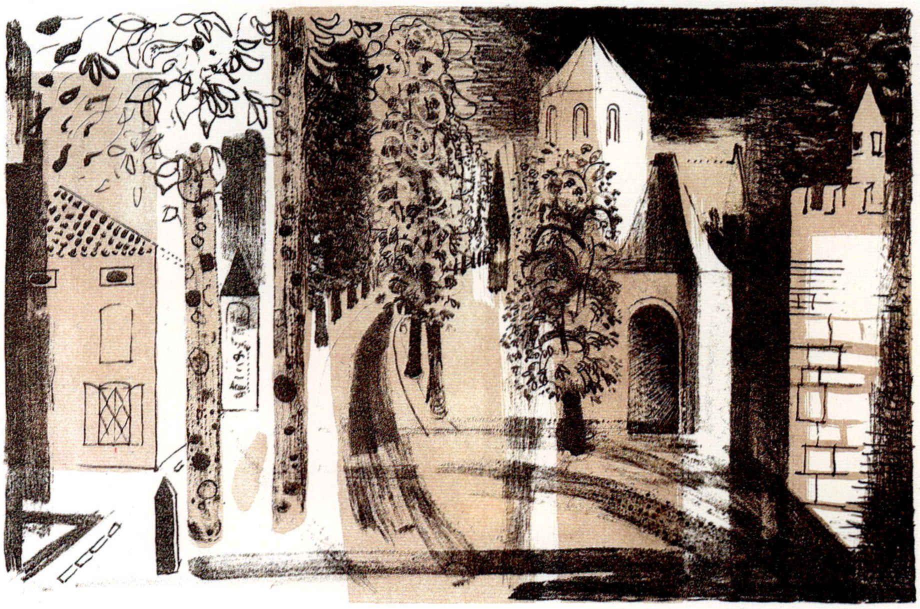
112

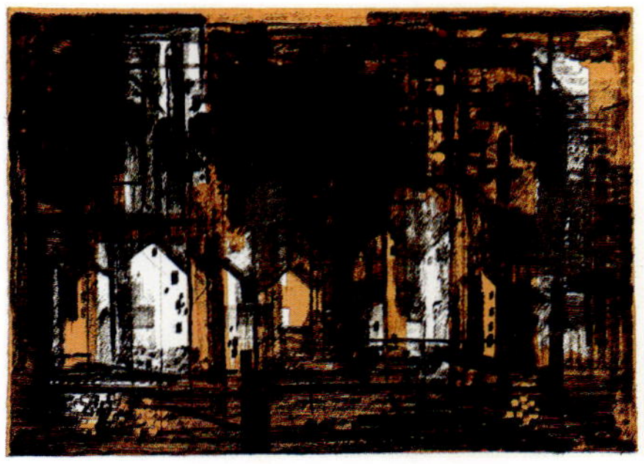
113

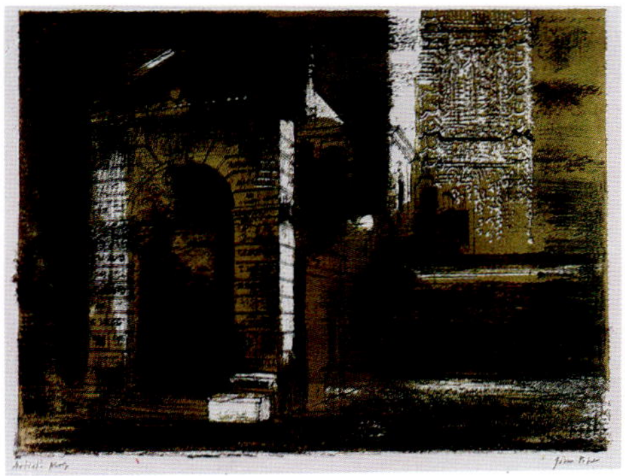
114

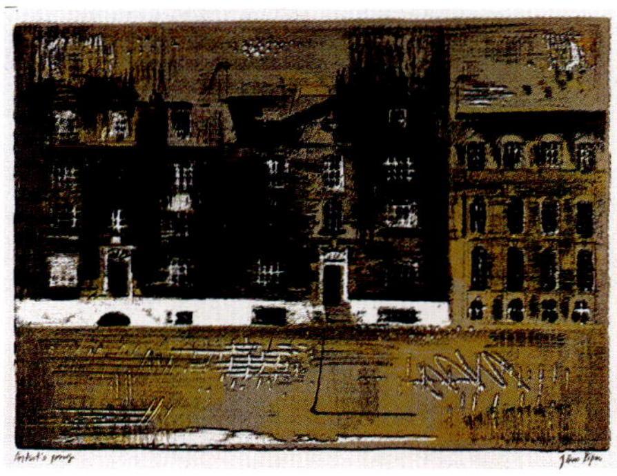
115

116
San Marco, Venice
Lithograph 637 × 462 ($25\frac{1}{8} \times 18\frac{3}{16}$)
Harley Brothers 1961
Curwen Press 1962
Barcham Green 300gsm, wmk 'Crisbrook Shield'
808 × 566 ($31\frac{13}{16} \times 22\frac{11}{16}$)
100 'John Piper' 10AP 2PP

Zinc and stone plates were used in combination, the main image being on stone and the colour added with zinc plates. One known black-and-white trial proof exists.

Tate Gallery

117
Brittany Beach
Lithograph 471 × 645 ($18\frac{9}{16} \times 25\frac{3}{8}$)
Curwen Studio 1961
Curwen Press 1962
Barcham Green 200gsm, wmk 'Crisbrook Shield'
575 × 809 ($22\frac{5}{8} \times 31\frac{7}{8}$)
75 'John Piper' 7AP 2HC 16UU

Sometimes incorrectly known as '*Beach in Brittany*'. Printer's blind stamp b.r. Repr. in Curwen (plate 28)

Leeds City Art Galleries; Leicestershire Museums, Arts and Record Service; Tate Gallery

118
San Zobenigo
Lithograph 644 × 444 ($25\frac{5}{16} \times 17\frac{7}{16}$)
Harley Brothers 1961
Curt Valentin Gallery 1961
J. Whatman 180gsm 795 × 575($31\frac{5}{16} \times 22\frac{5}{8}$)
50 'John Piper' various AP

Printer's blind stamp b.r. Zinc and stone plates were used in combination, the main image being on stone and the colour added with zinc plates. Four trial proofs – one brown, one black, one yellow and one signed 'John Piper' and marked 'trial proof for colour, not for sale' exist.

Victoria and Albert Museum

119
San Moisè, Venice
Lithograph 653 × 476 ($25\frac{11}{16} \times 18\frac{3}{4}$)
Harley Brothers 1961
Curt Valentin Gallery 1961
J. Whatman 180gsm, wmk 'J Whatman 1959 England' 794 × 575 ($31\frac{1}{4} \times 22\frac{5}{8}$)
50 'John Piper' various AP

Printer's blind stamp b.r. Zinc and stone plates were used in combination, the main image being on stone and the colour added with zinc plates. Two known trial proofs exist.

120
Anglesey Beach
Lithograph 560 × 445 ($22 \times 17\frac{1}{2}$)
Curwen Studio 1963
Galerie Wolfgang Ketterer 1963
Japon ancien (ed. A) and Arches (ed. B) 656 × 502 ($25\frac{13}{16} \times 19\frac{3}{4}$)
100 'John Piper' 13HC

Publisher's blind stamp b.r. One black-and-white trial proof exists. This print formed part of a portfolio of original lithographs by British artists (details of the other participating artists unknown) edited by Felix H. Man. The edition was divided into edition A, of 35 numbered with Roman numerals and printed on 'Japon'; edition B, of 65, numbered with Arabic numerals and printed on 'Arches', with 13 HC copies – 10 on 'Arches' and 3 on 'Japon'.

Tate Gallery (ed. B)

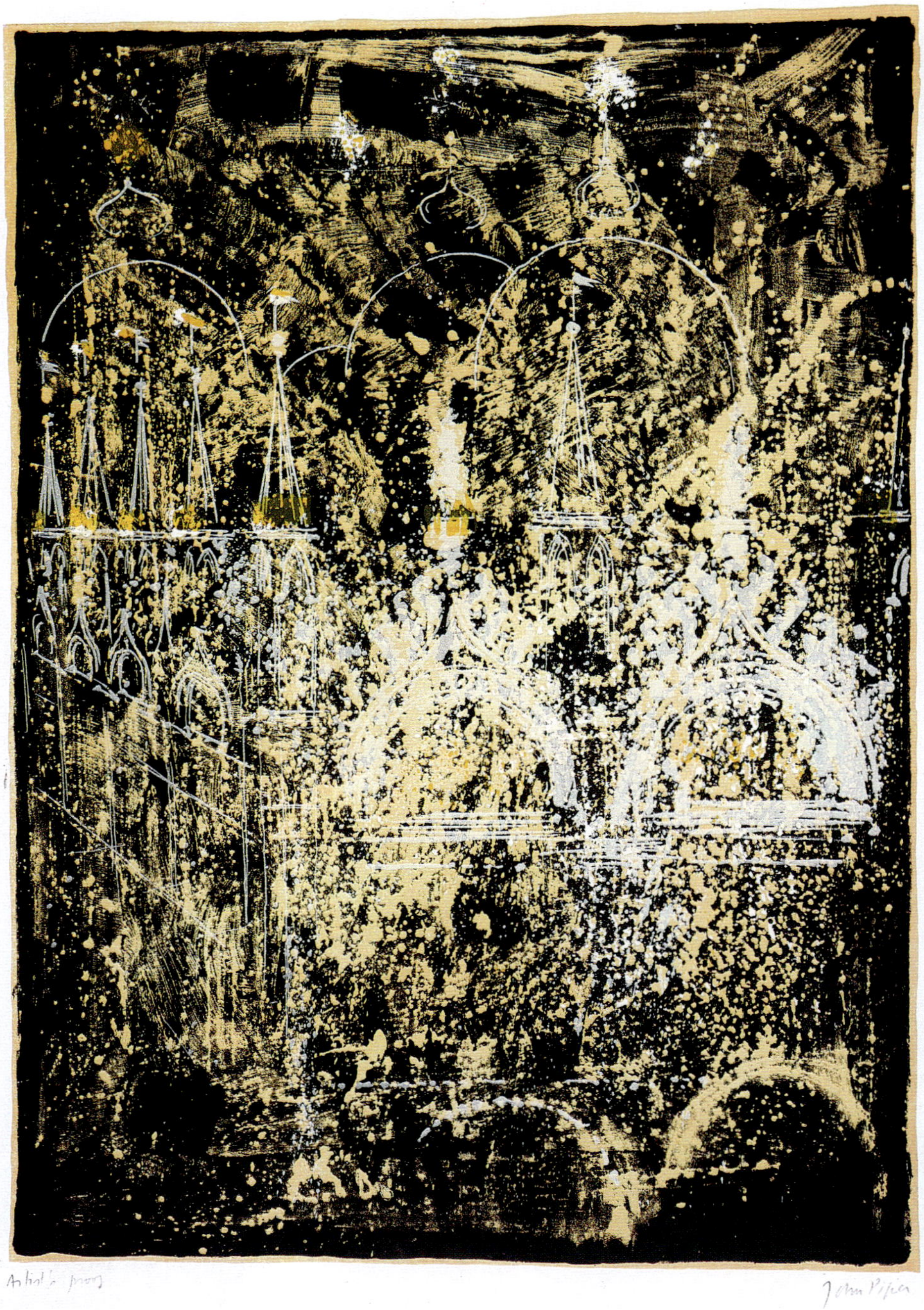

116

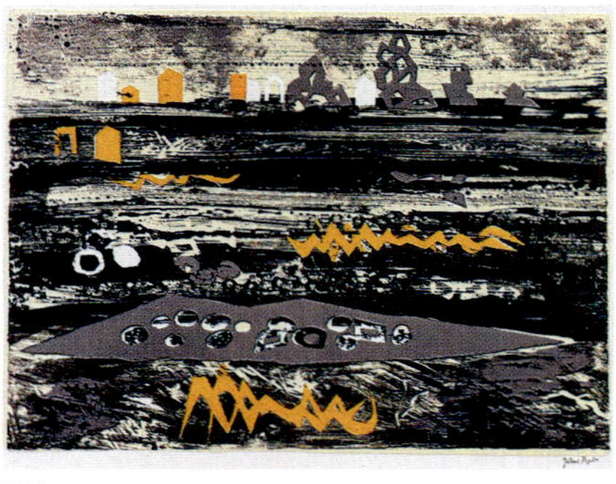

117

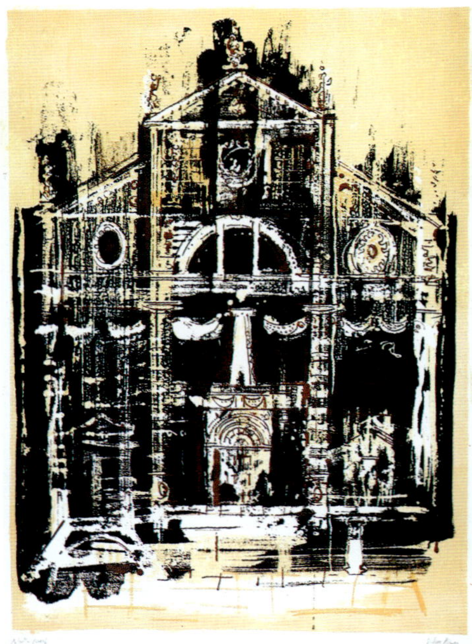

119

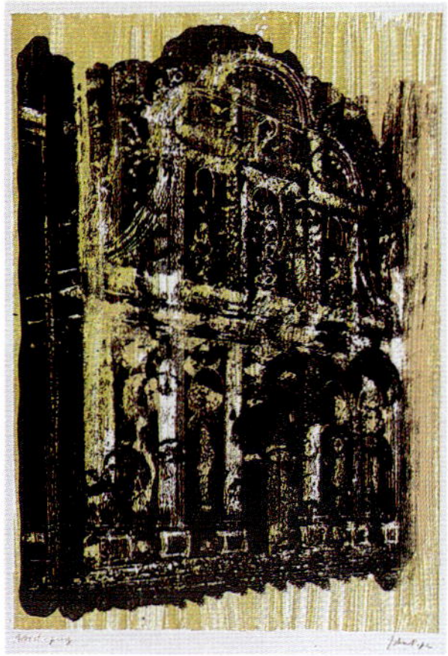

118

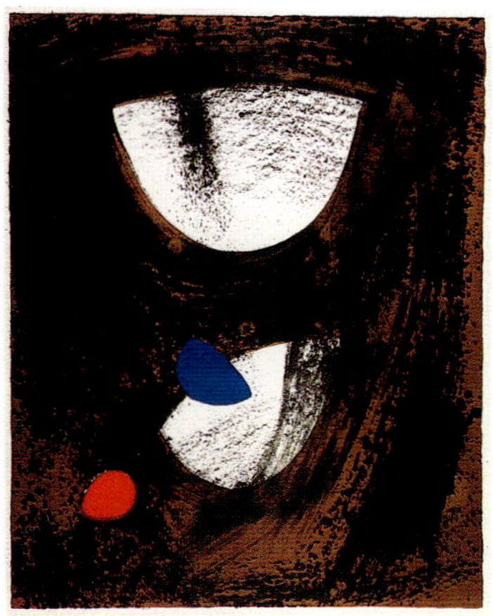

120

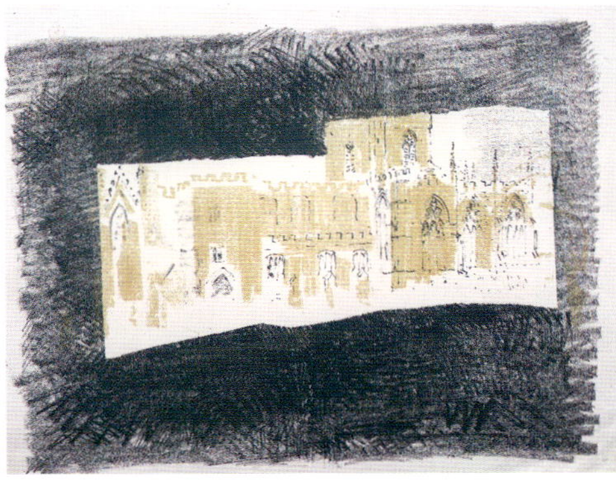

121

121
Edington, Wiltshire
Lithograph 530 × 698 (20 7/8 × 27 3/8)
Curwen Studio 1964
Unpublished
Crisbrook waterleaf 285gsm 572 × 804 (22 1/2 × 31 5/8)
Not issued as an edition Unsigned

Proofed as part of the portfolio, *A Retrospect of Churches* (Cats 122–45). The only known copy is in the Tate Gallery.

121A–145
A Retrospect of Churches, 1964

The *Retrospect of Churches* portfolio consists of twenty-five stone lithographs in a portfolio with a loose-leaf double page 567 × 778 (22 5/16 × 30 9/16) and one further stone lithograph glued to the portfolio's inside cover as a front end-paper. The portfolio also contains a title-page (with a foreword by John Betjeman) and a contents page (with details of edition and publication). Printed by Curwen Studio on Crisbrook Waterleaf 285gsm paper supplied by Barcham Green with the 'John Piper' watermark (some prints also have a watermark 'F.J. Head'), and published by Marlborough Fine Art. Although the project was commissioned and begun in the autumn of 1963 the first final proofs were made in 1964. The edition was numbered to 70 with five further copies marked A–E and two printer's proofs. All prints are signed 'John Piper' in pencil b.r.

The first twelve sets, numbered 1–12, were advertised as containing an original drawing by John Piper but with conflicting facts on this, it is unclear if this idea was carried out for some, or all or none of these twelve sets. One drawing of St Kew does exist, which was part of one these portfolios, but it cannot be established with accuracy if this was as a result of an inclusion as per the advertisement or not. It is possible too that all did have drawings but on reselling of these editions the drawings were retained by the owners, and hence no existing portfolios have drawings.

The portfolio is three-quarter-bound in leather; its size is 667 × 890 (26 1/4 × 35) and blocked on the cover in gold lettering on a leather square are 'John Piper' and 'A Retrospect of Churches'. Each print is presented in an individually numbered slipcase. Paper size: 595 × 820 (23 3/8 × 32 1/4) except for the front end-paper which is 303 × 424 (11 7/8 × 16 11/16).

A set of all the prints except Cat. 121A is in the Tate Gallery.

Foreword to *A Retrospect of Churches* by John Betjeman

In England and Wales there are over 20,000 parish churches. A large proportion of them are medieval in origin. Most of the rest are 18th century or Victorian. From a simple nave and chancel church in a farmyard (with the key kept half a mile away and bat droppings on the pews when you get in) to the most sumptuous town church (reeking of floor polish or incense according to the quality of the churchmanship) they represent the whole range of local history in glass and stone and wood. They display too the wide and many coloured varieties of building stone and peculiarities of local styles and building techniques until our own day of pre-fabrication. It is surprising that such loved and familiar and often beautiful buildings have inspired so few English artists when one thinks of how many foreign artists, principally Dutch, from the 17th century onwards painted their local churches. Rowlandson drew West Country churches as features of some of his landscapes. Turner delighted in abbeys particularly when they were in ruins. Constable painted Salisbury Cathedral. Cotman made etchings and water colours of Norfolk churches before etching the Romanesque churches of Normandy and these last belonged to the same period and style as their counterparts in England. Throughout the 19th century there were many local artists who made painstaking depictions of churches in their neighbourhood – the Rayner family in Derbyshire, the Buckler family in Wiltshire and West of it and in Essex. Then there were the people who must have made the sketches for Orlando Jewitt to engrave so meticulously on wood for the antiquarian publications of J. H. Parker of Oxford. 19th-century architects had attractive lithographs made of the more famous medieval village and town churches. These were done sometimes at the suggestion of the Camden Society, at other times to draw the attention of potential customers. Until towards the end of the century the Middle Pointed or Decorated style was chosen for illustration as this was considered by mid-Victorian church builders as the perfection of Gothic. Most architectural sketchers were interested in bringing out the virtues of a particular style. Indeed the Victorian pre-occupation with 'Norm', 'E.E.' 'Dec' and 'Perp' and the jargon of antiquaries which had turned looking at churches into scientific detective work and a search for dates may have put off artists from a sympathetic interpretation of English churches till the days when F. L. Griggs made his famous pencil sketches for the Highways and Byways series. Landscape artists instead concentrated on old cottages, parks, ruins, woods, fields and country lanes. Even the Pre-Raphaelites and their followers preferred decorating old and new churches with stained glass, hangings and mural paintings to depicting the churches themselves.

John Piper is the first English artist since Cotman to concentrate on churches and in particular those of England and Wales. His knowledge of them started as a boy when he was Honorary Local Secretary of the Surrey Archaeological Society. As a young man he made copies of medieval stained glass. He is a keen topographer and photographer and guide book writer and for these reasons has been into thousands of churches sketching and taking photographs. The more you look at churches the more you appreciate the work of all dates. If you are an artist and not just a specialist, you appreciate their varying atmospheres whether the vicar is high, or low or breezy or lazy or crazy. You notice too oddities of furnishing, hymn boards, oil lamps, electric lighting, pipes, wires and heating stoves. John Piper does not confine himself to one particular district or style of architecture. He enjoys the bold carving of the Normans on fonts and doors; the splendour of the great wool churches of flinty East Anglia and the towers and spires of the limestone belt stretching from Lincolnshire to Somerset. He likes to show what time does to churches and the effect of lichens on country churches and smoke on town ones and decay on both. He responds to Renaissance monuments and to the mighty bulk of Hawksmoor's East London churches which were built for post-Reformation merchants and sea-captains in days of growing commercial prosperity. He was the first artist to appreciate the originality and sense of scale of the great Victorian architects such as Street and Butterfield who had hitherto been dismissed as mere copiers of the Medieval. He was also the first to recognize the visual appeal of nonconformist chapels. He enjoys the shock tactics of a man like S. S. Teulon who went further than Butterfield in deliberately flouting Gothic conventions. The accompanying lithographs are the distillation of half a century's looking at churches.

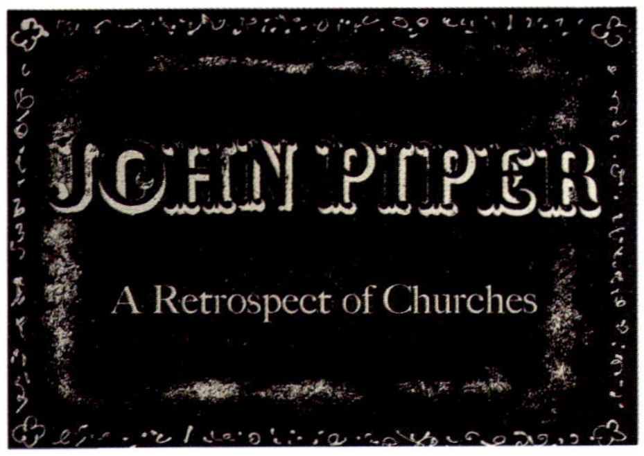

121A

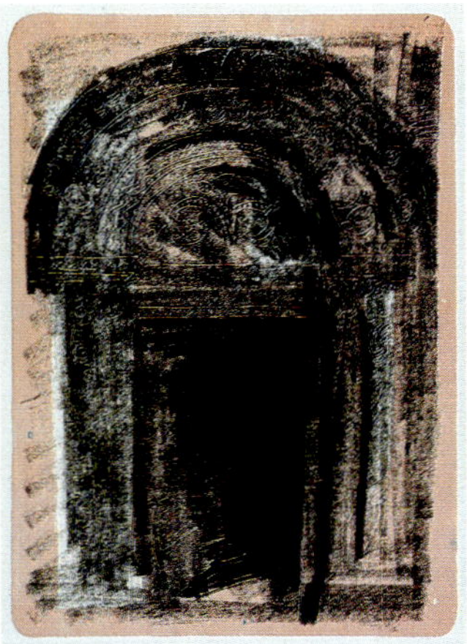
122

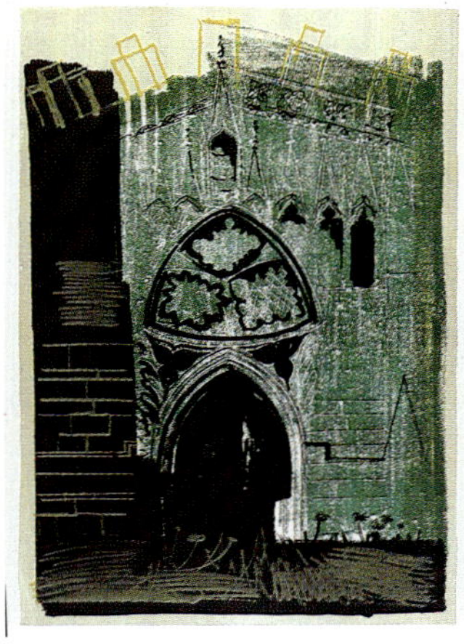
123

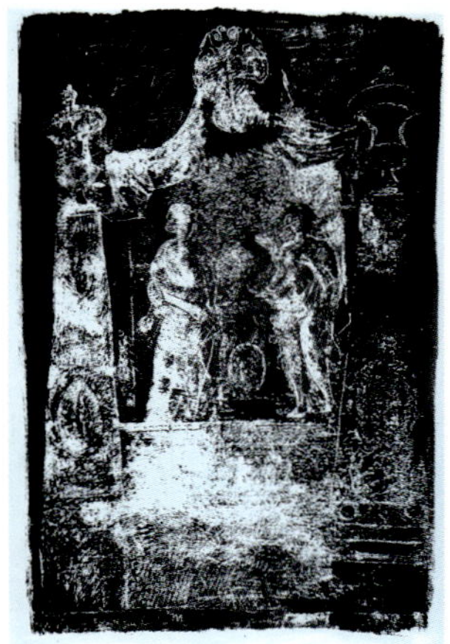
126

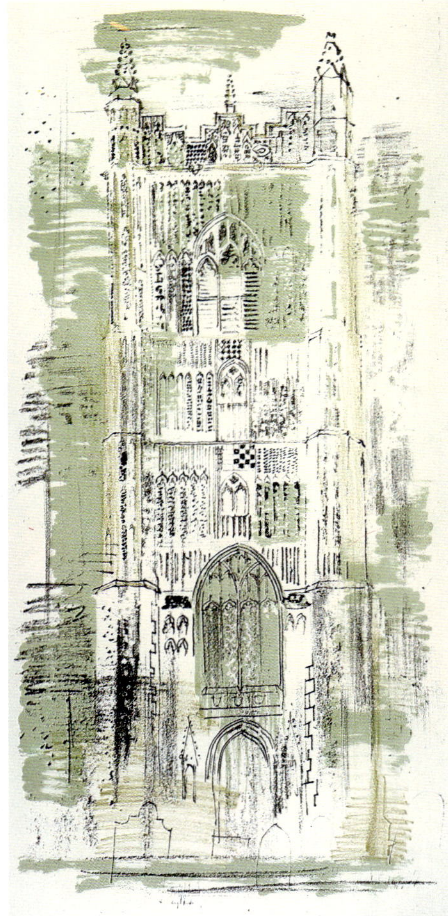
124

121A
A Retrospect of Churches: portfolio front end-paper
Plate I
303 × 424 ($11\frac{7}{8} \times 16\frac{11}{16}$)

122
Kilpeck, Herefordshire: the Norman south door
Plate II
726 × 517 ($28\frac{9}{16} \times 20\frac{3}{8}$)

123
Gaddesby, Leicestershire: medieval stonework
Plate III
672 × 472 ($26\frac{7}{16} \times 18\frac{9}{16}$)

Leicestershire Museums, Arts and Record Service

124
Redenhall, Norfolk: the tower
Plate IV
703 × 340 ($27\frac{11}{16} \times 13\frac{3}{8}$)

125
Warkton, Northamptonshire: monument by Vangelder, 1775
Plate V
693 × 490 ($27\frac{1}{4} \times 19\frac{1}{4}$)

Sometimes incorrectly known as *'Warkton, Northants'*

Albright-Knox Art Gallery

126
Exton, Rutland: monument by Grinling Gibbons, 1686
Plate VI
743 × 515 ($29\frac{1}{4} \times 20\frac{1}{4}$)

Albright-Knox Art Gallery

127
St Kew, Cornwall: church in a hilly landscape
Plate VII
504 × 702 ($19\frac{13}{16} \times 27\frac{5}{8}$)

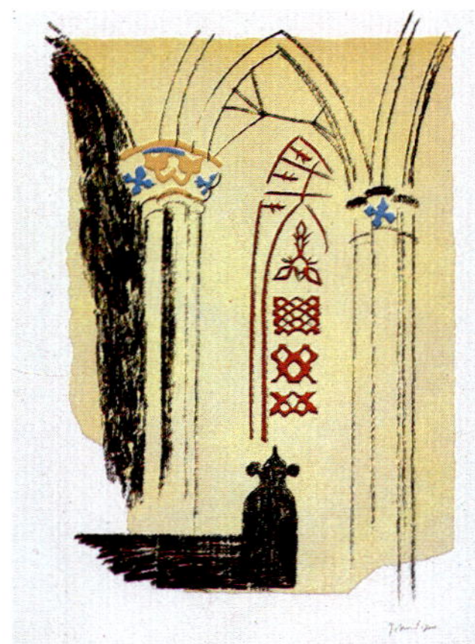
128

129

128
Llan-y-Blodwell, Shropshire: mid-19th-century furnishing and painting
Plate VIII
666 × 457 ($26\frac{3}{16} \times 18$)

Albright-Knox Art Gallery

129
Malmesbury, Wiltshire: the south porch
Plate IX
610 × 518 ($24 \times 20\frac{3}{8}$)

130
Tickencote, Rutland: the Norman chancel arch
Plate X
442 × 670 ($17\frac{3}{8} \times 26\frac{3}{8}$)

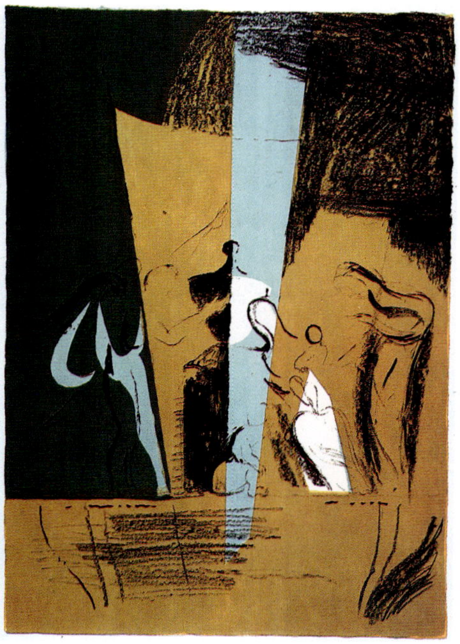

125

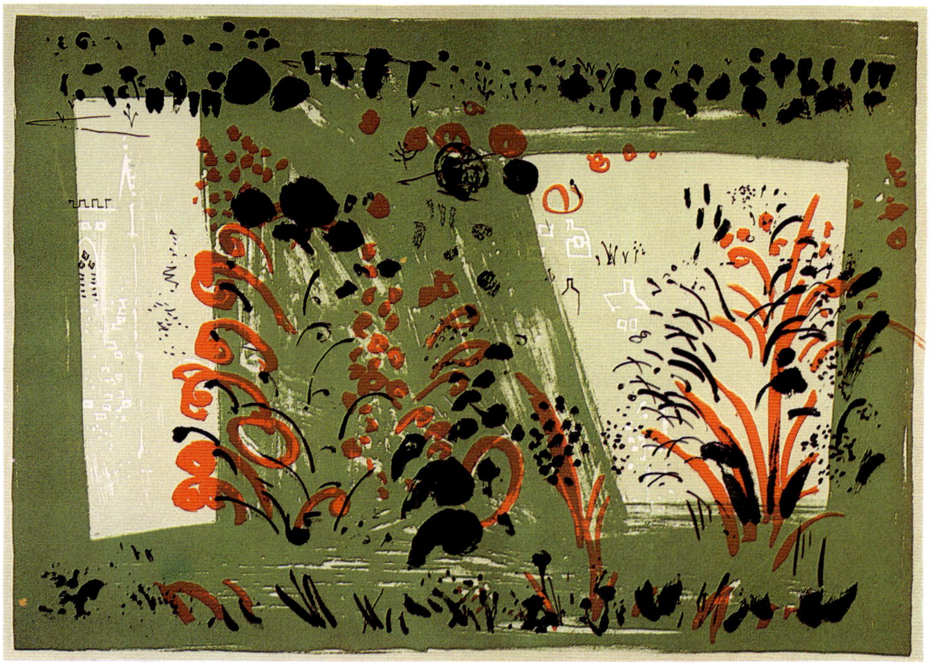

127

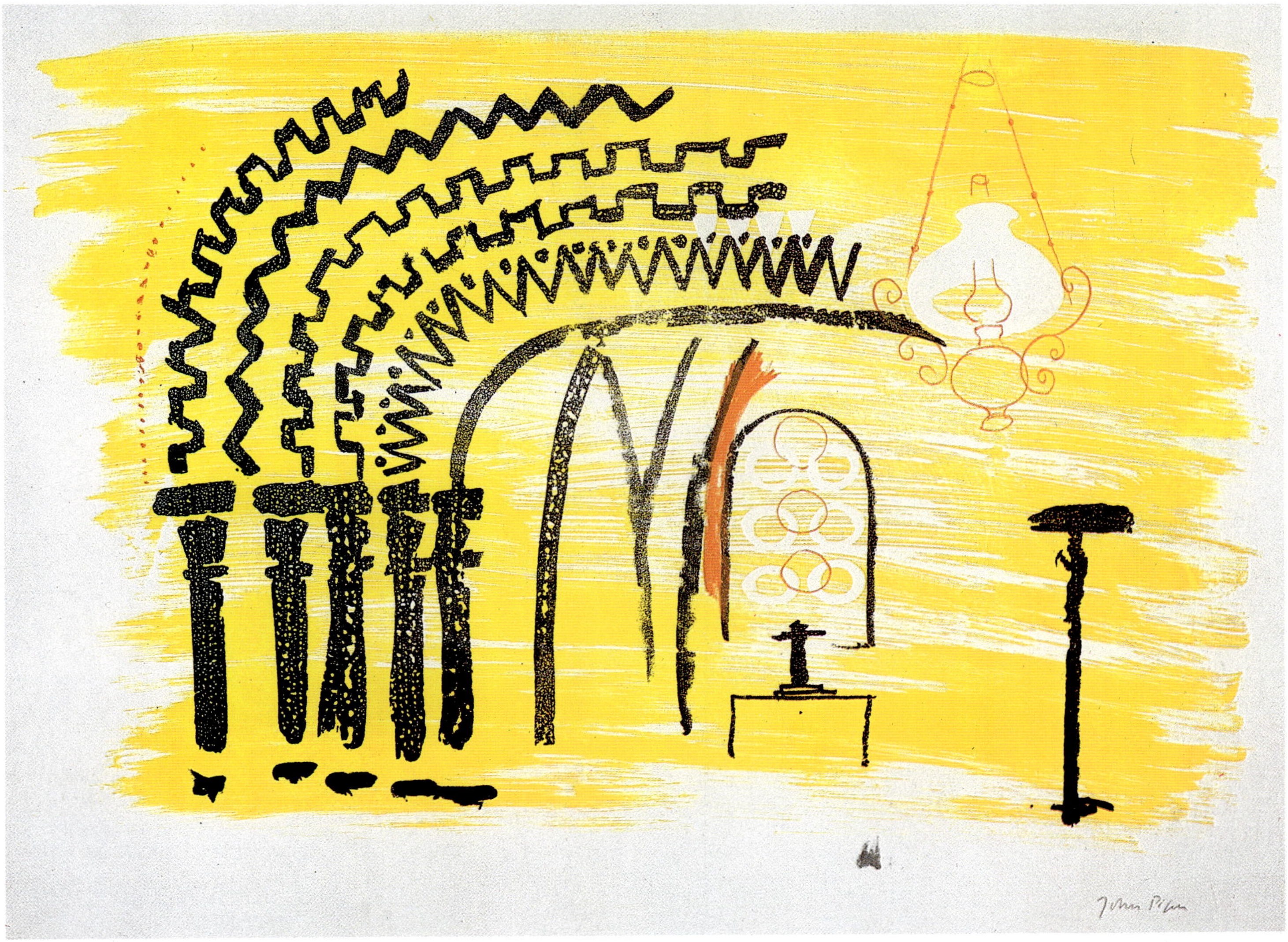

130

131
Rudbaxton, Pembrokeshire: 17th-century monument, 19th-century furnishings
Plate XI
464 × 644 (18$\frac{1}{4}$ × 25$\frac{3}{8}$)

Albright-Knox Art Gallery

132
Inglesham, Wiltshire: a rustic medieval interior
Plate XII
503 × 711 (19$\frac{13}{16}$ × 28)

133
Lewknor, Oxfordshire: textured walls, traceried windows
Plate XIII
529 × 708 (20$\frac{13}{16}$ × 27$\frac{7}{8}$)

Albright-Knox Art Gallery

134
Leckhampstead, Berkshire: a Victorian church, by S. S. Teulon
Plate XIV
673 × 470 (26$\frac{1}{2}$ × 18$\frac{1}{2}$)

135
Fotheringhay, Northamptonshire: medieval stone
Plate XV
485 × 687 (19$\frac{1}{8}$ × 27$\frac{1}{8}$)

136
St Nicholas, Liverpool: smoke-black dockland church
Plate XVI
681 × 450 (26$\frac{13}{16}$ × 17$\frac{3}{4}$)

Sometimes incorrectly known as '*St Nicholas Liverpool*'

137
Easton, Portland, Dorset: St George Reforne, an 18th-century church among the quarries
Plate XVII
638 × 502 (25$\frac{1}{8}$ × 19$\frac{3}{4}$)

Sometimes incorrectly known as '*St George Reforne, Easton, Portland, Dorset*'. Repr. in Ingrams/Piper (plate 21)

Albright-Knox Art Gallery

138
North Grimstone, Yorkshire (East Riding): the deposition – detail from the 12th-century font
Plate XVIII
729 × 533 (28$\frac{11}{16}$ × 21)

Albright-Knox Art Gallery

139
Gedney, Lincolnshire: a tower in the Fens
Plate XIX
772 × 515 (30$\frac{3}{8}$ × 20$\frac{1}{4}$)

140
Llangloffan, Pembrokeshire: the Baptist chapel
Plate XX
518 × 712 (20$\frac{3}{8}$ × 28)

Sometimes incorrectly known as '*Llangloffan*' or '*Llangloffan Baptist Chapel*'. Repr. in black-and-white in Curwen (plate 20) and West (illus.45)

Victoria and Albert Museum

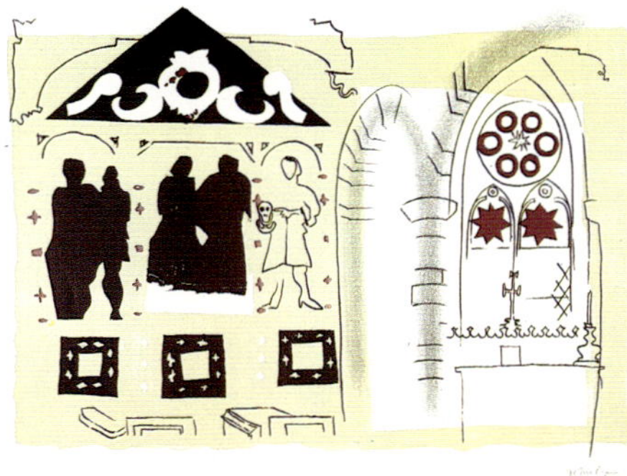
131

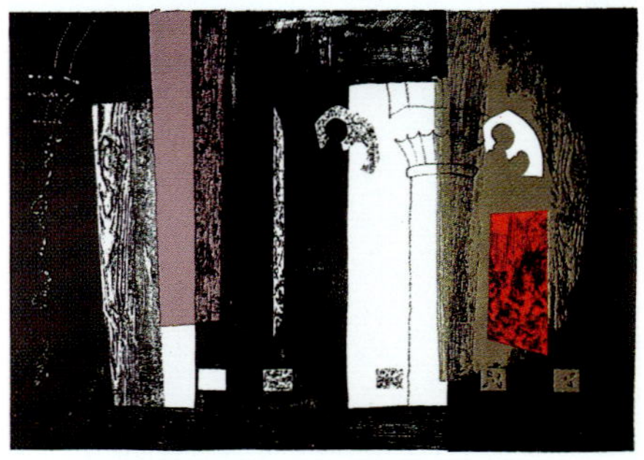
132

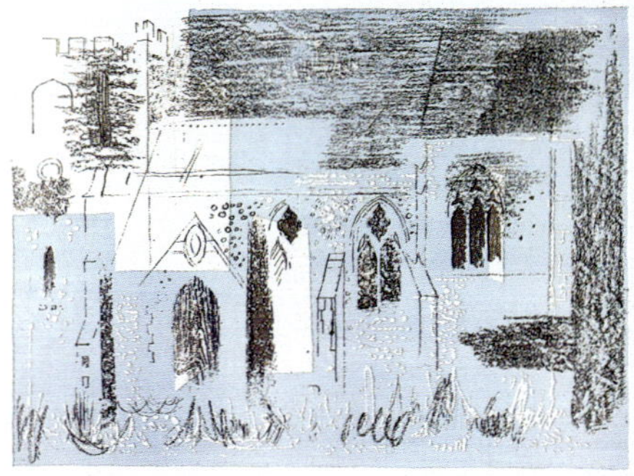
133

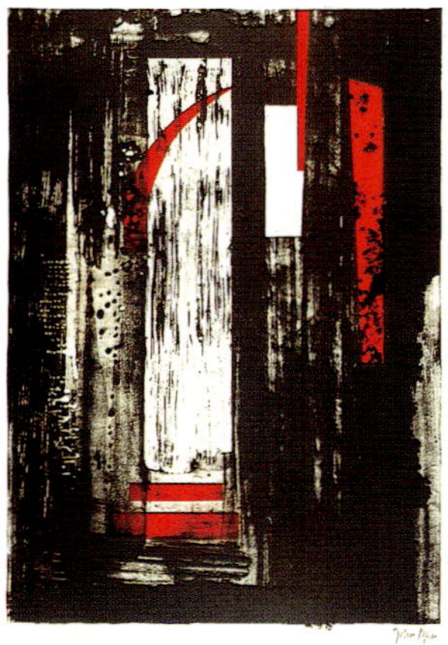
134

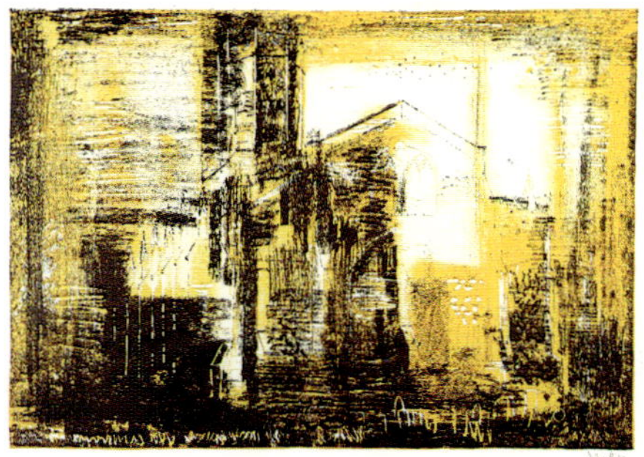
135

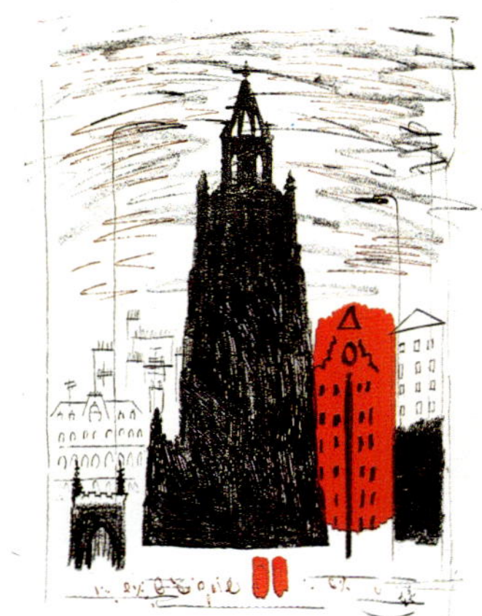
136

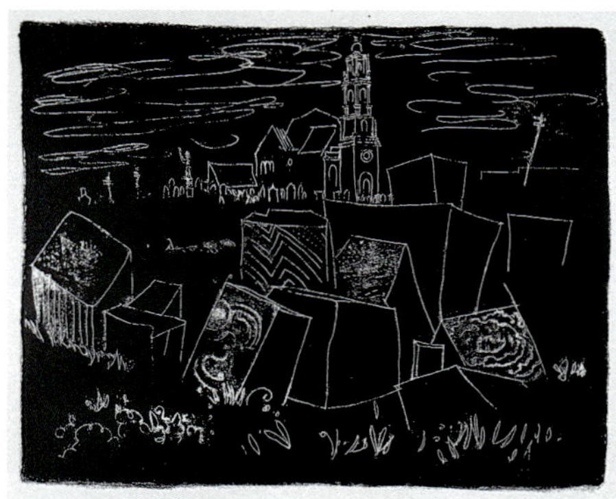
137

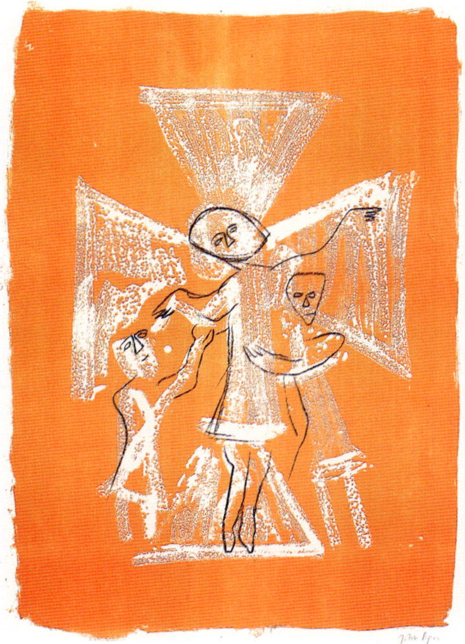

138

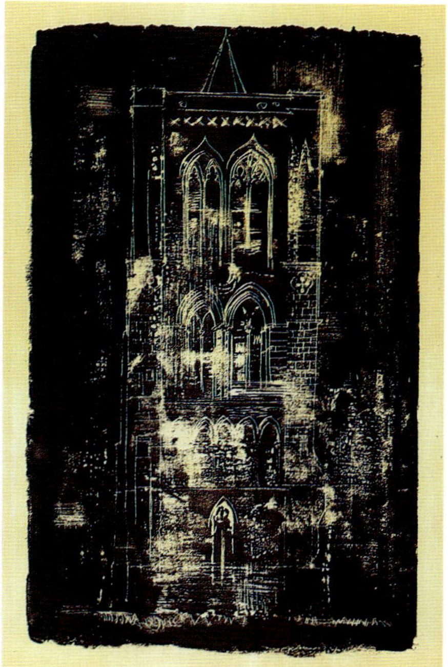

139

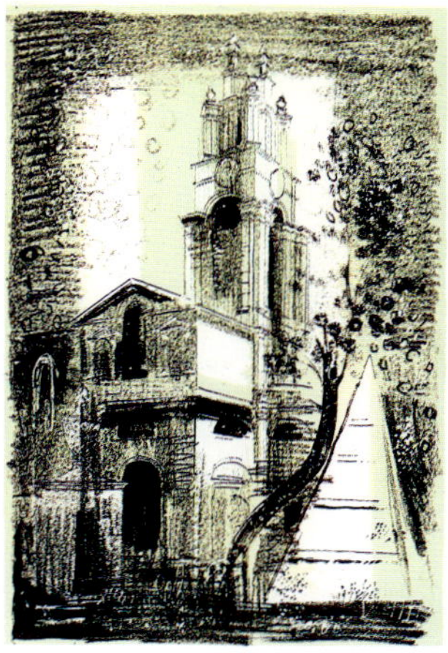

141

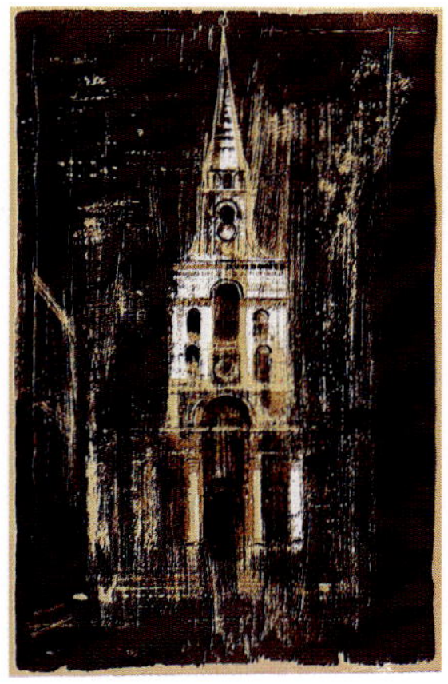

142

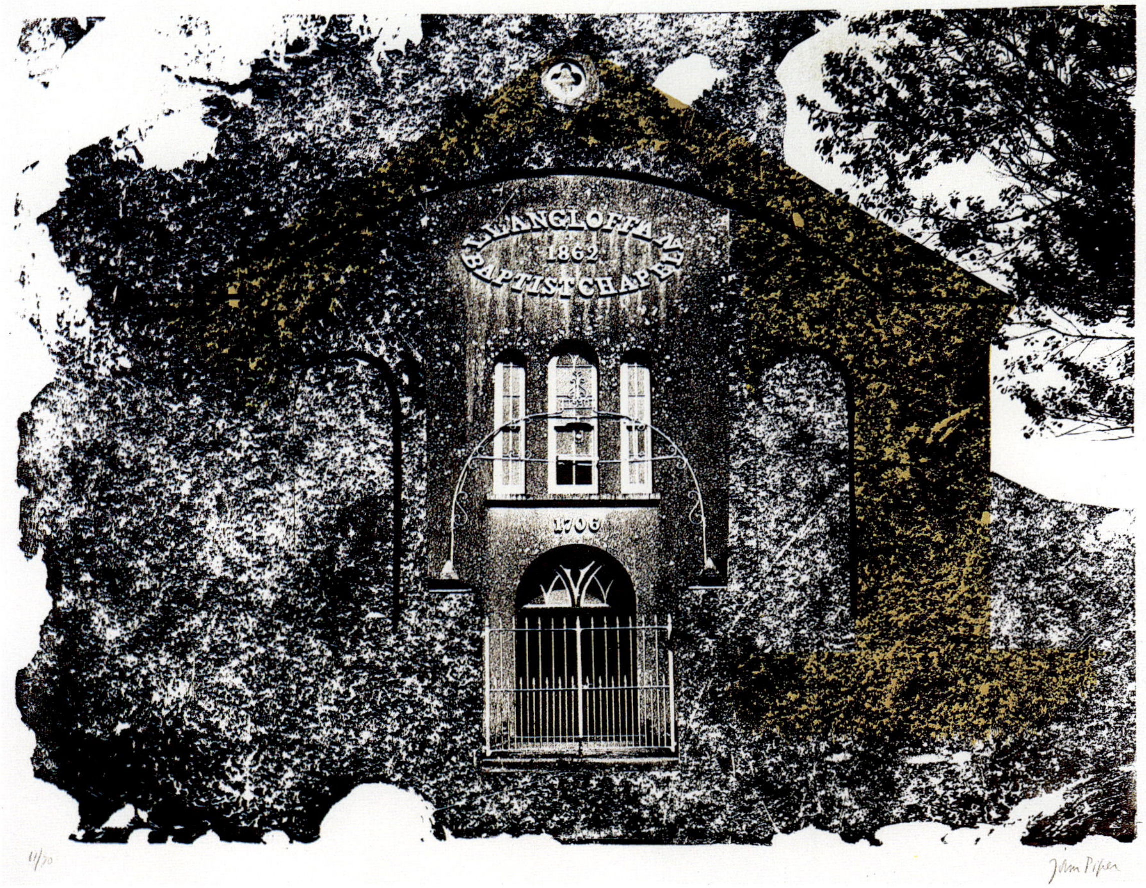

140

141
St Anne's, Limehouse, London, by Nicholas Hawksmoor
Plate XXI
708×479 (27⅞×18⅞)

142
Christ Church, Spitalfields, London, by Nicholas Hawksmoor
Plate XXII
716×470 (28³⁄₁₆×18½)

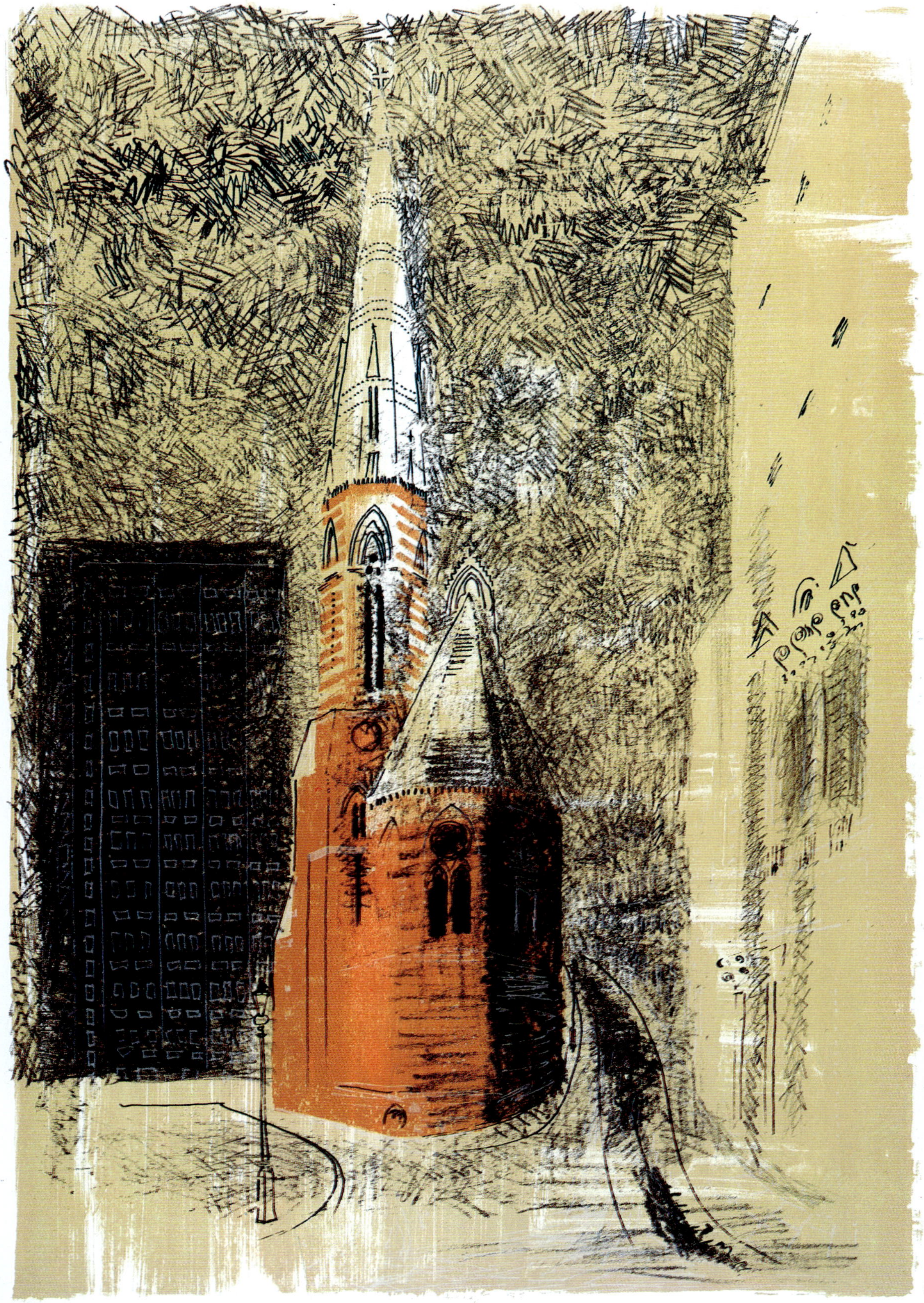

145

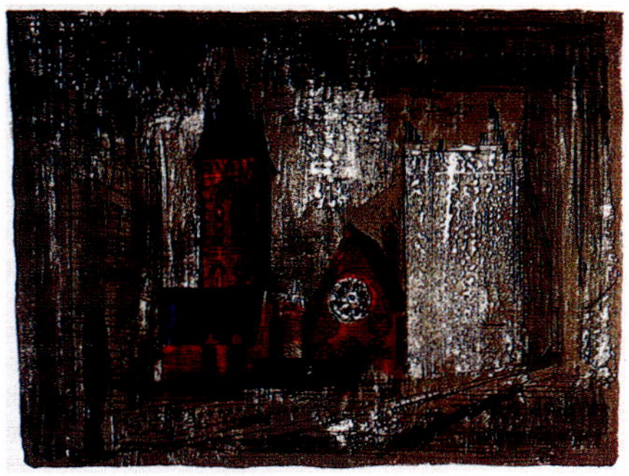

144

143
St Matthias, Stoke Newington, London, by William Butterfield
Plate XXIII
683×515 ($26\frac{7}{8}\times20\frac{1}{4}$)

144
St James the Less, Westminster, by G. E. Street
Plate XXIV
490×647 ($19\frac{1}{4}\times25\frac{7}{16}$)

145
St Mary's, Paddington, by G. E. Street
Plate XXV
695×486 ($27\frac{3}{8}\times19\frac{1}{8}$)

145A
[Venice]
Autolithograph 155×351 ($6\frac{1}{4}\times14$)
Unicorn Press at Royal College of Art 1965
Unpublished
Huntsman super white cartridge 280×390 ($11\times15\frac{3}{8}$)
Not issued as an edition Unsigned

Proofed as part of the book, *Venice* (Cats 146-71 or 146-71D or both). The only known copy has inscribed in pencil in the artist's hand t.c. '(unused) litho for Stokes'.

146-71D
Venice, March 1965
Venice by Adrian Stokes and John Piper is illustrated by John Piper with twenty-six autolithographs (thirty autolithographs for the second edition). The text is a revised version of the first edition, illustrated with photographs, published by Faber and Faber in 1945 as *Venice – an Aspect of Art* by Adrian Stokes.

Both editions printed by the Royal College of Art. The first edition bound and published by the Lion and Unicorn Press. The second edition bound and published in October by Duckworth and includes an extra lithograph (Cat. 171C), dust-jacket (Cat. 171A) and end-papers (Cats 171B, 171D). Both editions were unsigned, unnumbered, in an unspecified large print run and printed on Huntsman super white cartridge paper.

Book size: 241×197 ($9\frac{1}{2}\times7\frac{3}{4}$). Paper size: 239×194 ($9\frac{3}{8}\times7\frac{5}{8}$)

Bodleian Library (first edition); British Library (both editions); Cambridge University Library (both editions); National Library of Scotland (both editions); National Library of Wales (first edition); Trinity College Library, Dublin (second edition).

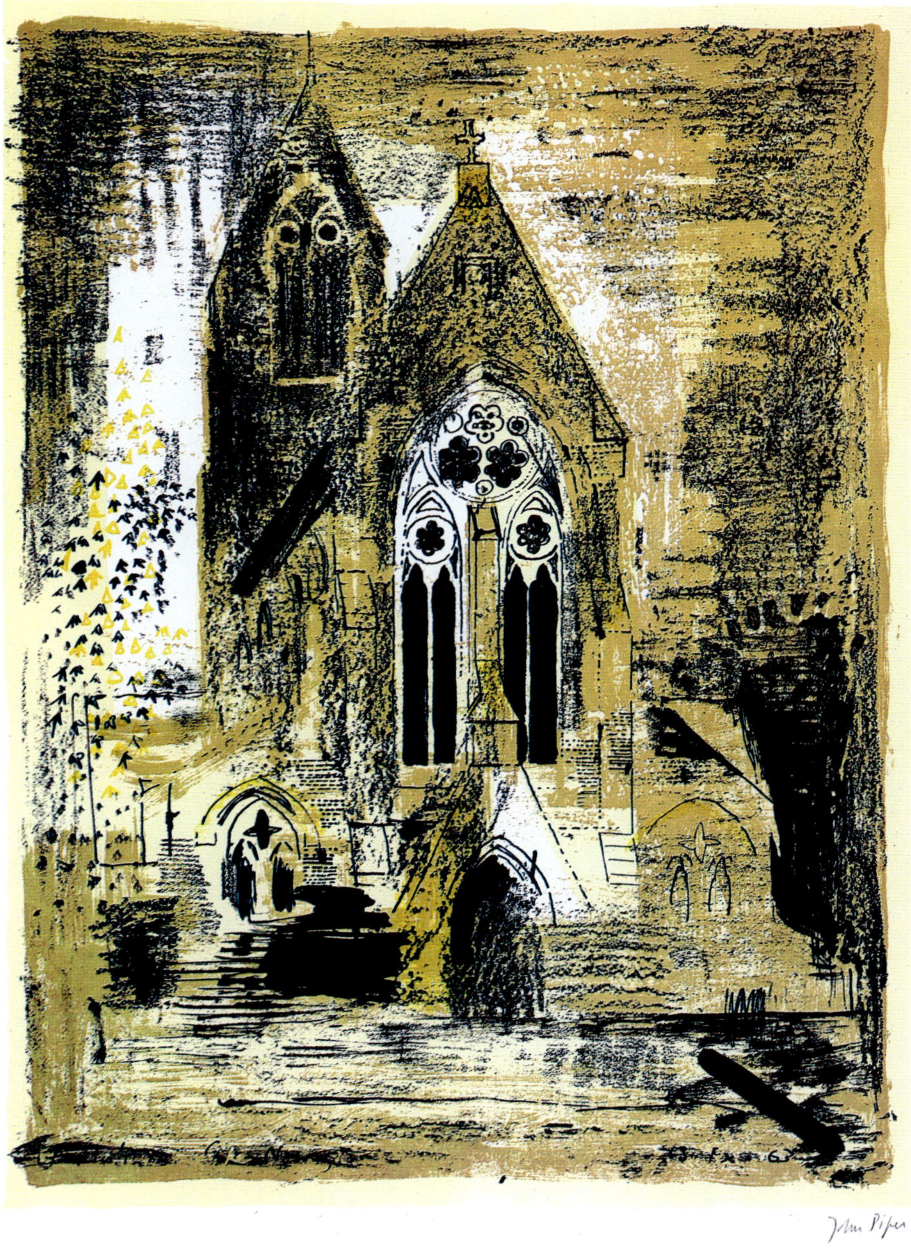

143

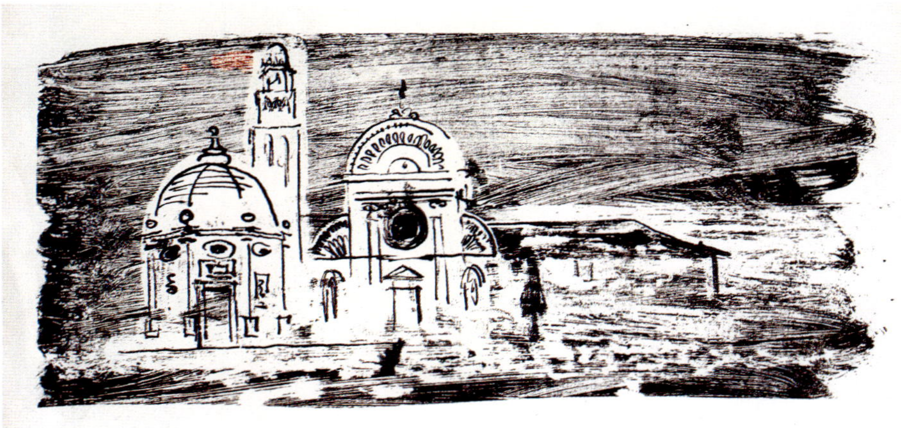

145A

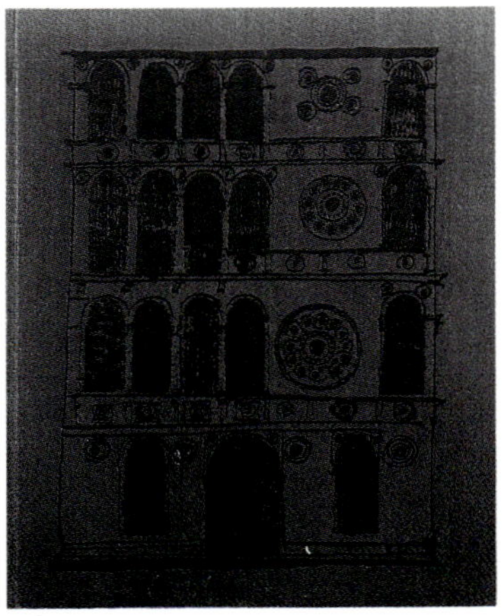

146

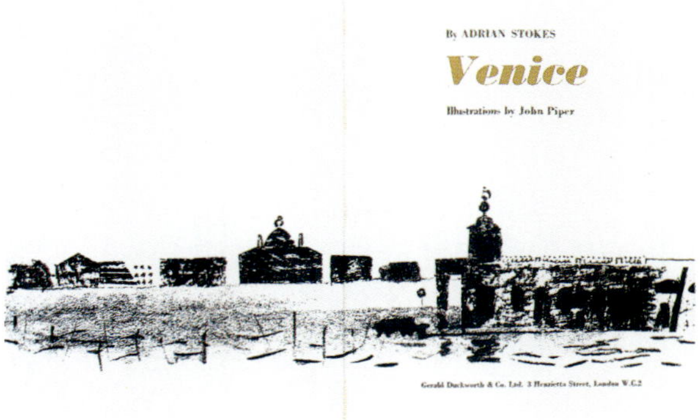

147

146
Palazzo Dario
Plate I, cover
210×150 ($8\frac{1}{4} \times 5\frac{7}{8}$)

147
The Dogana
Plate II, title-page
100×387 ($3\frac{5}{16} \times 15\frac{1}{4}$)

148
From the north, outside the Fondamenta Nuove
Plate III (pp.12 and 13)
239×387 ($9\frac{3}{8} \times 15\frac{1}{4}$)

149
The Salute
Plate IV (p.15)
239×194 ($9\frac{3}{8} \times 7\frac{5}{8}$)

150
The Giudecca
Plate V (pp.16 and 17)
70×388 ($2\frac{3}{4} \times 15\frac{5}{16}$)

151
Chiesa dell'Ospedaletto
Plate VI (p.19)
239×194 ($9\frac{3}{8} \times 7\frac{5}{8}$)

Repr. in Tate (p.28)

152
San Giorgio Maggiore
Plate VII (p.20)
64×194 ($2\frac{1}{2} \times 7\frac{5}{8}$)

153
San Marco
Plate VIII (pp.22 and 23)
239×388 ($9\frac{3}{8} \times 15\frac{5}{16}$)

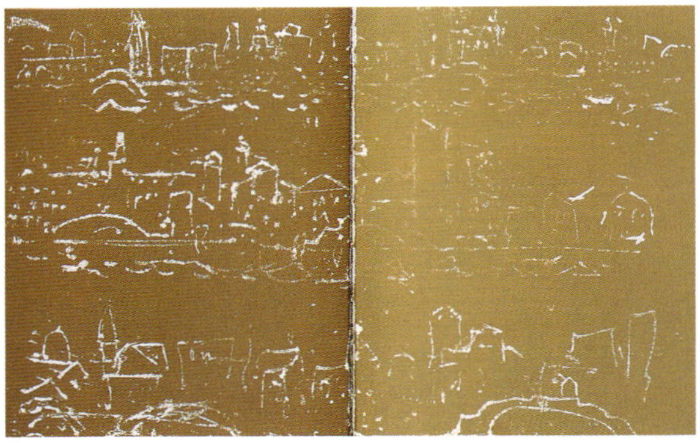

148

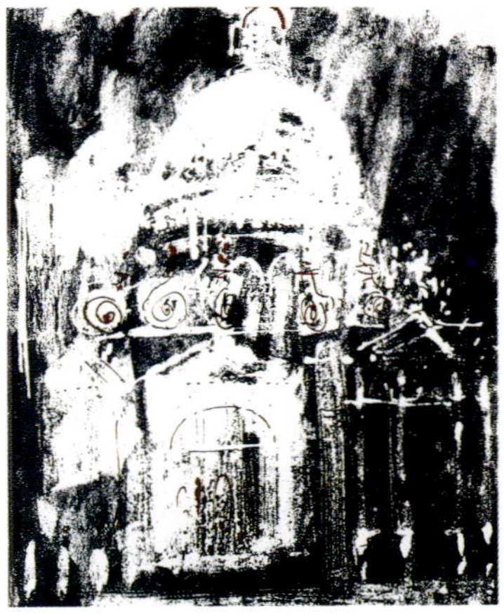

149

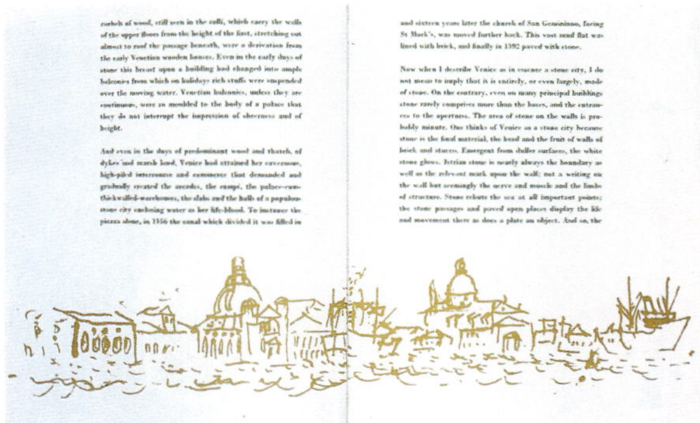

150

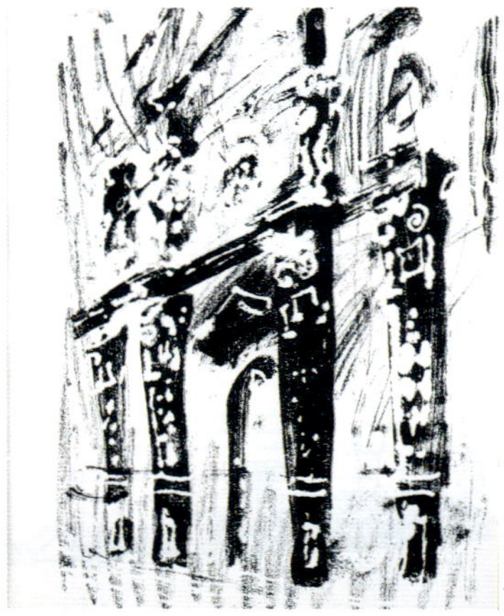

151

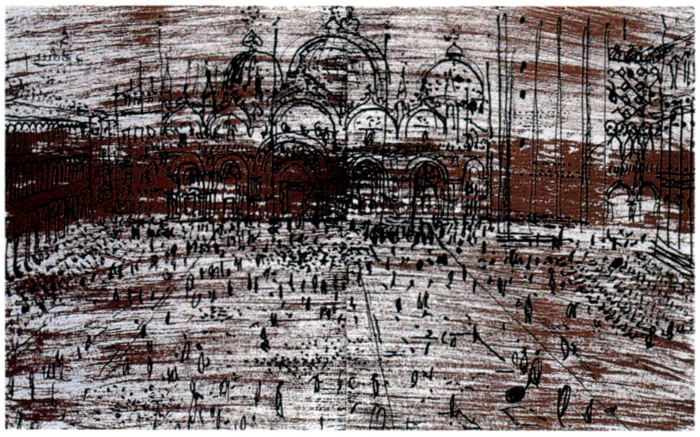

153

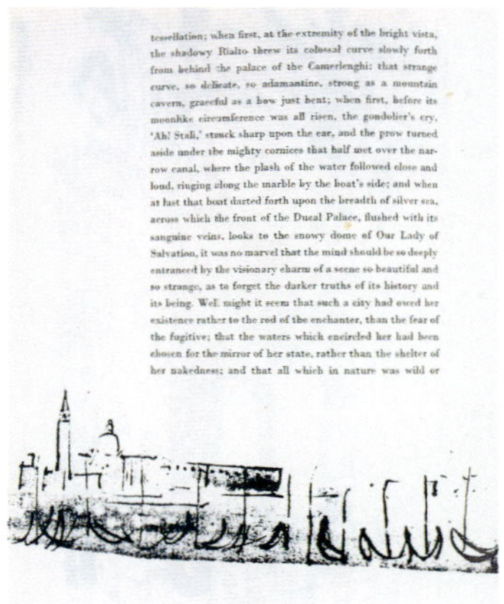

152

154
San Moisè
Plate IX (p.25)
239×194 ($9\frac{3}{8}$×$7\frac{5}{8}$)

155
The Piazza
Plate X (pp.26 and 27)
108×388 ($4\frac{1}{4}$×$15\frac{5}{16}$)

156
The Piazzetta
Plate XI (p.29)
239×194 ($9\frac{3}{8}$×$7\frac{5}{8}$)

157
Scuola di San Marco
Plate XII (pp.32 and 33)
239×388 ($9\frac{3}{8}$×$15\frac{5}{16}$)

158
San Stae
Plate XIII (p.35)
239×162 ($9\frac{3}{8}$×$6\frac{3}{8}$)

159
From the lagoon
Plate XIV (pp.36 and 37)
76×388 (3×$15\frac{5}{16}$)

160
Santa Maria Formosa
Plate XV (p.39)
134×194 ($5\frac{1}{4}$×$7\frac{5}{8}$)

161
From the lagoon
Plate XVI (p.41)
50×194 (2×$7\frac{5}{8}$)

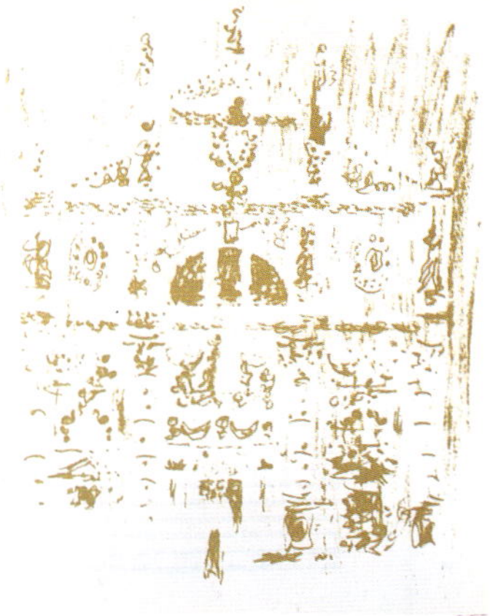

154

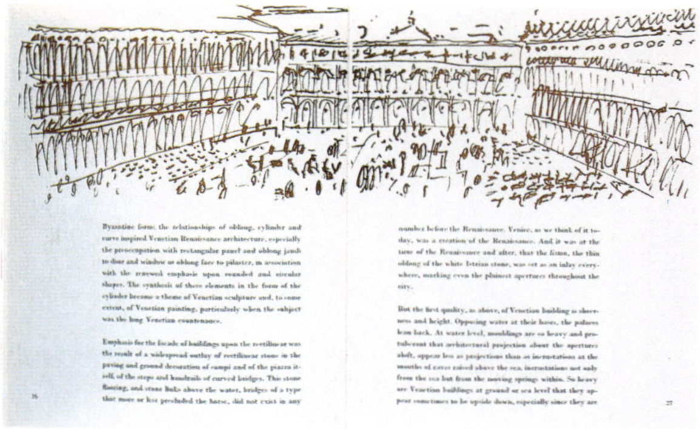

Byzantine form: the relationships of oblong, cylinder and curve inspired Venetian Renaissance architecture, especially the preoccupation with rectangular panel and oblong jamb to door and window or oblong face to pilaster, in association with the renewed emphasis upon rounded and circular shapes. The synthesis of these elements in the form of the cylinder became a theme of Venetian sculpture and, to some extent, of Venetian painting, particularly when the subject was the long Venetian countenance.

Emphasis for the facade of buildings upon the rectilinear was the result of a widespread outlay of rectilinear stone in the paving and ground decoration of campi and of the piazza itself, of the steps and handrails of curved bridges. This stone flooring, and stone links above the water, bridges of a type that more or less precluded the horse, did not exist in any

number before the Renaissance. Venice, as we think of it today, was a creation of the Renaissance. And it was at the time of the Renaissance and after, that the *listou*, the thin oblong of the white Istrian stone, was set as an inlay everywhere, marking even the plainest apertures throughout the city.

But the first quality, as above, of Venetian building is sheerness and height. Opposing water at their bases, the palaces lean back. At water level, mouldings are so heavy and protuberant that architectural projection about the apertures aloft, appear less as projections than as incrustations at the mouths of caves raised above the sea, incrustations not only from the sea but from the moving springs within. So heavy are Venetian buildings at ground or sea level that they appear sometimes to be upside down, especially since they are

155

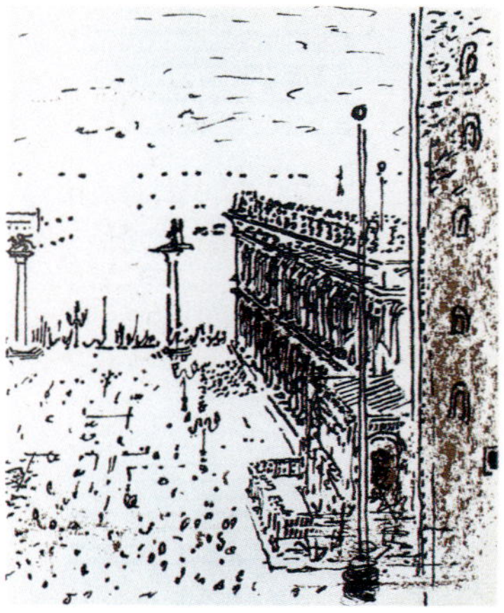

156

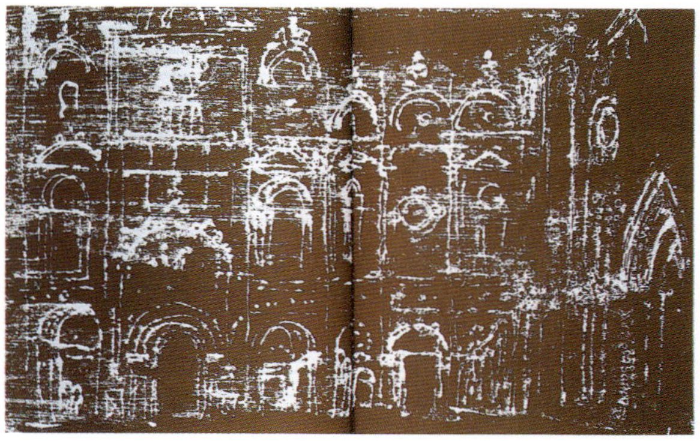

157

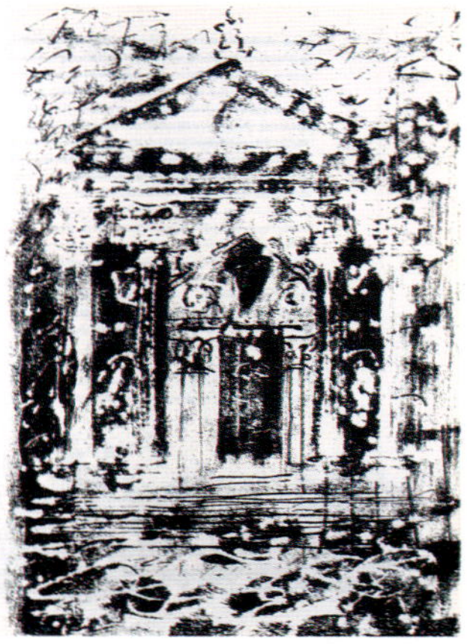

158

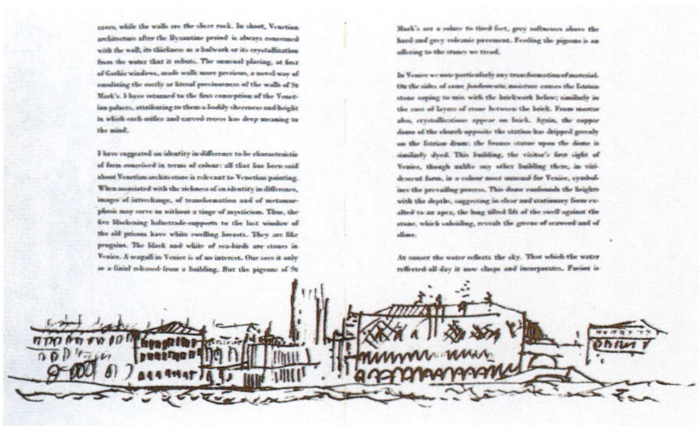

caves, while the walls are the sheer rock. In short, Venetian architecture after the Byzantine period is always concerned with the wall, its thickness as a bulwark or its crystallization from the water that it rebuts. The unusual placing, at first of Gothic windows, made walls more precious, a novel way of emulating the costly or literal preciousness of the walls of St Mark's. I have returned to the first conception of the Venetian palaces, attributing to them a bodily sheerness and height in which each orifice and carved recess has deep meaning to the mind.

I have suggested an identity in difference to be characteristic of form conceived in terms of colour: all that has been said about Venetian architecture is relevant to Venetian painting. When associated with the richness of an identity in difference, images of interchange, of transformation and of metamorphosis may serve us without a tinge of mysticism. Thus, the five blackening balustrade-supports to the last window of the old prisons have white swelling breasts. They are like penguins. The black and white of sea-birds are stones in Venice. A seagull in Venice is of no interest. One sees it only as a finial released from a building. But the pigeons of St Mark's are a solace to tired feet, grey softnesses above the hard and grey volcanic pavement. Feeding the pigeons is an offering to the stones we tread.

In Venice we note particularly any transformation of material. On the sides of some *fondamente*, moisture causes the Istrian stone coping to mix with the brickwork below; similarly in the case of layers of stone between the brick. From mortar also, crystallizations appear on brick. Again, the copper dome of the church opposite the station has dripped greenly on the Istrian drum: the bronze statue upon the dome is similarly dyed. This building, the visitor's first sight of Venice, though unlike any other building there, in viridescent form, in a colour most unusual for Venice, symbolizes the prevailing process. This dome confounds the heights with the depths, suggesting in clear and stationary form exalted to an apex, the long tilted lift of the swell against the stone, which subsiding, reveals the greens of seaweed and of slime.

At sunset the water reflects the sky. That which the water reflected all day it now clasps and incorporates. Fusion is

159

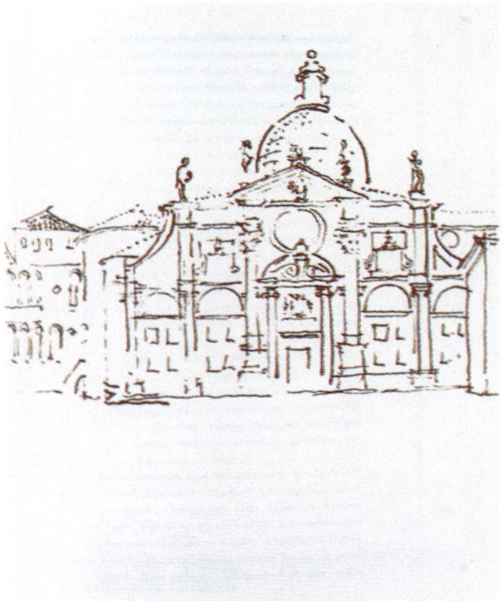

160

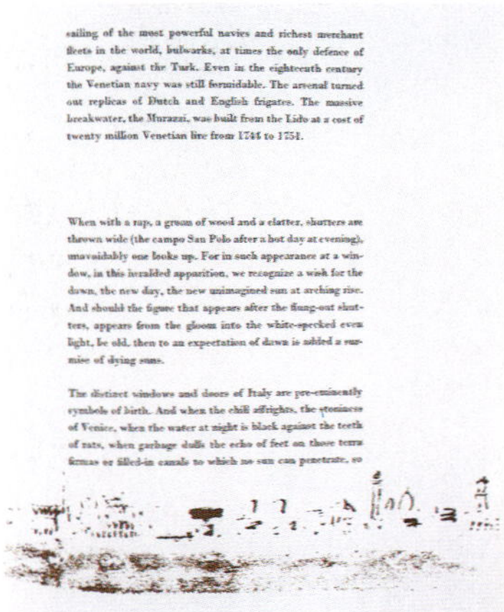

sailing of the most powerful navies and richest merchant fleets in the world, bulwarks, at times the only defence of Europe, against the Turk. Even in the eighteenth century the Venetian navy was still formidable. The arsenal turned out replicas of Dutch and English frigates. The massive breakwater, the Murazzi, was built from the Lido at a cost of twenty million Venetian lire from 1744 to 1751.

When with a rap, a groan of wood and a clatter, shutters are thrown wide (the campo San Polo after a hot day at evening), unavoidably one looks up. For in such appearance at a window, in this heralded apparition, we recognize a wish for the dawn, the new day, the new unimagined sun at arching rise. And should the figure that appears after the flung-out shutters, appears from the gloom into the white-specked even light, be old, then to an expectation of dawn is added a surmise of dying suns.

The distinct windows and doors of Italy are pre-eminently symbols of birth. And when the chill affrights, the stoniness of Venice, when the water at night is black against the teeth of rats, when garbage dulls the echo of feet on those terra firmas or filled-in canals to which no sun can penetrate, so

161

162
From the lagoon
Plate XVII (pp.42 and 43)
239 × 388 ($9\frac{3}{8} \times 15\frac{5}{16}$)

163
San Zaccaria
Plate XVIII (p.45)
239 × 167 ($9\frac{3}{8} \times 6\frac{9}{16}$)

164
From the lagoon
Plate XIX (pp.46 and 47)
104 × 375 ($4\frac{1}{8} \times 14\frac{3}{4}$)

165
Santa Maria dei Miracoli
Plate XX (p.49)
239 × 194 ($9\frac{3}{8} \times 7\frac{5}{8}$)

166
From the lagoon
Plate XXI (p.51)
104 × 194 ($4\frac{1}{16} \times 7\frac{5}{8}$)

167
Palazzo Manzoni-Angaran
Plate XXII (pp.52 and 53)
239 × 388 ($9\frac{3}{8} \times 15\frac{5}{16}$)

168
Side of the Palazzo Pesaro
Plate XXIII (p.55)
239 × 163 ($9\frac{3}{8} \times 6\frac{3}{8}$)

169
Base of the Campanile
Plate XXIV (pp.56 and 57)
140 × 388 ($5\frac{1}{2} \times 15\frac{5}{16}$)

Repr. in black-and-white in Tate (p.30)

170
Palazzo Pesaro
Plate XXV (p.59)
239 × 194 ($9\frac{3}{8} \times 7\frac{5}{8}$)

171
From the lagoon
Plate XXVI (pp.62 and 63)
239 × 388 ($9\frac{3}{8} \times 15\frac{5}{8}$)

171A
Venice: Untitled (dust-jacket)
2nd edition only
242 × 410 ($9\frac{9}{16} \times 16$)

171B
Venice: Untitled (front end-papers)
2nd edition only
238 × 385 ($9\frac{3}{8} \times 15\frac{1}{8}$)

The back end-paper is a reprint of the front end-paper with the left and right panels reversed and printed on to the board, paper unknown.
Kelpra Studio 1966

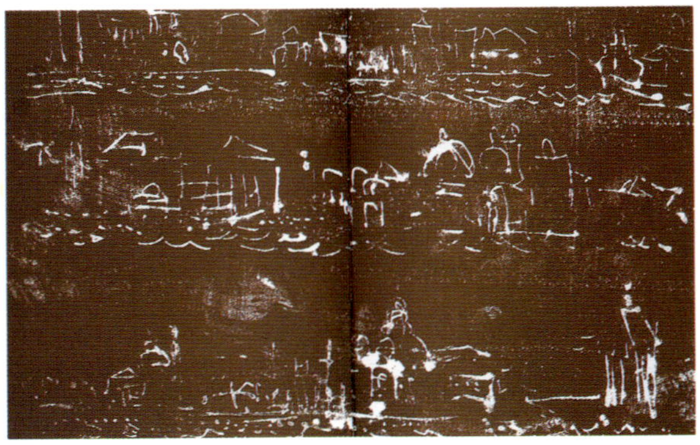
162

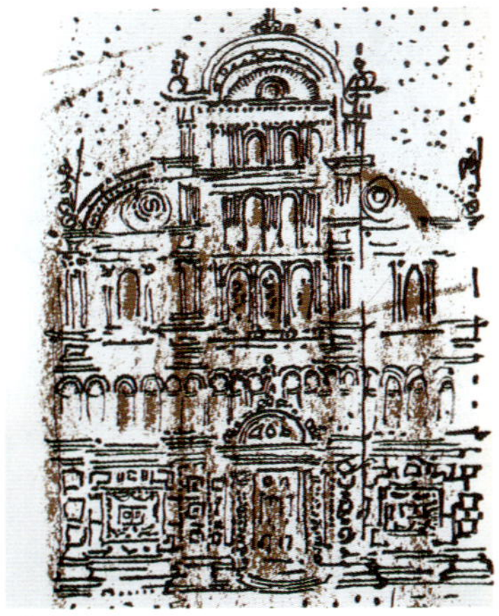
163

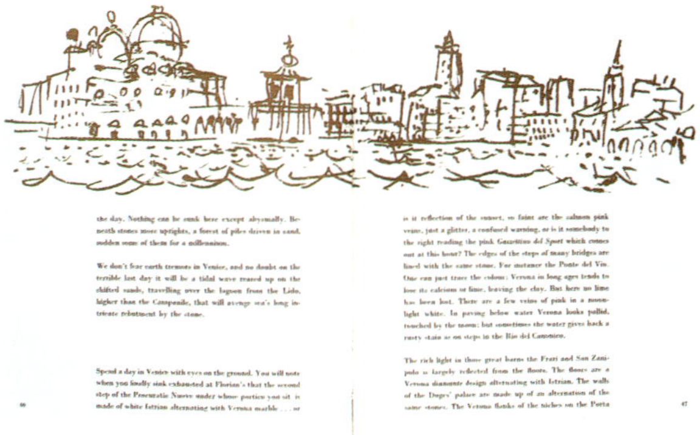
164

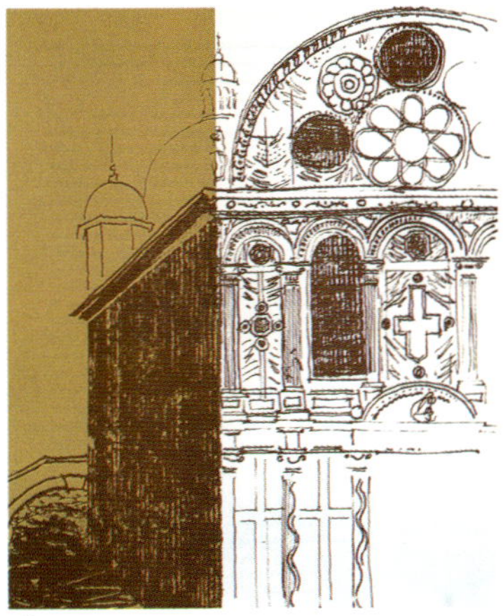
165

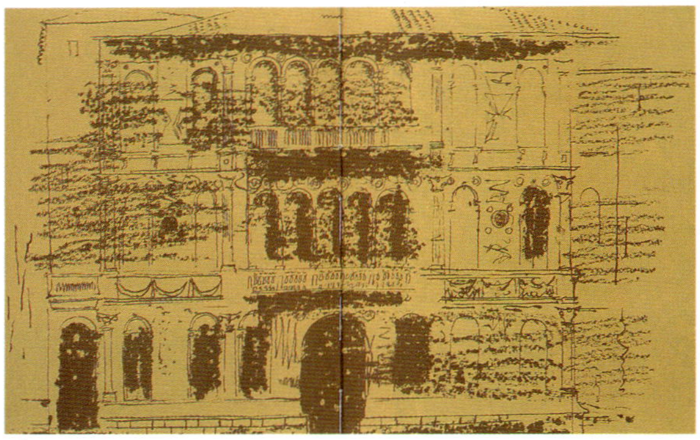
167

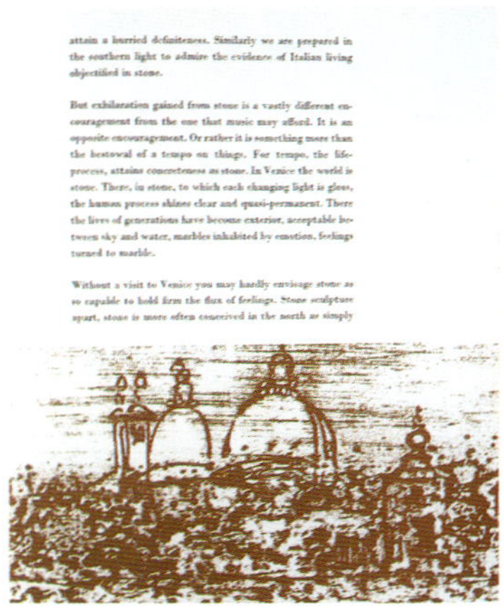
166

171C
Venice: Untitled (backpiece)
2nd edition only
76 × 190 ($3 \times 7\frac{1}{2}$)

171D
Venice: Untitled (back end-papers)
2nd edition only
238 × 385 ($9\frac{3}{8} \times 15\frac{1}{8}$)

The back end-paper is a reprint of the front end-paper with the left and right panels reversed and printed on to the board, paper unknown.

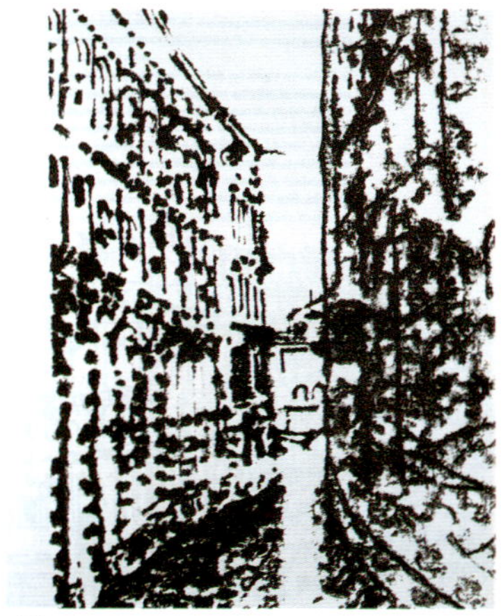
168

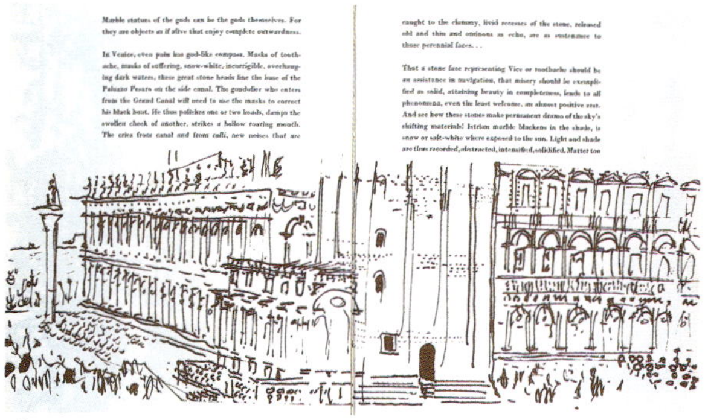

Marble statues of the gods can be the gods themselves. For they are objects as if alive that enjoy complete outwardness.

In Venice, even pain has god-like compass. Masks of toothache, masks of suffering, snow-white, incorrigible, overhanging dark waters, these great stone heads line the base of the Palazzo Pesaro on the side canal. The gondolier who enters from the Grand Canal will need to use the masks to correct his black boat. He thus polishes one or two heads, damps the swollen cheek of another, strikes a hollow roaring mouth. The cries from canal and from *calli*, new noises that are caught to the clammy, livid recesses of the stone, released old and thin and ominous as echo, are as sustenance to those perennial *faces*. . .

That a stone face representing Vice or toothache should be an assistance in navigation, that misery should be exemplified as solid, attaining beauty in completeness, lends to all phenomena, even the least welcome, an almost positive zest. And see how these stones make permanent drama of the sky's shifting materials! Istrian marble blackens in the shade, is snow or salt-white where exposed to the sun. Light and shade are thus recorded, abstracted, intensified, solidified. Matter too

169

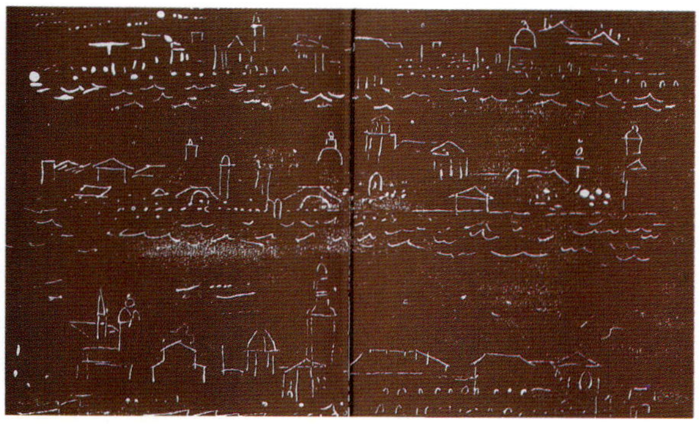

171

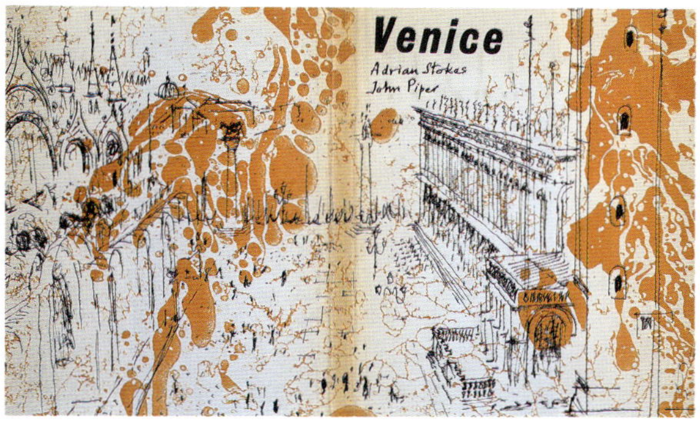

171A

170

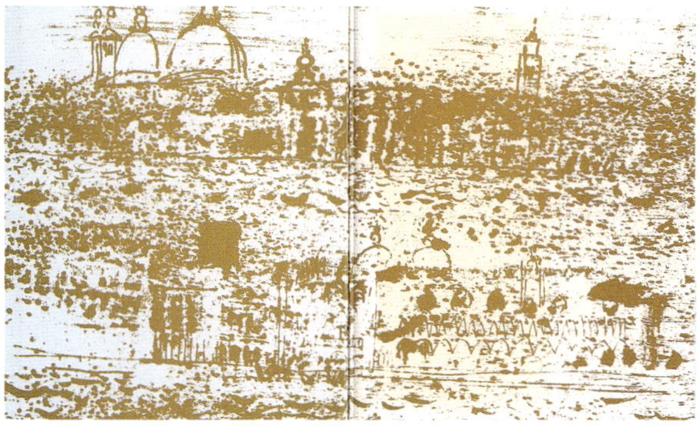

171B

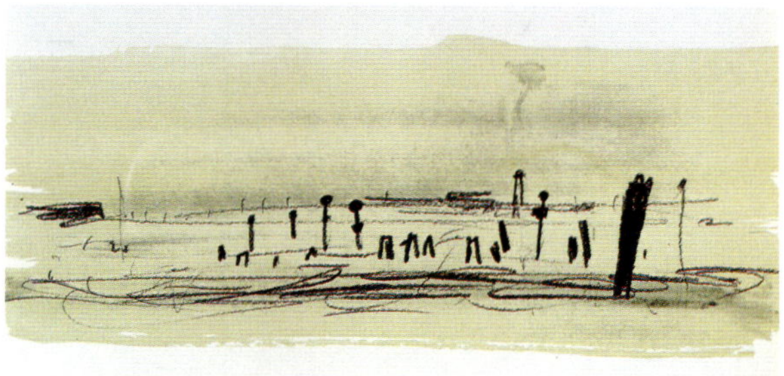

171C

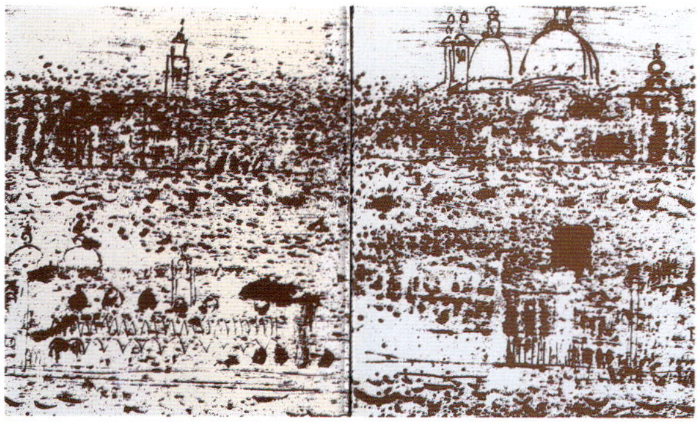

171D

172
Bethesda Baptist Chapel, Swansea
Lithograph 512 × 680 ($20\frac{3}{16} \times 26\frac{3}{4}$)
Curwen Studio 1966
Marlborough Fine Art 1966
Barcham Green 250gsm, wmk 'John Piper'
602 × 824 ($23\frac{11}{16} \times 32\frac{7}{16}$)
75 'John Piper' 7AP 2HC

Sometimes incorrectly known as *'Bethesda Chapel'* or *'Bethesda Church'*

Albright-Knox Art Gallery; Tate Gallery

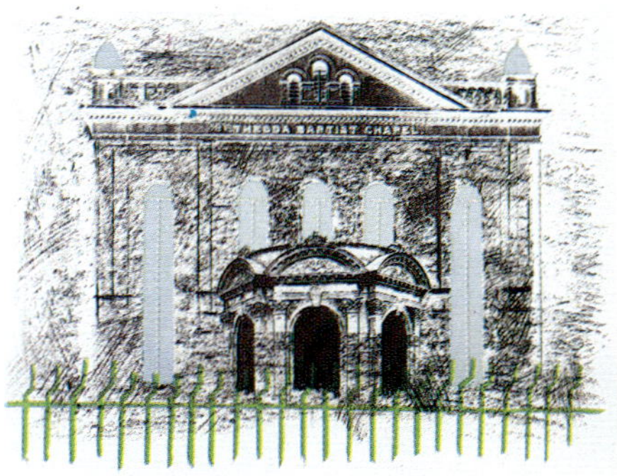

172

173
Crug Glas, Swansea
Lithograph 506 × 766 ($19\frac{15}{16} \times 30\frac{3}{16}$)
Curwen Studio 1966
Marlborough Fine Art 1966
Barcham Green 250gsm, wmk 'John Piper' and 'F. J. Head' 594 × 814 ($23\frac{3}{8} \times 32\frac{1}{16}$)
75 'John Piper' 10AP 2HC

Sometimes incorrectly known as *'Crug Glass'* or *'Crug Glas Chapel'* or *'Swansea Yellow'*

Albright-Knox Art Gallery; Tate Gallery

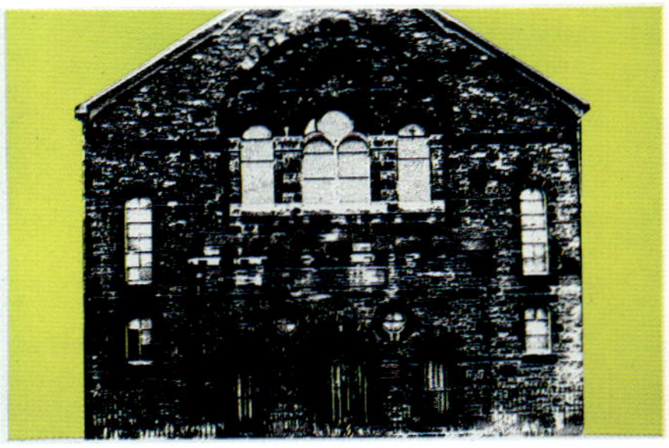

173

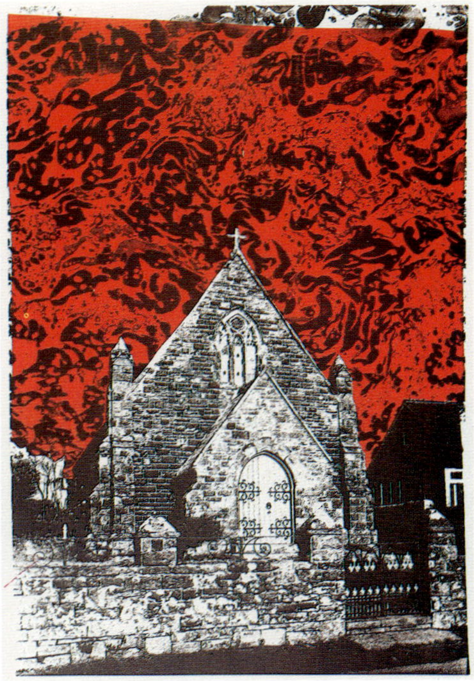

174

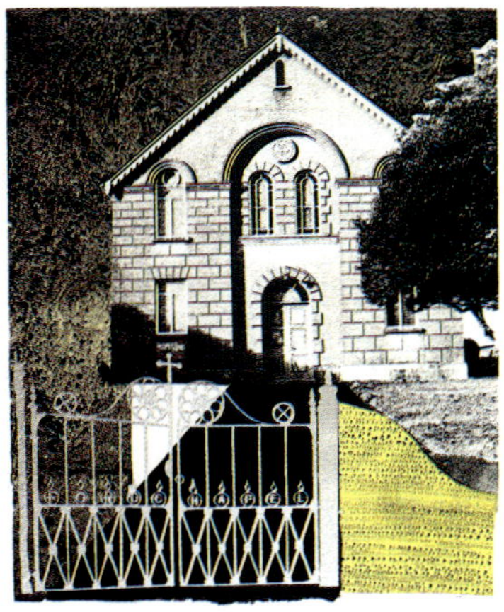

176

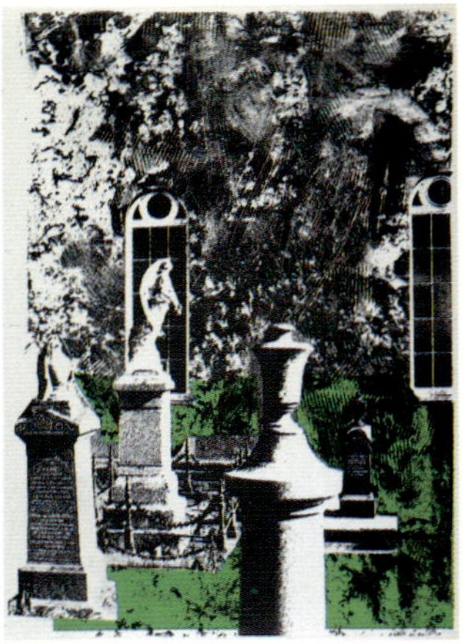

177

174
Newgate Chapel
Lithograph 752 × 512 ($29\frac{5}{8} \times 20\frac{1}{8}$)
Curwen Studio 1966
Marlborough Fine Art 1966
Barcham Green 250gsm, wmk 'John Piper'
813 × 590 ($32 \times 23\frac{1}{4}$)
75 'John Piper' 10AP 2HC

Sometimes incorrectly known as *'Newgate'* or *'Newgate Church'*

Albright-Knox Art Gallery

175 (detail Plate 4)
Swansea Chapel
Lithograph 693 × 516 ($27\frac{1}{4} \times 20\frac{5}{16}$)
Curwen Studio 1966
Marlborough Fine Art 1966
Barcham Green 250gsm, wmk 'John Piper'
810 × 592 ($31\frac{7}{8} \times 23\frac{7}{16}$)
75 'John Piper' 10AP 2HC

Sometimes incorrectly known as *'Swansea Blue'*

Albright-Knox Art Gallery; Scottish National Gallery of Modern Art; Tate Gallery

176
Penybont Ford Congregational Church
Screenprint 710 × 573 ($27\frac{15}{16} \times 22\frac{9}{16}$)
Kelpra Studio 1966
Marlborough Fine Art 1966
J. Green 233lbs 978 × 682 ($38\frac{1}{2} \times 26\frac{13}{16}$)
75 'John Piper' 10AP 5HC 5PP

Printer's stamp and no. '6625' on reverse

Albright-Knox Art Gallery; Tate Gallery

177
Dylwyn Church
Lithograph 773 × 539 ($30\frac{1}{2} \times 21\frac{1}{4}$)
Curwen Studio 1966
Marlborough Fine Art 1966
Barcham Green 250gsm, wmk 'John Piper' b.r.
817 × 592 ($32\frac{1}{4} \times 23\frac{1}{4}$)
75 'John Piper' 10AP 2HC

Sometimes incorrectly known as *'Dylwyn'*

Albright-Knox Art Gallery; Tate Gallery

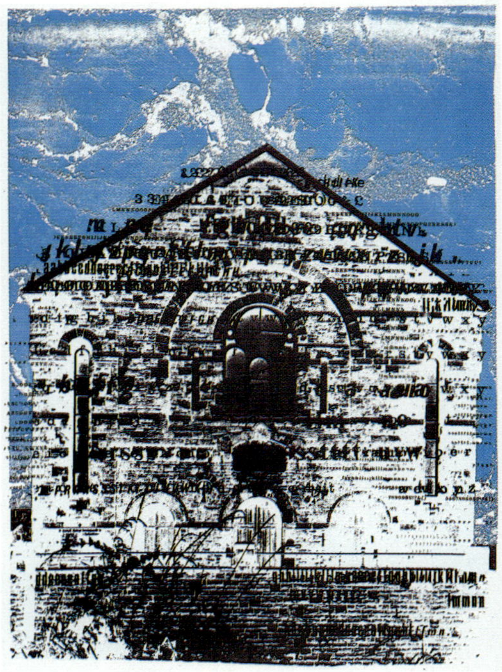

175

178
Ironbridge
Lithograph 482 × 643 ($19 \times 25\frac{5}{16}$)
Curwen Studio 1966
Friends of the Museum of Israel 1966
T. H. Saunders 120lbs 592 × 820 ($23\frac{5}{16} \times 32\frac{1}{4}$)
75 'John Piper' 10AP 2HC

Tate Gallery

179
Travel Notes: Devil's Bridge Waterfalls
Screenprint 747 × 509 ($29\frac{3}{8} \times 20$)
Kelpra Studio 1967
Marlborough Fine Art 1967
J. Green 233lbs 775 × 575 ($30\frac{1}{2} \times 22\frac{5}{8}$)
70 'John Piper' 10AP 5HC 5PP

Printer's stamp and no. '6907' on reverse

Tate Gallery

With a few prints of Cat. 181, Piper rotated the image 180 degrees so that the yellow figure b.r. was t.l. and then signed these prints in the normal way *ie* 'John Piper' b.r. and 'Artist's proof' b.l. The publishers also inform me that they have editioned, numbered prints in stock with the yellow figure t.l.

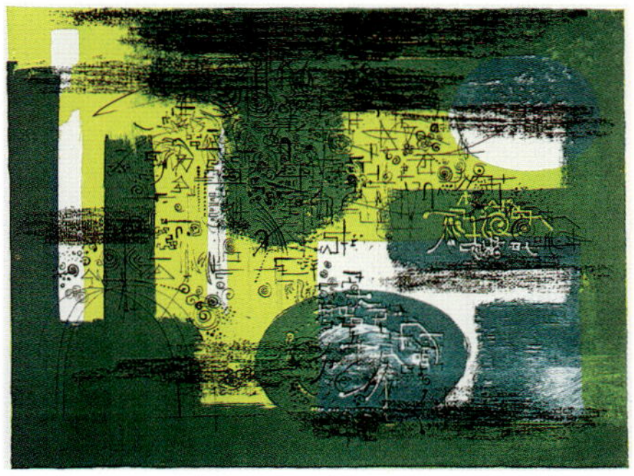

178

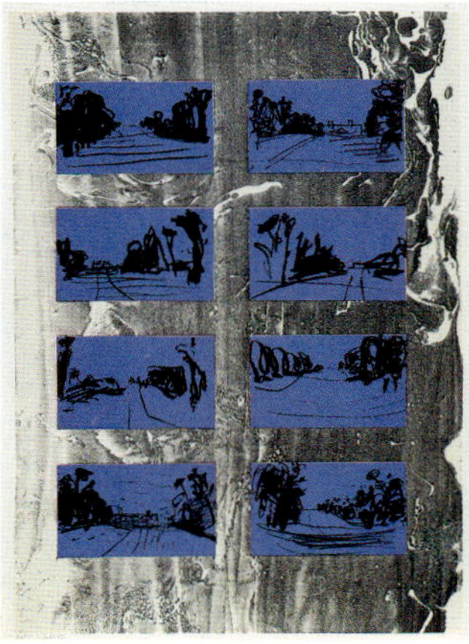

180

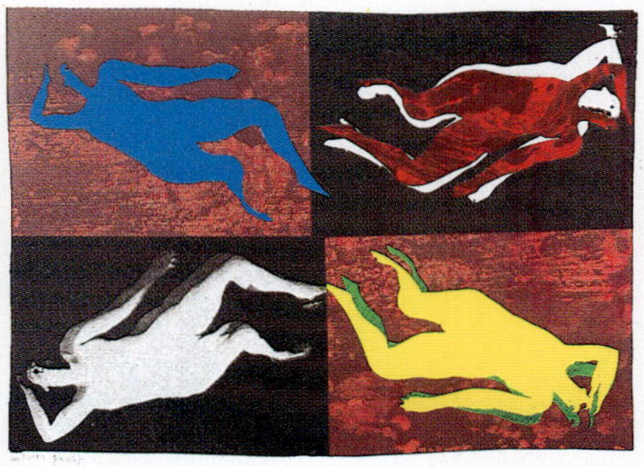

181

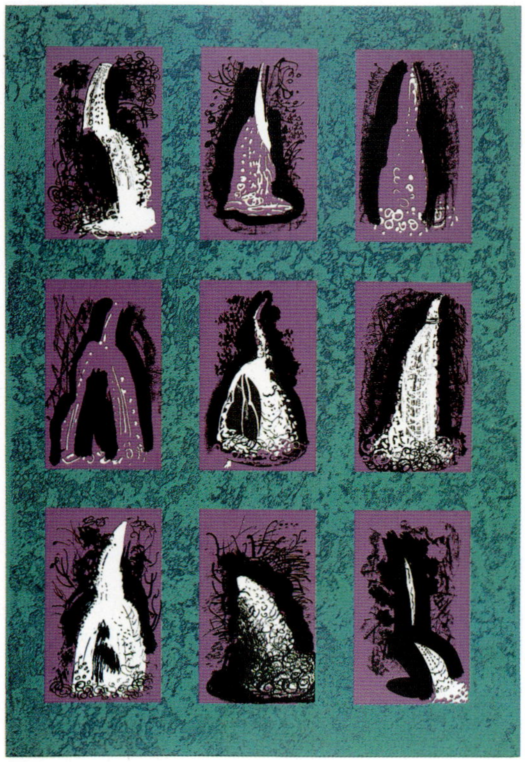

179

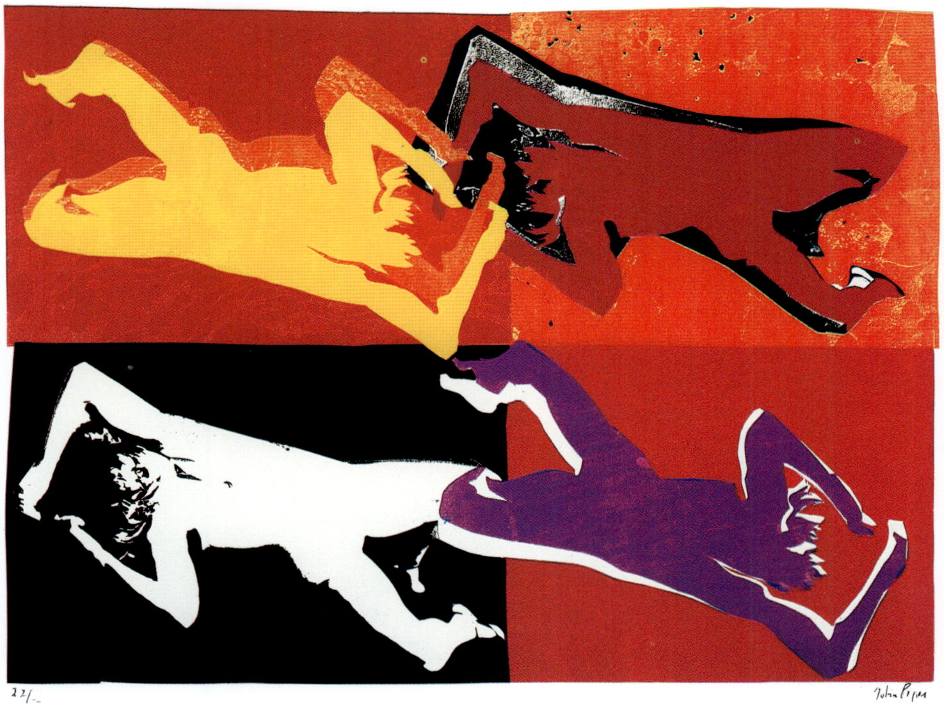

182

180
Travel Notes: Castle Ashby Avenue
Screenprint 747 × 535 ($29\frac{3}{8} \times 21\frac{1}{16}$)
Kelpra Studio 1967
Marlborough Fine Art 1967
J. Green 233lbs 775 × 575 ($30\frac{1}{2} \times 22\frac{5}{8}$)
70 'John Piper' 10AP 5HC 5PP

Printer's stamp and no. '6908' on reverse

Tate Gallery

181
Eye and Camera: Blue to Yellow
Screenprint 492 × 685 ($19\frac{3}{8} \times 26\frac{15}{16}$)
Kelpra Studio 1967
Marlborough Fine Art 1967
T. H. Saunders Imperial 140lbs 579 × 773 ($22\frac{3}{4} \times 30\frac{7}{16}$)
70 'John Piper' 10AP 5HC 5PP

Sometimes incorrectly known as *'Eye and Camera: Blue and Yellow'.* Three colour variations exist one in green, one in blue and one in red. Identical printer's stamp and no. as *Travel Notes: Castle Ashby Avenue* (Cat. 180). Repr. in black-and-white in *Kelpra Prints* (no. 176)

Tate Gallery

182
Eye and Camera: Flame Four
Screenprint 479 × 659 ($18\frac{7}{8} \times 25\frac{15}{16}$)
Kelpra Studio 1967
Marlborough Fine Art 1967
T. H. Saunders 140lbs 578 × 773 ($22\frac{3}{4} \times 30\frac{7}{16}$)
70 'John Piper' 10AP 5HC 5PP

Two colour variations exist, both with the figure reversed, one in green, the other in blue.

Tate Gallery

183
Eye and Camera: Yellow and Green
Screenprint 762 × 552 ($30 \times 21\frac{3}{4}$)
Kelpra Studio 1967
Marlborough Fine Art 1967
T.H. Saunders Imperial 140lbs 772 × 575 ($30\frac{3}{8} \times 22\frac{5}{8}$)
70 'John Piper' 10AP 5HC 5PP

Printer's stamp and no. '6910' on reverse

Tate Gallery

184
Florence Relief Landscape
Lithograph 445 × 622 ($17\frac{1}{2} \times 24\frac{1}{2}$)
Unknown 1967
Marlborough Fine Art and International Association of Art 1967
T.H. Saunders 120lbs 467 × 655 ($18\frac{3}{8} \times 25\frac{3}{4}$)
50 'John Piper' 5AP 2PP

Sometimes incorrectly known as *'Florence Flood Relief'* or '*Landscape*'. The artist believes the printing was done in Italy.

Tate Gallery

185
Montpellier-de-Didonne, Charente
Screenprint 768 × 560 ($30\frac{1}{4} \times 22$)
Kelpra Studio 1968
Marlborough Fine Art 1968
J. Green 233lbs 1027 × 686 ($40\frac{1}{2} \times 27$)
70 'John Piper' 10AP 5HC 5PP

Sometimes incorrectly known as *'Montpellier'* or *'Montpellier, Charente'*. Printer's stamp and no. '7026' on reverse

Guildhall Art Gallery; Tate Gallery

186
St Simon-de-Pelouaille, Charente
Screenprint 567 × 784 ($22\frac{5}{16} \times 30\frac{7}{8}$)
Kelpra Studio 1968
Marlborough Fine Art 1968
J. Green 233lbs 703 × 1038 ($27\frac{11}{16} \times 40\frac{7}{8}$)
70 'John Piper' 10AP 5HC 5PP

Printer's stamp and no. '7027' on reverse

Guildhall Art Gallery; Tate Gallery

187
St Raphael, Dordogne
Screenprint 580 × 788 ($22\frac{3}{4} \times 31$)
Kelpra Studio 1968
Marlborough Fine Art 1968
J. Green 233lbs 705 × 1050 ($27\frac{3}{4} \times 41\frac{1}{2}$)
70 'John Piper' 10AP 5HC 5PP

Printer's stamp and no. '7029' on reverse

Aberdeen Art Gallery and Museums; Guildhall Art Gallery; Tate Gallery

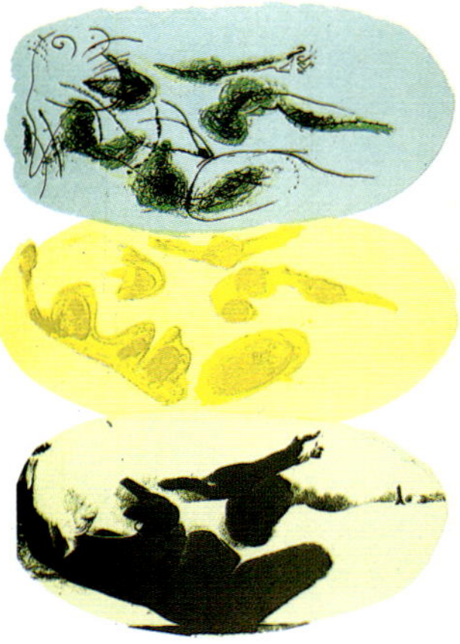
183

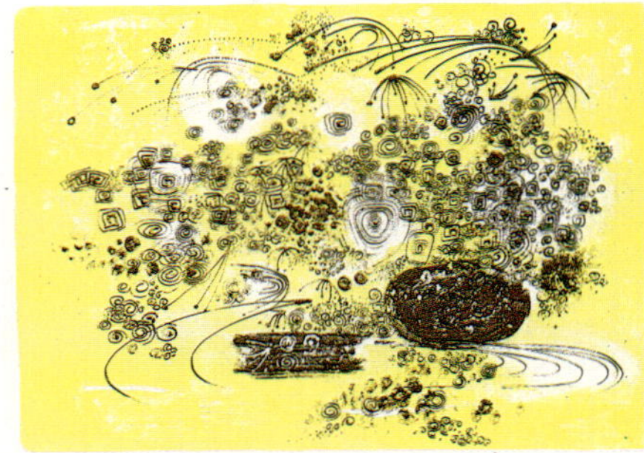
184

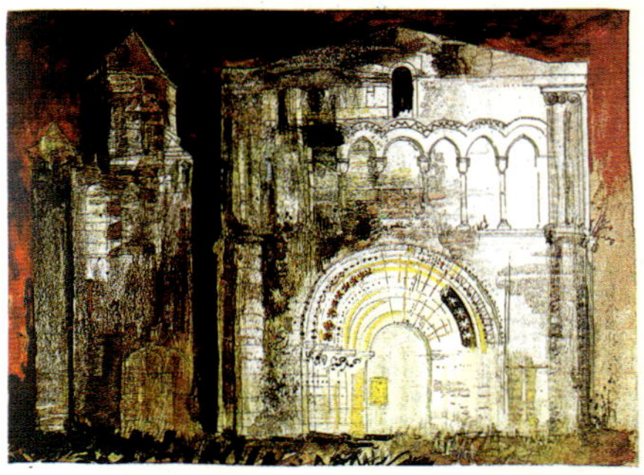
186

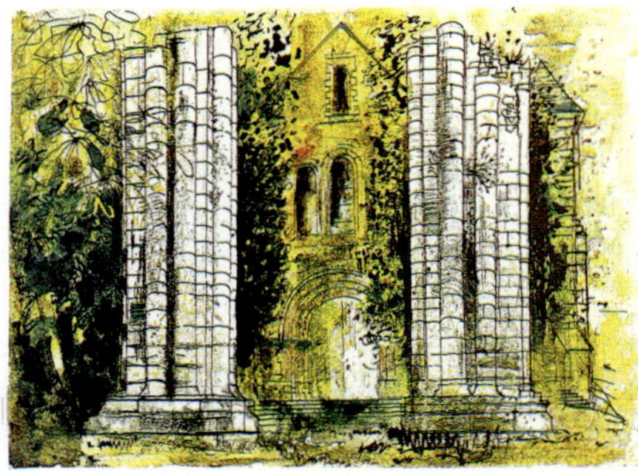
187

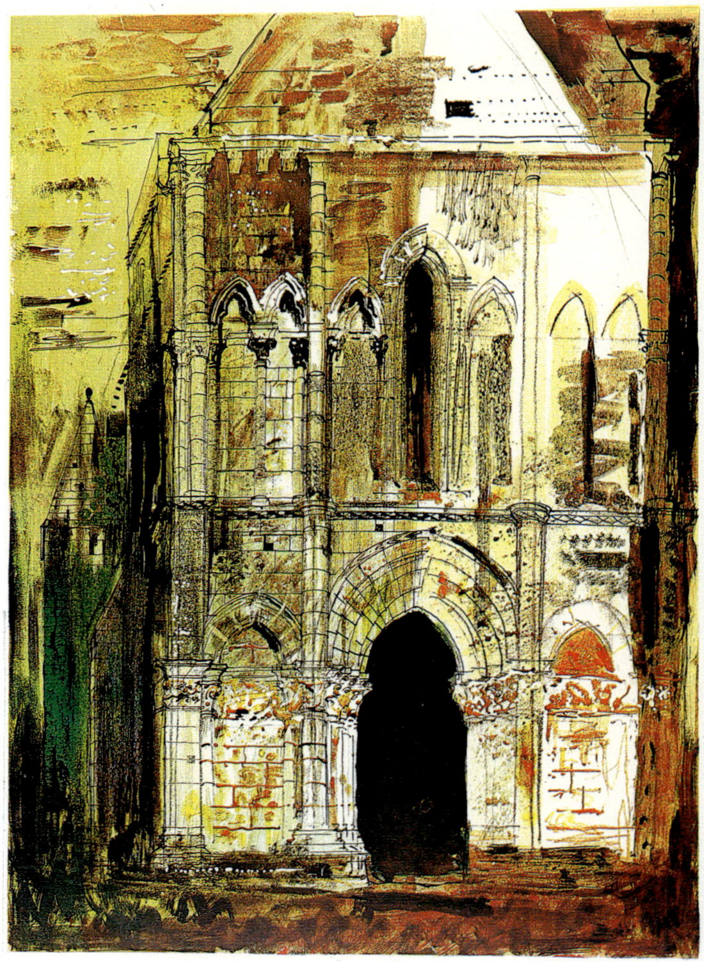
185

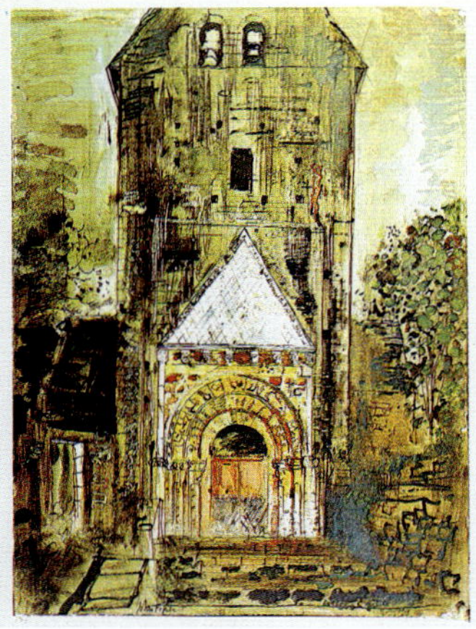

188

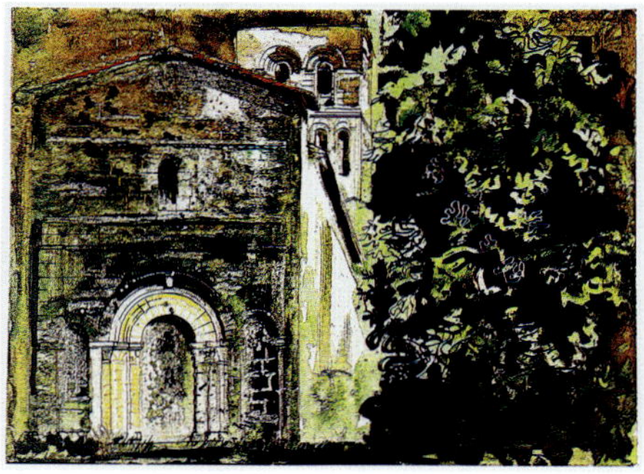

189

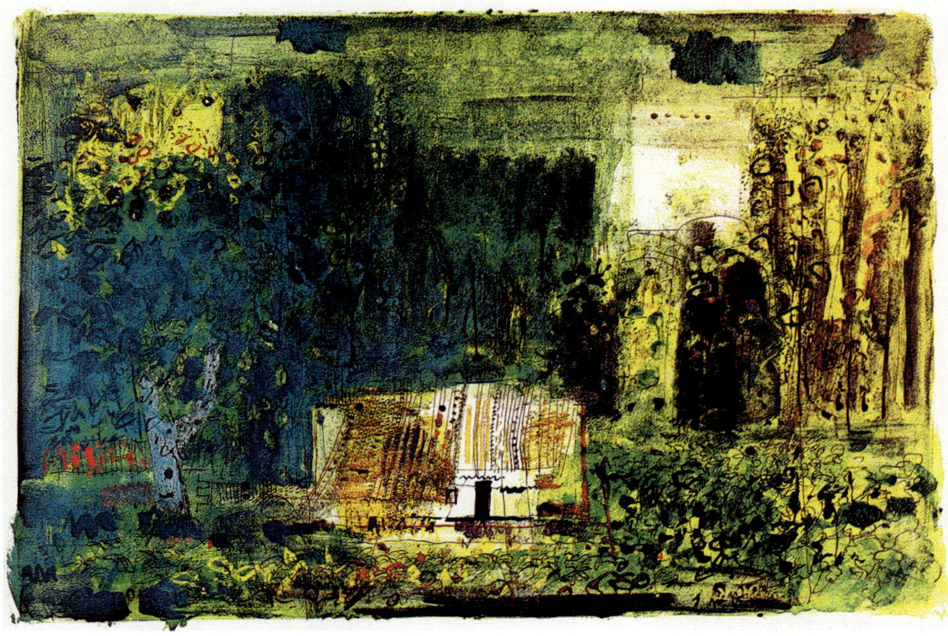

191

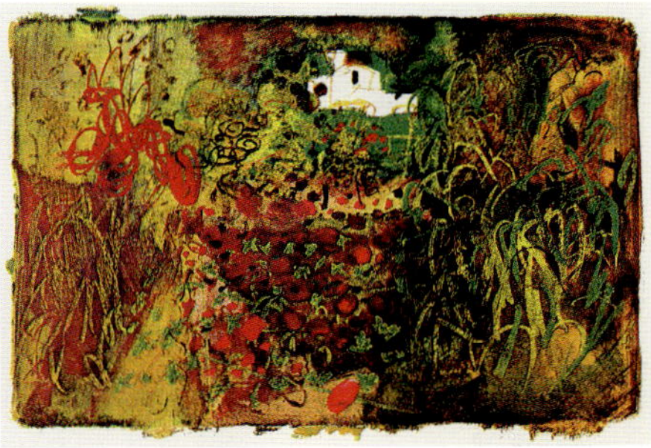

190

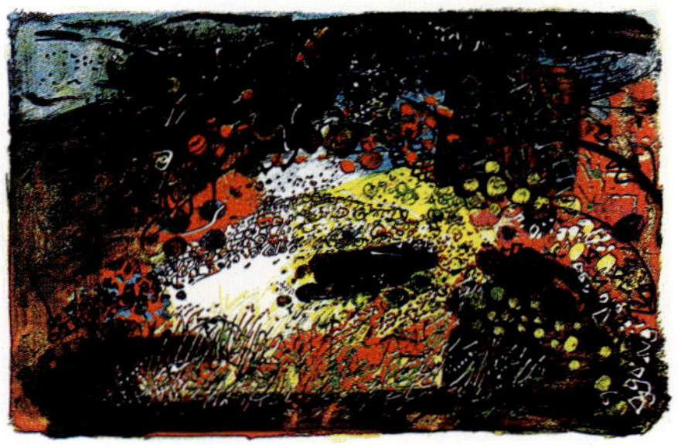

192

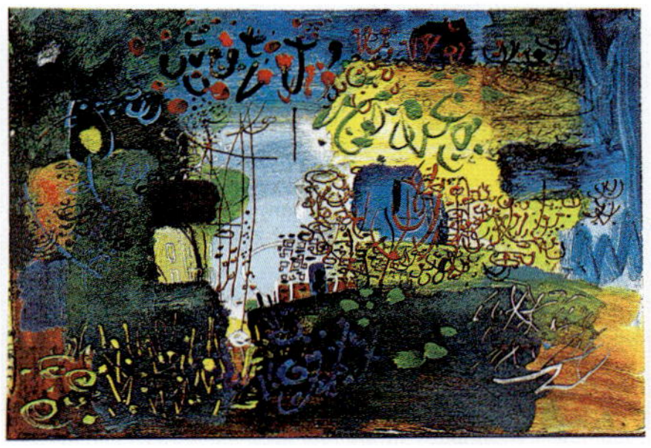

193

188
Besse, Dordogne
Screenprint 779×583 (30 11/16×22 7/8)
Kelpra Studio 1968
Marlborough Fine Art 1968
J. Green 233lbs 1022×706 (40 3/16×27 13/16)
70 'John Piper' 10AP 5HC 5PP

Some copies signed 'John Piper' in black crayon b.c. Printer's stamp and no. '7031' on reverse

Guildhall Art Gallery; Tate Gallery

189
La Chapelle St Robert, Dordogne
Screenprint 590×800 (23 1/4×31 1/2)
Kelpra Studio 1968
Marlborough Fine Art 1968
J. Green 233lbs 695×1022 (27 3/8×40 1/4)
70 'John Piper' 10AP 5HC 5PP

Sometimes incorrectly known as *'La Chapelle de St Robert, Dordogne'* or *'La Chapelle, St Robert'*

Guildhall Art Gallery; Leicestershire Museums, Arts and Record Service (Artworks Collection); Tate Gallery

190
Creysse, Dordogne
Screenprint 440×648 (17 1/4×25 1/2)
Kelpra Studio 1968
Marlborough Fine Art 1968
J. Green 233lbs 528×715 (20 3/4×28 1/8)
70 'John Piper' 10AP 5PP 5HC

Sometimes incorrectly known as *'Creysse '*. Printer's stamp and no. '7033' on reverse

Leicestershire Museums, Arts and Record Service (Artworks Collection); Tate Gallery

191
Woodman's Cottage, Charente
Screenprint 428×655 (16 7/8×25 3/4)
Kelpra Studio 1968
Marlborough Fine Art 1968
J. Green 233lbs 535×710 (21×28)
70 'John Piper' 10AP 5PP 5HC

Sometimes incorrectly known as *'Gamekeeper's Cottage, France'*, *'Mosnac, Charente '* or *'Mosnac, Dordogne'*. Printer's stamp and no. '7034' on reverse

Tate Gallery

192
Garn Fawr, Pembrokeshire
Screenprint 425×641 (16 3/4×25 1/4)
Kelpra Studio 1968
Marlborough Fine Art 1968
J. Green 233lbs 530×710 (20 7/8×28)
70 'John Piper' 10AP 5HC 5PP

Sometimes incorrectly known as *'Garn Fawr'*. Printer's stamp and no. '7032' on reverse

Tate Gallery

193
Near Newcastle Emlyn, Cardigan
Screenprint 435×634 (17 1/8×25)
Kelpra Studio 1968
Marlborough Fine Art 1968
J. Green 233lbs 518×717 (20 3/8×28 1/4)
70 'John Piper' 10AP 5HC 5PP

Sometimes incorrectly known as *'Emlyn, Newcastle'*. Printer's stamp and no. '7079' on reverse

Tate Gallery

194
Floirac
Screenprint 435 × 643 ($17\frac{1}{8} \times 25\frac{3}{8}$)
Kelpra Studio 1968
Marlborough Fine Art 1968
J. Green 233lbs 501 × 715 ($19\frac{3}{4} \times 28\frac{1}{8}$)
70 'John Piper' 10AP 5HC 5PP

Printer's stamp and no. '7080' on reverse

Tate Gallery

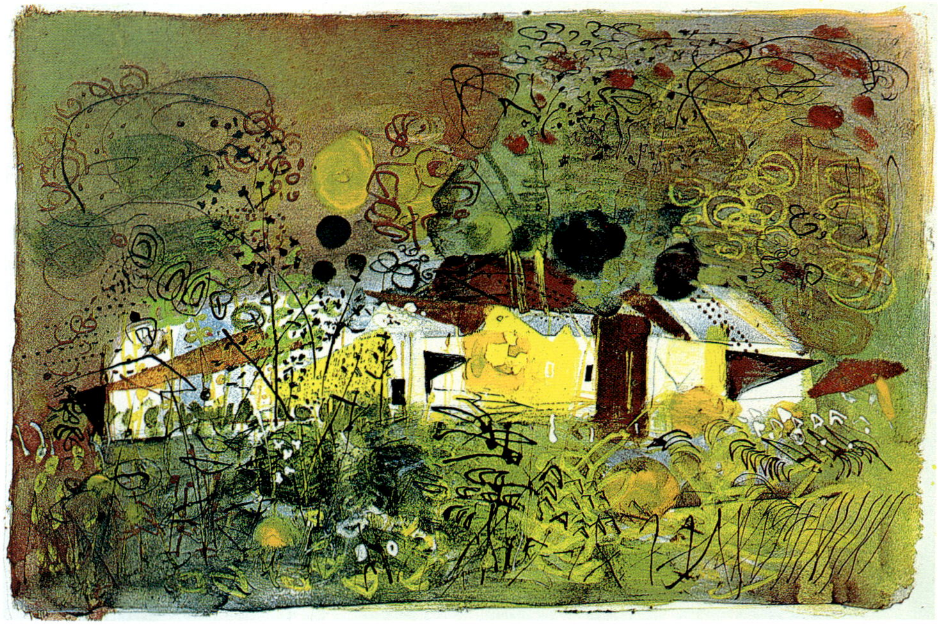
194

195
Moutou
Screenprint 431 × 650 ($17 \times 25\frac{5}{8}$)
Kelpra Studio 1968
Marlborough Fine Art 1968
J. Green 233lbs 431 × 650 ($17 \times 25\frac{5}{8}$)
70 'John Piper' 10AP 5HC 5PP

Sometimes incorrectly known as *'Eiollet, Charente'* or *'Moutu, near Carennac, Dordogne'* Some copies printed on paper 514 × 709 ($20\frac{1}{4} \times 27\frac{15}{16}$). Printer's stamp and no. '7081' on reverse

Tate Gallery

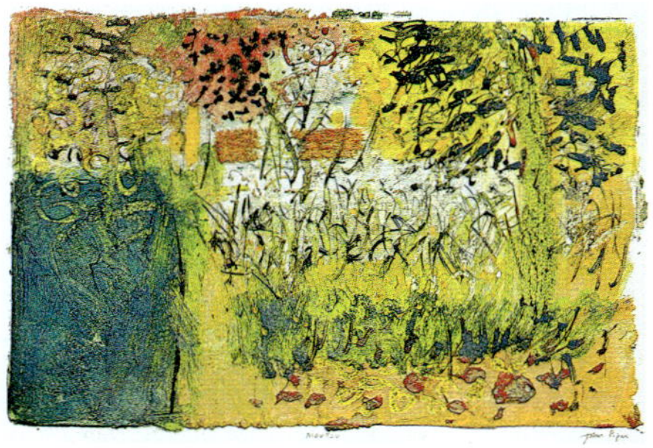
195

196
Jazenne, Charente
Screenprint 575 × 773 ($22\frac{5}{8} \times 30\frac{7}{16}$)
Kelpra Studio 1968
Marlborough Fine Art 1968
J. Green 233lbs 718 × 1030 ($28\frac{5}{16} \times 40\frac{9}{16}$)
70 'John Piper' 10AP 5HC 5PP

One known copy signed 'John Piper' b.l.

Guildhall Art Gallery; Leicestershire Museums, Arts and Record Service (Artworks Collection); Scottish National Gallery of Modern Art; Tate Gallery

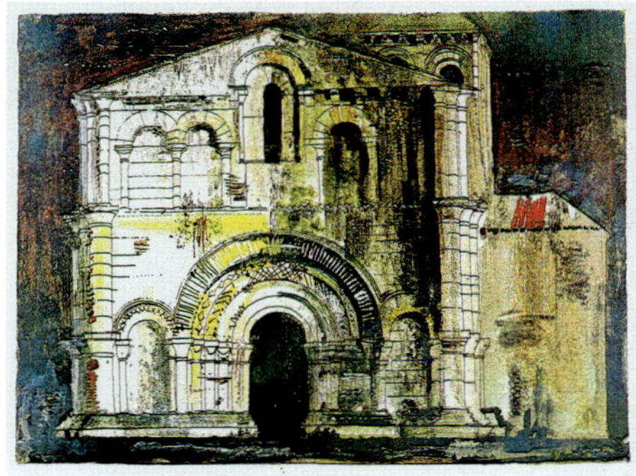
196

197
St Amand-de-Coly, Dordogne
Screenprint 580 × 774 ($22\frac{13}{16} \times 30\frac{7}{16}$)
Kelpra Studio 1968
Marlborough Fine Art 1968
J. Green 233lbs 702 × 1007 ($27\frac{5}{8} \times 39\frac{5}{8}$)
70 'John Piper' 10AP 5HC 5PP

Sometimes incorrectly known as *'St Amand de Coly'*. Printer's stamp and no. '7093' on reverse

Guidhall Art Gallery; Scottish National Gallery of Modern Art; Tate Gallery

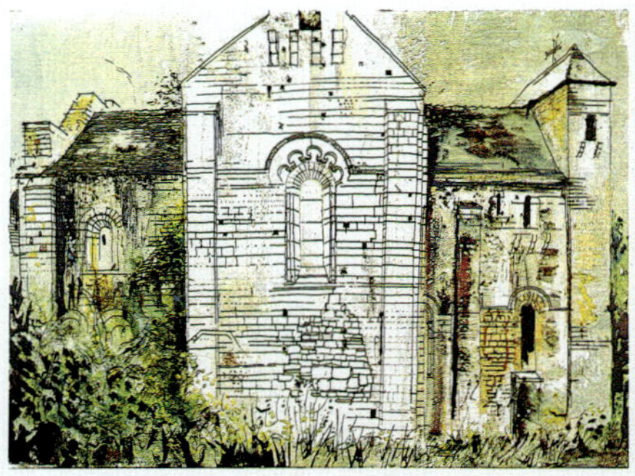
197

198
Welsh Landscape, Tretio
Screenprint 479 × 705 ($18\frac{7}{8} \times 27\frac{3}{4}$)
Kelpra Studio 1969
Marlborough Fine Art 1969
J. Green 233lbs 592 × 825 ($23\frac{5}{16} \times 32\frac{1}{2}$)
70 'John Piper' 10AP 5HC 5PP

Sometimes incorrectly known as *'Untitled, 1969'*. Some copies were printed without margins, and some with the date '1969', written b.r. by the artist. Some copies numbered out of a hundred. Printer's stamp and no. '7245' on reverse

Scottish National Gallery of Modern Art; Tate Gallery

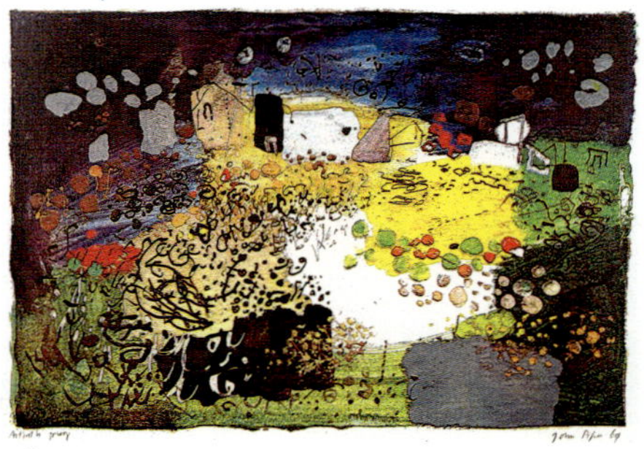
198

199
Foliate Head
Lithograph 389 × 266 ($15\frac{3}{8} \times 10\frac{3}{8}$)
Curwen Studio 1971
Unpublished
Cambridge 642 × 452 ($25\frac{1}{4} \times 17\frac{3}{4}$)
Not issued as an edition Unsigned

The print was to have been published by Leonard Appelbee, but did not get beyond the 'bon à tirer' state. The only known copy is in the Tate Gallery.

200
Caernarvon Castle I
Screenprint 494 × 753 ($19\frac{1}{2} \times 29\frac{5}{8}$)
Kelpra Studio 1971
Marlborough Fine Art 1971
J. Green 233lbs 599 × 868 ($23\frac{1}{2} \times 34\frac{1}{4}$)
70 'John Piper' 10AP 5HC 5PP

Printer's stamp and no. '7683' on reverse. Repr. in Ingrams/Piper (plate 129)

Sheffield Arts and Museums; Tate Gallery

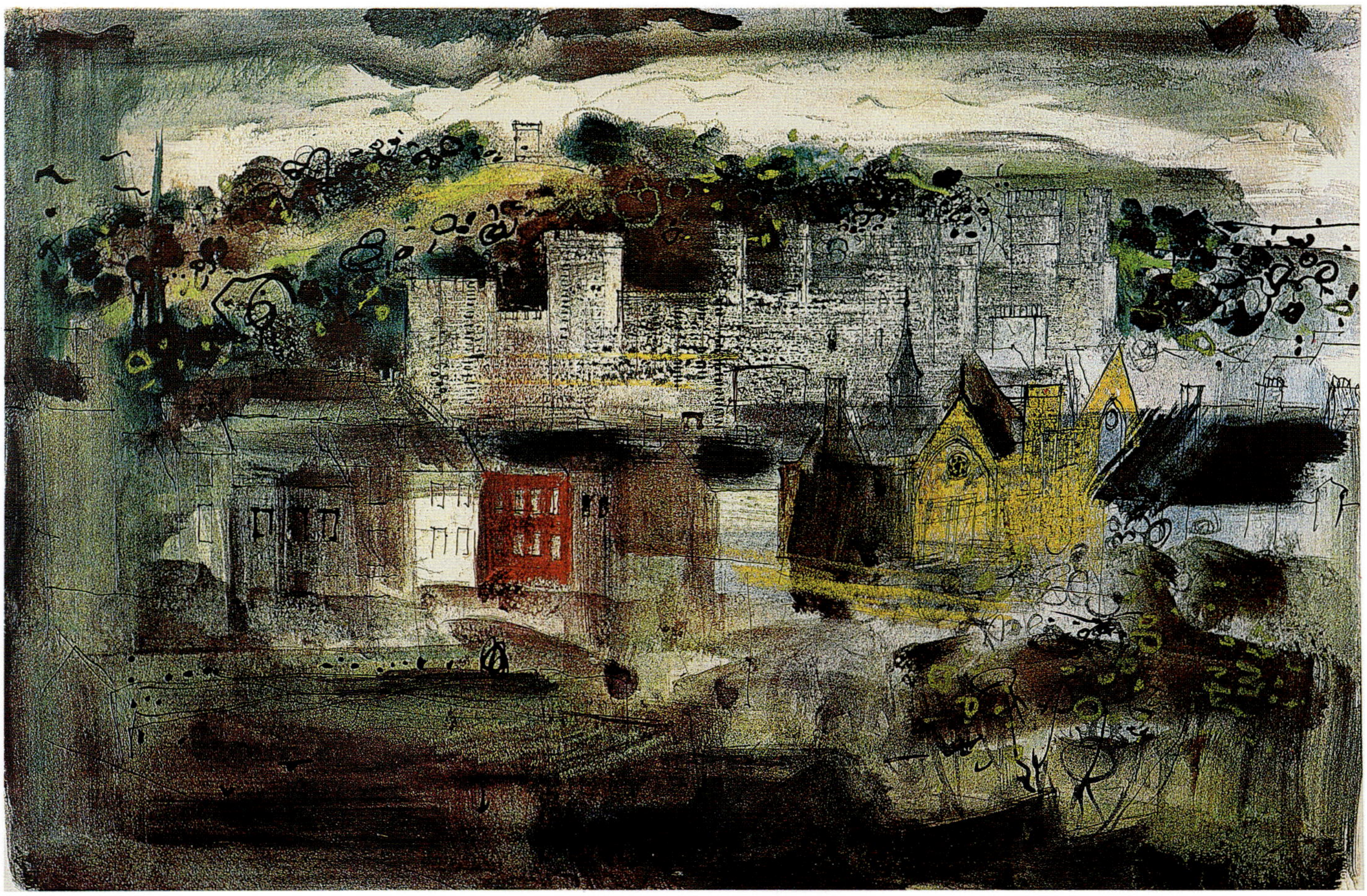

201

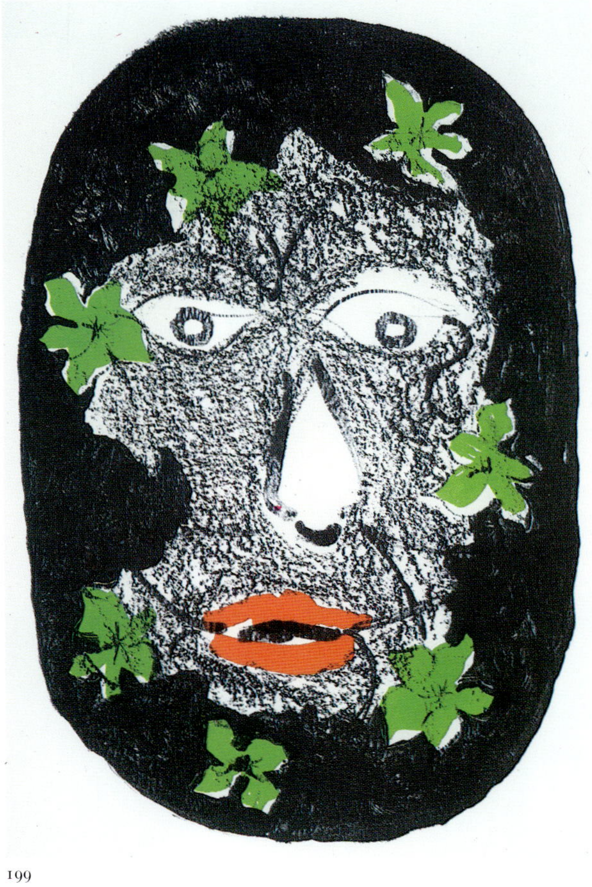

199

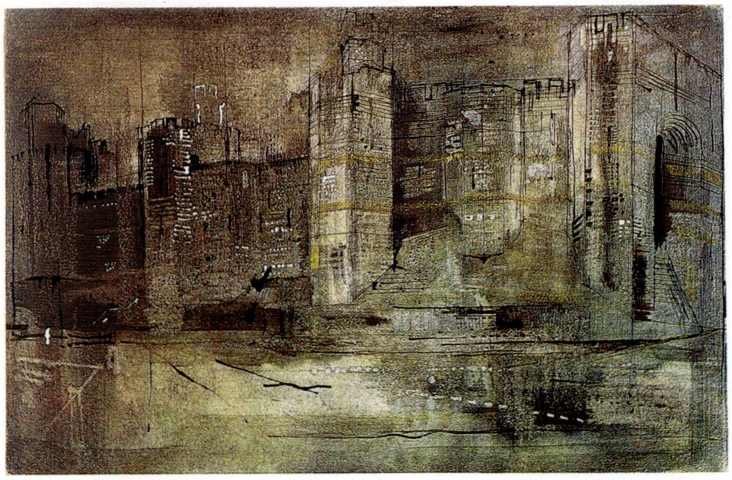

200

201
Caernarvon Castle II
Screenprint 493 × 750 (19⅜ × 29½)
Kelpra Studio 1971
Marlborough Fine Art 1971
J. Green 233lbs 602 × 868 (23¹¹⁄₁₆ × 34⅛)
70 'John Piper' 10AP 5HC 5PP

Printer's stamp and no. '7682' on reverse. Identical to the printer's stamp and no. of *Wymondham, Norfolk* (Cat. 205)

Tate Gallery

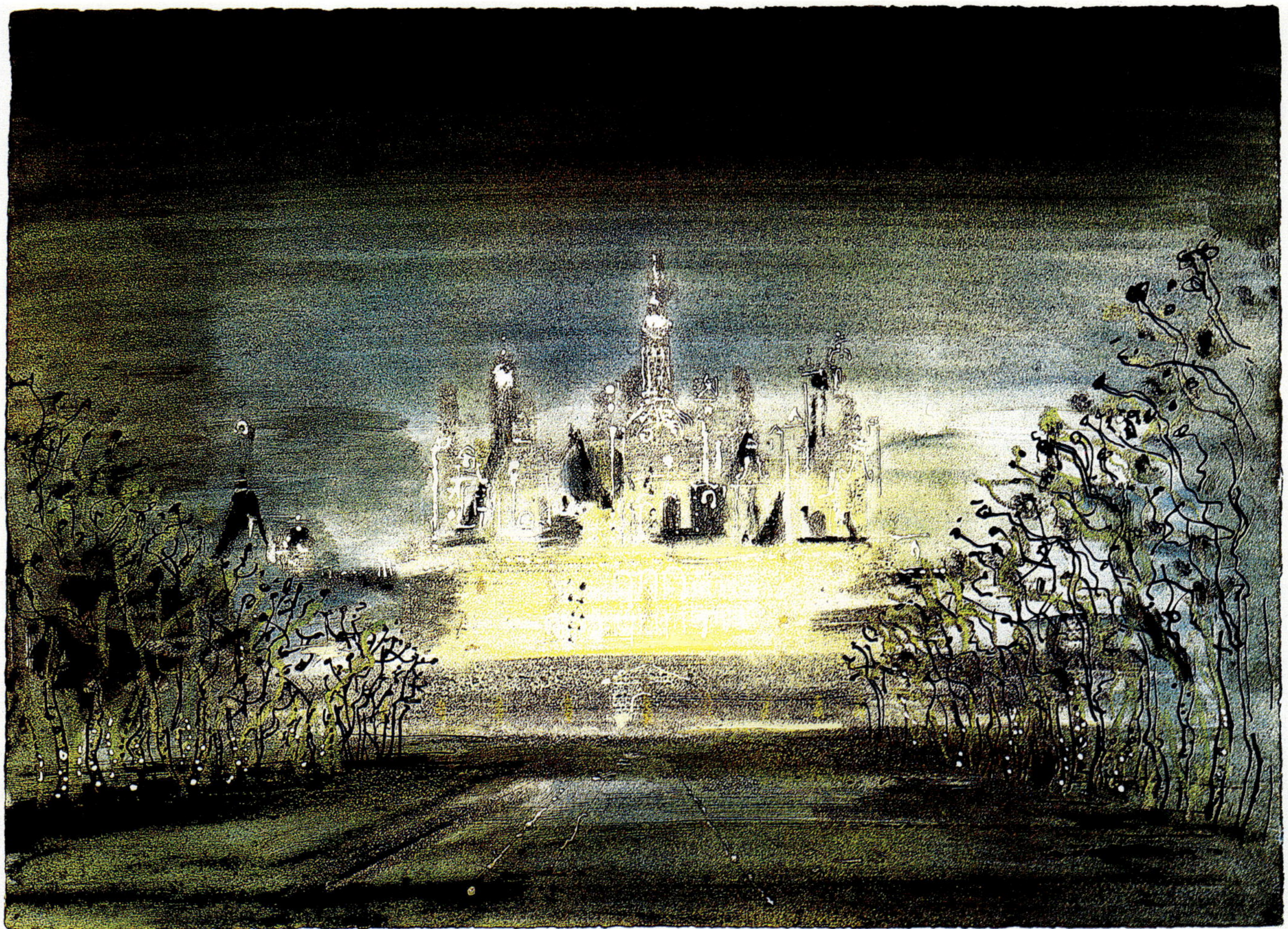

202

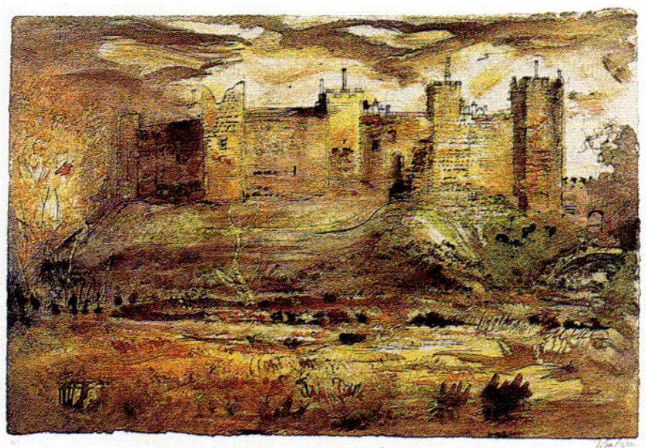

204

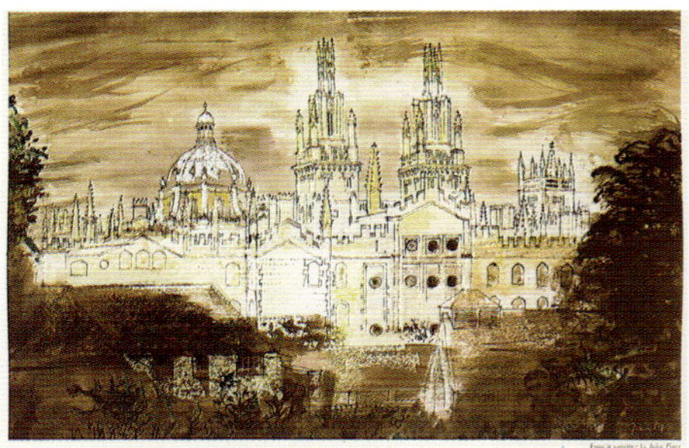

206

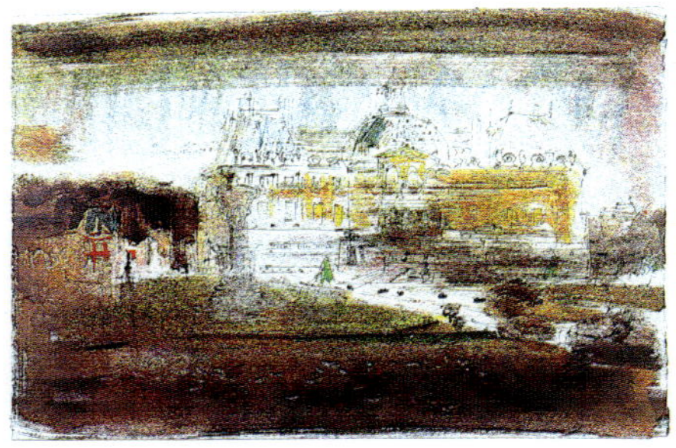

208

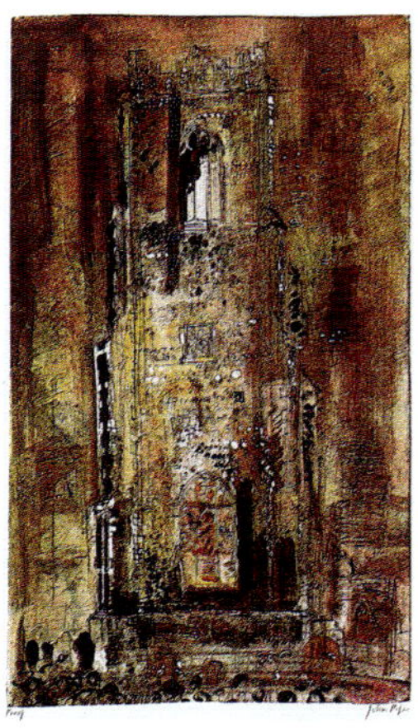

203

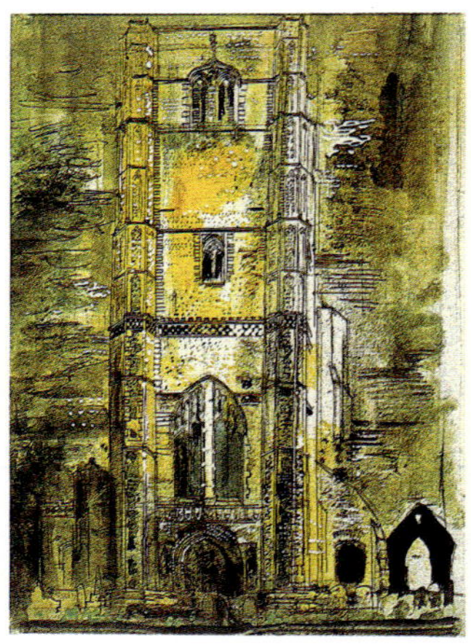

205

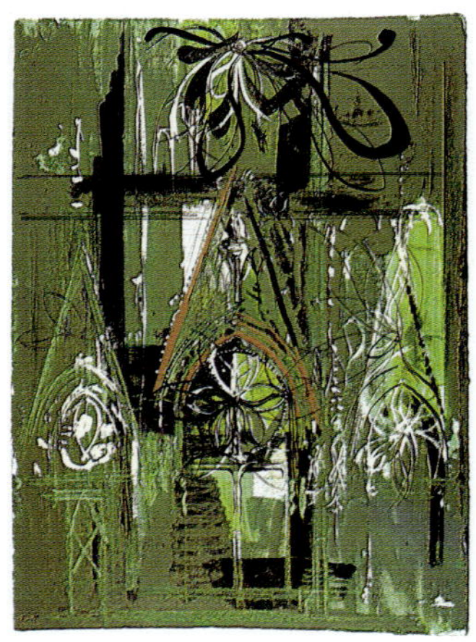

207

202
Chambord
Screenprint 500 × 680 ($19\tfrac{11}{16} \times 26\tfrac{3}{4}$)
Kelpra Studio 1971
Marlborough Fine Art 1971
Vélin Arches 300gsm 595 × 845 ($23\tfrac{3}{8} \times 33\tfrac{1}{4}$)
70 'John Piper' 10AP 5HC 5PP

Printer's stamp and no.'7806' on reverse

Tate Gallery

203
Corton Church, Suffolk
Screenprint 484 × 702 ($19\tfrac{1}{8} \times 27\tfrac{5}{8}$)
Kelpra Studio 1971
Marlborough Fine Art 1971
J. Green 233lbs 601 × 848 ($23\tfrac{9}{16} \times 33\tfrac{3}{8}$)
70 'John Piper' 10AP 5HC 5PP

Printer's stamp and no.'7735' on reverse

Tate Gallery

204
Framlingham Castle
Screenprint 474 × 703 ($18\tfrac{5}{8} \times 27\tfrac{5}{8}$)
Kelpra Studio 1971
Marlborough Fine Art 1971
J. Green 233lbs 597 × 845 ($23\tfrac{1}{2} \times 33\tfrac{1}{4}$)
70 'John Piper' 10AP 5HC 5PP

Printer's stamp and no.'7805' on reverse

Tate Gallery

205
Wymondham, Norfolk
Screenprint 766 × 560 ($30\tfrac{1}{8} \times 22\tfrac{1}{16}$)
Kelpra Studio 1971
Marlborough Fine Art 1971
Vélin Arches 300gsm 910 × 663 ($35\tfrac{13}{16} \times 26\tfrac{1}{8}$)
70 'John Piper' 10AP 5HC 5PP

Printer's stamp and no.'7682' on reverse. Identical to the printer's stamp and no. of *Caernarvon Castle II* (Cat.201)

Tate Gallery

206
View from the Upper Common Room, the Queen's College
Offset lithograph 298 × 462 ($11\tfrac{3}{4} \times 18\tfrac{3}{16}$)
Oxford University Press (OUP, Printing Division) 1971
Oxford University Press (OUP) 1972
Kent Drawing White 160gsm 761 × 560 ($29\tfrac{15}{16} \times 22\tfrac{1}{16}$)
1500 Unsigned

The black was printed in line and half-tone combined. The title and 'From a painting by John Piper' are printed centre and right respectively immediately below the image, which forms the upper half of the paper 'The Oxford Almanack', with the names of the University Officers and of the Heads of Colleges and Halls, occupying the lower half. The print was commissioned by *The Oxford Almanack*.

207
Abbeville, St Wolfrun
Screenprint 805 × 594 ($31\tfrac{11}{16} \times 23\tfrac{3}{8}$)
Kelpra Studio 1972
Marlborough Fine Art 1972
J. Green 233lbs 865 × 652 ($34\tfrac{1}{16} \times 25\tfrac{5}{8}$)
70 'John Piper' 10AP 5HC 5PP

Printer's stamp and no.'7990' on reverse

Leicestershire Museums, Arts and Record Service; Tate Gallery

208
Vaux-le-Vicomte
Screenprint 552 × 842 ($21\tfrac{3}{4} \times 33\tfrac{1}{8}$)
Kelpra Studio 1972
Marlborough Fine Art 1972
Vélin Arches 300gsm 700 × 1020 ($27\tfrac{9}{16} \times 40\tfrac{3}{16}$)
70 'John Piper' 10AP 5HC 5PP

Tate Gallery

209
Eye and Camera: Grey and Blue
Screenprint 508 × 700 ($20 \times 27\tfrac{9}{16}$)
Kelpra Studio 1972
Marlborough Fine Art 1972
Vélin Arches 300gsm 578 × 791 ($22\tfrac{3}{4} \times 31\tfrac{1}{8}$)
70 'John Piper' 10AP 5HC 5PP

Sometimes incorrectly known as *'Eye and Camera: Black and Grey – net-stocking, cross-legged'* or *'Eye and Camera: Grey Blue'*. Printer's stamp and no.'7985' on reverse

Tate Gallery

210
Eye and Camera: Blue and Red
Screenprint 508 × 702 ($20 \times 27\tfrac{5}{8}$)
Kelpra Studio 1972
Marlborough Fine Art 1972
Vélin Arches 300gsm 577 × 790 ($22\tfrac{11}{16} \times 31\tfrac{1}{8}$)
70 'John Piper' 10AP 5HC 5PP

Sometimes incorrectly known as *'Eye and Camera: Red and Blue'*. Printer's stamp and no.'7986' on reverse

Tate Gallery

211
Eye and Camera: Red and Black
Screenprint 508 × 702 ($20 \times 27\tfrac{5}{8}$)
Kelpra Studio 1972
Marlborough Fine Art 1972
Vélin Arches 300gsm 578 × 790 ($22\tfrac{3}{4} \times 31\tfrac{1}{16}$)
70 'John Piper' 10AP 5HC 5PP

Printer's stamp and no.'7987' on reverse

Tate Gallery

212 (detail Plate 3)
Eye and Camera: Multifigure
Screenprint 505 × 695 ($19\tfrac{7}{8} \times 27\tfrac{3}{8}$)
Kelpra Studio 1972
Marlborough Fine Art 1972
Vélin Arches 300gsm 575 × 776 ($22\tfrac{5}{8} \times 30\tfrac{9}{16}$)
70 'John Piper' 10AP 5HC 5PP

Printer's stamp and no.'7993' on reverse

Tate Gallery

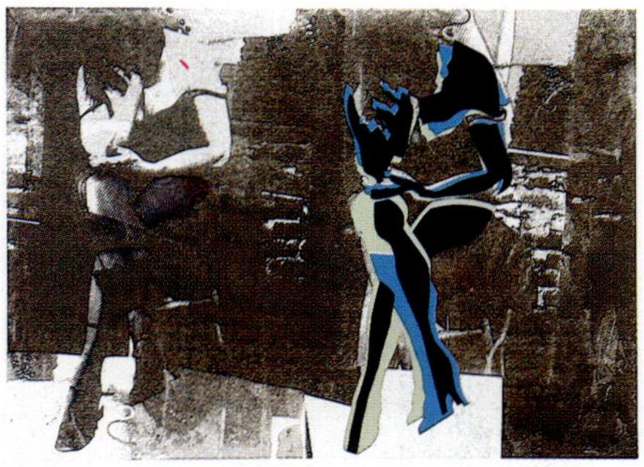

209

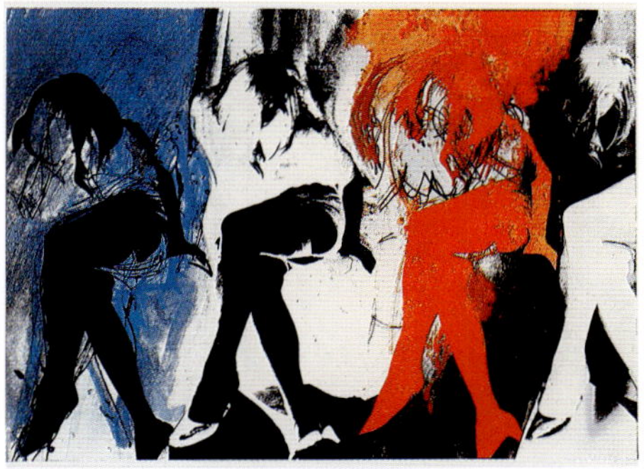

210

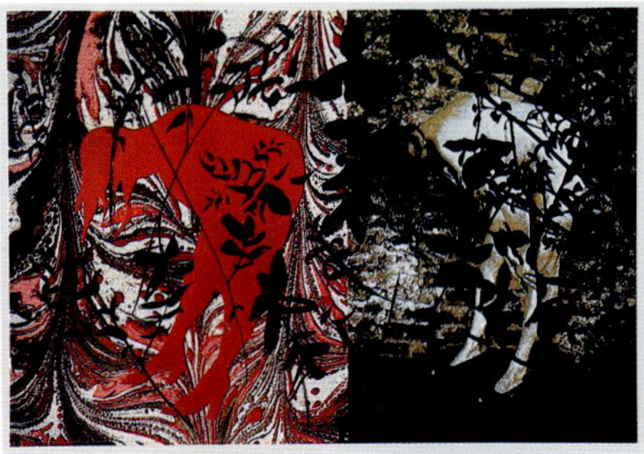

211

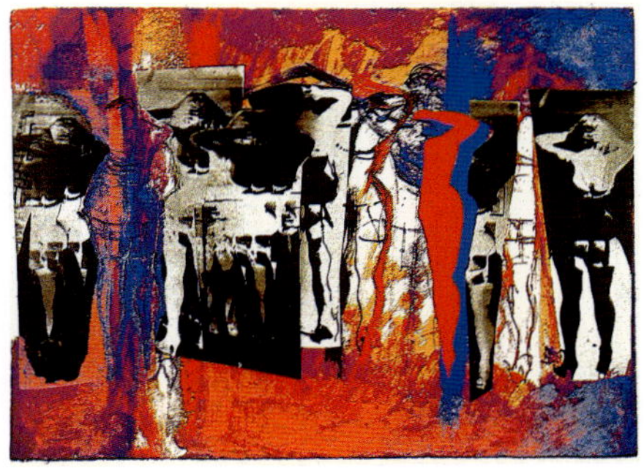

212

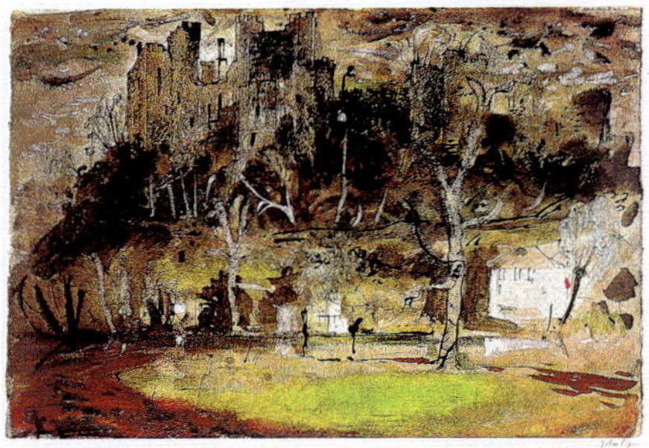

213

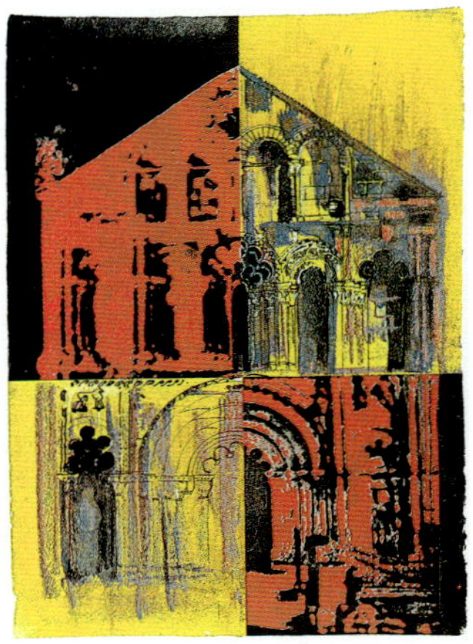

214

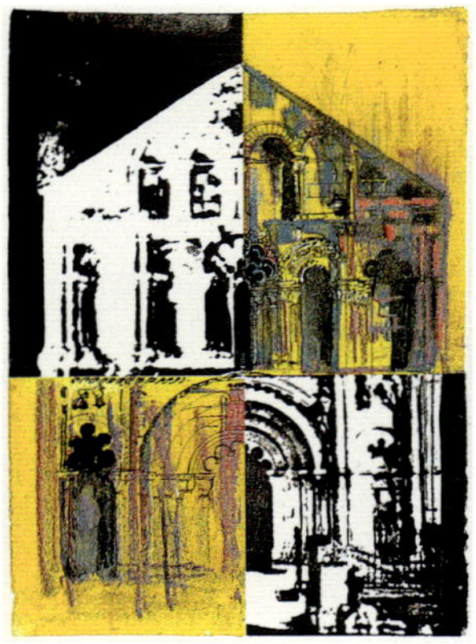

215

213
Ludlow Castle
Screenprint 546×798 ($21\frac{1}{2} \times 31\frac{7}{16}$)
Kelpra Studio 1972
Marlborough Fine Art 1972
Vélin Arches 300gsm 700×1020 ($27\frac{9}{16} \times 40\frac{1}{8}$)
100 'John Piper' 10AP 5HC 5PP

Printer's stamp and no.'7988' on reverse

Tate Gallery

214
Petit Palais: Pink and Yellow
Screenprint 780×573 ($30\frac{1}{16} \times 22\frac{9}{16}$)
Kelpra Studio 1972
Marlborough Fine Art 1973
Vélin Arches 300gsm 840×630 ($33\frac{1}{16} \times 24\frac{13}{16}$)
75 'John Piper' 5AP 1HC 2PP

Printer's stamp and no.'7992A' on reverse

Tate Gallery

215
Petit Palais: White and Yellow
Screenprint 780×573 ($30\frac{11}{16} \times 22\frac{9}{16}$)
Kelpra Studio 1973
Marlborough Fine Art 1973
Vélin Arches 300gsm 840×630 ($33\frac{1}{16} \times 24\frac{13}{16}$)
25 'John Piper' 5AP 1HC 2PP

Printer's stamp and no.'7992B' on reverse

Tate Gallery

216
Petit Palais: Yellow and Yellow
Screenprint 780×573 ($30\frac{11}{16} \times 22\frac{9}{16}$)
Kelpra Studio 1973
Marlborough Fine Art 1973
Vélin Arches 300gsm 840×630 ($33\frac{1}{16} \times 24\frac{13}{16}$)
25 'John Piper' 5AP 1HC 2PP

Printer's stamp and no.'7992C' on reverse

Tate Gallery

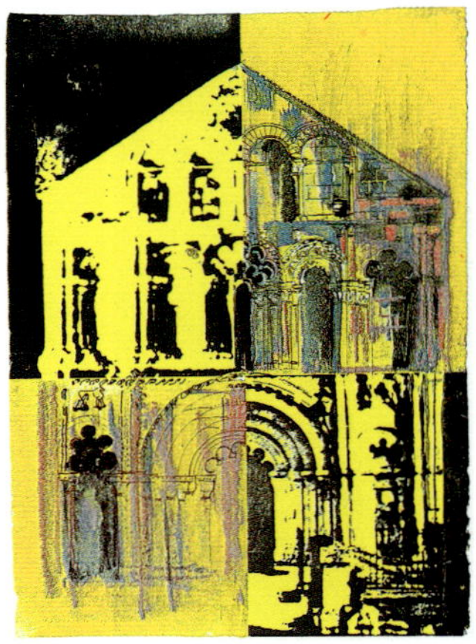

216

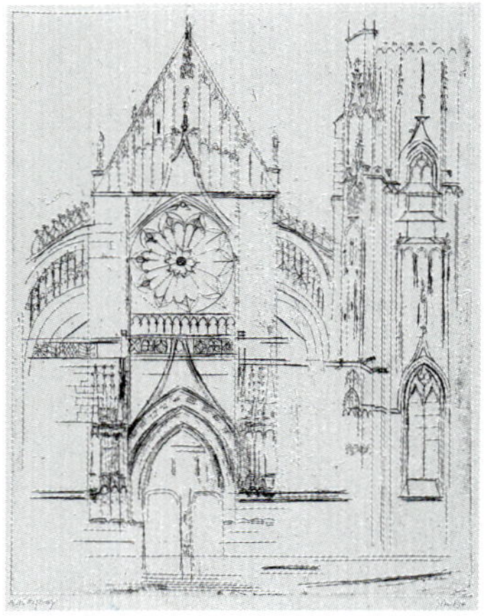

217

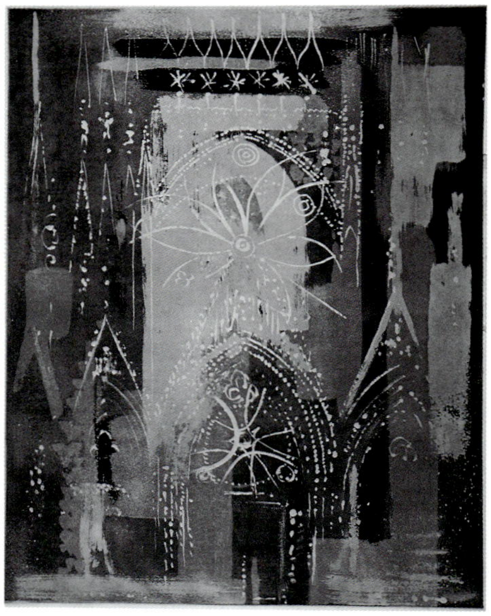

219

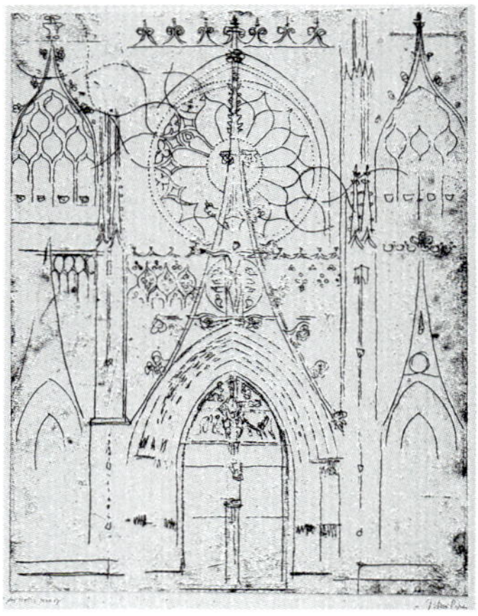

218

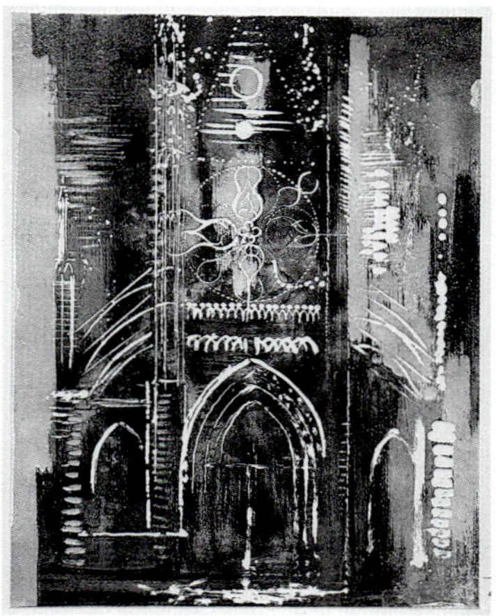

220

217
Clamecy, Burgundy
Line etching 688 × 537 ($27\frac{1}{8} \times 21\frac{1}{4}$)
Burleighfield House 1972
Pallas Gallery 1972
T. H. Saunders 150gsm 838 × 660 (33 × 26)
50 'John Piper' 5AP 5HC

A further six prints were hand-coloured in green, yellow and blue-grey gouache by the artist and numbered I/VI - VI/VI.

Rochdale Art Gallery; Tate Gallery

218
Notre-Dame-de-L'Epine, near Rheims
Intaglio etching 689 × 538 ($27\frac{1}{8} \times 21\frac{1}{4}$)
Burleighfield House 1972
Pallas Gallery 1972
T. H. Saunders 150gsm 839 × 660 (33 × 26)
50 'John Piper' 10AP 5HC

A further six prints were hand-coloured in green, yellow and blue-grey gouache by the artist and numbered I/VI - VI/VI.

Tate Gallery

219
Rheims Cathedral
Aquatint 686 × 543 ($27 \times 21\frac{5}{16}$)
Burleighfield House 1972
Pallas Gallery 1972
T. H. Saunders 150gsm 840 × 661 ($33\frac{1}{16} \times 26\frac{1}{16}$)
50 'John Piper' 15AP 5HC

A further six prints were hand-coloured in yellow and ochre gouache by the artist and numbered I/VI - VI/VI.

Glasgow Art Gallery and Museum; Tate Gallery

220
Eglise de Vernon, Normandy
Aquatint 690 × 540 ($27\frac{3}{16} \times 21\frac{3}{8}$)
Burleighfield House 1972
Pallas Gallery 1972
T.H.Saunders 150gsm 840 × 660 ($33\frac{1}{16} \times 26$)
50 'John Piper' 5AP 5HC

A further six prints were hand-coloured in ochre and blue-grey gouache by the artist and numbered I/VI - VI/VI.

Tate Gallery

221
Roof at Chambord
Screenprint 657 × 1050 ($25\frac{13}{16} \times 42\frac{5}{16}$)
Kelpra Studio 1973
Marlborough Fine Art 1973
Vélin Arches 300gsm 657 × 1050 ($25\frac{13}{16} \times 41\frac{5}{16}$)
70 'John Piper' in crayon b.r. 10AP 5HC 5PP

Sometimes incorrectly known as *'Chambord Rooftops'*

Tate Gallery

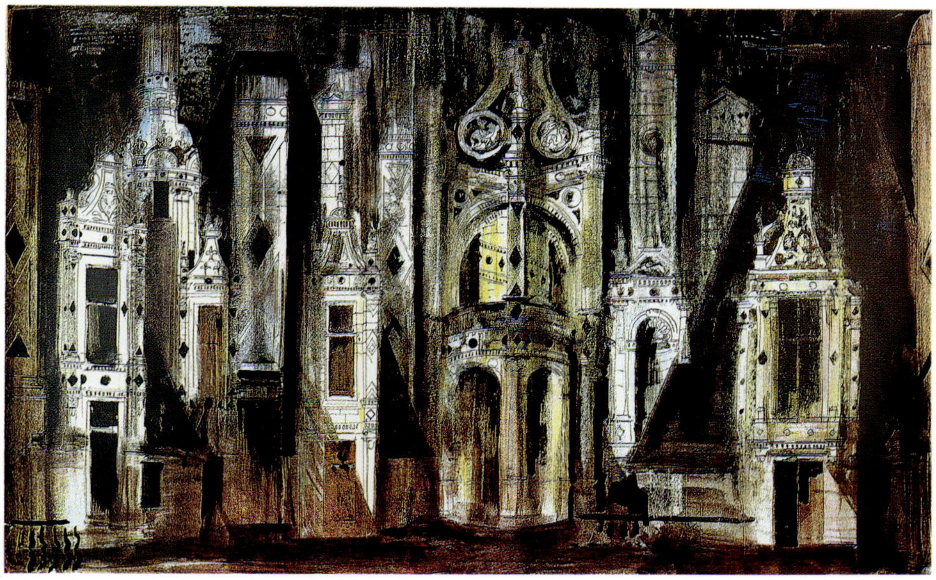

221

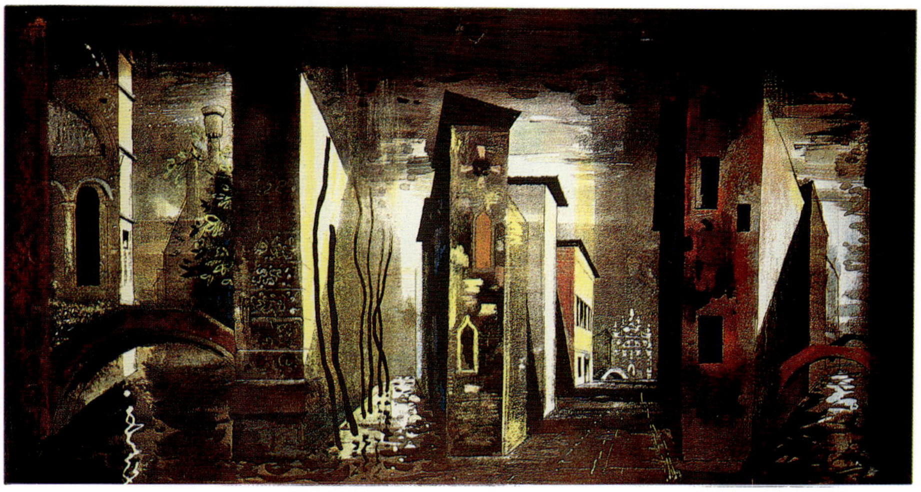

223

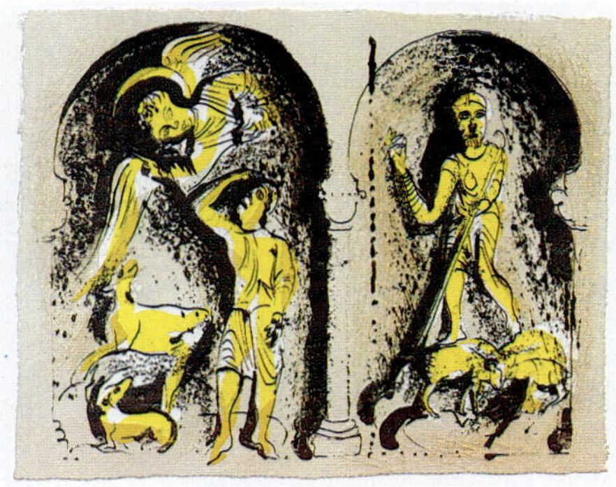

222

222
The Annunciation to the Shepherds
Lithograph 431 × 550 ($17 \times 21\frac{5}{8}$)
Curwen Studio 1973
Penwith Galleries 1973
Curwen-Saunders lithographic 580 × 795 ($22\frac{7}{8} \times 31\frac{1}{4}$)
90 'John Piper' 10AP 12HC (numbered 1-12) 2PP 2PUP

Glasgow Art Gallery and Museum; Tate Gallery

223
Venice Composition
Screenprint 556 × 1041 ($21\frac{7}{8} \times 41$)
Kelpra Studio 1973
Marlborough Fine Art 1973
Vélin Arches 300gsm 556 × 1041 ($21\frac{7}{8} \times 41$)
100 'John Piper' in white crayon b.r. 10AP 5HC 5PP

Sometimes incorrectly known as *'Venetian Backdrop'* or *'Venice Backdrop'*

Glasgow Art Gallery and Museum; Tate Gallery

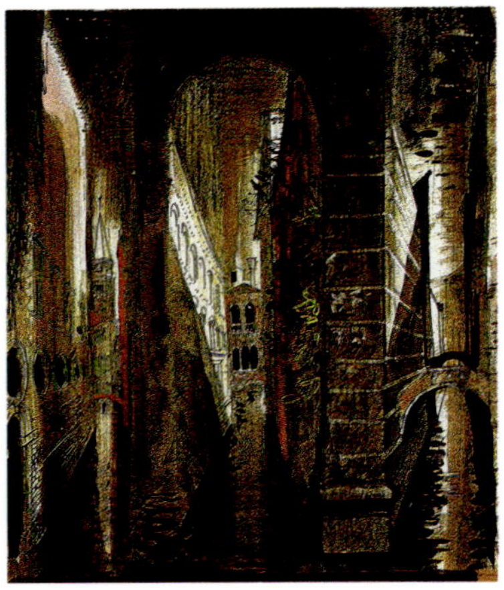

225

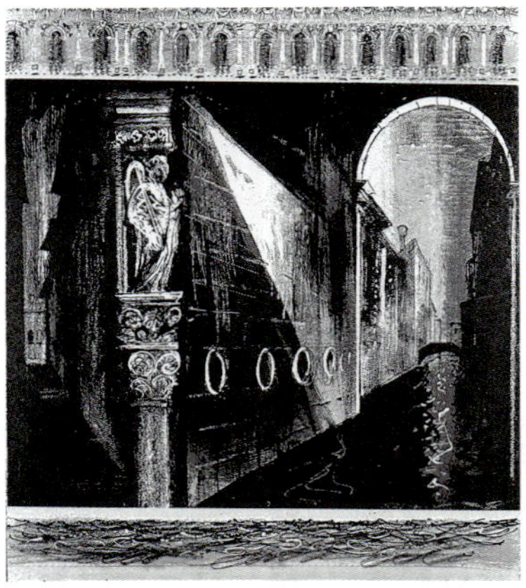

224

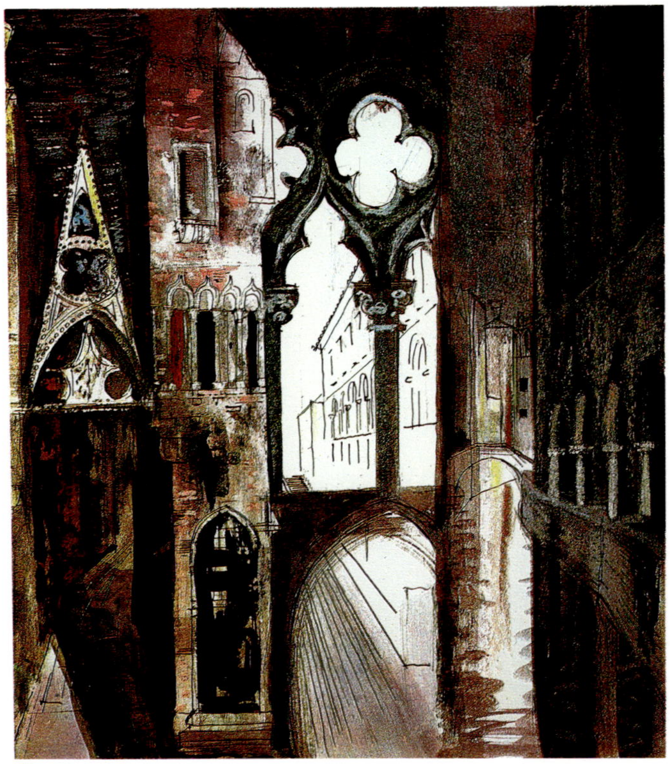

228

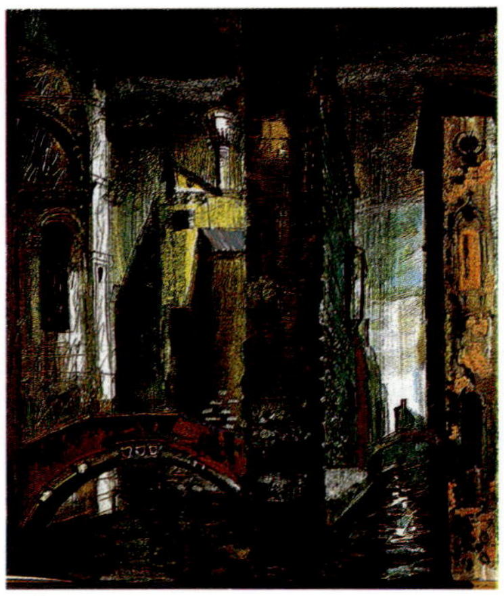

226

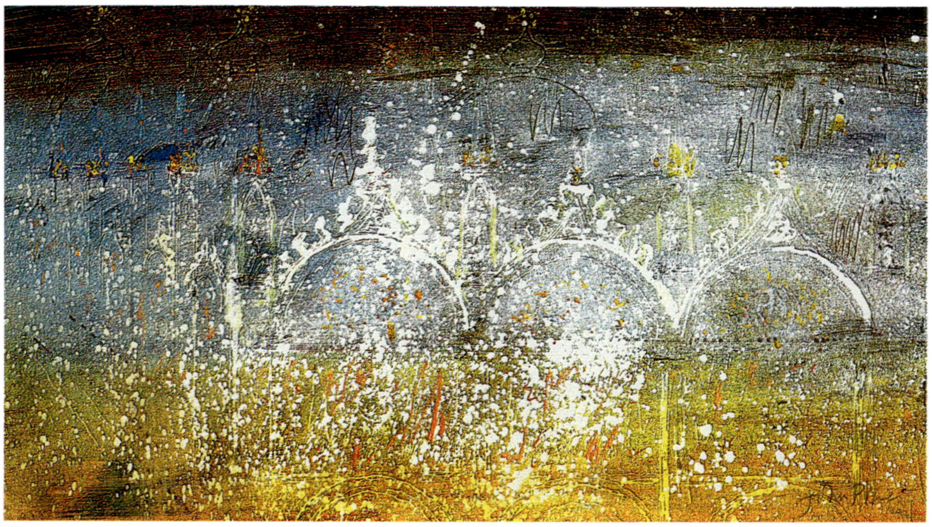

229

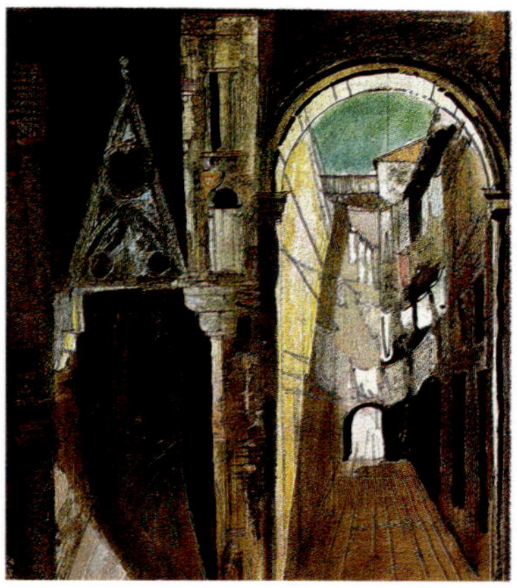

227

224-33
Death in Venice, 1973
The *Death in Venice* portfolio consists of ten screenprints (including side panels) from a selection of the sketches for the scenery of Benjamin Britten's opera, *Death in Venice*, which premiered at Aldeburgh, Suffolk in June 1973. Each portfolio contains: 2 side panels glued to the front and back of the specially designed cloth-bound portfolio; an introductory sheet with text by Myfanwy Piper (the librettist) and a contents page detailing the edition size and number, signed by the artist. Each screenprint (except both side panels) is numbered and signed by the artist. The edition size is 70. The first 30 copies of each image were presented in the clothbound portfolio and the remaining 40 sold individually, additional sets (marked A-J) being retained by the artist as artist's proofs. With the exception of the side panels in the sets, which were unsigned, all the prints were signed 'John Piper' b.r., some in crayon (images II, III, VII and VIII) and the remainder in pencil. The prints repr. have been used as the basis for the listing but it is probable that there are variations in the crayon and pencil signatures.

The graphics were screenprinted without margins on Grand Vélin Arches 300gsm paper by Kelpra Studio, bound by F. J. Randall and published by Marlborough Fine Art.

Tate Gallery (not side panels)

224
Death in Venice: side panel left
778 × 681 ($30\frac{5}{8} \times 26\frac{13}{16}$)

225
Death in Venice I
785 × 686 ($30\frac{15}{16} \times 27$)
Printer's stamp and no.'8162' on reverse

226
Death in Venice II
783 × 684 ($30\frac{13}{16} \times 26\frac{15}{16}$)
Printer's stamp and no.'8164' on reverse

227
Death in Venice III
783 × 686 ($30\frac{13}{16} \times 27$)
Printer's stamp and no.'8159' on reverse

228
Death in Venice IV
784 × 685 ($30\frac{7}{8} \times 27$)
Printer's stamp and no.'8161' on reverse

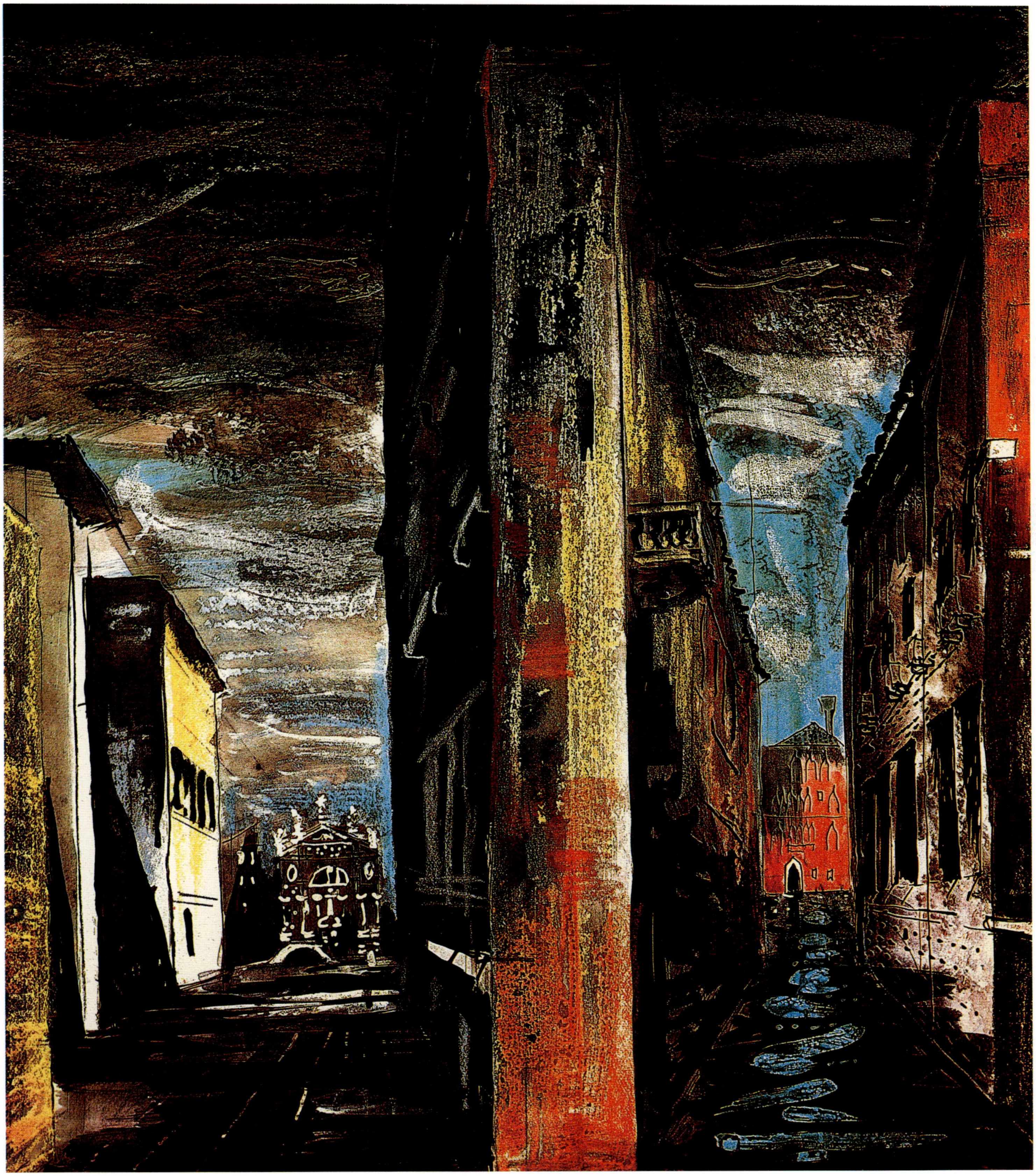

231

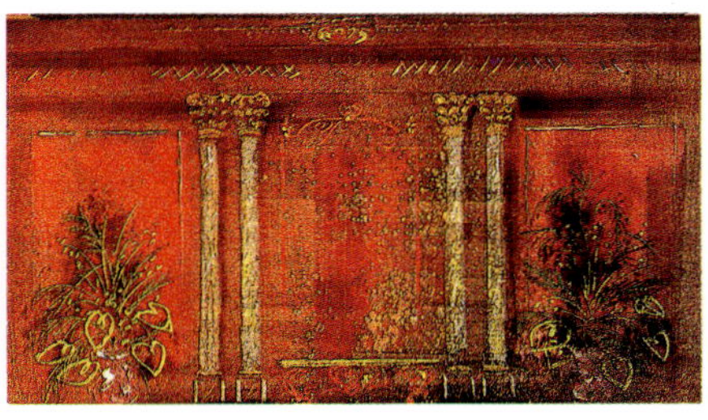

230

229
Death in Venice V
390×684 ($15\frac{3}{8} \times 26\frac{15}{16}$)
Printer's stamp and no.'8166' on reverse

230
Death in Venice VI
391×684 ($15\frac{3}{8} \times 26\frac{15}{16}$)
Printer's stamp and no.'8165' on reverse

231
Death in Venice VII
784×686 ($30\frac{7}{8} \times 27$)
Printer's stamp and no.'8160' on reverse

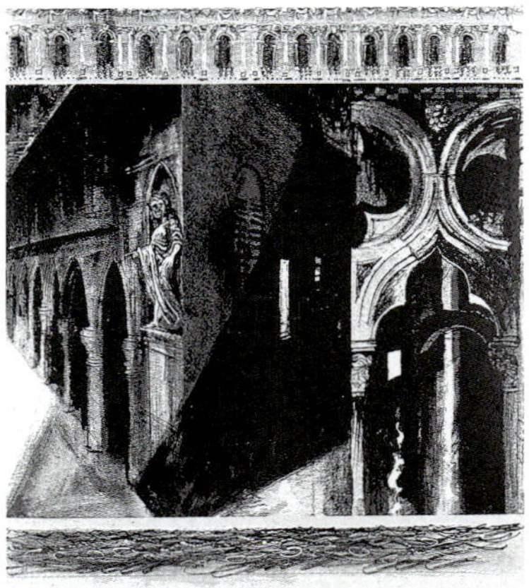

233

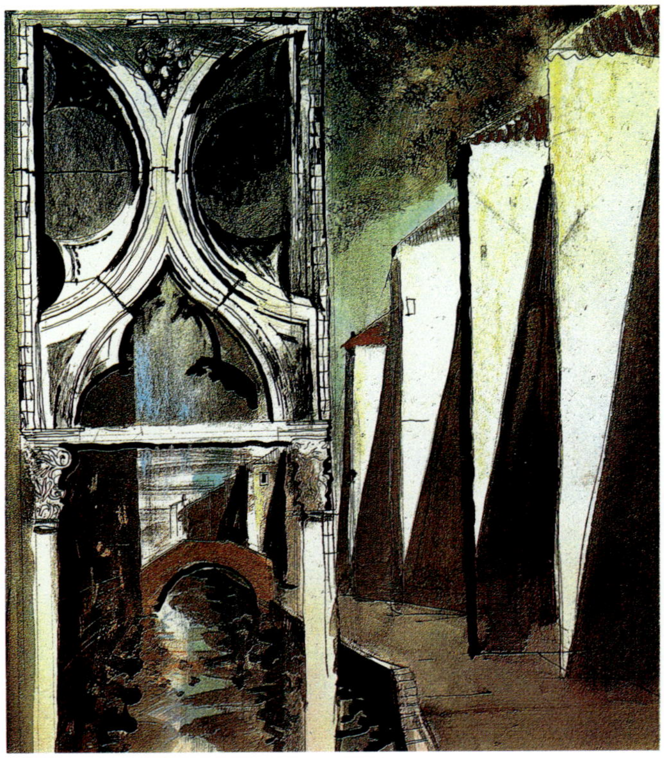

232

232
Death in Venice VIII
786 × 685 ($30\frac{15}{16} \times 27$)
Printer's stamp and no.'8163' on reverse

233
Death in Venice: side panel right
778 × 682 ($30\frac{5}{8} \times 26\frac{7}{8}$)

234
Eye and Camera: Marble, Red, Black etc. – lying figure reversed
Screenprint 699 × 457 ($27\frac{1}{2} \times 18$)
Kelpra Studio 1973
Marlborough Fine Art 1973
Vélin Arches 300gsm 768 × 585 ($30\frac{1}{4} \times 23$)
70 'John Piper' 10AP 5HC 5PP

Sometimes incorrectly known as *'Eye and Camera: Red and Blue II'*

Tate Gallery

235 (detail Plate 5)
Eye and Camera: Claret and Blue
Screenprint 477 × 701 ($18\frac{13}{16} \times 27\frac{5}{8}$)
Kelpra Studio 1973
Marlborough Fine Art 1973
Vélin Arches 300gsm 580 × 769 ($22\frac{13}{16} \times 30\frac{1}{4}$)
70 'John Piper' 10AP 5HC 5PP

Printer's stamp and no.'8152' on reverse

Tate Gallery

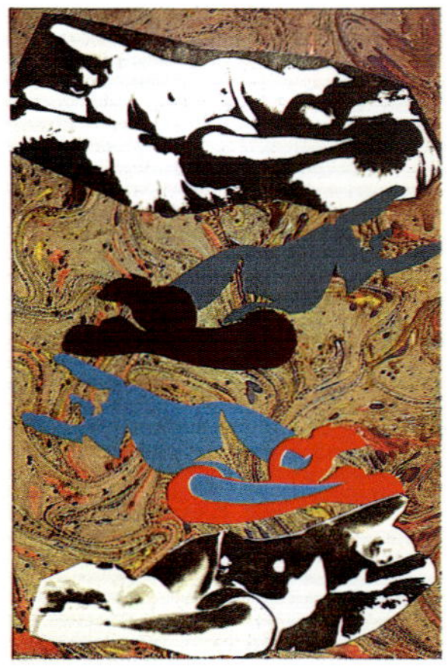

234

236
Three Somerset Towers
Screenprint 649 × 899 ($25\frac{9}{16} \times 35\frac{3}{8}$)
Kelpra Studio 1973
Marlborough Fine Art 1973
Vélin Arches 300gsm 705 × 960 ($27\frac{3}{4} \times 37\frac{3}{4}$)
70 'John Piper' 10AP 5HC 5PP

One trial proof with yellow replacing blue, and red replacing grey exists. Printer's stamp and no.'8176' on reverse

Sheffield Arts and Museums; Tate Gallery

237
Two Suffolk Towers
Screenprint 663 × 725 ($26\frac{1}{8} \times 28\frac{9}{16}$)
Kelpra Studio 1973
Marlborough Fine Art 1973
Vélin Arches 300gsm 701 × 768 ($27\frac{9}{16} \times 30\frac{1}{4}$)
70 'John Piper' 10AP 5HC 5PP

One trial state with a lighter background exists. Printer's stamp and no.'7991' on reverse

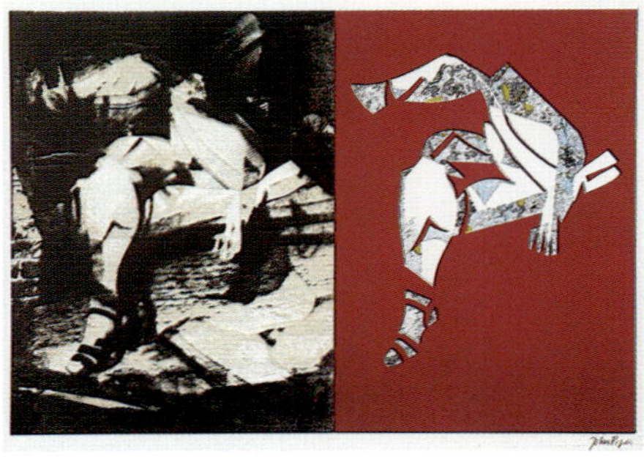

235

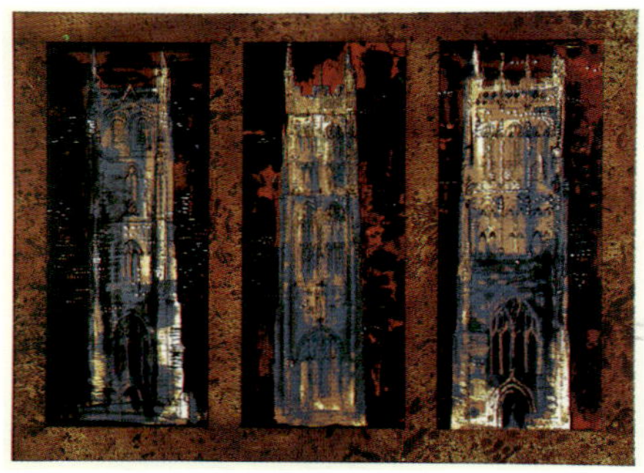

236

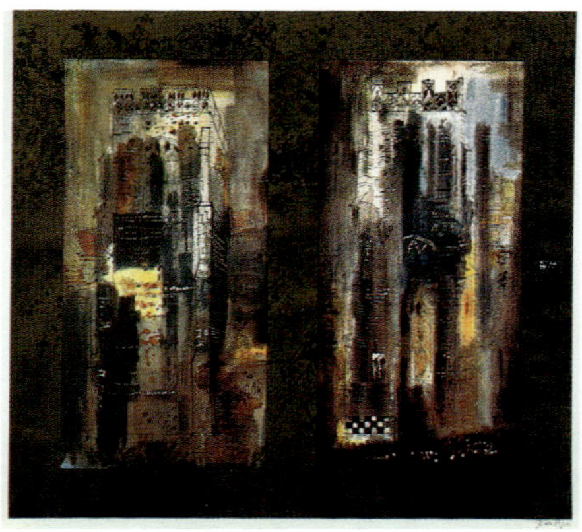

237

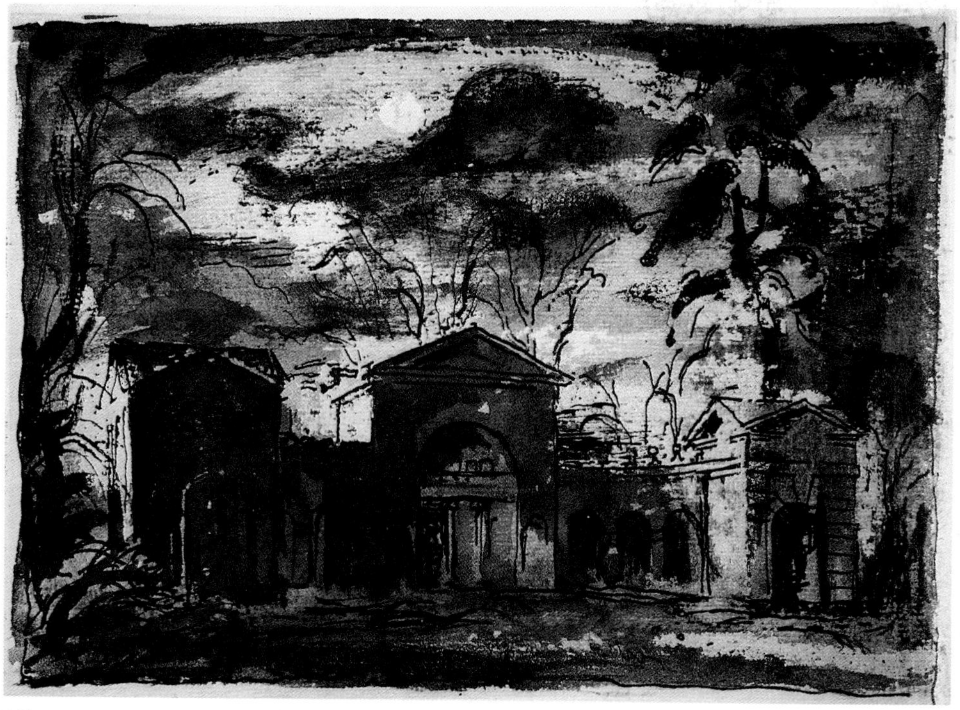

240

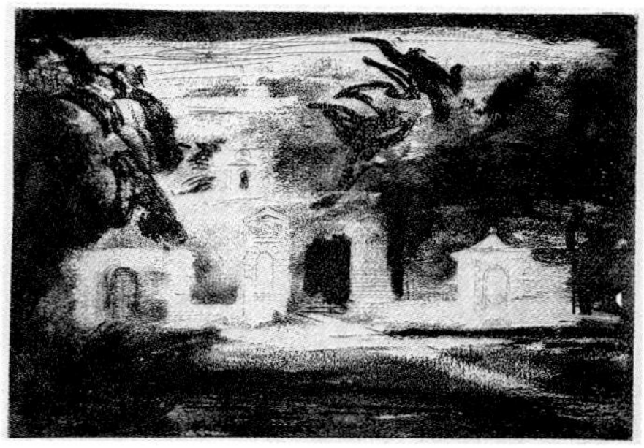

239

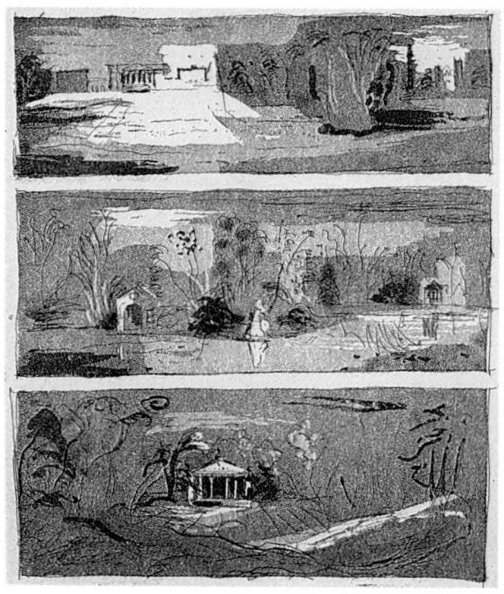

238

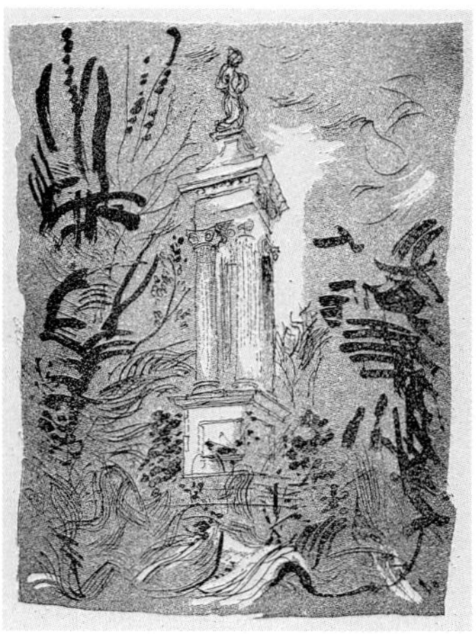

241

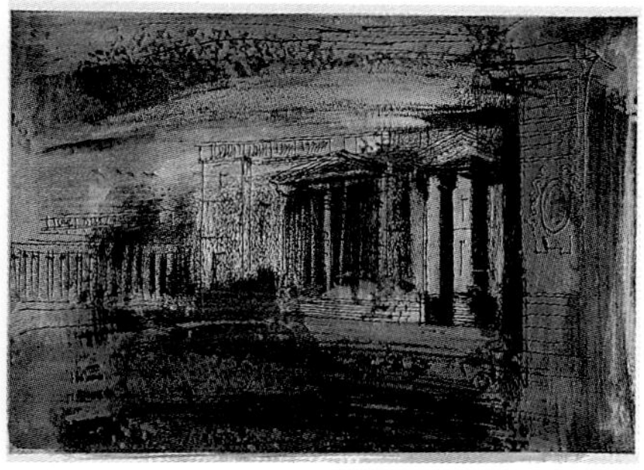

242

238
Stowe: Three Vistas
Aquatint 215 × 162 ($8\frac{7}{16} \times 6\frac{3}{8}$)
The artist *c.* 1975
Unpublished
Proofing paper 342 × 215 ($13\frac{7}{16} \times 8\frac{7}{16}$)
Not issued as an edition Unsigned

Sometimes incorrectly known as *'Stowe, Buckinghamshire: The House from the South, the Lake, the Temple of Concord'*

A number of hand-coloured versions and some proofs of the experimental plate exist. Repr. in Ingrams/Piper (plate 44, hand-coloured version)

239
Stowe
Etching 182 × 260 ($7\frac{1}{16} \times 10$)
The artist *c.* 1975
Unpublished
Proofing paper 252 × 280 ($9\frac{15}{16} \times 11$)
Not issued as an edition Unsigned

A number of proofs exist, most of which are overworked in pen and ink.

240
Stowe: Temple of Venus
Aquatint 164 × 224 ($6\frac{7}{16} \times 8\frac{13}{16}$) (plate)
The artist *c.* 1975
Unpublished
Proofing paper 225×233 ($9\frac{7}{8} \times 9\frac{1}{8}$)
Not issued as an edition Unsigned

A number of hand-coloured versions and some proofs of the experimental plates exist.

241
Stowe: Queen Caroline's Monument
Etching and aquatint 214 × 165 ($8\frac{7}{16} \times 6\frac{1}{2}$)
The artist *c.* 1975
Unpublished
Proofing paper 294 × 203 ($11\frac{9}{16} \times 8$)
Not issued as an edition Unsigned

A few proofs are known to exist.

242
Stowe: North Front
Aquatint 178 × 247 ($7 \times 9\frac{3}{4}$)
The artist *c.* 1975
Unpublished
Proofing paper 212 × 265 ($8\frac{3}{8} \times 10\frac{7}{16}$)
Not issued as an edition Unsigned

A number of hand-coloured versions and some proofs of the experimental plates exist.

243
Stowe: South Front
Aquatint 199 × 245 ($7\frac{13}{16} \times 9\frac{5}{8}$)
The artist *c.* 1975
Unpublished
Proofing paper 216 × 271 ($8\frac{1}{2} \times 10\frac{5}{8}$)
Not issued as an edition Unsigned

A number of hand-coloured versions and some proofs of the experimental plates exist.

244
Stowe: Two Vistas
Aquatint 192 × 263 ($7\frac{9}{16} \times 10\frac{3}{8}$)
The artist *c.* 1975
Unpublished
Proofing paper 258 × 368 ($10\frac{1}{8} \times 14\frac{7}{8}$)
Not issued as an edition Unsigned

A few proofs are known to exist.

245
Foliate Heads I
Screenprint 582 × 764 ($22\frac{7}{8} \times 30\frac{1}{16}$)
Kelpra Studio 1975
Marlborough Fine Art 1975
'Arches aquarelles satinées' 582 × 764 ($22\frac{7}{8} \times 30\frac{1}{16}$)
75 'John Piper' in yellow crayon b.r. 10AP 5HC 5PP

Printed without margins. Printer's stamp and no.'8280' on reverse

Tate Gallery

246
Foliate Heads II
Screenprint 582 × 764 ($22\frac{7}{8} \times 30\frac{1}{16}$)
Kelpra Studio 1975
Marlborough Fine Art 1975
'Arches aquarelles satinées' 582 × 764 ($22\frac{7}{8} \times 30\frac{1}{16}$)
75 'John Piper' in blue-white crayon b.r. 10AP 5HC 5PP

Printed without margins. Printer's stamp and no.'8281' on reverse

Tate Gallery

247
Horham, Suffolk
Screenprint 545 × 840 ($21\frac{7}{16} \times 33\frac{1}{16}$)
Kelpra Studio 1975
Marlborough Fine Art 1975
Vélin Arches 300gsm 615 × 895 ($24\frac{3}{16} \times 35\frac{1}{4}$)
70 'John Piper' 10AP 5HC 5PP

Tate Gallery

248
Whithorn Priory
Screenprint 603 × 905 ($23\frac{3}{4} \times 35\frac{5}{8}$)
Kelpra Studio 1975
Marlborough Fine Art 1975
Vélin Arches 300gsm 675 × 968 ($26\frac{9}{16} \times 38\frac{1}{8}$)
70 'John Piper' 10AP 5HC 5PP

The first print in the series *Five Scottish Chapels (in ruins)*

Tate Gallery

249
Ruined Chapel, Isle of Mull
Screenprint 634 × 836 ($24\frac{15}{16} \times 32\frac{15}{16}$)
Kelpra Studio 1975
Marlborough Fine Art 1975
Vélin Arches 300gsm 696 × 895 ($27\frac{3}{8} \times 35\frac{1}{4}$)
70 'John Piper' 10AP 5HC 5PP

Sometimes incorrectly known as *'Isle of Mull'*. The second print in the series *Five Scottish Chapels (in ruins)*. Printer's stamp and no.'8291' on reverse

Tate Gallery

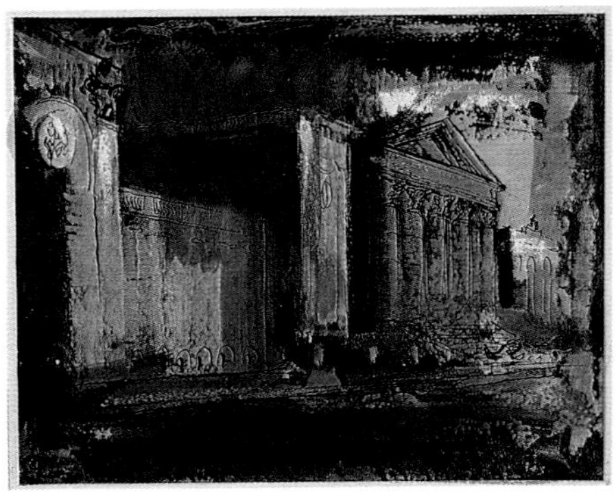

243

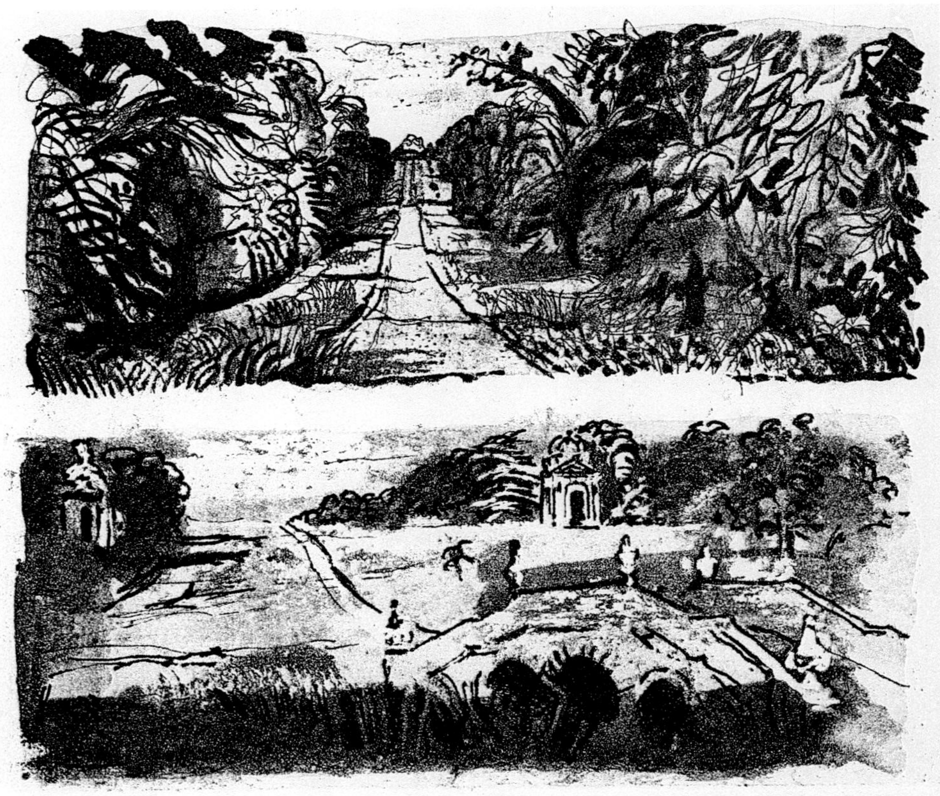

244

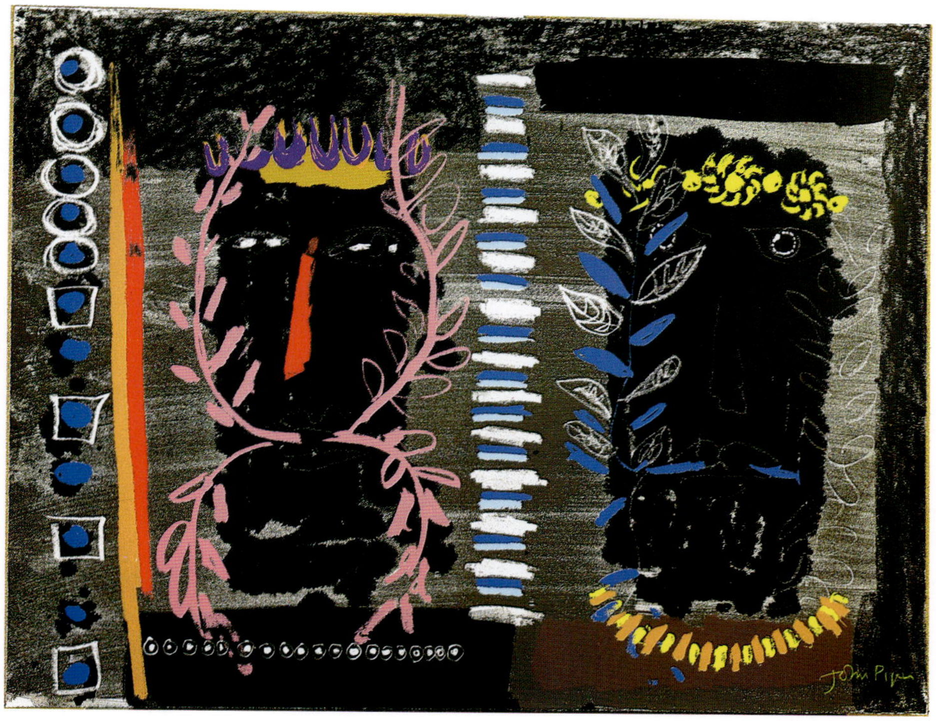

245

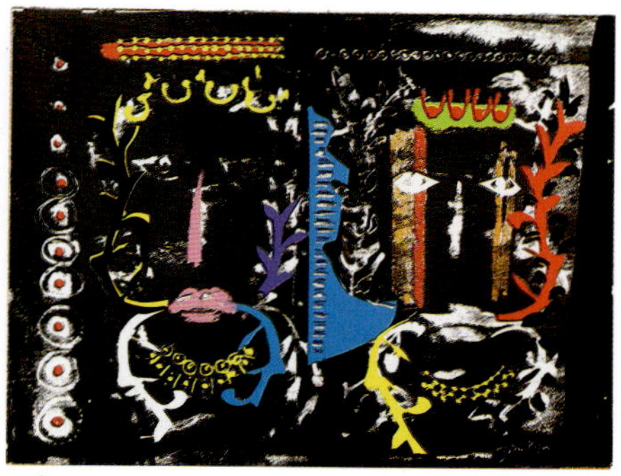

246

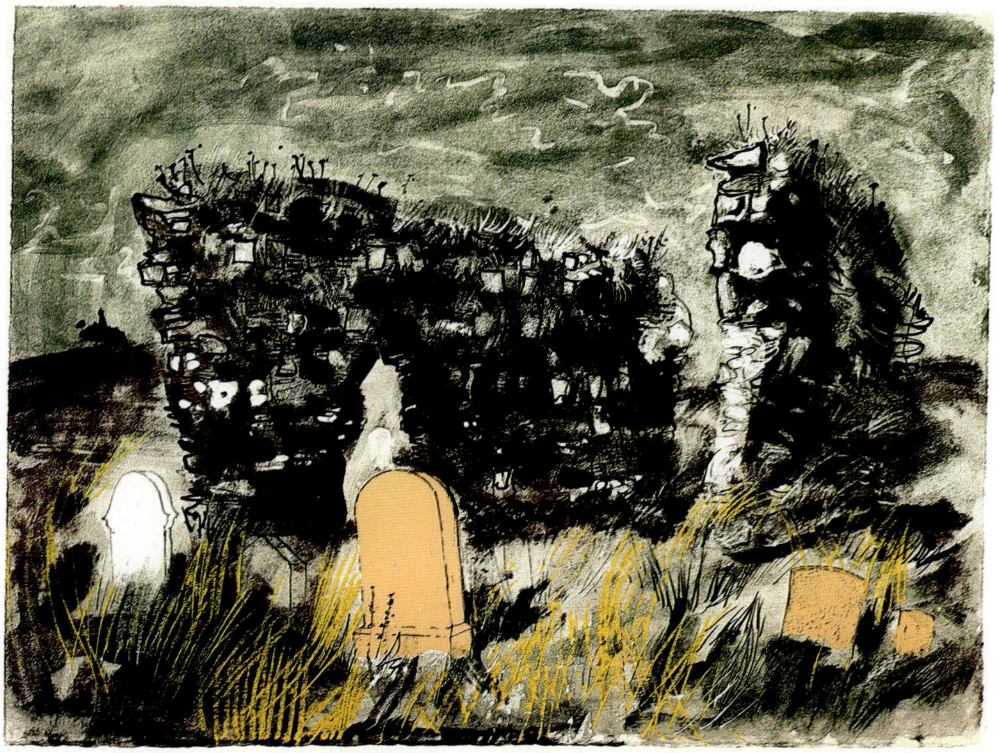

249

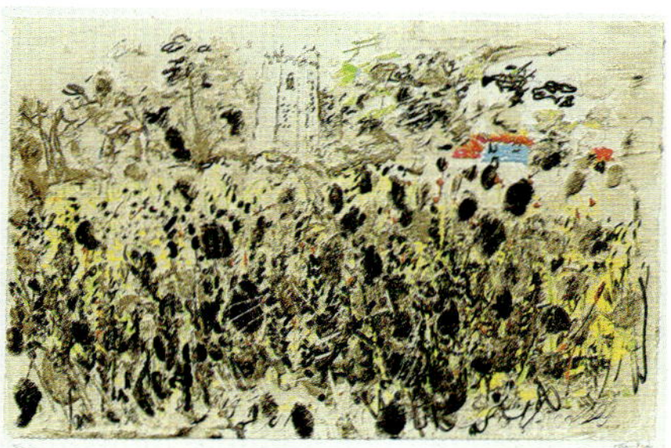

247

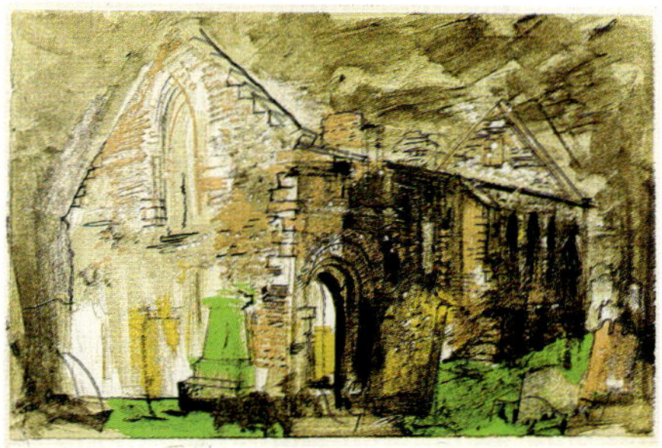

248

250
Skeabost, Skye
Screenprint 635 × 840 ($25 \times 33\frac{1}{16}$)
Kelpra Studio 1975
Marlborough Fine Art 1975
Vélin Arches 300gsm 700 × 902 ($27\frac{9}{16} \times 35\frac{1}{2}$)
70 'John Piper' 10AP 5HC 5PP

The third print in the series *Five Scottish Chapels (in ruins)*

Tate Gallery

251
Kilmory Chapel
Screenprint 634 × 840 ($24\frac{15}{16} \times 33\frac{1}{16}$)
Kelpra Studio 1975
Marlborough Fine Art 1975
Vélin Arches 300gsm 698 × 895 ($27\frac{1}{2} \times 35\frac{1}{4}$)
70 'John Piper' 10AP 5HC 5PP

Sometimes incorrectly known as *'Kilmory Chapel, Argyll'* or *'Kilmory Chapel, Napdale'*. The fourth print in the series *Five Scottish Chapels (in ruins)*. Printer's stamp and no.'8292' on reverse

Tate Gallery

252
Kirkmaiden
Screenprint 606 × 910 ($23\frac{13}{16} \times 35\frac{13}{16}$)
Kelpra Studio 1975
Marlborough Fine Art 1975
Vélin Arches 300gsm 673 × 970 ($26\frac{1}{2} \times 38\frac{3}{16}$)
70 'John Piper' 10AP 5HC 5PP

Sometimes incorrectly known as *'Kirkmaiden-in-Furness'*. The fifth print in the series *Five Scottish Chapels (in ruins)*

Tate Gallery

253
The Visitation
Lithograph 515 × 420 ($20\frac{1}{4} \times 16\frac{1}{2}$)
Burleighfield House 1975
Gallery Wolfgang Ketterer 1975
Arches 185gsm 563 × 479 ($22\frac{1}{8} \times 18\frac{7}{8}$)
90 'John Piper' 35AP (numbered I/XXXV-XXXV/XXXV) 5PP

Sometimes incorrectly known as '*Saints*' or '*Untitled (IAA Portfolio)*'

Part of a portfolio honouring the 1975 Holy Year and containing an introduction by Pope Paul VI, and a print by each of the following: Bargheer, Fuchs, Grieshaber, Piper, Schmidt-Rottluff, Scorcelli and Tot

Tate Gallery

254
Wiggenhall, St Peter
Lithograph 558 × 420 ($22 \times 16\frac{1}{2}$)
Burleighfield House 1975
International Association of Art (UK) 1975
Arches 185gsm 682 × 482 ($26\frac{7}{8} \times 19$)
75 'John Piper' 35AP (numbered I/XXXV-XXXV/XXXV)

The portfolio contained a print by each of the following: Robert Adams, Sandra Blow, Harvey Daniels, Terry Frost, Gertrude Hermes, Gordon House, Morris Kestleman, Robert Medley, Victor Pasmore, John Piper, Michael Rothenstein and Blair Hughes Stanton.

Tate Gallery

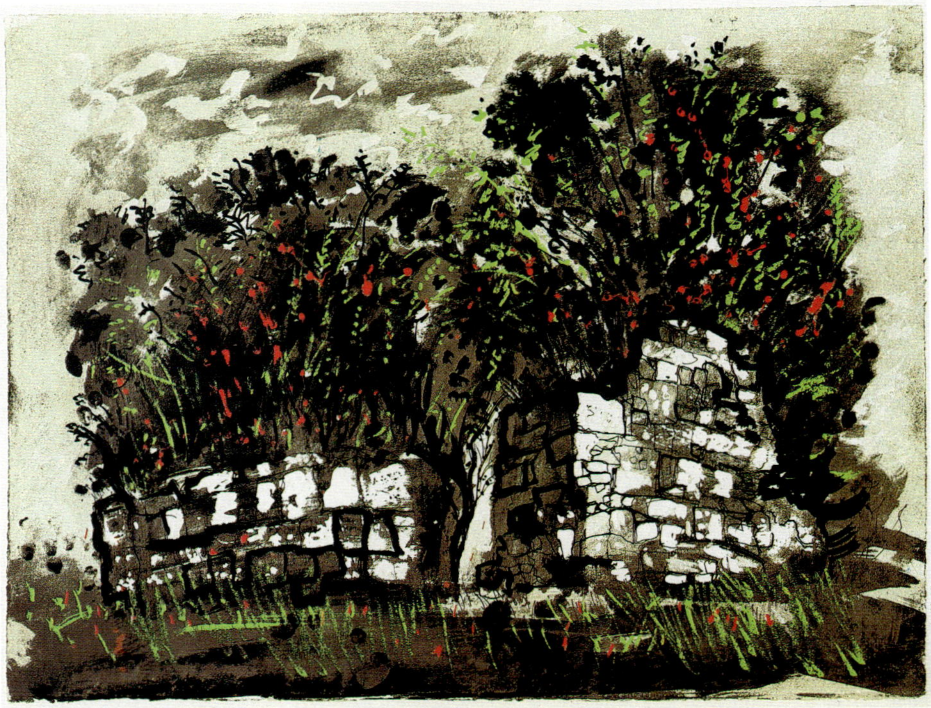

250

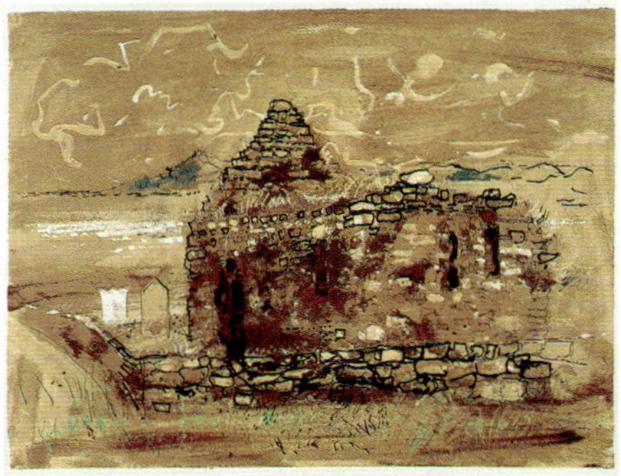

251

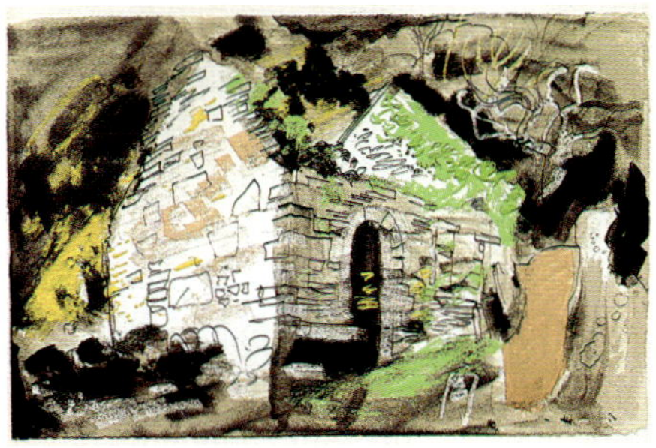

252

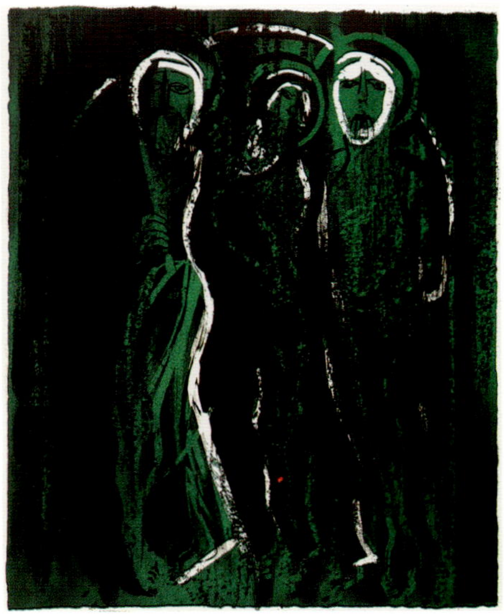

253

254

255
Magi, La Charité-sur-Loire, Ste Croix
Lithograph 231 × 337 ($9\frac{1}{8} \times 13\frac{1}{4}$)
Curwen Press *c.* 1976
Unknown *c.* 1976
Machine-made lithographic cartridge 381 × 565 ($15 \times 22\frac{1}{4}$)
Unspecified Unsigned

Sometimes incorrectly known as *'The Gifts of the Magi'* or *'Three Kings'*, *'Virgin and Child'*.

Proofed at Curwen Studio

256
Foliate Head
Lithograph 380 × 255 (15 × 10)
Curwen Studio 1976
Curwen Press 1976
T. H. Saunders 545 × 375 ($21\frac{7}{16} \times 14\frac{3}{4}$)
90 'John Piper' 10AP 2PP

Sometimes incorrectly known as *'Foliate Head: Pink and Blue'*

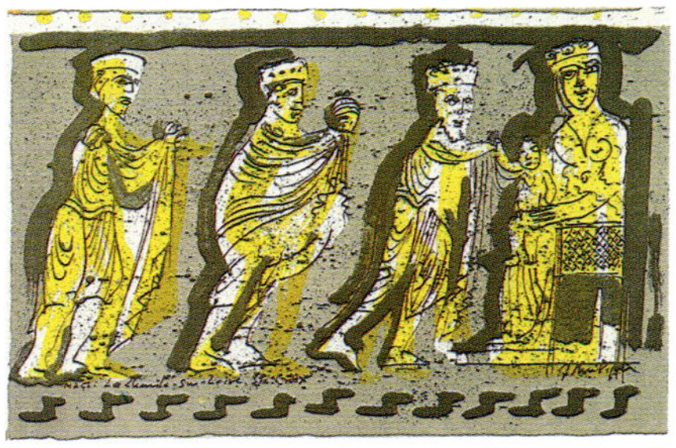

255

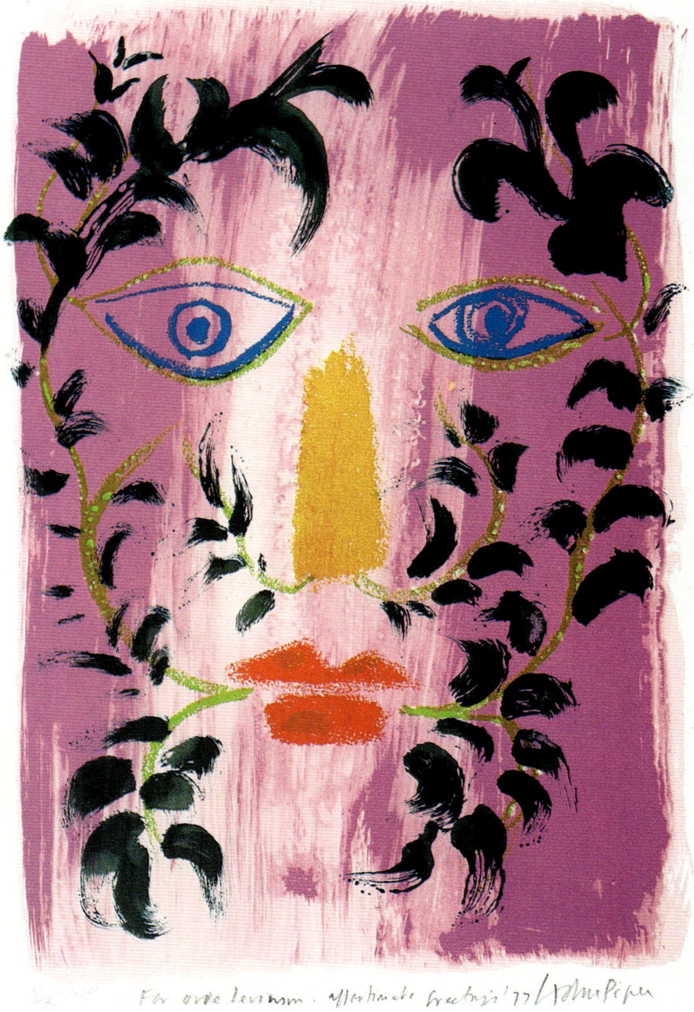

256

257
Clytha Castle
Lithograph 255 × 385 ($10\frac{1}{8} \times 15\frac{1}{8}$)
Curwen Studio 1976
Curwen Press 1976
Arches 369 × 485 ($14\frac{1}{2} \times 19\frac{1}{8}$)
90 'John Piper' 10AP 2PP

Further prints of this image, unsigned, unnumbered and in an unspecified large print run, were repr. by Curwen Press on Bockingford 90lbs, trimmed and bled off without a margin. They formed part of *Curwen Lithographs for those Special Occasions*, a brochure describing what a lithograph is and how to commission one.

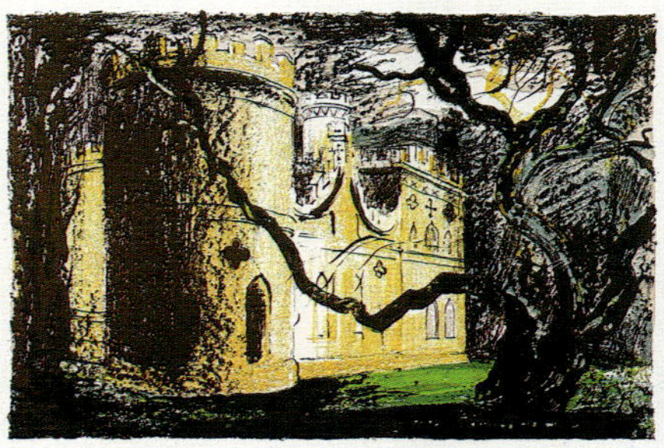

257

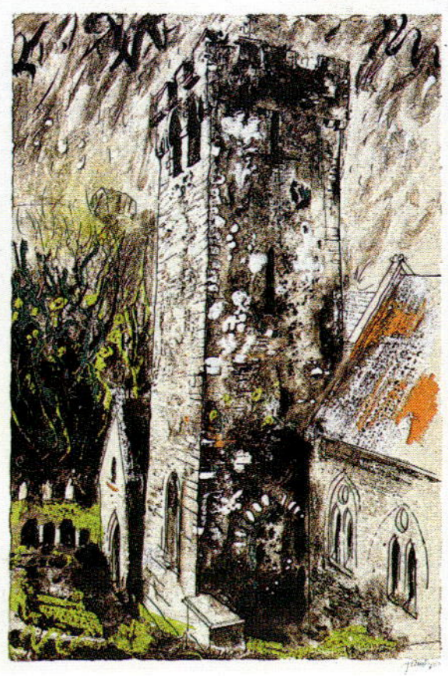

259

258
Avoncroft Museum
Lithograph 420 × 585 ($16\frac{1}{2} \times 23$)
Curwen Studio 1976
Avoncroft Museum of Buildings 1976
Curwen/Saunders lithographic 120lbs 572 × 763 ($22\frac{1}{2} \times 30\frac{1}{16}$)
75 'John Piper' 7AP 1PP

Donated by the artist to the Avoncroft Museum of Buildings, Stoke Heath, Bromsgrove, to assist with fund-raising

Avoncroft Museum of Buildings; Tate Gallery

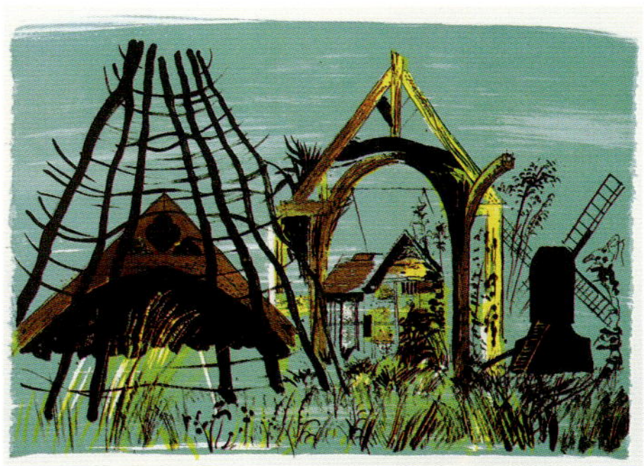

258

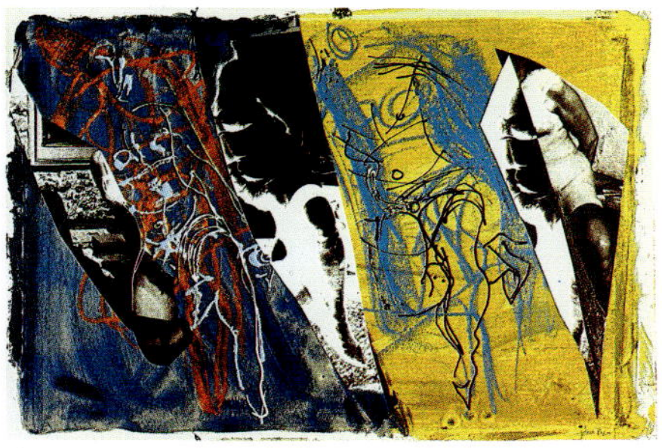

260

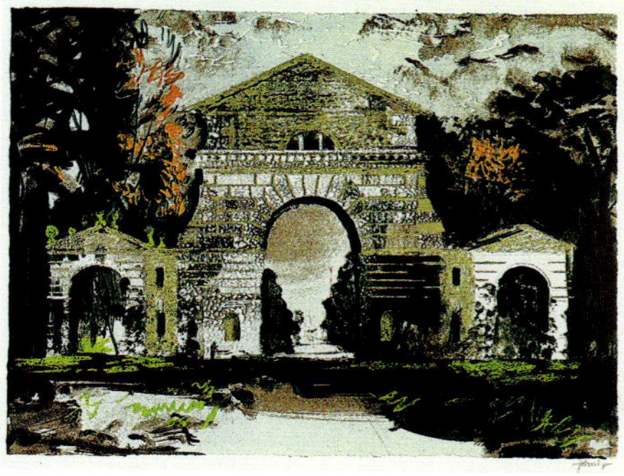

262

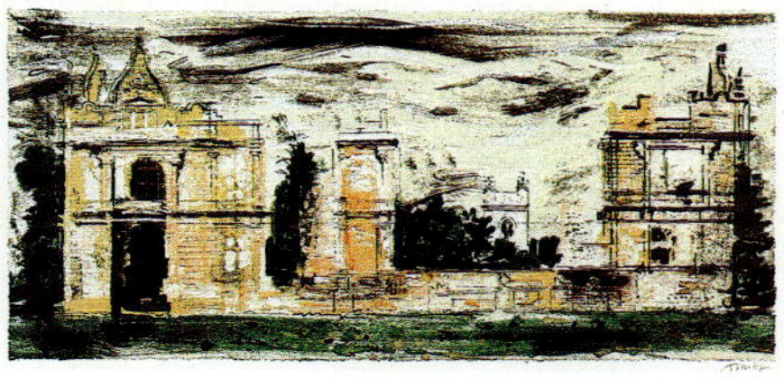

263

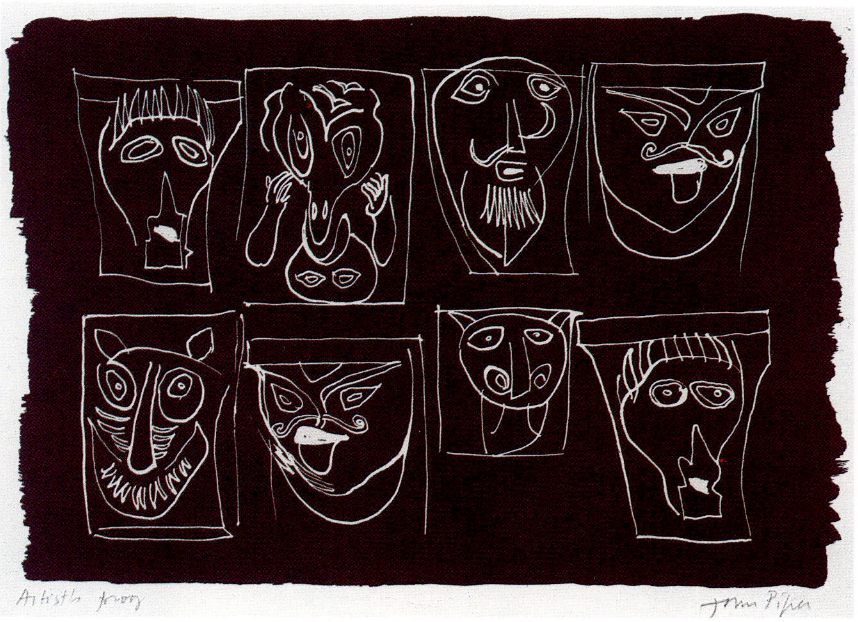

261

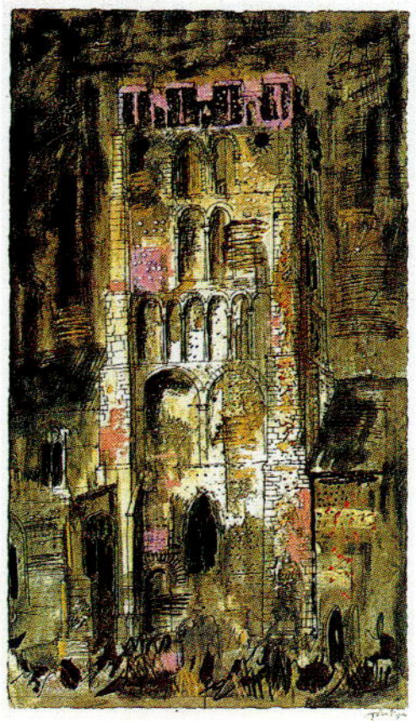

264

259
Castlemartin
Screenprint 920 × 610 ($36\frac{1}{4} \times 24$)
Kelpra Studio 1976
Marlborough Fine Art 1976
Vélin Arches 300gsm 1035 × 711 ($40\frac{3}{4} \times 28$)
70 'John Piper' 15AP 5HC 5PP

Printer's stamp and no. '8320' on reverse

Tate Gallery

260
Eye and Camera: Blue to Ochre
Screenprint 763 × 1111 ($30\frac{1}{16} \times 43\frac{3}{4}$)
Kelpra Studio 1976
Marlborough Fine Art 1976
Vélin Arches 300gsm 763 × 1111 ($30\frac{1}{16} \times 43\frac{3}{4}$)
75 'John Piper' in black crayon 10AP 5HC 5PP

Printer's stamp and no. '8326' on reverse. Repr. in black-and-white in Tate (illus. 161)

Tate Gallery

261
Corbels at Kilpeck
Screenprint 231 × 337 ($9\frac{1}{8} \times 13\frac{1}{4}$)
Charles Broome 1976
Friends of the Herefordshire Museums and Art Galleries 1976
Arches 185gsm 384 × 565 ($15\frac{1}{8} \times 22\frac{1}{4}$)
75 'John Piper' AP (Unknown)

Sometimes incorrectly known as *'Kilpeck'*, *'Kilpeck Corbels'* or *'Romanesque Corbels, Kilpeck, Herefordshire'*. Donated by the artist to raise money for Herefordshire Museums and Art Galleries. Repr. in black-and-white in Ingrams/Piper (back dust-jacket)

Herefordshire Museums and Art Galleries; Leicestershire Museums, Arts and Record Service

262
Holkham Gate, Norfolk
Screenprint 610 × 831 ($24 \times 32\frac{11}{16}$)
Kelpra Studio 1976
Marlborough Fine Art 1976
Vélin Arches 300gsm 726 × 938 ($28\frac{9}{16} \times 36\frac{15}{16}$)
70 'John Piper' 10AP 5HC 5PP

Printer's stamp and no. '8323' on reverse

Tate Gallery

263
Moreton Corbet
Screenprint 456 × 990 ($17\frac{15}{16} \times 39$)
Kelpra Studio 1976
Marlborough Fine Art 1976
'Vélin Arches' 300gsm 573 × 1085 ($22\frac{9}{16} \times 42\frac{3}{4}$)
70 'John Piper' 10AP 5HC 5PP

Printer's stamp and no. '8321' on reverse

Tate Gallery

264
South Lopham
Screenprint 914 × 520 ($36 \times 20\frac{7}{16}$)
Kelpra Studio 1976
Marlborough Fine Art 1976
Vélin Arches 300gsm 1032 × 625 ($40\frac{5}{8} \times 24\frac{5}{8}$)
70 'John Piper' 10AP 5HC 5PP

Printer's stamp and no. '8322' on reverse

Tate Gallery

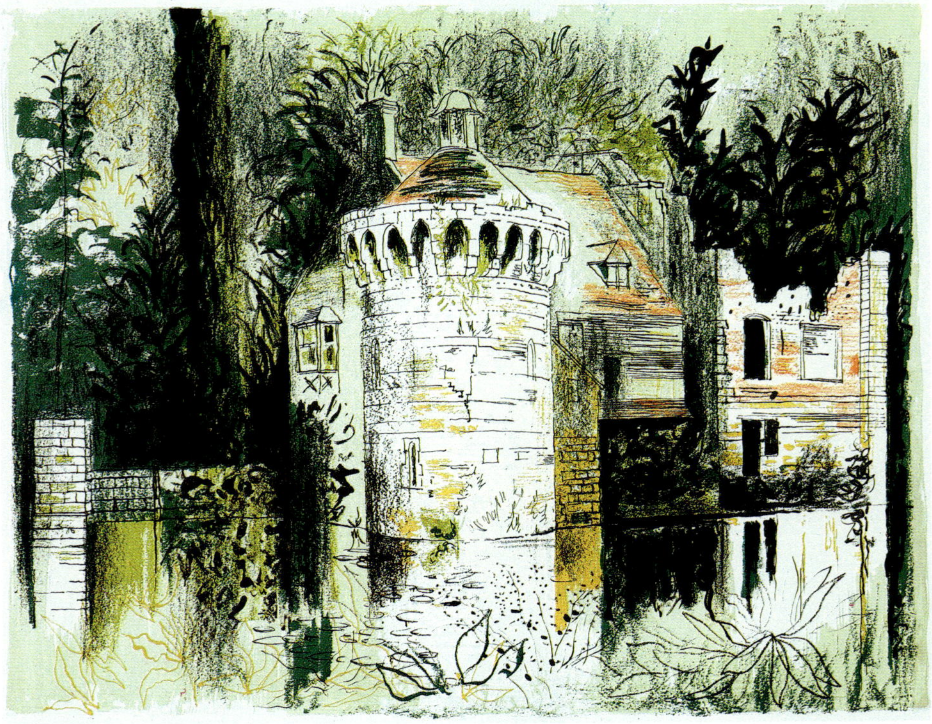

265

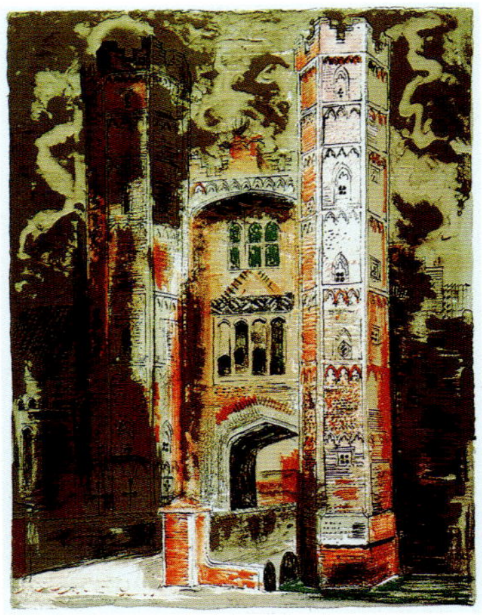

266

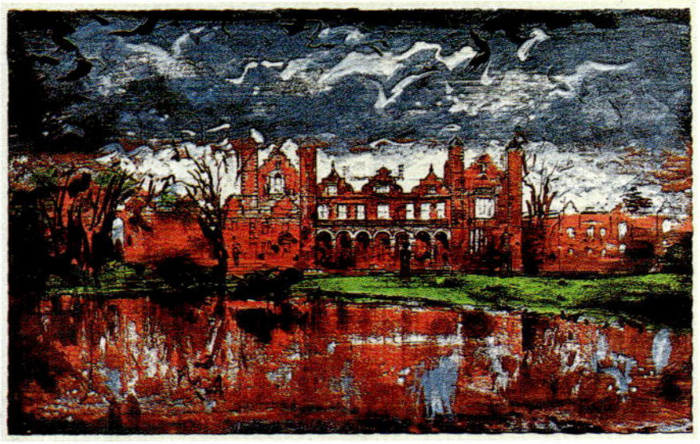

268

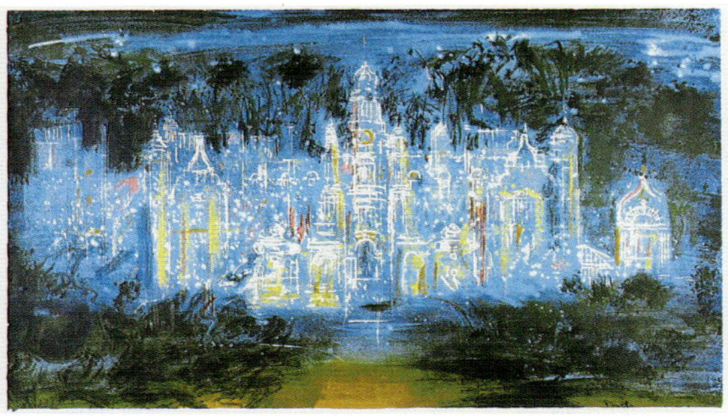

270

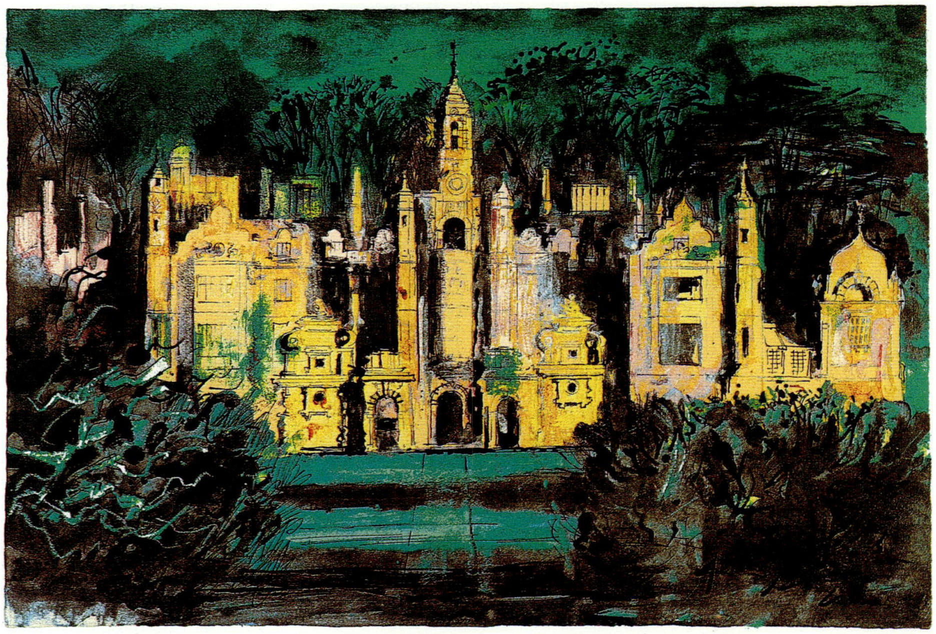

271

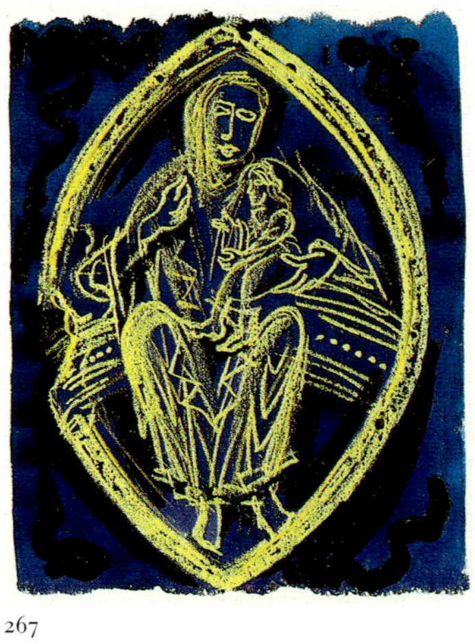

267

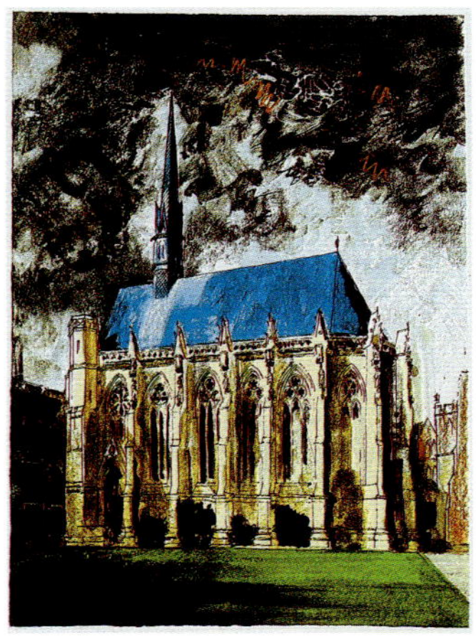

269

265
Scotney Castle, Kent
Lithograph 440 × 568 (17¼ × 22⅜)
Curwen Studio 1976
Christie's Contemporary Art and the National Trust 1977
T.H. Saunders 90lbs 480 × 609 (18⅞ × 24)
120 'John Piper' 12AP 2HC

Sometimes incorrectly known as '*Scotney Castle*'

266
Oxburgh Hall, Norfolk
Lithograph 575 × 442 (22⅝ × 17⁷⁄₁₆)
Curwen Studio 1977
Christie's Contemporary Art and the National Trust 1977
T.H. Saunders 90lbs 610 × 480 (24 × 18⅞)
120 'John Piper' 12AP 2HC

267
Virgin and Child
Lithograph 610 × 463 (24 × 18¼)
Curwen Studio 1977
Christie's Contemporary Art 1977
T.H. Saunders 120lbs 769 × 565 (30½ × 22½)
95 'John Piper' 5AP 2IC 2PP

Sometimes incorrectly known as '*Mother and Child*'

Tate Gallery

268
Capesthorne
Screenprint 640 × 1014 (25³⁄₁₆ × 39⅞)
Kelpra Studio 1977
Marlborough Fine Art 1977
Vélin Arches 300gsm 740 × 1120 (29⅛ × 44⅛)
75 'John Piper' 10AP 5HC 5PP

Sometimes incorrectly known as '*Capesthorne, near Macclesfield*'

Tate Gallery

269
Exeter College Chapel, Oxford
Screenprint 816 × 608 (32⅛ × 23⅞)
Kelpra Studio 1977
Marlborough Fine Art 1977
Vélin Arches 300gsm 931 × 709 (36⅝ × 27¹⁵⁄₁₆)
100 'John Piper' 10AP 5HC 5PP

Sometimes incorrectly known as '*Exeter Chapel*'. A percentage commission on sales was given to the Exeter College Junior Common Room (JCR) Art Collection. Printer's stamp and no.'8339' on reverse

Tate Gallery

270
Harlaxton (Blue)
Screenprint 574 × 1010 (22⁹⁄₁₆ × 39¾)
Kelpra Studio 1977
Marlborough Fine Art 1977
Vélin Arches 300gsm 694 × 1098 (27⁵⁄₁₆ × 43³⁄₁₆)
75 'John Piper' 10AP 5HC 5PP

Tate Gallery

271
Harlaxton Manor
Screenprint 460 × 680 (18⅛ × 26¾)
Kelpra Studio 1977
Marlborough Fine Art 1977
Vélin Arches 300gsm 570 × 781 (22⁷⁄₁₆ × 30¾)
70 'John Piper' 10AP 5HC 5PP

272-9
Victorian Dream Palaces, 1977
A portfolio of eight screenprints accompanied by a double-spread title-page containing an introduction by the artist and brief descriptions (not by the artist) of each 'Dream Palace'. The portfolio was published in an edition of 75 by Marlborough Fine Art and printed on Vélin Arches 300gsm paper by Kelpra Studio. The paper size is 605 × 775 (23¹³⁄₁₆ × 30½). All the screenprints are signed 'John Piper' in pencil b.r.

Sometimes incorrectly known as '*Victorian Dream Palaces and Other Buildings in Landscape*'

Tate Gallery

Introduction to *Victorian Dream Palaces* by the artist

An American journalist visiting an English country house in the middle of the nineteenth century wrote: 'With the whole visible horizon fenced in for the enjoyment of a household of which I was a temporary portion, and no enemy, except time and the gout, I felt as if I had been spirited into some castle of felicity and had not come by the royal stage coach at all.' (Quoted in Hewitt's Rural Life of England*). These 'castles of felicity' or 'dream palaces', whether they were inhabited by Fairy Princes or Princesses presiding with benevolence over the neighbourhood or by Wicked Ogres produced by the Industrial Revolution, reached the peak period of their construction in the 1870's. The peak period of their destruction is probably the 1970's, and this destruction was documented in a big exhibition at the Victoria and Albert Museum a couple of years ago. Those that I have visited and drawn still exist. Mark Girouard's book* The Victorian Country House *is an excellent guide to all these and many more.*

Notes to *Victorian Dream Palaces* not by the artist

The Royal Holloway College
The Royal Holloway College, Egham, Surrey, was begun in 1879, not as a country house but as a girls' college. Girton had been founded ten years before. Thomas Holloway was the founder. He had made a fortune out of pills and ointments, and also built the great Sanitorium nearby. The architect was W.H. Crossland, the model – more in detail than in shape, and not at all in colour – was Chambord. Holloway College is a great efflorescence of red brick which frequently astonishes unsuspecting motorists as they glimpse it through the trees hurrying towards Basingstoke along the A30.

Ettington Park
Ettington Park near Stratford-on-Avon was designed by John Pritchard and built, 1858-63. Influenced by the writings of John Ruskin the architect used bands of different-coloured stone, much sculpture, and wrought-iron screens in a Gothic arcade facing onto the forecourt. The grounds are planted in a rich Victorian style and the medieval church on the lawn completes the whole picturesque scene.

Wightwick Manor
Wightwick Manor, Wolverhampton, Staffordshire, is a particularly English kind of Dream Palace, built in Victorian Tudor half-timber, with some brick and stone in the base storey, the tower and chimneys. Edward Ould was the architect, and it was begun in 1887 for Theodore Mander, a member of the well known paint firm. Lived in by Manders ever since, the National Trust has owned it since 1937. There is a grand collection of pre-Raphaelite paintings and artefacts, including much by William Morris – wallpapers, furnishing fabrics and wall hangings – tiles by William de Morgan and stained glass by Kempe.

Harlaxton through the Gate
Harlaxton Manor near Grantham, Lincolnshire, is one of the great monuments of British architecture: big in size, big in scale, big in detail. It has the self-confident swagger of a great Elizabethan house, the grandeur and conviction of a Vanbrugh palace, but its final effect is wholly original. Built for a rich bachelor named Gregory, 1831-8, its architect was Anthony Salvin (joined later by William Burn). Recent research has shown that a year or so before the vast staircase inside was designed Salvin made a tour to look at south German Baroque. The house is a splendid adornment to the gently undulating south Lincolnshire landscape. It is now the European campus of Evansville University.

Milton Ernest Hall
Milton Ernest Hall near Bedford is the domestic masterpiece of William Butterfield, and was built for his brother in 1854-8 (it is said to have nearly ruined him). Beautifully thought out, to the last detail, with much use of varied marbles and metal work, it stands beside the slow Bedfordshire Ouse, and is now a comfortable Hotel. Original drawings for it by Butterfield hang in the hotel bar.

Shadwell Park
Shadwell Park near Thetford, Norfolk, is a private house in the possession of the Musker family, who have owned it since the end of the nineteenth century. A large addition to the east side, or entrance front, was made by S.S. Teulon in 1855-6 to a house by Edward Blore which had been built twenty years earlier. The wild, fantastic skyline of the Teulon addition, the Gothic and castellated details, the elaborate patterning of walls in dark Norfolk flint framed in pale stone are all fruits of that mid-nineteenth-century romanticism in building and decoration that followed the Great Exhibition of 1851.

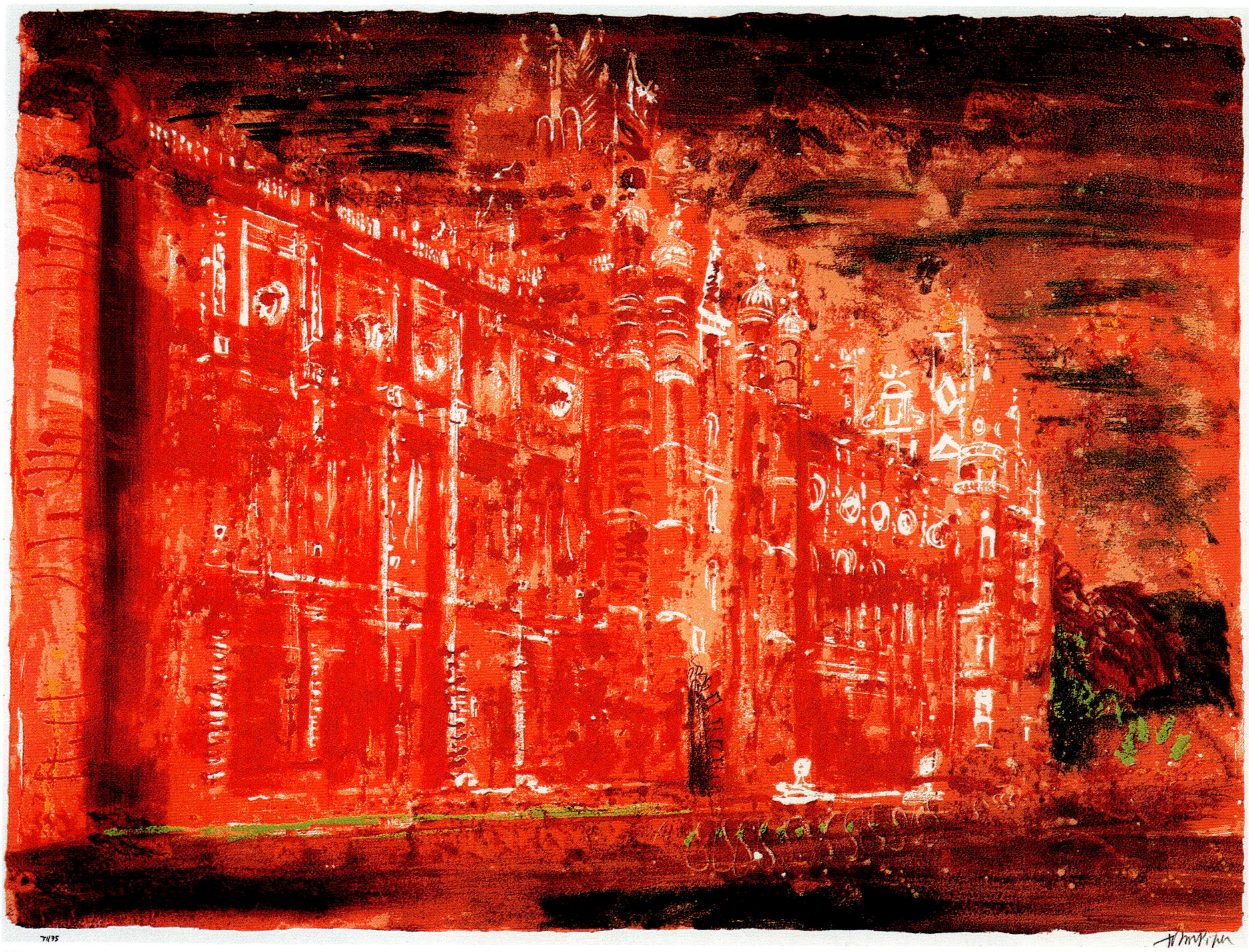

272

Kelham Hall
Kelham Hall, beside the Trent outside Newark, was built as a private house after a fire had destroyed its predecessor in 1857. It was commissioned by the Manners-Sutton family from George Gilbert Scott. The red brick with sandstone dressings, the hard Gothic mouldings, the clock tower with a spire above – a close relation of that at St Pancras – are all Scott signature tunes. 'The amazing silhouette', as Mark Girouard says, 'enriches the view for miles around'. The house had its own gas works, which also supplied the village. It became a Theological College early in this century, and is now the headquarters of the Nottinghamshire County Council.

Flintham Hall
Flintham Hall, Nottinghamshire, was a large Georgian house which was reconditioned as a classical Dream Palace for the Hildyard family in the early eighteen fifties. The architect was T. C. Hine of Nottingham, and the new work included a tall entrance tower, windows of an imaginative design and a big glass and iron conservatory in Crystal Palace style, with a Romeo and Juliet balcony of stone looking into it from a gallery in the splendid library.

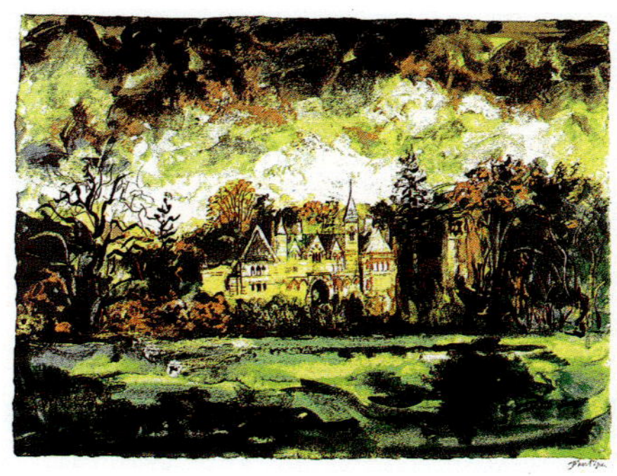

273

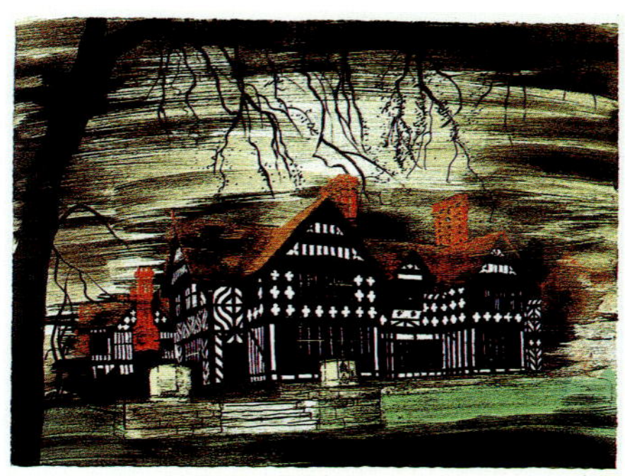

274

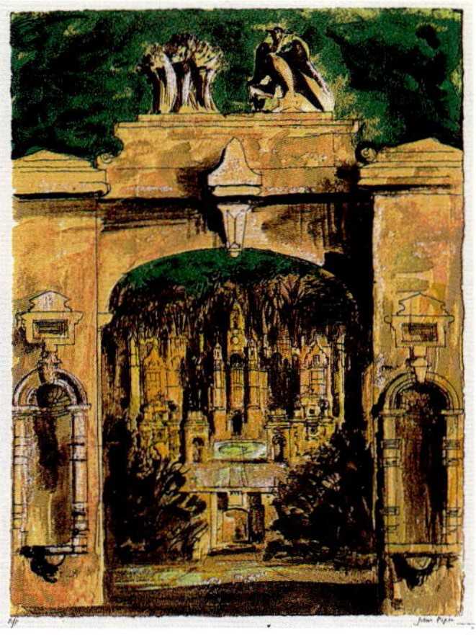

275

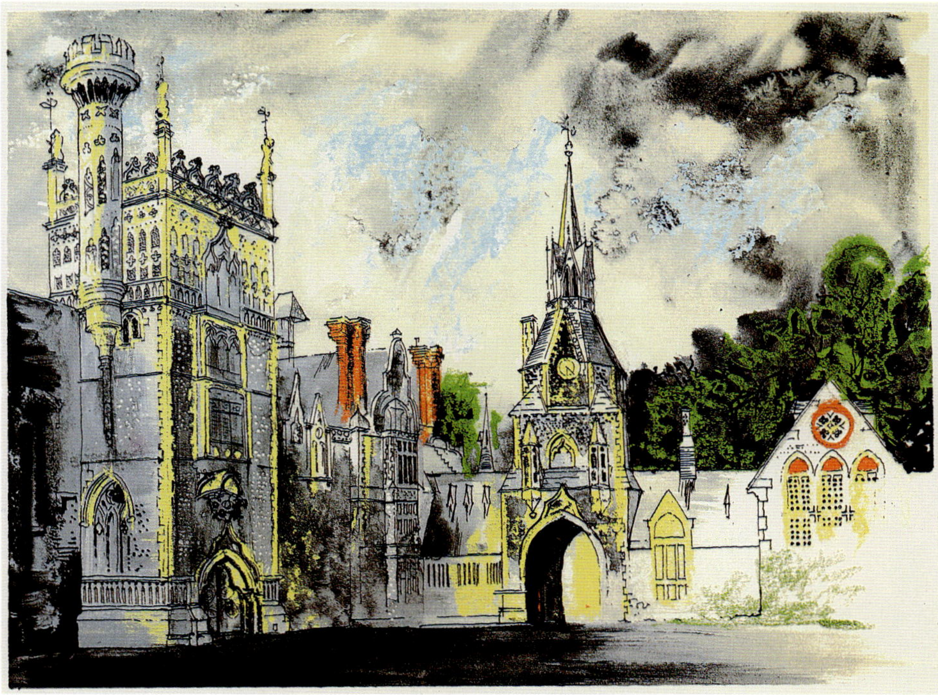

277

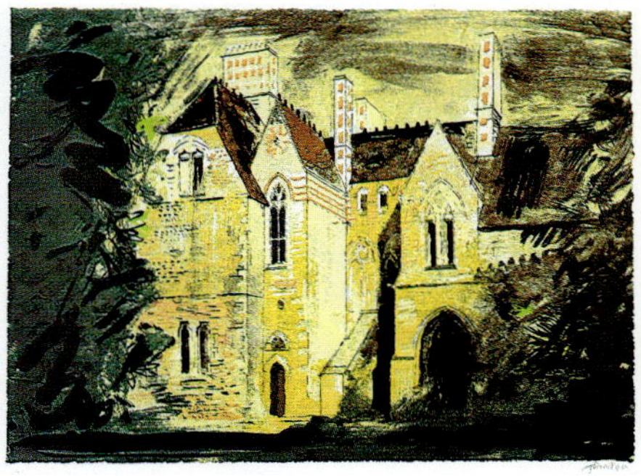

276

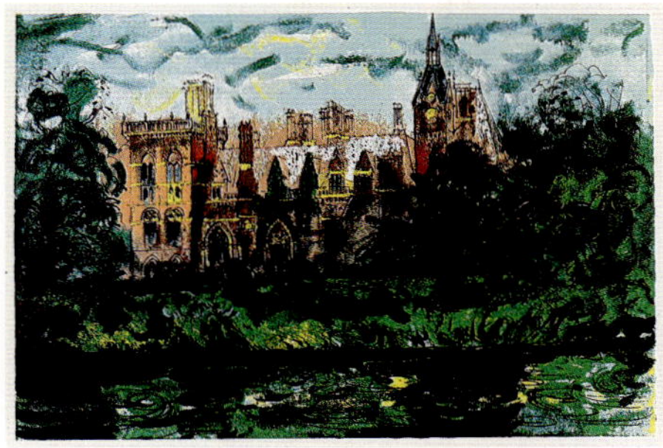

278

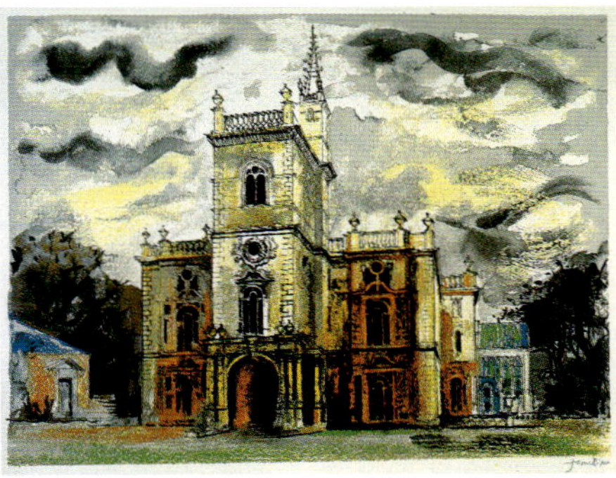

279

272
The Royal Holloway College
Plate I
529 × 700 (20$\frac{13}{16}$ × 27$\frac{9}{16}$)

Printer's stamp and no.'8342' on reverse

273
Ettington Park
Plate II
521 × 698 (20$\frac{1}{2}$ × 27$\frac{1}{2}$)

Printer's stamp and no.'8343' on reverse

274
Wightwick Manor
Plate III
522 × 702 (20$\frac{9}{16}$ × 27$\frac{5}{8}$)

Printer's stamp and no.'8345' on reverse

275
Harlaxton through the Gate
Plate IV
711 × 530 (28 × 20$\frac{7}{8}$)

Sometimes incorrectly known as '*Harlaxton Manor*'. Printer's stamp and no.'8344' on reverse

276
Milton Ernest Hall
Plate V
508 × 695 (20 × 27$\frac{3}{8}$)

Printer's stamp and no.'8347' on reverse

277
Shadwell Park
Plate VI
512 × 697 (20$\frac{3}{16}$ × 27$\frac{7}{16}$)

Printer's stamp and no.'8348' on reverse

278
Kelham Hall
Plate VII
467 × 694 (18$\frac{3}{8}$ × 27$\frac{5}{16}$)

Sometimes incorrectly known as '*Kelham*'. Printer's stamp and no.'8351' on reverse

279
Flintham Hall
Plate VIII
521 × 699 (20$\frac{1}{2}$ × 27$\frac{1}{2}$)

Sometimes incorrectly known as '*Flintham*'. Printer's stamp and no.'8350' on reverse

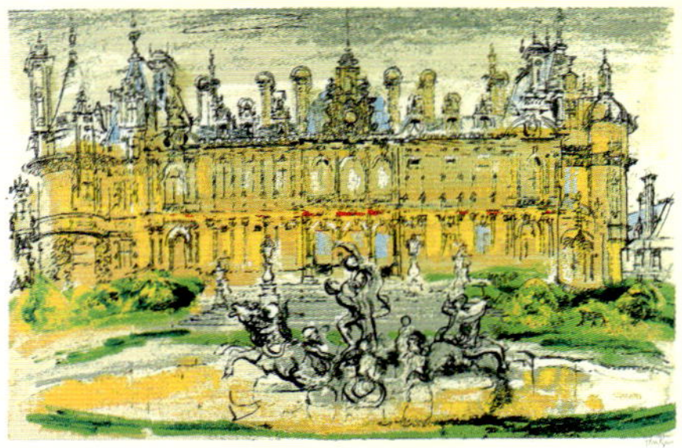

280

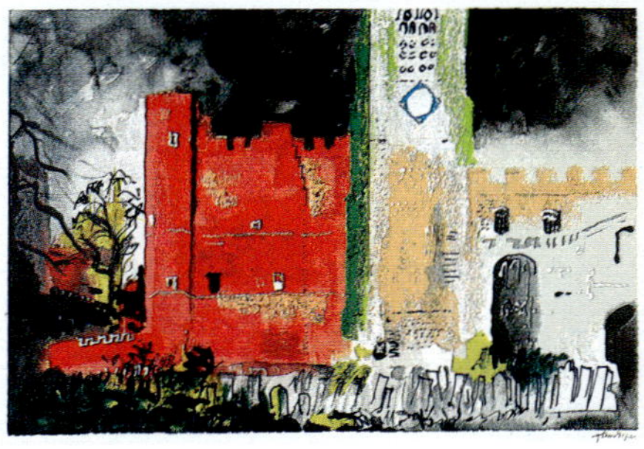

281

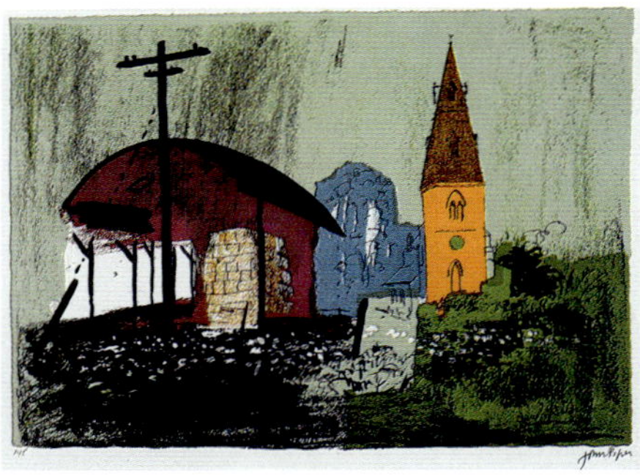

282

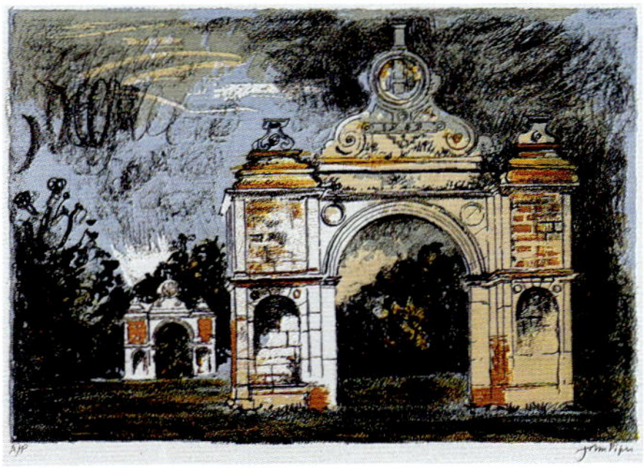

283

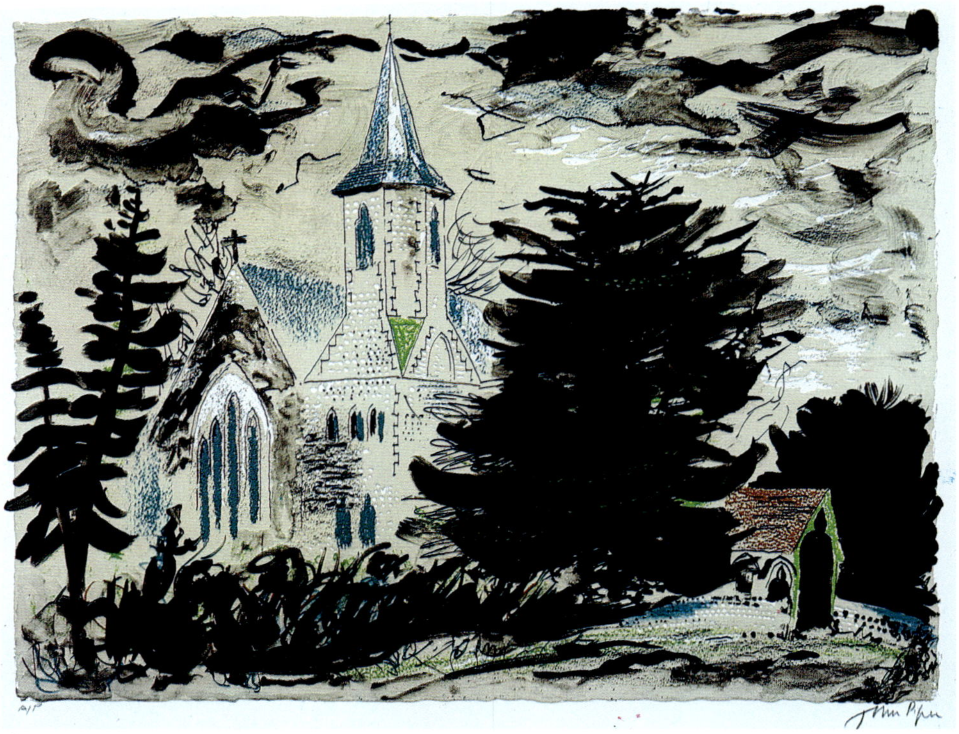

284

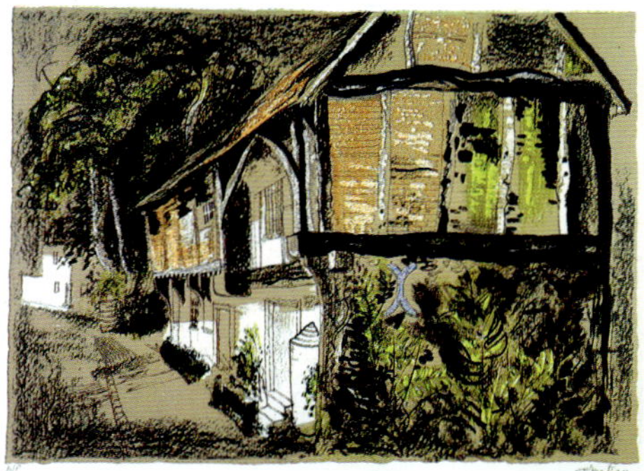

285

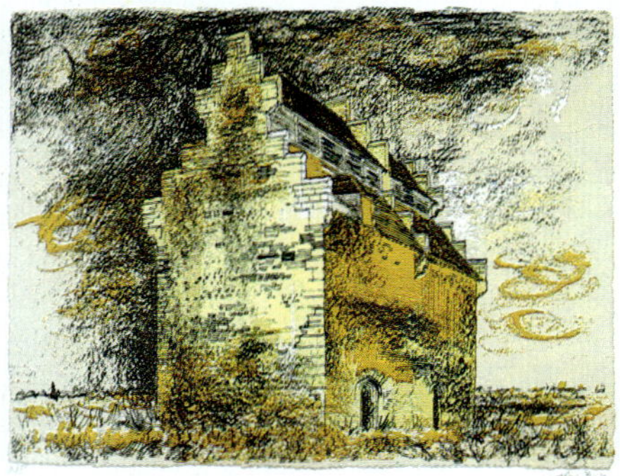

286

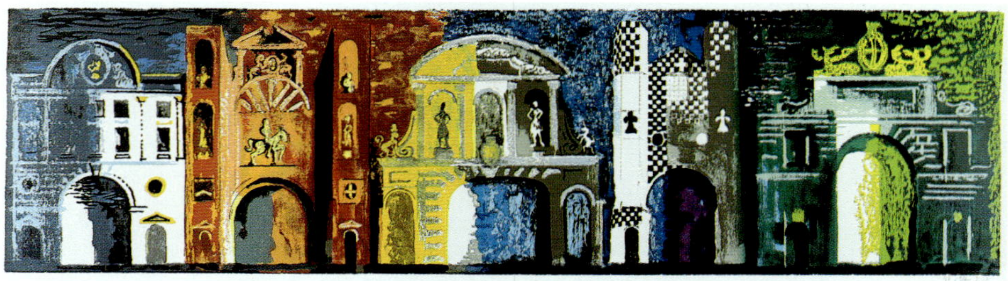

287

280
Waddesdon
Screenprint 640 × 986 ($25\frac{3}{16} \times 38\frac{3}{4}$)
Kelpra Studio 1977
Marlborough Fine Art 1977
Vélin Arches 300gsm 740 × 1070 ($29\frac{1}{8} \times 42\frac{1}{8}$)
75 'John Piper' 10AP 5HC 5PP

Sometimes incorrectly known as '*Waddesdon Manor, near Aylesbury*'. Printer's stamp and no.'8349' on reverse

Tate Gallery

281 (detail Plate 6)
Buckden in a Storm
Screenprint 576 × 847 ($22\frac{5}{8} \times 33\frac{3}{8}$)
Kelpra Studio 1977
Kelpra Editions 1978
Vélin Arches 300gsm 685 × 942 ($27 \times 37\frac{1}{16}$)
100 'John Piper' 10AP 5HC 5PP

Printer's stamp and no.'8383' on reverse

Tate Gallery

282
Seaton
Lithograph 423 × 599 (16⅝ × 23$\frac{9}{16}$)
Curwen Studio 1978
Orde Levinson 1978
T. H. Saunders 285gsm 570 × 774 (22$\frac{7}{16}$ × 30½)
75 'John Piper' 10AP 5PP

Publisher's blind stamp b.l.

Tate Gallery

283
Holdenby
Lithograph 422 × 603 (16⅝ × 23¾)
Curwen Studio 1978
Orde Levinson 1978
T. H. Saunders 285gsm 570 × 774 (22$\frac{7}{16}$ × 30½)
75 'John Piper' 10AP 5PP

Publisher's blind stamp b.l.

Tate Gallery

284
High Cross, Hampshire
Lithograph 412 × 550 (16¼ × 21⅝)
Curwen Studio 1978
Orde Levinson 1978
T. H. Saunders 285gsm 570 × 774 (22$\frac{7}{16}$ × 30½)
75 'John Piper' 10AP 5PP

Sometimes incorrectly known as *'High Cross'*. Publisher's blind stamp b.l.

Tate Gallery

285
Courthouse, Long Crendon, Buckinghamshire
Lithograph 422 × 580 (16½ × 22¾)
Curwen Studio 1978
Christie's Contemporary Art and The National Trust 1978
T. H. Saunders waterleaf 573 × 773 (22½ × 30½)
120 'John Piper' 12AP 2PP

Sometimes incorrectly known as '*The Courthouse*' or '*Courthouse, Long Crendon*'

286
Willington Dovecote, Bedfordshire
Lithograph 421 × 556 (16$\frac{9}{16}$ × 21⅞)
Curwen Studio 1978
Christie's Contemporary Art and The National Trust 1978
T. H. Saunders 120lbs 575 × 774 (22⅝ × 30$\frac{7}{16}$)
120 'John Piper' 12AP 2PP

Sometimes incorrectly known as *'Willington Dovecote'*

287
Five Gates of London
Screenprint 425 × 1598 (16$\frac{11}{16}$ × 62⅞)
Kelpra Studio 1978
Sedgwick Forbes 1978
Cuve 300gsm 513 × 1680 (20$\frac{3}{16}$ × 66⅛)
75 'John Piper' 10AP 5HC 5PP

Sometimes incorrectly known as *'Gates of London'*

Tate Gallery

288-314
Stones and Bones, 1978
A portfolio of twenty-seven screenprints including two end-papers, from a series of 11 unbound sheets folded into 44 pages and presented loose in a marbled half-bound leather folio box which is itself contained in a black slipcase. The 44 pages include 7 blank, a title-page, a contents page (signed and numbered by the artist) and two front end-page images – none of these 11 pages being paginated. Twenty-five images (of which some are diptychs and some cover a double page) occupy the remaining 33 pages, the majority of which are paginated. Some of these images are signed. In each case such details are listed according to the copy in the editor's possession, but these may not be applicable to other copies of the portfolio. The portfolio was screenprinted by Kelpra Studio and published by Kelpra Editions in 1978 in an edition of 50 with 10AP and 5PP. The type of paper used was 'Vélin Arches' 250gsm The paper size of all 11 pages is 505 × 700 (19⅞ × 27$\frac{9}{16}$). Certain images contain notes by the artist and quotations (from *The Old Glaciers of Switzerland and North Wales (1860)* by A. C. Ramsay FRS) all handwritten by the artist and printed as part of the plates – the image size given always includes these comments. *Stones and Bones* forms part of a series of unbound portfolios published by Kelpra Editions (other artists in the series are: Ian Tyson [1976], Joe Tilson [1976], Allen Jones [1977], Victor Pasmore [1977], Patrick Heron [1978], Gerd Winner [1978] and Gordon House [1978]).

The artist and publisher consider it a portfolio (although the contents page refers to the portfolio as a book) in which collectors can interchange the prints, displaying whichever they feel is appropriate to their mood.

Tate Gallery

288
Stones and Bones: front end-paper left
505 × 350 (19⅞ × 13¾)

289
Stones and Bones: front end-paper right
505 × 350 (19⅞ × 13¾)

This and the preceding image form a double-spread front end-paper.

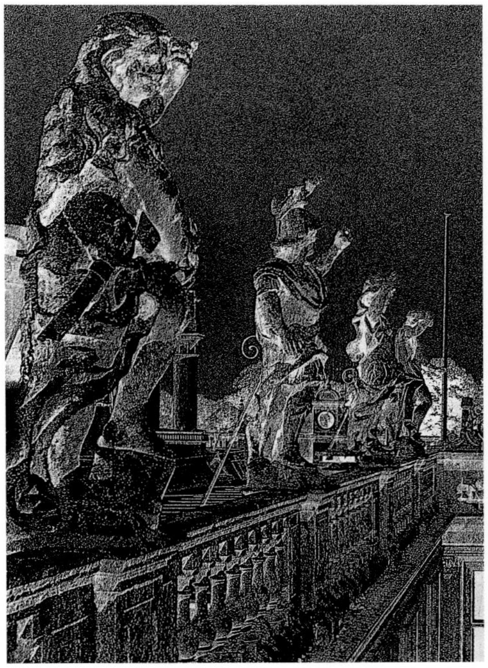
288

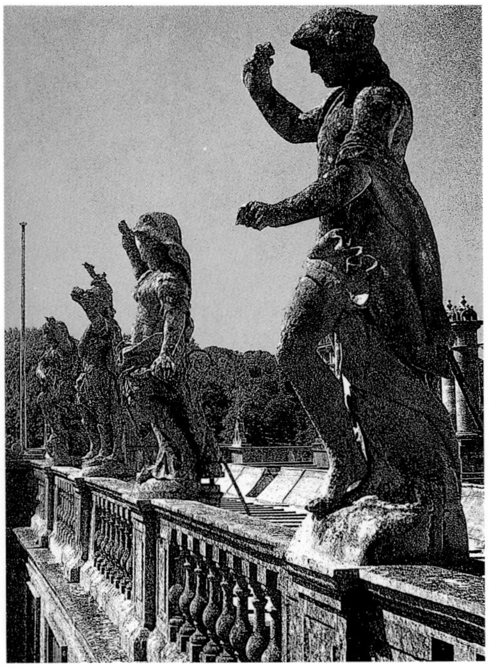
289

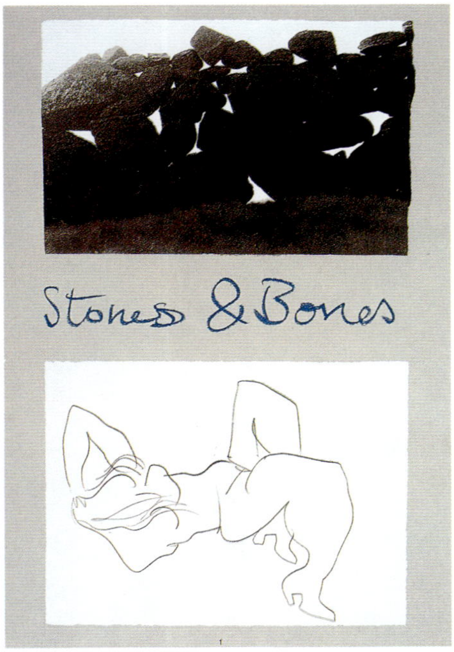

290

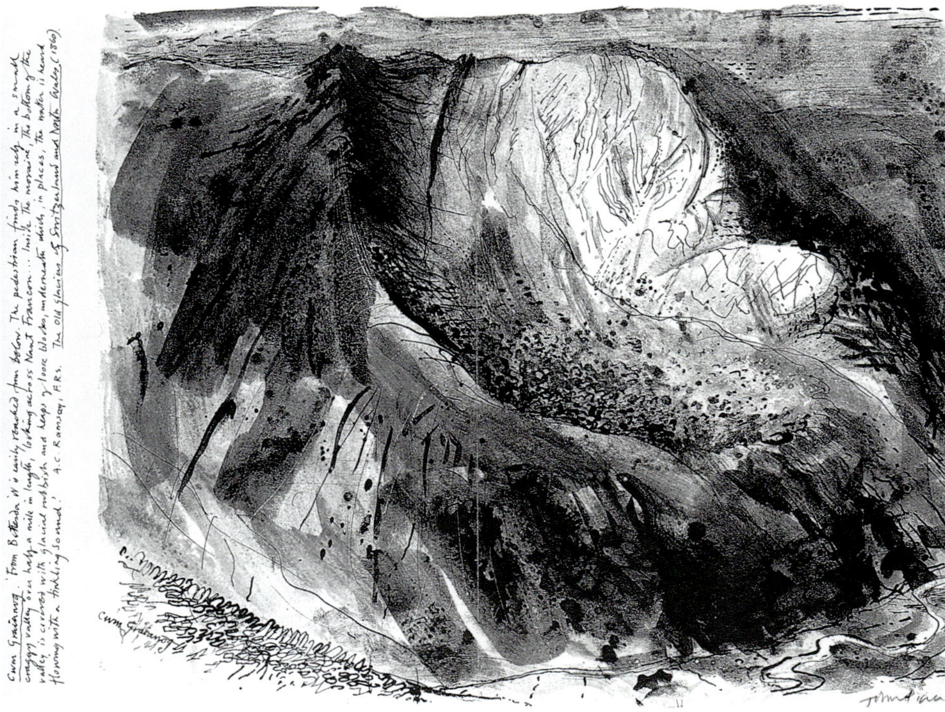

291

290
Stones and Bones I
460 × 273 ($18\frac{1}{8} \times 10\frac{3}{4}$)

A diptych, the two parts of which are separated by the title *Stones and Bones*. '1' printed b.c.

291
Stones and Bones II
505 × 684 ($19\frac{7}{8} \times 26\frac{15}{16}$)

Double-page spread, signed 'John Piper' . In the artist's hand are printed 'Cwm Graianog' b.l. and a Ramsay quotation printed left side: 'From Bethesda it is easily reached from below. The pedestrian finds himself in a small craggy valley over half a mile in length, looking across Nant Francon … Inside the moraine, the bottom of the valley is covered with glacial rubbish and heaps of loose blocks, underneath which, in places, the water is heard flowing with a tinkling sound.' Sometimes incorrectly known as '*Cwm Graianog Nant Ffrancon*'. Repr. in Elborn (p.69) and in *Kelpra Studio* (p.90)

292
Stones and Bones III
444 × 350 ($17\frac{1}{2} \times 13\frac{3}{4}$)

'4' printed b.c.
In the artist's hand b.l. is printed 'Groes Gosh Nant Ffrancon'

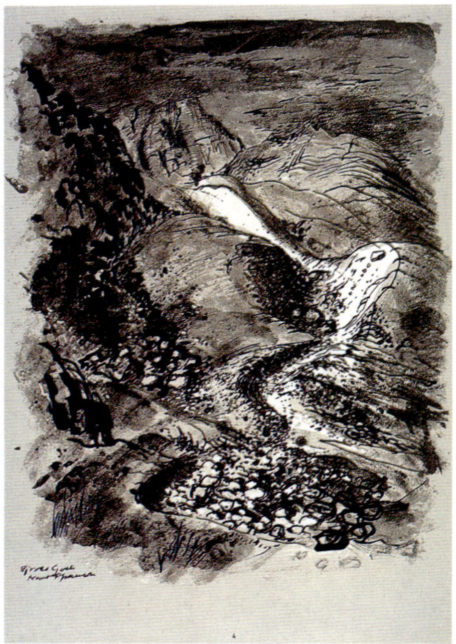

292

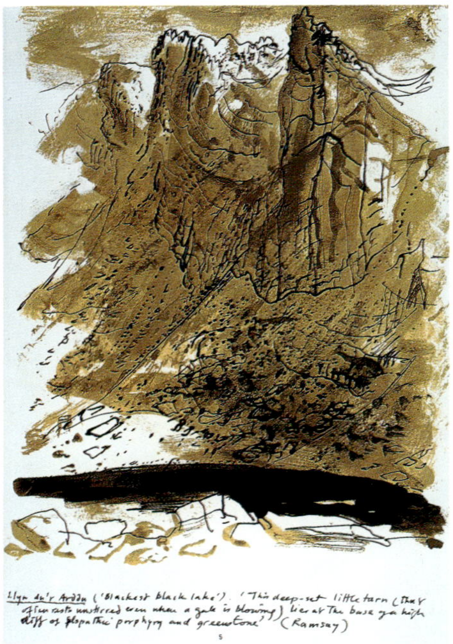

293

293
Stones and Bones IV
489 × 350 ($19\frac{1}{4} \times 13\frac{3}{4}$)

'5' printed b.c. In the artist's hand b.c. are printed 'Llyn du'r Arddu' ('Blackest black lake') and a Ramsay quotation: 'This deepset little tarn (that often rests unstirred even when a gale is blowing) lies at the base of a high cliff of felspathic porphyry and greenstone.' The title and English translation are not part of the Ramsay quotation.

294
Stones and Bones V
505 × 680 ($19\frac{7}{8} \times 26\frac{3}{4}$)

Double-page spread, signed 'John Piper' . In the artist's hand b.l. is printed a note by the artist: 'In Snowdonia, the shape and tilt of the big rocks near at hand often echoes the shape and tilt of distant mountains.'

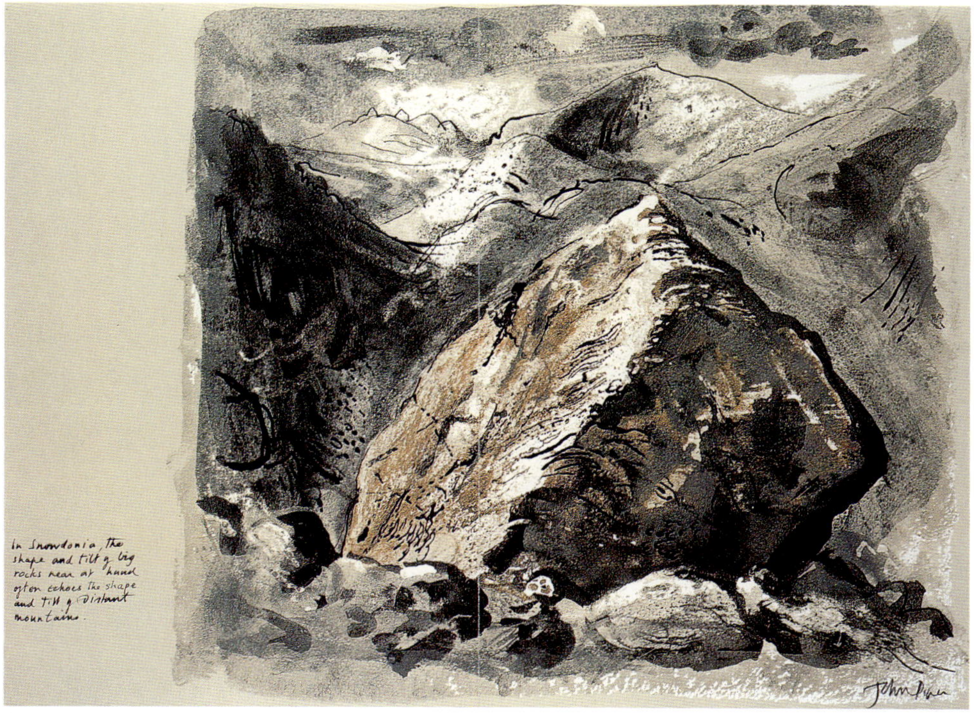

294

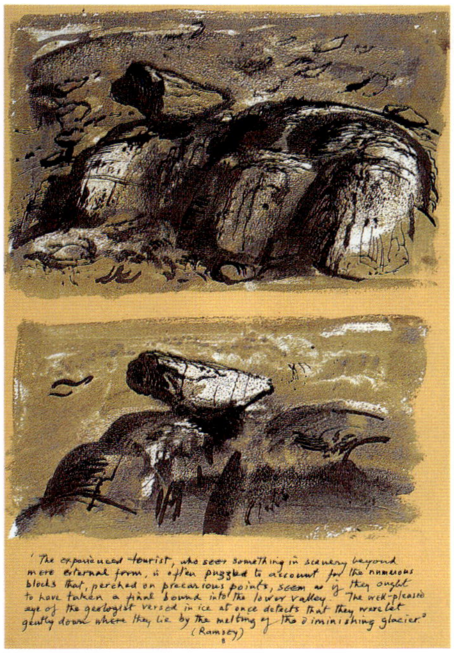

295

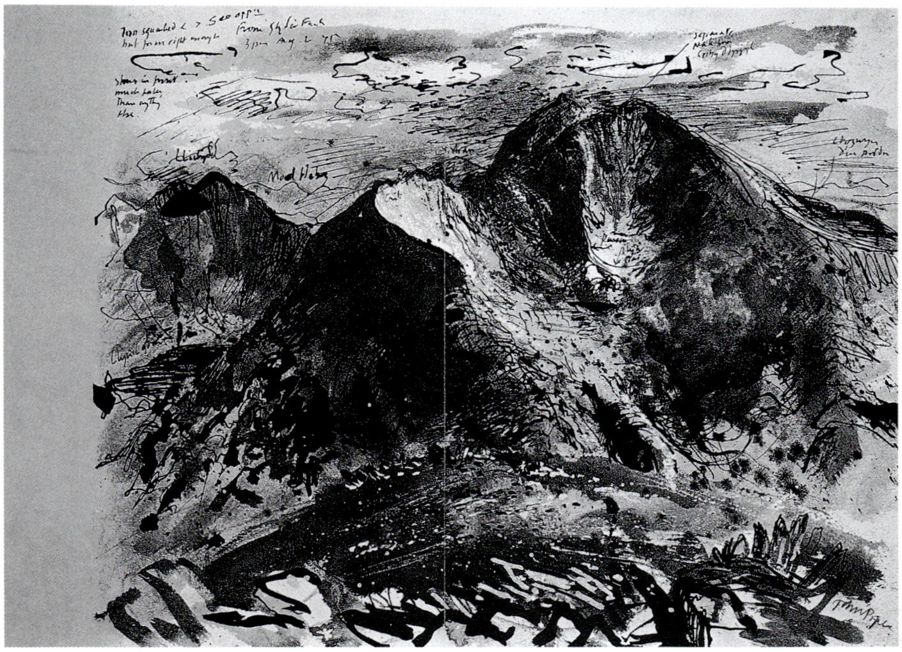

297

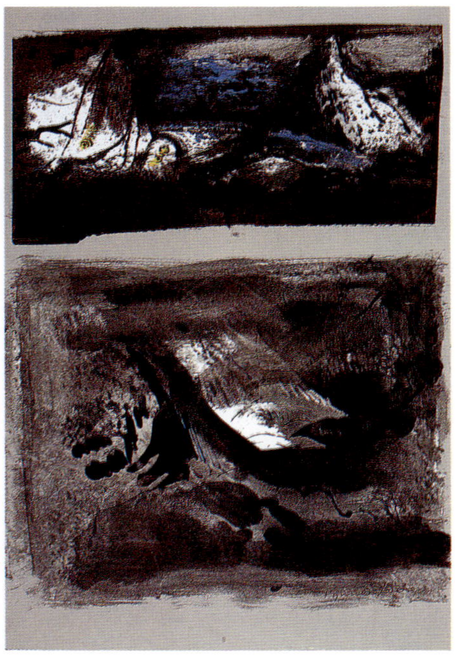

296

295
Stones and Bones VI
(diptych) 489×343 (19¼×13½)

In the artist's hand printed bottom is a Ramsay quotation: 'The experienced tourist, who sees something in scenery beyond mere external form, is often puzzled to account for the numerous blocks that, perched on precarious points, seem as if they ought to have taken a final bound into the lower valley. The well-pleased eye of the geologist versed in ice at once detects that they were let gently down where they lie by the melting of the diminishing glacier.' '8' printed b.c.

Sometimes incorrectly known as '*Rocks in Nant Ffrancon, North Wales*'. Repr. in black-and-white in Ingrams/Piper (plate 86)

296
Stones and Bones VII
(diptych) 454×350 (17⅞×13¾)

In the artist's hand b.r. is printed 'Fynnon Loer'. '9' printed b.c.

297
Stones and Bones VIII
505×622 (19⅞×24½)
Double-page spread, signed 'John Piper' . In the artist's hand printed in various positions over the entire image are notes and names written in telegraphic style.

Sometimes incorrectly known as '*Snowdon from the Glyders*'. Repr. in Elborn (p.70)

298
Stones and Bones IX
(diptych) 373 × 350 ($14\frac{11}{16} \times 13\frac{3}{4}$)

'12' printed b.c.

299
Stones and Bones X
(diptych) 467 × 327 ($18\frac{3}{8} \times 12\frac{7}{8}$)

'13' printed b.c.

300
Stones and Bones XI
505 × 700 ($19\frac{7}{8} \times 27\frac{9}{16}$)

Double-page spread, signed 'John Piper'. In the artist's hand b.l. is printed 'Moors of Cornwall: Kilman Tor beyond Trewartha Tor'.

301
Stones and Bones XII
480 × 350 ($18\frac{7}{8} \times 13\frac{3}{4}$)

In the artist's hand b.l. is printed 'Cheesewring'. '16' printed b.c.

302
Stones and Bones XIII
438 × 260 ($17\frac{1}{4} \times 10\frac{1}{4}$)

In the artist's hand b.l. is printed 'Men an tol'. '17' printed b.c.

303
Stones and Bones XIV
463 × 667 ($18\frac{1}{4} \times 26\frac{1}{4}$)

Double-page spread, signed 'John Piper'. In the artist's hand b.l. is printed 'Connemara'.

304
Stones and Bones XV
350 × 505 ($13\frac{3}{4} \times 19\frac{7}{8}$)

'20' printed bottom left, facing left

Sometimes incorrectly known as '*Dolmen near Login, Carmarthenshire 1977*'. Cats 304 and 305 are repr. (incorrectly, as one screenprint, with this image placed below Cat.305) in Ingrams/Piper (plate 126)

305
Stones and Bones XVI
350 × 505 ($13\frac{3}{4} \times 19\frac{7}{8}$)

'21' printed b.l., facing left

Sometimes incorrectly known as '*Dolmen near Login, Carmarthenshire 1977*'. Cats 304 and 305 are repr. (incorrectly, as one screenprint, with this image placed above Cat.304) in Ingrams/Piper (plate 126)

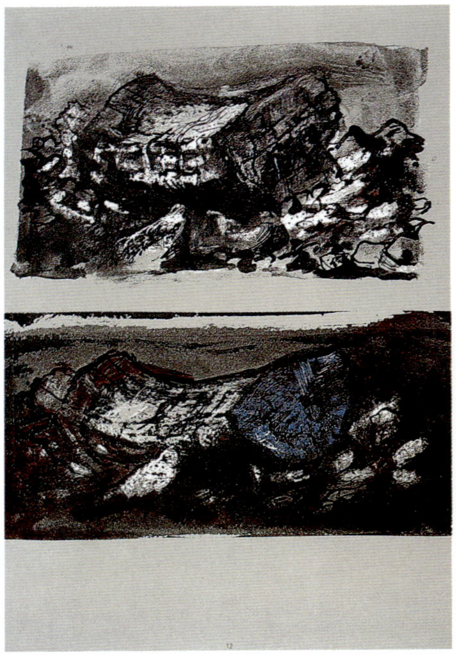

298

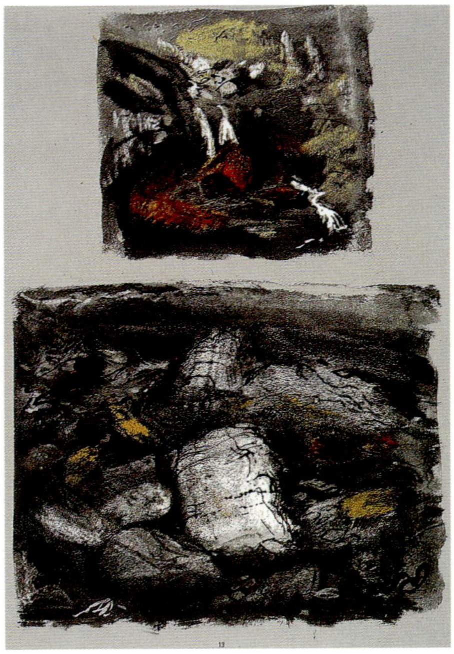

299

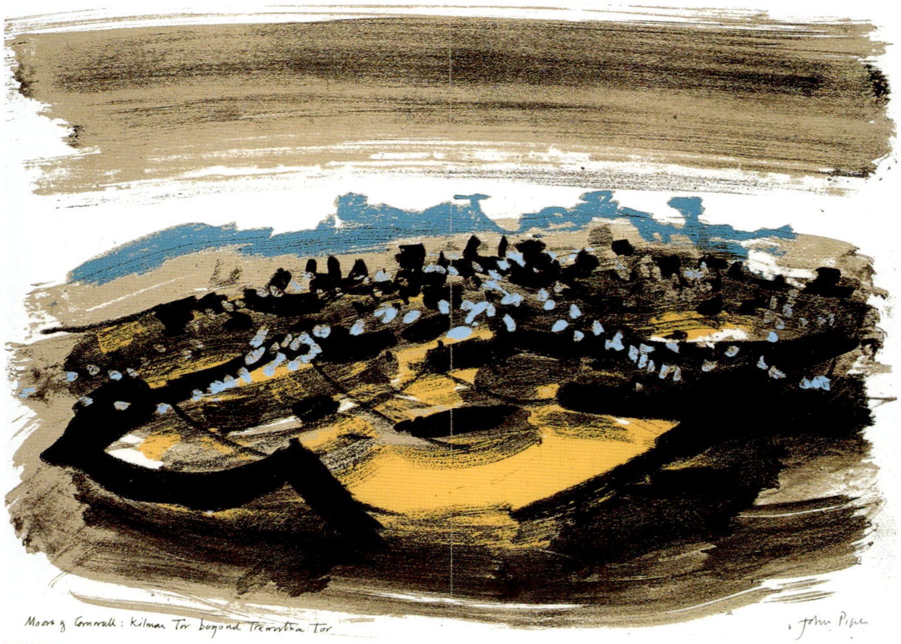

300

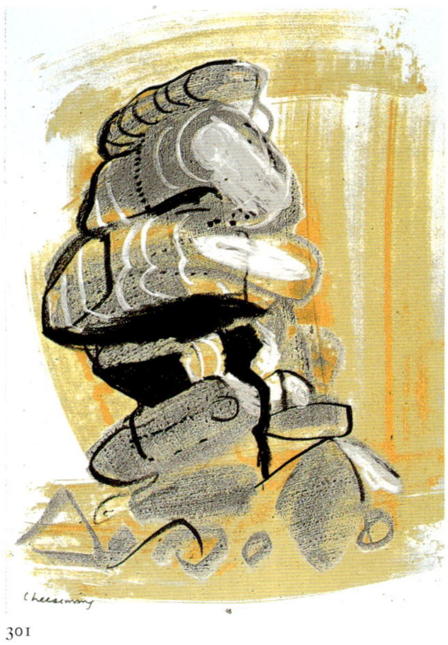

301

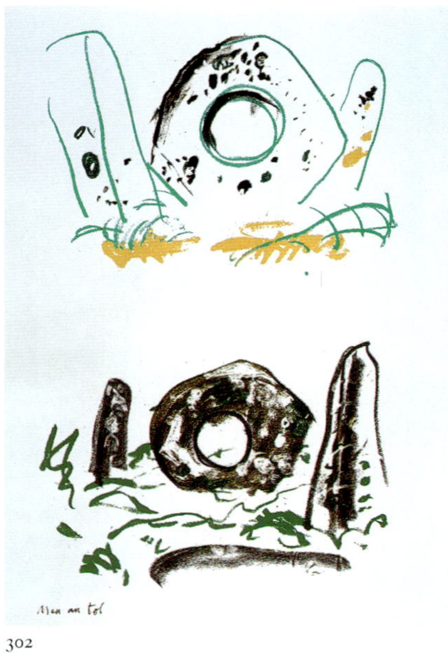

302

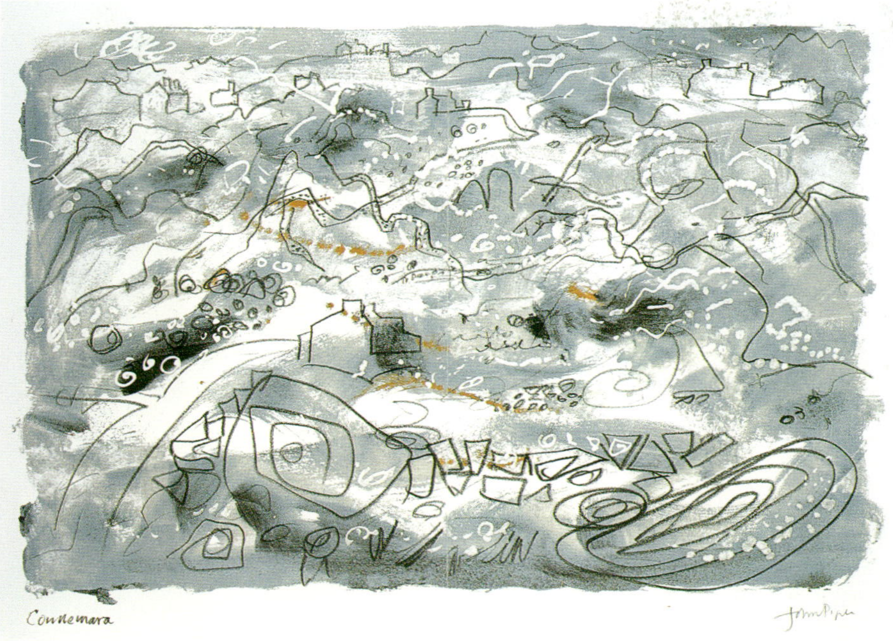

303

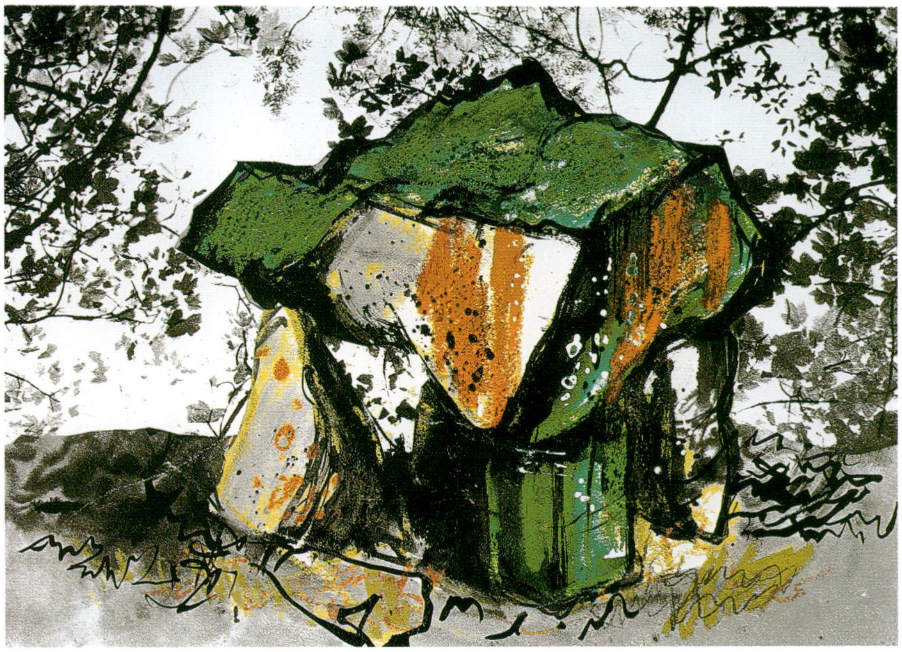

304

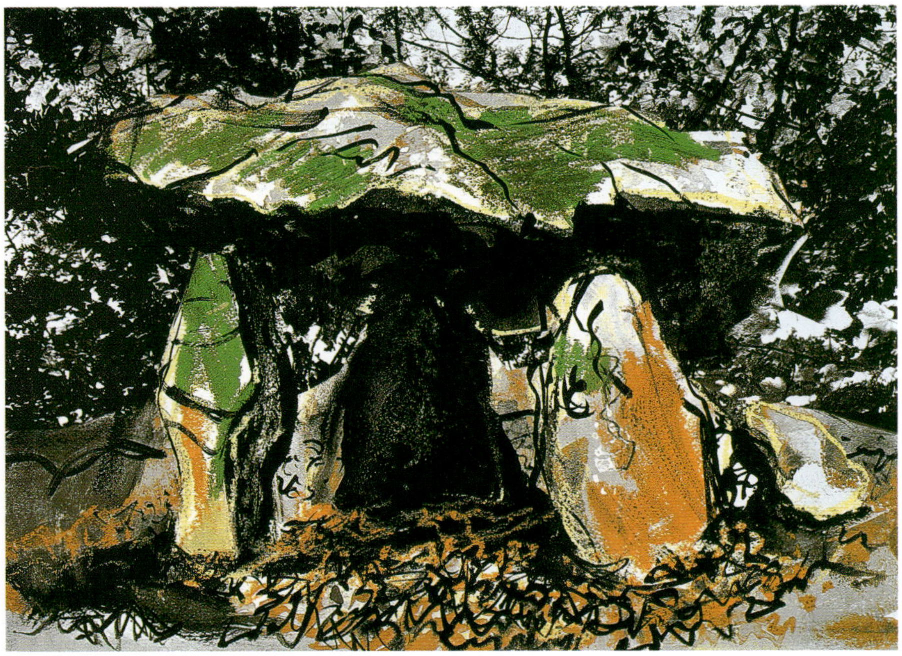

305

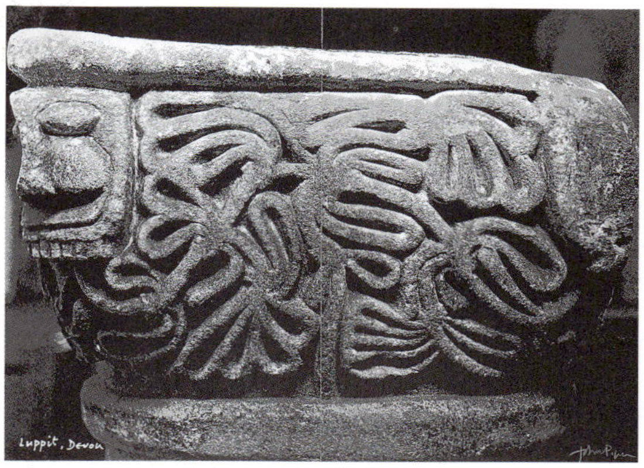

306

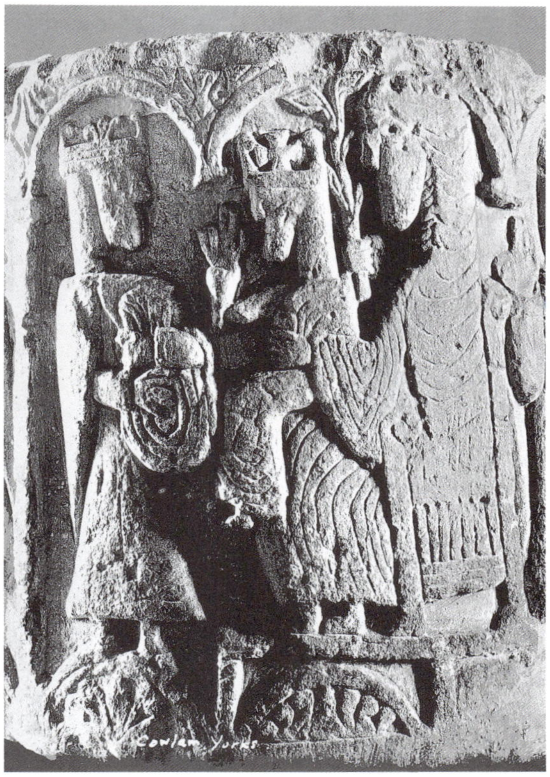

307

306
Stones and Bones XVII
505 × 700 (19⅞ × 27 9/16)

In the artist's hand b.l. is printed 'Luppit, Devon'. Double-page spread, signed 'John Piper' in yellow crayon b.r.

307
Stones and Bones XVIII
505 × 350 (19⅞ × 13¾)

In the artist's hand b.l. is printed 'Cowlam, Yorks'. '24' printed b.c.

308
Stones and Bones XIX
505×350 (19⅞×13¾)

In the artist's hand b.l. is printed 'Toller Fratrum, Dorset'. '25' printed t.l.

Sometimes incorrectly known as '*Detail of the font, Toller Fratrum, Dorset*'. Repr. in Ingrams/Piper (plate 25)

309 (detail Plate 2)
Stones and Bones XX
505×700 (19⅞×27$^{9}/_{16}$)

In the artist's hand b.r. is printed 'Boxted, Suffolk'. Double-page spread, signed 'John Piper' in black crayon b.r.

310
Stones and Bones XXI
505×286 (19⅞×11¼)

'28' printed b.r.

311
Stones and Bones XXII
505×350 (19⅞×13¾)

'29' printed b.r.

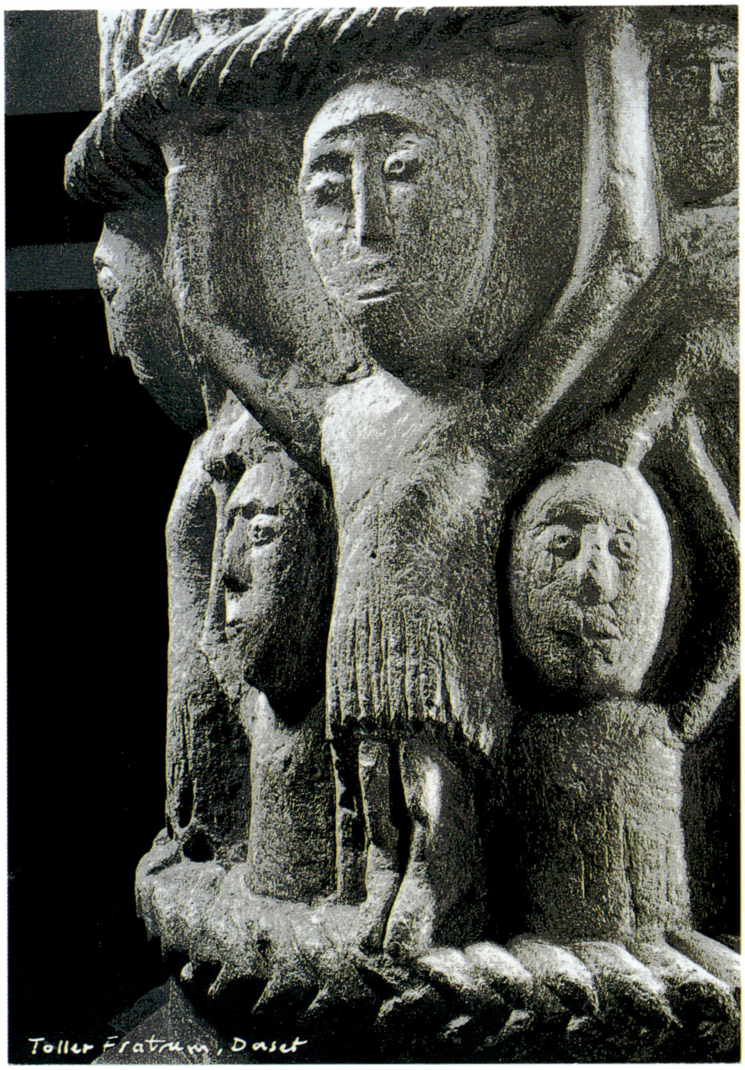

308

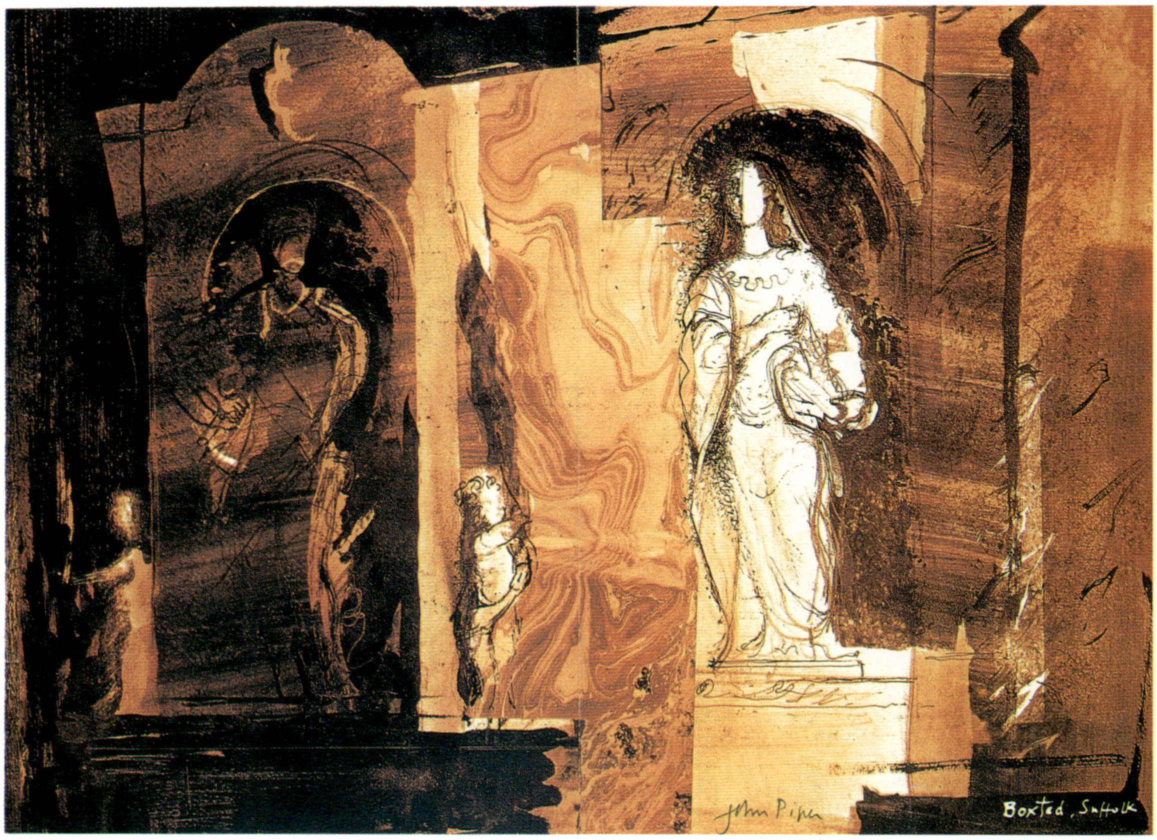

309

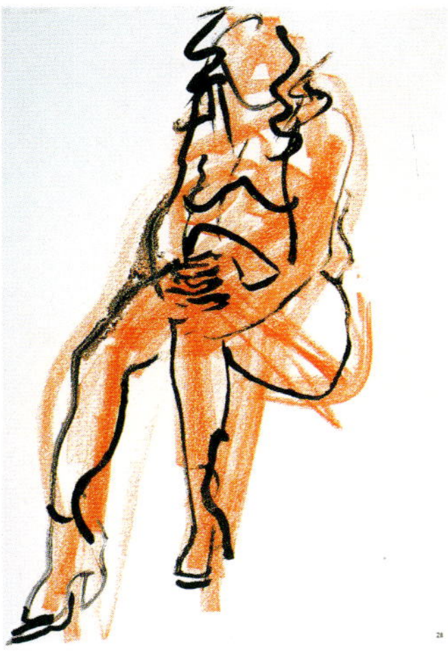

310

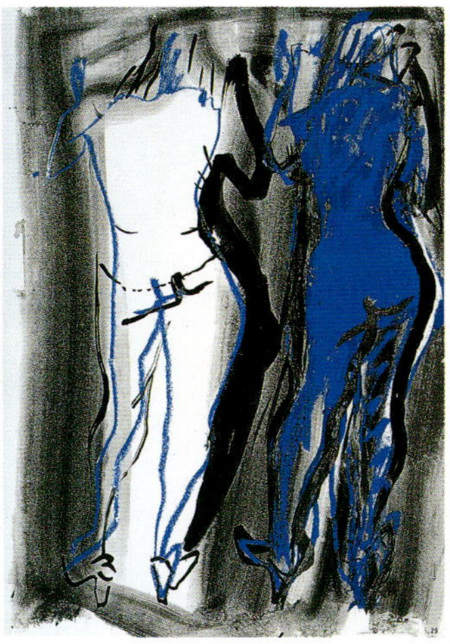

311

312
Stones and Bones XXIII
505 × 700 ($19\frac{7}{8} \times 27\frac{9}{16}$)

Double-page spread, signed 'John Piper' in pencil b.r.

313
Stones and Bones XXIV
350 × 505 ($13\frac{3}{4} \times 19\frac{7}{8}$)

'32' printed t.l., facing left

314
Stones and Bones XXV
489 × 324 ($19\frac{1}{4} \times 12\frac{3}{4}$)

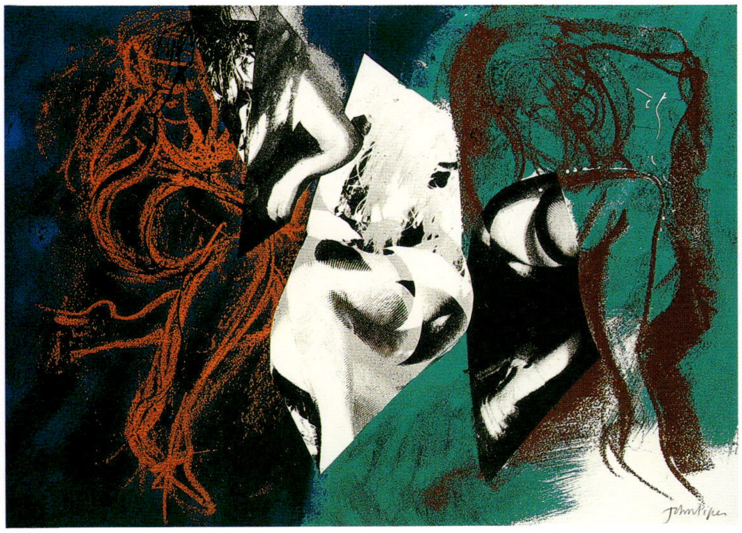

312

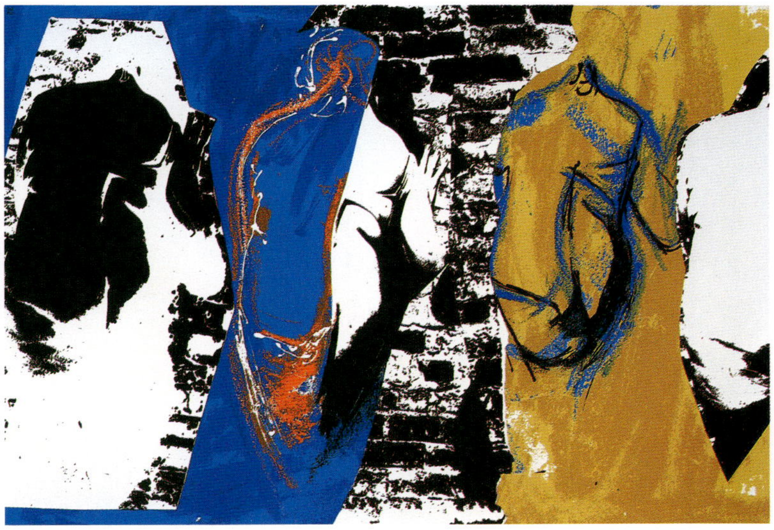

313

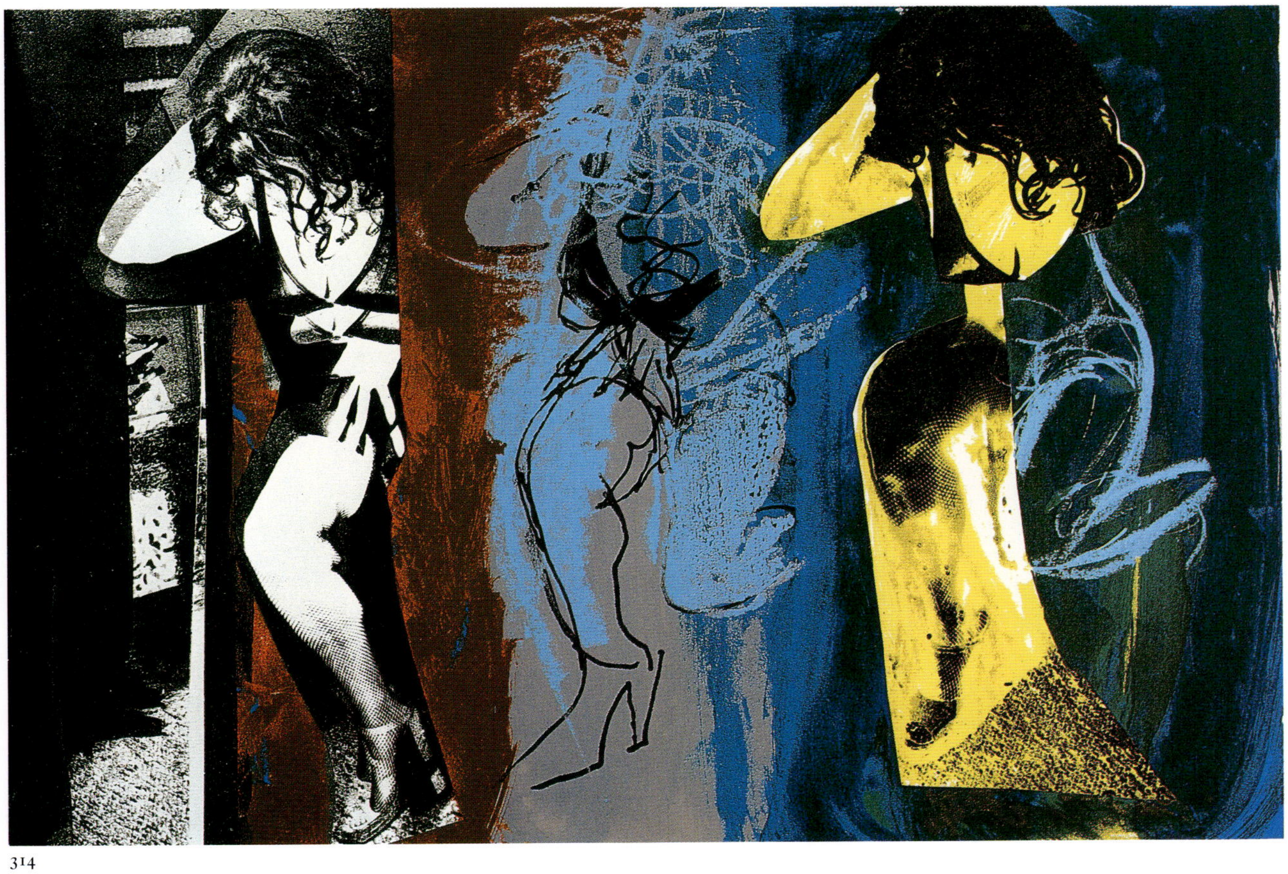

314

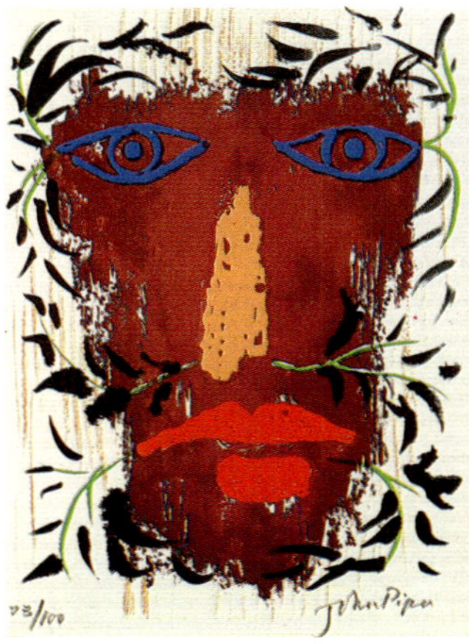

315

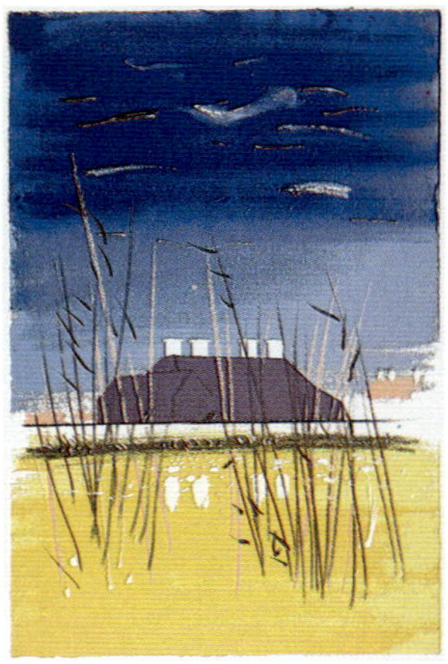

316

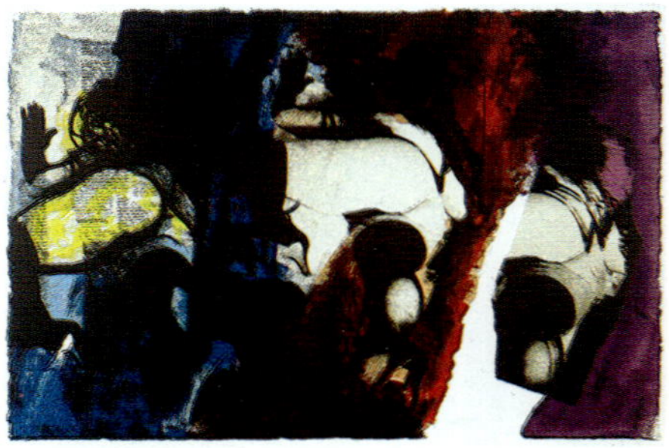

317

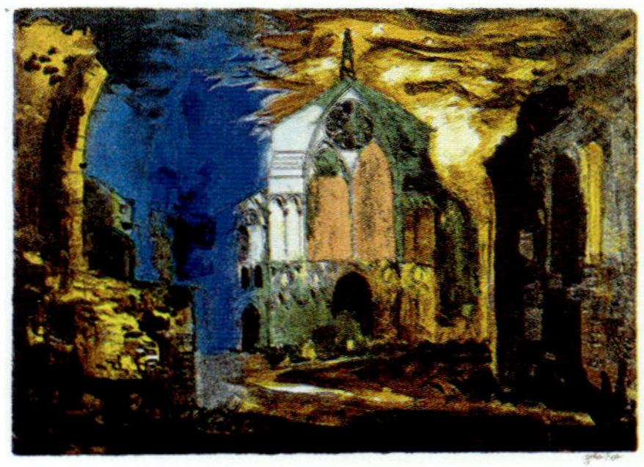

318

315
Foliate Head
Lithograph 248 × 185 ($9\frac{3}{4} \times 7\frac{1}{4}$)
Curwen Studio 1979
Martin Secker and Warburg 1979
T.H. Saunders 120lbs 248 × 185 ($9\frac{3}{4} \times 7\frac{1}{4}$)
100 'John Piper' 26AP (numbered A–Z)

The lithograph was tipped in as a frontispiece to West. The first 100 of an edition of 126 were numbered 1/100–100/100 and the remaining 26 lettered A–Z. Ten copies, numbered I–X, have the lithograph replaced by a watercolour of similar design on the same paper size and weight. In 1983, West was republished by Secker and Warburg with no original lithographs or watercolours.

316
Snape Maltings Concert Hall
Screenprint 766 × 510 ($30\frac{1}{8} \times 20\frac{1}{8}$)
Kelpra Studio 1979
Benson and Hedges 1979
Grand Vélin Arches 300gsm 910 × 642 ($35\frac{7}{8} \times 25\frac{1}{4}$)
150 'John Piper' 10AP 5HC 5PP

The edition of 150 was divided into 100 unsigned and unnumbered posters and 50 signed and numbered graphics. Printer's stamp and no.'8432' on reverse

317
Eye and Camera: Red, Blue and Yellow
Screenprint 400 × 605 ($15\frac{3}{4} \times 23\frac{7}{8}$)
Kelpra Studio 1980
Kelpra Editions and the Tate Gallery 1980
Grand Vélin Arches 300gsm 600 × 750 ($23\frac{5}{8} \times 29\frac{1}{2}$)
150 'John Piper' 15AP 5HC 5PP

Tate Gallery

318
Binham Abbey
Screenprint 552 × 769 ($21\frac{3}{4} \times 30\frac{1}{4}$)
Kelpra Studio 1981
Marlborough Fine Art 1981
Grand Vélin Arches 300gsm 665 × 879 ($26\frac{1}{8} \times 34\frac{5}{8}$)
70 'John Piper' 10AP 5PP

Sometimes incorrectly known as '*Binham Abbey, Norfolk*'. Printer's blind stamp b.r.

Tate Gallery

319
Clytha Castle Triptych
Screenprint 730 × 590 ($28\frac{3}{4} \times 23\frac{1}{4}$)
Kelpra Studio 1981
Marlborough Fine Art 1981
Grand Vélin Arches 300gsm 875 × 724 ($34\frac{1}{2} \times 28\frac{1}{2}$)
70 'John Piper' 10AP 5HC 5PP

Sometimes incorrectly known as '*Clytha Castle*'. Printer's blind stamp b.r.

Tate Gallery

320
East Barsham Manor
Screenprint 550 × 763 ($21\frac{5}{8} \times 30$)
Kelpra Studio 1981
Marlborough Fine Art 1981
Grand Vélin Arches 300gsm 670 × 880 ($26\frac{3}{8} \times 34\frac{5}{8}$)
70 'John Piper' 10AP 5PP

Printer's blind stamp b.r.

321
Stokesay Castle
Screenprint 545 × 770 ($21\frac{1}{2} \times 30\frac{1}{4}$)
Kelpra Studio 1981
Marlborough Fine Art 1981
Grand Vélin Arches 300gsm 655 × 878 ($25\frac{7}{8} \times 34\frac{1}{2}$)
70 'John Piper' 10AP 5HC 5PP

Printer's blind stamp b.r.

Tate Gallery

322
West Walton
Screenprint 556 × 768 ($21\frac{7}{8} \times 30\frac{1}{4}$)
Kelpra Studio 1981
Marlborough Fine Art 1981
Vélin Arches 300gsm 700 × 911 ($27\frac{9}{16} \times 35\frac{13}{16}$)
70 'John Piper' 10AP 5HC 5PP

Sometimes incorrectly known as '*West Walton, Norfolk*'. Printer's blind stamp b.r.

323
Wigmore Abbey Gateway
Screenprint 558 × 792 ($21\frac{15}{16} \times 31\frac{3}{16}$)
Kelpra Studio 1981
Marlborough Fine Art 1981
Grand Vélin Arches 300gsm 666 × 895 ($26\frac{1}{4} \times 35\frac{1}{4}$)
70 'John Piper' 10AP 5HC 5PP

Sometimes incorrectly known as '*Wigmore Abbey*'

324
Wymondham, Norfolk
Screenprint 557 × 766 ($21\frac{7}{8} \times 30\frac{3}{16}$)
Kelpra Studio 1981
Marlborough Fine Art 1981
Grand Vélin Arches 300gsm 702 × 910 ($27\frac{5}{8} \times 35\frac{13}{16}$)
70 'John Piper' 10AP 5HC 5PP

Printer's blind stamp b.r.

Tate Gallery

325
St Helen Hall
Screenprint 584 × 705 ($23 \times 27\frac{3}{4}$)
Kelpra Studio 1981
Marlborough Fine Art 1981
Grand Vélin Arches 300gsm 692 × 804 ($27\frac{1}{4} \times 31\frac{5}{8}$)
70 'John Piper' 10AP 5HC 5PP

Printer's blind stamp b.r.

Tate Gallery

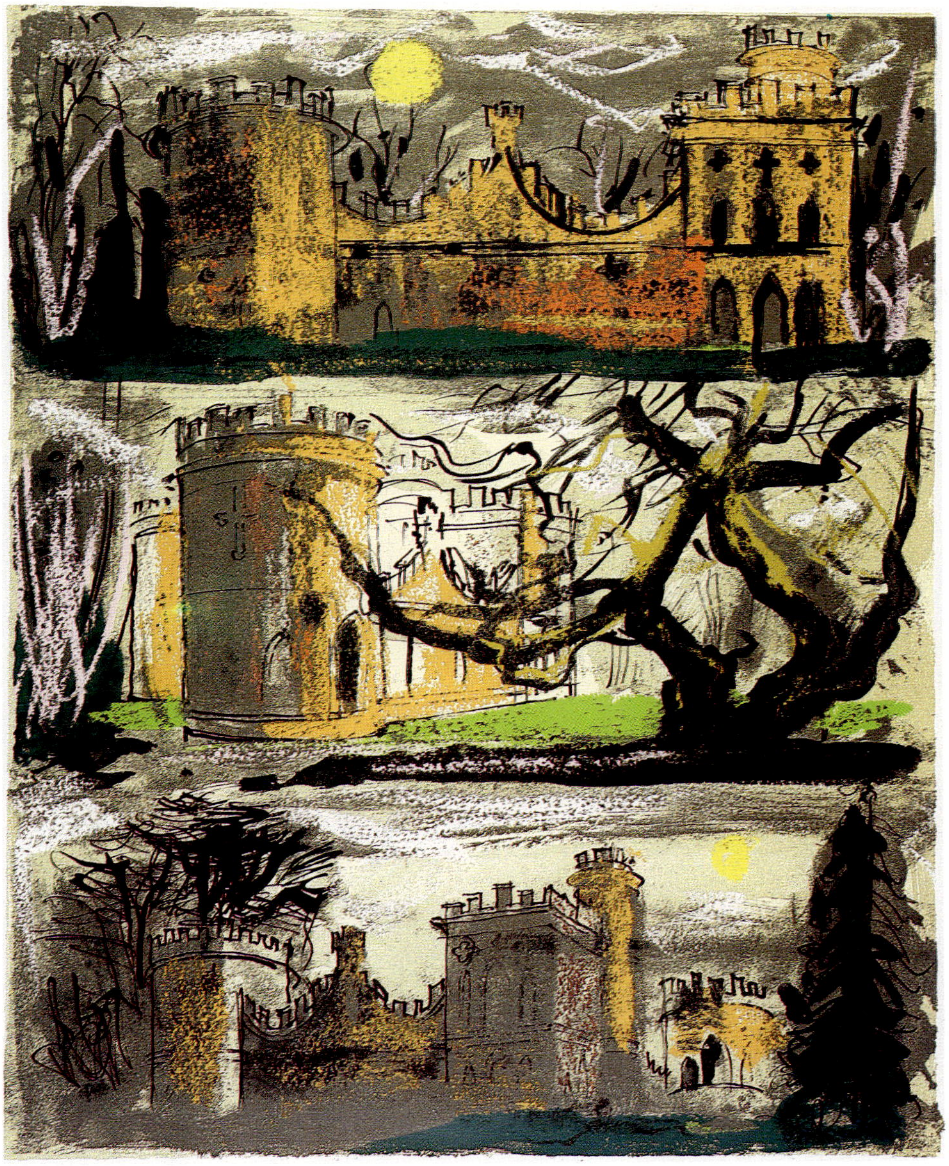

319

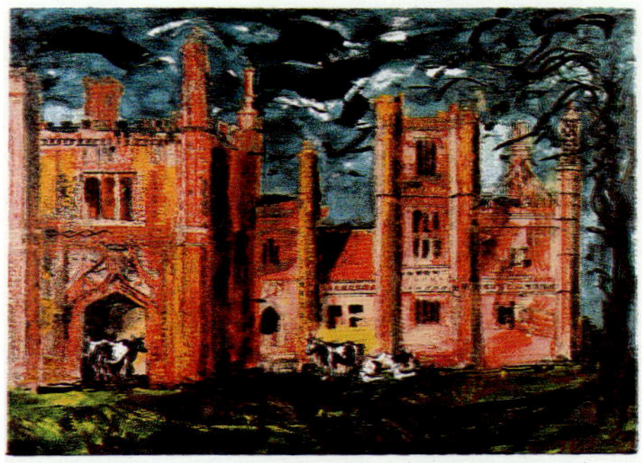

320

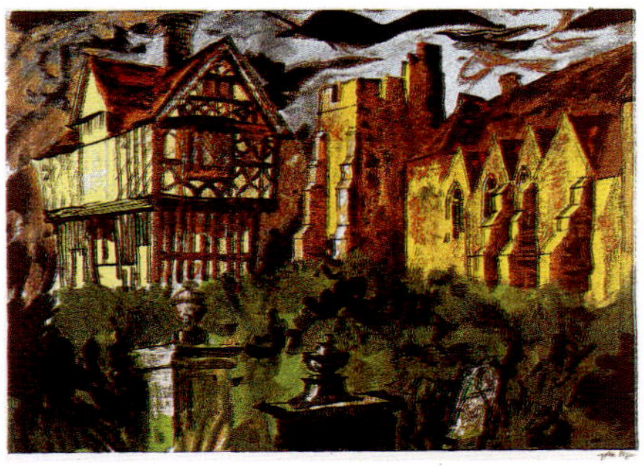

321

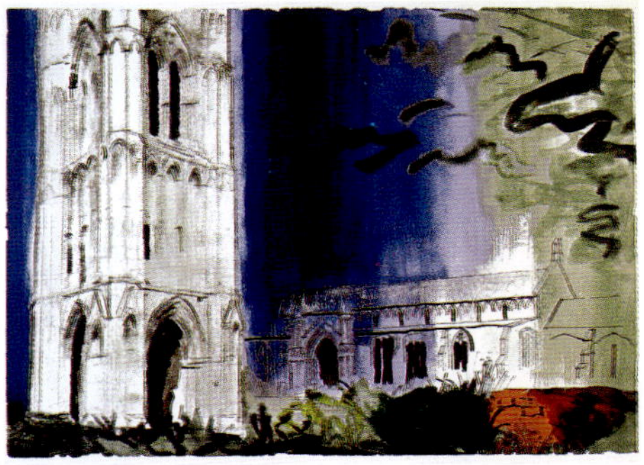

322

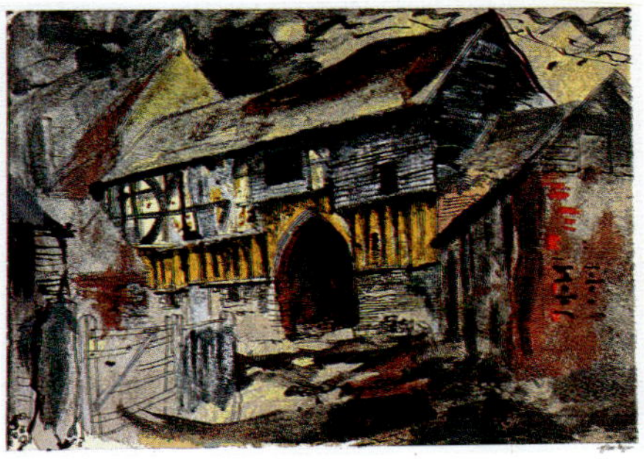

323

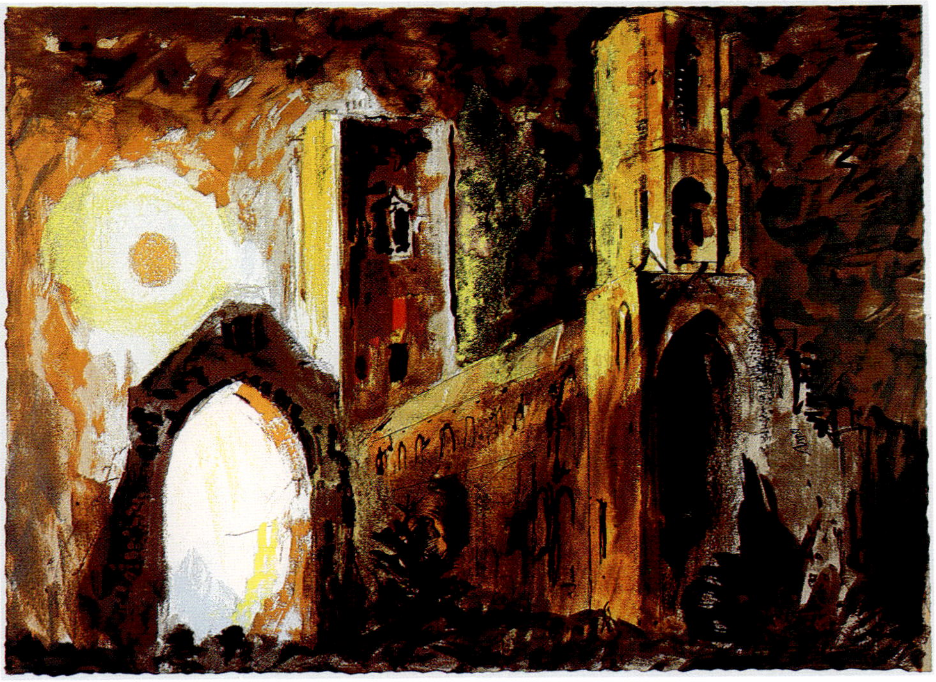

324

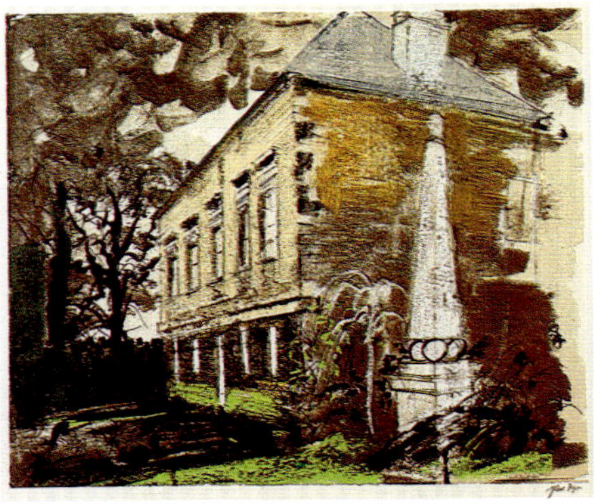

325

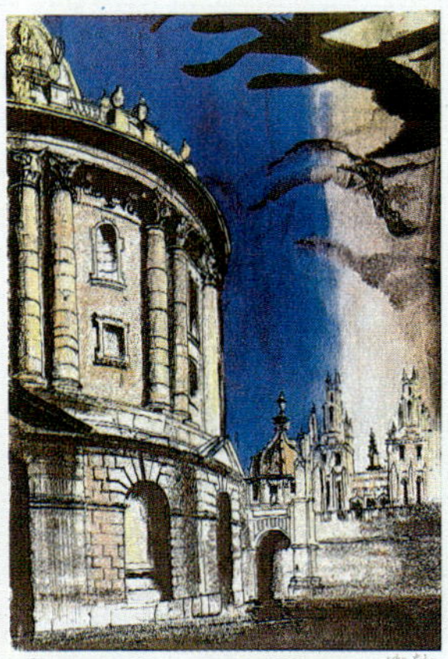

326

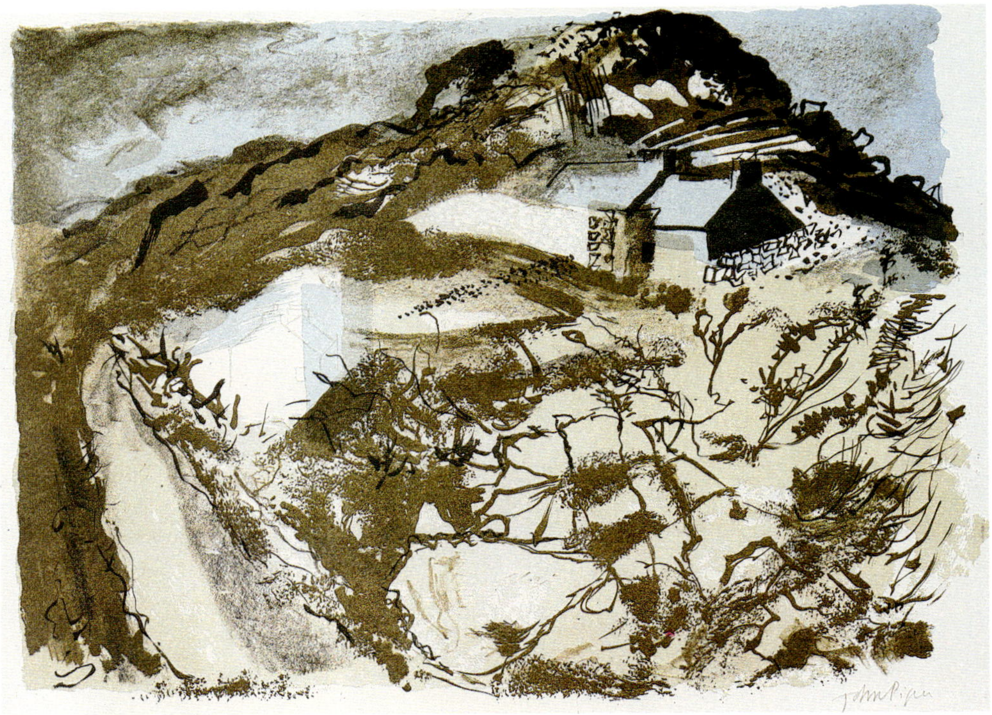

327

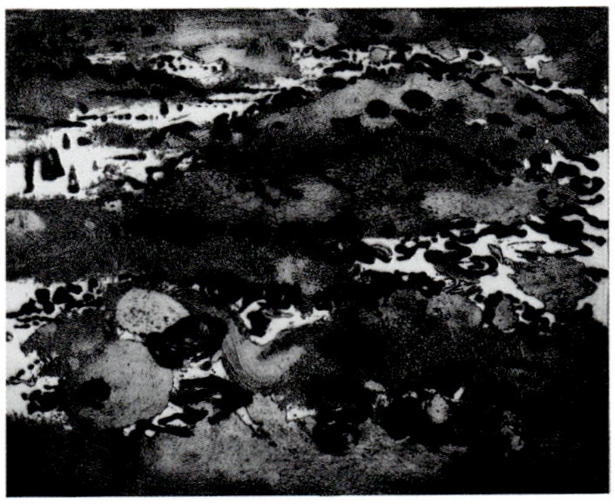

328

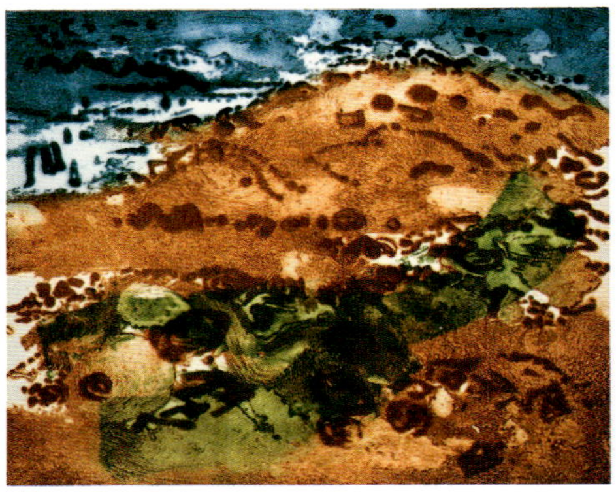

328A

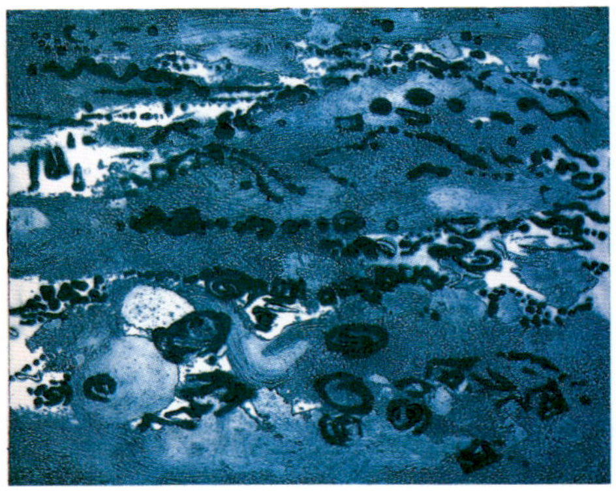

328B

326
Radcliffe Camera
Offset lithograph 530 × 356 ($20\frac{7}{8} \times 14$)
Senecio Press 1981
Oxford Museum of Modern Art 1981
Vélin Arches 160gsm, wmk 'Arches France' and Arches symbol 640 × 460 ($25\frac{3}{16} \times 18\frac{1}{8}$)
150 'John Piper' 40AP 5PP

Several trial proofs exist. Donated by the artist to the Appeal Fund for the Museum

327
Garn Fawr
Lithograph 385 × 535 ($15\frac{3}{16} \times 21\frac{1}{8}$)
Valerie Ewens 1981
Printmakers Council 1981
Vélin Arches Blancs 250gsm, wmk 'Arches France' 503 × 640 ($19\frac{3}{4} \times 25\frac{3}{16}$)
75 'John Piper' 8AP 2PP

The print forms part of a portfolio published to raise funds for the Printmakers Council. The other artists who donated editions of their work were: John Brunsdon, Jennifer Dickson, Anthony Gross, Gertrude Hermes, Marek Laczynski, Michael Rothenstein, Birgit Skiöld, Valerie Thornton and Julian Trevelyan.

328
Connemara I
Etching 265 × 324 ($10\frac{3}{8} \times 12\frac{3}{4}$)
Kelpra Studio 1981
Unpublished
Vélin Arches 300gsm 335 × 385 ($13\frac{3}{16} \times 15\frac{3}{16}$)
Not issued as an edition Unsigned

328A
Connemara II
Kelpra Studio 1981
Unpublished
Vélin Arches 300gsm 335 × 385 ($13\frac{3}{16} \times 15\frac{3}{16}$)
Not issued as an edition 'John Piper'

Signed 'AP' b.l.

328B
Connemara III
Kelpra Studio 1981
Unpublished
Vélin Arches 300gsm 335 × 385 ($13\frac{3}{16} \times 15\frac{3}{16}$)
Not issued as an edition 'John Piper'

Signed 'AP' b.l.

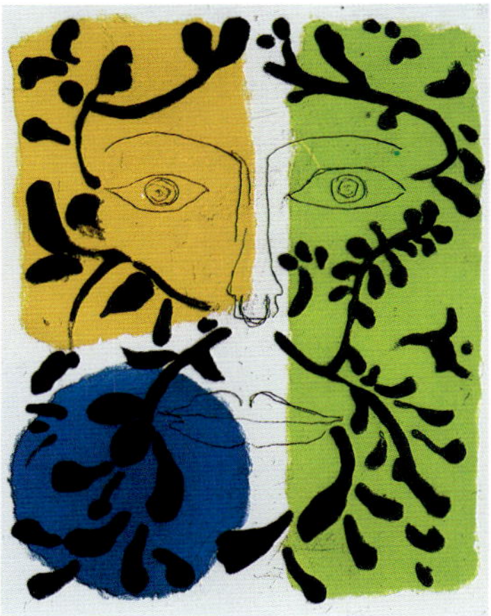

329

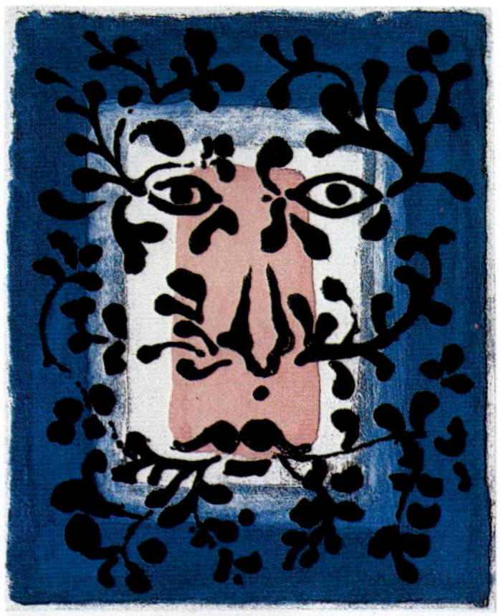

330

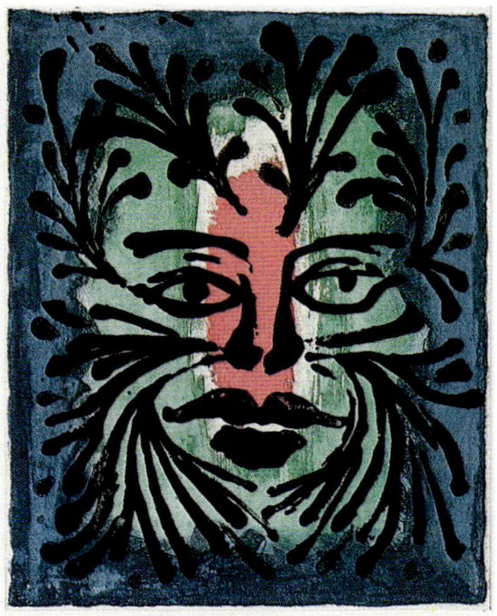

332

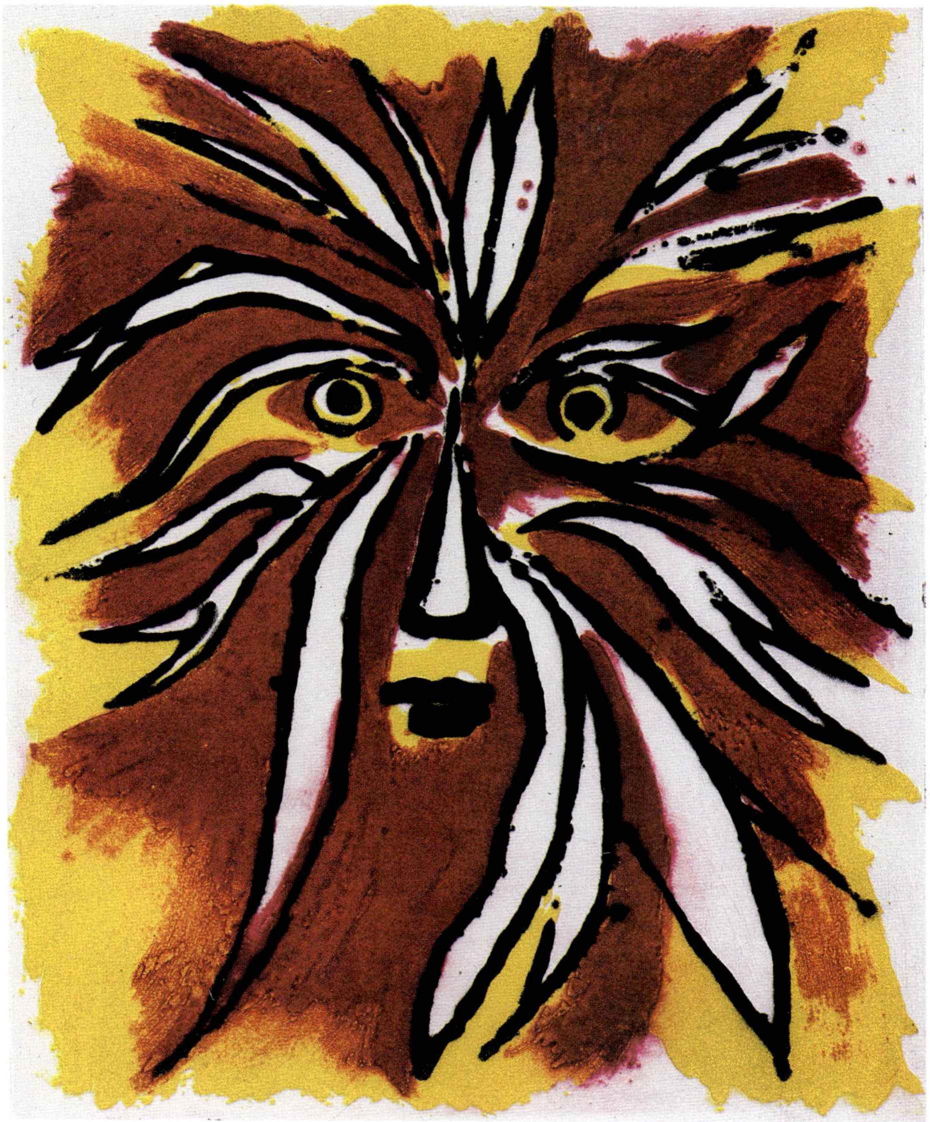

331

329
The Seasons: Spring
Etching 399×327 ($15\frac{11}{16} \times 12\frac{7}{8}$)
Kelpra Studio 1981
Christie's Contemporary Art 1981
Vélin Arches 300gsm 602×502 ($23\frac{11}{16} \times 19\frac{3}{4}$)
100 'John Piper' 10AP 5HC 5PP 2IC

The first print in the series *The Seasons*. Printed with a mixture of resin and carbonsodium powder producing both a relief and intaglio etching

330
The Seasons: Summer
Etching 399×327 ($15\frac{11}{16} \times 12\frac{7}{8}$)
Kelpra Studio 1981
Christie's Contemporary Art 1981
Vélin Arches 300gsm 602×502 ($23\frac{11}{16} \times 19\frac{3}{4}$)
100 'John Piper' 10AP 5HC 5PP 2IC

The second print in the series *The Seasons.* In 1985 a translation/interpretation of this image was woven as a tapestry by West Dean tapestry studios.

331
The Seasons: Autumn
Etching 399×327 ($15\frac{11}{16} \times 12\frac{7}{8}$)
Kelpra Studio 1981
Christie's Contemporary Art 1981
Vélin Arches 300gsm 602×502 ($23\frac{11}{16} \times 19\frac{3}{4}$)
100 'John Piper' 10AP 5HC 5PP 2IC

The third print in the series *The Seasons.* Printed with a mixture of resin and carbonsodium powder producing both a relief and intaglio etching

332
The Seasons: Winter
Etching 399×327 ($15\frac{11}{16} \times 12\frac{7}{8}$)
Kelpra Studio 1981
Christie's Contemporary Art 1981
Vélin Arches 300gsm 602×502 ($23\frac{11}{16} \times 19\frac{3}{4}$)
100 'John Piper' 15AP 5HC 5PP 2IC

The fourth print in the series *The Seasons*. Several trial proofs exist.

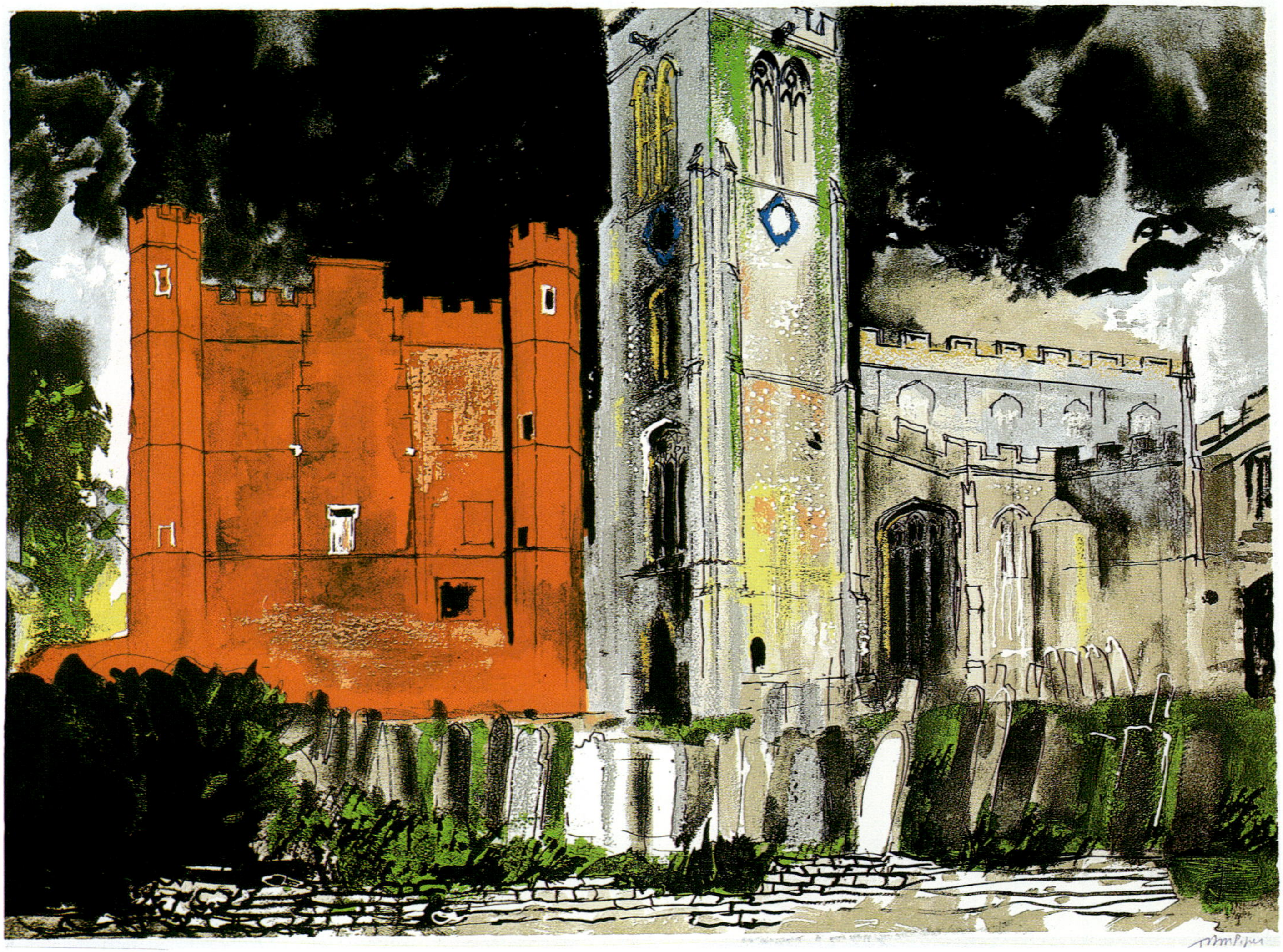

333

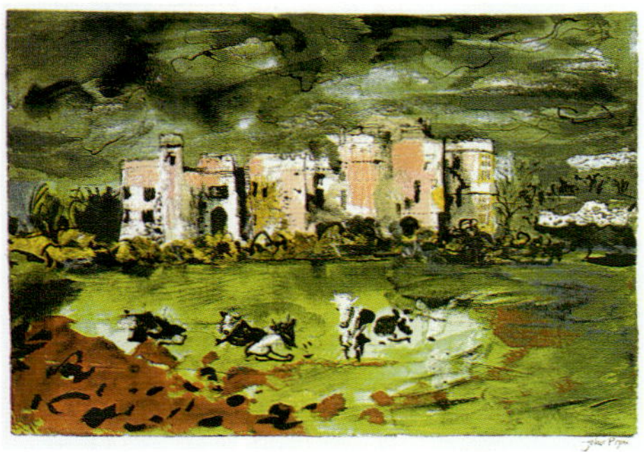

334

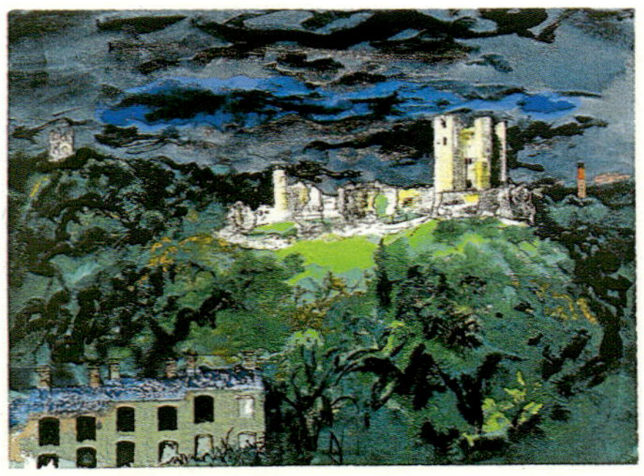

335

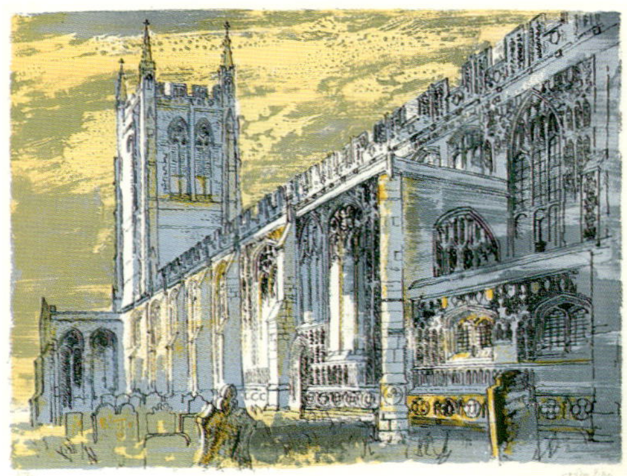

336

333
Buckden Palace, Cambridgeshire
Screenprint 576 × 778 ($22\frac{11}{16} \times 30\frac{5}{8}$)
Kelpra Studio 1982
Christie's Contemporary Art 1982
Vélin Arches 300gsm 719 × 925 ($28\frac{5}{16} \times 36\frac{3}{8}$)
100 'John Piper' 10AP 5HC 5PP 5IC

Sometimes incorrectly known as '*Buckden Abbey*' or '*Buckden in a Storm (2nd Version)*'

334
Carew Castle
Screenprint 446 × 645 ($17\frac{9}{16} \times 25\frac{3}{8}$)
Kelpra Studio 1982
Christie's Contemporary Art 1983
Vélin Arches 300gsm 544 × 745 ($21\frac{3}{8} \times 29\frac{3}{8}$)
100 'John Piper' 10AP 5HC 5PP 2IC

Printer's blind stamp b.r.

Tate Gallery

335
Conisbrough Castle, South Yorkshire
Screenprint 575 × 777 ($22\frac{5}{8} \times 30\frac{9}{16}$)
Kelpra Studio 1982
Christie's Contemporary Art 1982
Vélin Arches 300gsm 715 × 929 ($28\frac{3}{16} \times 36\frac{5}{16}$)
100 'John Piper' 10AP 5HC 5PP 2IC

Sometimes incorrectly known as '*Conisbrough Castle*'. Printer's blind stamp b.r.

336
Long Melford Church
Lithograph 467 × 615 ($18\frac{3}{8} \times 24\frac{1}{4}$)
Curwen Studio 1982
Canon Rubber Co 1982
T.H. Saunders 250gsm 560 × 775 ($22 \times 30\frac{1}{2}$)
275 'John Piper' 10AP

337-9
Grongar Hill, 1982
A book containing three autolithographs (two of which are triptychs) bound into a book with John Dyer's poem *Grongar Hill* (the text of the first edition, as it appeared in 1726 in *Savage's Miscellany*) and with a foreword by the artist.

The lithographs were printed by Curwen Studio on Vélin Arches paper and the text was set and printed by the Stourton Press, who also published the book.

All copies were numbered and signed by the artist. The edition of 175 was divided into a standard edition of 160 and a deluxe edition of 15. The deluxe edition was quarter-bound in leather and all the lithographs were mounted. A further 20 lithographs were sold individually and were signed and numbered 1/20–20/20 by the artist. The marbled cover of each book is different.

The images were drawn direct on to plastic plates by the artist. Paper size: 322×247 ($12\frac{11}{16} \times 9\frac{11}{16}$)

British Library; Cambridge University Library; National Library of Wales; National Library of Scotland

Foreword to *Grongar Hill* by the artist

On a first camping expedition to Pembrokeshire more than sixty years ago a friend and I were astonished by the Vale of Towy, between Llandeilo and Carmarthen. It was quite clearly the Promised Land – a wide, verdant, smiling, fertile, welcoming vale that Blake might have thought up, lying between ranges of highish hills that never become mountains; the perfect setting for classical landscapes with figures by Poussin and Claude, not to mention classical landscapes without figures by Alexander and J. R. Cozens and J. M. W. Turner. Here in a few miles between these pleasant towns the illustrations in the English aquatint books published between 1790 and 1825 or so blossom into life at every bend, as if not only some but all *of them had been done here.*

The green, partly wooded hills rise and fall happily on each flank, with a tower here or a hill and a whitewalled farm there in a shallow combe, and the centre of the vale is ornamented with beautifully shaped hillocks and echoing knolls, some with a house sunning itself on the south slope and with the Towy winding round the perimeter of its tree-girt grounds.

About twenty-five years later I returned, and found the Towy Vale quite unchanged. Dryslwyn Castle still on its knoll, Paxton's Tower on its hilltop and no 'development', no tourists, comparatively few motor-cars: only the single-line railway (rusty) that had been there for a hundred years anyway, and which must have startled some of the inhabitants when it first appeared as much as the one in the Derbyshire dales startled Ruskin. Between those two visits (in fact during the Hitler war) I had discovered Dyer's Grongar Hill, *which struck me as one of the best purely topographical poems in existence, because it is so visual. I did some drawings of the hill and the neighbourhood. Dyer, born in 1700, was trained as a painter. He is rather patronizingly referred to by Dr Johnson, and, positively criticized by silly old Gilpin for getting his foregrounds mixed up with his middle distances (or something) but was generally much praised, and still survives in many anthologies.*

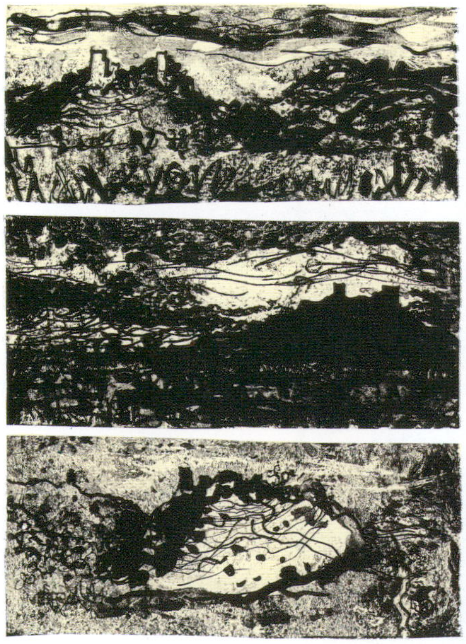

337

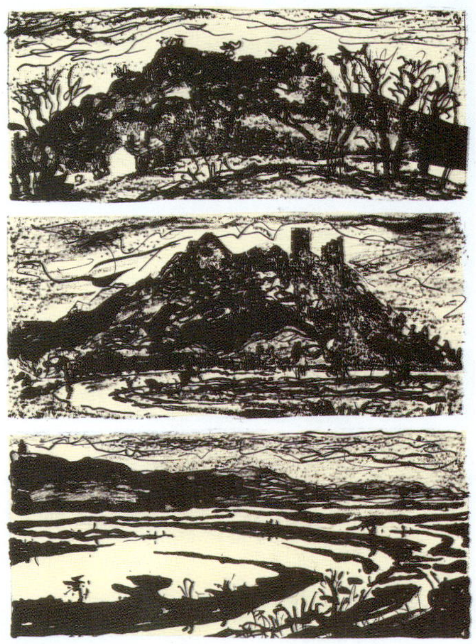

338

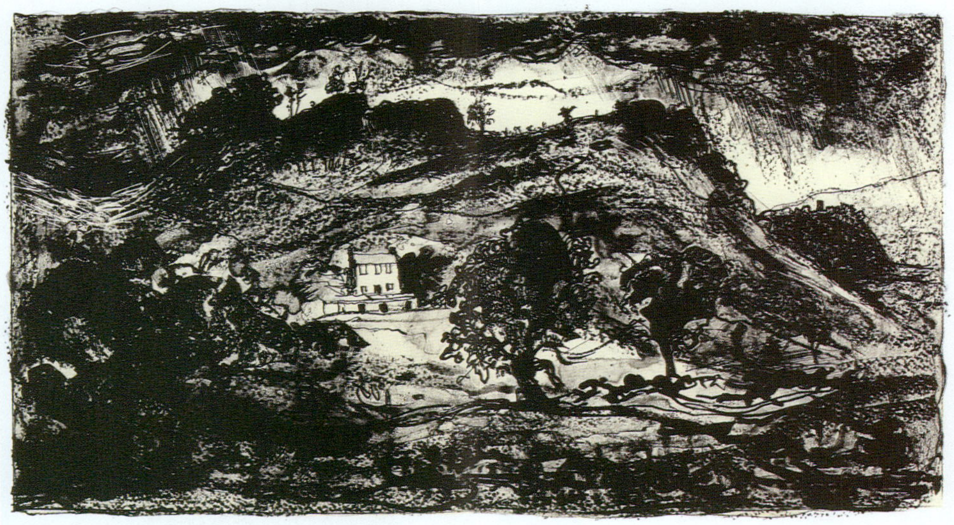

339

I have loved the poem ever since I first read it, and I return to it whenever I feel depressed about the country side getting spoilt. For Grongar and its surroundings have not been spoilt – they are almost as sylvan and undisturbed as they were when I was young, and the single-line railway track has not been made into a double one: it has been taken up, which I suppose would have pleased Ruskin, too.

337
Grongar Hill I
(facing stanza I)
226×161 ($8\frac{7}{8} \times 6\frac{3}{8}$)

Sometimes incorrectly known as '*Grongar Hill, Carmarthenshire*'. Repr. in Ingrams/Piper (plate 112)

338
Grongar Hill II
(facing stanza V)
229×165 ($9 \times 6\frac{1}{2}$)

339
Grongar Hill III
(centrefold following stanza VIII)
226×415 ($8\frac{7}{8} \times 16\frac{5}{16}$)

Sometimes incorrectly known as '*Grongar Hill, Carmarthenshire*'. Repr. in Ingrams/Piper (plate 111)

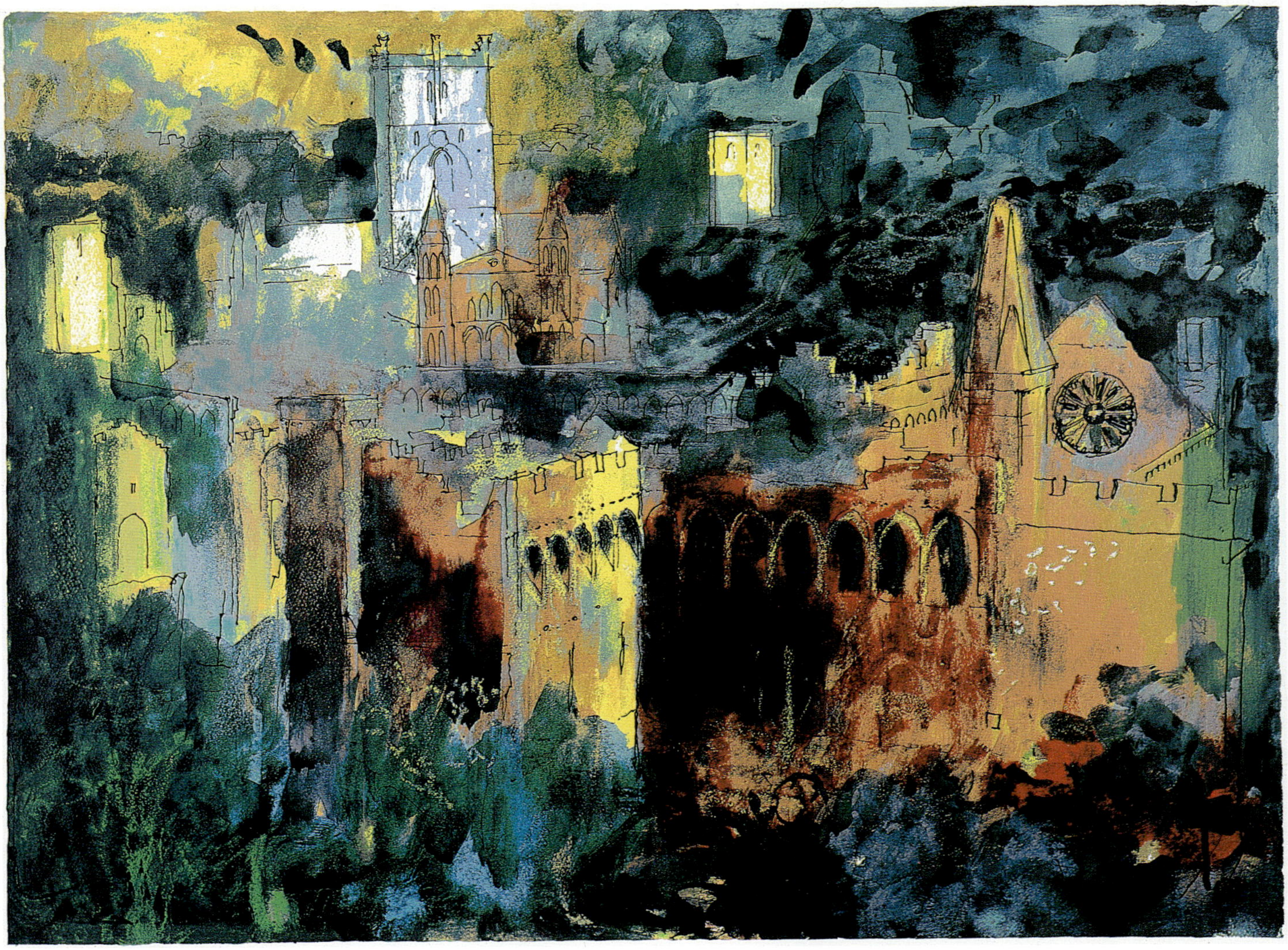

340

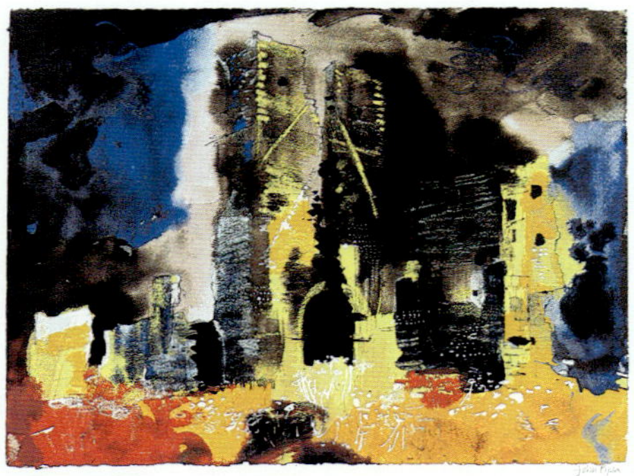

341

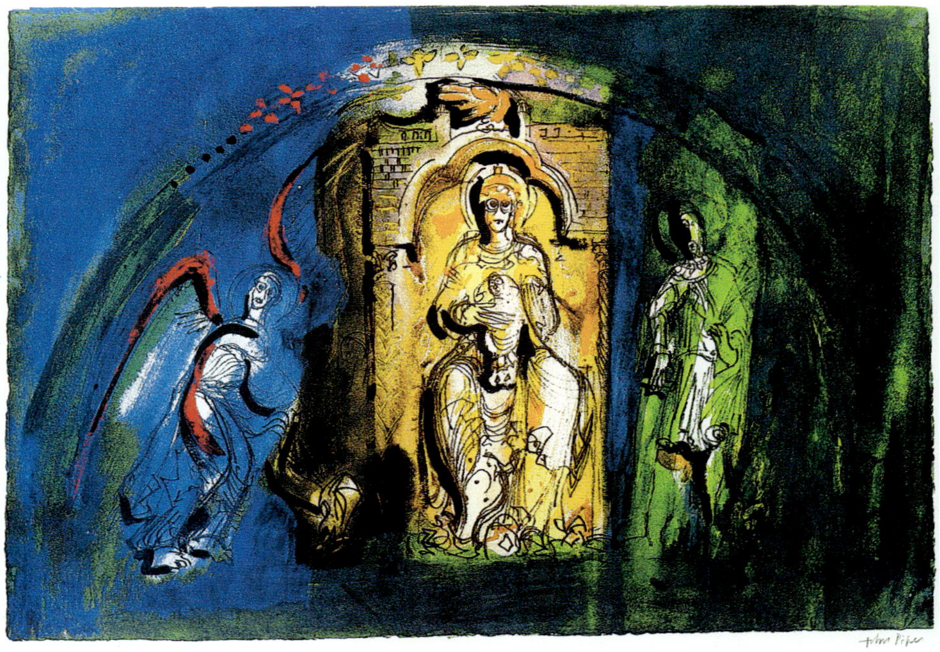

342

340
St David's, Dyfed
Screenprint 573 × 777 ($22\frac{9}{16} \times 30\frac{9}{16}$)
Kelpra Studio 1982
Christie's Contemporary Art 1982
Vélin Arches 300gsm 731 × 941 ($28\frac{3}{4} \times 37\frac{1}{16}$)
100 'John Piper' 10AP 5HC 5PP 5IC

341
Ruined Church, Bawsey
Screenprint 443 × 597 ($17\frac{1}{2} \times 23\frac{1}{2}$)
Kelpra Studio 1982
Christie's Contemporary Art 1983
Vélin Arches 300gsm 545 × 695 ($21\frac{1}{2} \times 27\frac{3}{8}$)
100 'John Piper' 10AP 5HC 5PP 5IC

Sometimes incorrectly known as '*Bawsey*'.
Printer's blind stamp b.r.

Tate Gallery

342
Donzy-le-Pré
Screenprint 439 × 650 ($17\frac{1}{4} \times 25\frac{5}{8}$)
Kelpra Studio 1982
Christie's Contemporary Art 1983
Vélin Arches 300gsm 545 × 752 ($21\frac{1}{2} \times 29\frac{1}{2}$)
100 'John Piper' 10AP 5HC 5PP 5IC

Sometimes incorrectly known as '*Colour Variations on a Romanesque Tympanum, Donzy-le-Pré*'.
Printer's blind stamp b.r.

343-8
Scotney Castle, Kent, 1982
This portfolio consists of six etchings, signed 'John Piper' in pencil b.r., and a title-page, in a green cloth folio with the title of the folio and the name of the artist printed on the front.

The etchings were printed by Kelpra Studio in 1982 and published by Kelpra Editions in 1983. The type of paper used was Vélin Arches 300gsm and each print has the printer's blind stamp b.r. Paper size: 302 × 494 ($11\frac{7}{8} \times 19\frac{1}{2}$). Image size: 213 × 406 ($8\frac{3}{8} \times 16$). Plate size: 215 × 406 ($8\frac{1}{2} \times 16$)

The edition size was 50 with 10AP and 5PP and the portfolio was bound by the Dorset Bookbinding Co, Wimborne.

343
Scotney Castle I

344
Scotney Castle II

345
Scotney Castle III

346
Scotney Castle IV

347
Scotney Castle V

348
Scotney Castle VI

343

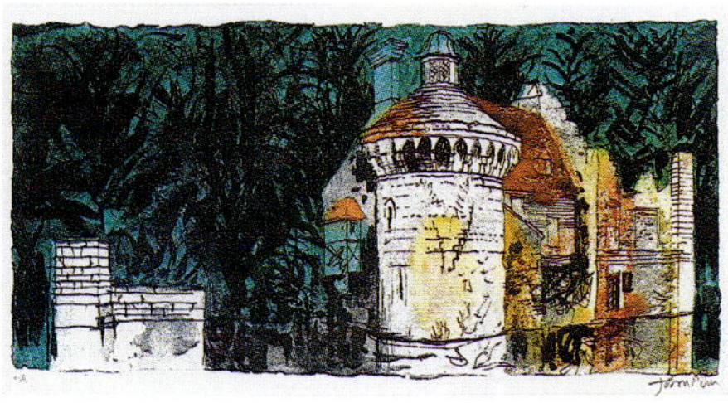
344

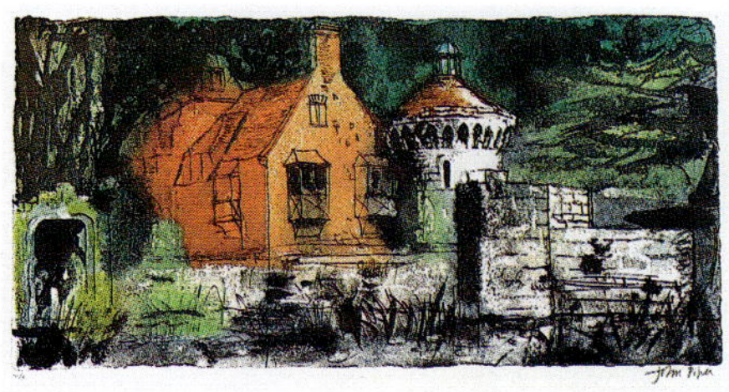
345

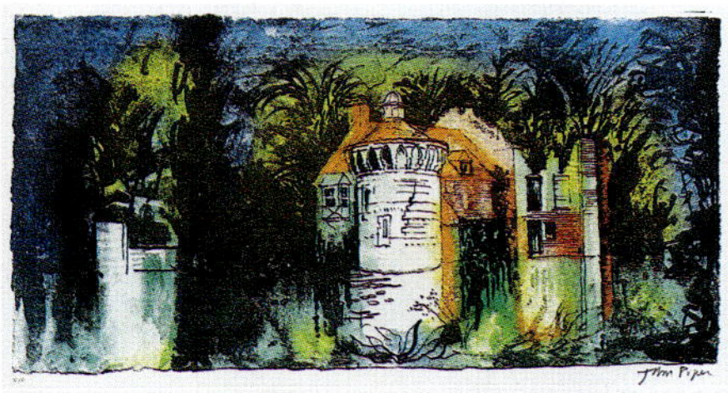
346

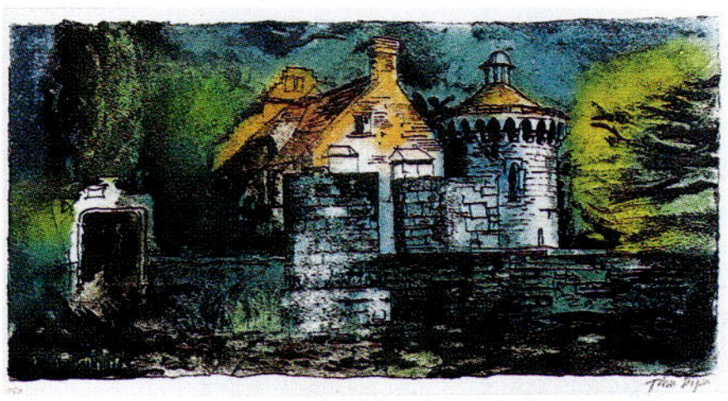
347

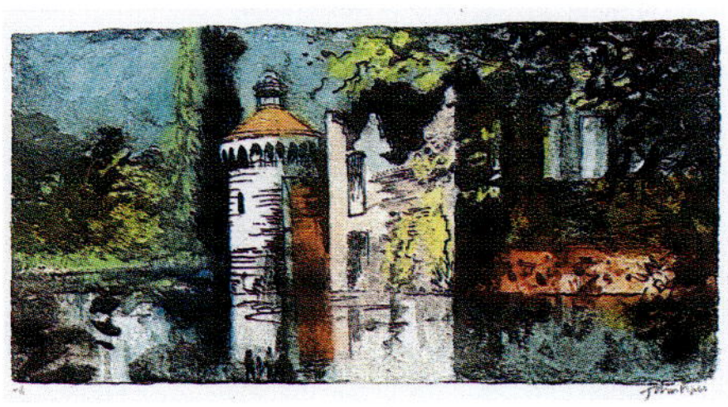
348

349
Babingley Church, Norfolk
Screenprint 445 × 597 ($17\frac{1}{2} \times 23\frac{1}{2}$)
Kelpra Studio 1983
Christie's Contemporary Art 1983
Vélin Arches 300gsm 555 × 698 ($21\frac{7}{8} \times 17\frac{1}{2}$)
100 'John Piper' 10AP 5PP 5IC

Sometimes incorrectly known as '*Babingley*'.
Printer's blind stamp b.r.

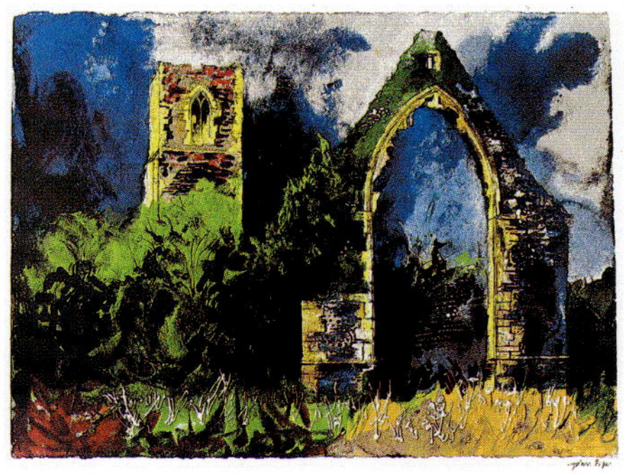
349

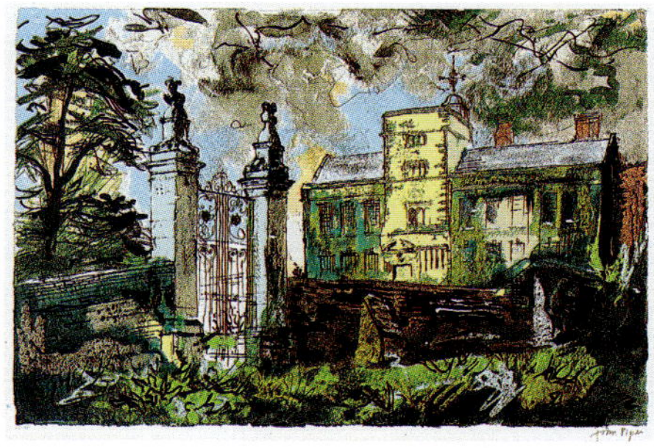
350

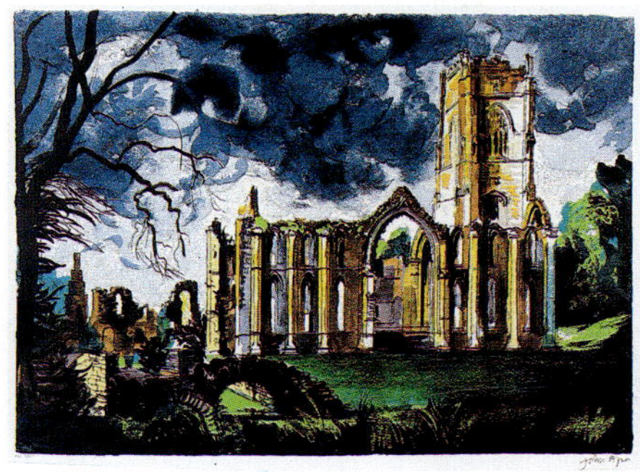
351

350
Canons Ashby, Northamptonshire
Screenprint 456 × 679 ($17\frac{15}{16} \times 26\frac{3}{4}$)
Kelpra Studio 1983
Christie's Contemporary Art and The National Trust 1983
Vélin Arches 300gsm 561 × 783 ($22\frac{1}{16} \times 30\frac{13}{16}$)
150 'John Piper' 10AP 12HC 5PP 3IC

Sometimes incorrectly known as '*Canon's Ashby*'.
Printer's blind stamp b.r.

Tate Gallery

351
Fountains Abbey, Yorkshire
Screenprint 451 × 623 ($17\frac{3}{4} \times 24\frac{1}{2}$)
Kelpra Studio 1983
Christie's Contemporary Art and National Trust 1983
Vélin Arches 300gsm 552 × 726 ($21\frac{3}{4} \times 28\frac{5}{8}$)
150 'John Piper' 10AP 12HC 5PP 3IC

Sometimes incorrectly known as '*Fountains Abbey*'

Tate Gallery

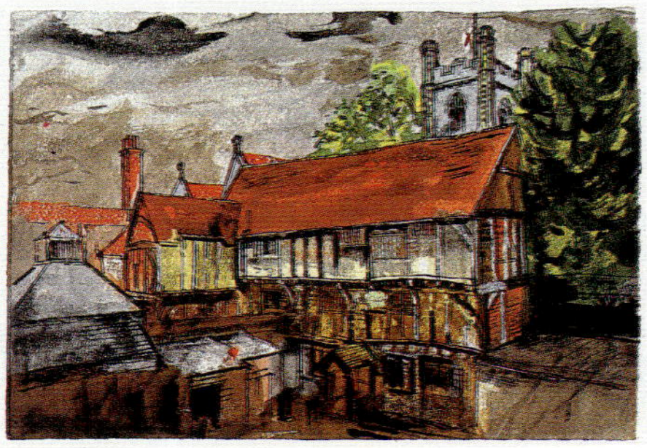

352

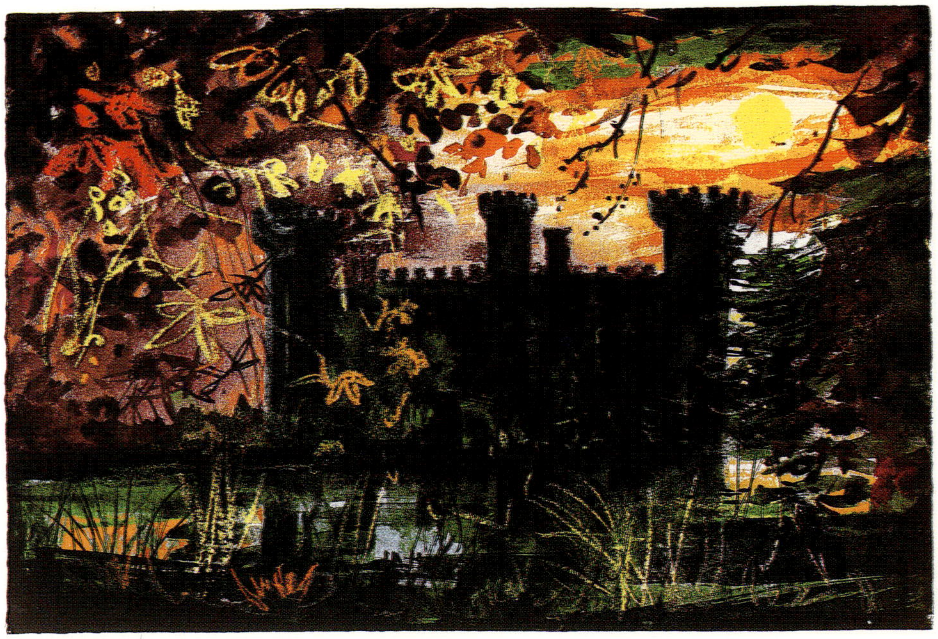

353

352
Chantry House, Henley
Screenprint 462 × 670 ($18\frac{3}{16} \times 26\frac{3}{8}$)
Kelpra Studio 1983
Century Gallery 1983
Vélin Arches 300gsm 568 × 782 ($22\frac{3}{8} \times 30\frac{13}{16}$)
100 'John Piper' 10AP 5HC 5PP 2IC

Sometimes incorrectly known as '*Chantry House*' or '*Henley Church*'

353
Eastnor Castle, Hereford
Screenprint 445 × 655 ($17\frac{1}{2} \times 25\frac{3}{4}$)
Kelpra Studio 1983
Marlborough Fine Art 1983
Vélin Arches 300gsm 546 × 752 ($21\frac{1}{2} \times 29\frac{5}{8}$)
70 'John Piper' 15AP 5PP

Sheffield Arts and Museums; Tate Gallery

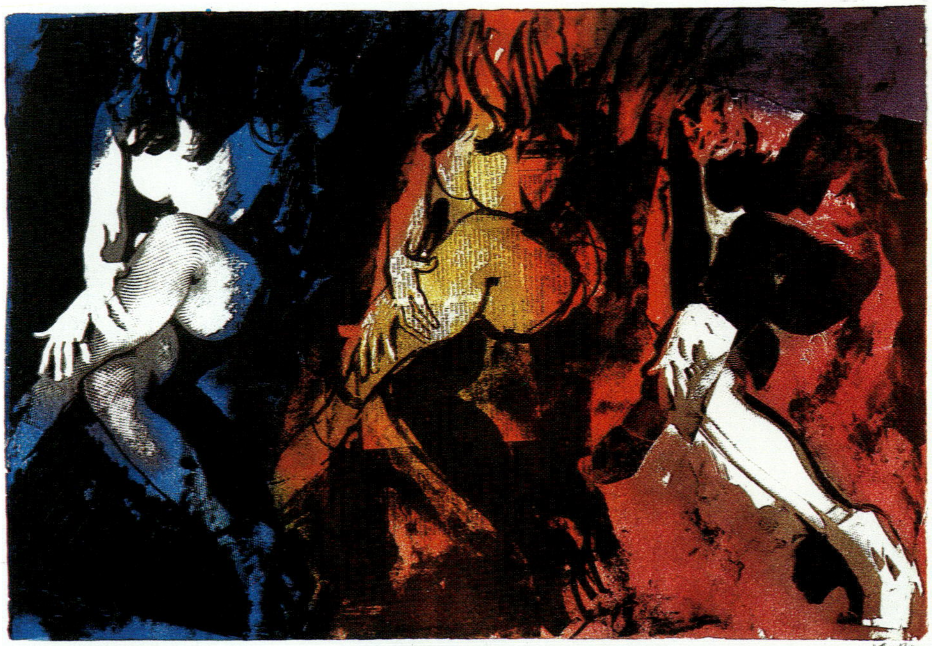

355

354-61
Eightieth Anniversary Portfolio, 1983
This portfolio consists of three etchings, four screenprints and one combined etching and screenprint and was published by Orde Levinson. All the prints are signed 'John Piper' in pencil b.r. and are presented in a cloth-bound portfolio, blocked on the cover with the artist's signature and the words '80th Anniversary Portfolio' in the artist's hand.

The standard edition was limited to 75, numbered 1/75-75/75, with 15 artist's proofs numbered I/XV-XV/XV and 10 dedication copies including exhibition copies. The standard edition was printed on Grand Vélin Arches 300gsm. Paper size: 560 × 760 (22 × 30). Each print (other than the deluxe edition) has the printer's blind stamp b.r.

A deluxe edition of 10, numbered 1/10 - 10/10, and two dedication copies were printed on Japon nacré 180gsm. Paper size: 560 × 765 ($22 \times 30\frac{1}{8}$). The deluxe edition portfolio was quarter-bound in leather.

The proofing and printing of the editions was by Kelpra Studio. The portfolios were made by Jane Rolo, London.

Modern Art Museum, Rio de Janeiro; Tate Gallery (Dedication editions)

354
Foliate Head
Plate I
Etching and screenprint 445 × 643 ($17\frac{5}{8} \times 25\frac{5}{16}$)

355
Eye and Camera
Plate II
Etching 451 × 665 ($17\frac{3}{4} \times 26\frac{3}{8}$)

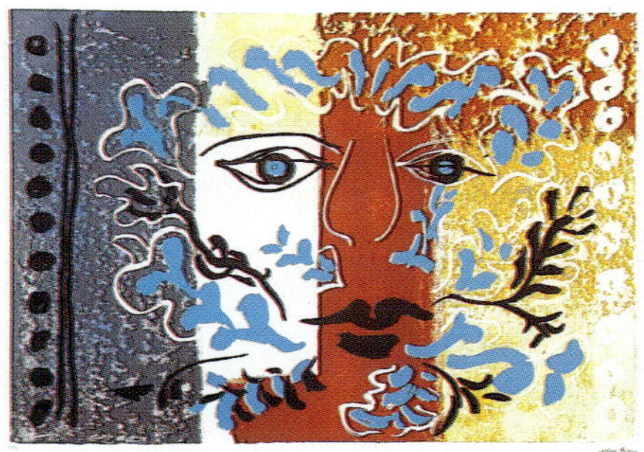

354

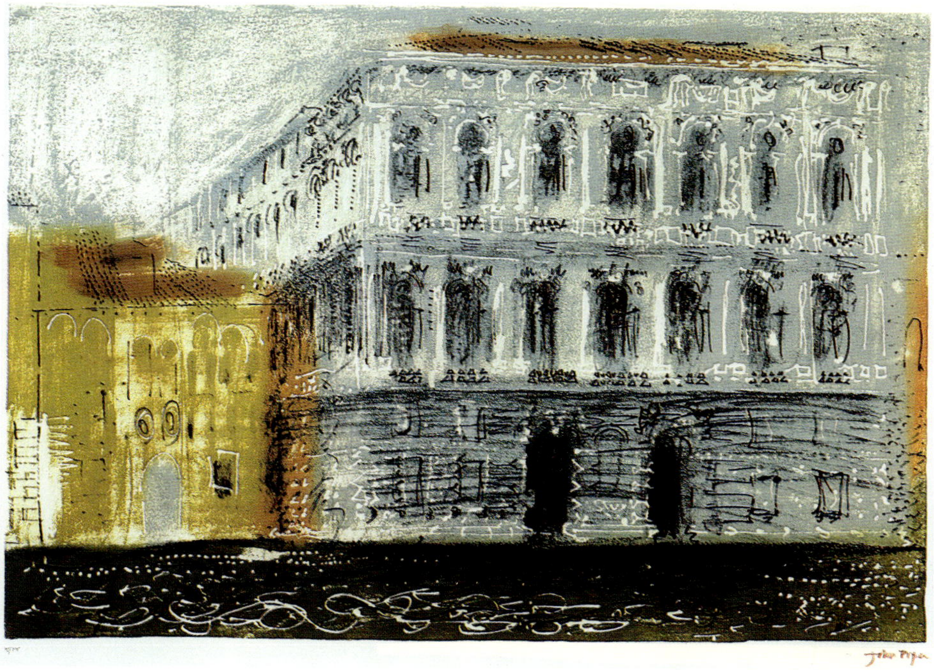
356

356
Palazzo Pesaro
Plate III
Etching 445 × 643 ($17\frac{1}{2} \times 25\frac{5}{16}$)

357
St Germain-de-L'Ivret
Plate IV
Screenprint 457 × 668 ($18 \times 26\frac{5}{16}$)

358
Blenheim Gates
Plate V
Etching 451 × 660 ($17\frac{3}{4} \times 26$)

359
Eastnor Castle
Plate VI
Screenprint 458 × 675 ($18 \times 26\frac{9}{16}$)

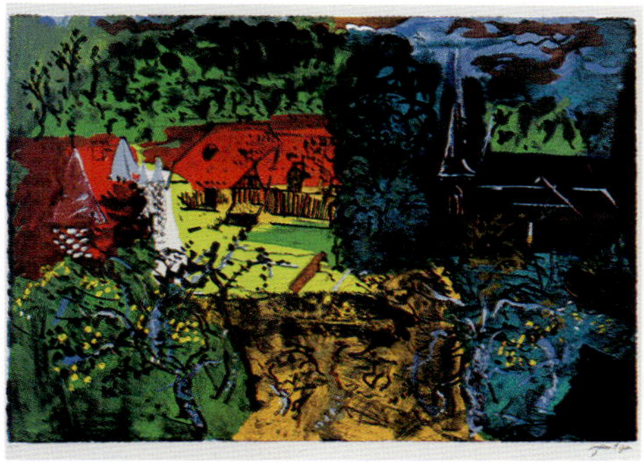
357

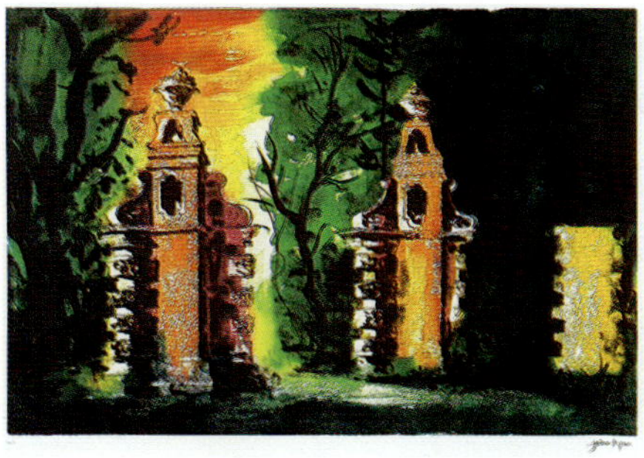
358

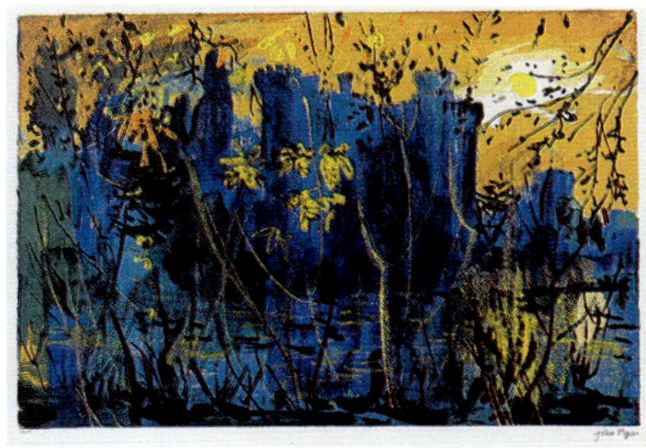
359

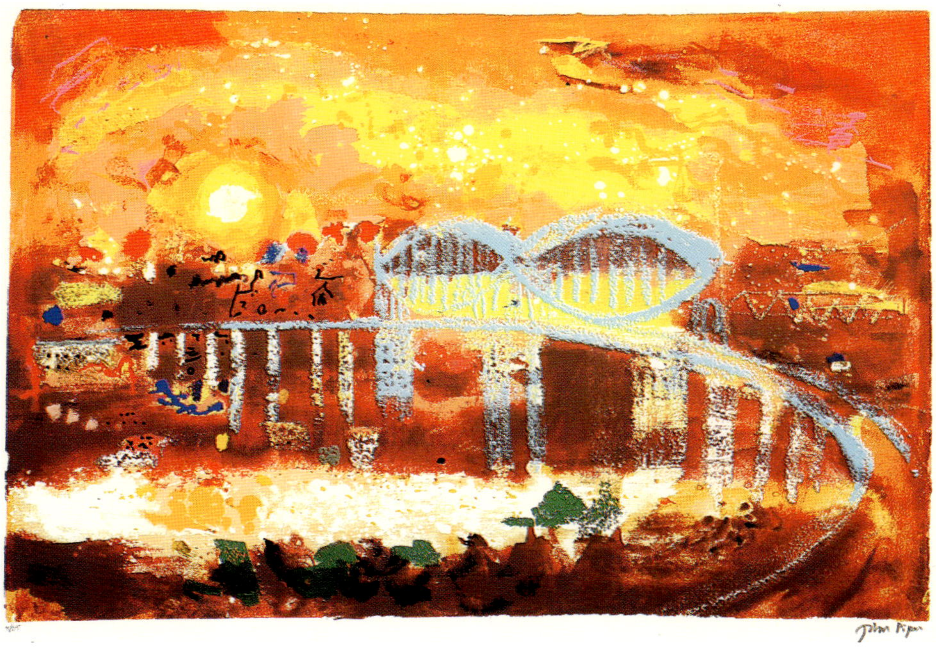
360

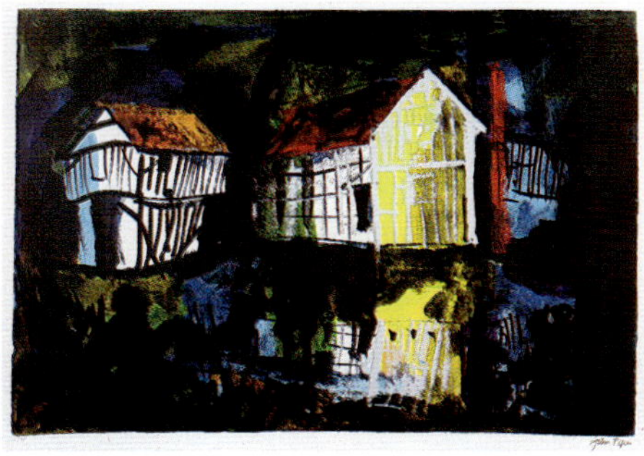
361

360
Saltash Bridge
Plate VII
Screenprint 455 × 680 ($17\frac{7}{8} \times 26\frac{3}{4}$)

361
Lower Brockhampton
Plate VIII
Screenprint 460 × 666 ($18\frac{1}{8} \times 26\frac{1}{4}$)

362
St Albans
Screenprint 508 × 597 (20 × 23½)
Kelpra Studio 1983
The Dean of St Albans 1983
Vélin Arches 300gsm 613 × 698 (24⅛ × 27½)
75 'John Piper' 10AP 5PP

Printer's blind stamp b.r.

363
Hautbois Church, Norfolk
Screenprint 445 × 630 ($17\frac{1}{2} \times 24\frac{13}{16}$)
Kelpra Studio 1983
Marlborough Fine Art 1983
Vélin Arches 300gsm 544 × 728 ($21\frac{7}{16} \times 28\frac{5}{8}$)
70 'John Piper' 15AP 5PP

Printer's blind stamp b.r.

364
Ivychurch, Romney Marsh
Etching and aquatint 450 × 615 (17¾ × 24¼)
Kelpra Studio 1983
Christie's Contemporary Art 1984
Vélin Arches 300gsm 545 × 760 (21½ × 30)
100 'John Piper' 10AP 5HC 3PP 2IC

Originally published as '*Ivychurch, Romney Marsh, Kent*'

365
Little Cressingham, Norfolk
Etching and aquatint 450 × 615 (17¾ × 24¼)
Kelpra Studio 1983
Christie's Contemporary Art 1984
Vélin Arches 300gsm 545 × 760 (21½ × 30)
100 'John Piper' 10AP 5HC 3PP 2IC

Originally published as '*Little Cressingham*'

366
Castlebythe
Screenprint 460 × 665 (18 × 26¼)
Kelpra Studio 1983
Christie's Contemporary Art 1983
Vélin Arches 300gsm 565 × 775 (22¼ × 30½)
100 'John Piper' 10AP 5HC 5IC

367
Dinton Folly
Screenprint 460 × 665 (18 × 26¼)
Kelpra Studio 1983
Christie's Contemporary Art 1984
Vélin Arches 300gsm 560 × 778 (22 × 30⅝)
100 'John Piper' 10AP 5HC 2PP 2IC

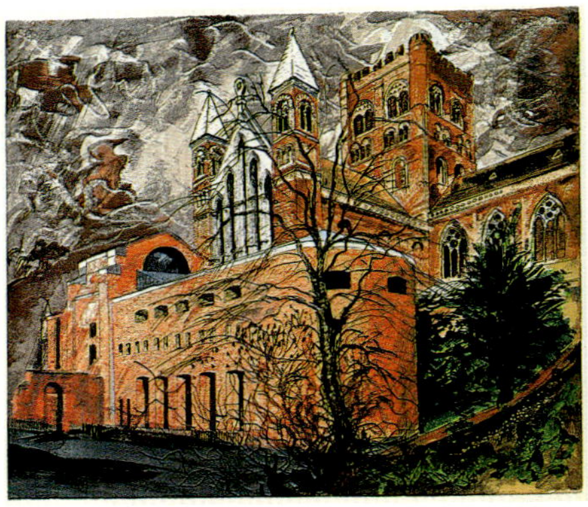
362

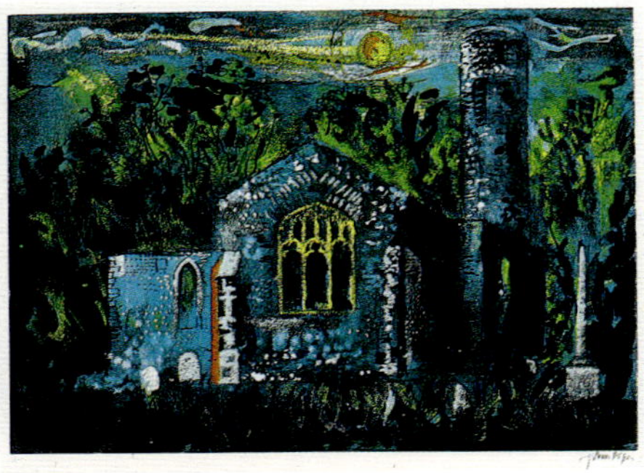
363

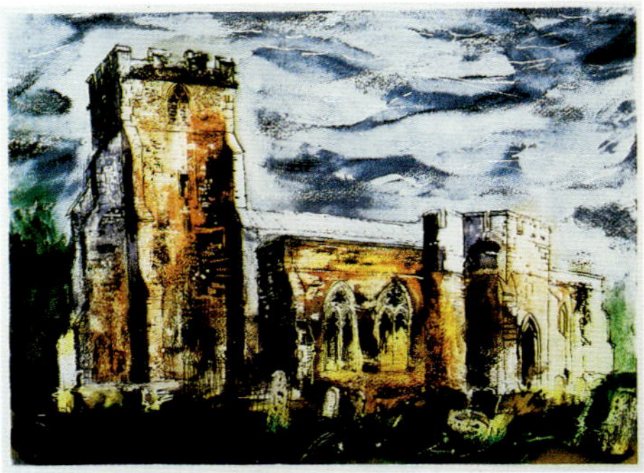
364

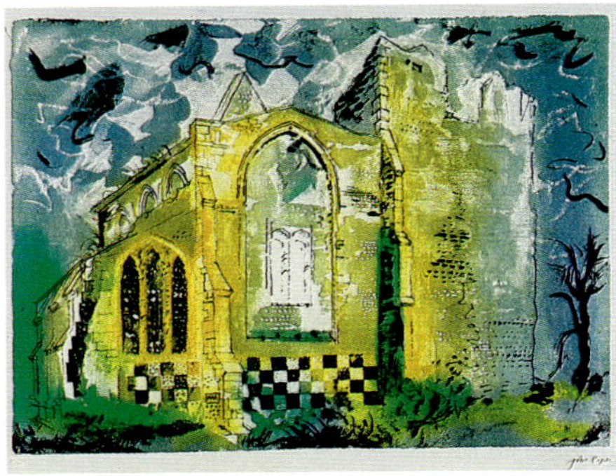
365

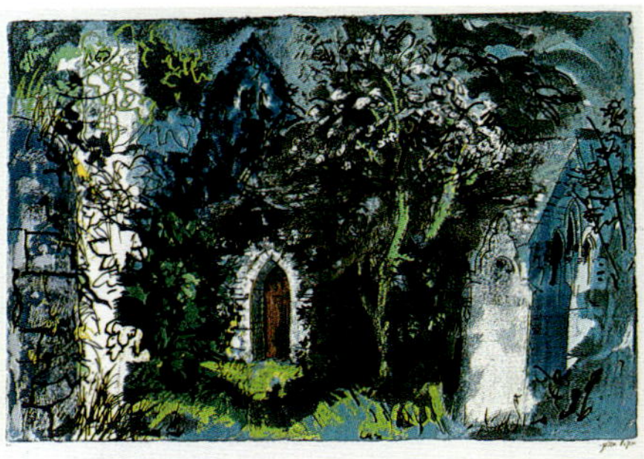
366

367

368
Foliate Head
Etching and screenprint 458 × 577 (18 × 22¾)
Kelpra Studio 1983
Christie's Contemporary Art 1984
Vélin Arches 300gsm 550 × 675 ($21\frac{5}{8} \times 26\frac{9}{16}$)
100 'John Piper' 10AP 5HC 2PP 2IC

369
Summer Garden, Fawley Bottom
Etching 388 × 575 (15¼ × 22½)
Kelpra Studio 1984
Kelpra Editions 1984
Vélin Arches 300gsm 522 × 700 (20½ × 27½)
85 'John Piper' 10AP 5PP

370
Clydey, Pembrokeshire
Screenprint 381 × 564 ($15 \times 22\frac{3}{16}$)
Kelpra Studio 1984
Marlborough Fine Art 1984
Vélin Arches 300gsm 500 × 667 ($19\frac{11}{16} \times 26\frac{1}{4}$)
70 'John Piper' 10AP 5PP

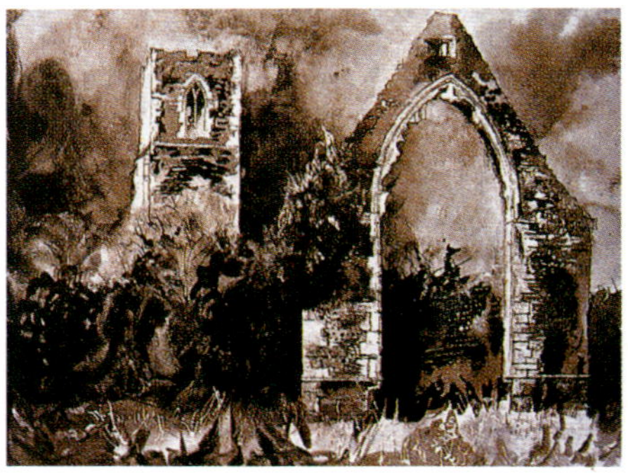
371

371
Babingley – Sepia Variation
Screenprint 445 × 595 (17¾ × 23⅜)
Kelpra Studio 1984
Christie's Contemporary Art 1984
BKF Rives 300gsm 560 × 680 (22 × 26¾)
50 'John Piper' 10AP 5HC 2PP 2IC

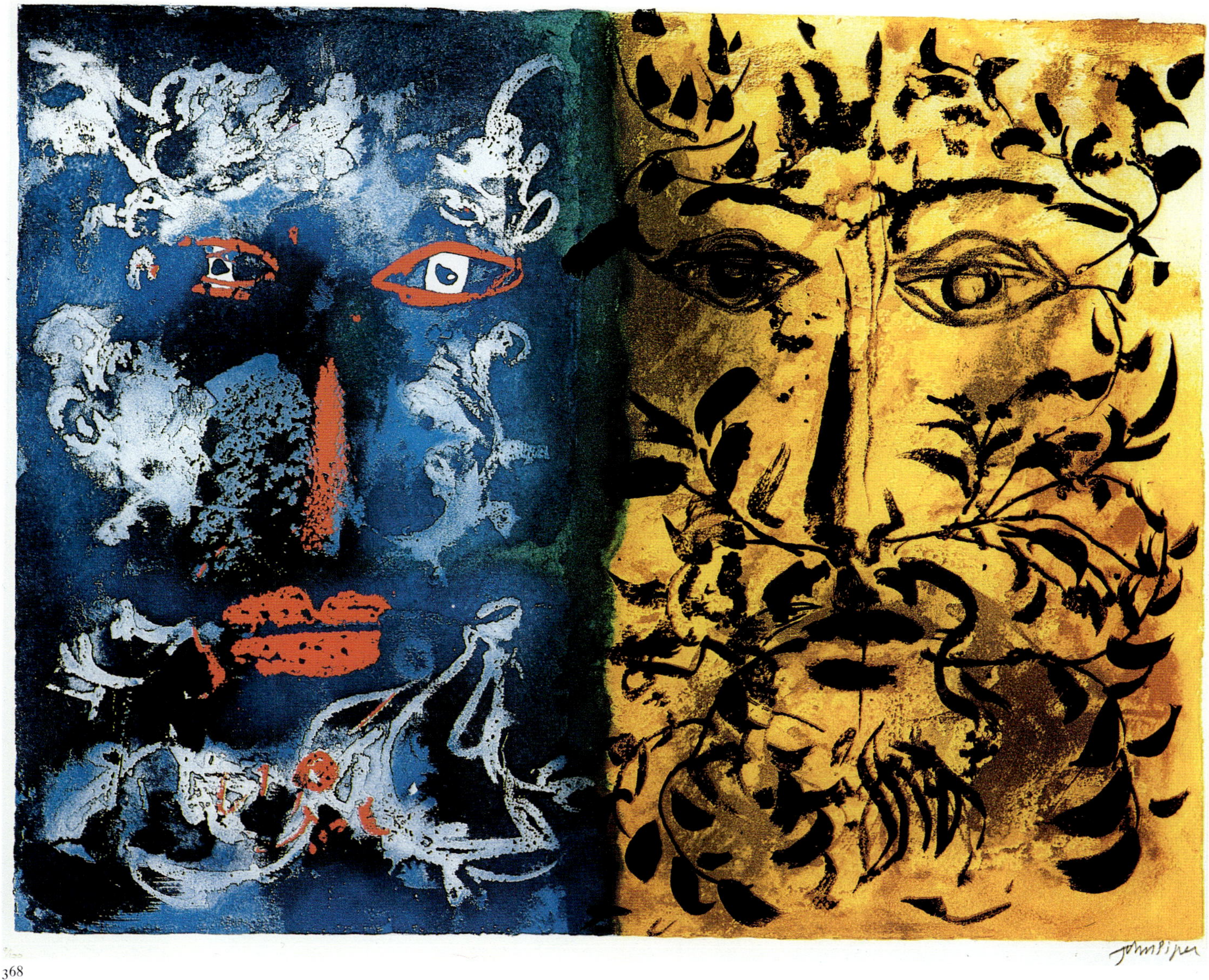

368

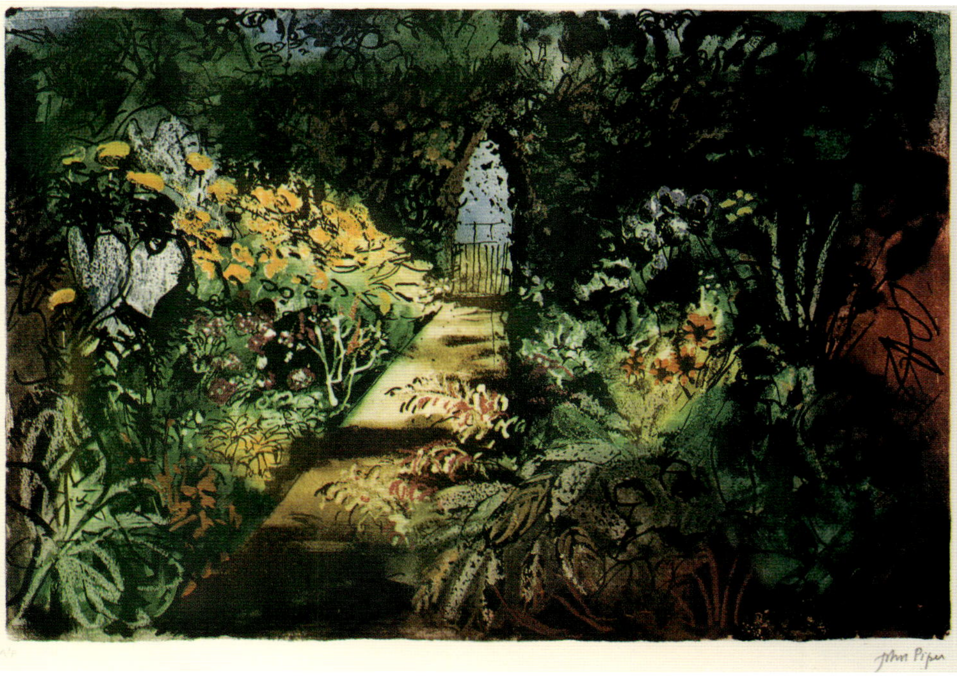

369

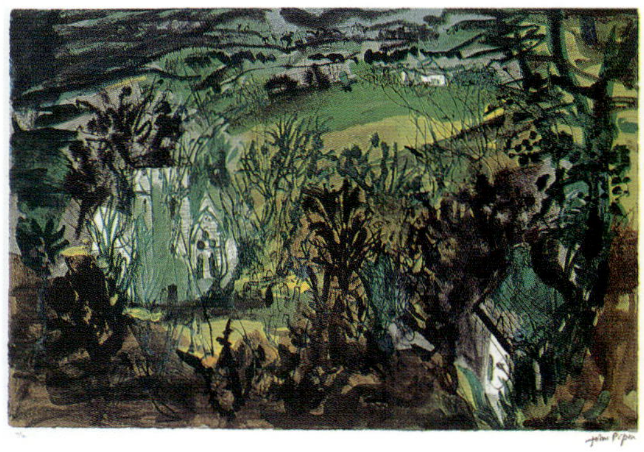

370

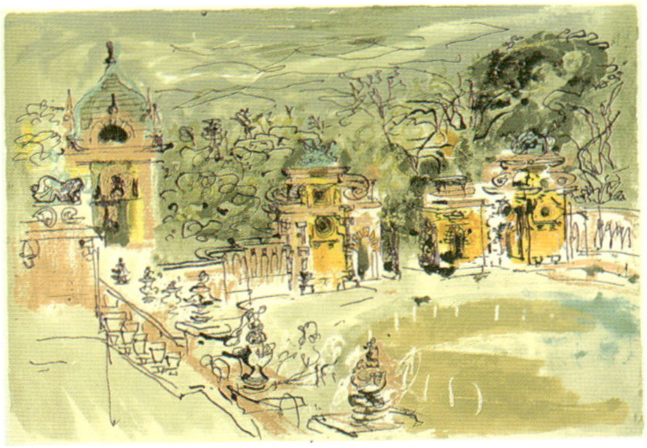

372

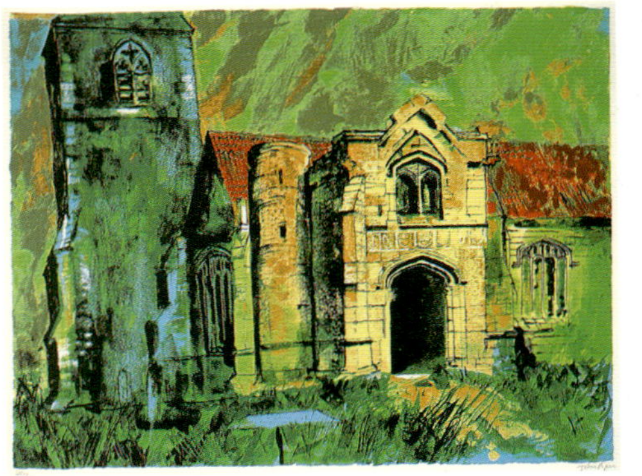

373

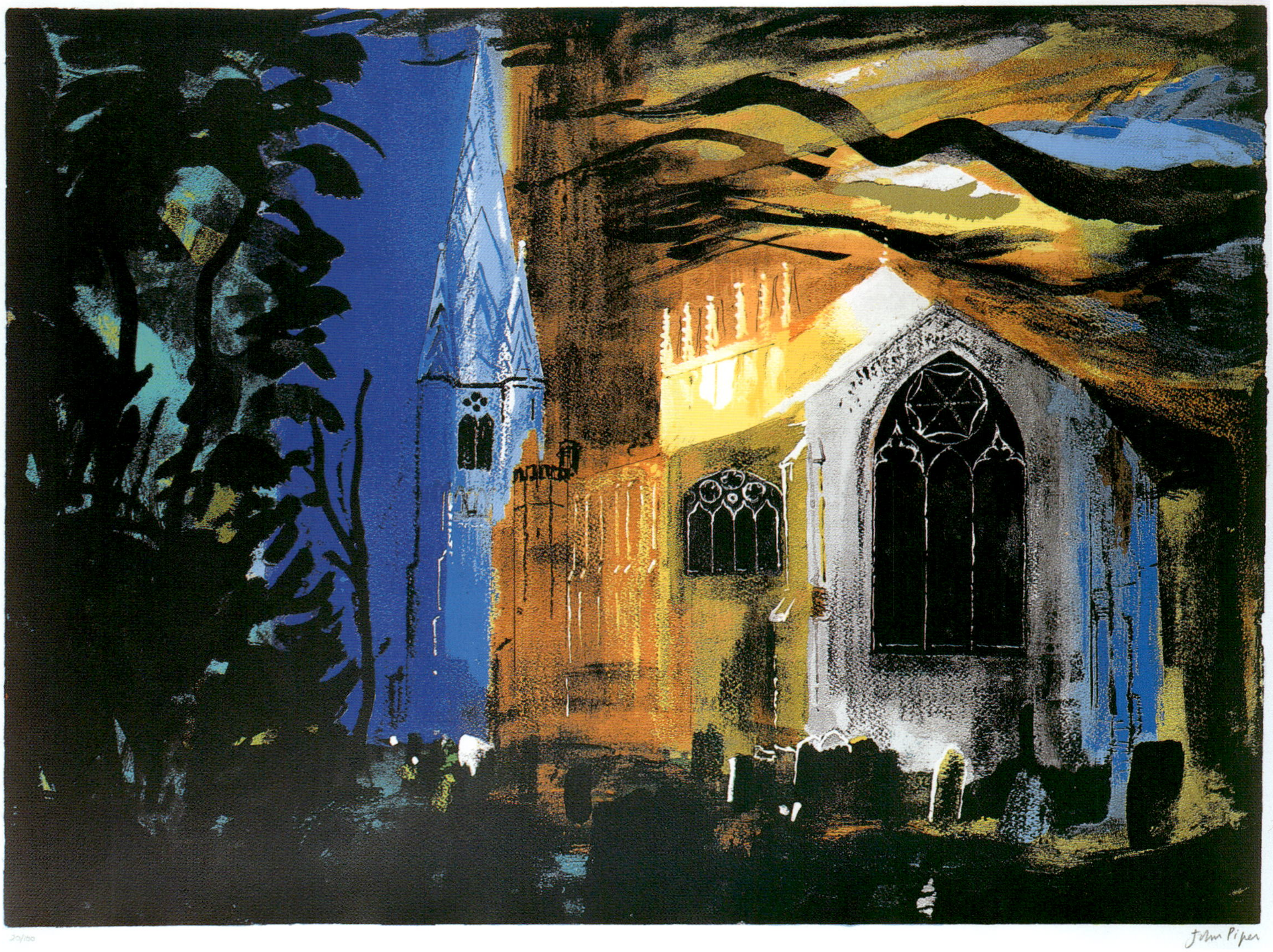

374

372
Harlaxton Hall
Screenprint 520 × 755 (20½ × 29¾)
Kelpra Studio 1984
Christie's Contemporary Art 1984
Vélin Arches 250gsm 660 × 890 (26 × 35)
90 'John Piper' 3AP 3HC 5PP

One known trial proof exists with a darker blue sky signed 'JP' b.l. and 'trial proof' b.r.

373
Holme, Nottinghamshire
Screenprint 500 × 660 (19¾ × 26)
Kelpra Studio 1985
Marlborough Fine Art 1985
Vélin Arches 300gsm 610 × 765 (24 × 30⅛)
70 'John Piper' 15AP 5PP

374
Long Sutton
Screenprint 605 × 825 (24 × 32½)
Kelpra Studio 1985
Christie's Contemporary Art 1985
Vélin Arches 300gsm 750 × 965 (29½ × 38)
100 'John Piper' 10AP 5HC 2PP 3IC

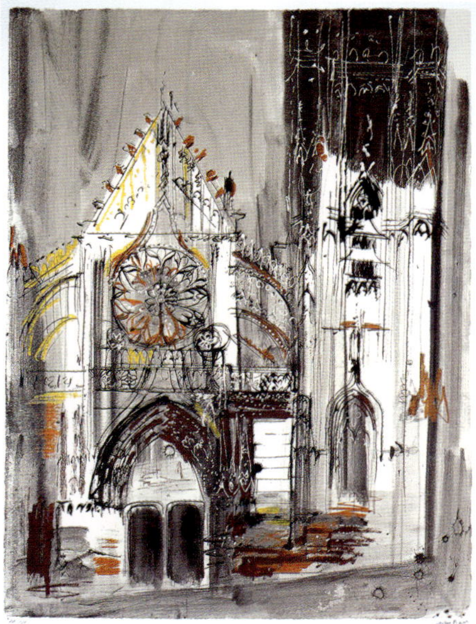

375

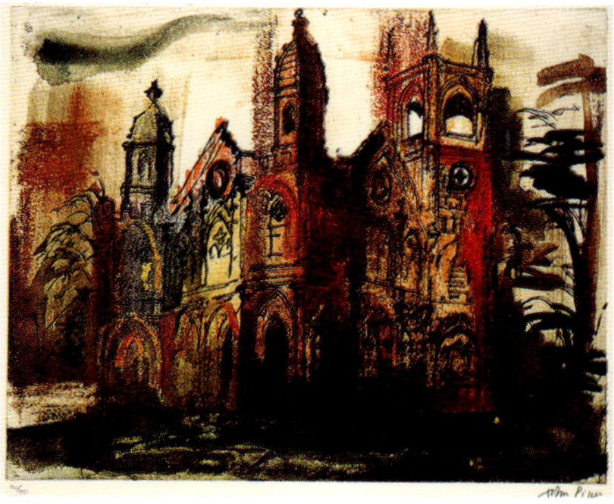

376

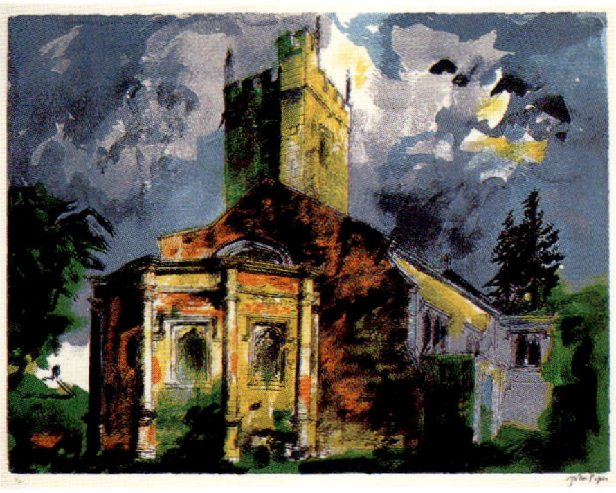

377

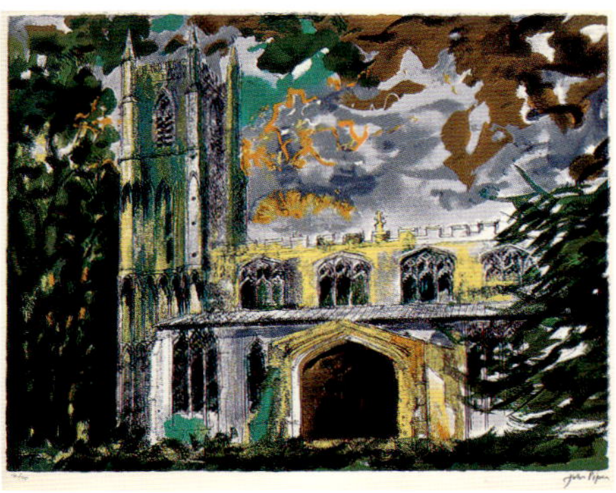

378

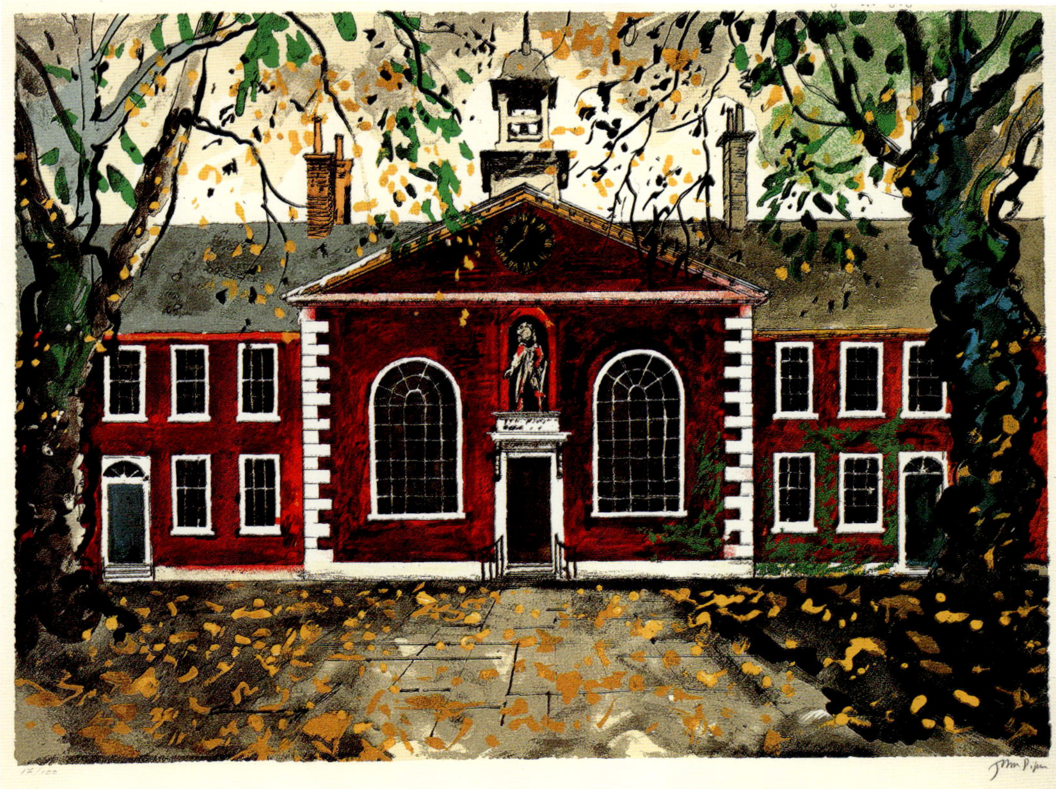

379

375
Clamecy, Burgundy
Screenprint 775 × 585 ($30\frac{1}{2} \times 23$)
Kelpra Studio 1985
Christie's Contemporary Art 1985
Vélin Arches 300gsm 910 × 710 ($35\frac{3}{4} \times 28$)
100 'John Piper' 10AP 5HC 2PP 3IC

376
Gothic Folly, Stowe
Etching 370 × 465 ($14\frac{9}{16} \times 18\frac{5}{16}$)
Kelpra Studio 1985
Marlborough Fine Art 1985
Vélin Arches 300gsm 540 × 622 ($21\frac{1}{4} \times 24\frac{1}{2}$)
70 'John Piper' 15AP 5PP

377
Sunningwell, Oxfordshire
Screenprint 505 × 655 ($19\frac{7}{8} \times 25\frac{3}{4}$)
Kelpra Studio 1985
Marlborough Fine Art 1985
Vélin Arches 300gsm 605 × 760 ($23\frac{13}{16} \times 29\frac{15}{16}$)
70 'John Piper' 15AP 5PP

378
Walsoken, Norfolk
Screenprint 505 × 665 ($19\frac{7}{8} \times 26\frac{3}{16}$)
Kelpra Studio 1985
Marlborough Fine Art 1985
Vélin Arches 300gsm 610 × 765 ($24 \times 30\frac{1}{8}$)
70 'John Piper' 15AP 5PP

379
The Geffrye Museum
Screenprint 462 × 633 ($18\frac{3}{16} \times 24\frac{15}{16}$)
Kelpra Studio 1985
Friends of the Geffrye Museum 1985
Vélin Arches 300gsm 564 × 739 ($22\frac{3}{16} \times 29\frac{1}{16}$)
100 'John Piper' 10AP 2PP

Sometimes incorrectly known as '*The Geffrye Museum in Autumn*'

380
Isle Abbots
Screenprint 685 × 460 (27 × 18)
Kelpra Studio 1986
CCA Galleries 1986
Vélin Arches 300gsm 790 × 560 (31 × 22)
100 'John Piper' 10AP 5HC 2PP 2IC

381
Ruishton
Screenprint 685 × 460 (27 × 18)
Kelpra Studio 1986
CCA Galleries 1986
Vélin Arches 300gsm 790 × 560 (31 × 22)
100 'John Piper' 10AP 5HC 2PP 2IC

382
Huish-Episcopi
Screenprint 790 × 560 (31 × 22)
Kelpra Studio 1986
CCA Galleries 1987
Vélin Arches 300gsm 685 × 460 (27 × 18)
100 'John Piper' 10AP 5HC 2PP 2IC

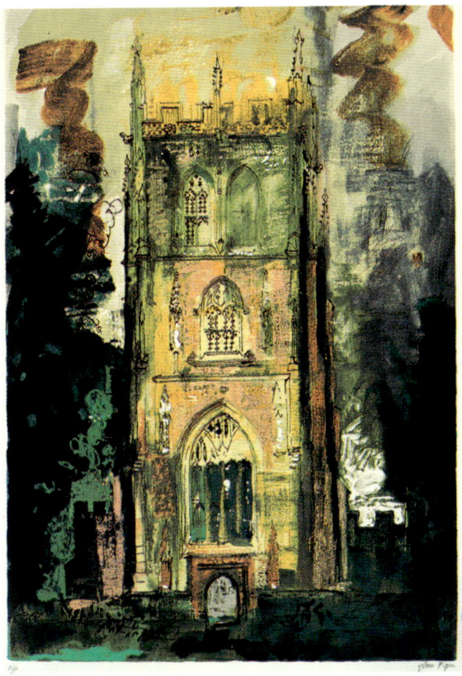

380

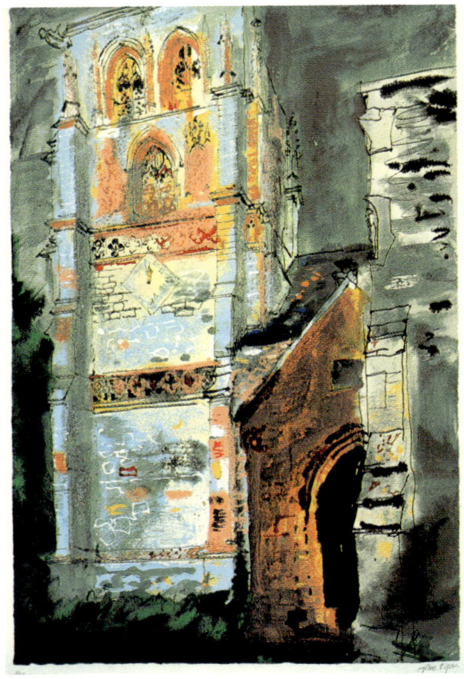

381

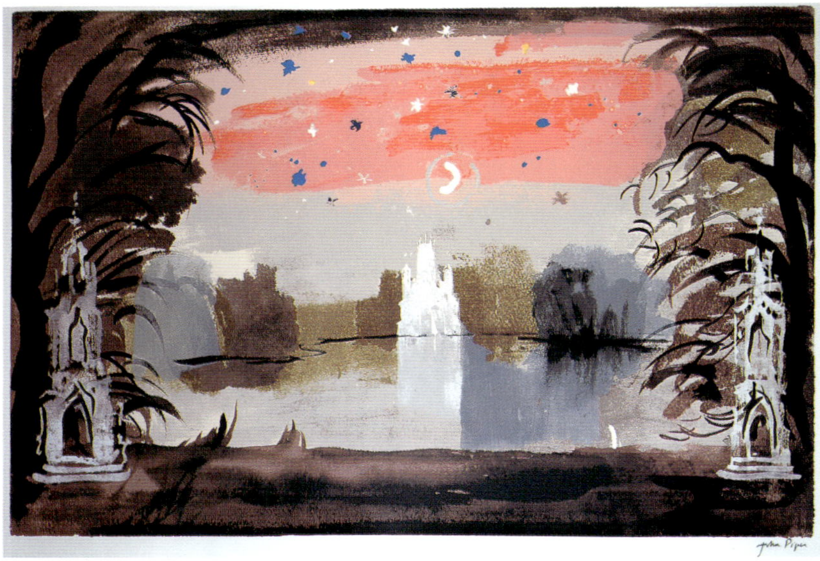

384

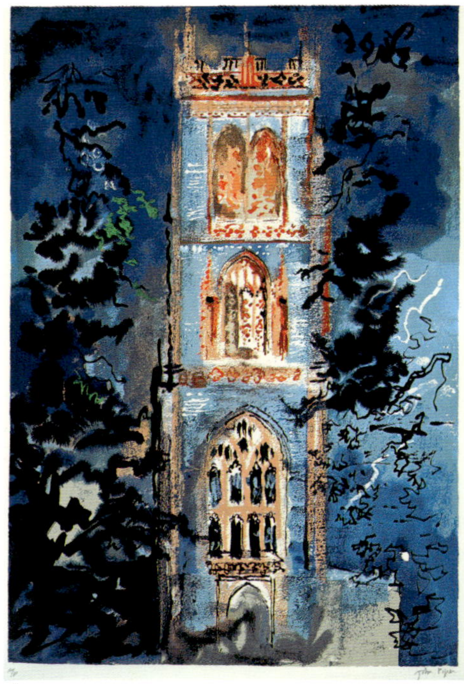

382

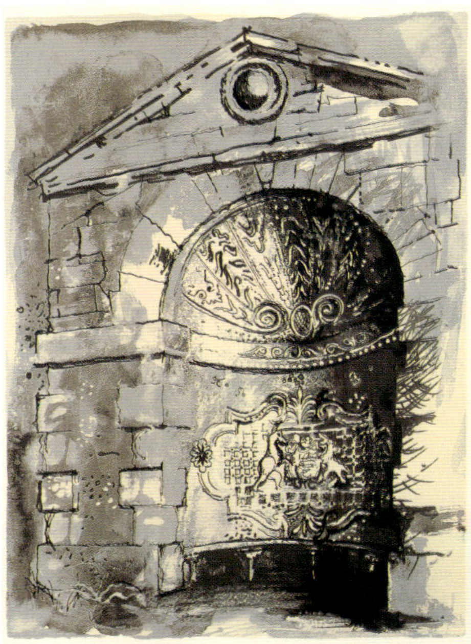

386

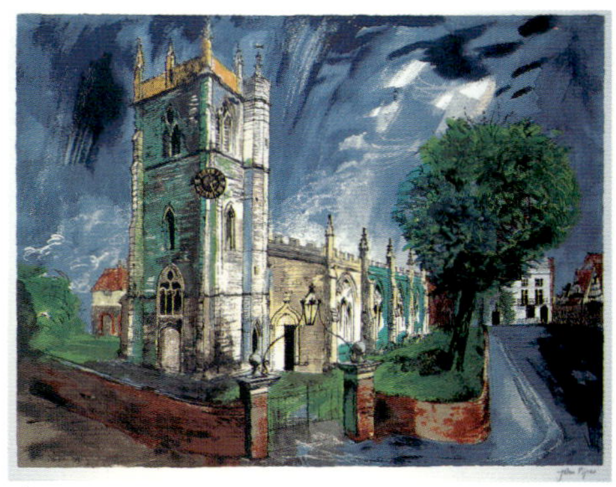

383

383
St Nicholas, Alcester
Screenprint 505 × 655 ($19\frac{7}{8} \times 25\frac{3}{4}$)
Kelpra Studio 1986
The Very Reverend Allan Shaw 1986
Vélin Arches 300gsm 688 × 840 ($27\frac{1}{8} \times 33\frac{1}{8}$)
100 'John Piper' 15AP 2PP

Sometimes incorrectly known as *'Alcester Church'*

384
The Quest
Screenprint 455 × 685 (18 × 27)
Kelpra Studio 1986
CCA Galleries 1986
Vélin Arches 300gsm 640 × 870 ($25\frac{1}{4} \times 34\frac{1}{4}$)
100 'John Piper' 10AP 5HC 2PP 2IC

385
Stansfield
Screenprint 860 × 450 ($33\frac{7}{8} \times 17\frac{3}{4}$)
Kelpra Studio 1986
CCA Galleries 1986
Vélin Arches 300gsm 1045 × 635 ($41\frac{1}{8} \times 25$)
100 'John Piper' 10AP 5HC 2PP 2IC

386
The Pebble Alcove, Stowe
Screenprint 615 × 453 ($23\frac{3}{4} \times 17\frac{7}{8}$)
Kelpra Studio 1986
Marlborough Fine Art 1986
Vélin Arches 300gsm 794 × 638 ($31\frac{1}{4} \times 25\frac{1}{8}$)
70 'John Piper' 15AP 5PP

387
Stowe, South of the House
Screenprint 455 × 570 ($17\frac{7}{8} \times 22\frac{7}{16}$)
Kelpra Studio 1986
Marlborough Fine Art 1986
Vélin Arches 300gsm 575 × 680 ($22\frac{5}{8} \times 26\frac{3}{4}$)
70 'John Piper' 15AP 5PP

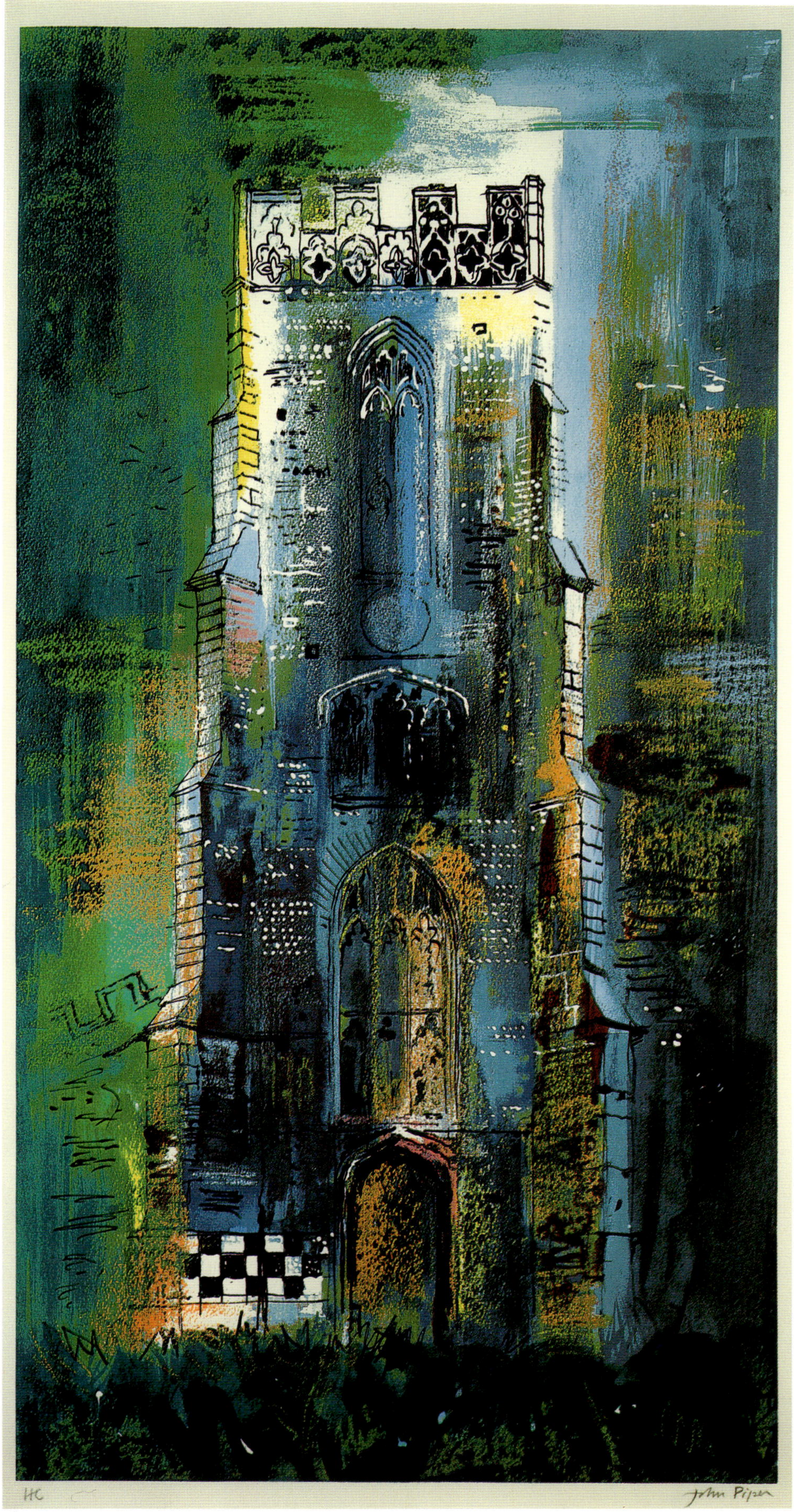

385

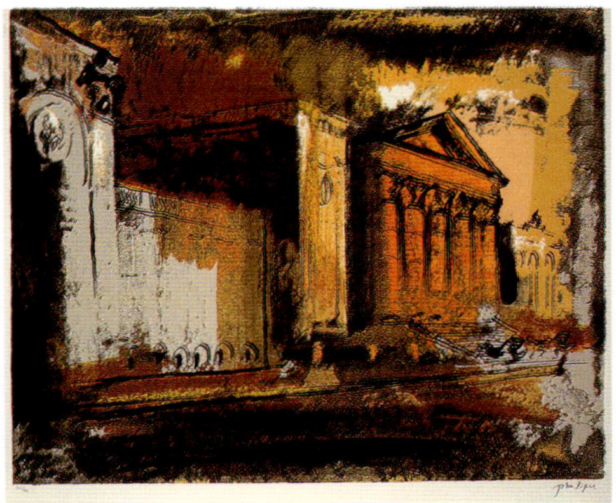

387

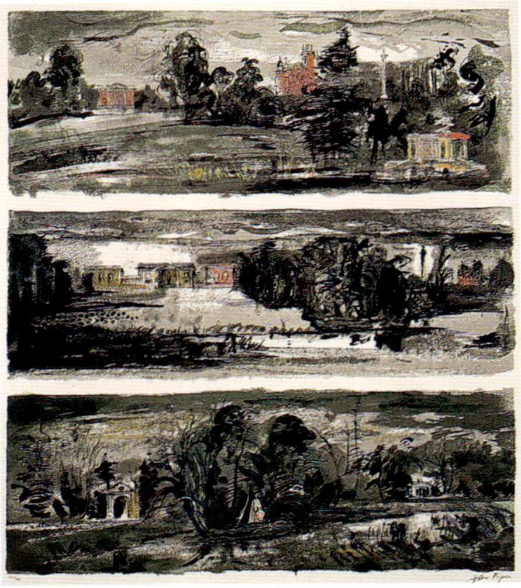

388

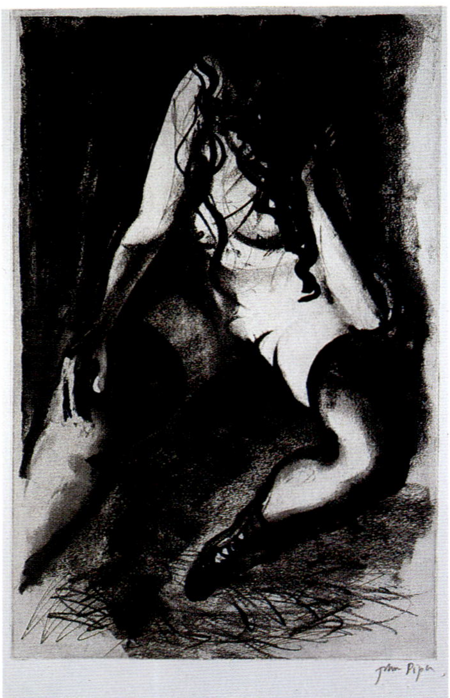

389

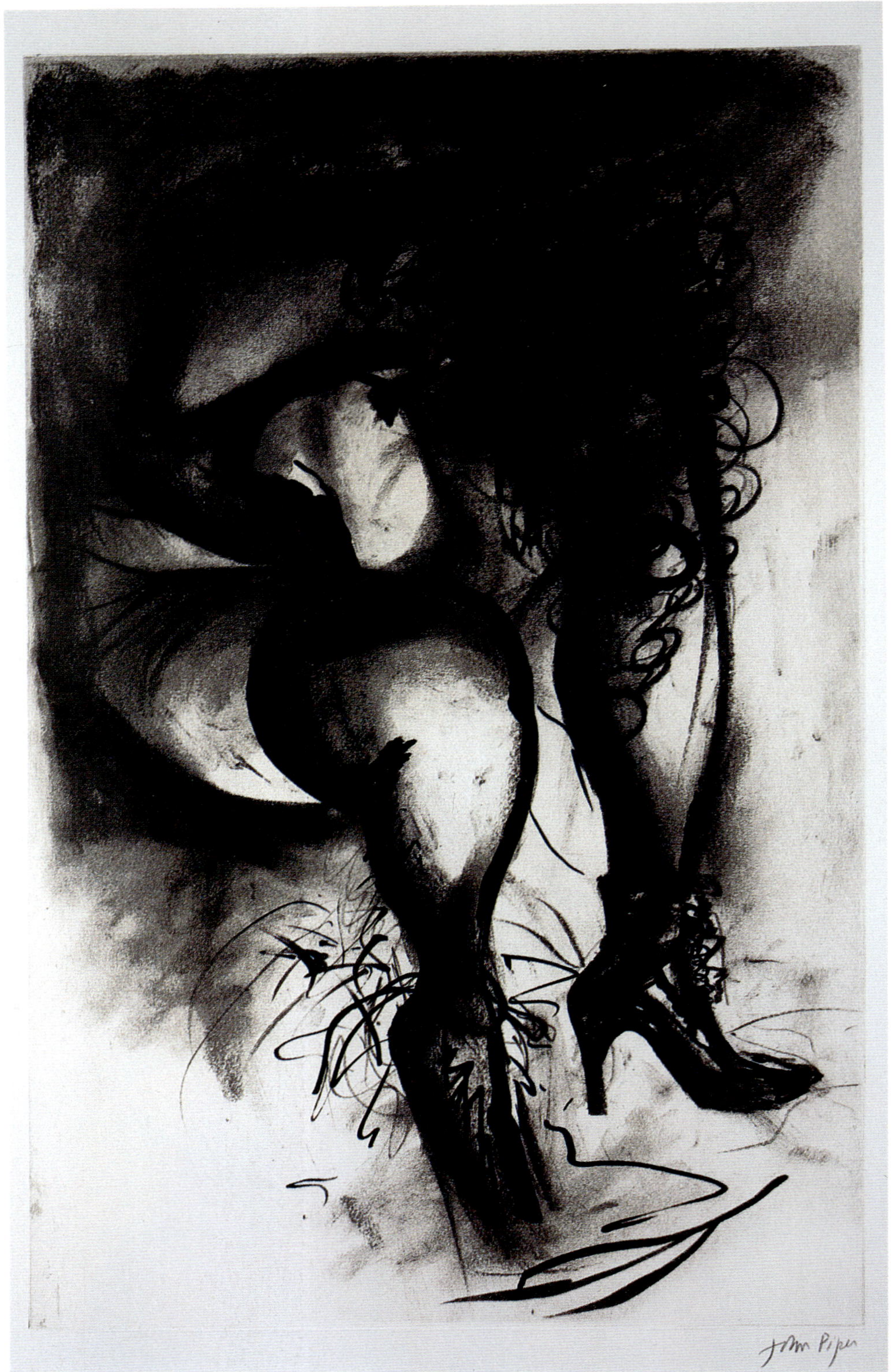

390

388
Stowe Triptych
Screenprint 615×545 ($24\frac{1}{4} \times 21\frac{5}{8}$)
Kelpra Studio 1986
Marlborough Fine Art 1986
Vélin Arches 300gsm 770×685 ($30\frac{1}{4} \times 27$)
70 'John Piper' 15AP 5PP

389
Nude I
Etching 495×320 ($19\frac{1}{2} \times 12\frac{5}{8}$)
Kelpra Studio 1986
Marlborough Fine Art 1986
Vélin Arches 300gsm 718×508 ($28\frac{1}{4} \times 20$)
70 'John Piper'. 15AP 5PP

390
Nude II
Etching and aquatint 492×320 ($19\frac{3}{8} \times 12\frac{5}{8}$)
Kelpra Studio 1986
Marlborough Fine Art 1987
Vélin Arches 300gsm 718×508 ($28\frac{1}{4} \times 20$)
70 'John Piper' 15AP 5PP

391
Dahlias and Ferns
Etching 405×550 ($16 \times 21\frac{3}{4}$)
Kelpra Studio 1987
CCA Galleries 1987
Vélin Arches 300gsm 590×710 ($23\frac{3}{4} \times 28$)
100 'John Piper' 10AP 5HC 2PP 2IC

392
Yellow Flowers
Etching and Aquatint 405×550 ($16 \times 21\frac{3}{4}$)
Kelpra Studio 1987
CCA Galleries 1987
Vélin Arches 300gsm 585×710 (23×28)
100 'John Piper' 10AP 5HC 2PP 2IC

Originally published as '*Blue Vase*'

393
Terrace with Morning Glories
Screenprint 490×680 ($19\frac{1}{4} \times 26\frac{3}{4}$)
Kelpra Studio 1987
Marlborough Fine Art 1987
Vélin Arches 300gsm 671×865 ($26\frac{1}{2} \times 34$)
70 'John Piper' 15AP 5PP

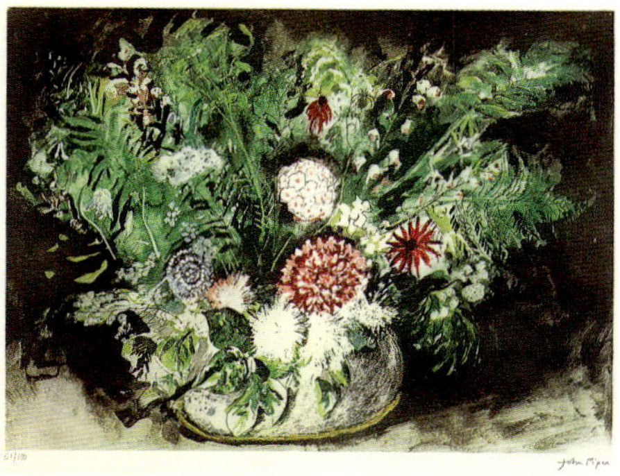
391

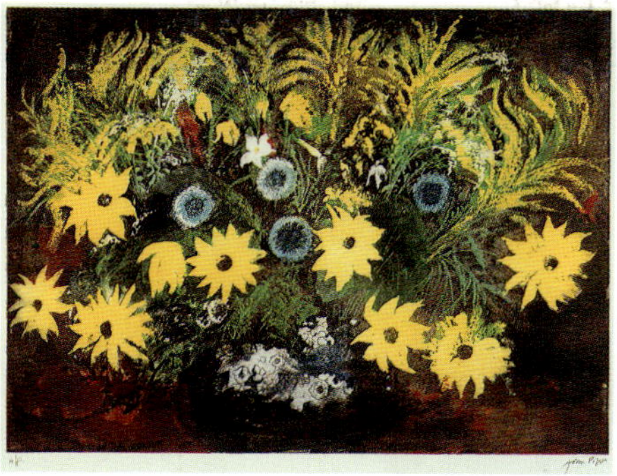
392

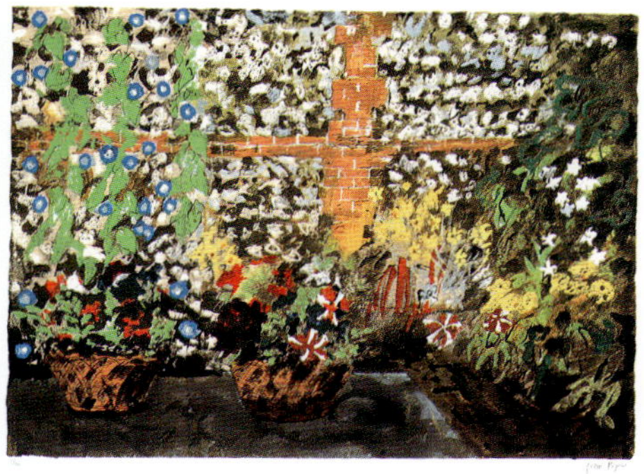
393

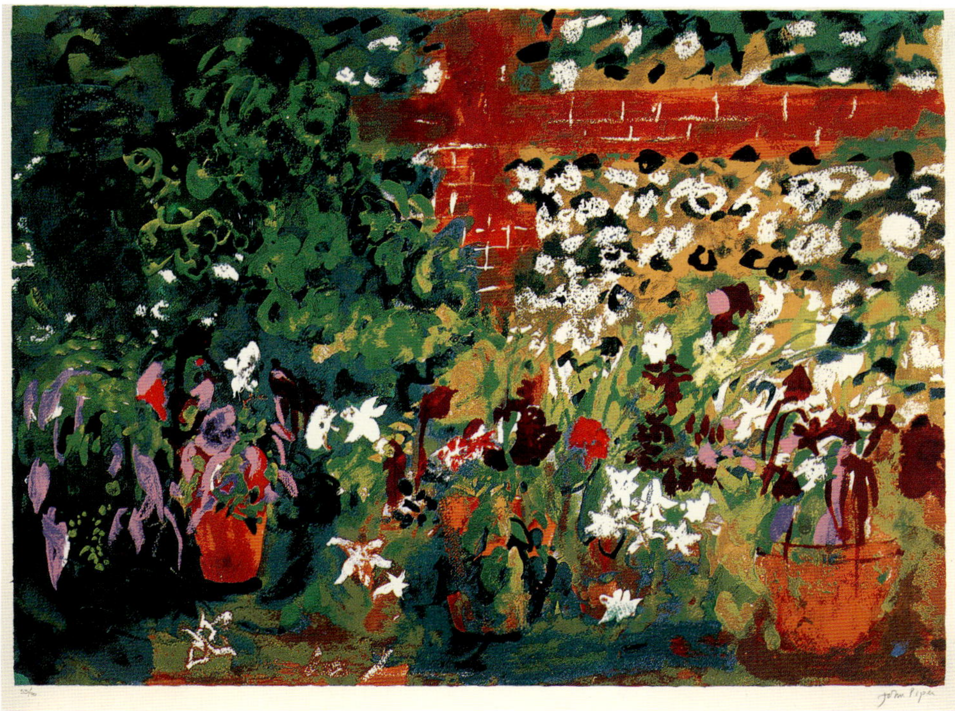
394

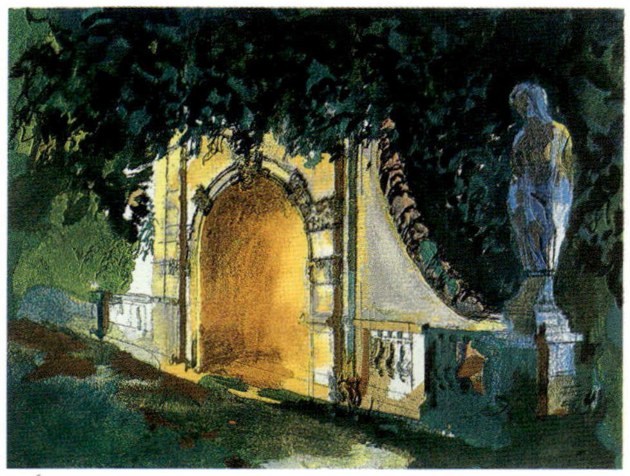
396

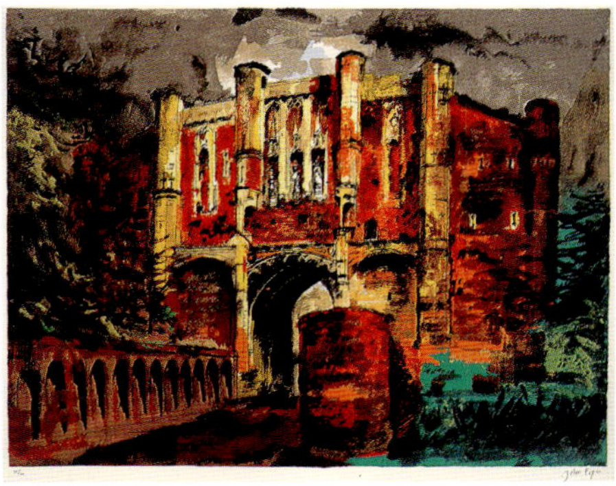
395

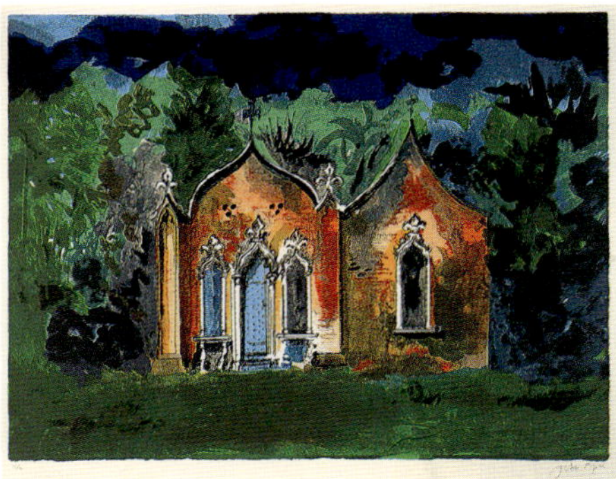
398

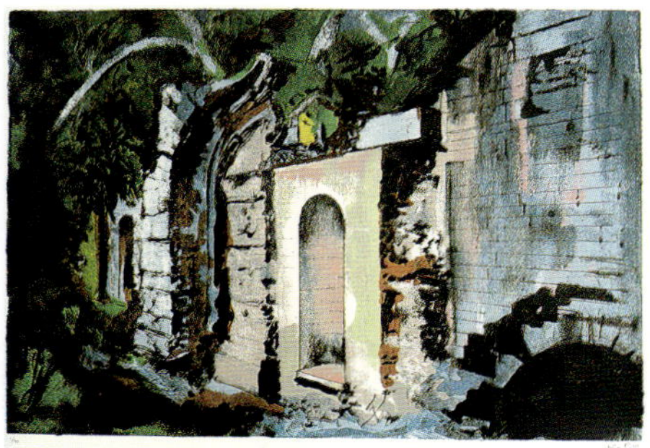
397

394
Terrace with Red Pots
Screenprint 490×670 ($19\frac{1}{4}\times26\frac{3}{8}$)
Kelpra Studio 1987
Marlborough Fine Art 1987
Vélin Arches 300gsm 673×852 ($26\frac{1}{2}\times33\frac{9}{16}$)
70 'John Piper' 15AP 5PP

One variant print with the brick wall printed in orange and signed 'John Piper' b.r. is known to exist.

395
Thornton Abbey Gateway
Screenprint 458×595 ($18\times23\frac{3}{8}$)
Kelpra Studio 1987
Marlborough Fine Art 1987
Vélin Arches 300gsm 642×595 ($25\frac{1}{4}\times30\frac{3}{4}$)
70 'John Piper' 15AP 5PP

396
The Grotto, Halswell, Somerset
Screenprint 455×605 ($17\frac{7}{8}\times23\frac{13}{16}$)
Kelpra Studio 1987
Marlborough Fine Art (London) 1987
Vélin Arches 300gsm 638×787 ($25\frac{1}{8}\times31$)
70 'John Piper' 15AP 5PP

397
Cascade Bridge, Halswell
Screenprint 462×673 ($18\frac{1}{4}\times26\frac{1}{2}$)
Kelpra Studio 1987
Marlborough Fine Art 1987
Vélin Arches 300gsm 648×855 ($25\frac{1}{2}\times33\frac{5}{8}$)
70 'John Piper' 15AP 5HC 5PP

398
The Red House, Painswick, Glos.
Screenprint 454×603 ($17\frac{7}{8}\times23\frac{3}{4}$)
Kelpra Studio 1987
Marlbrough Fine Art 1987
Vélin Arches 300gsm 633×782 ($24\frac{15}{16}\times30\frac{3}{4}$)
70 'John Piper' 15AP 5HC 5PP

399
Old Church of Mynachlogddu
Etching 395×534 ($15\frac{1}{2} \times 21$)
Kelpra Studio 1987
Orde Levinson 1987
Vélin Arches 300gsm 579×699 ($22\frac{3}{4} \times 27\frac{1}{2}$)
70 'John Piper' 15AP 2PP 1HC

Sometimes incorrectly known as '*Maenchlochlung*' or '*St Dogmael*'

400
Wild Bunch
Etching 535×395 ($21 \times 15\frac{1}{2}$)
Kelpra Studio 1987
Orde Levinson 1987
Vélin Arches 300gsm 711×561 (28×22)
70 'John Piper' 15AP 2PP 1HC

401
Llyn Teifi
Etching 396×578 ($15\frac{1}{2} \times 22\frac{3}{4}$)
Kelpra Studio 1987
Orde Levinson 1987
Vélin Arches 300gsm 579×745 ($22\frac{3}{4} \times 29\frac{5}{16}$)
70 'John Piper' 15AP 2PP 1HC

In 1989 a translation/interpretation of this image was woven as a tapestry by Ibenstein Weavers.

402
Ottery St Mary
Screenprint 570×760 ($22\frac{1}{2} \times 30$)
Kelpra Studio 1987
CCA Galleries 1988
Vélin Arches 300gsm 735×920 ($29 \times 36\frac{1}{2}$)
100 'John Piper' 10AP 5HC 2PP 2IC

403
Façade
Screenprint 450×585 ($17\frac{3}{4} \times 23$)
Kelpra Studio 1987
CCA Galleries 1988
Vélin Arches 300gsm 635×770 ($25 \times 30\frac{1}{4}$)
100 'John Piper' 10AP 5HC 2PP 2IC

404
Teffont Evias
Etching 530×397 ($20\frac{3}{4} \times 15\frac{1}{2}$)
Kelpra Studio 1988
Marlborough Fine Art 1988
Vélin Arches 300gsm 695×550 ($27\frac{1}{4} \times 21\frac{5}{8}$)
70 'John Piper' 15AP 5HC 5PP

Teffont Evias is the locally accepted name of the church of St Michael and All Angels.

405
Fawley Bottom
Screenprint 410×560 ($16\frac{1}{8} \times 22$)
Kelpra Studio 1988
Marlborough Fine Art 1989
Vélin Arches 300gsm 592×742 ($23\frac{1}{4} \times 29\frac{1}{4}$)
70 'John Piper' 15AP 5HC 5PP

Originally published as '*Fawley Bottom Farmhouse*'. Sometimes incorrectly known as '*Sebastian's Farm*'

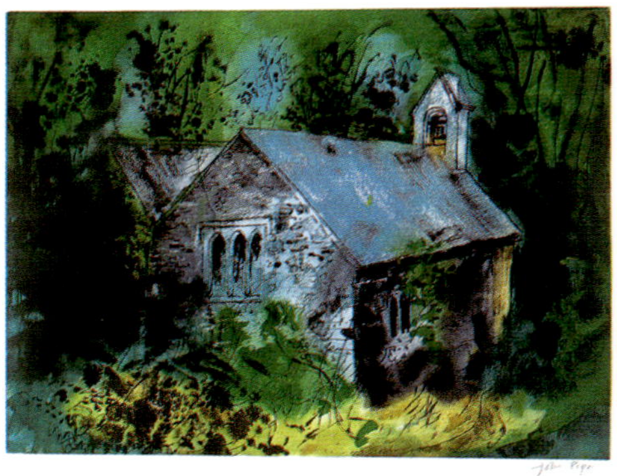
399

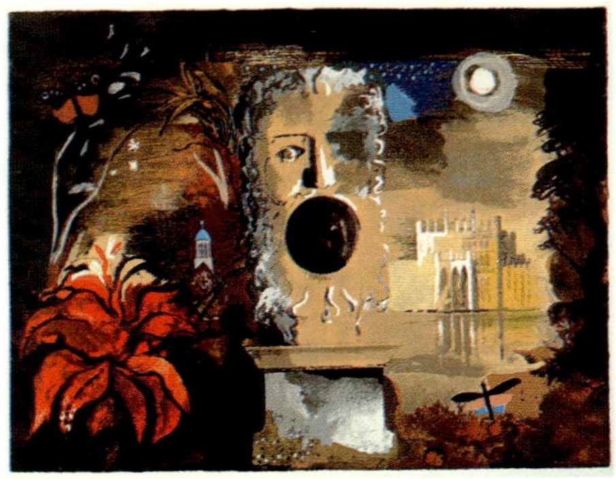
403

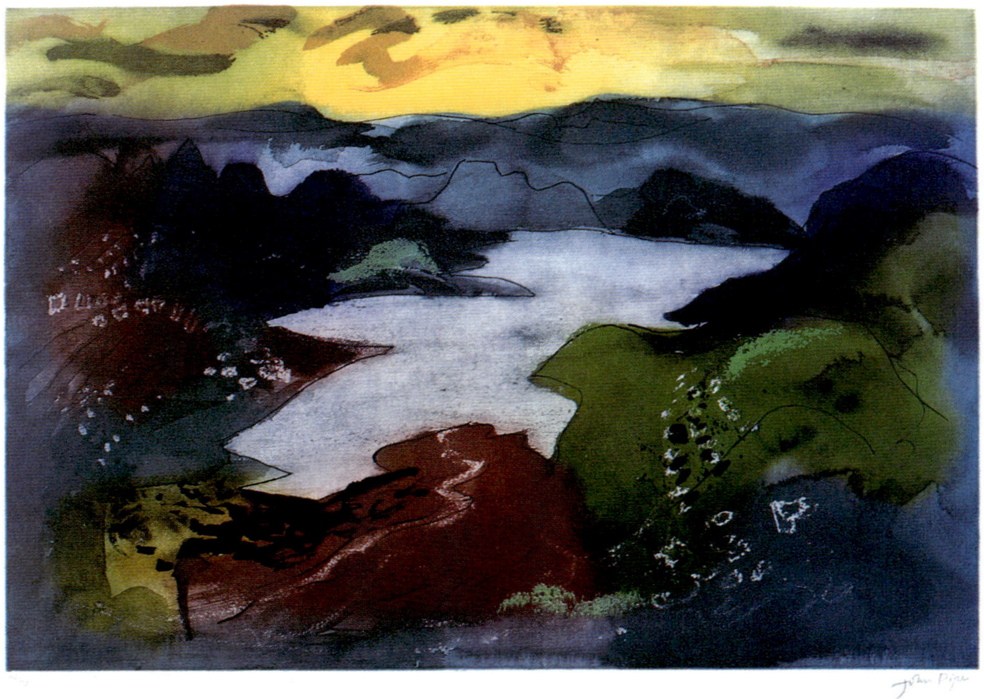
401

406
Kirkham Priory Gateway
Etching 400×520 ($15\frac{3}{4} \times 20\frac{1}{2}$)
Kelpra Studio 1988
CCA Galleries 1988
Vélin Arches 300gsm 570×675 ($22\frac{1}{2} \times 26\frac{1}{2}$)
100 'John Piper' 10AP 5HC 2PP 2IC

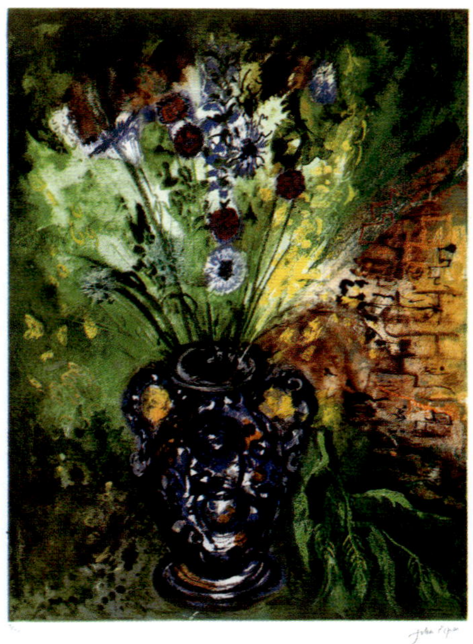
400

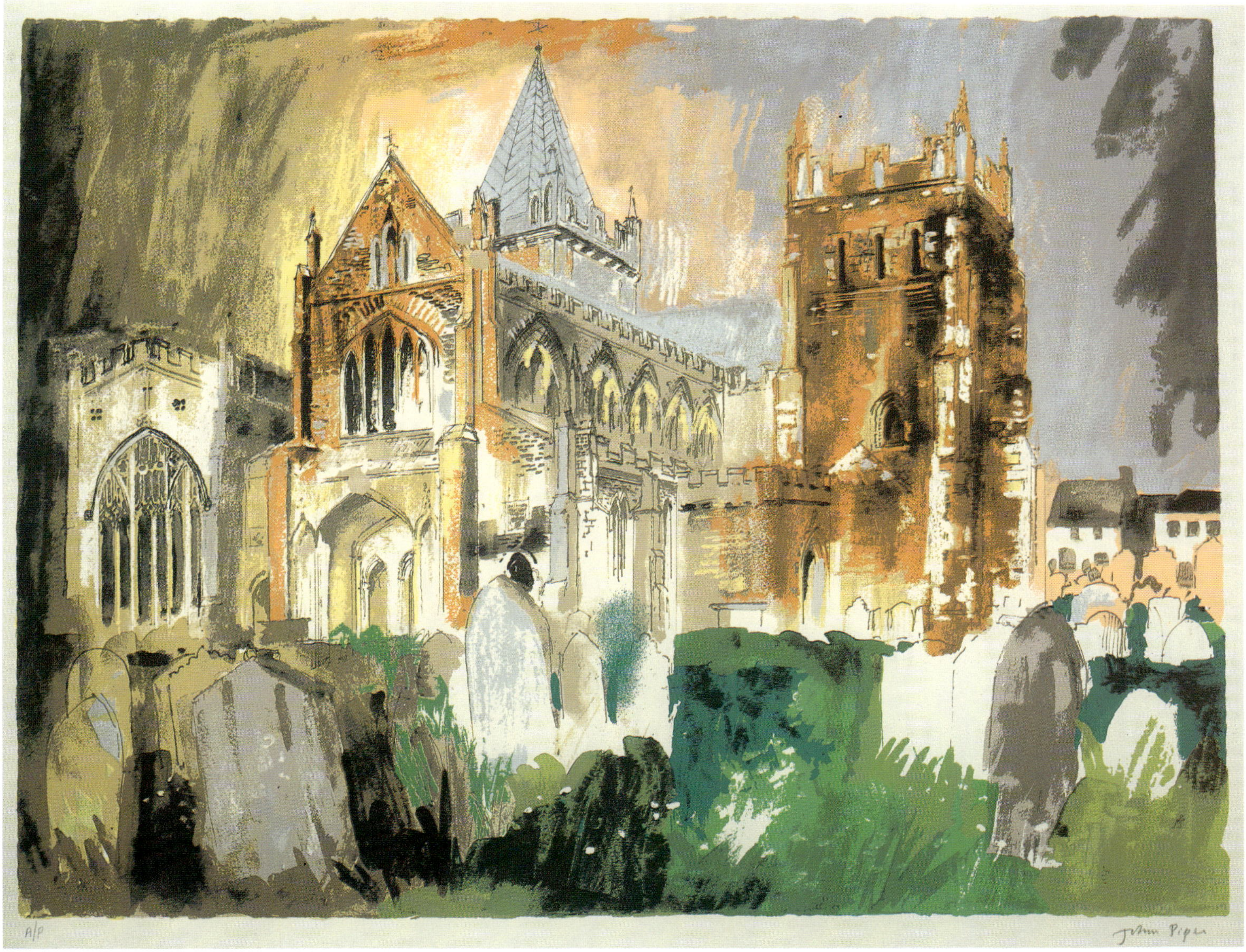

402

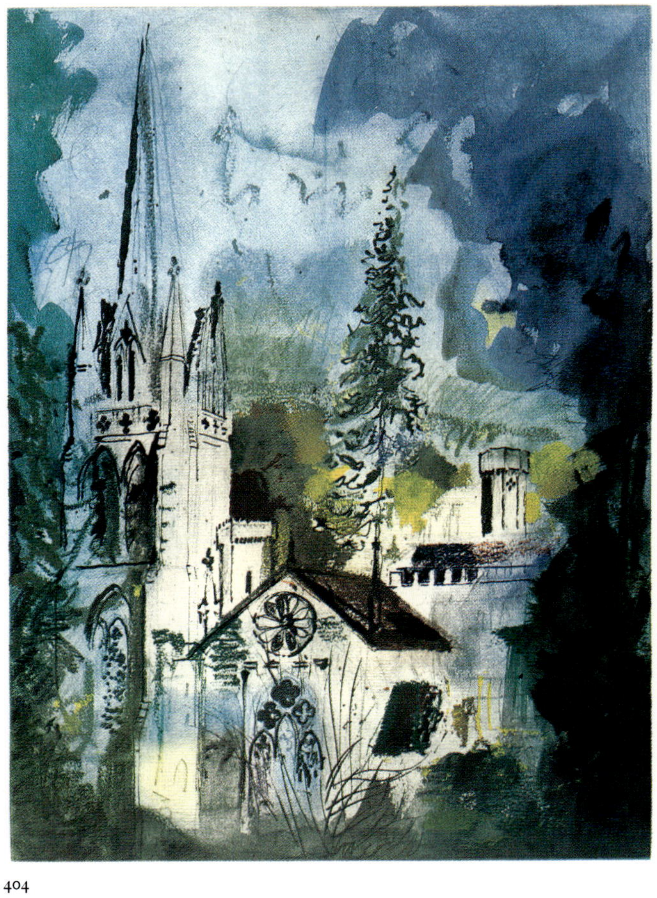

404

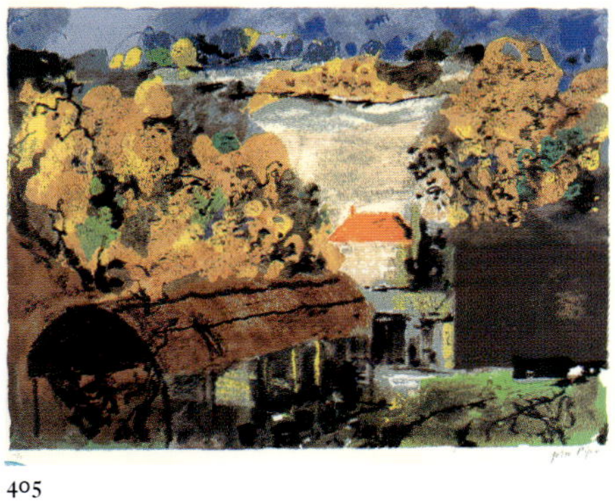

405

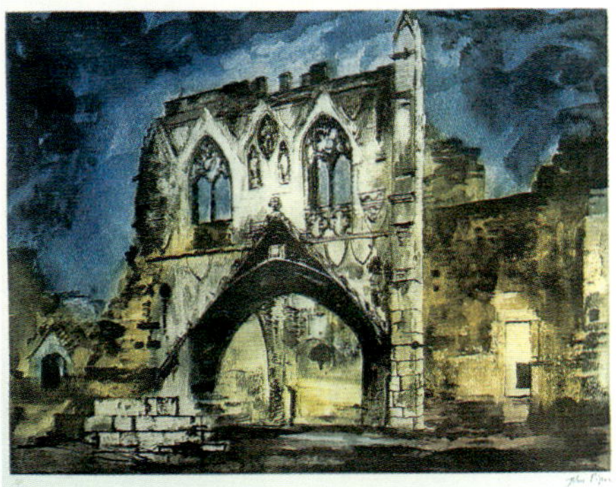

406

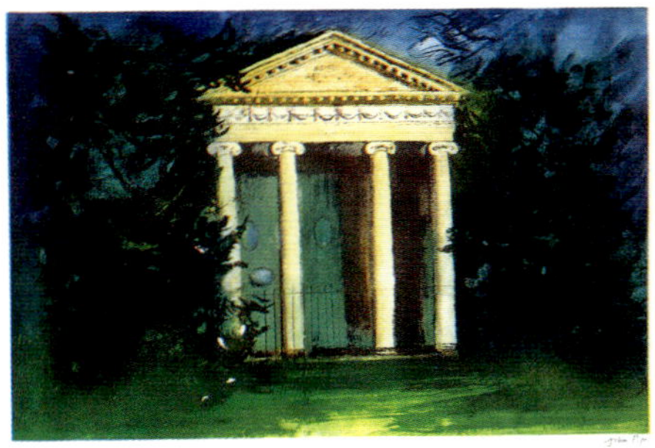
408

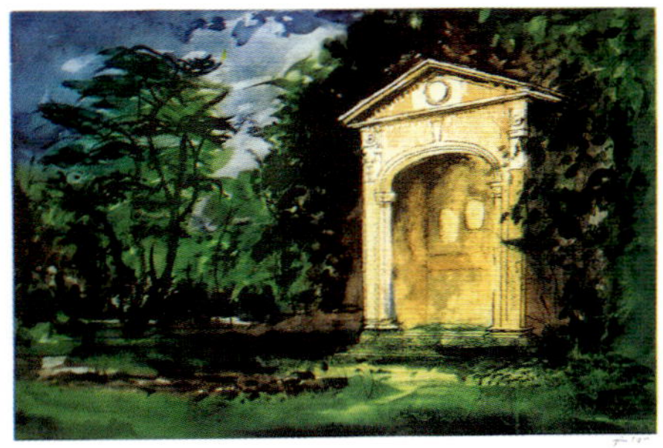
409

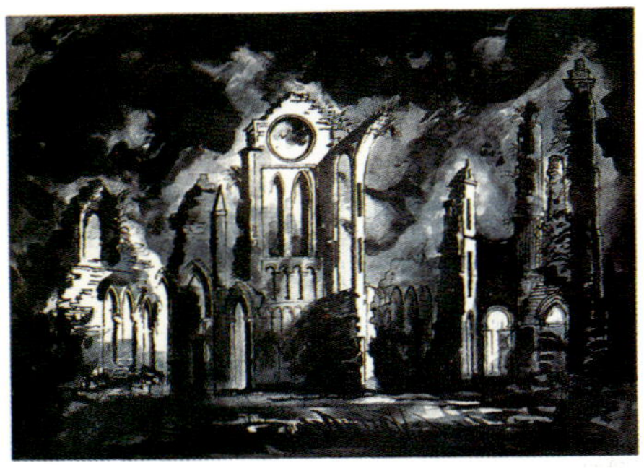
407

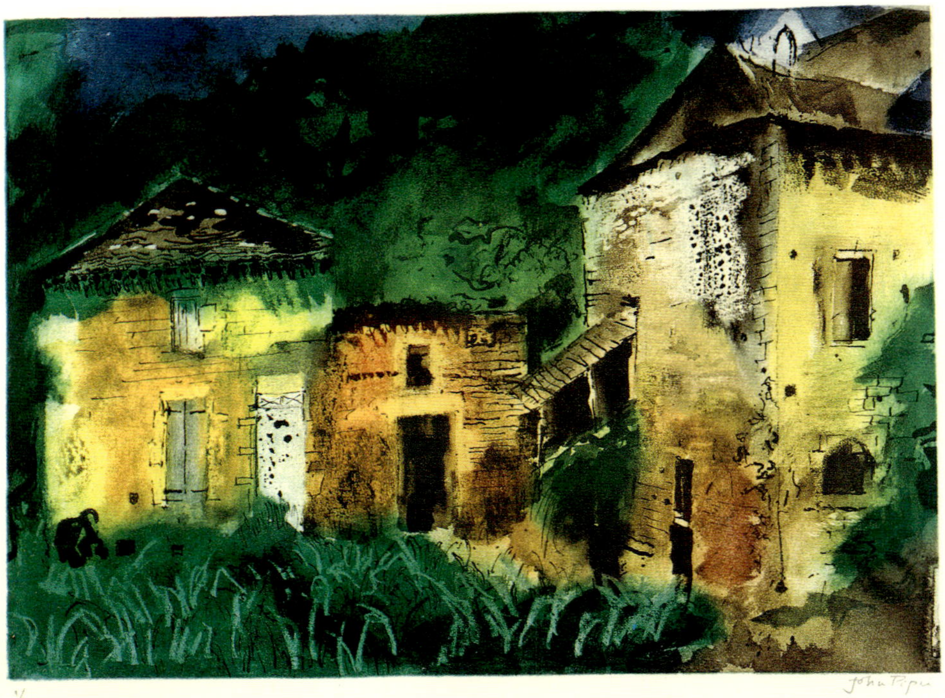
411

407
Abroath Abbey
Screenprint 398×557 (15¾×21⅞)
Kelpra Studio 1988
CCA Galleries 1988
Vélin Arches 300gsm 570×710 (22½×28)
100 'John Piper' 10AP 5HC 2PP 2IC

One variant print in black, signed 'John Piper' and probably a proof, is known to exist. Originally published as '*Abroath Remarkable Ruins*'

408
The Temple of Diana
Etching 400×595 (15¾×23½)
Kelpra Studio 1988
CCA Galleries 1988
Vélin Arches 300gsm 565×755 (22¼×29½)
100 'John Piper' 10AP 5HC 2PP 2IC

409
The Temple of Flora
Etching 400×595 (15¾×23½)
Kelpra Studio 1988
CCA Galleries 1988
Vélin Arches 300gsm 565×755 (22¼×29½)
100 'John Piper' 10AP 5HC 2PP 2IC

410
Flowers in a Black Pot
Etching and aquatint 520×394 (21½×15½)
Kelpra Studio 1988
Marlborough Fine Art 1988
Vélin Arches 300gsm 720×547 (28¼×21½)
70 'John Piper' 15AP 5PP

411
Les Junies
Etching and aquatint 402×560 (15⅞×22)
Kelpra Studio 1988
Marlborough Fine Art 1988
Vélin Arches 300gsm 566×712 (22¼×28)
70 'John Piper' 15AP 5PP

412
Hales, Norfolk
Etching and aquatint 400×590 (15¾×23¼)
Kelpra Studio 1989
Marlborough Fine Art 1989
Vélin Arches 300gsm 560×740 (22½×29½)
70 'John Piper' 15AP 5PP

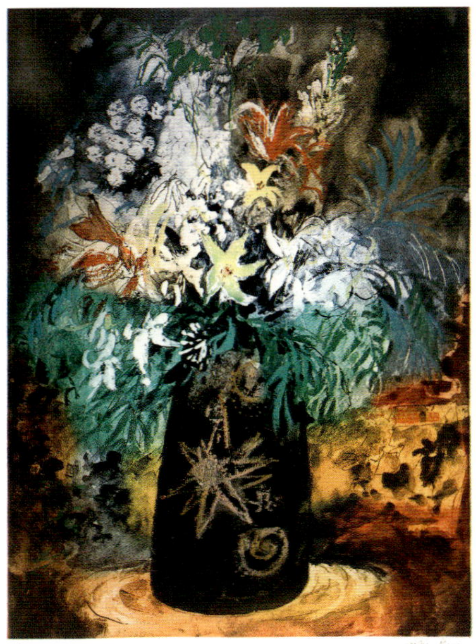
410

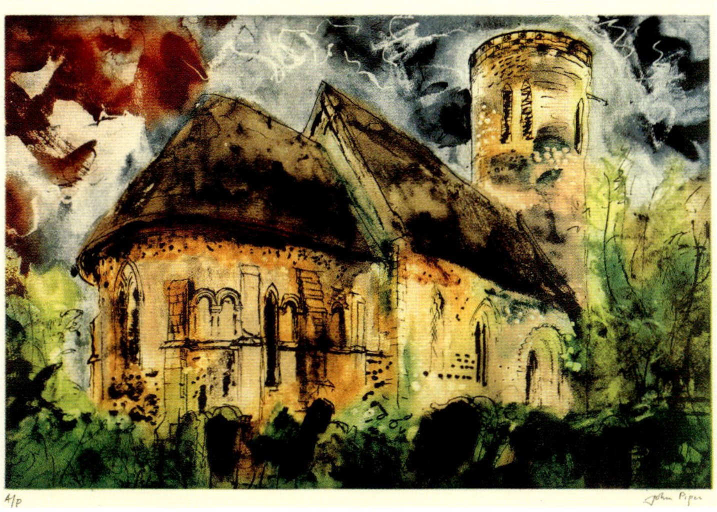

412

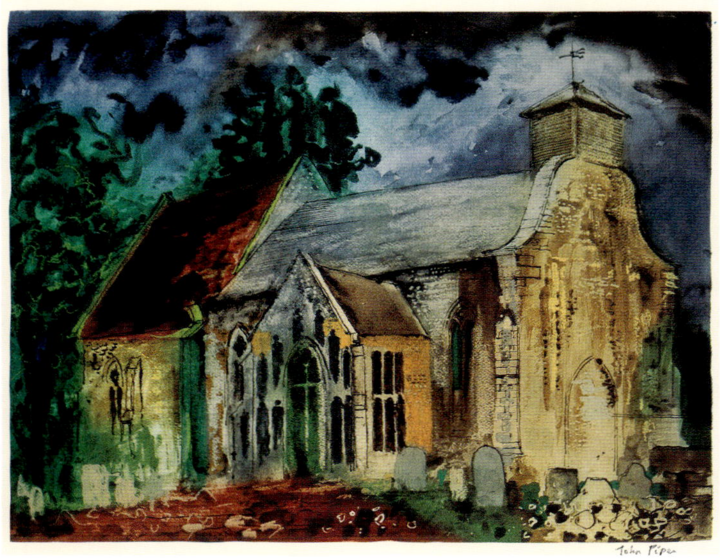

413

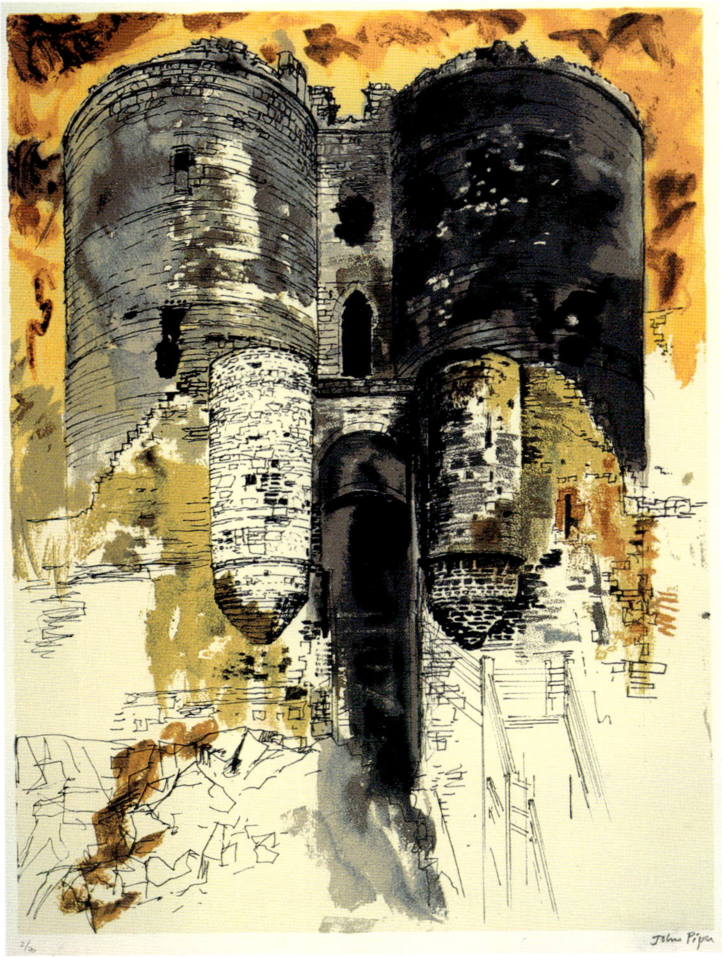

414

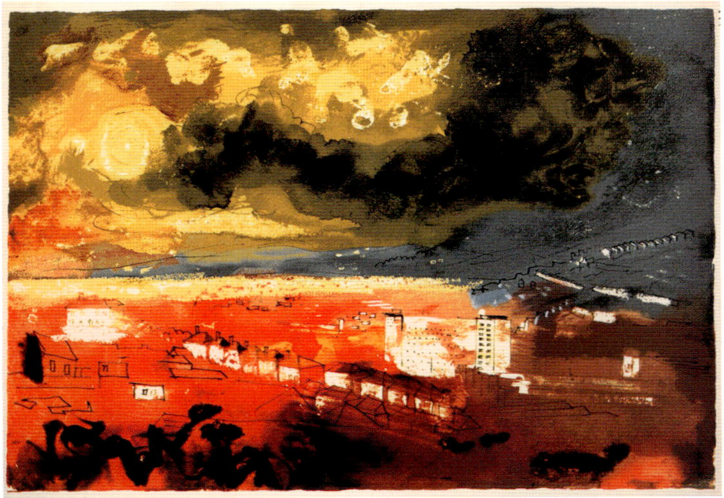

415

413
Bridgham Parish Church
Etching and aquatint 398×522 ($15\frac{11}{16} \times 20\frac{5}{8}$)
Kelpra Studio 1989
Marlborough Fine Art 1989
Vélin Arches 300gsm 570×680 ($22\frac{3}{8} \times 26\frac{3}{4}$)
70 'John Piper' 10AP 5PP

Sometimes incorrectly known as '*Norfolk Church*'

414
Harlech Castle
Screenprint 611×460 ($24\frac{1}{16} \times 18\frac{1}{16}$)
Kelpra Studio 1989
Marlborough Fine Art 1989
Vélin Arches 300gsm 795×643 ($31\frac{1}{4} \times 25\frac{1}{4}$)
70 'John Piper' 15AP 5PP

415
Swansea West
Screenprint 410×610 ($16\frac{1}{8} \times 24$)
Kelpra Studio 1989
Marlborough Fine Art 1989
Vélin Arches 300gsm 595×790 ($23\frac{3}{16} \times 31\frac{1}{8}$)
70 'John Piper' 15AP 5PP

416
Blenheim Bridge
Screenprint 420 × 595 ($16\frac{1}{2} \times 23\frac{1}{2}$)
Kelpra Studio 1988
CCA Galleries 1989
Vélin Arches 300gsm 600 × 780 ($23\frac{5}{8} \times 30\frac{3}{4}$)
100 'John Piper' 10AP 5HC 2PP 2IC

417
Blenheim Palace
Screenprint 455 × 870 ($18 \times 34\frac{1}{4}$)
Kelpra Studio 1988
CCA Galleries 1988
Vélin Arches 300gsm 655 × 1045 ($25\frac{3}{4} \times 41\frac{1}{8}$)
100 'John Piper' 10AP 5HC 2PP 2IC

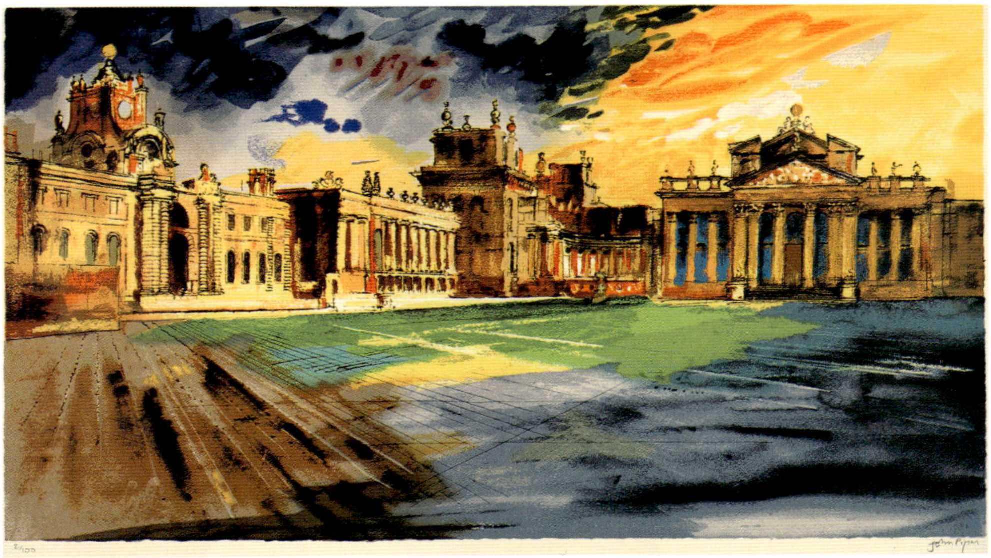

417

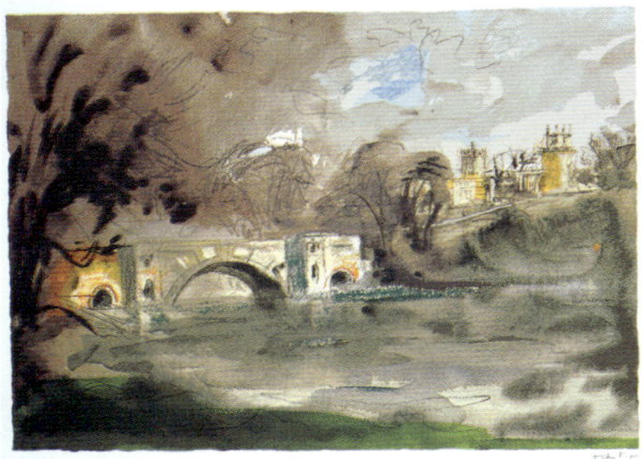

416

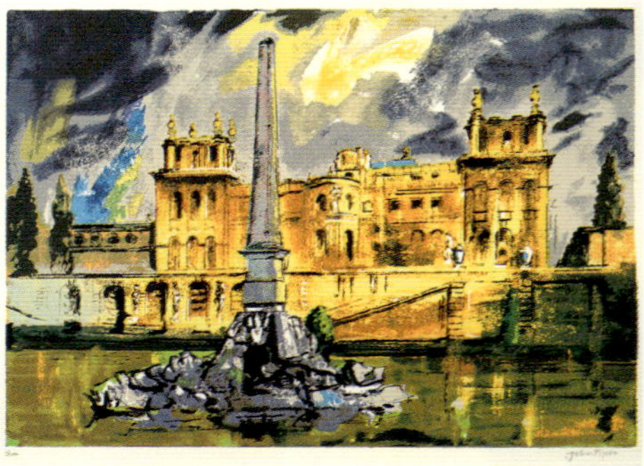

418

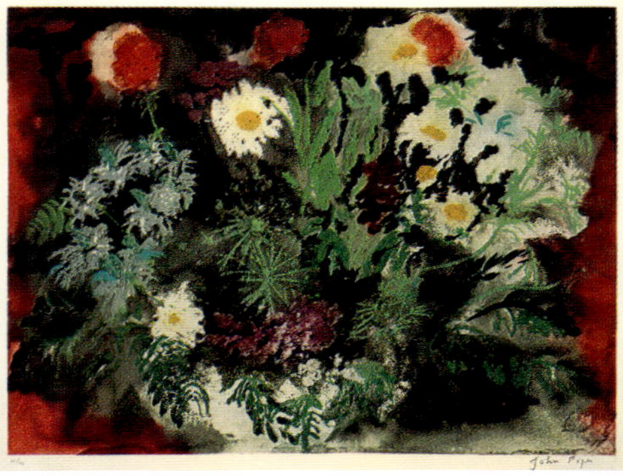

419

418
Duchêne Fountain, Blenheim
Screenprint 598 × 420 ($23\frac{1}{2} \times 16\frac{1}{2}$)
Kelpra Studio 1989
CCA Galleries 1989
Vélin Arches 300gsm 780 × 583 ($30\frac{7}{8} \times 22\frac{7}{8}$)
100 'John Piper' 10AP 5HC 2PP 2IC

Sometimes incorrectly known as '*Blenheim Fountain*'

419
Late Summer Flowers
Etching and aquatint 410 × 545 ($16 \times 21\frac{1}{2}$)
Kelpra Studio 1989
Marlborough Fine Art 1989
Vélin Arches 300gsm 585 × 710 (23 × 28)
70 'John Piper' 15AP 5PP

420
Sunflowers
Etching and aquatint 414 × 548 ($15\frac{7}{8} \times 21\frac{1}{2}$)
Kelpra Studio 1989
National Art-Collections Fund (NACF) 1989
Vélin Arches 300gsm 580 × 705 ($22\frac{3}{4} \times 27\frac{3}{4}$)
70 'John Piper' 15AP 5PP

421
Inglesham
Lithograph 380 × 565 ($15 \times 22\frac{1}{4}$)
Curwen Studio 1989
The Society for the Protection of Ancient Buildings (SPAB) 1989
Lana 300gsm 542 × 715 ($21\frac{5}{16} \times 28\frac{1}{8}$)
100 'John Piper' AP (unknown)

Donated to raise funds for the SPAB in memory of John Betjeman. The image was also repr. on the award certificate 'The John Betjeman Award' given by the SPAB. Some artist's proofs and printer's proofs were printed (estimated at 10) but the exact figure is not known.

422
Swansea East
Screenprint 410 × 600 ($16\frac{1}{2} \times 23\frac{5}{8}$)
Kelpra Studio 1989
Marlborough Fine Art 1989
Vélin Arches 300gsm 595 × 782 ($23\frac{3}{8} \times 30\frac{3}{4}$)
70 'John Piper' 15AP 5PP

423 (detail Plate 7)
Waddesdon
Screenprint 422 × 570 ($16\frac{5}{8} \times 22\frac{1}{2}$)
Kelpra Studio 1989
Marlborough Fine Art 1989
Vélin Arches 300gsm 608 × 753 ($24 \times 29\frac{5}{8}$)
70 'John Piper' 15AP 5PP

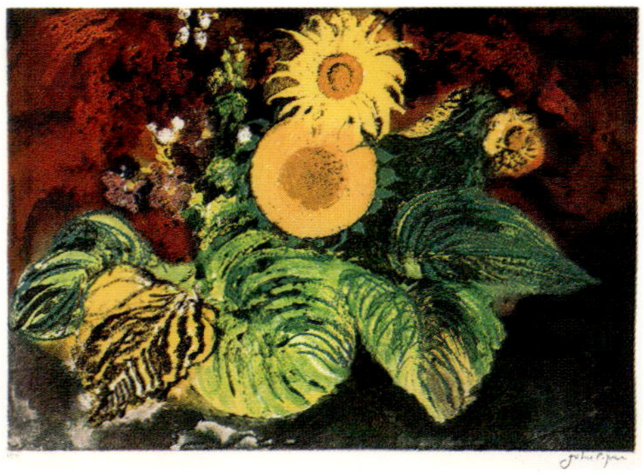

420

424
Street Scene in *Don Giovanni*
Screenprint 292 × 495 ($11\frac{1}{2} \times 19\frac{1}{2}$)
Kelpra Studio 1989
Glyndebourne Productions Limited 1989
Vélin Arches 300gsm 475 × 675 ($18\frac{3}{4} \times 26\frac{1}{2}$)
70 'John Piper' 15AP 5PP

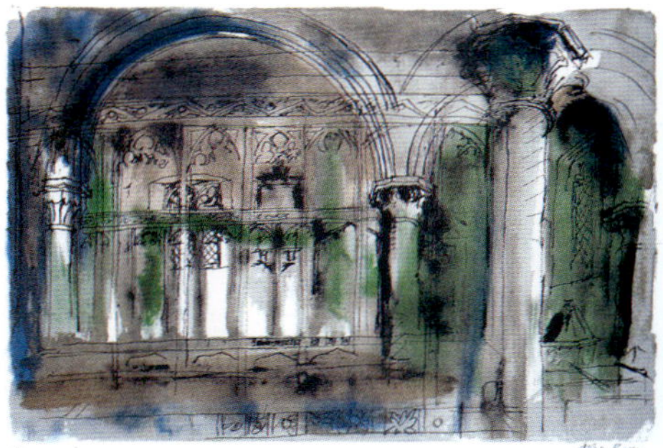

421

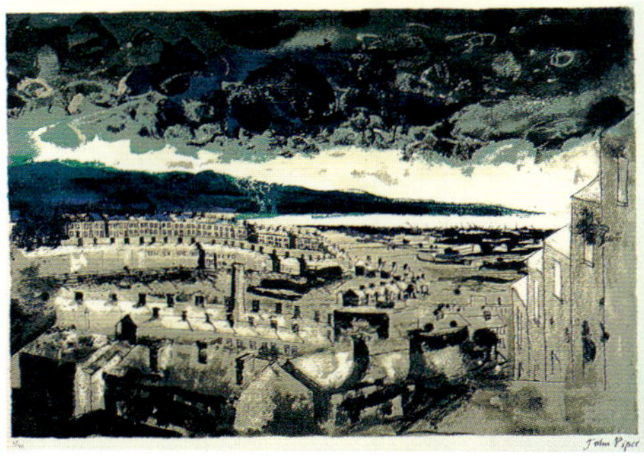

422

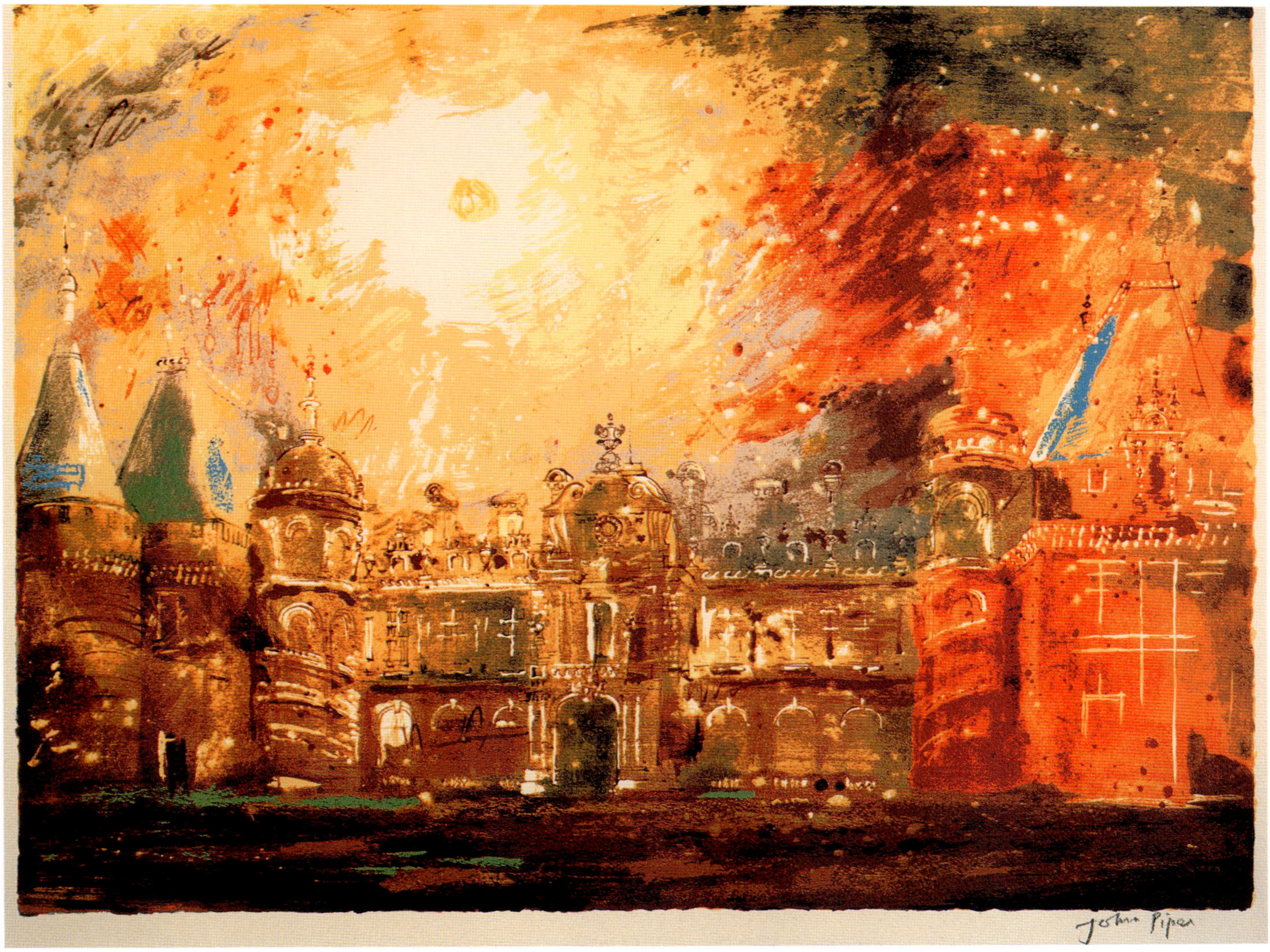

423

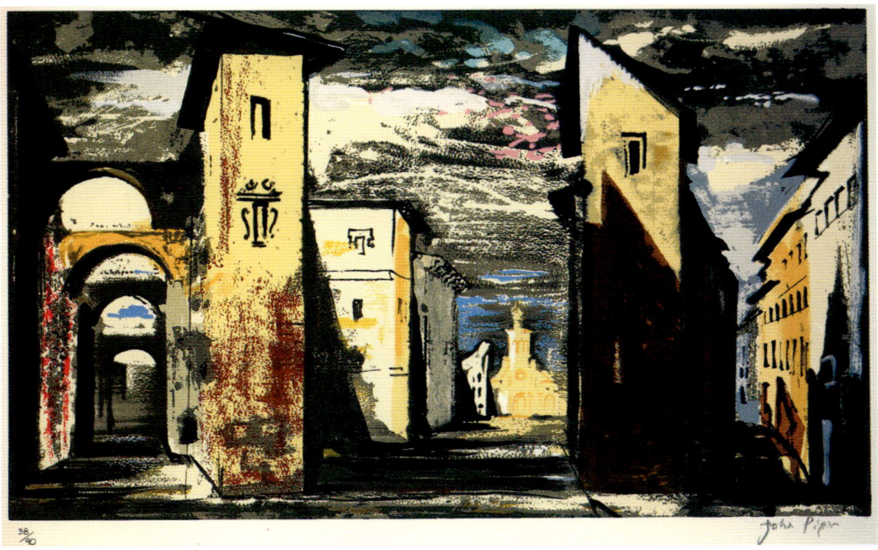

424

425
Alpilles
Etching and aquatint 407×613 (16×24¼)
Kelpra Studio 1989
Marlborough Fine Art 1990
Vélin Arches 300gsm 580×769 (22¾×30¼)
70 'John Piper' 15AP 5PP

426
Locmariaquer, Brittany
Etching and aquatint 410×615 (16¼×24½)
Kelpra Studio 1990
Marlborough Fine Art 1990
Vélin Arches 300gsm 580×769 (22¾×30¼)
70 'John Piper' 15AP 5PP

427
Halifax
Screenprint 380×597 (15×23½)
Kelpra Studio 1990
Nicholas Fisher 1990
Vélin Arches 300gsm 565×780 (22¼×30¾)
70 'JP' 15AP 5PP

Each print was initialled 'JP' by the artist.

428
Ceres and Proserpine
Etching and aquatint 420×555 (16½×21¾)
Kelpra Studio 1990
Marlborough Graphics Ltd 1990
Vélin Arches 300gsm 605×737 (23¾×29)
70 'JP' 15AP 5PP

Each print was initialled 'JP' by the artist.

429 (detail Plate 8)
Blue Hydrangea
Screenprint 405×545 (16×21½)
Kelpra Studio 1990
Marlborough Graphics Ltd 1990
Vélin Arches 300gsm 590×730 (23¼×28¾)
70 'JP' 15AP 5PP

Each print was initialled 'JP' by the artist.

430
Ottery St Mary
Screenprint 406×540 (16×21¼)
Kelpra Studio 1990
Marlborough Graphics Ltd 1991
Vélin Arches 300gsm 587×724 (23×28½)
70 'John Piper' and 'John Piper JECP' 15AP 5PP

Some prints were signed 'John Piper' and, when the artist felt he could not sign each print himself, he had a block-stamp made with the letters 'John Piper JECP'. Each print was then, under the artist's supervision, block-stamped in ink 'John Piper JECP'.

431
Manorbier, Dyfed
Screenprint 406×540 (16×21¼)
Kelpra Studio 1990
Marlborough Graphics Ltd 1991
Vélin Arches 300gsm 590×720 (23¼×28¼)
70 'John Piper JECP' 15AP 5PP

Each print was, under the artist's supervision, block-stamped in ink 'John Piper JECP'. Originally published as '*Kidwelly Castle, Wales*'. Sometimes incorrectly known as '*The Manor House*'

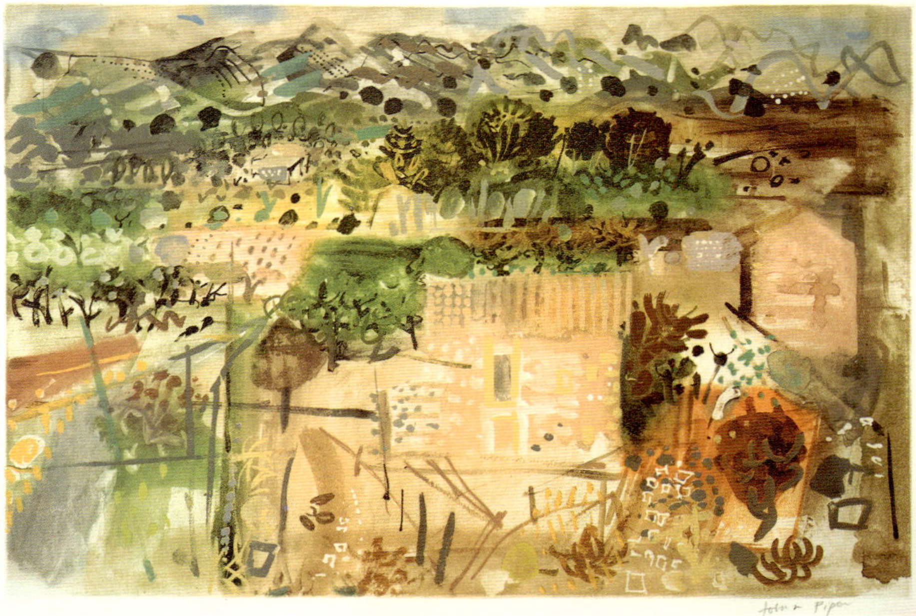
425

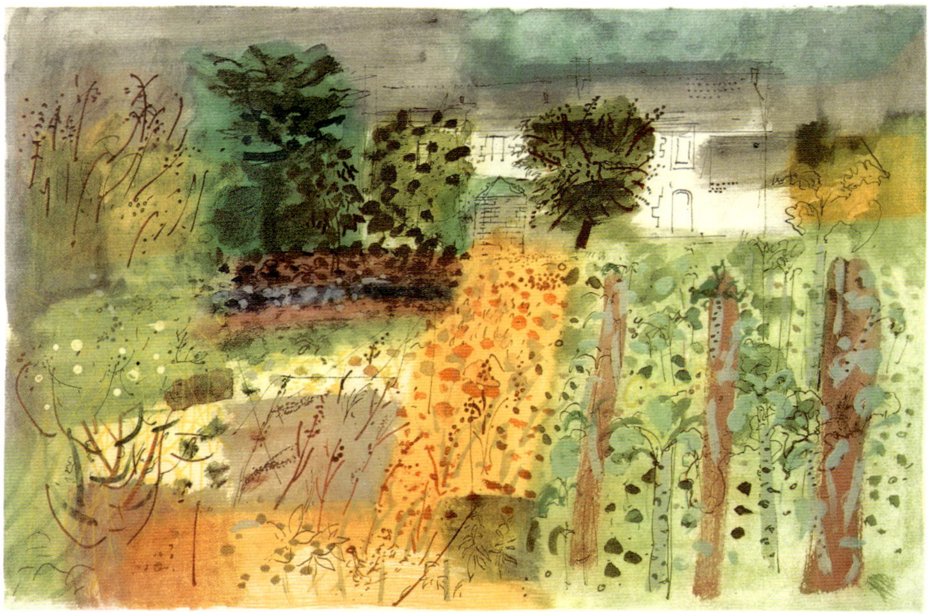
426

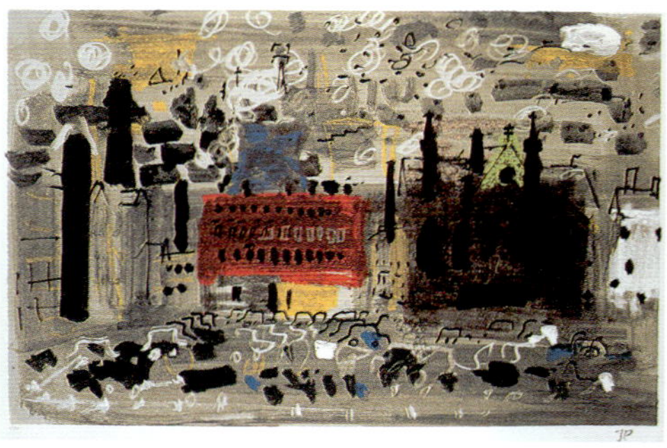
427

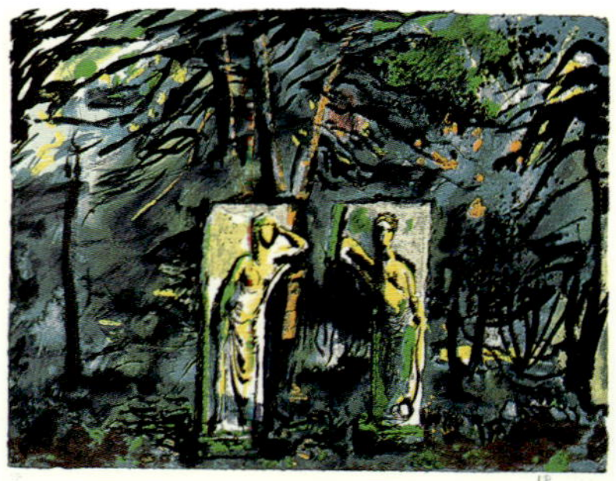
428

432
Pyrton Manor
Screenprint 455×750 (18×29½)
Kelpra Studio 1990
CCA Galleries 1991
Vélin Arches 300gsm 645×945 (25¼×37)
70 'John Piper JECP' 15AP 5PP

Each print was, under the artist's supervision, block-stamped in ink 'John Piper JECP'

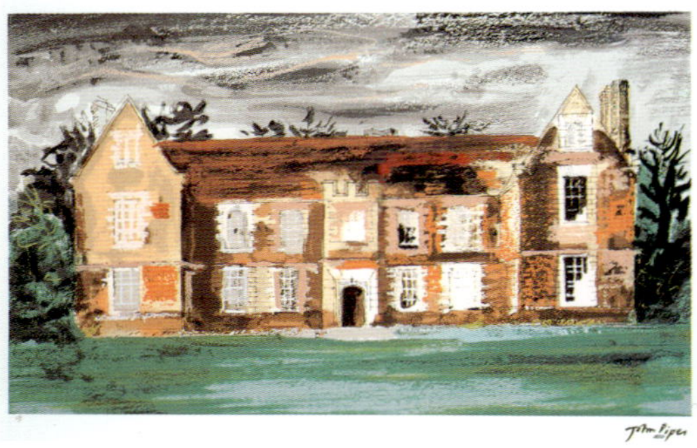
432

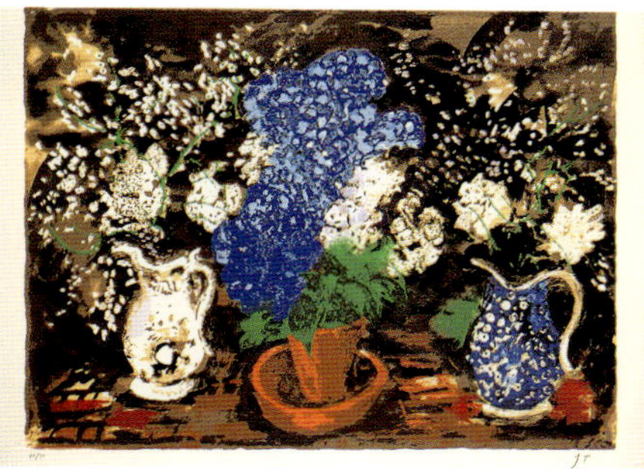

429

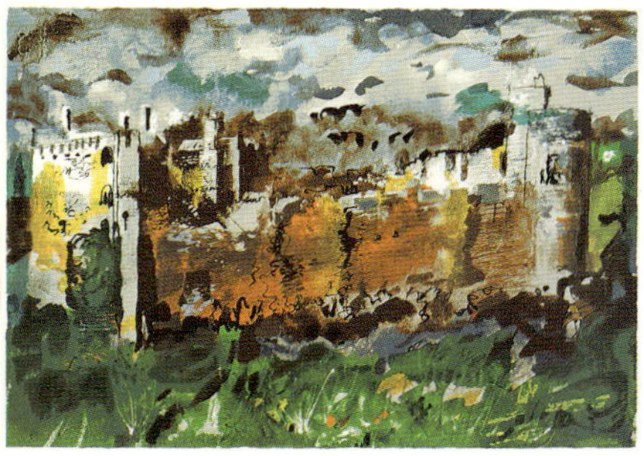

431

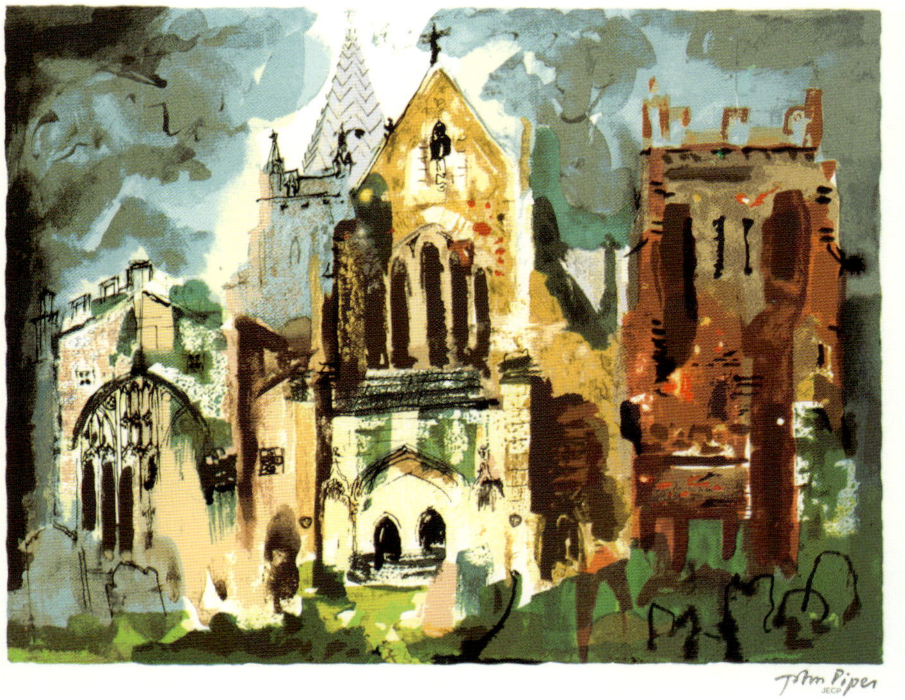

430

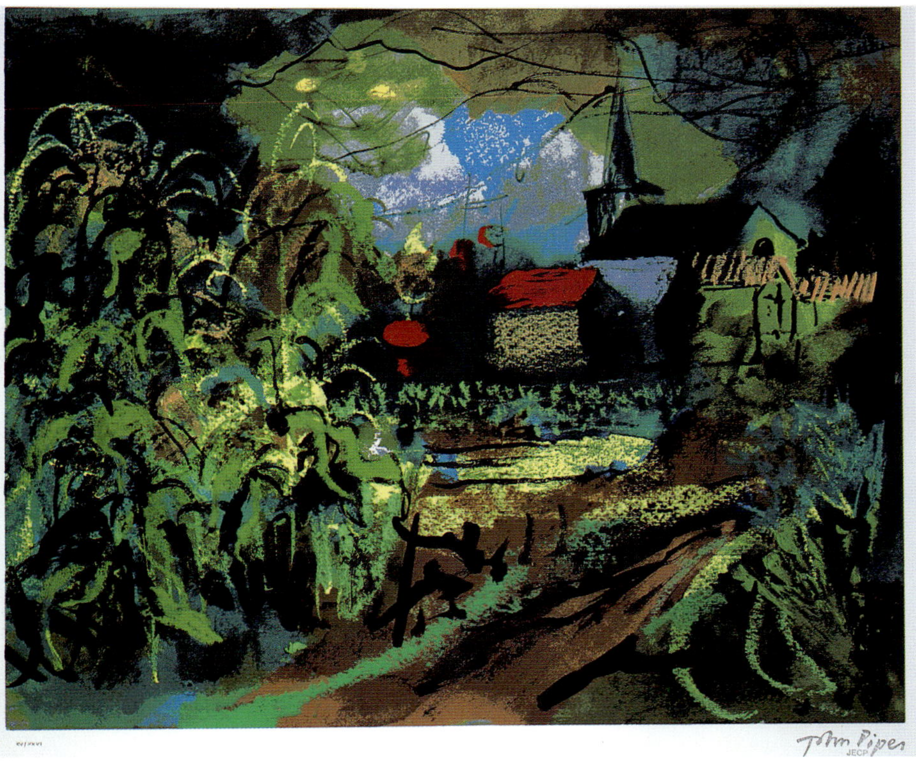

433

433
Boissy-en-Dronais
Screenprint 420 × 520 (16½ × 20½)
Kelpra Studio 1990
The Hope and Optimism Foundation SA 1991
Vélin Arches 300gsm 600 × 700 (23½ × 27½)
200 'John Piper JECP' 26AP 5PP

Each print was, under the artist's supervision, block-stamped in ink 'John Piper JECP'.

National Gallery of Gibraltar; Tate Gallery

Part of the *Hope and Optimism Portfolio*, an ongoing portfolio (at the time of going to press), in which a leading artist from every country in the world was nominated to participate. Piper represented England with this print.

The portfolio (to October 1995 with completed images) contained a print by each of the following: Alexandra Vassilikian (stateless); Houra Niati (Algeria); Vivienne Littlejohn (Australia); Franz West (Austria); Mounir Islam (Bangladesh); Mark Maynard (Barbados); Dacos (Belgium); Sharon Wilson (Bermuda); Ana Maria Pacheco, Sergio de Moraes, Andrea Christina Las (Brazil); Yuly Mintchev (Bulgaria); David Alexander, Will Gorlitz, Otis Tamasauskas (Canada); Beaudry-Leduc (Quebec); Xin Ying (China); Ofelia Rodriquez (Colombia); Upokoina D. George (Cook Islands); Ivan Komárek (Czechoslovakia); Jiri George Dokoupil (Czech Republic); Lars Ravn (Denmark); Adly Rizqallah, Hussein El Geballi (Egypt); Robert Ballagh (Eire); John Piper (England); Outi Heiskanen (Finland); Robert Combas (France); Walter Dahn (West Germany); Hubertus Giebe (East Germany); Atta Kwami (Ghana); Mario Finlayson (Gibraltar); Yiannis Goupzis (Greece); Helgi Thorgils Fridjonsson (Iceland); Krishen Khanna, Krishna Reddy (India); Dia Azzawi (Iraq); Rivka Friedman (Israel); Frederic Bruly Bouabre (Ivory Coast); Judith Salmon (Jamaica); Eizo Sakata, Fumio Kitaoka (Japan); Maurice Boots (Jersey); Rima Farah (Jordan); John Diang'a (Kenya); Walid Mustafa (Kurdistan); Ali Omar Ermes (Libya); Gast Michels (Luxembourg); Alfred Chircop (Malta); Neermala Luckeenarain (Mauritius); Leticia Ocharan (Mexico); Marina Abromovic (Montenegro); Mehdi Qotbi, Tibari Kantour (Morocco); Themba Massala (Namibia); Nuche Kaji Bajracharaya (Nepal); Rob Scholte (The Netherlands); Kura te Waru Rewiri (New Zealand); Bruce Ovobrakpeya (Nigeria); Noelene Pasisi (Niue); Guttorm Guttormsgaard (Norway); Leila Shawa (Palestine); Alberto Quintanilla (Peru); Fil Delacruz (Philippines); Josef Szajna (Poland); Henrique Silva (Portugal); Ali Hassan (Qatar); Patricia Seznec (Réunion); Faisal Samra (Saudi Arabia) John Bellany (Scotland); Iba N'Diaye (Senegal); Goh Ee Choo (Singapore); Miloslav Moucha (Slovakia); Jose Ciuha (Slovenia); Philippa Hobbs (South Africa); Austin Hleza (Swaziland); Lars-Gosta Lundberg (Sweden); Ghassan Al-Sibai (Syria); Lin Chin Lin (Taiwan); Leon Golub, Mark Kostabi, Michael Rubin, Robert Longo, MANUAL, Andres Serrano (United States of America); Andrei Roiter (USSR); Sandro Chia (Vatican City); Glen Sujo (Venezuela); Harry Holland (Wales); Cheri Samba (Zaire); Gabriel Ellison (Zambia); Helen Leiros (Zimbabwe).

The signatures nos 1–2 were used by Piper for all his prints until he became ill at the end of 1989. He then began signing with the initials JP (nos 3–4) and then with his fuller initials (5–6) for Cats 427–9 and part of Cat.430. With the failing of his health in late 1990 he designed a single block-stamp with his name 'John Piper' and below this his initials 'JECP' (no.7) for Cats 430–3.

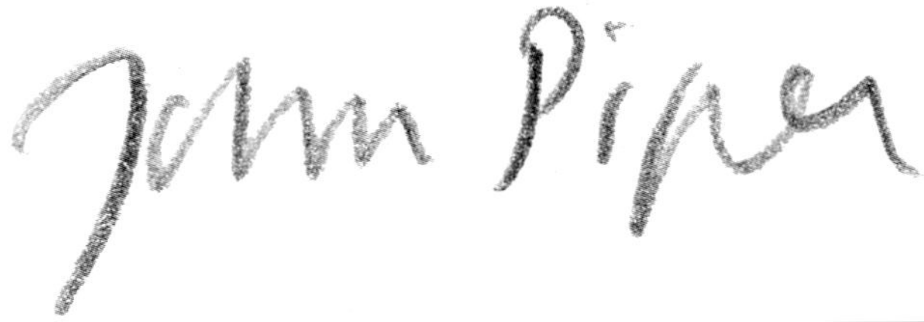

1

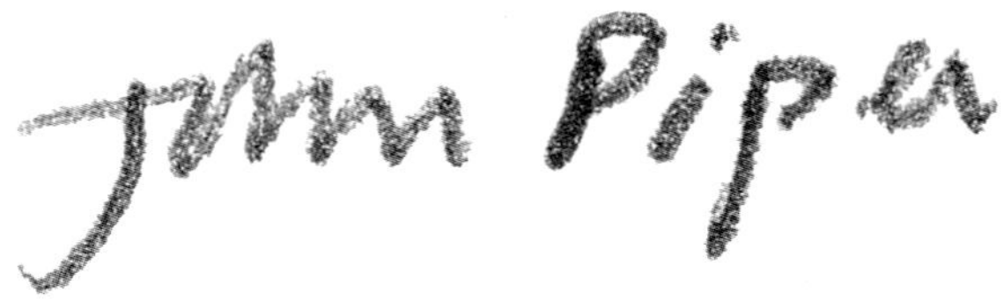

2

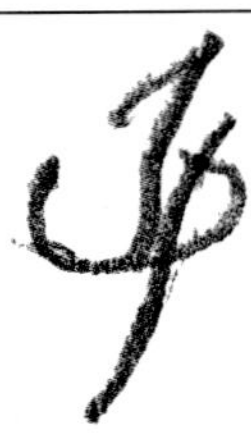

3

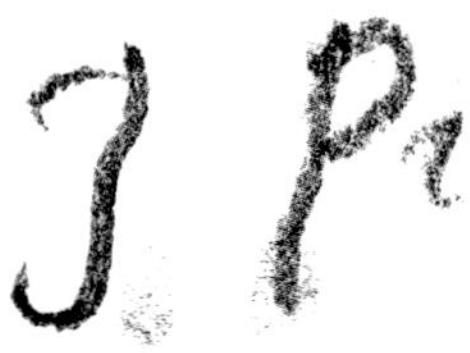

4

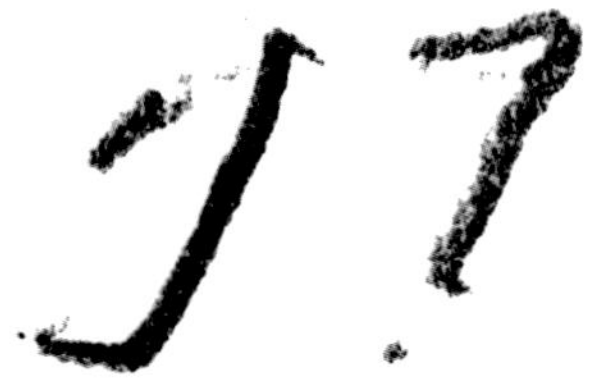

5

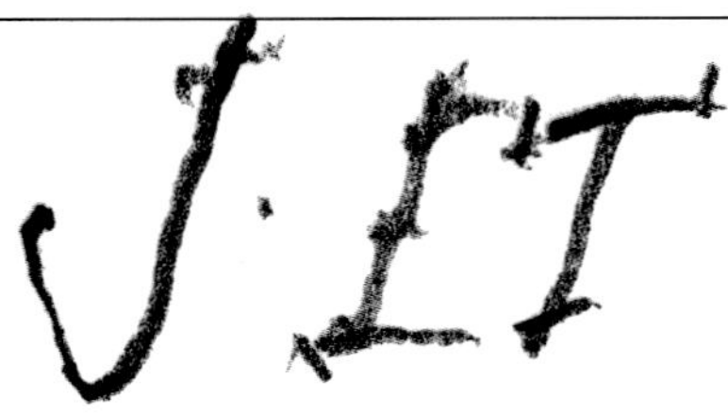

6

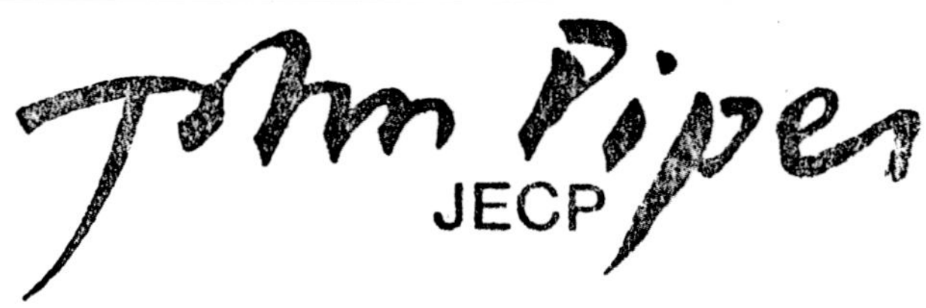

7

Index of Prints

A dagger (†) or an asterisk (*) before the title indicates that the print is a book illustration or part of a portfolio respectively. These prints are also listed under the name of the publication in 'Illustrations by John Piper: Books, Articles, Pamphlets, Almanacs, Film Posters, Records and Compact Discs' on pp.154-60, and under the portfolio title in the list of 'Portfolios' on p.150. Prints which were created as part of a portfolio or a book illustration but were not published are, however, not classified as part of that portfolio or book illustration and do not have the corresponding dagger or asterisk.

'*Venice Fantasy*' catalogued in West (plate 13) as a silkscreen is an oil and '*Romanesque tympanum with hanging lamp, Rowlstone, Herefordshire*', catalogued in Ingrams/Piper (plate 26) as a print is a gouache, thus neither is listed. The reference to '*York Minster*' in *Kelpra Prints* and in *Kelpra Studio* as a screenprint published in 1969 is incorrect. Neither Chris Prater nor the artist can recall the print nor have any copies been traced.

The mention of 'detachable lithographs specially prepared for this book' in *Castell Caernarfon*, HMSO,1969, refers to lithographic reproductions from gouaches. '*Cwm Idwal*', 1949, allegedly an undiscovered graphic, is a lithographic reproduction. There are a further seven known lithographic reproductions some of which are signed by the artist. The first three were undertaken as fund-raising exercises. The first is '*Dorchester Abbey*', *c.*1965, published by Dorchester Abbey, Dorchester-on-Thames in an edition of around 2000 of which 50 were signed by the artist, none of them numbered. The second and third are '*Rural Reading*' and '*Reading Townscape*', 1976, published by Reading Borough Council. These two collotypes are reproductions from the two tapestries of the same name in the Reading Council and were published in editions of 250, 75 of which were signed by the artist, none of which were numbered. The fourth is the '*[Romeo and Juliet Balcony]*', where the poster design for the 1976 production of *Romeo and Juliet* at Merton College, Oxford was reproduced in an unsigned, unnumbered edition of 300. The fifth was published in 1980 by the Cavendish Collection and titled '*Llangloffan*'. It was published in an edition of 750, some of which were signed b.r. but not numbered, and bears the blind stamps 'F.A.T.G.' (Fine Arts Trade Guild) b.l. and of Cavendish Collection also b.l. The sixth and seventh form part of (but were not bound in) the deluxe edition of the book *John Piper's Stowe*, 1983 published by the Hurtwood Press in association with the Tate Gallery in a total edition of 300 copies, 1-50 comprising the deluxe edition. The prints are titled: '*The Palladium Bridge*' and '*Stowe, The Oxford Bridge*'. Each print and each book (of the deluxe edition) was signed in ink, but not numbered, by the artist. Copies 51-300 did not contain prints but a few spare prints were signed by the artist. In 1987 Coventry Cathedral Gift Shop commissioned '*Cathedral Ruins*', from a watercolour by Piper, in an edition of 500. These were reproductions and woven as silk ribbon pictures 300 × 210 (11⅞ × 8¼) by J. & J. Cash Ltd and signed in the mount by Piper b.r. and numbered b.l.

Piper's reference in Ingrams/Piper (p.15) to making his 'first lithograph' while at the Royal College of Art is incorrect. Piper left the Royal College in 1928, and no known lithographs exist before then. The reference is probably to Cat.5, dated 1929, which was lithographed using the presses of the Royal College of Art.

Prints created prior to 1984 and discovered after the publication of the first edition of this book (*sc.* Cats 4A-B, 5A-D, 11A, 57A-C, 67A-B, 85A, 87A-C, 101A, 145A) are incorporated at the year of creating, where known. Cat.171D, an omission, is reproduced immediately after Cat.171C, while the omissions Cats 71A and 121A are reproduced immediately before Cats 72 and 121 respectively. Works forming part of a book or portfolio and proofed as such (always as spares in case of damage or loss), but never incorporated, have been listed immediately prior to the relevant publication, *eg* Cats 11, 121, 145A.

Variants are not given separate entries but are detailed under other comments where they are clearly known to be experimental proofs and were discussed with the artist. Only on one occasion have I given separate entries to variants and this is with *Connemara* (Cats 328, 328A, 328B). Here Cats 328A and 328B were discovered after the death of the artist and therefore could not be discussed with him and the known prints were signed. Furthermore, they are in colour as opposed to being a black-and-white version of a colour image. I simply cannot be sure whether or not they are variants and decided it best to give them separate entries as it may have been the artist's intention to create a series in different colours.

Abbreviations

A	Aquatint
Al	Autolithograph
E	Etching
E & A	Etching and aquatint
E & S	Etching and screenprint
L	Lithograph
S	Screenprint
W eng	Wood engraving
W	Woodcut

CAT. NO.	TITLE	YEAR OF PRINTING	MEDIUM
207	Abbeville, St Wolfrun	1972	S
407	Abroath Abbey	1988	S
7	Abstract Composition	1936	Al
3	[Adam and Eve]	*c.* 1923	W eng
67A	† [Adam and Eve's Garden]	1947	Al
425	Alpilles	1989	E & A
120	Anglesey Beach	1963	L
222	Annunciation to the Shepherds, The	1973	L
42	† Approach to Gordale Scar, Yorkshire	1944	Al
39	† At Lewknor, Oxfordshire	1944	Al
54	† Attingham, Shropshire	1944	Al
57C	† Avebury Restored	1944	Al
1	[Avenue]	*c.* 1923	W eng
258	Avoncroft Museum	1976	L
349	Babingley Church, Norfolk	1983	S
371	Babingley – Sepia Variation	1984	S
169	† Base of the Campanile	1965	Al
17	† Bedford Square	1939	E & A
188	Besse, Dordogne	1968	S
172	Bethesda Baptist Chapel, Swansea	1966	L
318	Binham Abbey	1981	S
416	Blenheim Bridge	1988	S
358	* Blenheim Gates	1983	E
417	Blenheim Palace	1988	S
429	Blue Hydrangea	1990	S
433	Boissy-en-Dronais	1990	S
53	† Bolsover Castle, Derbyshire	1944	Al
413	Bridgham Parish Church	1989	E & A
15	† Brighton from the Station Yard	1939	E & A
11	Brighton Street	1939	E & A
117	Brittany Beach	1961	L
11A	Brunswick Square	1939	E & A
16	† Brunswick Terrace	1939	E & A
281	Buckden in a Storm	1977	S
333	Buckden Palace, Cambridgeshire	1982	S
89	† Bullslaughter Bay, Pembrokeshire I	1954	Al
91	† Bullslaughter Bay, Pembrokeshire II	1954	Al
25	Byland Abbey, Yorkshire	*c.* 1940	E & A
200	Caernarvon Castle I	1971	S
201	Caernarvon Castle II	1971	S
350	Canons Ashby, Northamptonshire	1983	S
102	Canterbury Cathedral	1956	Al
268	Capesthorne	1977	S
334	Carew Castle	1982	S
397	Cascade Bridge, Halswell	1987	S
366	Castlebythe	1983	S
259	Castlemartin	1976	S
58	† Castles on the Ground, The (dust-jacket)	1946	L
59	† Castles on the Ground I, The	1946	Al
60	† Castles on the Ground II, The	1946	Al
61	† Castles on the Ground III, The	1946	Al
62	† Castles on the Ground IV, The	1946	Al
63	† Castles on the Ground V, The	1946	Al
64	† Castles on the Ground VI, The	1946	Al
65	† Castles on the Ground VII, The	1946	Al
66	† Castles on the Ground VIII, The	1946	Al
428	Ceres and Proserpine	1990	E & A
202	Chambord	1971	S
352	Chantry House, Henley	1983	S
21	† Chapel of St George, The, Kemp Town	1939	E & A
189	Chapelle St Robert, Dordogne, La	1968	S
111	Château de Taillebourg	1958	L
27	† Cheltenham	1940	Al
47	† Chicheley Hall, Buckinghamshire	1944	Al
151	† Chiesa dell'Ospedaletto	1965	Al

CAT. NO.	TITLE	YEAR OF PRINTING	MEDIUM
142	* Christ Church, Spitalfields, London, by Nicholas Hawlsmoor	1964	L
217	Clamecy, Burgundy	1972	E
375	Clamecy, Burgundy	1985	S
370	Clydey, Pembrokeshire	1984	S
81	Clymping Beach	1953	L
257	Clytha Castle	1976	L
319	Clytha Castle Triptych	1981	S
5	Coldkitchen Farm	1929	L
6	Coldkitchen Farm	1930	W
335	Conisbrough Castle, South Yorkshire	1982	S
328	Connemara I	1981	E
328A	Connemara II	1981	E
328B	Connemara III	1981	E
261	Corbels at Kilpeck	1976	S
203	Corton Church, Suffolk	1971	S
285	Courthouse, Long Crendon, Buckinghamshire	1978	L
190	Creysse, Dordogne	1968	S
173	Crug Glas, Swansea	1966	L
391	Dahlias and Ferns	1987	E
224	* Death in Venice: side panel left	1973	S
225	* Death in Venice I	1973	S
226	* Death in Venice II	1973	S
227	* Death in Venice III	1973	S
228	* Death in Venice IV	1973	S
229	* Death in Venice V	1973	S
230	* Death in Venice VI	1973	S
231	* Death in Venice VII	1973	S
232	* Death in Venice VIII	1973	S
233	* Death in Venice: side panel right	1973	S
57A	† Devizes: In Long Street	1944	Al
57B	† Devizes: The Market Place	1944	Al
367	Dinton Folly	1983	S
147	† Dogana, The	1965	Al
342	Donzy-le-Pré	1982	S
82	Dryslwyn Castle	1953	L
90	† Dryslwyn Castle	1954	Al
418	Duchêne Fountain, Blenheim	1989	S
177	Dylwyn Church	1966	L
43	† Easegill, Lancashire	1944	Al
320	East Barsham Manor	1981	S
359	* Eastnor Castle	1983	S
353	Eastnor Castle, Hereford	1983	S
137	* Easton, Portland, Dorset: St George Reforne, an 18th-century church among the quarries	1964	L
121	Edington, Wiltshire	1964	L
220	Eglise de Vernon, Normandy	1972	A
87	Elizabethan Dance	*c.* 1954	L
93	† Elizabethan Love Songs I	1955	Al
94	† Elizabethan Love Songs II	1955	Al
95	† Elizabethan Love Songs III	1955	Al
96	† Elizabethan Love Songs IV	1955	Al
97	† Elizabethan Love Songs V	1955	Al
98	† Elizabethan Love Songs VI	1955	Al
99	† Elizabethan Love Songs VII	1955	Al
100	† Elizabethan Love Songs VIII	1955	Al
34	† English, Scottish and Welsh Landscape (dust-jacket)	1944	Al
273	* Ettington Park	1977	S
269	Exeter College Chapel, Oxford	1977	S
126	Exton, Rutland: monument by Grinling Gibbons, 1686	1964	L
355	* Eye and Camera	1983	E
210	Eye and Camera: Blue and Red	1972	S
260	Eye and Camera: Blue to Ochre	1976	S

CAT. NO.	TITLE	YEAR OF PRINTING	MEDIUM
181	Eye and Camera: Blue to Yellow	1967	S
235	Eye and Camera: Claret and Blue	1973	S
182	Eye and Camera: Flame Four	1967	S
209	Eye and Camera: Grey and Blue	1972	S
234	Eye and Camera: Marble, Red, Black etc.– lying figure reversed	1973	S
212	Eye and Camera: Multifigure	1972	S
211	Eye and Camera: Red and Black	1972	S
317	Eye and Camera: Red, Blue and Yellow	1980	S
183	Eye and Camera: Yellow and Green	1967	S
403	Façade	1987	S
4A	[Farmhouse]	*c.* 1923	W eng
5B	[Farmyard Gate]	*c.* 1929	W
405	Fawley Bottom	1988	S
78	Ffynnon Loer	*c.* 1950	A
88	† Figures from a Seal	1954	A
2	[Figures in a Landscape]	*c.* 1923	W eng
12	† First Avenue Hotel, Hove, The	1939	E & A
287	Five Gates of London	1978	S
279	* Flintham Hall	1977	S
194	Floirac	1968	S
184	Florence Relief Landscape	1967	L
410	Flowers in a Black Pot	1988	E & A
199	Foliate Head	1971	L
256	Foliate Head	1976	L
315	Foliate Head	1979	L
354	* Foliate Head	1983	E & S
368	Foliate Head	1983	E & S
83	Foliate Heads I	1953	L
84	Foliate Heads II	1953	L
245	Foliate Heads I	1975	S
246	Foliate Heads II	1975	S
28	Font and Tortoise Stove: Britwell Salome	1940	L
135	* Fotheringhay, Northamptonshire: medieval stone	1964	L
351	Fountains Abbey, Yorkshire	1983	S
204	Framlingham Castle	1971	S
113	French Village under a Cliff: St Véran	*c.* 1958	L
159	† From the lagoon	1965	Al
161	† From the lagoon	1965	Al
162	† From the lagoon	1965	Al
164	† From the lagoon	1965	Al
166	† From the lagoon	1965	Al
171	† From the lagoon	1965	Al
148	† From the north, outside the Fondamenta Nuove	1965	Al
123	* Gaddesby, Leicestershire: medieval stonework	1964	L
327	Garn Fawr	1981	L
192	Garn Fawr, Pembrokeshire	1968	S
139	* Gedney, Lincolnshire: a tower in the Fens	1964	L
379	Geffrye Museum, The	1985	S
150	† Giudecca, The	1965	Al
85A	Gloriana Street Scene	1953	L
376	Gothic Folly, Stowe	1985	E
38	† Grongar Hill, Carmarthenshire	1944	Al
337	† Grongar Hill I	1982	Al
338	† Grongar Hill II	1982	Al
339	† Grongar Hill III	1982	Al
396	Grotto, Halswell, Somerset, The	1987	S
67B	† [Hafod]	1947	Al
55	† Hafod, Cardiganshire	1944	Al
412	Hales, Norfolk	1989	E & A
427	Halifax	1990	S
29	Hall Place, Botallack, Fowey, Cornwall	*c.* 1943	A

CAT. NO.	TITLE	YEAR OF PRINTING	MEDIUM
30	Hall, The, Trecarrel, Cornwall	*c.* 1943	E
85	Hampton Court	1953	L
270	Harlaxton (Blue)	1977	S
372	Harlaxton Hall	1984	S
271	Harlaxton Manor	1977	S
275	* Harlaxton through the Gate	1977	S
414	Harlech Castle	1989	S
363	Hautbois Church, Norfolk	1983	S
284	High Cross, Hampshire	1978	L
283	Holdenby	1978	L
262	Holkham Gate, Norfolk	1976	S
373	Holme, Nottinghamshire	1985	S
247	Horham, Suffolk	1975	S
382	Huish-Episcopi	1986	S
110	Île-d'Elle	1958	L
421	Inglesham	1989	L
132	* Inglesham, Wiltshire: a rustic medieval interior	1964	L
10	Invention in Colour	1937	Al
178	Ironbridge	1966	L
380	Isle Abbots	1986	S
364	Ivychurch, Romney Marsh	1983	E & A
196	Jazenne, Charente	1968	S
411	Junies, Les	1988	E & A
278	* Kelham Hall	1977	S
19	† Kemp Town	1939	E & A
251	Kilmory Chapel	1975	S
122	* Kilpeck, Herefordshire: the Norman south door	1964	L
86	King's College, Cambridge, from Trinity	1953	L
51	† Kirby Hall, Northamptonshire	1944	Al
406	Kirkham Priory Gateway	1988	E
252	Kirkmaiden	1975	S
52	† Knole, Kent	1944	Al
5C	[Landscape]	*c.* 1929	W
419	Late Summer Flowers	1989	E & A
134	* Leckhampstead, Berkshire: a Victorian church, by S. S. Teulon	1964	L
133	* Lewknor, Oxfordshire: textured walls, traceried windows	1964	L
365	Little Cressingham, Norfolk	1983	E &A
140	* Llangloffan, Pembrokeshire: the Baptist chapel	1964	L
128	* Llan-y-Blodwell, Shropshire: mid-19th-century furnishing and painting	1964	L
401	Llyn Teifi	1987	E
425	Locmariaquer, Brittany	1990	E & A
336	Long Melford Church	1982	L
374	Long Sutton	1985	S
361	* Lower Brockhampton	1983	S
213	Ludlow Castle	1972	S
255	Magi, La Charité-sur-Loire, Ste Croix	*c.* 1976	L
129	* Malmesbury, Wiltshire: the south porch	1964	L
431	Manorbier, Dyfed	1990	S
430	Manor House, The	1991	S
5A	Marepond Farm	1929	W eng
68	† Market Place at Devizes, The	1948	Al
48	† Mereworth Castle, Kent	1944	Al
23	† Metropole Hotel from the West Pier, The	1939	E & A
276	* Milton Ernest Hall	1977	S
18	† Mixed Styles: Regency-Victorian-Modern	1939	E & A
185	Montpellier-de-Didonne, Charente	1968	S

CAT. NO.	TITLE	YEAR OF PRINTING	MEDIUM
263	Moreton Corbet	1976	S
195	Moutou	1968	S
193	Near Newcastle Emlyn, Cardigan	1968	S
174	Newgate Chapel	1966	L
92	† Niton, Isle of Wight	1954	Al
138	* North Grimstone, Yorkshire (East Riding): the deposition – detail from 12th-century font	1964	L
218	Notre-Dame-de-L'Epine, near Rheims	1972	E
389	Nude I	1986	E
390	Nude II	1986	E & A
8	Nursery Frieze I	1936	Al
9	Nursery Frieze II	1936	Al
399	Old Church of Mynachlogddu	1987	E
71A	† On the Making of Gardens (cover)	1949	Al
72	† On the Making of Gardens I	1949	Al
73	† On the Making of Gardens II	1949	Al
74	† On the Making of Gardens III	1949	Al
75	† On the Making of Gardens IV	1949	Al
76	† On the Making of Gardens V	1949	Al
77	† On the Making of Gardens VI	1949	Al
402	Ottery St Mary	1987	S
430	Ottery St Mary	1990	S
266	Oxburgh Hall, Norfolk	1977	L
146	† Palazzo Dario	1965	Al
167	† Palazzo Manzoni-Angaran	1965	Al
170	† Palazzo Pesaro	1965	Al
356	* Palazzo Pesaro	1983	E
44	† Park Place, Berkshire	1944	Al
109	Parthenay	1958	L
386	Pebble Alcove, Stowe, The	1986	S
176	Penybont Ford Congregational Church	1966	S
214	Petit Palais: Pink and yellow	1972	S
215	Petit Palais: White and yellow	1973	S
216	Petit Palais: Yellow and yellow	1973	S
105	Petworth Park Gate	c.1958	L
155	† Piazza, The	1965	Al
156	† Piazzetta, The	1965	Al
35	† Pistyll Cain, North Wales	1944	Al
4	Pond, The	c.1923	W eng
87A	† [Prometheus I]	1954	Al
87B	† [Prometheus II]	1954	Al
87C	† [Prometheus III]	1954	Al
432	Pyrton Manor	1990	S
384	Quest, The	1986	S
326	Radcliffe Camera	1981	L
124	Redenhall, Norfolk: the tower	1964	L
398	Red House, Painswick, Glos. The	1987	S
20	† Regency Square	1939	E & A
14	† Regency Square from the West Pier	1939	E & A
121A	Retrospect of Churches: portfolio front end-paper	1964	L
219	Rheims Cathedral	1972	A
40	† Rievaulx Abbey, Yorkshire	1944	Al
4B	[Road, The]	c.1923	W Eng
221	Roof at Chambord	1973	S
272	* Royal Holloway College, The	1977	S
13	† Royal Pavilion, The	1939	E & A
131	* Rudbaxton, Pembrokeshire: 17th-century monument, 19th-century furnishings	1964	L
249	Ruined Chapel, Isle of Mull	1975	S
341	Ruined Church, Bawsey	1982	S
26	Ruined Cottage near Roman Wall	c.1940	E & A

CAT. NO.	TITLE	YEAR OF PRINTING	MEDIUM
381	Ruishton	1986	S
362	St Albans	1983	S
197	St Amand-de-Coly, Dordogne	1968	S
141	* St Anne's, Limehouse, London, by Nicholas Hawksmoor	1964	L
22	† St Bartholomew's Church	1939	E & A
340	St David's, Dyfed	1982	S
357	* St Germain-de-L'Ivret	1983	S
325	St Helen Hall	1981	S
144	* St James the Less, Westminster, by G.E. Street	1964	L
127	* St Kew, Cornwall: church in a hilly landscape	1964	L
145	* St Mary's, Paddington, by G.E. Street	1964	L
143	* St Matthias, Stoke Newington, London, by London, by William Butterfield	1964	L
383	Saint Nicholas, Alcester	1986	S
136	* St Nicholas, Liverpool: smoke-black dockland church	1964	L
187	St Raphael, Dordogne	1968	S
186	St Simon-de-Pelouaille, Charente	1968	S
360	* Saltash Bridge	1983	S
149	† Salute, The	1965	Al
152	† San Giorgio Maggiore	1965	Al
153	† San Marco	1965	Al
116	San Marco, Venice	1961	L
154	† San Moisè	1965	Al
119	San Moisè, Venice	1961	L
158	† San Stae	1965	Al
165	† Santa Maria dei Miracoli	1965	Al
160	† Santa Maria Formosa	1965	Al
163	† San Zaccaria	1965	Al
118	San Zobenigo	1961	L
265	Scotney Castle, Kent	1976	L
343	* Scotney Castle I	1982	E
344	* Scotney Castle II	1982	E
345	* Scotney Castle III	1982	E
346	* Scotney Castle IV	1982	E
347	* Scotney Castle V	1982	E
348	* Scotney Castle VI	1982	E
157	† Scuola di San Marco	1965	Al
329	Seasons, The: Spring	1981	E
330	Seasons, The: Summer	1981	E
331	Seasons, The: Autumn	1981	E
332	Seasons, The: Winter	1981	E
282	Seaton	1978	L
49	† Seaton Delaval, Northumberland	1944	Al
277	* Shadwell Park	1977	S
168	† Side of the Palazzo Pesaro	1965	Al
5D	[Siena]	c.1929	W
250	Skeabost, Skye	1975	S
316	Snape Maltings Concert Hall	1979	S
264	South Lopham	1976	S
79	Stair Hole, Lulworth	c.1950	A
385	Stansfield	1986	S
321	Stokesay Castle	1981	S
80	Stonehenge	1950	E & A
288	* Stones and Bones: front end-paper left	1978	S
289	* Stones and Bones: front end-paper right	1978	S
290	* Stones and Bones I	1978	S
291	* Stones and Bones II	1978	S
292	* Stones and Bones III	1978	S
293	* Stones and Bones IV	1978	S
294	* Stones and Bones V	1978	S
295	* Stones and Bones VI	1978	S
296	* Stones and Bones VII	1978	S
297	* Stones and Bones VIII	1978	S

CAT. NO.	TITLE	YEAR OF PRINTING	MEDIUM
298	* Stones and Bones IX	1978	S
299	* Stones and Bones X	1978	S
300	* Stones and Bones XI	1978	S
301	* Stones and Bones XII	1978	S
302	* Stones and Bones XIII	1978	S
303	* Stones and Bones XIV	1978	S
304	* Stones and Bones XV	1978	S
305	* Stones and Bones XVI	1978	S
306	* Stones and Bones XVII	1978	S
307	* Stones and Bones XVIII	1978	S
308	* Stones and Bones XIX	1978	S
309	* Stones and Bones XX	1978	S
310	* Stones and Bones XXI	1978	S
311	* Stones and Bones XXII	1978	S
312	* Stones and Bones XXIII	1978	S
313	* Stones and Bones XXIV	1978	S
314	* Stones and Bones XXV	1978	S
46	† Stonesfield, Oxfordshire	1944	Al
71	Stone Wall, Anglesey	*c.* 1949	L
239	Stowe	*c.* 1975	E
242	Stowe: North Front	*c.* 1975	A
241	Stowe: Queen Caroline's Monument	*c.* 1975	E & A
243	Stowe: South Front	*c.* 1975	A
387	Stowe, South of the House	1986	S
240	Stowe: Temple of Venus	*c.* 1975	A
238	Stowe: Three Vistas	*c.* 1975	A
388	Stowe Triptych	1986	S
244	Stowe: Two Vistas	*c.* 1975	A
424	Street Scene in *Don Giovanni*	1989	S
50	† Sudbrooke Park, Richmond, Surrey	1944	Al
369	Summer Garden, Fawley Bottom	1984	E
104	Sunflowers	*c.* 1957	L
420	Sunflowers	1989	E & A
103	Sunflowers at Marignac	1956	L
377	Sunningwell, Oxfordshire	1985	S
112	Surgères	1958	L
69	Sutton Waldron	1948	L
175	Swansea Chapel	1966	L
422	Swansea East	1989	S
415	Swansea West	1989	S
108	Syleham	1958	L
45	† Talland Church, Cornwall	1944	Al
404	Teffont Evias	1988	E
408	Temple of Diana, The	1988	E
409	Tempe of Flora, The	1988	E
393	Terrace with Morning Glories	1987	S
394	Terrace with Red Pots	1987	S
395	Thornton Abbey Gateway	1987	S
236	Three Somerset Towers	1973	S
106	Three Somerset Towers I	*c.* 1958	L
107	* Somerset Towers II	1958	L
130	* Tickencote, Rutland: the Norman chancel arch	1964	L
37	† Tomen-y-Mur and Roman Amphitheatre, North Wales	1944	Al
180	Travel Notes: Castle Ashb Avenue	1967	S
179	Travel Notes: Devil's Bridge Waterfalls	1967	S
41	† Trawsfynnydd, Merioneth	1944	Al
31	Trecarrel Chapel, Cornwall	*c.* 1943	E & A
237	Two Suffolk Towers	1973	S
101	University Museum, The (Founded 1855)	1955	L
57	† Vanished Fonthill, Wiltshire	1944	Al
208	Vaux-le-Vicomte	1972	S
145A	† [Venice]	1965	Al

CAT. NO.	TITLE	YEAR OF PRINTING	MEDIUM
223	Venice Composition	1973	S
171D	† Venice: Untitled (back end-papers)	1965	Al
171C	† Venice: Untitled (backpiece)	1965	Al
171A	† Venice: Untitled (dust-jacket)	1965	Al
171B	† Venice: Untitled (front end-papers)	1965	Al
206	View from the Upper Common Room, the Queen's College	1971	L
267	Virgin and Child	1977	L
253	Visitation, The	1975	L
280	Waddesdon	1977	S
423	Waddesdon	1989	S
378	Walsoken, Norfolk	1985	S
125	* Warkton, Northamptonshire: monument by Vangelder, 1775	1964	L
101A	[Waterloo Bridge]	1955	Al
36	† Weathercote Cave, Yorkshire	1944	Al
198	Welsh Landscape, Tretio	1969	S
24	Welsh Waterfall	*c.* 1939	E & A
114	Westminster School I	1961	L
115	Westminster School II	1961	L
322	West Walton	1981	S
56	† West Wycombe Park, Buckinghamshire	1944	Al
248	Whithorn Priory	1975	S
254	Wiggenhall, St. Peter	1975	L
274	* Wightwick Manor	1977	S
323	Wigmore Abbey Gateway	1981	S
400	Wild Bunch	1987	E
286	Willington Dovecote, Bedfordshire	1978	L
67	Windsor Castle	*c.* 1948	L
191	Woodman's Cottage, Charente	1968	S
205	Wymondham, Norfolk	1971	S
324	Wymondham, Norfolk	1981	S
70	Yarnton Monument, Oxon.	1948	L
33	Yatton, Herefordshire	*c.* 1943	E & A
32	Yatton, Herefordshire (Interior)	*c.* 1943	E & A
392	Yellow Flowers	1987	E & A

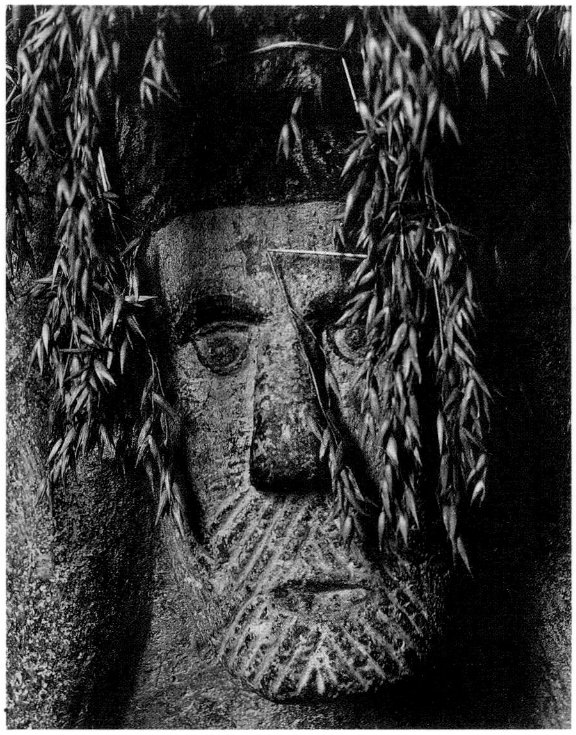

John Piper, *Harvest Festival*, date unknown

Incorrect Titles

Titles which are simply misspelt, *eg* 'Bottallack' for Botallack (Cat.29) or 'Sutton Walden' for Sutton Waldron (Cat.69) are not included.

Original published titles which were subsequently altered by the artist, or altered by the author from the first edition upon suggestion from third parties and discussion with the artist, are listed here, in inverted commas, as incorrect titles, although clearly at the time of publication they were not incorrect.

YEAR	CAT. NO.	TITLE OTHER TITLE/S
*c.*1923	2	[Figures in a Landscape] 'Figure Composition 1'
1936	7	Abstract Composition 'Abstract'/'Abstract Still Life'
1939	11	Brighton Street 'Brighton Street, Sussex'
	15	Brighton from the Station Yard 'Brighton from the Station Yard with St Peter's'
	21	The Chapel of St George, Kemp Town 'St George, Kemptown'/'St George Kemptown, Brighton, Sussex'
	22	St Bartholomew's Church 'St Bartholomew'
1940	28	Font and Tortoise Stove: Britwell Salome 'The Font'
*c.*1943	29	Hall Place, Botallack, Fowey, Cornwall 'Botallack Chapel, Near Fowey, Cornwall'
	30	The Hall, Trecarrel, Cornwall 'Launceston'/'Chapel near Launceston'
	31	Trecarrel Chapel, Cornwall 'Farmyard Chapel, Trecarrel, Cornwall'/'Trecarrel Chapel, Lezant, Cornwall'
	33	Yatton, Herefordshire 'Chapel at Yatton, Herefordshire'/'Yatton Chapel, Herefordshire'
1948	70	Yarnton Monument, Oxon 'Interior with Red Curtains'/'Yarnton Waldron'
*c.*1949	71	Stone Wall, Anglesey 'A Wall in Anglesey'
1953	81	Clymping Beach 'Clymping'
	82	Dryslwyn Castle 'The Golden Valley'
	85	Hampton Court 'Royal Residence'
1954	86	King's College, Cambridge, from Trinity 'View of Cambridge'
	88	Figures from a Seal 'Cretan Seal'/'Figures from Ancient Seals'
	89	Bullslaughter Bay, Pembrokeshire I 'Bullslaughter Bay I'
	91	Bullslaughter Bay, Pembrokeshire II 'Bullslaughter Bay II'
	92	Niton, Isle of Wight 'Niton'
1956	103	Sunflowers at Marignac 'Sunflowers'/'Church and Sunflowers'
*c.*1958	105	Petworth Park Gate 'Holland Park Gateway'/'Park Gates'/'Petworth Park, Sussex, Entrance Gates'
1958	106	Three Somerset Towers I 'Three Somerset Towers' (black version)'
	108	Syleham 'Syleham Church, Suffolk'
1961	114	Westminster School I 'Westminster School (A)'
	115	Westminster School II 'Westminster School (B)'
	117	Brittany Beach 'Beach in Brittany'
1964	125	Warkton, Northamptonshire: monument by Vangelder, 1775 'Warkton, Northants'
	136	St Nicholas, Liverpool: smoke-black dockland church 'St Nicholas, Liverpool'
	137	Easton, Portland, Dorset: St George Reforne, an 8th-century church among the quarries 'St George Reforne, Easton, Portland, Dorset'
	140	Llangloffan, Pembrokeshire: the Baptist chapel 'Llangloffan'/'Llangloffan Baptist Chapel'
1966	172	Bethesda Baptist Chapel, Swansea 'Bethesda Chapel'/'Bethesda Church'
	173	Crug Glas, Swansea 'Crug Glas Chapel'/'Crug Glass'/'Swansea Yellow'
	174	Newgate Chapel 'Newgate'/'Newgate Church'
	175	Swansea Chapel 'Swansea Blue'
	177	Dylwyn Church 'Dylwyn'
1967	181	Eye and Camera: Blue to Yellow 'Eye and Camera: Blue and Yellow'
	184	Florence Relief Landscape 'Florence Flood Relief'/'Landscape'
1968	185	Montpellier-de-Didonne, Charente 'Montpellier'/'Montpellier, Charente'
	189	La Chapelle St Robert, Dordogne 'La Chapelle de St Robert, Dordogne'/'La Chapelle, St Robert'
	190	Creysse, Dordogne 'Creysse'
	191	Woodman's Cottage, Charente 'Gamekeeper's Cottage, France'/'Mosnac, Charente'/'Mosnac, Dordogne'
	192	Garn Fawr, Pembrokeshire 'Garn Fawr'
	193	Near Newcastle Emlyn, Cardigan 'Emlyn, Newcastle'
	195	Moutou 'Eiollet, Charente'/'Moutou, near Carennac, Dordogne'
	197	St Amand-de-Coly, Dordogne 'St Amand de Coly'

YEAR	CAT. NO.	TITLE / OTHER TITLE/S
1969	198	Welsh Landscape, Tretio 'Untitled, 1969'
1972	209	Eye and Camera: Grey and Blue 'Eye and Camera: Black and Grey - net-stocking, cross-legged'/'Eye and Camera: Grey Blue'
	210	Eye and Camera: Blue and Red 'Eye and Camera: Red and Blue'
1973	221	Roof at Chambord 'Chambord Rooftops'
	223	Venice Composition 'Venetian Backdrop'/'Venice Backdrop'
	234	Eye and Camera: Marble, Red, Black etc.- lying figure reversed 'Eye and Camera: Red and Blue II'
c.1975	238	Stowe: Three Vistas 'Stowe, Buckinghamshire: The House from the South, the Lake, the Temple of Concord'
1975	249	Ruined Chapel, Isle of Mull 'Isle of Mull'
	251	Kilmory Chapel 'Kilmory Chapel, Argyll'/'Kilmory Chapel, Napdale'
	252	Kirkmaiden 'Kirkmaiden-in-Furness'
	253	The Visitation 'Saints'/'Untitled (IAA Portfolio)'
1976	255	Magi, La Charité-sur-Loire, Ste Croix 'The Gifts of the Magi'/'Three Kings, Virgin and Child'
	256	Foliate Head 'Foliate head: Pink and Blue'
	261	Corbels at Kilpeck 'Kilpeck'/'Kilpeck Corbels'/'Romanesque Corbels, Kilpeck, Herefordshire'
	265	Scotney Castle, Kent 'Scotney Castle'
	267	Virgin and Child 'Mother and Child '
1977	268	Capesthorne 'Capesthorne, near Macclesfield'
	269	Exeter College Chapel, Oxford 'Exeter Chapel'
	272-9	Victorian Dream Palaces 'Victorian Dream Palaces and Other Buildings in Landscape'
	275	Harlaxton through the Gate 'Harlaxton Manor'
	278	Kelham Hall 'Kelham'
279		Flintham Hall 'Flintham'
	280	Waddesdon 'Waddesdon Manor, near Aylesbury'
1978	284	High Cross, Hampshire 'High Cross'
	285	Courthouse, Long Crendon, Buckinghamshire 'The Courthouse'/'Courthouse, Long Crendon'
	286	Willington Dovecote, Bedfordshire 'Willington Dovecote'
	287	Five Gates of London 'Gates of London'
	291	Stones and Bones II 'Cwm Graianog Nant Ffrancon'
	295	Stones and Bones VI 'Rocks in Nant Ffrancon, North Wales'
	297	Stones and Bones VIII 'Snowdon from the Glyders'

YEAR	CAT. NO.	TITLE / OTHER TITLE/S
	304-5	Stones and Bones XV, XVI 'Dolmen near Login, Carmarthenshire 1977'
	308	Stones and Bones XIX 'Detail of the font, Toller Fratrum, Dorset'
1981	318	Binham Abbey 'Binham Abbey, Norfolk'
	319	Clytha Castle Triptych 'Clytha Castle'
	322	West Walton 'West Walton, Norfolk'
	323	Wigmore Abbey Gateway 'Wigmore Abbey'
1982	333	Buckden Palace, Cambridgeshire 'Buckden Abbey'/'Buckden in a Storm (2nd Version)'
	335	Conisbrough Castle, South Yorkshire 'Conisbrough Castle'
	337	Grongar Hill I 'Grongar Hill, Carmarthenshire'
	339	Grongar Hill III 'Grongar Hill, Carmarthenshire'
	341	Ruined Church, Bawsey 'Bawsey'
	342	Donzy-le-Pré 'Colour Variations on a Romanesque Tympanum, Donzy-le-Pré'
1983	349	Babingley Church, Norfolk 'Babingley'
	350	Canons Ashby, Northamptonshire 'Canon's Ashby'
	351	Fountains Abbey, Yorkshire 'Fountains Abbey'
	352	Chantry House, Henley 'Chantry House'/'Henley Church'
	364	Ivychurch, Romney Marsh 'Ivychurch, Rommey Marsh, Kent'
	365	Little Cressingham, Norfolk 'Little Cressingham'
1985	379	The Geffrye Museum 'The Geffrye Museum in Autumn'
1986	383	St Nicholas, Alcester 'Alcester Church'
1987	392	Yellow Flowers 'Blue Vase'
	399	Old Church of Mynachlogddu 'Maenchlochlung'/'St Dogmael'
1988	405	Fawley Bottom 'Fawley Bottom Farmhouse'/'Sebastian's Farm'
	407	Abroath Abbey 'Abroath Remarkable Ruins'
1989	413	Bridgham Parish Church 'Norfolk Church'
	418	Duchêne Fountain, Blenheim 'Blenheim Fountain'
1990	431	Manorbier, Dyfed 'Kidwelly Castle, Wales'/'The Manor House'

Portfolios

The generic titles *Five Scottish Chapels (in ruins)* (Cats 248-52) and *The Seasons* (Cats 329-32) are series titles and do not refer to any official portfolios.

Where John Piper was invited to participate, along with other artists, in a portfolio, *eg* Cats 26, 433, these are not listed here.

CAT. NO.	PLATE NO.	TITLE
121A-145	I-XXV	*A Retrospect of Churches* Lithographs, 1964
121A	I	A Retrospect of Churches: portfolio front end-paper
122	II	Kilpeck, Herefordshire: the Norman south door
123	III	Gaddesby, Leicestershire: medieval stonework
124	IV	Redenhall, Norfolk: the tower
125	V	Warkton, Northamptonshire: monument by Vangelder, 1775
126	VI	Exton, Rutland: monument by Grinling Gibbons, 1686
127	VII	St Kew, Cornwall: church in a hilly landscape
128	VIII	Llan-y-Blodwell, Shropshire: mid-19th-century furnishing and painting
129	IX	Malmesbury, Wiltshire: the south porch
130	X	Tickencote, Rutland: the Norman chancel arch
131	XI	Rudbaxton, Pembrokeshire: 17th-century monument, 19th-century furnishings
132	XII	Inglesham, Wiltshire: a rustic medieval interior
133	XIII	Lewknor, Oxfordshire: textured walls, traceried windows
134	XIV	Leckhampstead, Berkshire: a Victorian church, by S. S. Teulon
135	XV	Fotheringhay, Northamptonshire: medieval stone
136	XVI	St Nicholas, Liverpool: smoke-black dockland church
137	XVII	Easton, Portland, Dorset: St George Reforne, an 18th-century church among the quarries
138	XVIII	North Grimstone, Yorkshire (East Riding): the deposition – detail from the 12th-century font
139	XIX	Gedney, Lincolnshire: a tower in the Fens
140	XX	Llangloffan, Pembrokeshire: the Baptist chapel
141	XXI	St Anne's, Limehouse, London, by Nicholas Hawksmoor
142	XXII	Christ Church, Spitalfields, London, by Nicholas Hawksmoor
143	XXIII	St Matthias, Stoke Newington, London, by William Butterfield
144	XXIV	St James the Less, Westminster, by G. E. Street
145	XXV	St Mary's, Paddington, by G. E. Street
224-33	I-XX	*Death in Venice* Screenprints, 1973
224	I	Death in Venice: side panel left
225	II	Death in Venice I
226	III	Death in Venice II
227	IV	Death in Venice III
228	V	Death in Venice IV
229	VI	Death in Venice V
230	VII	Death in Venice VI
231	VIII	Death in Venice VII
232	IX	Death in Venice VIII
233	X	Death in Venice: side panel right
272-9	I-VIII	*Victorian Dream Palaces* Screenprints, 1977
272	I	The Royal Holloway College
273	II	Ettington Park
274	III	Wightwick Manor

CAT. NO.	PLATE NO.	TITLE
275	IV	Harlaxton through the Gate
276	V	Milton Ernest Hall
277	VI	Shadwell Park
278	VII	Kelham Hall
279	VIII	Flintham Hall
288-314	I-XXVII	*Stones and Bones* Screenprints, 1978
288	I	Stones and Bones: front end-paper left
289	II	Stones and Bones: front end-paper right
290	III	Stones and Bones I
291	IV	Stones and Bones II
292	V	Stones and Bones III
293	VI	Stones and Bones IV
294	VII	Stones and Bones V
295	VIII	Stones and Bones VI
296	IX	Stones and Bones VII
297	X	Stones and Bones VIII
298	XI	Stones and Bones IX
299	XII	Stones and Bones X
300	XIII	Stones and Bones XI
301	XIV	Stones and Bones XII
302	XV	Stones and Bones XIII
303	XVI	Stones and Bones XIV
304	XVII	Stones and Bones XV
305	XVIII	Stones and Bones XVI
306	XIX	Stones and Bones XVII
307	XX	Stones and Bones XVIII
308	XXI	Stones and Bones XIX
309	XXII	Stones and Bones XX
310	XXIII	Stones and Bones XXI
311	XXIV	Stones and Bones XXII
312	XXV	Stones and Bones XXIII
313	XXVI	Stones and Bones XXIV
314	XXVII	Stones and Bones XXV
343-8	I-VI	*Scotney Castle, Kent* Etchings, 1982
343	I	Scotney Castle I
344	II	Scotney Castle II
345	III	Scotney Castle III
346	IV	Scotney Castle IV
347	V	Scotney Castle V
348	VI	Scotney Castle VI
354-61	I-VIII	*Eightieth Anniversary Portfolio* Etchings, Screenprints, Etching and Screenprint, 1983
354	I	Foliate Head (Etching and screenprint)
355	II	Eye and Camera (Etching)
356	III	Palazzo Pesaro (Etching)
357	IV	St Germain-de-L'Ivret (Screenprint)
358	V	Blenheim Gates (Etching)
359	VI	Eastnor Castle (Screenprint)
360	VII	Saltash Bridge (Screenprint)
361	VIII	Lower Brockhampton (Screenprint)

Printers

(London, unless otherwise stated)

A. Alexander and Sons
Cats 11, 11A, 12-23, 88

The Artist
Cats 1, 2, 3, 4, 4A, 4B, Betchworth: 5, 5B, 5C, 5D; Fawley Bottom: 24, 25, 26, 29, 30, 31, 32, 33, 78, 79, 80, 238, 239, 240, 241, 242, 243, 244

Artists International Association (AIA)
Cat.28

Baynard Press
Cats 58-66

Jesse Broad and Co Ltd, Manchester
Cats 87A-87C

Charles Broome, Hereford
Cat.261

Burleighfield House, Loudwater, near High Wycombe
Cats 217, 218, 219, 220, 253, 254

Butler and Tanner, Frome and London
Cats 57A-C, 67A-B

Central School of Arts and Crafts
Cats 69, 70, 71

Chromoworks
Cats 87, 102

W. S. Cowell, Ipswich
Cats 93-100

Curwen Press
Cats 7, 10, 27, 34-46, 47-57, 101A, 255

Curwen Studio
Cats 114, 115, 117, 120, 121, 121A, 122, 123, 124, 125, 126, 127, 128, 129, 130, 131, 132, 133, 134, 135, 136, 137, 138, 139, 140, 141, 142, 143, 144, 145, 172, 173, 174, 175, 177, 178, 199, 222, 256, 257, 258, 265, 266, 267, 282, 283, 284, 285, 286, 315, 336, 337-9, 421

Dropmore Press
Cats 71A-7, 72-7

Valerie Ewens
Cat.327

Harley Brothers, Edinburgh
Cats 86, 105, 106, 107, 108, 109, 110, 111, 112, 113, 116, 118, 119

Kelpra Studio
Cats 176, 179, 180, 181, 182, 183, 185, 186, 187, 188, 189, 190, 191, 192, 193, 194, 195, 196, 197, 198, 200, 201, 202, 203, 204, 205, 207, 208, 209, 210, 211, 212, 213, 214, 215, 216, 221, 223, 224, 225, 226, 227, 228, 229, 230, 231, 232, 233, 234, 235, 236, 237, 245, 246, 247, 248, 249, 250, 251, 252, 259, 260, 262, 263, 264, 268, 269, 270, 271, 272, 273, 274, 275, 276, 277, 278, 279, 280, 281, 287, 288, 289, 290, 291, 292, 293, 294, 295, 296, 297, 298, 299, 300, 301, 302, 303, 304, 305, 306, 307, 308, 309, 310, 311, 312, 313, 314, 316, 317, 318, 319, 320, 321, 322, 323, 324, 325, 328, 328A, 328B, 329, 330, 331, 332, 333, 334, 335, 340, 341, 342, 343, 344, 345, 346, 347, 348, 349, 350, 351, 352, 353, 354, 355, 356, 357, 358, 359, 360, 361, 362, 363, 364, 365, 366, 367, 368, 369, 370, 371, 372, 373, 374, 375, 376, 377, 378, 379, 380, 381, 382, 383, 384, 385, 386, 387, 388, 389, 390, 391, 392, 393, 394, 395, 396, 397, 398, 399, 400, 401, 402, 403, 404, 405, 406, 407, 408, 409, 410, 411, 412, 413, 414, 415, 416, 417, 418, 419, 420, 422, 423, 424, 425, 426, 427, 428, 429, 430, 431, 432, 433

Knapp, Drewett and Sons, Kingston-upon-Thames
Cat.68

Marshall Press
Cat.5A

Mercury Press
Cat.6

Mourlot Frères, Paris
Cats 81, 82, 83, 84, 89-92, 103, 104

Oxford University Press (Printing Division), London and Oxford
Cats 101, 206

Royal College of Art
Cats 85, 85A, 145A, 146-71, 146-71D

Senecio Press, Charlbury
Cat.326

Waterlow and Sons
Cats 8, 9

Unknown
Cats 67, 184

Publishers

(London, unless otherwise stated)

Architectural Press
Cats 58-66, 68

The Artist
Cats 1, 2, 3, 4, 4A, 4B, 5B, 5C, 5D

Artists International Association (AIA)
Cat.28

Avoncroft Museum of Buildings, Bromsgrove
Cat.258

Benson and Hedges
Cat.316

British Travel and Holidays Association
Cat.102

Canon Rubber Co
Cat.336

CCA Galleries
Cats 380, 381, 382, 384, 385, 391, 392, 402, 403, 406, 407, 408, 409, 416, 417, 418, 432

Century Gallery, Henley-on-Thames
Cat.352

Christie's Contemporary Art
Cats 267, 329, 330, 331, 332, 333, 334, 335, 340, 341, 342, 349, 364, 365, 366, 367, 368, 371, 372, 374, 375

Christie's Contemporary Art and The National Trust
Cats 265, 266, 285, 286, 350, 351

Comforts Fund for Women and Children of Soviet Russia (Mrs Martin and Mary Wykeham)
Cat.26

Contemporary Arts Trust, Kings College JCR, Cambridge (Michael Jaff and Martin Newell for the Trust)
Cat.86

Contemporary Lithographs
Cats 7, 8, 9

Paul Cornwall-Jones
Cats 114, 115

Cupid Press, Barham Manor, Suffolk
Cats 93-100

Curt Valentin Gallery, New York
Cats 81, 103, 108, 118, 119

Curwen Press
Cats 116, 117, 256, 257

Dropmore Press
Cats 71A-7, 72-7

Duckworth
Cats 12-23, 146-71D

Prints in Public Collections

At the time of publication, the editor has received no confirmation of the existence of graphics in public collections other than those in the list below. The editor is acquainted with private individuals and corporations who hold large collections of Piper's prints and would be happy to transmit this information to interested parties, where permission is so granted.

For book illustrations the reader is also referred to other major libraries.

An asterisk (*) indicates that the graphic is held at more than one public institution.

Brazil
Rio de Janeiro
Modern Art Museum
Cats 354*, 355*, 356*, 357*, 358*, 359*, 360*, 361*

Canada
Ottawa
National Gallery of Canada/Galerie Nationale du Canada
Cats 69*, 70*

Eire
Dublin
Trinity College Library
Cats 12*-23*, 34*-46*, 57A*-C*, 58*-66*, 67A*-B*, 68*, 72*-7*, 88*-92*, 93*-100*, 146*-71D*

Gibraltar
National Gallery, John MacIntosh Building
Cat.433

Great Britain

Aberdeen
Aberdeen Art Gallery and Museums
Cats 103*, 107*, 187*

Aberystwyth
National Library of Wales
Cats 12*-23*, 27*, 34*-46*, 57A*-C*, 58*-66*, 67A*-B*, 68*, 72*-7*, 88*-92*, 93*-100*, 146*-71*, 146*-71D*, 337*-9*

Birmingham
Birmingham Museum and Art Gallery
Cat.19*

Cambridge
Cambridge University Library
Cats 10*, 12*-23*, 27*, 34*-46*, 57A*-C*, 58*-66*, 67A*-B*, 68*, 72*-7*, 88*-92*, 93*-100*, 146*-71*, 146*-71D*, 337*-9*

Edinburgh
National Library of Scotland
Cats 12*-23*, 27*, 34*-46*, 57A*-C*, 58*-66*, 67A*-B*, 68*, 72*-7*, 88*-92*, 93*-100*, 146*-71*, 146*-71D*, 337-9*
Scottish National Gallery of Modern Art
Cats 7*, 112, 175*, 196*, 197*, 198*

Glasgow
Glasgow Art Gallery and Museum
Cats 107*, 219*, 222*, 223*

Harrogate
Harrogate Museums and Art Gallery Service
Cat.70*

Hereford
Herefordshire Museums and Art Galleries
Cat.261*

Leeds
Leeds City Art Galleries
Cats 108, 117*

Leicester
Leicestershire Museums, Arts and Record Service
Cats 85, 103*, 105*, 109, 117*, 123*, 207*, 261*
Leicestershire Museums, Arts and Record Service (Artworks Collection)
Cats 189*, 190*, 196*

Lincoln
Lincolnshire Recreational Services: Usher Gallery
Cat.84

London
Arts Council Collection
Cats 12*-23*, 70*, 86
British Council
Cats 20*, 69*, 70*
British Library
Cats 10*, 12*-23*, 27*, 34*-46*, 47-57, 57A*-C*, 58*-66*, 67A*-B*, 68*, 72*-7*, 88*-92*, 93*-100*, 146*-71*, 146*-71D*, 337*-9*
British Museum
Cats 7*, 12*-23*, 26, 28*, 34*-46*
Guildhall Art Gallery
Cats 185*, 186*, 187*, 188*, 189*, 196* 197*
Tate Gallery
Cats 8*, 9*, 10*, 34*-46*, 82, 114, 115, 116, 117*, 120, 121, 121A, 122, 123*, 124, 125* 126*, 127, 128*, 129, 130, 131*, 132, 133*, 134, 135, 136, 137* 138*, 139, 140*, 141, 142, 143, 144, 145, 172*, 173* 175*, 176* 177*, 178, 179, 180, 181, 182, 183, 184, 185* 186*, 187*, 188*, 189*, 190*, 191, 192, 193, 194, 195, 196*, 197*, 198*, 199, 200*, 201, 202, 203, 204, 205, 207*, 208, 209, 210, 211, 212, 213, 214, 215, 216, 217*, 218, 219*, 220, 221, 222*, 223*, 225, 226, 227, 228, 229, 230, 231, 232, 234, 235, 236*, 245, 246, 247, 248, 249, 250, 251, 252, 253, 254, 258*, 259, 260, 262, 263, 264, 267, 268, 269, 270, 272, 273, 274, 275, 276, 277, 278, 279, 280, 281, 282, 283, 284, 287, 288, 289, 290, 291, 292, 293, 294, 295, 296, 297, 298, 299, 300, 301, 302, 303, 304, 305, 306, 307, 308, 309, 310, 311, 312, 313, 314, 317, 318, 319, 321, 324, 325, 334, 341, 350, 351, 353*, 354*, 355*, 356*, 357*, 358*, 359*, 360*, 361*, 433
Victoria and Albert Museum
Cats 7*, 8*, 9*, 12*-8*, 20*-1*, 23*, 25, 28*, 29, 30, 67, 70*, 83*, 87, 101, 103*, 107*, 118, 140*

Manchester
City Art Gallery
Cats 69*, 83*, 105*

Oxford
Bodleian Library
Cats 10*, 12*-23*, 27*, 34*-46*, 57A*-C*, 58*-66*, 67A*-B*, 68*, 72*-7*, 88*-92*, 93*-100*, 146*-71*

Rochdale
Rochdale Art Gallery
Cat.217*

Sheffield
Sheffield Arts and Museums
Cats 200*, 236*, 353*

Stoke Heath, Bromsgrove
Avoncroft Museum of Buildings
Cat.258*

Wakefield
Wakefield Museums, Galleries and Castles
Cat.71*

United States of America

Buffalo
Albright-Knox Art Gallery
Cats 70*, 125*, 126*, 128*, 131*, 133*, 137*, 138*, 172*, 173*, 174, 175*, 176*, 177*

Detroit
Detroit Institute of Arts
Cat.69*

New York
Museum of Modern Art
Cats 12*-23*, 34*-46*, 58*-66*, 69*, 70*, 71*

Washington
The Phillips Collection
Cat.53

Illustrations by John Piper:

Books, Articles, Pamphlets, Almanacs, Film Posters, Records and Compact Discs

Below is a comprehensive catalogue of book/article/pamphlet/almanac/film poster/record and compact disc illustrations by John Piper. Those considered by the artist to be original autolithographic works have their entries printed in bold type and are documented and illustrated in the Catalogue. They are also separately indexed at the end of this list (see pp.159-60 below). The many publications, such as exhibition catalogues and magazines, which reproduce images not originally intended to illustrate a text are not included, for example Cat.6 *Coldkitchen Farm*. However, *Invention in Colour*, Cat.10, is listed, as it was created especially for the magazine (see no.6 below).

On occasion Piper would create an original Christmas Card for publishers. No known list exists and the only known one found is that for Penguin, 1955 (no.97 below).

The order of the entries are books (alphabetical by author), then the following (chronologically by date): article, pamphlet, almanac, film poster, record and compact disc illustrations. Undated book illustrations appear after the last entry.

The illustrations by Piper are listed at the end of the entries and only to avoid confusion in certain cases is it stated 'by Piper'. For example, in no.187 below, Jennifer Sherwood, *A Guide to the Churches of Oxfordshire*, the photographs and watercolour illustrations are by Piper.

It is sometimes difficult to distinguish when Piper was asked to illustrate an article and where there was some personal connection and involvement or when his work was used as one of a few or many illustrations in a book. When in doubt I have included the notation in this section and not in books about Piper, my main criteria being the difference between the use of Piper's work in an article on him or on art in general and the use of Piper's work to illustrate an article or where there is a feeling, an impression, which also contains a personal link to the artist or shared feeling.

The reference in the S. John Woods article 'John Piper as a Topographical Illustrator' (appearing in *Image*, 1949, no.70 below) to autolithographs by Piper appearing in *The Ambassador*, 1949 in fact refers to two plates used from Cats 47-57. *International Textiles* had changed its name to *The Ambassador* by the time it lent the plates for the Woods article.

Very few of the film poster designs by Piper exist and I have only been able to trace references to three in 1943. I would welcome further information on them and on any other items not listed.

Books/Articles etc not seen by the author or untraceable, but referenced in correspondence to or from Piper or other writings are listed under the appropriate year and preceded by an asterisk (*).

1921

1. John Piper, *Wind in the Trees*, Horseshoe Publishing Co, Bristol. Line drawing illus.

1924

2. John Piper, *The Gaudy Saint and other poems*, Horseshoe Publishing Co, Bristol. Six line drawing illus.

1925

3. Charles A. Piper, *Sixty-Three, Not Out: A Book of Recollections*, Curwen Press, London (privately printed). Nineteen ink drawing illus.

1936

4. John Piper, 'England's Early Sculptors', *Architectural Review*, Vol.80, October, pp.157-62. Illus.

5. *Modern Travel for Modern People*, Imperial Airways, London. Advertising pamphlet design

---

1937

6. 'Invention in Colour': autolithograph by John Piper. *Signature*, No.6, July, frontispiece (*sc.* Cat.10)

1938

7. John Piper, *Oxon*, Batsford, London ('Shell Guide' series). Line drawing illus. and end-paper design. [2nd edition, Faber and Faber, 1953 (see no.82 below)

8. John Piper, 'The Nautical Style', *Architectural Review*, Vol.83, January, pp.1-14. Illus.

1939

9. John Piper, *Brighton Aquatints*, Duckworth, London, containing twelve black-and-white aquatints of modern Brighton with short descriptions by the artist and an introduction by Lord Alfred Douglas. Text printed at the Curwen Press, London; aquatints printed by A. Alexander and Sons Ltd, London (*sc.* Cats 12-23)

10. John Piper, 'London to Bath', *Architectural Review*, Vol.85, May, pp.229-46. Illus.

11. John Betjeman, 'The Seeing Eye, or: How to Like Everything', *Architectural Review*, Vol.86, November, pp.201-4. Eight illus.

12. *Curwen Press News-Letter*, No.16. Three-colour lithograph design by Piper on cover

---

1940

13. C. Day Lewis, *Poems in Wartime*, Jonathan Cape, London. Line drawing illus. on the cover and the title-page, printed by Alden Press, Oxford

14. *Horizon*, January (Vol.1, No.1). Cover design by Piper

15. John Betjeman, 'Cheltenham', *Signature*, No.13, January, pp.33-7, containing a fold-out 'lithographic panorama', *Cheltenham*, between pp.36 and 37. Printed at the Curwen Press, London (*sc.* Cat.27)

16. John Piper, 'Grey Tower and Panelled Pew', *The Listener*, 1st February, pp.216-18. Four illus.

17. 'Fully licensed: [in praise of the ordinary public house]', *Architectural Review*, Vol.87, March, pp.87-100. Illus. incl. photos by Piper

18. John Piper, 'Decrepit Glory', *Architectural Review*, Vol.LXXXVII, June, pp.207-10. Six illus.

19. 'Towers in the Fens'. *Architectural Review*, November, pp.131-4. Illus. incl. eight photos by Piper.

20. *John Betjeman, *The Architecture of Noncorformity* (Vol.88), photographs by Piper (mentioned in correspondence with the BBC for use on the Welsh TV series 'Cympas', 13th April, 5th May 1960)

1941

21. John Piper, 'John Piper at the A.A.', (extracts from 'Buildings in English Art'), *Architect and Building News*, Vol.CLXVI, 9th May, p.85. Two illus.

22. *Architect and Building News*, Vol.168, 19th December, pp.170-1. Two illus.

1943

23. Osbert Sitwell, *Selected Poems: Old and New*, Duckworth, London. Front dust-jacket design, printed by the Riverside Press, Edinburgh

24. John Piper, 'A Cubist Folk Art', *Architectural Review*, Vol.94, July, pp.21-2. Five colour drawings

25. John Piper, 'The Gratuitous Semicircle', *Architectural Review*, Vol.XCIV, October, pp.112-13. Four drawings

26. John Piper, 'Some Old Friends', *Architectural Review* ('Colour in Building' series), November, pp.139-41. Illus. incl. seven drawings

27. John Piper, 'Colour and Display', *Architectural Review* ('Colour in Building' series), Vol.XCIV, December, pp.168-71. Illus. incl. nine drawings

28. *Painted Boats*, Director: Charles Crighton, Ealing Film Studios. Film poster

29. *Pink String and Sealing Wax*, Ealing Film Studios. Film poster

*30. *The Bells Go Down*, Ealing Film Studios. Film poster. An unverified reference attributes this poster to Piper.

31. John Betjeman and Geoffrey Taylor (eds), *English, Scottish and Welsh Landscape 1700-c.1860*, Frederick Muller, London ('New Excursions into English Poetry' series, eds W.J.Turner and Sheila Shannon), containing thirteen colour autolithographs including the dust-jacket. Printed at the Curwen Press, London (*sc.* Cats 34-46)

32. Revd Francis Kilvert, *Kilvert's Diary, 1870-1879: selections from the diary of the Revd Francis Kilvert* (chosen, ed. and with an introduction by William Plomer), Readers Union, Jonathan Cape, London. Line drawing illus. on the title-page and as the frontispiece, printed by the Alden Press, Oxford

33. John Piper, 'Topographical Letter from Norwich', *Cornhill*, Vol.161, No.961, January, pp.9-18. Illus.

34. John Piper, 'Blandford Forum', *Architectural Review* ('Colour in Building' series), Vol.96, July, pp.21-3. Illus. incl. eleven drawings

35. John Piper, 'Warmth in the West', *Architectural Review*, Vol.96, September, pp.89-91. Illus. incl. eight drawings

36. John Piper, 'Flint', *Architectural Review*, Vol.96, November, pp.149-51. Illus. incl. seven drawings

37. John Piper, 'Topographical Letter from Devizes', *Cornhill*, Vol.161, No.963, November, pp.190-5. Illus. incl. three colour autolithographs (*sc.* Cats 57A-C)

38. John Piper, 'The Colour of English Country Houses', *International Textiles*, No.8, containing eleven colour autolithographs bound in an eight-page pamphlet accompanying *International Textiles*. Printed at the Curwen Press, London (*sc.* Cats 47-57)

1945

39. *Henry Green, *Loving*, Hogarth Press, London. Cover design by Piper

40. Palinurus, *The Unquiet Grave: A Word Cycle*, Hamish Hamilton, London (revised edition). Collage, lithographed at the Curwen Press, Plaistow, on the front dust-jacket

41. John Piper, 'Shops', *Architectural Review*, Vol.97, March, pp.89-91. Three illus.

42. John Piper, 'Colour in the Picturesque Village', *Architectural Review*, Vol.97, May, pp.130, 149-50. Six illus.

43. John Piper, 'St Marie's Grange', *Architectural Review*, Vol.98, October, pp.90-3. Two illus.

44. John Piper, 'Introduction to Middlesbrough', *Cornhill*, Vol.161, No.966, December, pp.430-3. One illus.

45. Sir Osbert Sitwell, *Left Hand, Right Hand* (an autobiography in 5 volumes, 1945-50), Macmillan, London [I, *Cruel Month* (1945); II, *The Scarlet Tree* (1946); III, *Great Morning* (1948); IV, *Laughter in the Next Room* (1949); V, *Noble Essences* (1950)]. Drawings and paintings repr. throughout the books

---

1946

46. Sir Thomas Browne, *The Last Chapter of Urne Buriall* (ed. by John Carter, Will Carter). Rampant Lion Press, Cambridge. Printed in a limited edition of 175 copies. Cover and title-page designs printed by the Rampant Lion Press, Cambridge

47. Walter de la Mare, *The Traveller*, Faber and Faber, London. Four colour drawings, lithographed by T.E. Griffiths at the Baynard Press

48. Myfanwy Evans (ed.), *The Pavilion: a contemporary collection of British art and architecture*, I.T. Publications, London. Two copies of medieval stained-glass windows, lithographed by T.E. Griffiths, pp.15-17

49. Sir Osbert Sitwell, *The Scarlet Tree*, Macmillan, London. Reproductions of paintings and drawings

50. John Piper, 'The Market Square', *Architectural Review* ('Colour in Building' series), Vol.99, May, pp.153-5. Four illus.

51. J.M. Richards, *The Castles on the Ground*, Architectural Press, London, December, containing nine colour autolithographs including the dust-jacket and the frontispiece. Printed at the University Press, Glasgow; lithographs printed at the Baynard Press, London (*sc.* Cats 58-66). 2nd edition, 1973 (see no.145 below)

52. John Piper, 'A Wool Country', *The Ambassador*, No.5, pp.61-72. Eleven illus. incl. the cover design

---

1947

53. Norman Hancock, *An Innocent Grows Up*, J.M. Dent, London. Collage lithographed on the dust-jacket and as the frontispiece

54. Michael Sadleir, *Forlorn Sunset*, Constable, London. Two-colour lithograph on the dust-jacket and as the frontispiece, printed by T. and A. Constable Ltd, University Press, Edinburgh

55. Evelyn Waugh, *Scott-King's Modern Europe*, Chapman and Hall, London. Dust-jacket design

56. Geoffrey Grigson. 'Kubla Khan in Wales', *Cornhill*, Vol.162, Spring. Four illus. incl. two autolithographs (*sc.* Cats 67A-B)

1948

57. Geoffrey Grigson, *An English Farmhouse and its Neighbourhood*, Max Parrish & Co, London ('Studies in Composition and Tradition' series, ed. by John Piper). Double-spread cover design, produced by Rotogravure, Leiden, Holland

58. John Piper, *Buildings and Prospects*, Architectural Press, London, containing a colour autolithograph, *The Market Place at Devizes*, tipped in as the double-spread frontispiece and title-page, and repr. on the double-spread dust-jacket with one minor colour change. Printed by Knapp, Drewett and Sons Ltd, Kingston-on-Thames (*sc.* Cat.68)

59. John Piper, *Designs of Lucretia* in *The Rape of Lucretia: a symposium*, ed. by Ronald F.H. Duncan, Bodley Head, London. Eight colour lithographic reproductions of the original designs incl. the frontispiece which is repr. on the front dust-jacket. Incl. the *'Designs of Lucretia'* by John Piper and a symposium discussion comprising Benjamin Britten, Ronald Duncan, John Piper, Henry Boys, Eric Crozier and Angus McBean

60. John Piper and John Betjeman (eds), *Murray's Buckinghamshire Architectural Guide*, John Murray, London. Dust-jacket design

61. William Sansom, *South: Aspects and Images from Corsica, Italy and Southern France*, Hodder and Stoughton, London. Wrapper design, printed by Hazell, Watson and Viney Ltd, Aylesbury

62. Sir Osbert Sitwell, *Great Morning*, Macmillan, London. Reproductions of paintings and drawings

63. *'The Artist and the Country Life', *Country Life*, January. Illus. with Piper reproductions

64. *Britain Today*, No.144, April. One illus. design for 'The Quest' facing p.39

65. *Britain Today*, No.148, October. Two illus. set designs for 'Job – A Masque for Dancing' facing p.37

66. John Piper, 'Pattern and Colour from English Slate Engravings', *The Ambassador*, No.9, pp.67-80. Fifty illus.

1949

67. John Piper and John Betjeman (eds), *Murray's Berkshire Architectural Guide*, John Murray, London. Dust-jacket design and four line drawing illus.

68. Sir George Sitwell, *On the Making of Gardens*, with an introduction by Sir Osbert Sitwell, Dropmore Press, London, September, containing six line-block autolithographs (*sc.* Cats 71A, 72-7)

69. Sir Osbert Sitwell, *Laughter in the Next Room*, Macmillan, London. Reproductions of paintings and drawings

70. S. John Woods, 'John Piper as a Topographical Illustrator', *Image: a quarterly of the visual arts*, London, No.2, Autumn, pp.3–18. Six line tint reproductions, incl. Cats 53, 54

I am not sure if the reproductions of *Bolsover Castle* and *Attingham* (*sc.* Cats 53–4) are reproductions or second editions of the plates from the 1944 publication *The Colour of English Country Houses* (*sc.* Cats 47–57). I tend to suspect the latter, given time factors, deterioration of plates etc.

71. 'Stonehenge' (Reassessment, 5) *Architectural Review*, September, Vol.106, pp.177–82. Illus. incl. seven photos by Piper

72. John Piper, 'Book Illustration and the Painter-Artist', *Penrose Annual*, Vol.XLIII, pp.52–4. Six illus.

1950

73. Elisabeth Inglis-Jones, *Peacocks in Paradise: the story of a house – its owners and the Elysium they established there, in the mountains of Wales, in the 18th century*, Faber and Faber, London. Front dust-jacket design

74. T.D. Kendrick, *British Antiquity*, Methuen, London. Front dust-jacket design, printed by Ebenezer Bayliss and Son, The Trinity Press, Worcester

75. John Piper, *Romney Marsh*, Penguin Books, Harmondsworth ('King Penguin' series, No.55). One line drawing illus., sixteen halftones in colour and sixteen in black-and-white

76. Edith Sitwell, *Façade and other poems, 1920–1935* (with an introductory essay by Jack Lindsay), Gerald Duckworth, London. Curtain design for the concert performance of 'Façade' repr. on the dust-jacket, printed by The Riverside Press, Edinburgh

77. 'Britain's Road Back', *Fortune*, May. Colour halftone from a pen and wash drawing on the cover

1951

78. John Piper and John Betjeman, *Shropshire*, Faber and Faber, London ('Shell Guide' series). Title-page drawing and eight illus.

79. William Wordsworth, *A Guide through the District of the Lakes in the North of England*, with an introduction by W.M. Merchant, Rupert Hart-Davis, London. Ten line-block lithographs from pen and collage drawings, two of which are repr. on the front dust-jacket, printed by William Clowes and Sons Ltd, London and Beccles

1952

80. John Betjeman, *First and Last Loves*, John Murray, London. Title-page design, repr. on the double-spread dust-jacket, and twenty-four illus. from drawings and collages, printed by William Clowes and Sons Ltd, London and Beccles

81. Moelwyn Merchant (ed.), *Wordsworth's Guide to the Lakes*, Rupert Hart-Davis, London. Line illus.

1953

82. John Piper, *Oxfordshire (not including the City of Oxford)*, Faber and Faber, London ('Shell Guide' series), 2nd edition. Line drawing illus. 1st edition, 1938 (see no.7 above)

83. Arthur Raistrick, *Dynasty of Ironfounders: the Darbys and Coalbrookdale*, Longmans, Green and Co, London. Front dust-jacket and frontispiece designs, printed by Spottiswoode and Ballantyne and Co, London

84. John Piper and John Betjeman, 'Glories of English Craftsmanship – Electricity and Old Churches', *Time and Tide*, Vol.34, No.49, December, pp.1582–3. Line drawing illus.

85. John Piper, 'What they stand for', *The Ambassador* (Coronation Edition), pp.40–52

1954

86. John Betjeman, *Poems in the Porch*, SPCK, London. Eight line drawing illus. incl. one on the front cover

87. Edwin Muir, *Prometheus* ('Ariel Poem' series), Faber and Faber, London. Three autolithographs printed by Jesse Broad and Co Ltd, Manchester, all on commercial printing paper. The print run size was approximately 500. None of the prints were signed by the artist, who however on occasion signed the front cover of the book. Each book was sent out in a light green/grey envelope on which were printed the title, author, illustrator, publisher and price. Book size: 212 × 146 (8⅜ × 5¾). Envelope size: 170 × 232 (6 × 9¼) (*sc.* Cats 87A–C)

88. Janet Stone (compiler), *Edward Sydney Woods, 94th Bishop of Lichfield: some appreciations*, Victor Gollancz, London. Two illus., one of which is engraved on wood by Reynolds Stone

89. Glyndebourne Festival Programme Book, Glyndebourne Productions Ltd, London. Reproduction for set design for *Don Giovanni*, p.45

90. John Piper, 'Portland Stone, Portland Colours', *The Ambassador*, No.6, pp.80–94. Seventeen illus. incl. the cover design

1955

91. Julian Duguid, *The Blue Triangle*, Hodder and Stoughton, London. Dust-jacket design, printed by Richard Clay and Co Ltd, Bungay

92. John Hadfield (ed.), *Elizabethan Love Songs*, The Cupid Press, Barham Manor, Suffolk, containing eight colour autolithographs printed by W.S. Cowell Ltd, Ipswich. A limited edition of 660 copies signed and numbered by the artist (*sc.* Cats 93–100)

93. S. John Woods, *John Piper: Paintings, Drawings and Theatre Designs, 1932–1954*, Faber and Faber, London, in a standard edition containing four autolithographs printed by Mourlot Frères, Paris in 1954, and an aquatint tipped in as the frontispiece, printed by A. Alexander and Sons Ltd, London, also in 1954. Embossed on the hardback front cover is a *Foliate Head* design repr. from a drawing by Piper (*sc.* Cats 88–92)

94. John Piper and John Betjeman (eds), *Murray's Lancashire Architectural Guide*, John Murray, London. Dust-jacket design

95. *The Installation of Electricity in Churches*, Central Council for the Care of Churches, London, pp.4–6. 'Drawings illustrating how not to do it'

96. *The University Museum (Founded 1855)*, Oxford University Press (OUP), Oxford. A print commissioned for *The Oxford Almanack* (*sc.* Cat.101)

97. Christmas Card, Penguin Books (*sc.* Cat.101A)

98. **Recording Britain*, drawings by Piper mentioned in correspondence

1956

99. *David Bell, *The Artist in Wales*, Harrap, London. Cover illus. by Piper

100. *Benjamin Britten, *The Turning of the Screw*. Cover design

101. Colin Graham, *The English Opera Group, 1946–1956*. Cover design

102. David Verey, *Wiltshire*, Faber and Faber, London, 2nd edition ('Shell Guide' series). Front end-paper drawing. 3rd edition, 1968, by John Piper and J.H. Cheetham, has no graphic illus.

103. *The John Piper Windows*, Oundle School, Oundle. Three line drawing illus.

104. *Illustration for John Betjeman poem in the *Saturday Book*, Hutchinson, London

1958

105. John Betjeman (ed.), *Collins' Guide to English Parish Churches, including the Isle of Man*, Collins, London. Line drawing illus. 2nd and 3rd editions, 1968 and 1980 respectively (see nos 132 and 164 below)

106. Basil F.L. Clarke, *Anglican Cathedrals outside the British Isles*, with a foreword by John Betjeman, SPCK, London. Front dust-jacket design, printed by Morrison and Sibb Ltd, London

107. *The House of Whitbread*, Whitbread Group of Companies, Spring. Front and back dust-jacket design

1959

108. Yvonne Mitchell, *The Bed-Sitter*, A. Barker, London. Front dust-jacket design

109. Bertrand Russell, *The Wisdom of the West*, ed. by Paul Foulkes, Macdonald, London. Ten colour illus. from collages

1960

110. Ronald F.H. Duncan, *Judas*, Anthony Blond, London, March. In two

editions: one limited to 500 numbered and signed copies by the author and the artist. Eight black-and-white collotypes from collages, printed at Chiswick Press on Matt Grosvenor Litho

111. * Nicholas d'Eglise Thomas, *Guide to Prehistoric England*, Batsford, London. Cover design

112. Ivan Sanderson and Sacheverell Sitwell, *A Century of Sanderson, 1860–1960*, Arthur Sanderson and Sons Ltd, London. Cover design

113. **BBC Yearbook*. Front and back-cover illus.

114. **Vickers Magazine*, special supplement on lithography, July. Examples of Piper's work incl.

1961
115. *Bertrand Russell, *The History of Western Philosophy*, Penguin, Harmondsworth. Colour plates by Piper

116. John Piper, 'Serenissima', *Architectural Review*, Vol.129, May, pp.301–3. One illus.

1962
117. Robin Fedden, *The Enchanted Mountains: a quest in the Pyrenees,* John Murray, London. Three-colour lithographic reproduction as the frontispiece, by Butler and Tanner Ltd, Frome and London

118. Gilbert White (ed.), *The Natural History of Selborne*, with an introduction and notes by W. S. Scott, Folio Society, London. Twelve illus. incl. the frontispiece, printed by Richard Clay and Co, Bungay

119. *A set of illustrations of English racecourses for *Sports Illustrated* magazine, New York

1963
120. *D. F. Bickmore, G. E. Blackman, M. A. Shaw, *The Atlas of Britain and Northern Ireland*, Clarendon Press, Oxford. End-papers by Piper

1964
121. *Basil Clarke and John Betjeman, *English Churches*, Vista Books, London. Cover photographs by Piper

122. William Golding, *The Spire*, Faber and Faber, London. Front dust-jacket design, printed by R. Mac Lehose and Co Ltd, Glasgow

1965
123. René Huyghe (ed.), *Art and Mankind: Larousse Encyclopedia of Modern Art*, Hamlyn Publishing Group Ltd, London (originally published by Librairie Larousse, Paris, 1961). 'St Mary le Port, Bristol, 1940', repr. p.371

124. Kenneth Lindley, *Of Graves and Epitaphs*, Hutchinson, London. Frontispiece and end-paper designs: drawings by Piper engraved on wood by Lindley and reused in *Urns and Angels: an anthology of epitaphs*, 1965 (see no.125 below)

The original correspondence between Piper and Hutchinson in 1962 was for a book entitled *Over My Dead Body*, to include an introduction and frontispiece by Piper with possibly other literary and pictorial material

125. Joyce and Kenneth Lindley, *Urns and Angels: an anthology of epitaphs*, Pointing Finger Press, Swindon, a limited edition of 22 copies. Wood engravings reused from *Of Graves and Epitaphs*, 1965 (see no.124 above)

126. James Morris, *Oxford*, Faber and Faber, London. Two-colour lithographic reproduction as the frontispiece

127. Adrian Stokes and John Piper, *Venice*, Lion and Unicorn Press at the Royal College of Art, London, March, containing six colour and twenty two-tone autolithographs (*sc.* Cats 146–71) (2nd edition, Duckworth, 1965 (see no.128 below))

128. Adrian Stokes and John Piper, *Venice*, Duckworth, London, October, 2nd edition, containing eight colour and twenty-four two-tone autolithographs incl. the dust-jacket and the end-papers (*sc.* Cats 146–71, as no.127 above, plus 171A, 171B, 171C and 171D). (1st edition, Lion and Unicorn Press, Cambridge, 1965, see no.127 above)

1966
129. Edmund Blunden, *The Great Church of the Holy Trinity, Long Melford.* Cover design

130. *Flower in Praise: 2, 3, 4 September 1966*, Chichester Cathedral. Two-colour halftone used as the cover design and throughout the text

1967
131. *Cathedral of Christ the King*, Souvenir publication, Liverpool Cathedral. Illus. of the Lantern Tower

1968
132. John Betjeman (ed.), *Collins' Pocket Guide to English Parish Churches*, Collins, London, 2nd edition (2 Vols). Dust-jacket design and ten line drawing illus. in the introduction. (1st edition, 1958, see no.105 above; 3rd edition, 1980, see no.164 below)

133. Basil F. L. Clarke, 'Street's Yorkshire churches and contemporary criticism' in *Concerning architecture: essays on architectural writers and writing presented to Nikolaus Pevsner* (ed. J. Summerson), Allen Lane, London, pp.209–25, notes on contemporary criticism by Basil F.L. Clarke. Nine black-and-white photos by Piper

134. Photographs by Piper illustrating 'The Rural Cradle of a Revolution', Bodfan Gruffyd, *Country Life*, 11th January

1969
135. Arnold J. Taylor, *Castell Caernarfon*, HMSO, Cardiff, published on the occasion of the Investiture of the Prince of Wales. Three reproductions from gouaches

136. Ronald S. Thomas, *The Mountains* (with a descriptive note by the artist), The Chilmark Press, New York; also at the Rampant Lion Press, Cambridge, in a limited edition of 350 numbered copies, of which 110 are signed, specially bound and with an extra set of wood engravings. Ten drawings by Piper engraved on wood by Reynolds Stone

137. *100 Hymns for Today*, Melody Editions, London. Cover design printed by William Clowes and Sons Ltd, London

1970
138. *A History of Lincolnshire*, Darwen Finlayson Ltd, Henley-on-Thames. Six photographs by Piper

139. *Oxfordshire Historic Churches Appeal*, Pergamon Press, Oxford, for the appeal by Robert Maxwell MC. Line drawing cover illustration

1971
140. Wilhelmine Harrod (ed.), *Norfolk Country Churches and the Future*, The Norfolk Society, Norwich. Colour halftone from a drawing on the cover

141. Alun Hoddinott, *The Tree of Life*, Oxford University Press, Oxford. Cover design

142. *View from the Upper Common Room, the Queen's College*, Oxford University Press (OUP), Oxford. A print commissioned for *The Oxford Almanack* (*sc.* Cat.206)

1972
143. Anne Ridler, *The Jesse Tree*, Lyrebird Press, London, in a limited edition of 100 numbered and signed copies and a paperback edition, No.3 in the series 'PL: Editions Poetry London'. Cover design, frontispiece (omitted in the paperback edition) and nine black-and-white illus., printed by the University Press, Oxford

1973
144. Jan Morris, *Heaven's Command: an Imperial Progress*, Faber and Faber, London. Double-spread dust-jacket; frontispiece and title-page illus. repr. from a painting. The illus. of 'Serzincote House' was reused in the Penguin paperback, 1979

145. J. M. Richards, *The Castles on the Ground: The Anatomy of Suburbia*, John Murray, London, 2nd edition, with a new introduction. Jacket design, incorporating one new image, and eight offset lithographic illus. of which four are new. 1st edition, 1946 (see no.51 above)

1974
146.* Design for the cover of John Cornforth's enquiry into country houses for the British Tourist Authority

147. *Death In Venice*, Benjamin Britten, Decca Records, London. Cover design for the booklet accompanying the opera

148. Poster reproduction of *Virgin and Child* (Cat.267) as the poster for the Victoria and Albert Museum Christmas Print Fair, 9th November–21st December

1975

149. *John Hanbury Sparrow, *Santa Maria della Salute*, Cambridge. Verse illus. by Piper, originally published 1973

150. *Chichester 900*, with a preface by Walter Hussey, Chichester Cathedral, Chichester. Double-spread colour cover design from a drawing, printed by Chichester Press Ltd, Chichester

1976

151. Henry Thorold (ed.), *Lincolnshire Churches: Their Past and Their Future*, Lincolnshire Old Churches Trust. Seven halftone illus. and nine black-and-white photographs from paintings incl. one in colour on the cover

152. William Shakespeare, *Romeo and Juliet*, directed by Simon Wallis, Merton College Gardens, Merton College, Oxford, May. Poster design commissioned by Nicholas Cranfield, titled *[Romeo and Juliet Balcony]* and repr. in a limited unsigned, unnumbered edition of 300

153. **Betjeman*, The Open University, Milton Keynes. Two Piper works repr. from *John Piper* (John Betjeman, Penguin, 1944)

154. *Festival Programme*, Llanddewibrefi Arts Festival. Black-and-white halftone from a painting on the cover

1977

155. *India Love Poems*, translated by Tambimuttu, Paradine, New York; Lyrebird Press, London ('PL: Editions Poetry London' series, No.4), a collectors' edition of 200 signed and numbered copies, incl. 40 accompanied by a signed original drawing. Eighteen colour reproductions lithographed by Senecio Press, Oxford and printed by the Rampant Lion Press

156. 'English Village and French Village: Weston Zoyland and Essoyes', *Architype* (Bristol University Student Architecture Magazine), No.3. Two line drawing illus.

157. 'Herefordshire – 3', *Vole*, No.1, pp.38-9. Four photos

1978

158. Peter Porter, *Les Très Riches Heures*, The Keepsake Press ('Keepsake Poem' 36), Richmond. Edition of 180 copies, 12 signed by the author and artist. One line drawing

159. Roger Pringle and Christopher Hampton (eds), *A Selection from Poems for Shakespeare* (Vols I-VI), Globe Playhouse Publications, London, a limited edition of 500 copies. Title-page design and one line drawing illustration on the end-papers

1979

160. W.H.Hudson, *A Shepherd's Life*, London. Engravings of Piper originals by Reynolds Stone

161. *Walton, *Troilus and Cressida – Vocal Score*, Oxford University Press, Oxford. Cover design

162. **Aldeburgh Festival of Music and the Arts*, Aldeburgh – Snape Maltings Foundation Ltd. Cover design

163. *Composition*, Reading University Fine Art Department Magazine, Spring. Illus. photostatically repr. from drawings, incl. the cover

1980

164. John Betjeman (ed.), *Collins' Guide to Parish Churches of England and Wales, including the Isle of Man*, Collins, London, 3rd edition. Ten line drawings in the introduction. lst and 2nd editions, 1958 and 1968 respectively (see nos 105 and 132 above)

165. Jean Corke, John Blatchly, John Fitch (eds), *Suffolk Churches*, Suffolk Historic Churches Trust, Lavenham, Sudbury, 3rd edition. Black-and-white halftone from a drawing as the frontispiece

166. *More Hymns for Today*, Hymns Ancient and Modern Ltd, Melody Editions, London. Cover design printed by William Clowes and Sons Ltd, Beccles

1981

167. John Betjeman, *Church Poems*, John Murray, London. Eighteen line drawing illus., one repeated on the dust-jacket, printed by W. and J. MacKay Ltd, Chatham. Limited edition of 100 signed by the artist and quarter-bound in leather

168. Ronald Blythe (ed.), *Places: an Anthology of Britain*, Oxford University Press, Oxford. Nine black-and-white illus. incl. the dust-jacket, title-page and end-papers, printed by University Press, Oxford

169. Eric Mottram, *A Book of Herne, 1975-1981*, Arrowspire Press, Colne. The etching *The Seasons: Spring* (*sc.* Cat.329), repr. as the front dust-jacket design

170. June Osborne, *Stained Glass in England*, Frederick Muller Ltd, London. Three colour plates of windows by Piper

171. *Cardiff Festival of Music*, Cardiff, 28th November–12th December. Programme front cover

172. *British Council at the Frankfurt Book Fair. Repr. on cover of the programme

173.*Programme for the 'Golden Jubilee Gala', English National Opera. Cover design by Piper

1982

174. John Dyer, *Grongar Hill*, Stourton Press, London, with a foreword by the artist, containing three two-tone lithographs. Printed at the Curwen Studio, London (*sc.* Cats 337-9)

175. Peter Moore, *Crown in Glory: A Celebration of Craftmanship – Studies in Stained Glass*, Jarold and Sons Ltd, Norwich. Watercolour of stained glass from Salisbury Cathedral on the cover

176. *Quarto*, No.25, January–February. Line drawing illus. of Little Moreton Hall, Cheshire on the cover

177. *Poetry London/Apple Magazine*, No.2. Cover design and a halftone from a collage repr. between pp.48 and 49 to accompany the poem *Hands*, by Brian Guinness

1983

178. John Evans (ed.), *Aldeburgh Festival of Music and the Arts*, Snape Maltings Foundation Ltd, Aldeburgh. Front and back cover illus.

179. *John Mortimer. *Paradise Postponed*, Penguin, Harmondsworth. Jacket illus.

180. John Piper and Mark Girouard, *John Piper's Stowe*, Hurtwood Press, Westerham, Kent in association with the Tate Gallery, London. Standard edition of 250 and a deluxe edition of 50. Two offset lithographs, photomechanically repr. from watercolours, namely 'Stowe: The Oxford Bridge' and 'Stowe: The Palladian Bridge' were signed by Piper b.r. and were included with the deluxe edition of 50.

1984

181. *Dylan Marlais Thomas, *Deaths and Entrances*, Gwasg Gregynoy, Newtown, Powys. Poems edited by W. Davies, illus. by Piper. Originally published London, 1946. A new edition of 290 copies. Colour frontispiece and seven double-page colour illus. by Piper. A run on of approximately 20 of Piper's illus. for the book, unsigned and unnumbered, were sold individually.

1986

182. *Catharine Arnold, *Lost Time*, Hodder and Stoughton, London. 'Canon's Ashby 1983' repr. as front cover illus.

183. Moelwyn Merchant, *Confrontation of Angels*, Oxford University Press and Christopher Davies Ltd. Front cover and two black-and-white illus.

184. *A tribute to Peter Pears 1910-1986*, Royal Opera House, London, 3rd November. Cover Illus. Given in aid of the Aldeburgh Appeal. Conductor: Simon Rattle

1988

185. Rona Campbell, *The Hedge*, Cover-point Publications, London. Front and back cover illus.

186. *Books on Art and Architecture 1988-1989* (catalogue), Faber and Faber, London. Front cover

1989

187. Jennifer Sherwood, *A Guide to the Churches of Oxfordshire*, Robert Dugdale in association with Oxfordshire Historic Churches Trust. Front and back cover. Incl. photographs and watercolour illus.

188. Henry Thorold, *Lincolnshire Churches Revisited*, Michael Russell Ltd. Photographs by Peter Burton and Piper

189. Alun Hoddinott. *Symphony No.6, Op.166; Op.105 No.2; Op.90; Op.119.* Chandos Records Ltd, Colchester. CD front cover. Symphony No.6 dedicated to John Piper; Selection of poems for Op.90 – a contemplation of flowers – chosen by Myfanwy Piper

1990

190. Benjamin Britten, *Les Illuminations*; *Serenade*, *Nocturne*, Nimbus Records, Monmouth. CD front cover

191. Benjamin Britten, *Spring Symphony Op.44*, Chandos Records Ltd, Colchester. CD front cover

192. William Mathias, *Church and Choral Music*, Nimbus Records, Monmouth. CD front cover

1990/91

193. *Annual Catalogue 1990/91*, Decca Records, London. Front and back cover illus.

1991

194. Benjamin Britten, *Holiday Diary*, Virgin Classics Ltd, London. CD front cover

195. Benjamin Britten, *The Young Person's Guide to the Orchestra*; *Sea Interludes*, *Courtly Dances*, *Suite on English Folk Tunes*, Nimbus Records, Monmouth. CD front cover

1993

196. Bruce Metzger and Michael Coogan (eds), *The Oxford Companion to the Bible*, Oxford University Press, Oxford. Baptistry windows, Coventry Cathedral repr. as front cover

197. Alun Hoddinott, *Orchestral Music*, Nimbus Records, Monmouth. CD front cover

198. William Mathias, *Organ Music*, Nimbus Records, Monmouth. CD front cover

1994

199. Andrew Sanders, *The Short History of English Literature*, Clarendon Press, Oxford. Front cover illus.

Undated/Unknown

200. *Safwn Gnybwlch/Save Snowdonia*, appeal booklet, Ferens Art Gallery, Kingston upon Hull. Cover illus.

Autolithographic Illustrations

CAT. NO.	PL. NO.	TITLE
10		*Invention in Colour* Autolithograph, 1937 (from *Signature*, No.6, July 1937)
12-23		*Brighton Aquatints* Aquatints, 1939 Author: John Piper
12	I	The First Avenue Hotel, Hove
13	II	The Royal Pavilion
14	III	Regency Square from the West Pier
15	IV	Brighton from the Station Yard
16	V	Brunswick Terrace
17	VI	Bedford Square
18	VII	Mixed Styles: Regency-Victorian-Modern
19	VIII	Kemp Town
20	IX	Regency Square
21	X	The Chapel of St George, Kemp Town
22	XI	St Bartholomew's Church
23	XII	The Metropole Hotel from the West Pier
27		*Cheltenham* Autolithograph, 1940 (from: *Signature*, No.13, January 1940)
34-46		*English, Scottish and Welsh Landscape* Autolithographs, 1944 (verse chosen by John Betjeman and Geoffrey Taylor)
34		Untitled (dust-jacket)
35	I	Pistyll Cain, North Wales
36	II	Weathercote Cave, Yorkshire
37	III	Tomen-y-Mur and Roman Amphitheatre, North Wales
38	IV	Grongar Hill, Carmarthenshire
39	V	At Lewknor, Oxfordshire
40	VI	Rievaulx Abbey, Yorkshire
41	VII	Trawsfynnydd, Merioneth
42	VIII	Approach to Gordale Scar, Yorkshire
43	IX	Easegill, Lancashire
44	X	Park Place, Berkshire
45	XI	Talland Church, Cornwall
46	XII	Stonesfield, Oxfordshire
47-57		*The Colour of English Country Houses* Autolithographs, 1944 (enclosed as a separate pamphlet in *International Textiles*, No.8)
47	I	Chicheley Hall, Buckinghamshire
48	II	Mereworth Castle, Kent
49	III	Seaton Delaval, Northumberland
50	IV	Sudbrooke Park, Richmond, Surrey
51	V	Kirby Hall, Northamptonshire
52	VI	Knole, Kent
53	VII	Bolsover Castle, Derbyshire
54	VIII	Attingham, Shropshire
55	IX	Hafod, Cardiganshire
56	X	West Wycombe Park, Buckinghamshire
57	XI	Vanished Fonthill, Wiltshire
57A-C		'Topographical Letter from Devizes', Autolithographs, 1944 (from: *Cornhill*, Vol.161, No.963, November 1944)
57A		Devizes: In Long Street
57B		Devizes: The Market Place
57C		Avebury Restored

CAT. NO.	PL. NO.	TITLE
58-66		*The Castles on the Ground* Autolithographs, 1946 Author: J. M. Richards
58		The Castles on the Ground (dust-jacket)
59	I	The Castles on the Ground I
60	II	The Castles on the Ground II
61	III	The Castles on the Ground III
62	IV	The Castles on the Ground IV
63	V	The Castles on the Ground V
64	VI	The Castles on the Ground VI
65	VII	The Castles on the Ground VII
66	VIII	The Castles on the Ground VIII
67A-B		['Kubla Khan in Wales'] Autolithographs, 1947 (from: *Cornhill*, Vol.162, No.970, Spring 1947)
67A		[Adam and Eve's Gate]
67B		[Hafod]
68		*The Market Place at Devizes* Autolithograph, 1948 (frontispiece to: John Piper, *Buildings and Prospects*)
71A-77 **72-7**		*On the Making of Gardens* (deluxe edition) *On the Making of Gardens* Autolithographs, 1949 Author: Sir George Sitwell
71A		On the Making of Gardens (cover, deluxe edition only)
72	I	On the Making of Gardens I
73	II	On the Making of Gardens II
74	III	On the Making of Gardens III
75	IV	On the Making of Gardens IV
76	V	On the Making of Gardens V
77	VI	On the Making of Gardens VI
88-92		John Piper: *Paintings, Drawings and Theatre Designs 1932-54* Aquatint and Autolithographs, 1954 Author: S. John Woods
88		Figures from a Seal (frontispiece) (Aquatint)
89		Bullslaughter Bay, Pembrokeshire I (Autolithograph)
90		Dryslwyn Castle (Autolithograph)
91		Bullslaughter Bay, Pembrokeshire II (Autolithograph)
92		Niton, Isle of Wight (Autolithograph)
93-100		*Elizabethan Love Songs* Autolithographs, 1955 Editor: John Hadfield
93		Elizabethan Love Songs I
94		Elizabethan Love Songs II
95		Elizabethan Love Songs III
96		Elizabethan Love Songs IV
97		Elizabethan Love Songs V
98		Elizabethan Love Songs VI
99		Elizabethan Love Songs VII
100		Elizabethan Love Songs VIII

CAT. NO.	PL. NO.	TITLE
101A		[Waterloo Bridge] Autolithograph, 1955 Christmas Card for Penguin Books
146-71 **146-71D**		*Venice* Autolithographs 1965 *Venice* Autolithographs 1965 (2nd edition) Authors: Adrian Stokes and John Piper
146	I	Palazzo Dario
147	II	The Dogana
148	III	From the north, outside the Fondamenta Nuove
149	IV	The Salute
150	V	The Giudecca
151	VI	Chiesa dell'Ospedaletto
152	VII	San Giorgio Maggiore
153	VIII	San Marco
154	IX	San Moisè
155	X	The Piazza
156	XI	The Piazzetta
157	XII	Scuola di San Marco
158	XIII	San Stae
159	XIV	From the lagoon
160	XV	Santa Maria Formosa
161	XVI	From the lagoon
162	XVII	From the lagoon
163	XVIII	San Zaccaria
164	XIX	From the lagoon
165	XX	Santa Maria dei Miracoli
166	XXI	From the lagoon
167	XXII	Palazzo Manzoni-Angaran
168	XXIII	Side of the Palazzo Pesaro
169	XXIV	Base of the Campanile
170	XXV	Palazzo Pesaro
171	XXVI	From the lagoon
171A	–	Venice (dust-jacket) (2nd edition only)
171B	–	Venice (front end-papers) (2nd edition only)
171C	–	Venice (backpiece) (2nd edition only)
171D	–	Venice (back end-papers) (2nd edition only)
337-9		*Grongar Hill* Autolithographs, 1982 Author: John Dyer
337		Grongar Hill I
338		Grongar Hill II
339		Grongar Hill III

Exhibitions

A combined list of one-man exhibitions, indicated by an asterisk (*) before the venue, and group exhibitions. Exhibitions devoted entirely to prints are listed in bold type.

The information is arranged as follows:
Exhibition venue, city, title of exhibition, date. Exhibition details (if available).

Where an organiser holds an exhibition at a venue the name of the organiser is listed followed by the words 'at' and the exhibition venue. For example, no.294 below: Louis Grosse Ltd at Coventry Cathedral, Coventry.

Where a title is not known but a close approximation can be made from information to hand then this title is placed in square brackets, for example, no.91 below.

Within each year exhibitions are placed chronologically by month and then date. Where a date can be estimated this is given a *circa* (*c.*) listing and placed immediately after the nearest month or year as appropriate. Where the year is known but not the date, the entry is placed alphabetically at the end of that year. Exhibitions where no year can be estimated are placed alphabetically at the end of the list.

Where correspondence to or from the artist indicates an exhibition but no confirmation of it has been found, the information is listed and preceded by a dagger (†) prior to the entry number.

The details always relate to Piper. Thus the listing under no.256 below of 'Coventry Cathedral vestments and designs' are those by Piper.

Generally, unless complete specific venues and dates are known, travelling exhibitions are listed once, under the entry of first venue.

The known firework displays are listed at the end.

All known information is listed. The author would welcome further information, especially where entries are incomplete.

1927

1. Arlington Gallery, London. *Wood engravings* (with David Birch)

1931

2. Heal and Son, Mansard Annexe, London. *An Exhibition of water colours, offsets from stage designs not previously exhibited* (with Patrick Millard, Eileen Holding and Clarice Mofart)

3. New Burlington Galleries, London, *The London Group: 29th Exhibition*

1932

4. New Burlington Galleries, London, *The London Group: 30th Exhibition*

1933

5. New Burlington Galleries, London, *The London Group, 31st Exhibition*

6. Zwemmer Gallery, London

1934

7. Leicester Galleries, London, *13th exhibition of the Seven and Five Society*

1935

8. Experimental Theatre, Finchley Road, London

9. Zwemmer Gallery, London, *The Seven and Five Society*

1936

10. Alex Reid and Lefèvre, London, *Abstract and concrete: an international exhibition of abstract painting and sculpture today,* The first English International exhibition of abstract art, organised by Nicolette Gray, in co-operation with *AXIS*. Toured to Oxford, Liverpool, Newcastle and Cambridge

11. Duncan Miller Ltd, London, *Modern Pictures for modern rooms: an exhibition of abstract art in contemporary settings*

12. Everyman Cinema, Hampstead, London, *Abstract art: Barbara Hepworth, Arthur Jackson, Henry Moore, Ben Nicholson, John Piper*

13. New Burlington Galleries, London, *The London Group, 34th Exhibition*

1937

14. Artists International Association (AIA), London, *1937 Exhibition: unity of artists for peace, democracy, and cultural development*

15. Fine Art Society, Minto House, Edinburgh

16. Leicester Galleries, London, *The London Group*

17. London Gallery, London, *Exhibition of constructive art*

18. London Gallery, London, *Surrealist objects and poems*

19. New Burlington Galleries, London, *The London Group: 36th Exhibition*

20. Thomas Agnew and Sons, London, *An exhibition of paintings in connexion with a scheme to provide a permanent gallery for the constant display of works by contemporary painters and sculptors*

1938

21. Cooling Galleries, London, *Paintings, drawings and scupture chosen by the London Group*

22. Guildhall, Gloucester, *Realism and Surrealism: an exhibition of several phases of contemporary art*

23. Leicester Galleries, London, *Lithographs in colour*

24. *London Gallery, London, *John Piper; paintings, collages and drawings*

25. Salon d'Automne, Palais de Chaillot, Paris, *L'Art anglais indépendent contemporain*

1939

26. Leicester Galleries, London, *Selected paintings, drawings and pottery lent by the Contemporary Art Society*

27. London Gallery, London, *Living art in England*

28. Tate Gallery, London, *Mural Painting in Great Britain 1919–1939*

1940

29. *Leicester Galleries, London, *Paintings and Watercolours by John Piper*, March

30. Alex Reid and Lefèvre, London, *Art of today: some trends in British painting*

31. Alex Reid and Lefèvre, London, *Modern English Painting, Recent Works*

32. National Gallery, London

1941

33. Temple Newsam, Leeds, *Works by John Piper, Henry Moore and Graham Sutherland*, 25th July–28th September

34. National Gallery, London, *War pictures at the National Gallery*

1941–2

35. Temple Newsam, Council for the Encouragement of Music and the Arts, Leeds. Selections from the 1941 Temple Newsam exhibition touring to Leicester, Harrogate, Brighton and Wakefield

1942

36. Alexander Postan Fine Art, London, *Aspects of Abstract Art in England 1935–42*

37. Alex Reid and Lefèvre, London

38. London Museum, London, *New Movements in art: contemporary work in England, an exhibition of recent paintings and sculpture*

39. Ministry of Information, London, *War drawings by British artists*

40. National Gallery, London

1943
41. Council for the Encouragement of Music and the Arts, London

42. Royal Academy, London, *The London Group: fifth wartime exhibition*

1943–4
43. Council for the Encouragement of Music and the Arts, London

1944
44. Ministry of Information, London, *War Pictures by British Artists*

45. Redfern Gallery, London, *French and English paintings*

1945
46. 28 Avenue des Champs-Élysées, Paris, *Quelques contemporains Anglais*. Organised by the British Council.

47. Buchholz Gallery, New York, *Contemporary British Artists: Ivon Hitchens, Henry Moore, Paul Nash, John Piper*

48. *Leicester Galleries, *The Sitwell Country: Derbyshire domains, backgrounds to an autobiography*

49. National Gallery

50. Roland Browse and Delbanco, London, March–April

51. Royal Academy, London, *Exhibition of National War Pictures*

1946
52. Albright-Knox Art Gallery, Buffalo; Worcester Art Museum, Massachusetts; Cleveland Museum of Art; Art Gallery of Toronto; City Art Museum of St Louis, Missouri; California Palace of the Legion of Honour, San Francisco, *Contemporary British Art*, The British Council (touring exhibition), Autumn of 1946 to 6th August 1947

53. Arts Council, London, *British Painting 1939 to 1945*

54. Associated American Artists Inc, New York Galleries

55. *Leicester Galleries, London, *John Piper: stage designs for Benjamin Britten's opera The Rape of Lucretia*

1947
56. *Leicester Galleries, London, *New paintings and drawings by John Piper*, December

57. British Council, Cairo

58. British Council Sweden (touring exhibition)

1948
59. *Buchholz Gallery (Curt Valentine), New York, *John Piper*, 3rd–21st February

60. Redfern Gallery, London, Colour Prints by the Society of Painters and Printers, 30th November–31st December

1949
61. Victoria and Albert Museum, London, *Special exhibition of paintings by John Piper for the British Embassy in Rio de Janeiro*

1950
62. *Buchholz Gallery (Curt Valentine), New York, *John Piper: Recent Work*, 17th October–4th November

63. Birmingham Museum and Art Gallery, *Six contemporary British painters*

64. British Council, London

65. Cincinnati Art Museum, Cincinnati, *Six English Moderns: Piper, Sutherland, Hepworth, Tunnard, Moore, Nicholson*

66. Whitechapel Art Gallery, London, *Painter's Progress*

1951
67. *Philadelphia Art Alliance, Philadelphia, *John Piper; oils, gouaches, watercolours*, 6th February–4th March

68. *Leicester Galleries, London, *Stones and Flowers: An exhibition of new paintings by John Piper*, November

69. Festival of Britain, Main Vista, Festival Gardens, Battersea. Exhibition based on drawings of architectural subjects made during the previous twenty years (with Osbert Lancaster)

1952
70. Arts Council, Cambridge

1953
71. *Aldeburgh Festival, Suffolk, *Paintings 1932–52*

72. Arts Council Gallery, Cambridge, *John Piper, Retrospective Exhibition*. Toured to the Cecil Higgins Museum, Bedford

73. *Arts Council (Welsh Committee), *Paintings and Drawings by John Piper*

74. National Museum of Wales, Cardiff, *British Romantic Painting in the Twentieth Century*. Toured to Aberystwyth and Swansea

1954
75. Redfern Gallery, London

1954–5
76. 13th–25th October, Ottawa; 29th October–12th November, Rothesay NB; 19th November–3rd January, 1955, Wolfville NS; 10th–17th January, Amherst NS; 24th January–18th February, Sackville NB; 25th February–14th March, Charlottetown PEI; 22nd March–15th April, Halifax NS; 25th April–5th May, Fredericton NB, and Western Galleries, *British Watercolours*. Organised by Commonwealth Society of Artists

1955
77. Rochester Art Center, Minnesota, and the Saint Paul Gallery and School of Art, *Mirror to Man*, 6th February–3rd March. Travelled to Saint Paul Gallery: 6th–30th March. Organised as a result of the art project for the new building of the Mayo Clinic

78. *Curt Valentine Gallery, New York, *John Piper*, 15th February–12th March

79. Zwemmer Gallery, London, April

80. Oxford Art Society, *c.*April

81. American Federation of Arts, New York, *World at Work*, 1st May 1955–1st May 1956. Touring exhibition

82. *Leicester Galleries, London, *The recent work of John Piper*, 19th May–9th June

83. Bristol Old Vic Company at the Royal West of England Academy, Bristol, *The Art of the Theatre*, May

84. Epsom College, Surrey, [*Centenary Founders Day Exhibition*], 11th June

85. Franz Bader Inc, Washington DC, October

86. Washington University, School of Fine Arts, Saint Louis, International Invitational Prints Exhibition, 2nd November–23rd November

87. St John's College, York, 26th November–10th December

88. Arts Council, London, *A Small Anthology of Modern Stained Glass*. Toured to the Aldeburgh Festival, Aldeburgh, Suffolk, and elsewhere (with Patrick Reyntiens).

89. Arts Council, London, *Some Twentieth-Century paintings from the collection of Peter Pears and Benjamin Britten*

90. Carnegie Institute, Pittsburgh. An International Exhibition of Contemporary Painting and Sculpture

91. Leicester Galleries, London, [*Etchings in colour*]

***c.*1955–6**
92. Arts Council (touring exhibition), *Some 20th Century Watercolours*, Exhibition closed end of June 1956

1956
93. Wintringham Boys' Grammar School, Grimsby, 14th January–14th February

94. Society of the Four Arts, Palm Beach, Florida, January

95. Royal Scottish Academy, Edinburgh, *10 English Painters, 1925–1955*, *c.*February (exhibition closed 19th February). Organised by Arts Council (Scottish Committee)

96. Bladon Gallery, Andover, Hampshire, [*Annual Summer Exhibition of Paintings and Sculpture*], 6th May–8th July

97. The Century Museum, New York, *John Piper Prints*, 16th July–16th August

98. Leicester Galleries, London, August

99. Stockton, Co Durham, August

100. Art Gallery of Toronto, 23rd–30th September

101. Amsterdam Municipal Museum, Amsterdam, [*Modern Textiles*], October-12th November. Travelled to Recklinghausen Museum (see no.112 below)

102. *Kunstzaal Magdalene Sothmann, Amsterdam, *John Piper*, 24th October–24th November

103. Ashmolean Museum Department of Fine Art, Oxford, [*Exhibition of the work of staff and visitors to the School*], 26th November

104. Redfern Gallery, London, [*French and English Lithographs in colour*], December

105. Aldeburgh Festival, Suffolk, *Theatre Models*

106. Contemporary Art Society at the Tate Gallery, London, *The Seasons*

107. *Durlacher Bros, New York, *John Piper*

108. St John's College, York

109. Scarborough Public Libraries Museums and Art Galleries

110. University of Durham, Durham, [*Stained Glass exhibition*]

111. Zwemmer Gallery, London, [*New Editions Group exhibition*]

1957
112. Recklinghausen Museum, Ruhr, [*Modern Textiles*], 20th January–24th February

†113. Corcoran Gallery, Washington DC, [*Exhibition of Contemporary British art organisied by Silberman Galleries*], 31st January–3rd March. Travelled to Brooklyn Museum, New York, Albright-Knox Art Gallery, Buffalo, La Jolla Art Center, California

114. *Durlacher Brothers, New York, John Piper, 26th February–23rd March

†115. Ohana Gallery, Venice, *International Exhibition of Sculpture in Venetian Glass*, 19th April–18th May. Organised by the Italian Institute with the Centro Studio Pittori Arte del Vetro of Venice and in co-operation with 'La Voce degli Italiani' of London

116. Charing Cross Tube Station, London, Dennis Lennon, [*Fund-raising exhibition*], July. Organised by the Architects and Designers in association with the Historic Churches Preservation Trust

117. Zwemmer Gallery, London, *John Piper, Michael Rothenstein*, *c.*August

118. Guildford Repertory Theatre, Guildford, [*Theatre design*], 5th–6th October. Incl. Piper's designs for *Don Giovanni* and *The Magic Flute*

119. *Leicester Galleries, London, *New paintings and watercolours by John Piper*, October–November

120. Zwemmer Gallery, London, [*New Editions Group exhibition*], opened on 22nd November

121. Wildenstein Gallery, New York, [*Fourth international Hallmark art award exhibition*], opened on 3rd December

122. Institute of Contemporary Arts, London, *Picture Fair*, *c.*Christmas

123. Arthur Jeffress Pictures, London

124. Art Rental Gallery, Washington DC, [*Opening exhibition*]

125. Castle Museum, Norwich, [*Watercolours from the end of the 19th century until the present day*]. The Third Watercolours exhibition

126. Howard Roberts Studio and Gallery, Cardiff

127. Masque Bookshop, London. Included *Gloriana* costume designs and other drawings

128. National Book League, London, [*Ballet exhibition*]. Included model set of *Prince of the Pagodas*

1957-8
129. Guildford House, Guildford, *Contemporary English Theatre Design*, 30th September 1957–30th August 1958. An Arts Council touring exhibition

130. Arts Council, London. Probably part of the touring exhibition under no.129 above

---

1958
131. John Lewis and Company Ltd, Southampton, *c.*March-April

132. Redfern Gallery, London, [*Contemporary religious art*], April

133. Bear Lane Gallery, Oxford, opened 6th May

134. *Midland Group Gallery, Nottingham, [*One man exhibition*], 24th May–14th June. A Midland Group of Artists exhibition, in association with the Arts Council of Great Britain

135. Aldeburgh Festival in conjunction with Norwich Exhibition Committee, *Drawings by Contemporary British Artists*, June

136. Edinburgh Festival, *Lithograph Exhibition*, *c.*August. Toured to Glasgow (see no.138 below)

137. Trafford Gallery, [*Mixed exhibition*], August-September

138. Glasgow Art Gallery, [*Lithograph exhibition*], November

139. Central Council for the Care of Churches, *The Church and the Artist*. Touring exhibition.

140. Zwemmer Gallery, London

***c.*1958**
141. *[*Exhibition of the cartoon of the window for the Plymouth Church*]

1958-9
142. Carnegie Institute, Pittsburgh, *1958 Pittsburg International Exhibition of Contemporary Painting and Sculpture*, 4th December 1958–8th February 1959

1959
143. Smithsonian Institute, Washington DC, *Art in Craftmanship*, opened 10th January. Organised by British Artist Craftsmen Ltd. Toured the USA and Canada

144. *Michaelis School of Fine Art, Cape Town, [*John Piper's Lithographs and Watercolours*], 31st March–16th April. Toured to Port Elizabeth and Johannesburg

145. *Midland Group Gallery, Nottingham, 2nd–23rd May. Midland Group of Artists in association with the Arts Council

146. Howard Roberts Studio and Gallery, Cardiff, [*Third anniversary exhibition*], September

147. St Margaret's Convent, East Grinstead, [*An exhibition of ecclesiastical art, ancient and modern*], 4th–8th November

148. *Leicester Galleries, London, *New Paintings and Gouaches by John Piper*, November

149. Stone Gallery, Newcastle upon Tyne, *c.*December

150. Institute of Contemporary Arts, London, *Picture Fair*, *c.*Christmas

151. Cardiff, British Architects' Conference

152. College Art Departments compiled by M. E. Foulkes, [*Costume designs*]. A touring exhibition

153. Edinburgh, Arts Council (Scottish Committee). A touring exhibition

154. São Paulo, *São Paulo Theatre Biennale*. Organised by the British Council, toured to Rio de Janeiro and Santiago

155. Stratford, Ontario, the Shakespeare Festival, in association with the International Theatre Institute. Set designs for *Prince of the Pagoda* and costume design for *Gloriana*

1960

156. Art Gallery, Northampton, *Art Alive*, 5th March–9th April

157. Vancouver Art Gallery, BC, with the help of the International Association of Art Critics, *Do You own a Contemporary Painting?*, 26th March–2nd April. A feature of the exhibition was '25 pictures by 25 British artists' including Piper

158. Reid Gallery, London, *Famous Contemporary English Draughtsmen*, April

159. South London Art Gallery, Camberwell Borough Council, *Fifty Years of Lithography by the Senefelder Group 1910-1960*, 24th April–14th May

160. *Arthur Jeffress Gallery, London, *Paintings and Watercolours of Venice by John Piper*, 31st May–24th June

161. Canaletto Gallery, Grand Union Canal, [*Opening exhibition*], June. With P. Greenham, V. Pitchforth, Lord Methuen. J. Bratby, D. Lindle, P. Berrisford, P. Coker, H. Bird, A. Newton, L. Cole, C. Wright

162. The Silk Mill at Albert Hall, London, [*Fabrics based on the designs of contemporary artists*], June. With Osbert Lancaster and Fulco Verdura

163. College of Art Gallery and Wheatstone Hall, Gloucester, *John Piper. Lynn Chadwick: exhibition of paintings and sculpture*, 1st September–1st October

164. Victoria and Albert Museum, London, *Mural Art Today*, October. The Society of Mural Painters at the Musuem

165. Zwemmer Gallery, London, [*Christmas Exhibition*]

166. The Silk Mill at Albert Hall, London, [*Fabrics based on the designs of contemporary artists*] (with Osbert Lancaster and Fulco Verdura)

167. Arthur Sanderson and Sons Ltd, London, [*Exhibition opening Berners Street building and marking centenary of Sandersons*]

168. Arts Centre, Shrewsbury

169. Appunto Gallery, Rome

170. National Gallery of Modern Art, Edinburgh

171. Northampton, *Art Now*

172. Smithsonian Institution, Washington DC, *British Artist Craftsmen*

1961

173. University of Nottingham Department of Fine Art, University Art Gallery, *Shakespeare in Art*, 11th January–11th February. Set and designs of *Midsummer Night's Dream* by Piper

174. Reading, *Modern Stained Glass*, January. An Arts Council touring exhibition to March

175. Leicester Galleries, London, [*New Year exhibition*], *c.*January

176. *Bear Lane Gallery, Oxford, *New Paintings of Brittany*, 5th May–7th June

177. Zwemmer Gallery, London, [*summer show*], May–June

178. Zwemmer Gallery, London, *New Editions*, July

179. New Metropole Arts Centre, Folkestone, [*Opening exhibition*], 2nd August

180. Reid Gallery, London, opened 6th September

181. Guildford, Surrey, [*Exhibition in L. Jonleigh's studio in aid of the Cancer Relief Fund*], 23rd–24th September

182. Temple Newsam House, Leeds, [*Glass exhibition*], October–8th November

183. *Durlacher Brothers, New York, *John Piper*, 31st October–25th November

184. Arts Council Gallery, London, November

185. Walker Art Gallery, Liverpool, *The Third John Moores Liverpool Exhibition*, Autumn

186. Institute of Contemporary Arts, London, *Picture Fair*, *c.*Christmas

187. Midland Group Gallery, Nottingham, [*Opening exhibition of new gallery*], Midland Group of Artists

1962

188. The Design Centre, Haymarket, London, [*Canberra/Oriana exhibition*], 15th January–10th February. The Council of Industrial Design in association with P&O Orient Lines – features furniture, furnishings and articles of equipment designed or selected for the two ships

189. Guildford, [*Exhibition linked to Yvonne Arnaud Appeal for Guildford's riverside theatre*], 3rd–24th March. Model of stage design for *The Midsummer Night's Dream*

190. Laing Galleries, Toronto, [Gouaches], April

191. St George's Gallery in association with Trust Houses Ltd, [*Autographic Print Competition*], *c.*April

192. Arthur Jeffress Gallery, *Paintings and Watercolours of Rome by John Piper*, 1st–25th May

193. Royal Watercolour Society Galleries, *The Graven Image*, London, May. Toured the United Kingdom for twelve months

194. Tate Gallery, London, *c.*May–June

195. Dorchester Abbey Friends Festival, [*Exhibition of stained glass*], 26th May–2nd June. With Nutyens, Haywood, Rutherford

196. Zappeion Hall, Athens, *Stage performance for mass audiences*, 16th–25th June. International Festival of Public Performance

197. Chichester Antiques Ltd Art Galleries, *The Painter and the Stage*, 21st July–4th August

198. Friends of Ponds Home for Spastics, Great Missenden Branch [*Fund-raising exhibition*], 29th–30th September

199. *Keel Picture Loan Collection Exhibition*, October

200. Landry Gallery, New York, *Coventry*, December. With recent aquisitions from Sutherland, Moore, Ernst, Jawlensky

201. Alfred Hecht, London

202. Arts Council (Welsh Committee) and the Lake District Art Gallery Trust, *Seven Modern British Painters*

203. Brighton Art Gallery and Museum, Brighton, *The Painter's Brighton*

204. Ind Coope Ltd, Burton-on-Trent, [*Exhibition from Ind Coope collection of Modern Paintings*]

205. National Museum of Wales, Cardiff, organised by the Welsh Committee of the Arts Council of Great Britian, *British art and the modern movement 1930-1940*

1963

206. South London Art Gallery, Camberwell Borough Council, *Prominent British Printmakers*, 16th February–7th March

207. *Marlborough Fine Art, New London Gallery, London, *John Piper: Recent Work*, March-April

1964

208. *Marlborough Fine Art, New London Gallery, *John Piper: Retrospective Exhibition*, March

209. Bladon Gallery, Andover, Hampshire, [*Annual Summer Exhibition of Paintings and Sculpture*], 3rd May–6th July

210. Bear Lane Gallery, Oxford, *John Piper and Kenneth Lee*, 4th–29th May

211. Branson Studio, Wiltshire, *Ramsbury Festival of Art and Music*, 13th June–5th July

212. *Prebendal House of Llandaff Cathedral, *John Piper in Wales* (retrospective exhibition), opened 16th June. Arts Council (Welsh Committee) in conjunction with the Llandaff Festival Committee. A touring exhibition

213. *Howard Roberts Gallery, Cardiff, *John Piper*, 18th June–18 July

214. Adam House, Edinburgh, [*Exhibition of sacred art*], 17th–29th August. Edinburgh International Festival in association with Grail book and art centre

215. Donald Pass Gallery, Chester, *Religious Themes by the Younger Generation*, 30th November–23rd December

216. City Art Gallery, Bradford, [*Exhibition of three local collections*], December

†**217.** Ash Barn, Stroud

218. *Marlborough Fine Art, London

219. National Museum of Wales, Cardiff, *London Group Jubilee Exhibition*. An Arts Council touring exhibition. Travelled to New Museum and Art Gallery, Doncaster and Southampton Art Gallery

220. *School of Fine Art, The University of Reading, Reading

1965

221. University of Exeter Arts Festival, March

222. Cafe Royal, London, [*Cafe Royal Centenary exhibition 1865-1965*], 10th June–9th July

223. Hambledon Gallery, Blandford Forum, *c.*June

224. *Baukunst, Cologne, *John Piper: Ölbilder, Aquarelle, Gouachen, Collagen, Kirchenfensterentwürfe*, 24th September–19th November

225. Torquay, *Devon Guild of Craftsmen Exhibition*, 25th September–16th October

226. Budapest, [*Stage designs*], opened October. A British Council touring exhibition

227. Leicester Galleries, London, November

228. Marlborough Fine Art, London, *Art in Britian 1930-40 centred around the Axis, Circle, Unit One*

229. School of Applied Art, Cologne, *Ten British Scene Painters*. A British Council touring exhibition

***c.*1965-75**

230. Camden Studios, London, *Exhibition of Contemporary Art*. A fund-rasing exhibition for medical aid for Vietnam

1966

231. Marlborough Fine Art, London, *Nolan – Piper – Richards*, April-May

232. *Aldeburgh Festival, Aldeburgh, *John Piper, Suffolk Churches and Landscapes*, June

233. Herbert Art Gallery and Museum, Coventry, [*Alfred Herbert centenary exhibition*], September

234. Howard Roberts Gallery, London

235. Wright Hepburn Gallery, London

1967

236. Bretton Hall Training College, Wakefield, [*Exhibition of church yards*], January. Toured to School of Advanced Architectural Studies, York

237. University of York Fine Arts Society, [*Recent Christian Art*], 14th–18th March. Drawings for the Chichester tapestry

238. Marlborough Fine Art, London, *[Designs and studies for Church commissions including Liverpool Cathedral]*, April (with Ceri Richards)

239. *University Art Gallery, Nottingham, [*Design for the Chichester Cathedral Tapestry*], 19th May–17th June

240. *Reading Museum and Art Gallery, Reading, *Retrospective Exhibition*, 7th June–3rd July

241. Usher Gallery, City of Lincoln Libraries, Museum and Art Gallery in association with Marlborough Fine Art, July

242. *Royle Publications Ltd, London, summer. A touring retrospective exhibition

243. David Paul Design Group, Chichester, *c.*August-September

244. *Brook Street Gallery, London, *Studies from Sketch Books 1940-60*

245. City Art Gallery, Wakefield

246. Graves Art Gallery, Sheffield, *'In our view': some paintings and sculpture bought by Hans and Elspeth Juda between 1931-1967*

247. *Graves Art Gallery, Sheffield, *Retrospective Exhibition*

248. *Ulster Museum, Belfast, *John Piper: Retrospective*. Toured to Marlborough Fine Art, London and Richard Demarco Gallery, Edinburgh

1968

249. *New Metropole Arts Centre, Folkestone, [*Retrospective exhibition*], February. Could have toured from no.247 above

250. Chichester Cathedral, Chichester, *Church 68*, 19th July

251. *Cecil Higgins Art Gallery, Bedford, *John Piper*, 28th September–26th October

252. Newbury combined Parishes Arts Council, Parish Church of St George, [*Stained glass*], October (with Pierre Fourmantroux, Alfred Fisher, Brian Thomas, Charles Norris, John Heyward)

253. Camden Town Centre, London

254. Council of Industrial Design, London [*Competition for souvenirs of the investiture of the Prince of Wales*]. Reproduction of Piper's painting of Caernarvon Castle entered by the Ministry of Public Buildings and Works

255. *Hambledon Gallery, Blandford Forum, *John Piper: life drawings*

256. Louis Grosse Ltd, London, [*Exhibition of church art, running concurrently with the Lambeth Conference*]. Coventry Cathedral vestments and designs

†**257.** The Minories, Colchester, *Object and Owner*

258. Sonning, Reading, [*Exhibition of ecclesiastical art*]. Tapestry and drawings for Chichester Cathedral

1969

259. *Hamet Gallery, London, *John Piper-Gouaches-Watercolours*, 3rd February–1st March

260. Angel Hotel, Guildford, Guildford Festival of Arts, [*Paintings, drawings and sculpture*], 7th–16th March

261. Morley College Exhibition Gallery, [*Opening exhibition*], March

262. *Cathedral Arts Festival, Manchester, *John Piper*, 27th April–11th May

263. *Marlborough Fine Art, New London Gallery, London, *John Piper, European Topography 1967-1969, Oil paintings and Gouaches*, May-June

264. *Bear Lane Gallery, Oxford, *John Piper*, 28th June–26th July

265. *Derwent College, University of York, *John Piper*

266. QE2, Cunard-Marlborough London Gallery, on board QE2

1970

267. *Chapter House, York Minster, [*Screenprints*], April–May. Exhibition based on thirteen of Piper's pictures

268. *Bladon Society of Arts and Crafts, Bladon Gallery, Andover, *John Piper*, 23rd April–14th July

269. Hayward Gallery, London, *Kelpra Prints*, 17th June–7th July

270. Arts Council of Great Britain in association with Earls Barton Church, Northampton, [*Exhibition celebrating the church tower's millenium*], 1st–30th August

271. *Pieter Wenning Gallery, Johannesburg, *John Piper*, opened 6th October

272. AIA Gallery, London, [*Retrospective of the work of the AIA as it closes the Gallery*], October

273. *Arts Centre, New Metropole, Folkestone, *John Piper Retrospective Exhibition*, 24th October–22nd November

274. Century Galleries, Sonning, Reading, *John Piper*

275. *Hambledon Gallery, Blandford Forum, *Landscapes and churches*

276. International Art Fair, Kunsthalle, Basle

277. *Newcastle Festival, *Retrospective Exhibition*

278. *University of York, [*Screenprints*] Exhibition based on thirteen of Piper's pictures. Probably preceded or travelled from York, no.267 above

279. Wright Hepburn Gallery, [*Theatre designs*]

1971

280. Fuji Television Gallery, Tokyo, *John Piper, Ceri Richards*, 10th–30th June

281. *William Weston Gallery, *Lithographs by John Piper*, June

282. *Arundel Art Centre, Arundel, *John Piper*. Festival Exhibition

283. Brighton Festival Exhibition. Exhibition of aquatints

284. Lichfield, *Festival Exhibition*

285. Welsh Arts Council, *Worship* (third in a series of exhibitions on Art and Society). A touring exhibition which included Cardiff, Bolton, Hull

1972

286. Church of England Chaplaincy in the University of York, opened 28th January

287. Royal Academy Diploma Galleries, London, *British Decorative Arts 1840-1940*, February-April

288. *Marlborough Fine Art, London, *John Piper: oil paintings, gouaches and ceramics*, March–April

289. Folio Society Ltd, London, [*Exhibition marking the Society's 25th anniversary*], opened 27th March

290. *Lincoln Cathedral, Lincoln, *John Piper*, (Part of the festival marking the Cathedral's 900 years of existence), opened 5th May

291. Fischer Fine Art, London, *A Journey into the Universe of Art*, May–June

292. *Kidderminster Art Gallery, Kidderminster, *John Piper – Paintings and Graphics*, 5th–19th August

293. *Fermoy Art Gallery, King's Lynn, *John Piper*. Proceeds donated to the Church of St Mary Restoration Fund, Long Sutton, Lincolnshire

294. Louis Grosse Ltd at Coventry Cathedral, Coventry

295. *Oundle School, Oundle, Peterborough, *John Piper*

296. Pallas Gallery, London

297. Wandsworth School, London, [*Exhibition of pictures illustrating a book of poems by Edwin Muir*]

298. Whitechapel Art Gallery, London, *Painting and drawing in Britain 1940-1949*. A touring exhibition

1973

299. Whitworth Art Gallery, Manchester, *British Artists in Europe* (part of the Fanfare for Europe celebrations), January

300. *Marjorie Parr Gallery, London, *John Piper*, 25th January–24th February

301. *Gadsby Gallery, Leicester, *John Piper* (Lithographs, screen prints and small oils), 10th April–12th May

302. Louis Grosse Ltd at St Edmundsbury Cathedral, opened 3rd May

303. *Pieter Wenning Gallery, Johannesburg, *John Piper*, May

304. *Kederminster Library, Langley, Buckinghamshire, [*Exhibition as part of the celebrations of the 350th anniversary of the founding of the Library; also fund-raising for same*], opened 1st July

305. *Fine Art Gallery, The Gallery Upstairs, Reading, *Originals and Graphics by John Piper*, 10th November–1st December

306. New Metropole Arts Centre, Folkestone, *Some Aspects and Influences of the Medieval and Renaissance Worlds*, 10th November–16th December

307. Marlborough Gallery, London, opened November

308. Curwen Prints Ltd at the Camden Arts Centre, London, [*Lithography done at the Curwen Studio since 1958*], opened 13th December

309. *Turnpike Gallery, Leigh, Lancashire, *John Piper; oil paintings, drawing, gouaches, watercolours and ceramics*. Toured to Burnley

310. *Arts Council (Welsh Committee), National Museum of Wales, Cardiff, *John Piper*

311. *Barry Cronan Fine Art, London, *John Piper*

312. *Compendium Galleries, Birmingham, *John Piper*

313. Lincoln Cathedral, Lincoln, [*Exhibition demonstrating the work of artists and craftsmen in the Cathedral over the centuries*]. A loan of stained glass

314. *Playhouse Gallery, Harlow, *John Piper*

315. Tate Gallery, London, [*Works from John Piper, Ceri Richards, Graham Sutherland, Barbara Hepworth marking their 70th birthdays*]

*c.*1974

316. Fischer Fine Art, London, *Architecture in Painting – from Canaletto to John Piper*

317. Weald of Kent Preservation Society, [*Art exhibition*]

1974

318. Selwood Galleries, Frome, Somerset, 23rd February–16th March

319. *Buxton Mill Galleries, Norwich, Norfolk, *John Piper*, 5th–27th April

320. Marjorie Parr Gallery, London, July

321. Leicester Galleries, London, *Summer Exhibition*

322. Marlborough Fine Art, London, *XX Century Drawings and Watercolours*, September-October

323. Pieter Wenning Gallery, Johannesburg, 29th September–30th November

324. Arts Council (Scottish Committee), Edinburgh Festival, *Art Then: Eight English Artists 1924-40*

325. Norwich Arts Council

326. Roland, Browse and Delbanco, London

327. Talbot Rice Art Centre, Edinburgh, *Aspects of Abstract Painting in Britain 1910-1960*, touring to Galerie Herve Alexandre, Brussels; Galerie Bargera, Cologne

1974-5

328. Welsh Arts Council, *Photographs of Wales*, 19th August–7th September, Arts Centre, Aberystwyth. Toured to Parc Howard, Llanelli, 14th–28th September; Queen's University, Belfast, 2nd–23rd November; Beaford Centre, N. Devon, 9th December 1974–3rd January 1975; Durham Light Infantry Museum and Arts Centre, 11th January–2nd February; University Sherman Theatre, Cardiff, 8th–26th April; Royal Institute of British Architects, London, 7th–17th May; The Ulster Museum, Belfast, 24th May–14th June; Oriel Bangor, 28th June–19th July

*c.*1975

329. Victoria and Albert Museum, London, *British Art and Design in the Thirties*

1975

330. *University of Birmingham, Library Gallery, opened 28th January

331. *Prouds Pty Ltd, Sydney, [*Ceramics by Piper*], opened 17th April

332. Galerie Aziza, *The British Season*, April–May. Toured to France, Switzerland, the USA and Canada

333. Llanddewibrefi Arts Festival, [*Art Exhibition*], May

334. Delahaye Gallery, Cirencester, Glos., [*Artists working with Architectural Subjects*], 16th June–14th July. Marked European Architectural Heritage Year

335. *Marlborough Fine Art, London, *John Piper*, September–October

336. Aldeburgh Festival, Marland Gallery, Aldeburgh, Suffolk. *Death in Venice* portfolio exhibited

337. *Bohun Gallery, Henley-on-Thames, Oxon, *John Piper: eye and camera*

338. Bonython Art Gallery, Sydney

339. Galeria Wolfgang Ketterer, Munich, *Anno Santo*

340. Midhurst, West Sussex

341. *Selective Eye Gallery, Jersey, *John Piper*

1976

342. Sheffield Polytechnic School of Art and Design, [*Photographs*], January

343. Brighton Festival, [*Designs for the opening night firework display and for the Sky Painting*], 4th–16th May

344. Portsmouth Theatre Royal Society, at the City Art Gallery, Portsmouth, [*Theatre set and costume designs*], 4th–27th June. A fund-raising exhibition

345. *Gallery Kasahara, Osaka, *John Piper*, 12th–24th July

346. Bohun Gallery, Henley-on-Thames, Oxon, *Small Paintings*, *c.*October

†347. JPL Fine Arts, London, Card Game, 1st–31st December

348. Hereford Cathedral, [*Church artists*]

349. *Marjorie Parr Gallery, London, *John Piper*

350. *Orde Levinson Fine Art at Nedbank Ltd, Johannesburg, *John Piper*. Toured to Durban, Cape Town

1977

351. Victoria and Albert Museum, London, *Tonic to the Nation,* closed 3rd April

352. Western Australia Art Gallery, Perth, *Perth International Survey of Drawing*, opened 3rd May

353. Bohun Gallery, Henley-on-Thames, Oxon, 26th November–25th December

354. *Abbot Hall Gallery, Kendal, *John Piper*

355. *Arts Centre Gallery, University College of Wales, Aberystwyth, *John Piper*

356. Arts Council (Welsh Committee), Chapter Arts Centre, Cardiff, *Selling Dreams: British and American film posters 1890-1976*

357. Fieldborne Galleries, London, *Art in Religion*

358. *Hambledon Gallery, Blandford Forum, *John Piper*

359. *Marlborough Fine Art, London, *John Piper, Victorian Dream Palaces, and Other Buildings in Landscape*

360. Tate Gallery, London, *Artists at Curwen: a celebration of the gifts of artists' prints from the Curwen studio*

1977-8

361. *Imperial War Museum, London [*Piper as Official War Artist*], 6th October 1977–29th January 1978

362. New Art Centre, London, *Artists as Illustrators*, opened December 1977

1978

363. Arts Council, London, *Print Techniques*, opened January

364. *University College Central Hall, Cardiff (Cardiff Festival of 20th Century Music), *John Piper: Early and Recent Pictures*, 27th February–11th March

365. *University of Tennessee and the Hunter Museum, Chattanooga, Tennessee, *Retrospective Exhibition*, *c.*March

366. *Aldeburgh Festival, New Gallery, Snape Maltings Foundation, Suffolk, *John Piper*, 8th–25th June. Exhibition to open new recital room

367. Festival of the City of London, International Exhibition of Stained Glass at the Royal Exchange, London, *Glass/Light*, 18th July–30th August

368. *Glynn Vivian Art Gallery and Museum, Swansea, *John Piper: Swansea Festival*, 6th October–4th November

369. *Llantarnam Grange Art Centre, Cwmbran, Gwent, *Paintings by John Piper*, 25th November–9th December

370. *Bohun Gallery, Henley-on-Thames, Oxon, *John Piper*

371. *Rye Art Gallery, Rye, Sussex, *John Piper*

372. *St Edmund's Art Centre, Salisbury, *John Piper*

1978-9

373. Arts Council, *The Mechanised Image*, opened March. Toured for a year, including Portsmouth, Sheffield, Hull, Belfast, scheduled to visit Paris

374. National Museum of Wales, Cardiff, 23rd December 1978–11th February 1979

1979

375. *Arts Council, Museum of Modern Art, Oxford and The Minories, Colchester, *John Piper: 50 Years of Work: Paintings, Drawings and Photographs, 1929-79*, 20th May–24th June, Oxford; 30th June–29th July, Colchester

†376. *Farnsfield Gallery, Nottinghamshire, *c.*July-August

377. Mostyn Art Gallery, Llandudno, *The Native Land (a Celebration of the Landscape of North Wales by Artists working from the 18th Century to the Present Day)* (opening exhibition), 28th July–15th September

378. Hessisches Landesmuseum, Darmstadt, *Das Bild in Glas*, 3rd October–11th November

379. Victoria and Albert Museum, London, *Photography in Printmaking*, Autumn

380. Canterbury Cathedral, Canterbury, *Church Buildings: an exhibition of paintings and prints: John Piper, John Ward, John Doyle*

1979-80

381. Arts Council in association with the Victoria and Albert Museum at Hayward Gallery, London, *Thirties-British Art and Design before the War*, 24th October–13th January 1980

382. Atkinson Art Gallery, Southport, *The Seven and Five Society 1920-35*. Toured to Cardiff, Colchester, London and Penzance

1980

383. University of Evansville-British Campus, Harlaxton College, Grantham, Lincolnshire, opened 8th May

384. *Bohun Gallery, Henley-on-Thames, Oxon, *John Piper*

385. *Manchester Cathedral Regimental Chapel, Manchester, *John Piper*

386. The Minories, Colchester, *Designs for Opera*

387. *Rufford Craft Centre, Ollerton, *John Piper*

388. Tate Gallery, London, *Kelpra Studio: The Rose and Chris Prater Gift, Artists' Prints 1961-1980*

1980-1

389. Victoria Art Gallery, Bath, *Leeds Paintings*. Toured to Huddersfield Art Gallery; Herbert Art Gallery and Museum, Coventry; Harris Museum and Art Gallery, Preston; Cooper Gallery, Barnsley; Usher Gallery, Lincoln; Bolton Museum and Art Gallery

1981

390. *Maclean Gallery, London, *The Sitwells' Montegufoni*, 28th January–20th February

391. Fieldborne Galleries, London, *Music and Musicians*, opened 18th March

392. CCA Galleries, London, [*Printmakers' Council Portfolio*], 11th–30th May

393. Acme Gallery, London, *Artists for Nuclear Disarmament*, 12th–30th May

394. *Dorchester Galleries in association with Marlborough Fine Art, Dorchester Abbey, Dorchester, Oxon, *John Piper*, 21st June–4th July

395. Grahamstown, South Africa, *1820 Settlers National Monument Foundation Festival*, 11th–18th July

396. Bohun Gallery, Henley-on-Thames, Oxon, [*Drawings exhibition*], 10th–29th October

1981-2

397. *Marlborough Fine Art, London, *John Piper: Tudor Picturesque, Other Buildings and Landscapes*, December 1981–January 1982

398. Imperial War Museum, London, *Neo-Romantic Watercolours*

1982

399. *Solomon Gallery, Dublin, *Paintings by John Piper*, 11th January–3rd February

400. *Blackman Harvey, Kettle's Yard, Cambridge, *John Piper – Graphics*, 20th February–20th March

401. *Michael Parkin Fine Art, London, *John Piper; Tambimuttu – India Love Poems*, 22nd April–7th May. Celebrated the Festival of India

402. Centre International du Vitrail, Chartres, *New British Glass & Vitrail Français Contemporain*, 20th June–31st October

403. Arnolfini, Bristol, *Prophecy and Vision*, opened 3rd September

404. *Dan Klein, London, in conjunction with the Fulham Pottery Ltd, London, *New Ceramics by John Piper*, 10th–27th November

405. Ellingham Mill Art Society, Suffolk. Fund-raising exhibition

406. Kettle's Yard, Cambridge, *Circle: Constructive art in Britian 1934-40*

407. *Newlyn Art Gallery, Newlyn, *Solo exhibitions: John Piper*

408. Tate Gallery, London, [*Exhibition marking the Festival of India*] (with Tagore, Jamoni Roy, Amrita Sher-Gil)

1982-3

409. *Kettle's Yard, Cambridge, *John Piper – Painting in Coloured Light and related works*, 2nd December 1982–9th January 1983

410. *Johannesburg Art Gallery, Johannesburg, *John Piper and English Neo-Romanticism* (touring exhibition)

411. *National Museum of Wales, Cardiff (in association with The 1820 Foundation and the South African National Gallery), *John Piper and English Neo-Romanticism*. Toured to London during 1983

1983

412. *Bohun Gallery, Henley-on-Thames, Oxon, *John Piper – recent paintings and ceramics*, 14th May–9th June. Exhibition marking John Piper's 80th birthday

413. *Festival Gallery and Gallery 44, Aldeburgh, Suffolk, *John Piper: The Britten-Pears Collection, and John Piper Ceramics* (in conjunction with the Fulham Pottery Ltd and Dan Klein Ltd), 10th–26th June

414. *Olympus Gallery, London, *John Piper: The Romantic Landscape: Photographs 1936-1983*, opened 30th November

415. Austin/Desmond Fine Art, Ascot, *Aspects of Modern British Art 1920-1960*

416. *Fermoy Centre, King's Lynn, *John Piper: watercolours of Windsor*

417. Fischer Fine Art London, in conjunction with the National Museum of Wales, Cardiff, *The British Neo-Romantics 1935-1950*

418. Marlborough Fine Art, London

1983-4

419. *Marlborough Fine Art, London, *Romantic Places*, 25th November 1983–14th January 1984

420. *Tate Gallery, London, *John Piper*, 30th November 1983–22nd January 1984

421. *CCA Galleries, London, *John Piper*

422. *Marlborough Fine Art, New York

423. Redfern Gallery, London

1984

424. *New Grafton Gallery, London, *80th Birthday Exhibition of John Piper*, 15th February–10th March

425. *Christie's Contemporary Art in conjunction with King George VI Art Gallery, Port Elizabeth, *John Piper – 60 Years of Graphics*, 6th March–24th April; King George VI Art Gallery, 9th May–10th June; National Gallery, Cape Town, also touring to Pretoria, Pietermaritzburg and Kimberley

426. *Long Gallery, Englefield House, *An Exhibition of Paintings and Ceramics by John Piper*, 9th–24th March

†**427.** *Fosse Gallery, Stow on the Wold, [*Drawings*], April-May

428. *Lichfield Festival Exhibition, Englefield House, *Piper's Churches*, July

429. *Arundel Festival, Arun Art Centre, *John Piper*, 25th August–29th September

430. Poor Priest Hospital, [*Canterbury Festival*], 22nd September–13th October

431. *Marlborough Fine Art, London, *John Piper*, 7th–29th December

432. Austin/Desmond Fine Art, Ascot, *Aspects of Modern British Art II 1910-1965*

433. Redfern Gallery, London, *British Prints 1914-1945*

1984-5

434. Oxfordshire County Council, Museum of Oxford, Oxford, [Contemporary British ceramics], July–August 1984. Then toured to Southampton Museum and Art Gallery, Bristol City Museum and Art Gallery, Leeds City Museum (Temple Newsam House), Leicester Museum and Art Gallery, Birmingham City Museum and Art Gallery, Sheffield Museum and Art Gallery, Norwich Museum and Art Gallery

1985

435. Buckinghamshire County Museum, Aylesbury, opened 21st March

436. The Kayler Fine Arts Gallery, Exeter, *c.*November

437. *Henley Festival of Music and the Arts, Henley-on-Thames, Oxon

1986

438. *Marlborough Graphics Gallery, London, *John Piper*, February

439. Marlborough Fine Art, London, *Studies of the Nude*, 18th March–2nd May

440. *Chelmsford Cathedral, Chelmsford, [*Piper exhibition for the Chelmsford, Cathedral Festival*], 9th May–17th May

441. *Marsham Street Gallery, London, *John Piper*, 14th–17th May

442. *National Theatre, London, *John Piper*, 9th June–19th July

443. Beaux Arts Gallery, Bath, *John Piper and Edward Piper*, 16th–30th June

†**444.** Easton Rooms, Rye Art Gallery, Rye, Sussex, [*Exhibition to celebrate the 21st anniversary of the Rye Art Gallery*], September

445. *Jersey Art Centre, St Helier, *John Piper*, 30th September–17th October. Toured to The Coach House Gallery, St Peter Port, Guernsey, 26th October–14th November

†**446.** Leeds City Art Gallery, Temple Newsam House, Leeds, *Angels of Anarchy and Machines for Making Clouds, Painting and Sculpture in Britian in the 30's*, 9th October–7th December

447. Austin/Desmond Fine Art, Ascot, *Aspects of Modern British Art IV*

448. *Waddington Galleries, London, in association with James Kirkman, London, *John Piper*

1987

449. Laing Art Gallery, Newcastle and Northern Centre for Contemporary Art, Sunderland, *2D 3D Art and Craft made and designed for the Twentieth century*, 14th January–8th March. Exhibition of Piper's *Foliate Heads*. Reduced version toured to Crafts Council Gallery, London

450. Royal Academy, London, *British Art in the Twentieth Century: The Modern Movement*, 15th January–5th April

451. Goodman Gallery, Sandton, in association with Waddington Galleries, London and James Kirkman, London, *John Piper*, 7th February–7th March

452. Staatsgalerie, Stuttgart, *British Art in the Twentieth Century: The Modern Movement*, 8th May–9th August,

453. Barbican Art Gallery, London, *A Paradise Lost: The Neo-Romantic Imagination in Britain 1935–55*, 21st May–19th July

454. Arts Centre, University of Warwick, Warwick, *To build a Cathedral*, 25th May–12th July. Celebrates the 25th Anniversary of the consecration of Coventry Cathedral

455. Aldeburgh Festival Gallery, Suffolk, *Aldeburg Festival*, 12th–28th June

456. Peter Pears Gallery, Aldeburgh, (selected by John Piper), 12th–28th June

457. *Marlborough Graphics Gallery, London, *John Piper: recent prints*, 1st September–2nd October

458. Marlborough Fine Art, London, *John Piper – Georgian Arcadia*, 16th September–16th October

459. Chichester Cathedral, Chichester, *The Glass of Vision*, September

460. *CCA Galleries, London, *John Piper*, October

461. Bohun Gallery, Henley-on-Thames, Oxon, *Recent Gouaches and Prints*, 9th May–4th June

462. *Natalie Knight Gallery, Johannesburg, *John Piper – Exhibition of Paintings, Graphics, and Tapestries*

463. Redfern Gallery, London, *Landscape and Figure*

1988

464. New Ashgate Gallery, Farnham, Surrey, *Paintings-Prints-Tapestry-Ceramics-Jewellery*, 31st January–5th March (with Edward Piper, David Leach, Keiko Hasagawa, Audrey Dryden-Brownlee)

465. *Gallery Deux Têtes, Toronto, *John Piper*, 26th March–9th April

466. Arun Art Centre, Arundel, *Great Graphics*, 30th April–28th May

467. *Marlborough Graphics, London, *John Piper and Bill Jackling: prints*, 3rd May–24th June

468. *Hugo Barclay Gallery, Brighton, *John Piper*, 6th–28th May

469. Redfern Gallery, London, *Spring Exhibtion: Modern Prints*, *c.*May

470. Greys Gallery, Gosforth, Newcastle upon Tyne, June–July

471. *Waddington Galleries, London, in association with James Kirkman, London, John Piper, 22nd June–16th July

472. *Oxford Gallery, Oxford, *John Piper*, 27th June–27th July

473. Bohun Gallery, Henley-on-Thames, Oxon, *Artists by themselves – an exhibition of self-portraits*, 11th November–6th December

474. Albemarle Gallery, London. *Nine Neo-Romantic Artists*

475. Austin/Desmond Fine Art, London, *The Best of Modern British Art*

476. Austin/Desmond Fine Art, Ascot, *Aspects of Modern British Art VI*

477. CCA Galleries, London, *Selection of work by Henry Moore and his contemporaries*

478. Lefèvre Gallery, London, *Mother and Child* (in aid of Birthright)

479. Manchester City Art Gallery, Manchester, *Out of Clay*

480. Royal College of Art, London, *Exhibition Road: Painters at the Royal College of Art*

481. Williamson Art Gallery and Museum, Birkenhead, *Artists of Wirral*

1988–9

482. *Williamson Art Gallery and Museum, Birkenhead, *John Piper: a birthday tribute*, 1st December 1988–8th January 1989

1989

483. Century Gallery, Henley-on-Thames, Oxon, *Modern British Tapestries*, 17th March–11th April

484. *Arts Club, *John Piper – etchings and screenprints*, 8th May–11th June

485. *Marlborough Graphics, London, *John Piper: rare prints*, 20th June–4th August

486. Harewood Gallery, London, *Images of Paradise*, (in aid of Survival International), 24th June–19th September

487. Tate Gallery, Liverpool, *World War Two*, 26th September–19th November

†**488**. *Concourse Gallery, Barbican Centre, London, [*John Piper exhibition in connection with Alun Hoddinott's 60th birthday*], October

489. Austin/Desmond Fine Art, London, *Post-War British Prints*

490. Bar Convent Museum, York, *Michael Sadler Gift Collection*

491. Beaux Arts Gallery, Bath, *Beaux Arts Collections*

492. *CCA Galleries, London, *John Piper: Graphics*

493. National Museum of Wales, Cardiff, *Derek Williams Bequest*

494. Royal Scottish Academy, Edinburgh, *Royal Scottish Society of Painters in Watercolours Annual Exhibition*

1990

495. Walker Art Gallery, Liverpool, *The Artist at War: Second World War Paintings and Drawings from the Walker Art Gallery's Collection*, 10th February–1st April

496. *Oriel 31 Touring Exhibition, *John Piper in Wales*, Davies Memorial Gallery, Powys, 14th July–21st August; National Museum of Wales, Cardiff, 1st September–27th October; Oriel Mostyn, Llandudno, 10th November–8th December

497. *Pembroke College, Oxford, [*Exhibition of John Piper's work to mark the opening of the new building*], Summer. From the collection of Mr and Mrs Robert Lewin, donated to Pembroke College

498. Waterman Fine Art, London, *Summer Show*

499. York City Art Gallery, *York through the eyes of the Artist*, August–September

500. *Bohun Gallery, Henley-on-Thames, Oxon, *John Piper: Paintings and Graphic Works*, 12th October–27th November

501. *Trumpington Gallery, Cambridge, *John Piper – Master Prints*, 5th–8th December

502. Beaux Arts Gallery, Bath, *Tribute to Peter Fuller*

503. *CCA Galleries, Cambridge, *John Piper, Graphics*

504. *CCA Galleries, Farnham, Surrey, *John Piper and Modern British Printmaking*

505. CCA Galleries, London, *John Piper: The Master Prints*

506. CCA Galleries, London, *Modern Masters*

507. Crane Kalman Gallery, London, *A Selection of British Paintings*

508. Lynne Stern Art Consultancy and Gallery, London, *Work by Contemporary British Artists*

1991

509. *Marlborough Graphics, London, *John Piper – Six Decades of Printmaking*, 27th February–13th April

510. *Beaux Arts Gallery, Bath, *John Piper*, previewed 13th April

511. Bohun Gallery, Henley-on-Thames, Oxon, *Water's Edge-Paintings, Watercolours and Prints to coincide with the Henley Royal Regatta*, 21st June–16th July

512. *CCA Galleries, Cambridge, *John Piper, Graphics*

513. *Marlborough Graphics, London

514. Railings Gallery, London, *John Piper: Exhibition of original prints*

515. *Tate Gallery, London, *John Piper: New Displays*. Annual display from the collection in one room

1991-2
516. *Berkeley Square Gallery, London, *John Piper: Prints, Drawings and Watercolours*

517. Curwen Gallery, London, *British Printmakers*

518. Lamont Gallery, London, *Contemporary Master Graphics*

519. Roy Miles Gallery, London, *British Month*

520. Smith's Galleries, London, *The 2nd Green Contemporary Art Sale*

521. Waddington Galleries, London, *British Art from 1930*

1992
522. Consulate Hotel, St Helena, *Exhibition of Contemporary Prints by British Artists*, March

523. *Old Speech Room Gallery, Harrow School, Harrow on the Hill, *John Piper – screenprints*, 7th May–11th June. Catalogue and Introduction by Carolyn Leder; sections include a chronology, graphic work and a glossary

524. William Weston Gallery at the 20th Century British Art Fair, The Royal College of Art, London, *20th-Century British Masters: lithographs, etchings and woodcuts*, 23rd–27th September

525. *Bohun Gallery, Henley-on-Thames, Oxon, *John Piper: Foliate Heads*, 5th November–1st December

526. Ashmolean Museum, Oxford, *Watercolours and Drawings from the Robert and Rena Lewin gift to the Ashmolean*

527. *CCA Galleries, Cambridge, *John Piper, Graphics*

528. *CCA Galleries, Farnham, Surrey, *John Piper*

529. CCA Galleries, London, *20th Century British Print Makers*

530. Glynn Vivian Art Gallery, Swansea, *The Painter in Glass*, (part of the the Swansea Festival)

531. *Linda Goodman Gallery, Sandton

532. Music Theatre Gallery, London, *10 British Painters of the 20th Century*

1992-3
533. *Berkeley Square Gallery, London, *Piper's Country: prints and watercolours*, 4th December 1992–23rd January 1993

1993
534. *Pallant House, Chichester, *John Piper and the Stage*, 6th February–3rd April

535. *Woburn Festival, High Wycombe, *John Piper: Theatre Designs*, 25th September–23rd October

536. Century Gallery, Henley-on-Thames, Oxon, *John Piper*, 17th October–1st November

537. Berkeley Square Gallery, London, *New Acquisitions 1993*

538. Bodilly Galleries, Cambridge

539. *CCA Galleries, Bath. Toured to CCA Galleries, Avon, *John Piper*

540. *CCA Galleries, Farnham, Surrey, *John Piper, Master Graphics*

541. *CCA Galleries, London, *John Piper*

542. *Oxford Gallery, Oxford

543. Wales Art Centre, Fishguard

1993-4
544. Beaux Arts Gallery, London, *John Piper: Oils and Watercolours*

1994
545. *Waddington Galleries, London, in association with James Kirkman, London, *A Retrospective – Works from the Artist's Studio*, 12th January–5th February

546. Marlborough Graphics, London, at Art 94: The London Contemporary Art Fair, Business Design Centre, *John Piper*, 19th–23rd January

547. *Pallant House, Chichester, *The Chichester Tapestry*, 22nd January–19th February

548. Finsbury Art Group, Finsbury Town Hall. Toured to Lambeth Town Hall, *Two Stages*, 26th June–13th July

549. *Bohun Gallery, Henley-on-Thames, Oxon, *John Piper: Gouches and Prints*, 14th October–29th November

550. *CCA Galleries, Cambridge, *John Piper, Paintings, Tapestries and Prints*

551. *CCA Galleries, London, *John Piper, Oil on Paper, Tapestries and Prints*

552. CCA Galleries, London, *New Acquisitions*

553. *CCA Galleries, Oxford, *John Piper, Master Prints*

554. Venue Unknown, [*Church Buildings and exhibition of prints and paintings*] (with John Ward and John Doyle)

555. National Museum of Wales, Cardiff, Welsh Arts Council, *Art in Wales in the 20th Century: The Early Years 1900-1956*. Toured throughout Wales

1994-5
556. *Berkeley Square Gallery, London, *John Piper: From his studio*, 8th December 1994–12th February 1995'

1995
557. Bohun Gallery, Henley-on-Thames, Oxon, *John Piper: Collectors' Prints*, 1st–25th April

558. Pallant House, Chichester, West Sussex, *The Flowers of Peace: British Art and Design in 1945*, 6th June–19th August

559. CCA Galleries, London, *John Piper and the Neo-Romantic Tradition*, 14th June–8th July

560. CCA Galleries, Oxford, *John Piper and his contemporaries*, 19th October–4th November

Undated
561. Ferens Art Gallery, Kingston upon Hull, *Save Snowdonia*

Firework displays

1965
562. Hyde Park fireworks display, London, 26th August

1976
563. Brighton Festival, Brighton, *c.*May

1977
564. Queen's Silver Jubilee firework display for the London Celebrations Committee, Hyde Park, 9th June

1979
565. Tate Gallery firework display at the opening of the Tate extension, 24th May

Designs by John Piper: Sets, Stained Glass and Tapestries

'A designer may understand tapestry thoroughly, may be learned in its history and contemporary practise and possibilities, but design remains design until someone's imagination brings it to life in the new medium. I have had the pleasure – thrill is really a more appropriate word – of seeing this happen with my own designs for the stage, for colour reproduction, for stained-glass and for tapestry. It is always exciting for an artist to see his work successfully realised.'[1]

Below is a chronologically detailed yearly list of the set designs, stained-glass and tapestry designs by John Piper. Each entry has a sequential numeric reference and after this reference number, in square brackets, is an indication of the category: [s] for set designs, [sg] for stained-glass and [t] for tapestry, in that order.

All entries are listed according to the year of commission unless otherwise stated.

When a tapestry or stained-glass design is in effect a diptych or triptych created in the same year only one entry number has been used, for example Hereford (no.102 below). Where it was a series of commissions over a number of years, as is usually the case with the stained glass, separate entries have been used and cross referenced.

Although the tapestry and set designs are as complete as possible, information for the stained glass, especially sizes, is difficult to obtain. As this is the first attempt to collate all Piper's designs, errors are bound to appear and the author would welcome any further information.

Set Designs

The fabric designs, including vestments and scarves, are not included in this listing. The Sadler's Wells Ballet is now known as the Birmingham Royal Ballet. Myfanwy Evans is the widow of John Piper and has been credited here, as in the theatre programmes, under her maiden name.

The set designs are listed as follows:
Title of entertainment/play/opera, production company, town
Piper's contribution, any further details

Stained Glass

The stained-glass works are catalogued according to the year of commission except for the panels which are catalogued according to the year of completion. The information for each stained-glass work is arranged as follows:
Title,[2] Interpreter in glass, Place of installation,[3] Size,[4]
Classification. Other comments

Within each year of installation, commissions of the same year are listed alphabetically according to their titles *eg* nos 51, 53 below. Commissions completed in a single year are listed before those spread out over a number of years. Where a year of commission is not known precisely an approximate date is given and this is indicated by the letter *c.* (for *circa*) before the year.

Also catalogued are all the known stained-glass panels, seven in the estate of the artist (nos 16, 38, 41, 42, 105, 107 below) and the rest in the Victoria and Albert Museum (nos 23, 30, 32, 33, 43 below) and all the known designs and cartoons for stained-glass works, including those which have not yet been interpreted in glass.

All works are in glass unless otherwise stated. The exceptions are nos 58 and 60 below which are in fibreglass.

It is noted that while the mosaics and murals of Piper may bear a resemblance to the stained-glass works they are not listed here, for the reason that they are not stained glass but also as my enquiries have yielded little information about them other than that there were commissions in 1938, 1943, 1949, 1955 and two in 1958.

Tapestries

The tapestries are catalogued as follows:
Title;[5] Commissioner, town; weaver, town; edition;[6] Size[7]
Comments[8]

There exist for all of the tapestries either specially created cartoons or works in other media (*eg* gouache) on which they were based.

Since the 1950s the Dovecot Studios are also known as Edinburgh Tapestry Company. The West Dean Tapestry Studio is part of The Edward James Foundation.

For information on *Cathedral Ruins*, a silk-ribbon picture, see introductory text to the 'Index of Prints', on p.143.

1 *Master weavers: tapestries from the Dovecot Studios 1912–80* [catalogue for exhibition held at the Royal Scottish Academy, Edinburgh August-September 1980], Canongate, Edinburgh. Foreword by John Piper
2 With *Brittany Beach I* and *II*, 1961 already so named I have added *III* to the third one (nos 41–3 below).
3 Where one venue has had more than one commission (*eg* St Andrew Parish Church, Plymouth (no.27 below)), only the first commission contains in the commentary a cross-reference to all subsequent commissions at the same venue. All subsequent commissions (indicated by an asterisk (*)) contain a reference to the first commission only.
4 Approximately in cm (in) if known
5 Where a title is not known or not given, I have given it the most appropriate title based on information supplied and have placed this title in square brackets.
6 Unique pieces have no listing under this section. The letters AP are used to indicate the number of proofs.
7 cm (in)
8 Where an editioned tapestry is in a public collection, this is indicated with the name and place of exhibition.

1937
1 [s]. *Trial of a Judge*, Group Theatre, Unity Theatre, London
Scenery and Costumes. Play by Stephen Spender; produced by Rupert Doone

1942
2 [s]. *Façade*, Oxford University Press, Aeolian Hall, London
Front-of-stage cloth. An 'entertainment' by Edith Sitwell and William Walton

1942–3
3 [sg]. *[Design for the Merton Priory Civic Restaurant]*, not interpreted, Arts Council of Great Britain, London
A gouache 122×122 (48×48) of this work is known to exist.

1943
4 [s]. *The Quest*, Sadler's Wells Ballet, New Theatre, London
Scenery and costumes. Choreography by Frederick Ashton; music by William Walton. World Premiere

1945
5 [s]. *Oedipus Rex*, Old Vic Theatre Company, New Theatre, London
Scenery. Drama by Sophocles, translated by W.B.Yeats; produced by Michel Saint-Denis

1946
6 [s]. *The Rape of Lucretia*, Glyndebourne Opera Company, Glyndebourne
Scenery and costumes. Opera by Benjamin Britten, produced by Eric Crozier. Restaged: English Opera Group, Royal Opera House, London in 1947

1947
7 [s]. *Albert Herring*, English Opera Group, Glyndebourne, June and Royal Opera House, London, October
Scenery and costumes. Opera by Benjamin Britten; produced by Frederick Ashton

8 [s]. *The Rape of Lucretia*, English Opera Group, Royal Opera House, London, October.
Scenery and costumes. Opera by Benjamin Britten; produced by Eric Crozier
Restaging of the 1946 Glyndebourne production

1948
9 [s]. *Job*, Royal Ballet and Sadler's Wells Ballet, Royal Opera House, London
Scenery and costumes. Music by Vaughan Williams; choreography and produced by Ninette de Valois
Originally designed by Gwen Raverat but redesigned by Piper

10 [s]. *Simone Boccanegra*, Sadler's Wells Opera, Covent Garden, London
Scenery with John Moody. Opera by Verdi; produced by John Moody

1949
11 [s]. *Sea Change*, Sadler's Wells Theatre Ballet and the Gaiety Theatre, Dublin, Royal Opera House, London
Scenery and costumes. Ballet by John Cranko; music by Sibelius; choreographed by John Cranko. World Premiere

1951
12 [s]. *Harlequin in April*, Sadler's Wells Theatre Ballet and Sadler's Wells Theatre, Royal Opera House, London
Scenery and costumes. Ballet by John Cranko; music by Richard Arnell; choreographed by John Cranko. Ballet commissioned for the Festival of Britain. World Premiere

13 [s]. *Comattimento di Tancredi e Clorinda*, English Opera Group, Lyric Theatre, Hammersmith, London
Scenery and costumes. Opera-ballet choreography by Walter Gore; music by Monteverdi

14 [s]. *Don Giovanni*, Glyndebourne Festival Opera, Glyndebourne
Scenery and costumes. Opera by Mozart; produced by Carl Ebert

15 [s]. *Billy Budd,* Covent Garden Opera, Royal Opera House, London
Scenery and costumes. Opera by Benjamin Britten; produced by Basil Coleman. Commissioned by the Arts Council of Great Britain for the Festival of Britain. World Premiere

16 [sg]. *Two Heads,* Patrick Reyntiens, Piper estate
Panel 57.2 × 57.2 (22½ × 22½). A study for the Oundle commission, no.22 below

1952
17 [s]. *Dancing*, Kenton Theatre, Henley-on-Thames, Oxon
Scenery and costumes. Ballet by John Cranko; music by George Shearing

1953
18 [s]. *The Shadow*, Sadler's Wells Ballet, Royal Opera House, London
Scenery and costumes. Ballet by and choreographed by John Cranko; music by Dohnanyi

19 [s]. *Gloriana*, Covent Garden Opera, Royal Opera House, London
Scenerey and costumes. Opera by Benjamin Britten; produced by Basil Coleman. Commissioned by the Royal Opera House in honour of the coronation of Queen Elizabeth II. World Premiere

20 [s]. *The Pearl Fishers*, Sadler's Wells Opera, Royal Opera House, London
Scenery. Opera by Bizet; produced by Basil Coleman

1954
21 [s]. *The Turn of the Screw*, English Opera Group, Venice Opera House, Venice
Scenery and costumes. Opera by Benjamin Britten; produced by Basil Coleman

1954-6
22 [sg]. *Nine figures of Christ*, Patrick Reyntiens, Oundle School, Oundle
Installed at the Chancel Apse in three windows as: *The Way*, *The Truth*, *Life*; *The True Vine*, *The Living Bread*, *The Water of Life*; *The Judge*, *The Teacher*, *The Shepherd*. Three designs for these works exist: a drawing in pen and pencil and a gouache, both *c.*1954, and both 40.6 × 66.4 (16 × 26¼) and both in the Victoria and Albert Museum, London and a watercolour, 91.5 × 76.2 (36 × 30) with the Governing Body of Oundle School. There exists also in the artist's estate a cartoon for *The True Vine*, a gouache on a photograph, *c.*1954, 396.5 × 56 (126 × 22).

1955
23 [sg]. *Christ between St Peter and St Paul,* Patrick Reyntiens, Victoria and Albert Museum, London
Panel, 85.5 × 58.5 (33⅝ × 23)

1956
24 [s]. *The Magic Flute*, Covent Garden Opera Company, Royal Opera House, London
Scenery and costumes with Alix Stone. Opera by Mozart; produced by Christopher West

1957
25 [s]. *The Prince of Pagodas*, Royal Ballet, Covent Garden, London
Scenery. Ballet by John Cranko, choreographed by John Cranko; music by Benjamin Britten. World premiere

26 [s]. *Less than Kind*, Arts Theatre, London
Set. Play by Derek Monsey. Directed by Yvonne Mitchell

1957-62
27 [sg]. *The Instruments of Passion and the Cross of St Andrew,* Patrick Reyntiens, St Andrew Parish Church, Plymouth
Installed in the Tower (Astor Memorial Window), one of six stained-glass windows installed at this church between 1957 and 1968 (nos 46, 51, 53, 64, 65 below)

1958
28 [s]. *Il Ballo delle Ingrate*, English Opera Group, Aldeburgh
Scenery and costumes. Opera by Monteverdi; produced by John Cranko

29 [s]. *Reflection*, Edinburgh Festival, Edinburgh
Set and costumes. Ballet by John Cranko

30 [sg]. *Christ between St Peter and St Paul,* Patrick Reyntiens, Victoria and Albert Museum, London
Panel, 82.5 × 56 (32½ × 22)

1959
31 [s]. *The Turn of the Screw*, ITV television production, London
Scenery. Opera by Benjamin Britten; libretto by Myfanwy Evans

32 [sg]. *[Scale model for Coventry Cathedral Baptistry window]*, Patrick Reyntiens, Victoria and Albert Museum, London
Panel, in two parts, in wood and stained glass each 193 × 218.5 (76 × 86) and 173.4 × 214.7 (68¼ × 84½)

33 [sg]. *[Trial panel for Coventry Cathedral Baptistry window]*, Patrick Reyntiens, Victoria and Albert Museum, London
Panel, 128 × 47 (47½ × 18½)

1959-60
34 [sg]. *Abstract Composition*, Patrick Reyntiens, Arthur Sanderson & Sons Ltd showrooms, London, 640.5 × 976 (252 × 384)
Installed beside the main staircase

1959-62
35 [sg]. *Holy Spirit*, Patrick Reyntiens, Coventry Cathedral, Coventry
Installed in the Baptistry window
A watercolour cartoon, *c.*1959, 139.6 × 69.8 (55 × 27½) for a panel of the window is in the possession of the Warwick District Council Art Gallery and Museum

1959-64
36 [sg]. *Four Miracles* (North Side); *Four Parables* (South Side), Patrick Reyntiens, Eton College, Buckinghamshire
Installed on the North Side in four windows east to west: *The Raising of Lazarus*, *The Stilling of the Waters*, *The Feeding of the Five Thousand*, *The Miraculous Draught of Fishes*
Installed on the South Side in four windows east to west: *The Light under a Bushel*, *The House Built on a Rock and the House Built on Sand*, *The Lost*

Sheep, Seed Sown on Good Ground and Seed sown on Stony Ground
In both sides the proposition is presented in the the lower half of the windows and its resolution is presented in the upper half.

1960
37 [s]. *A Midsummer Night's Dream*, Aldeburgh Festival Opera, Aldeburgh Festival, Jubilee Hall, Aldeburgh
Scenery and costumes (assisted by Carl Toms). Opera by Benjamin Britten; produced by John Gielgud
Restaged: Covent Garden Opera Company, Royal Opera House, London in 1961

37A [s]. *Abélard and Héloïse*, Art Theatre, London
Set. Play by Ronald Duncan. Produced by Hugh Hunt

38 [sg]. *The Elect and the Damned,* Patrick Reyntiens, Piper estate
Panel

1960–1
39 [sg]. *Old and New Testament Prophets*, Patrick Reyntiens, All Hallows Church, Wellingborough
One (Helen Wells Chapman Memorial Window) of three windows installed at this church between 1960 and 1969 (nos 45, 68 below)

1961
40 [s]. *A Midsummer Night's Dream*, Covent Garden Opera Company, Royal Opera House, London, February
Scenery and costumes (assisted by Carl Toms). Opera by Benjamin Britten; produced by John Gielgud
Restaging of the 1960 Aldeburgh production

1961
41 [sg]. *Brittany Beach Scene I*, Patrick Reyntiens, Piper estate
Panel, 117.2×162.2 (46⅛×63⅞) (nos 42, 43 below)

*42 [sg]. *Brittany Beach Scene II*, Patrick Reyntiens, Piper estate
Panel, 115.6×159.4 (45½×62¾) (no.42 above)

*43 [sg]. *Brittany Beach Scene III*, Patrick Reyntiens, Victoria and Albert Museum, London
Panel, 120×160 (47¼×63) (no.42 above)

1961–2
44 [sg]. *The Supper at Emmaus*, Patrick Reyntiens, Llandaff Cathedral, Llandaff
Installed in the Chancel window

1963
45 [sg]. *Abstract Composition,* Patrick Reyntiens, All Hallows Church, Wellingborough
Installed in the Tower (Rose Window) as one of three windows installed at this church between 1960 and 1969 (nos 39 above, 67 below)

*46 [sg]. *The Four Elements*, Patrick Reyntiens, St Andrew Parish Church, Plymouth
Installed in the Tower (Lady Astor Memorial Window), one of six stained-glass windows installed at this church between 1957 and 1968 (no.27 above)

1963–4
47 [sg]. *Flames,* Patrick Reyntiens, St Mark's Church, Woodthorpe, Sheffield
Installed in the West window

1964
48 [sg]. *Abstract Composition*, Patrick Reyntiens, St Woolo's Cathedral, Newport
Installed in the Rose Window, Chancel

49 [sg]. *Foliate Heads*, Patrick Reyntiens, Forte Crest Hotel (formerly Wessex Hotel), Winchester
Installed as one screen divided into twelve panels each with a different foliate head

1965–6
50 [sg]. *Abstract Designs*, Patrick Reyntiens, St Mary's Church, Swansea
Installed in the Lady Chapel in two windows

*51 [sg]. *St Catherine's Wheel and Symbols of the Four Evangelists*, Patrick Reyntiens, St Andrew Parish Church, Plymouth
Installed in the St Catherine Chapel Window, South Aisle, one of six stained-glass windows installed at this church between 1957 and 1968 (no.27 above). A design, mixed media with collage, 77.5×47 (30½×18½), 1965 for this work (or no.25 above) exists.

52 [sg]. *Symbols of the Stigmata,* Patrick Reyntiens, Nuffield College Chapel, Nuffield College, Oxford
Installed in the North window is the design symbolising *The Five Wounds* and in the East and West windows the *Angels of Light and Darkness* are symbolised.

*53 [sg]. *Symbols of the Virgin*, Patrick Reyntiens, St Andrew Parish Church, Plymouth
Installed in the Lady Chapel Window, North Aisle, one of six stained-glass windows installed at this church between 1957 and 1968 (no.27 above). A design, mixed media with collage, 77.5×47 (30½×18½), 1965, for this work (or no.51 above) exists.

54 [sg]. *Holy Trinity*, Patrick Reyntiens, Metropolitan Cathedral of Christ the King, Liverpool (12,500 foot square)
Installed in the Tower lantern and perimeter walls.

1966
55 [sg]. *Emblems of St Peter: the fishing boat, the keys, the cockerel, a keyhole,* Patrick Reyntiens, St Peter's Church, Babraham, Cambs.
Installed in the Chancel window. A design, gouache with collage, 57.8×38.5 (22¾×15¼), *c.*1965, exists in the Victoria and Albert Museum, London.

56 [sg]. *Foliate Cross with Symbols of the Stigmata*, Patrick Reyntiens, All Saints' Church, Misterton
Installed in the left-hand East window

57 [t]. *The Chichester Tapestry,* Dean and Chapter of Chichester Cathedral, Pinton Frères, near Aubusson, the tapestry is in seven strips, the outer four are 450×92 (177×36¼) each, and the central three 450×117 (177×46) each. The tapestries hang behind the High Altar. Commissioned in 1963, the work depicts the Trinity, surrounded by the four natural elements and the symbols of the four Evangelists. A trial proof of one section of the design is at Pallant House, Chichester.

1966–7
58 [sg]. *Memorials*, Patrick Reyntiens, Malsis School, Keighley
Installed in two ranges of seventeen windows in the Chancel. Each window is a Memorial individually dedicated to the former pupils and the master who died inWorld War II and bears their names and service emblems.

1967
59 [sg]. *Tree, River of Life* and *Blue Grass,* David Gillespie Associates, All Saints' Church, Clifton, Bristol
Installed in fibreglass in three windows. *Tree* and *River of Life* were installed in the Baptistry window, *Blue Grass* was installed in the Side Aisle. A design of the Bapistry window, mixed media with collage, 91.5×79.5 (36×31⅜), 1967, exists.

1967–8
60 [sg]. *Abstract Compositions*, Patrick Reyntiens, St Margaret's Church, Westminster, London
Installed in eight Nave windows

1968
61 [sg]. *Abstract Composition*, David Gillespie Associates, St Mathew's Church, Southcote, Reading
Installed in two windows in fibreglass

62 [sg]. *Heaven*, Patrick Reyntiens, St Paul's Church, Bledlow Ridge, Bucks.
Installed in a West window

63 [sg]. *River of Life*; *Tree of Life*, Patrick Reyntiens, The Cathedral, Christchurch, New Zealand
Two lancets

*64 [sg]. *The Creation and the Trinity* , Patrick Reyntiens, St Andrew Parish Church, Plymouth
Installed in the North Transept window, one of six stained-glass windows installed at this church between 1957 and 1968 (no.27 above). A design, mixed media with collage, 76.6×49.8 (30⅛×19⅝), 1967, for this work exists.

*65 [sg]. *Music and Inspiration*, Patrick Reyntiens, St Andrew Parish Church, Plymouth
Installed in the North Transept (Dr Harry Moreton Memorial Window), one of six stained-glass windows installed at this church between 1957 and 1968 (no.27 above).

66 [t]. *[Piper Tapestry]*, Newcastle upon Tyne Civic Centre, Newcastle upon Tyne, Pinton Frères, near Aubusson, 610×244 (240×96)
Currently hanging in the Civic Centre Banqueting Hall, Newcastle upon Tyne

1968–9
67 [sg]. *1666 Great Fire of London*, *1715 Fire in Thames Street* and *1940 Destroyed on the first Night of the Blitz*, Patrick Reytiens, Bakers' Hall, Harp Lane, London
Three commemorative windows representing the three occasions on which the buildings were destroyed by fire

1969
68 [sg]. *Abstract Composition*, Patrick Reytiens, All Hallows Church, Wellingborough
One of three windows (Constance Elizabeth Chapman Memorial Window) installed at this church between 1960 and1969 (nos 39, 68 above)

69 [sg]. *Abstract Compositions*, Patrick Reyntiens, George VI Memorial Chapel, Windsor Castle
Installed as two windows

70 [sg]. *Emblems of St Paul*, Patrick Reyntiens, St Paul's Church, Pishill, Oxon
Installed as one window

1970
71 [sg]. *Abstract Compositions*, Patrick Reyntiens, The Chapel, Churchill College, Cambridge
Installed as eight windows

72 [sg]. *The Resurrection*, Patrick Reytiens, St Bartholomew's Church, Nettlebed, Oxon
Installed in the Chancel (Dr Williams Memorial Window), one of two stained-glass windows installed at this church between 1970 and 1976 (no.94 below)

73–5 [t]. *Piper Tapestries* comprising: *[Piper Tapestry I]*, 274.5×274.5 (108×108), *[Piper Tapestry II]*, 274.5×274.5 (108×108), *[Piper Tapestry III]*, 274.5×610 (108×240), The Court of the Grocers' Company, London, Pinton Frères, near Aubusson
All three tapestries hang in the Piper Room. Proofs of the design are in the possession of the Grocers' Company

1970–1
76 [sg]. *Tree of Life*, Patrick Reyntiens, St Giles', Totternhoe, Beds.
Installed as the Chancel window

1973
77 [s]. *Owen Wingrave*, Royal Opera, Royal Opera House, London
Scenery. Opera by Benjamin Britten; libretto by Myfanwy Evans; produced by Colin Graham

78 [s]. *Death in Venice*, English Opera Company, Snape Maltings Concert Hall, Snape, near Aldeburgh.
Scenery. Opera by Benjamin Britten; libretto by Myfanwy Evans; produced by Colin Graham
Restaged: English Opera Group, Royal Opera House, London, October 1973 and Venice, Brussels, Edinburgh, New York. Revived The Maltings and Covent Garden 1975

79 [t]. *The Fruits of the Earth*, Rothschild Inter-Continental Bank, London, Pinton Frères, near Aubusson, 194×440 (75½×169¼)
Used to hang in the Executive Floor, Ebbgate House, Barclays de Zoete Wedd Ltd, London, present whereabouts unknown

80–1 [t]. *[Science]* and *[Humanities]*, University of the Witwatersrand, Johannesburg, Pinton Frères, near Aubusson, 251×601 (98¾×236¼) each
Hanging in the Warternweiler Library. Presented as a gift to the University on the occasion of its Golden Jubilee in 1972 by the Building Industry in South Africa. The proposed subjects were *Science and Technology* and *The Humanities* respectively, with an added referential subject of the quotation '... Sweet are the uses of adversity ... Sermons in stones and good in everything', *As You Like It*, Shakespeare, Act 2 Scene 1.
The two maquettes of the tapestries were given as a gift by Piper to the University and are displayed in the Vice-Chancellor's office.

1973–4
82 [sg]. *The Life of St Andrew*, Patrick Reyntiens, St Andrew's Church, Wolverhampton
Installed in the West window. A design, watercolour on paper, 34.3×73.8 (13½×29), 1973 for this work exists.

83 [sg]. *Tree of Life*, Patrick Reyntiens, Washington National Cathedral, Washington DC
Installed in the Tower (Churchill Memorial Window)

1974
84 [sg]. *[A sword dividing the cloak with a hand reaching up to take the lower half]*, Patrick Reyntiens, St Martin's Church, Sandford St Martin, Oxon
Installed as one window. A design, watercolour on paper, 60.9×15.2 (24×6), 1974 for this work exists.

1975
85 [sg]. *In commemoration* , Patrick Reyntiens, St Mary's Church, Turville, Bucks.
Installed as one window in commemoration of the deconsecration of St Saviour's, Turville Heath in 1972. A design, a gouache, 30.5×48.0 (12×18⅞), 1975 for this work exists.

86 [t]. *Foliate Head*, Orde Levinson, Oxford, Ibenstein Weavers, Dordabis, 10, 2AP, 152.5×213.5 (60×84)
Signature and edition number woven into the front b.r.
Exhibited *John Piper Retrospective*, Tate Gallery, 1983. Collection of Wolfson College, Oxford (Library)

87–8 [t]. *Rural Reading* and *Reading Townscape,* Reading Borough Council, Pinton Frères, near Aubusson, 289.6×244 (114×96) each
Both tapestries hang in the Kennet Room at the Civic Offices, Reading

89 [t]. *Five Gates of the City of London*, Sedgwick Forbes, London, Dovecot Studios, Edinburgh
244×910.5 (96×360)
Hangs in the offices of Sedgwick Group plc, London

90 [t]. *Foliate Heads*, Barry Cronan Fine Art Ltd, London; Robert Wallace, London; 18, 164×222 (64½×87½)
Signature woven b.l. Signed and numbered by the artist on a label, then sewn onto the back of each tapestry

91 [t]. [*Brighton Fantasia*], Property Services Agency, Croydon, for the British Embassy, Helsinki, Pinton Frères, near Aubusson, 233.5×454 (91$^{15}/_{16}$×178¾)
Although commissioned for the embassy in Helsinki it was never displayed there. In 1982 the Property Services Agency gave the tapestry to the Government Art Collection and from 1982 to 1995 it was displayed at the British Embassy, Caracas. In 1995 it was returned to the Government Art Collection, London.

1976
92 [sg]. *Representing a text from the gospels, John XII 13*, Patrick Reyntiens, St Peter's Church, Wolvercote, Oxon
Installed in the South Aisle (Bellamy Memorial Window)

93 [sg]. *Tree of Life*, Patrick Reyntiens, St Mary's Church, Fawley, Bucks.
Installed as one window (Anthonly Hartley Memorial Window)

94 [sg]. *Tree of Life*, Patrick Reyntiens, St Bartholomew's Church, Nettlebed, Oxon
Installed in the South Aisle (Peter Fleming Memorial Window), one of two stained-glass windows installed at this church between 1970 and 1976 (no.72 above). A design, watercolour on paper, 77.5×43.8 (30½×17¼), 1976 and a cartoon, mixed media with collage, 228.7×144.8 (90×57), 1976 for this work exists, the latter in the stained-glass Museum, Ely.

95 [t]. *Foliate Head: blue to yellow*, Orde Levinson, Oxford, Ibenstein Weavers, Dordabis, 6, 2AP, 91.5×152.5 (36×60)
Signature and edition number woven into the front b.r. and b.l. respectively

1977

96 [s]. *What the Old Man does is Always Right*, Fishguard Music Festival, Fishguard, Pembrokeshire
Scenery. Opera by Alun Hoddinott; libretto by Myfanwy Evans; produced by John Moody assisted by Euros Lewis. World Premiere

97 [sg]. *The Life of St Paul*, Patrick Reyntiens, Thorpe Tilney Hall, Thorpe Tilney, Lincolnshire
Installed as four semi-circular windows (*Stoning of St Stephen; Conversion of St Paul; St Paul's shipwreck on Malta* and *St Paul's execution*) in the base of the dome of the Garden Pavilion

98 [sg]. *Tree of Life* and *River of Life*, Patrick Reyntiens, The Chapel, Charing Cross Hospital, London
Installed as two windows

1978

99 [t]. *[Sussex University Tapestry]*, Sussex University, Falmer, Dovecot Studios, Edinburgh, 112×1158.4 (44½×456)
Hangs in the Meeting House, Sussex University.The design is based on psalm 46.

1978-80

100 [sg]. *The Light of the World* and *Composition based on a tympanum at Neuilly-en-Donjon, Allier*, Patrick Reyntiens, The Chapel, Robinson College, Cambridge
Installed in the Chancel and the Antechapel respectively. A cartoon for *The Light of the World*, gouache, 122×122 (48×48), *c.*1978 exists in the collection of Robinson College.

1979

101 [sg]. *Benjamin Britten Memorial Window*, Patrick Reyntiens, Church of St Peter and St Paul, Aldeburgh, Suffolk
Originally known as *Britten's Church Operas*. Installed as one window. The operas are *The Prodigal Son, Curlew River* and *The Burning Fiery Furnace*. A watercolour cartoon 381×188 (150×74), 1979 exists and a watercolour sketch 66×42 (26×16½) is in the Britten-Pears Foundation.

102 [t]. *The Tree of Life,* comprising from l. to r.: *The Tree in Eden*, *The Tree in Zion*, *The Tree in Heaven*, The Dean and Chapter of Hereford Cathedral, Hereford, Ibenstein Weavers, Dordabis, 277×190.5 (109×75) each
All three tapestries hang in the South Transept of the Cathedral. The tapestries are sometimes referred to as *The Tree of Disobedience*, *The Tree of Obedience* and *The Tree of Life*.
Commissioned to commemorate 1300 years of Christianity at Hereford

1981

103 [sg]. *Foliate Heads*, Patrick Reyntiens, The School, Henley Road, Ipswich
Installed in the library as four circular windows each representing one of the Seasons

1982

104 [sg]. [*Archaeological sites and finds*] , Patrick Reyntiens, The Museum, Long Street, Devizes
Installed as one window, illustratating some of the archaeological sites and finds of north Wiltshire as well as the woolly-headed thistle with some prehistoric objects in the Devizes Museum

105 [sg]. *The Nativity*, David Walsley, Piper estate, 186.2×81.4 (73¼×32)
Panel, installed in 1995/6 (no.123 below).

106 [sg]. *The Annunciation*, Patrick Reyntiens, St Peter and St Paul, Abington, Northants.
Installed as one window and based on a Botticelli painting. A design, watercolour on paper, 59×43.8 (23¼×17¼), 1982 for this work exists.

107 [sg]. *The Four Seasons*, Patrick Reyntiens, Piper estate
Panel, 115×159.4 (45¼×62¾)

1983

108 [t]. *Foliate Head – blue to brown*, Orde Levinson, Oxford, Ibenstein Weavers, Dordabis, 10, 2AP, 152.5×213.5 (60×84)
Signature and edition number woven into the back b.r. and b.l. respectively
Collection of Magdalen College, Oxford (Magdalen Centre, Oxford Science Park)

1984

109 [s]. *Owen Wingrave*, Royal Opera, Snape Maltings Concert Hall, Snape, near Aldeburgh
Scenery. Opera by Benjamin Britten; libretto by Myfanwy Evans; produced by Colin Graham

110 [sg]. [Unknown], St John's Hospital, Lichfield

111 [t]. *Long Sutton, Lincolnshire*, Barry Cronan Fine Art Ltd, London, R.Dutt, Calcutta, 25, 168×208 (66×82)
Signed and numbered by the artist on a label, then sewn onto the back of each tapestry

1985

112. [sg]. [*The Piper Window*], Patrick Reyntiens, St Paul's Church, Jarrow, Tyne and Wear, 1585×360 (625×141¾)
Installed in the Lancet window in the North Wall Saxon Chancel. The design modelled on the Leningrad manuscript of Bede's Ecclesiastical History

113 [t]. *Foliate Head*, John Piper, Henley-on-Thames, Oxon, West Dean Tapestry Studio, Chichester, 108×88 (42½×34⅝)
A translation/interpretation of the etching *The Seasons: Summer* (*sc.* Cat.330)

1986

114 [t]. *Foliate Head,* Orde Levinson, Oxford, Ibenstein Weavers, Dordabis, 12, 2AP, 122×122 (48×48)
Signature and edition number woven into the back b.r. and b.l. respectively
Collection of Magdalen College, Oxford (Magdalen Centre, Oxford Science Park)

115-18 [t]. *Foliate Head: The Seasons*, comprising: *Foliate Head: Spring* 135×167 (53¼×65¾), *Foliate Head: Winter* , 138×168 (54¼×66¼, *Foliate Head: Summer*, 138×164 (54¼×64½), *Foliate Head: Autumn*, 135×166 (53¼×65⅜)
Royal Surrey County Hospital, Guildford, West Dean Tapestry Studio, Chichester
All four hang in the Hospital Chapel.

1987

119 [sg]. *Tree of Life*, Gage Chapel, St Peter's Church, Firle, East Sussex, 2905×1405 (585½×968⁵⁄₁₆)

1988

120 [t]. *Sunflowers*, Barclays de Zoete Wedd, London, West Dean Tapestry Studio, Chichester, 184×243 (72⅜×95⅝)
Hangs at Head Office, Lombard Street.

1989

121 [t]. *Welsh Lake*, Orde Levinson, Oxford, Ibenstein Weavers, Dordabis, 8, 2AP, 152.5×213.5 (60×84)
Signature and edition number woven into the back b.r. and b.l. respectively
A translation/interpretation of the etching *Llyn Teifi* (*sc.* Cat.401)

1990

122 [t]. *Foliate Head*, Private Collection, West Dean Tapestry Studio, Chichester, 136×205 (53½×80⅝)

1995

123 [sg]. *The Nativity*, St Mary, The Virgin, Iffley
Myfanwy Piper was approached regarding the donation of the stained-glass panel (no.105 above) for St Mary's West Window and she readily agreed.

Written Works by and Interviews with John Piper

Books (written or edited), articles, essays, reviews, prefaces, broadcasts and lectures by and interviews with the artist, including unpublished works.

This is a combined list of all items written by John Piper presented chronologically by year. In each year the order of categorisation is: books, articles, and then interviews (by date).

Untraceable items which appear in Piper's correspondence are listed at the end of this section, in order of books, then articles, then interviews. Thereafter appears a list of proposed publications for which no manuscript exists, either because none were done or they are now lost. These items are dated from correspondence to the year in which the proposal for the publication was first made.

Where the date of an interview is not known, but the date (or year of publication in the case of a book) is then this date is given in order of day, month and year where known.

All items have been seen by the author except those prefixed with an asterisk (*).

Books
This section lists all books written or edited by Piper and are listed according to the title, publisher.

Piper was since 1938 associated with the Shell Guides series – as an editor (initially with John Betjeman, later alone) and as photographer and illustrator. All the Shell Guides are co-authored with John Betjeman unless otherwise stated and unless otherwise stated all Shell Guides contain photographic illustrations by John Piper. Owing to questions of space, where a Shell Guide has been republished without any major alterations, it is listed under the year of first publication only, with all republications indicated in this entry of first publication only. There is no cross-referencing to later (or earlier) publications.

Articles
This section includes all articles and sections of books, as well as forewords, afterwords and introductions by Piper, and symposiums in which Piper participated.

The order of listing is title, publication details, date, page number/s. Place of publication for periodicals and newspapers is London unless otherwise stated. After the title I have indicated what the writing related to, *eg* book or exhibition review.

Between the late 1920s and 1950s Piper contributed articles, reviews and illustrations to periodicals such as the *Athenaeum*, *The New Statesman and Nation*, *The Spectator*, *Horizon*, *The Saturday Review*, *London Mercury*, *New Leader*, *House and Garden*. From the 1st December 1939 to 26th May 1944 he wrote regularly for *The Spectator* as their art critic. Although all known contributions are included, it is acknowledged that this list may be incomplete. The author would welcome assistance from anyone having information on other writings by Piper.

Interviews
These include interviews with the artist, broadcasts and lectures.

The order of these is as follows:
Date, title, interviewer, medium, place

1921
1. *Wind in the trees*, Horseshoe Publishing Co, Bristol. Line drawings by Piper

---

1924
2. *The gaudy saint, and other poems*, Horseshoe Publishing Co, Bristol. Six vignettes: line drawings by Piper

---

1931
3. Grant, Duncan, 'Weekly notes on art', review of Cooling Galleries exhibition, *The Listener*, 24th June, pp.1058-9

4. 'Flower, vase and larder in English art', 'Weekly notes on art', *The Listener*, 16th September, pp.452-3

1933
5. 'Younger English painters – I', *The Listener*, 22nd March, pp.450-2

6. 'Younger English painters – II', *The Listener*, 29th March, pp. 490-2

7. 'The Epstein exhibition', *The New Statesman and Nation*, 6th May, pp.570-1

8. 'Interpreting Ruskin', book review of *John Ruskin* by Wilenski, *The New Statesman and Nation*, 17th June, p.800

9. 'Interviewing artists', book review of *Artists at work* by Casson, *The New Statesman and Nation*, 15th July, p.84

10. Foreword to the exh. cat. *New paintings by Ivon Hitchens*, Lefèvre Gallery, London, October, p.[1]

11. 'Contemporary English drawing', *The Listener*, 11th October, pp.541-3

12. 'December galleries', *The New Statesman and Nation*, 16th December, pp.809-10

13. 'Recent paintings of Edward Wadsworth', *Apollo*, 18th December, pp.386-7

1935
14. 'Picasso at the Tate', *AXIS*, No.1, January, pp.27-8

15. 'Recent books: *Plastic redirections in twentieth century painting* by J. J. Sweeney and *The modern movement in painting* by T. W. Earp', *AXIS*, No.2, April, pp.30-1

16. 22nd January, 'To unemployed listeners', John Hilton with John Piper, Radio broadcast, BBC

1936
17. With Geoffrey Grigson, 'England's climate', *AXIS*, No.7, Autumn, pp.5-9

18. *'England's early sculptors' (text by John Piper; photos by John Piper and Myfanwy Evans), *Architectural Review*, October, Vol.80, pp.157-62, plus four leaves of plates

19. 7th November, 'The Autumn galleries', Television broadcast, BBC

20. 18th November, 'Some further exhibits described by Mr Piper', Television broadcast, BBC

1937
21. 'Lost: a valuable object', pp.69-73; and 'English early sculptors', pp.116-25 in *The painter's object*, ed. by Myfanwy Evans, Gerald Howe, London. Illus. of works by Piper, pp.68, 71
Reprinted 1954 in S. J. Wood, *John Piper: Paintings, Drawings and Theatre Designs, 1932-1954*, Faber and Faber, London; reprinted 1970 by Arno Press; reprinted *John Piper: 50 years of his work*, exh. cat. for retrospective exhibition at the Museum of Modern Art, Oxford, 20th May–24th June, 1979

22. 'Lithographs by Eric Ravilious of shop fronts', *Signature*, No.5, March, p.48, plus three leaves of plates

23. 'Died April 1st 1837: John Constable', *Architectural Review*, April, Vol.81, pp.149-50, plus one plate

24. 'Recent watercolours by Paul Nash', *Town Flats and Country Cottages*, May

25. 'Modern Painters and Sculptors as Illustrators', book review, *Signature*, No.6, July, pp.50-2

26. 'Aspects of modern drawing', *Signature*, No.7, November, pp.33-41, plus three leaves of plates

27. 'Pre-history from the air', *AXIS*, No.8, Early Winter, pp.4-8

28. 13th January, 'London Galleries', Television broadcast, BBC

29. 27th January, 'Art and modern architecture: a discussion between John Piper and Serge Chermayeff', Television broadcast, BBC

30. 10th February, 'London Galleries', Television broadcast, BBC

31. 24th February, 'Modern art and stage design', John Piper and Robert Medley, Television broadcast, BBC

32. 10th March, 'John Piper and W. Staite Murray', Television broadcast, BBC

33. 24th March, 'John Piper and a group of young artists', Television broadcast, BBC

1938

34. *Shell Guides: Oxfordshire, not including the city of Oxford*, Batsford, London.
Reissued Faber and Faber, London, 1953

35. *'The nautical style', *Architectural Review*, January, Vol.83, pp.1-14, plus one plate, photos by Piper and J. M. Richards

36. 'English sea pictures', *The Listener*, 28th July, pp.180-1

37. 'Abstraction on the beach', *XXe Siècle*, July/August/September (1ère année, No.3), p.41. Extract reprinted in exh. cat. to *John Piper*, Tate Gallery, London, 1983, p.37

38. 'The art of the early crosses', *Country Life*, 28th August, pp.218-19

39. 'Henry Fuseli, R.A. 1741-1825', *Signature*, No.10, November, pp.1-14, plus four leaves of plates

40. 'Architectural deportment', reviews of *A miniature history of the English house* by J. M. Richards and *Pillar to post* by O. Lancaster, *The New Statesman and Nation*, 10th December, pp.1000, 1002

41. 'Notes on wall objects old and new', *Decoration*, No.30, Winter, pp.39-43

42. 10th January, 'A trip to the seaside by Myfanwy Evans and John Piper', Television broadcast, BBC

1939

43. *Brighton Aquatints: twelve original aquatints of modern Brighton*; with short descriptions by the artist; and an Introduction by Lord Alfred Douglas, Duckworth, London, twelve full-page black-and-white original aquatints. In the deluxe edition the images were all hand-coloured (*sc.* Cats 12-23)

44. *Devon – A Shell Guide*, John Betjeman and Brian Watson, J. Betjeman (ed.), Faber and Faber, London (originally published under Betjeman, 1936)

45. *Sailing on the South Coast – A Shell Guide*, K. Adlard Coles, J. Piper and J. Betjeman (eds), Faber and Faber, London. Reprinted 1947. Revised edition: *Pocket Pilot for the South Coast*: 1950, third revised edition: 1962, fourth revised edition: 1968, reprinted: 1973, fifth revised edition: 1977, sixth edition, revised and edited by Captain J. O. Coote: 1982

46. 'London: l'architecture Londonienne depuis 1800', *Cahiers d'Art*, Vol.14, Nos 1-4, pp.92-103

47. *'London to Bath: a topographical and critical survey of the Bath road', written and illus. by Piper, *Architectural Review*, May, Vol.85, pp.229-46

48. 'Barbarous Wales', review of *Welsh life in the eighteenth century* by Sir L. Twiston Davies and R. Edwards, *The New Statesman and Nation*, 9th December, pp.868, 870

1940

49. *'Grey tower and panelled pew: John Piper looks at English country churches and makes drawings of them specially for The Listener', *The Listener*, 1st February, pp.216-18. Four illus.

50. *'Fully licensed – in praise of the ordinary public house', *Architectural Review*, March, Vol.87, pp.87-100. Illus. incl. photos by Piper

51. *'Decrepit glory: a tour of Hafod', *Architectural Review*, June, Vol.87, pp.207-10, plus one plate. Six illus. by Piper

52. 'Round the art exhibitions', *The Listener*, 6th June, p.1100

53. 'The art of the stuccador', *The Listener*, 5th September, p.353

54. *'Towers in the Fens', *Architectural Review*, November, pp.131-4, plus two plates. Illus. incl. eight by Piper

1941

55. *'John Piper at the AA', extracts from a paper entitled 'Buildings in English art', *Architect and Building News*, 9th May, Vol.166, p.85. Two illus. by Piper

56. 'The Euston Road Group', *The Listener*, 29th May, pp.771-2

57. 'Victorian painting', *The Listener*, 20th November, p.698

58. *['Buckland House'; 'Towcester – screen to Racecourse'], *Architect and Building News*, 19th December, Vol.168, pp.170-1. Two illus. by Piper

1942

59. *British romantic artists*, Collins, London ('Britain in pictures series'). Republished in *Aspects of British art*, ed. by W. J. Turner, Collins, London, 1947 and republished in *Labrys*, Vol.9, November 1983, pp.3-37

60. 'S. H. Grimm: watercolour painter (Art)', *The Listener*, 12th March, p.341

61. 'John Sell Cotman, 1782-1842', *Architectural Review*, July, Vol.92, pp.9-12

62. 'Notes from a Yorkshire journal', *The Geographical Magazine*, December, pp.364-7

1943

63. *Correspondence with Michael Sandler for proposed book entitled *Art History, Criticism and Prophesy*

63. Foreword to the exh. cat. *The artist and the Church*, organised by CEMA, London, pp.3-4

65. 'Stanley Spencer', *Britain Today*, January, No.81, p.24

66. 'A Cubist folk art', *Architectural Review*, July, Vol.94, pp.21-2. five drawings by Piper, photos incl. some by Piper

67. 'Colour reproduction and the cheap book (Art)', *The Listener*, 22th July, p.104

68. 'The gratuitous semicircle', *Architectural Review*, October, Vol.94, pp.112-13. Illus. incl. four drawings by Piper

69. 'Some old friends. (Colour in building series)', *Architectural Review*, November, Vol.94, pp.139-41. Illus. incl. seven drawings by Piper

70. 'Colour and display. (Colour in building series)', *Architectural Review*, December, Vol.94, pp.168-71. Illus. incl. nine drawings by Piper

1944

71. 'Colour and texture. (Colour in building series)', *Architectural Review*, February, Vol.95, pp.30, 51-2

72. 'Blandford Forum. (Colour in building series)', *Architectural Review*, July, Vol.96, pp.21-3. Illus. incl. eleven drawings by Piper

73. 'Warmth in the west', *Architectural Review*, September, Vol.96, pp.89-91. Illus. incl. eight drawings by Piper

74. 'Topographical letter from Norwich [illus. with notes for painting]', *Cornhill Magazine*, January, Vol.161, No.961, pp.9-18, plus four pp. of plates, eight line drawings, four pen and wash

75. 'Flint', *Architectural Review*, November, Vol.96, pp.149-51. Illus. incl. seven illus. by Piper

76. 'Topographical letter from Devizes', *Cornhill Magazine*, November, Vol.161, No.963, pp.190-5, plus four pages of plates, four line drawings in text, three colour lithos

77. Myerscough-Walker, B., 'Modern art explained by modern artists (Part III)', *The Artist*, May, Vol.27, No.3, pp.65-7

1945

78. With James Boswell and Giles, *The Artist and the Public*, The Army Bureau of Current Affairs, No.96, 2nd June. Piper's contribution is titled 'The Practical Business of Painting'

79. 'Seaton Delaval', *Orion: a miscellany*, No.1, pp.43-7

80. 'The English tradition of draughtsmanship', *The Listener*, 8th February

81. *'Shops', *Architectural Review*, March, Vol.97, pp.89-91. Three illus. by Piper

82. *'Colour in the picturesque village', *Architectural Review*, May, Vol.97, pp.130, 149-50. Six illus. by Piper

83. 'Renaissance Britain' (Art)', *The Listener*, 26th July, p.104

84. *'St Marie's Grange: first home of A.W.N. Pugin', *Architectural Review*, October, Vol.98, pp.90-3. Two illus. by Piper

85. 'Introduction to Middlesbrough', *Cornhill Magazine*, December, Vol.161, No.966, pp.430-3, plus four pages of plates. One illus. from a watercolour by Piper

86. 'Coloured pictures', *The Listener*, 6th December, pp.663-4

1946

87. *'A wool country: colour in the Cotswolds', *The Ambassador*, No.5, pp.61-72. Ten illus. by Piper, plus cover design

88. 'Georgian London (Art)', *The Listener*, 28th March, p.408

89. 'Exeter replanned', review of *Exeter phoenix* by T. Sharp, *The New Statesman and Nation*, 20th April, pp.288-9

90. *'The market square. (Colour in building series)', *Architectural Review*, May, Vol.99, pp.153-5. Four illus. by Piper

91. 'The artist and the Church', *Cymry 'r Groes: a Quarterly Magazine*, July, Vol.2, No.1, pp.25-32

92. 'Religion inspires a modern artist', on Graham Sutherland's *Crucifixion* in the Church of St Matthew, Northampton, *Picture Post*, 21st December, pp.13-15

1947

93. 'Post-Reformation sculpture', review of *English church monuments, 1510-1840*, by K. A. Esdaile, *The New Statesman and Nation*, 8th March, p.160

94. 'Pleasing decay', *Architectural Review*, September, Vol.102, pp.85-94

95. 'Sickert: painter-critic', *The Listener*, 4th September, p.396

96. 'English painting at the Tate [exhibition review]', *Burlington Magazine*, October, Vol.89, p.285

97. 'A new Bath guide', *The Listener*, 27th November, p.946

1948

98. *Buildings and prospects*, Architectural Press, London. Illus. comprise three halftones of drawings, four halftones of paintings, one line drawing and dust-jacket

99. With John Betjeman (eds), *Murray's Buckinghamshire architectural guide*, John Murray, London. Dust-jacket designed by Piper
This was the first of a series of guide books in which Piper and John Betjeman were the editors and then the general editors. Piper was associated with these series – as an editor (initially with John Betjeman, later alone) as photographer and illustrator. The general format was around 112 pages with some 180 illustrations, arranged chronologically and from the earliest times to the present. See also no.107 below

100. (ed.), *Studies in composition and tradition*, M. Parrish, London

101. Introduction to the exh. cat. for his own one-man exhibition, Buchholz Gallery, New York, 3rd–21st February

102. 'Designs of Lucretia', p.67 in *The Rape of Lucretia: a symposium*; ed. by Ronald F. H. Duncan; with texts by Benjamin Britten, Ronald Duncan, John Piper *et al* and a symposium discussion comprising Benjamin Britten, Ronald Duncan, John Piper, Henry Boys, Eric Crozier and Angus McBean, Bodley Head, London. Also contains eight colour lithographs from the original designs by Piper, most full page. Three fold out to 38.1 cm (15 in) wide. One reproduction on the front dust-jacket

103. 'Design for The Quest', *Britain Today*, April, No.144. One illus. facing p.39

104. *'Pattern and colour from English slate engravings; collected, coloured and described by John Piper', *The Ambassador*, No.9, pp.67-80. fifty illus.

105. 'Bath, Edinburgh, and art historians (Art)', *The Listener*, 1st July, p.28

106. *'Job: a masque for dancing – set designs', *Britain Today*, October, No.148. Two illus. facing p.37

1949

107. With John Betjeman (eds), *Murray's Berkshire architectural guide*, John Murray, London. Dust-jacket designed by Piper

108. Foreword in *The drawings of Henry Fuseli*, by Paul Ganz, M. Parrish, London, pp.7-10

109. *'Book illustration and the painter-artist', *Penrose Annual*, Vol.43, pp.52-4, plus four pages of tipped-in lithographs from illus. by Piper. Six illus.

110. *'S. John Woods. – Portrait of the artist', *Art News and Review*, 16th July, Vol.11, No.12, p.1

111. *'Stonehenge (Reassessment, 5)', *Architectural Review*, September, Vol.106, pp.177-82. Illus. incl. seven photos by Piper

1950

112. *Romney Marsh*, illus. and described by John Piper, Penguin Books, Harmondsworth (King Penguin Books, No.55). One line drawing, sixteen halftones in colour, sixteen in black-and-white

113. 'Picturesque travel illustrated', *Signature*, No.11 (new series), pp.3-19, plus four leaves of plates. Incl. a wood engraving by Reynolds Stone from a drawing by Piper

1951

114. *Shell Guides: Shropshire*, with John Betjeman (eds), Faber and Faber, London. Rewritten see no.182 below

115. 'Advertising films intelligently', *The Penrose Annual*, Vol.45, pp.33-4

116. Quotes from Piper in the exh. cat. for his own exhibition at the Philadelphia Art Alliance, Philadelphia, opened 4th March

1952

117. *Gloucestershire – A Shell Guide*, Anthony West and David Verey, John Piper (eds), Faber and Faber (new edition, originally published under Betjeman 1939). Rewritten see no.175 below

118. *The West Coast of Scotland – A Shell Guide*, Stephen Bone, J. Piper and J. Betjeman (eds), Faber and Faber, London

119. 'Aquatint and lithography, review of *Scenery of Great Britain and Ireland in aquatint and lithography, 1770-1860, from the Library of J. R. Abbey*, *Signature*, No.16 (new series), pp.50-1

1953

120. *'What they stand for', *The Ambassador*, Special Coronation Edition, pp.40-52

121. 'Electricity and old churches' (with John Betjeman), *Time and Tide*, 5th December

122. Preface to *Etching and engraving: Techniques and the modern trend*, by J. Buckland Wright, The Studio, London

1954

123. *Northumberland – A Shell Guide*, Thomas Sharp, J. Piper and J. Betjeman (eds), Faber and Faber, London (second edition, first published 1937 under Betjeman), third edition 1969

124. *'Portland stone – Portland colours: textures and shades of the island and its treasure', *The Ambassador*, No.6, pp.80–91. Sixteen illus. by Piper plus cover design

1955

125. *A small anthology of Modern Stained Glass*, selected by and with introduction by Piper, The Arts Council of Great Britain, London

126. *Herefordshire – A Shell Guide*, David Very, John Betjeman, John Piper (eds), Faber and Faber, London

127. *Murray's Lancashire Architectural Guide*, John Piper, John Betjeman (eds), John Murray, London. Dust-jacket design

128. *Poems in the Porch*, with John Betjeman, SPCK, London

129. *The Installation of Electricity in Churches*, with John Betjeman, The Church Information Board

130. 'The world of Paul Nash', review of *Paul Nash: the portrait of an artist*, by A. Bertram, *The New Statesman and Nation*, 8th October, pp.434, 436

131. 30th March 'John Piper' documentary, by John Read, incl. interviews with Piper, Television broadcast, BBC

1956

132. *Wiltshire – A Shell Guide*, David Verey, John Piper and John Betjeman (eds), Faber and Faber, London. first published 1935 under Betjeman

133. 'Master of all arts', review of *In search of Diaghilev* by R. Buckle, *The New Statesman and Nation*, 11th February, pp.158–9

134. 'The card and the charmer, review of *William Nicholson* by L. Browse, *The New Statesman and Nation*, 1st August, p.138

1957

135. *Norfolk – A Shell Guide*, Wilhelmine Harrod and the Revd C. F. L. Linnell, John Piper and John Betjeman (eds), Faber and Faber, London. Reprinted in 1964 (second edition); 1966 (third edition); 1969; 1982 (fourth edition, contains no illus. by Piper)

136. Correspondence with Faber and Faber, London, regarding proposed book, *Stained Glass*, with Patrick Reyntiens. Cancelled due to cost

137. 'Abstraction to creation' in *A tribute to Evie Hone and Mainie Jellett*, Stella Frost (ed.), Browne and Nolan, Dublin, pp.43–5

138. 'Good to steal from', review of *Index to the story of my days* by Edward Gordon Craig, *The New Statesman and Nation*, 5th October, p.436

1958

139. *Film Commentary for the British Transport Commission

1959

140. Correspondence with William Heinemann Ltd, London, regarding proposed book entitled *A New Microcosm of London* with John Betjeman and Osbert Lancaster. Not realised

141. 'The Flowering of the Romantics', *The Observer*, 12th July, p.8

142. 'On [Gerald Manley] Hopkins as a Draughtsman', *The Journals and Papers of Gerald Manley Hopkins*, Humphrey House (ed.)(completed by Graham Storey), Oxford University Press, London, pp.454–5. Piper was also responsible for the preparation of Hopkins' sketches in Appendix I

1960

143. *Mid-Wales: Brecon, Radnor and Montgomery – A Shell Guide*, David Verey, John Piper and John Betjeman (eds), Faber and Faber, London

144. *Suffolk – A Shell Guide*, Norman Scarfe, John Piper (eds), Faber and Faber, London. Reprinted 1966, 1976, 1982 (paperback), republished 1988, The Alastair Press, Suffolk

1961

145. *'Serenissima', *Architectural Review*, May, Vol.129, pp.301–3. One illus. by Piper

146. 'Predicament', *London Magazine*, July, pp.81–2

1962

147. Correspondence with Anthony Gishford, regarding proposed book on Benjamin Britten, to incl. contributions from Piper. Cancelled due to Gishford's illness

148. 'The eyes have it. (Pleasure in reading)', *The Times*, 1st February, p.13

149. 24th May, 'Woman's Hour', interviewed by Cecilia Ococks, discussing Coventry Cathedral's stained glass, Radio broadcast, BBC

1963

150. *Oxfordshire – A Shell Guide*, John Piper, John Betjeman (eds), Faber and Faber, London

151. *Rutland – A Shell Guide*, W. G. Hoskins, John Piper (eds), Faber and Faber, London

152. *South-West Wales: Pembrokeshire and Camarthenshire – A Shell Guide*, Vyvyan Rees, John Piper (eds), Faber and Faber, London. Second edition: 1976, reprinted in paperback: 1982

153. Spender, Stephen, 'A talk with John Piper', *Encounter*, May, Vol.20, No.5, pp.59–61

1964

154. *Cornwall – A Shell Guide*, John Betjeman and John Piper (eds), Faber and Faber, London

155. *Worcestershire – A Shell Guide*, J. Lees-Milne, John Piper and John Betjeman (eds), Faber and Faber, London. Republished 1968

156. *'In Town Today', interviewed by Nan Winton, Radio broadcast, BBC

157. Barber, Noël, *Conversations with painters*, Collins, London, pp.57–68

1965

158. *Lincolnshire – A Shell Guide*, Jack Yates and Henry Thorold, John Piper and John Betjeman (eds), Faber and Faber, London

159. Correspondence with Leslie Frewin Publishers Ltd, London, regarding *The Painter and Stained Glass*, a proposed work of 30,000 words which Piper abandoned (letter dated 1st February 1966)

160. 25th November, 'British art in the thirties', Radio broadcast, BBC

1966

161. 'The artist and his work', *The Christian Science Monitor*, Boston, Mass., 16th February

162. *'Ivor Herbert, Insight Interview', *Evening News*, November

163. *Dorset – A Shell Guide*, Michael Pitt-Rivers, John Piper and John Betjeman (eds), Faber and Faber, London

1967

164. *The Isle of Wight – A Shell Guide*, Pennethorne Hughes, John Piper and John Betjeman (eds), Faber and Faber, London

165. Foreword to exh. cat. *John Piper: Designs for the Chichester Cathedral Tapestry*, exhibition at Nottingham University Art Gallery, 19th May–17th June

166. 'The Liverpool lantern', *Studio International*, June, Vol.173, No.890, pp.294–5

167. Review of *Madocks and the Wonders of Wales*, by Elisabeth Beazley, *Architectural Review*, Vol.141, June, p.407

1968

168. *Essex – A Shell Guide*, Norman Scarfe, John Piper (eds), Faber and Faber, London

169. *Northamptonshire and the Soke of Peterborough – A Shell Guide*, Juliet Smith, John Piper (eds), Faber and Faber, London. Second impression with corrections: 1972

170. *Wiltshire – A Shell Guide*, John Piper and J. H. Cheetham, Faber and Faber, London

171. *Stained glass: art or anti-art*, with J. H. Cheetham, Studio Vista, London, Reinhold, New York. Reprinted in *John Piper: Painting in coloured glass*, 1982, and extracts reprinted in *Labrys*, Vol.9, November 1983, pp.39–47

1969

172. *Kent – A Shell Guide*, Pennethorne Hughes, John Piper (eds), Faber and Faber, London

173. Foreword to exh. cat. *European Topography, 1967–1969*, Marlborough Fine Art, London, May–June

174. [Francis Hodgkins], unpublished, with Myfanwy Piper, Piper Archives

1970

175. *Gloucestershire – A Shell Guide*, David Verey, John Piper (eds), Faber and Faber, London. New edition of no.117 above

176. *Leicestershire – A Shell Guide*, W. G. Hoskins, John Piper (eds), Faber and Faber, London

177. 4th October, interview and film for 'A Chapel at Churchill', Anglia Television

178. 4th December, interview on work for Coventry Cathedral for 'Art and Design: Stained Glass', BBC Radio 4 (Schools)

1971

179. *Mid Western Wales – A Shell Guide, Cardiganshire and Merioneth*, Vyvyan Rees, John Piper (eds), Faber and Faber, London

180. *North Wales – A Shell Guide*, Elisabeth Beazley, Lionel Brett, John Piper (eds), Faber and Faber, London

1972

181. 'Strange Presences', review of *Henry Moore: Sculpture and Drawings 1921-1969* by Robert Melville, Thames and Hudson, London, *Architectural Review*, Vol.151, March, p.195

1973

182. *Shropshire – A Shell Guide*, Michael Moulder, John Betjeman, John Piper (eds), Faber and Faber, London. A rewrite of no.114 above

183. 'Adrian Stokes', obituary, *Architectural Review*, March, Vol.153, pp.209-10

184. 'Paul Nash – photographer', review of Tate Gallery exhibition, *Architectural Review*, July, Vol.154, pp.62-3

1974

185. 13th December, excerpts from interviews with British Information Services used in 'Death in Venice' at the time of the opera's opening in New York, Radio broadcast, WNYC, New York (and other radio stations)

1975

186. 'Completion of Queen's Gate – the results, article by the assessors', with others, *Building Design*, August, No.261, pp.9-12

187. *5th October, interview for Thames Television (recorded 21st August)

188. 11th December, unpublished interview with Orde Levinson, Fawley Bottom Farmhouse, near Henley-on-Thames

1976

189. 'Colouring light', review of *Stained glass* by Lawrence Lee, George Seddon and Francis Stephens, *The Guardian*, 28th October, p.15

190. Banham, Mary, and Bevis Hillier, 'A painter's funfair: interview with John Piper, artist, designer'. With Osbert Lancaster of the Grand Vista, Battersea Pleasure Gardens, *A tonic to the nation*, Thames and Hudson, London, pp.123-5

1977

191. *Surrey – A Shell Guide*, Bruce Watkin, John Piper (eds), Faber and Faber, London. No illus. by Piper

192. 'Herefordshire – 3', *Vole*, No.1, pp.38-9. Five photos by Piper

193. 'Place of the month: the Fens', *Vole*, No.3, pp.43-52. Four photos by Piper

194. Foreword to exh. cat. *Victorian Dream Palaces, and Other Buildings in Landscape*, Marlborough Fine Art, London

195. 29th March, interview with British Information Service, New York, for programme in honour of Sir William Walton, Radio broadcast WNYC, New York

196. Berthoud, Roger, 'The painter who likes working with craftsmen', News International Newspaper Ltd, November

1978

197. *East Sussex – A Shell Guide*, W. S. Mitchell, John Piper (eds), Faber and Faber, London

198. *Staffordshire – A Shell Guide*, Henry Thorold, John Piper (eds), Faber and Faber, London

199. 'Rev. Dr Victor Kenna', obituary, with W. M[oelwyn] M[erchant], *The Times*, 16th August, p.14

200. Foreword in *Glass Light*, compiled by Martin Harrison, Thorn Lighting Ltd, Borehamwood

201. 18th November, interviewed by Gary Power, Richard Swift and Emma Cunningham, unpublished. First published 1979, see no.205 below

1979

202. 'Art or anti-art', in *Architectural stained glass*; ed. by B. Clarke, John Murray, London, pp. 53-7. Piper's work with stained glass also covered

203. *Warwickshire – A Shell Guide*, Douglas Hickman, John Piper (eds), Faber and Faber, London

204. Margetts, Martina, 'A Piper Portfolio', *Crafts*, January-February, pp.34-9

205. Power, Gary, with Richard Smith and Emma Cunningham, 'John Piper, interviewed, 18th November 1978', *Composition: University of Reading fine Art Department*, Spring, pp.31-46

1980

206. *County Durham – A Shell Guide*, Henry Thorold, John Piper (eds), Faber and Faber, London

207. *Devon – A Shell Guide*, Ann Jellicoe and Roger Mayne, John Piper (eds), Faber and Faber, London. A rewrite of no.44 above

208. Foreword in *Epitaphs from Oxfordshire*, by Patricia Utechin, Robert Dugdale, Oxford. Second edition, Robert Dugdale in association with the Oxfordshire Historic Churches Trust, Oxford: 1990

209. Foreword to exh. cat. *Master weavers: tapestries from the Dovecot Studios 1912-80*, Royal Scottish Academy, Edinburgh, 15th August–14th September, Canongate, Edinburgh. Pipers' tapestries listed but not exhibited

1981

210. *Buckinghamshire – A Shell Guide*, Bruce Watkin, John Piper (eds), Faber and Faber, London

211. 'The Dream' goes to Glyndebourne: John Higgins talks to John Piper, first designer of Britten's opera', interviewed by John Higgins, *The Times Preview*, 19th-25th June

212. Interviewed by John Read, Music and Arts Department, BBC, and filmed by Jane Coles for 'In the Making' series, BBC Television

213. *Interviewed and filmed for 'The Other Side of Me', TVS

1982

214. *Hertfordshire – A Shell Guide*, R. M. Healey, John Piper (eds), Faber and Faber, London

215. 21st February, interviewed by Angela Levin; photographed by Brian Moody, 'A Room of my own', *Observer Magazine*

1983

216. *Piper's Places: John Piper in England and Wales*, with Richard Ingrams, Chatto and Windus, London

217. *Cambridgeshire – A Shell Guide*, Norman Scarfe, John Piper (eds), Faber and Faber, London

218. Foreword in John Piper, *John Piper's Stowe*, commentary by Mark Girouard, Hurtwood Press in association with the Tate Gallery, London

219. Foreword to exh. cat. 'Ceramics', *The Britten-Pears Collection*, John Evans (ed.), Aldeburgh Festival of Music and the Arts, Aldeburgh, 10th-26th June

220. 27th February, *Time with Betjeman*, interview, Television broadcast, BBC

221. 16th October. *John Piper*, 'South Bank Show', interviewed by Melvyn Bragg, Television broadcast, LWT

222. 24th November, 'Through a glass colourfully, The Times Profile', interviewed by John Fuller, *The Times*, p.10

223. 25th November, 'The Arbitrary Eye – A Photographic Discourse between John Piper and Paul Joyce', *British Journal of Photography*, pp.1239ff.

224. Interviews recorded with BBC for broadcast on Radio 3 in November at the time of his retrospective at the Tate Gallery

225. Hughes, Graham, 'John Piper', *Arts Review Year Book*, pp.42–3

1984

226. *Nottinghamshire – A Shell Guide*, Henry Thorold, John Piper (eds), Faber and Faber, London

227. 'The life of a Laureate: John Betjeman, 1906-1984', obituary, with Roy Fuller, *The Sunday Times*, 20th May, p.5

228. Foreword in *Modern Stained Glass in British Churches*, by Mark Angus, Mowbray, London and Oxford

229. Short description by Piper of his chapel window in *St John's Hospital, Lichfield: A Short History*, by Howard Clayton

230. *1st July, 'Romantic vision of a pagan believer', interviewed by Sebastian Faulks

231. **Glyndebourne: a celebration*, interviewed by J. Higgins (ed.)

1987

232. *A Painter's Camera*, Tate Gallery Publications, London

233. 'Working with Printers' in *John Piper: The Complete Graphic Works. A Catalogue Raisonné 1923-1983*, by Orde Levinson, Faber and Faber, London. Republished in the present book

234. 'A note on equipment', *The Painters Object*

235. 'Mapping out British Culture', essay in exh. cat. *A Paradise Lost: The Neo-Romantic Imagination in Britain, 1935-1955*, Barbican Art Gallery, London, 21st May–19th July, in association with Lund Humphries, London

1988

236. 'John Piper: Neo-Romanticism In The 1980s', interviewed by Peter Fuller, *Modern Painters*, Vol.1, No.2, pp.17-22. Republished in 1993, see no.241 below

237. 10th December, *An English Romantic*, Peter Fuller, *The Independent Magazine*

238. 'Piper's Prime', interviewed by Jane Ashby, 'Limited Edition', *Oxford Times Colour Supplement*, Christmas, No.26, p.32

1989

239. Quoted in exh. cat. *John Piper: the Master Prints*, CCA Galleries, London

1990

240. 'Interview with John Piper', interviewed by Ian Simpson, *The Artist*, November

1993

241. 'John Piper', interviewed by Peter Fuller in *Modern Artists*, John McDonald (ed.), Methuen, London, pp.254-63

Undated/Unknown

244. Foreword in *Stained Glass in England: 1150-1550*, by Brian Coe, W.H. Allen and Co Ltd, London. Perhaps *c.*1967

245. Extracts from *Romney Marsh*, pp.27, 28 in unknown book

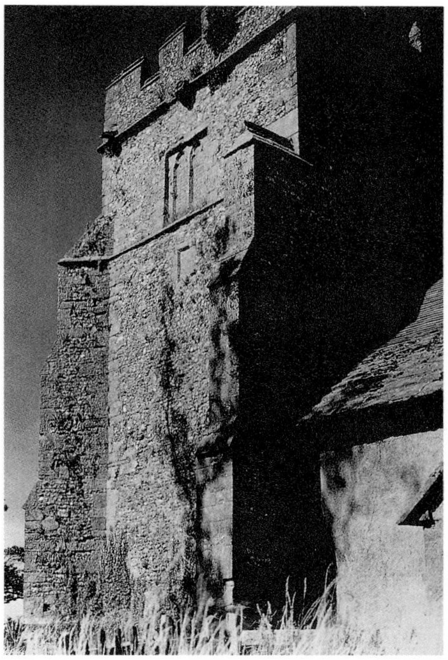

John Piper, *Tower of Hamsey*, Sussex, 1939

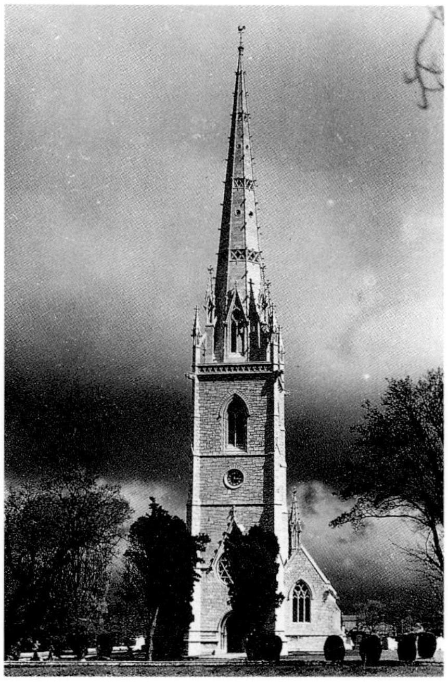

John Piper, *The 'marble church' Bedelwyddan, Flintshire*, 1971

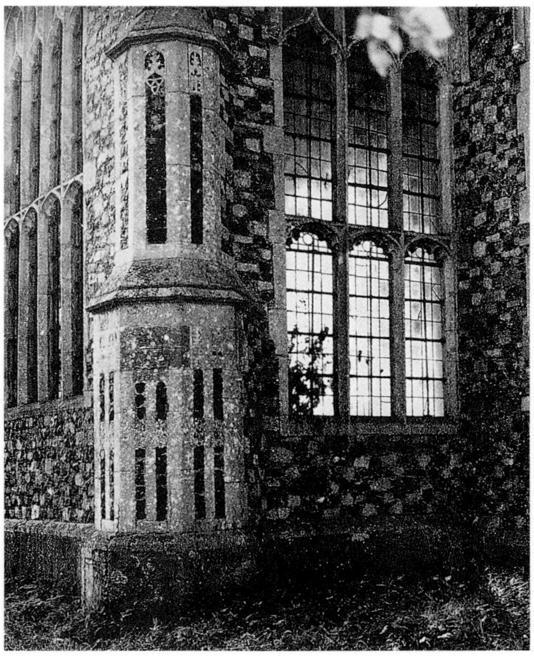

John Piper, *The Window at Gipping*, Suffolk, 1968

Writings about John Piper

Books, periodicals and newspaper articles about the artist, including dissertations and dedications.

Place of publication for periodicals and newspapers is London unless otherwise stated.

These are arranged by year and then by author (in alphabetical order), title, publisher, place of publication, page details (if applicable). Items which have no listed author are arranged alphabetically by title or publisher at the end of each year section and indicated by [AU].

I have indicated, where applicable, after the titles what the writings related to, *eg* review or preface. All known reviews are included, but the author acknowledges that this section is probably incomplete and would welcome any information on it.

Articles not seen by the author or untraceable, but referenced in correspondence to or from Piper are listed under the appropriate year and preceded by an asterisk (*).

1935

1. Porteous, Hugh Gordon, 'Piper and abstract possibilities', *AXIS*, No.4, November, pp.14–16

2. Wescher, Herta, 'John Piper', *AXIS*, No.4, November, pp.12–13

1937

3. Martin, J.L., with B.Nicholson and N. Gabo (eds), *Circle: international survey of constructive art*, Faber and Faber, London

1940

4. McGreevy, Thomas, Leicester Galleries: John Piper, Henry Lamb, review of 1940 exhibition, 'In the world's art centres', *The Studio*, May, Vol.119, No.566, p.184

5. Sitwell, Osbert, review of *Brighton Aquatints*, *The Listener*, 4th January

6. Tayler, Herbert, 'Found: a valuable object' – 'Brighton Aquatints', a book review, *Architectural Review*, February, Vol.87, p.6

1941

7. Hendy, Philip, Foreword to catalogue of an exhibition at Temple Newsam, Leeds, 25th July–28th September

8. [AU], 'Exhibitions at Temple Newsam', review of touring CEMA exhibition selected from Temple Newsam exhibition which commenced Leicester, December, *Apollo*, December, Vol.34, pp.157–60

1942

9. Gordon, Jan, review of the 1941–2 CEMA touring group exhibition, 'London commentary', *The Studio*, April, Vol.123, No.589, pp.114–15

10. Leeds, T.T, 'Art for the people', review of the 1941–2 CEMA touring group exhibition, *The Studio*, March, Vol.123, No.588, p.81

11. Thomas, Trevor, 'Moore – Piper – Sutherland exhibition', review of 1941 group exhibition at Temple Newsam, *The Museums Journal*, February, Vol.41, No.11, pp.259–61

1943

12. Lehman, John (ed.), Dance critic, 'English ballet finds a patron', *The Penguin New Writing*, 17, April–June, pp.129–38

13. [G.P.], 'British Romantic artists', review of the 1942 book by Piper, *Journal of the Royal Society of Arts*, 20th August, Vol.91, No.4646, p.528

14. [AU], 'The Quest', notes on the decor *Arabesque*, Oxford University Ballet Club, Trinity term

1944

15. Betjeman, John, *John Piper*, Penguin Books (Penguin Modern Painters Series), Harmondsworth

16. Seddon, Richard, 'Artists of note: John Piper', *The Artist*, Tenterden, January, Vol.26, No.5, pp.110–12

17. [AU], 'Perspex', review of the 1944 Redfern Gallery group exhibition, 'Current shows and comments', *Apollo*, January, Vol.39, No.228, pp.1–2

1945

18. Baxendall, D.K., '*John Piper* by John Betjeman', review of the book, Penguin Modern Painters Series, *The Museums Journal*, October, Vol.45, No.7, pp.124–5

19. Hussey, Christopher, 'The twilight of the great house', review of the 1945 one-man exhibition of paintings by John Piper at the Leicester Galleries, *Country Life*, 26th January, Vol.97, p.153

20. Newton, Eric, *War through artists' eyes*, John Murray, London, pp.78, 85

21. Russell, John, 'John Piper', *Magazine of Art*, April, Vol.38, No.4, pp.144–7

1946

22. Hoffman, Edith, '*John Piper* by John Betjeman', book review, 'The Literature of Art', *Burlington Magazine*, January, Vol.88, p.25

23. Lansdale, Nelson, 'The Old Vic brings new art', article on the set designs for 'Oedipus', *Art News*, May, Vol.45, No.3, pp.48–9, 69

24. Wallis, N.A.D., 'The Penguin Modern Painters – John Piper', review of John Betjeman's book, *Journal of the Royal Society of Arts*, 18th January, Vol.94, p.130

1947

25. Cronache, H.A., 'Londra: Una mostra di John Piper', *Emporium*, Bergamo, February, Vol.105, No.626, p.85

26. Ironside, Robin, *Painting since 1939*, British Council, London

27. [AU], 'English Painters at the Tate', *Burlington Magazine*, October

1948

28. Preston, Stuart, 'Spotlight on: Koerner, Piper (and other artists)', review of the 1948 one-man exhibition at the Buchholz Gallery, *Art News*, February, Vol.46, No.12, pp.29, 49

29. Reed, Judith Kaye, 'Piper, Modern English', review of the 1948 one-man exhibition at the Buchholz Gallery, *Art Digest*, New York, February, Vol.22, No.10, p.11

30. [AU], 'Stage design', *Vogue*, September, pp.86–7, 110, 112, 116

1949

31. Grigson, Geoffrey, 'John Piper's England', *The Listener*, 28th April, p.274

32. Hendy, Philip, review of the 1949 one-man exhibition at Leicester Galleries, 'English watercolours', *Britain Today*, February, No.154, pp.37–40

33. Hussey, Christopher, 'Murals for Rio de Janeiro by John Piper at the Victoria and Albert Museum', review of the 1949 one-man exhibition at the V&A, *Country Life*, 2nd December, Vol.106, pp.1649–50

34. Woods, S.John, 'John Piper as a Topographical Illustrator', *Image: a quarterly of the visual arts*, No.2, Autumn, pp.3–18

35. Woods, S.John, 'Portrait of the artist', *Art News and Review*, 15th November

36. [AU], 'Romantic opera 1949', review of Piper's sets for the New York production of 'The Rape of Lucretia', *Art News*, January, Vol.47, No.9, p.24

1950

37. Cater, J., Foreword to catalogue for the exhibition *John Piper: Recent Work*, Buchholz Gallery, New York, 17th October–4th November

38. Hendy, Sir Philip, 'John Piper', *Britain Today*, February, No.166, pp.37–40

1951

39. Barry, Gerald, 'The Festival gardens are taking shape' in 'The Festival is Britain's', *Picture Post*, 6th January, Vol.50, No.1, p.17

40. Cranko, John, 'Beach inspired Sea Change', an article on the ballet 'Sea Change', *Dance and Dancers*, March, Vol.2, No.3, p.10

41. Hope-Wallace, Philip, 'Billy Budd', *Picture Post*, 22nd December, pp.30–2

42. Hussey, Christopher, 'The Festival gardens', *Country Life*, 15th June, Vol.109, pp.1898, 1900, 1902

43. Klark, Austen, 'Billy Budd: a musical event of more than usual importance is Britten's "Billy Budd"', *Bandwagon*, November

44. Savarus, Albert, 'John Piper crée les décors du "Billy Budd" de Britten', *Les Beaux-Arts*, Brussels, 7th December, p.5

45. Williams, Peter, 'Decor' in 'Harlequin in April', *Dance and Dancers*, July, Vol.2, No.7, pp.14–15

46. [AU], 'An all-men opera set on board ship: Benjamin Britten's Billy Budd', *Illustrated London News*, 8th December, p.929 (chiefly illus.)

47. [AU], 'A new English Opera wins its spurs [Billy Budd]', *The Tatler*, 19th December, p.8

48. [AU], 'Billy Budd: the first performance of Benjamin Britten's fifth opera at Covent Garden', *The Sphere*, 8th December, p.388 (chiefly illus.)

49. [AU], 'Glyndebourne: Don Giovanni', *Opera*, September, Vol.2, No.10, pp.508–13, 520–1

50. [AU], 'John Piper', *The Sunday Times*, 9th December, p.8

1952

51. Cowper, Anthony, 'John Piper – Design for ballet, 1', *Dance and Dancers*, February, Vol.3, No.2, p.8

52. Lancaster, Karen, 'John Piper as a designer for the theatre', *Adelphi*, Vol.29, No.1, pp.19–25

53. [M.S.], 'Stage and artist in the television era: 1952 cross section', *Art News*, February, Vol.50, No.10, pp.22–5, 59. Incl. two illus. of the sets for Billy Budd

54. Woods, S.John, 'John Piper – Portrait of the artist, No.99', *Art News and Review*, 15th November, Vol.4, No.21, p.1

55. [AU], 'Billy Budd: The story. First impressions by Winton Dean, Scott Goddard, Fred Goldbeck', *Opera*, January, Vol.3, No.21, pp.4–16

56. [AU], 'Romantic realist', *Time*, New York, 1st December, pp.54, 57

1953

57. Britten, Benjamin, *Winter Words*, song cycle after poems by Thomas Hardy and dedicated to John and Myfanwy Piper

58. Commander, John, Foreword to cat. of the exhibition *Paintings and Drawings 1935–1952*, Cambridge, Arts Council of Great Britain

59. Corathiel, Elizabeth H.C., 'John Piper (Creative artists in the theatre, 6)', *Theatre World*, July, Vol.49, No.342, pp.16–18

60. Goddard, Scott, 'Daring designs for "Gloriana"', *News Chronicle*, 9th June

61. Muller, Robert, '"Gloriana" is born', *Picture Post*, 13th June, pp.67–8

62. Spender, Stephen, 'English artists vs. English painting', *Art News*, November, Vol.52, No.7, pp.14–17, 46–9

63. [AU], '"Gloriana" at the Royal Opera', *Music and Musicians*, July, p.9

64. [AU], 'Presented in a gala performance before Her Majesty on June 8: Britten's coronation opera "Gloriana"', *Illustrated London News*, 13th June, pp.987–9

1954

65. Commander, John, 'John Piper: scenografo di Britten', *La Biennale di Venezia*, Venice, September-October, No.22, p.33

66. [AU], 'Personalities and events of the week: people in the public eye. To be a trustee of the Tate Gallery: Mr John Piper [portrait]', *Illustrated London News*, 4th December, Vol.225, p.102

1955

67. Alloway, Lawrence, 'Romantic summer', review of the 1955 Leicester Galleries one-man exhibition, 'Summer events: London', *Art News*, Summer, Vol.54, No.4, p.69

68. Clarke, Mary, *The Sadler's Wells ballet: a history and an appreciation*, Adam and Charles Black, London, pp.19, 21, 176, 177, 225, 279

69. Cooper, Douglas, 'An interim report on the work of John Piper', review of *John Piper: Paintings, Drawings and Theatre Designs*, by S.John Woods, *Times Literary Supplement*, 17th June, p.336

70. Fairfield Porter, 'John Piper', review of 1955 Curt Valentin one-man exhibition, *Art News*, February, Vol.53, No.10, p.60

71. Seddon, Richard, 'John Piper: an interim report', book review of *John Piper: Paintings, Drawings and Theatre Designs*, by S.John Woods, *The Studio*, December, Vol.150, No.753, pp.187–91

72. Vernis, 'John Piper', review of the 1955 one-man exhibition at Leicester Galleries, 'International Studio', *Connoisseur*, August, Vol.136, No.547, p.41

73. Woods, S.John, Foreword to catalogue for the exhibition *John Piper* at Curt Valentin Gallery, New York, 15th February–12th March

74. Woods, S.John, *John Piper: Paintings, Drawings and Theatre Designs 1932–1954*, Faber and Faber, London

1956

75. [C., H.], *The John Piper windows executed for Oundle School Chapel by Patrick Reyntiens*, Nene Press, Oundle School

*76. Foulkes, M.E., article on John Piper's designs, Saint Luke's College, Exeter, 14th October

77. Hussey, Christopher, 'New windows at Oundle', *Country Life*, 2nd August, Vol.120, p.248

*78. Ireland, Ben L., letter requesting John Piper's assistance with research for Masters degree, Kansas State College, Kansas, 31st May

79. West, Christopher, 'The Magic Flute in 1956', *Opera*, January, Vol.7, No.1, pp.8–13

80. [AU], 'Stained glass at Oundle', *Architectural Review*, August, Vol.120, pp.118–19

81. [AU], 'Wintringham Boys Grammar School shows John Piper's work', two local press reports, 14th January and 14th February

1957

82. Schuyler, James, 'John Piper', review of the 1957 one-man exhibition at Durlacher Bros, 'Reviews and previews', *Art News*, March, Vol.56, No.1, p.9

83. Young, Vernon, 'John Piper', review of the 1957 one-man exhibition at Durlacher Bros, *Arts*, March, Vol.31, No.6, p.53

84. [AU], 'The Piper painting', article on the hospital commission, *Guy's Hospital Gazette*, 27th April, p.1

85. [AU], 'The Prince of the Pagodas', *The Times*, 2nd January, p.3

86. [AU], 'The rectangle in Mr. John Piper's recent paintings', review of the exhibition of paintings and watercolours at Leicester Galleries, London

1958

87. Innes, John, 'Scots artists put prints on world show', *The Dispatch*, 1st February

*88. Whittick, H., letters to John Piper concerning Arlington and Chichester memorial for proposed article, *The Monumental Journal*, 15th and 22nd September

89. [AU], 'How Piper makes a mural in mosaics', *The Times*, 4th December, p.3. Concerning a mural for BBC Television Centre

1959

90. Merchant, W. Moelwyn, 'Measure for measure' (Chapter 15) in *Shakespeare and the artist*, Oxford University Press

91. Meville, Robert, review of the 1960 Arthur Jeffress one-man exhibition, 'Exhibitions', *Architectural Review*, September, Vol.128, pp.222-4

92. Mock, Jean Yves, 'Piper and Ben Shahn at the Leicester Galleries', 'Notes from London and Paris', *Apollo*, December, Vol.70, pp.188-9

93. Shipp, Horace, 'Modernism in service', review of the 1960 one-man exhibition at Arthur Jeffress, 'Current shows and comments', *Apollo*, July, Vol.72, p.2

94. Whittet, G.S., review of the 1960 one-man exhibition at Arthur Jeffress, 'London commentary', *The Studio*, September, Vol.160, No.809, pp.108-9

1960

95. [AU], report on school visit to John Piper, *Eton College Chronicle*, 17th November

1961

*__96__. Baynes, Ken, letter to John Piper concerning *Graphis* feature on stained glass, Zurich, 18th October

97. Preston, Stuart, 'New York' incl. review of the 1961 one-man exhibition at Durlacher Bros, 'Current and forthcoming exhibitions', *Burlington Magazine*, December, Vol.103, p.526

98. Raynor, Vivien, 'John Piper', review of the 1961 one-man exhibition at Durlacher Bros, *Arts Magazine*, December, Vol.36, No.3, p.53

99. Swenson, Gene R., 'John Piper', review of the 1991 one-man exhibition at Durlacher Bros, 'Reviews and previews', *Art News*, November, Vol.60, No.7, p.17

100. Warrack, John, 'A Midsummer Night's Dream, Covent Garden, February 2', *Opera*, March, Vol.12, No.3, pp.201-5

101. [AU], 'Shakespeare by Benjamin Britten: "A Midsummer Night's Dream" at the Royal Opera House, Covent Garden', *Illustrated London News*, 4th February, p.19

102. [AU], 'A Midsummer Night's Dream', *Music and Musicians*, March, p.15

103. [AU], 'A Midsummer Night's Dream: Britten's latest opera at Covent Garden', *The Sphere*, 11th February, pp.214-15

1962

104. Coberman, David, 'Philip Rance and John Piper', 'Galleries and Museums', *Vogue*, 6th June

*__105__. Cowen, Charles, letter to John Piper regarding transparencies of Coventry window magazine article, *Home Magazine*, 12th October

*__106__. Driberg, Tom, 'Coventry's New Cathedral – Is It All Its Admirers Have Claimed?', incl. remarks about John Piper's window, *Evening Standard*, 18th May

107. Goodden, Wyndham, 'Details from Coventry', incl. illus. of vestments by Piper, *Design*, December, No.168, pp.38-50

108. Hope, Alice, 'Modern art in an old cowshed', *Daily Telegraph*, 2nd April, p.9

*__109__. Jackson, Enid, letter to John Piper, regarding photographs to be used for article, *Embroidery*, 26th March

110. Jordan, R. Furneaux, 'Coventry Cathedral', *The Studio*, August, Vol.164, No.832, pp.54-7

111. Russell, John, 'John Piper', 'The world of art: London letter', *Art in America*, New York, Fall, Vol.50, No.3, pp.110-13

112. Russell, John, 'The glass: a great blaze of individual genius', review of Piper's stained glass in Coventry Cathedral, *The Sunday Times Colour Section*, 20th May, pp.16-18

113. Whittet, G.S., 'London commentary: the R.A., Armitage, Tindle and others', review of the 1962 one-man exhibition at Arthur Jeffress, *The Studio*, July, Vol.164, No.831, p.34

114. [AU], 'British avant-garde in the 1930s', review of the 1962 exhibition *British art and the modern movement* at the National Museum of Wales, *The Times*, 17th October, p.18

115. [AU], 'Cathedral Church of St Michael, Coventry', *Architectural Review*, July, Vol.132, pp.36-42

116. [AU], 'The Cathedral of St Michael, Coventry', *Builder*, London, 25th May, pp.1067-85, (p.1074 texts, p.1075 illus. of Baptistry window)

1963

117. Melville, Robert, 'Exhibitions', review of the 1963 one-man exhibition at Marlborough Fine Art, *Architectural Review*, June, Vol.133, p.439

118. Mullins, Edwin, 'How are the elders faring?', review of the 1963 Marlborough 'New London' one-man exhibition, *Apollo*, April, Vol.77, No.14, p.324

119. Petersen, Valerie, 'John Piper', 'Reviews and previews', review of the 1962 Landry Gallery one-man exhibition, *Art News*, February, Vol.61, No.10, p.12

120. Roberts, Keith, 'London', 'Current and forthcoming exhibitions', incl. a review of the 1963 one-man exhibition at Marlborough Fine Art, *Burlington Magazine*, April, Vol.105, p.178

121. Tillim, Sidney, 'John Piper', review of the 1962 one-man exhibition at Landry Gallery, New York, 'In the Galleries', *Arts Magazine*, February, Vol.37, No.5, pp.45-6

1964

*__122__. Bamford, Joan, letter to John Piper requesting assistance with *Country Fair* article, 19th June

123. Burr, James, 'From neglect: round the London galleries', review of the 1964 Marlborough Fine Art 'New London' retrospective exhibition, *Apollo*, March, Vol.79, No.25, p.238

*__124__. Green, D.J.N., interview request for article in *Warwickshire and Worcestershire and Birmingham Illustrated*, English Counties Periodicals Ltd, Leamington Spa, 31st December

*__125__. Hadfield, John, letter requesting John Piper's participation in a proposed book about stained glass, George Rainbird Book Design and Production, London, 16th July

126. Lynton, Norbert, 'Pied Piper', *New Statesman*, 27th March, Vol.67, No.1724, pp.500, 502

127. Melville, Robert, Preface to catalogue for the Piper exhibition at Marlborough New Gallery, London, March

128. Roberts, Keith, 'London', 'Current and forthcoming exhibitions', review of the 1964 Marlborough Fine Art 'New London' retrospective exhibition, *Burlington Magazine*, May, Vol.106, pp.243-4

129. Rykwert, Joseph, 'Mostre a Londra', review of the 1964 Marlborough Fine Art 'New London' retrospective exhibition, *Domus*, Pisa, June, No.415 (English text)

130. [AU], 'Mr Piper's art in retrospect', review of the 1964 Marlborough Fine Art 'New London' retrospective exhibition, *The Times*, 28th March, p.5

1965

131. Barrett, Cyril, 'Art in Britain 1930-40, centred around Axis, Circle, Unit One', review of the 1965 group exhibition Axis, Circle and Unit One, at Marlborough Fine Art, *Kunstwerk*, Stuttgart, July, Vol.19, No.1, pp.12-15

*__132__. Bruce-Milne, Marjorie, letters to John Piper, regarding article in *The Christian Science Monitor*, 15th November

133. Graham, Rigby, *Romantic book illustration in England 1943-1955*, Private Libraries Association, Pinner, Middlesex

134. Piper, Myfanwy, 'Back in the thirties', *Art and Literature*, No.7, Winter, p.136

135. Piper, Myfanwy, 'John Piper', Preface in German to catalogue for Piper exhibition at Baukunst, Cologne, 24th September–19th November

136. [AU], 'Piper's Pyrotechnics', review of John Piper's design for Hyde Park fireworks display, *Daily Mail*, 26th August

1966

137. Bruce-Milne, Marjorie, 'Nature impels John Piper's art', *The Christian Science Monitor*, Boston, Mass., 16th February, p.4

138. Mullins, Edwin, 'Weaving a work of modern art', article on Chichester Cathedral tapestry, *Weekend Telegraph*, 23rd September, pp.35–7

139. Thompson, David, 'London commentary: concentric circles', review of the 1964 Marlborough Fine Art 'New London' retrospective exhibition, *Studio International*, June, Vol.171, No.878, pp.269–70

1967

140. Driberg, Tom, 'At 63 still the prolific Piper', *Evening Standard*, 7th September, p.7

141. Gibberd, Frederick, 'The coloured glass', section about Piper and Reynteins' stained glass, *Metropolitan Cathedral of Christ The King, Liverpool*, Architectural Press, London, pp.69–74

142. Gordon, Alastair, 'Art in the modern manner', review of the 1967 touring one-man exhibition, *Connoisseur*, June, Vol.165, p.128

143. Hodges, Paul, R. T., 'John Piper: studies for the Chichester Cathedral tapestry', *Arts Review*, 2nd September, Vol.19, No.17, p.314

144. Hussey, W., *The Pictorial History of Chichester Cathedral*, Pitkin Pictorials, London, pp.12–13

145. Mills, John Fitzmaurice, 'The new Liverpool Metropolitan Cathedral', *Connoisseur*, December, Vol.166, pp.225–31

146. Reichardt, Tony, Preface to catalogue for the Marlborough Fine Art Retrospective, Sheffield

147. Reyntiens, P., 'The Metropolitan Cathedral of Christ the King, Liverpool, England', incl. an article on the Cathedral glass, *Architectural Design*, June, Vol.37, pp.256–64

148. [AU], Souvenir publication to commemorate the consecration of the Cathedral of Christ the King, Liverpool, *English Counties Periodicals*, Leamington Spa

1968

149. Peter, John, 'A note on John Piper's towers and churches', *Malahat Review*, Victoria BC, No.6, April, pp.62–72. Text followed by 8pp. of plates

150. Harrison and Sons Ltd, Leaflet to accompany a series of postage stamps celebrating British Painting, incl. John Piper, 12th August

1969

151. Burr, James, 'Divergent directions: London Galleries', review of the 1969 one-man Marlborough exhibition, *Apollo*, June, Vol.89, No.88, p.472

1970

152. Eveleigh, John, Introduction to catalogue for the *Retrospective Exhibition* at The Arts Centre, New Metropole, Folkestone, 24th October–22nd November

153. Lucie-Smith, Edward, and Patricia White, *Art in Britain, 1969–70*, Dent, London

154. Master of the Worshipful Company of Bakers, *Master's appeal for the John Piper windows in Bakers Hall* (fold-out leaflet), The Company, London

1971

155. Buckle, Richard, 'Variations on a theme of Titian (1)', *Art and Artists*, August, Vol.6, No.5, pp.46–9

156. [AU], Introduction to catalogue for the exhibition *Lithographs by John Piper* at William Weston Gallery, June

1972

157. Blakeston, O., 'John Piper', review of the 1972 Marlborough Fine Art one-man exhibition, *Arts Review*, 25th March, Vol.24, No.6, p.166

158. Burr, James, 'Purely for pleasure', review of the 1972 Marlborough Fine Art one-man exhibition, *Apollo*, April, Vol.95, No.122, p.327

159. Denvir, Bernard, 'London letter', review of the 1972 Marlborough Fine Art one-man exhibition, *Art International*, Lugano, May, Vol.16, No.5, p.39

160. Evan, Anthony, 'Piper currency', review of the 1972 Marlborough Fine Art one-man exhibition, *The Spectator*, 25th March, p.487

161. Gaunt, William, 'Adventures with John Piper', review of the 1972 Marlborough Fine Art one-man exhibition, *The Times*, 5th April, p.7

162. Graham, Rigby, 'John Piper as book illustrator', *American Book Collector*, Plainfield, NJ, January, Vol.22, No.4, pp.10–20

163. Jacques, Clive, 'John Piper', review of the 1972 one-man exhibition at the Yarrow, Oundle School, *Arts Review*, 21st October, Vol.24, No.21, p.654

164. Roberts, Keith, 'London', incl. review of the 1972 Marlborough Fine Art one-man exhibition, 'Current and forthcoming exhibitions', *Burlington Magazine*, May, Vol.114, p.354

165. [AU], 'The Wartenweiler Library: a brochure published on the occasion of the official opening …', University of the Witwatersrand, Johannesburg, 14th February

166. [AU], 'This artist has designs on life', review of the Witwatersrand University Library tapestry, *Rand Daily Mail*, Johannesburg, 26th January, p.7

1973

167. Arber, Nick, 'John Piper', review of the 1973 one-man exhibition at Turnpike Gallery, Leigh, Lancs, *Arts Review*, 28th July, Vol.25, No.15, p.518

168. Blyth, Alan, 'Death in Venice: Aldeburgh Festival', *Opera*, August, Vol.24, No.8, pp.688–91

169. Gilmour, Pat, 'Graphics', article on John Piper and the autographic print, *Arts Review*, 7th April, Vol.25, No.7, p.223

170. Gilmour, Pat, 'John Piper: Death in Venice', review of the 1973 one-man exhibition at Marlborough Graphics, *Arts Review*, 17th November, Vol.26, No.5, p.785

171. Graham, Rigby, 'John Piper', Introduction and other notes for a catalogue to an exhibition of *Paintings, Drawings and Prints and Illustrated Books by John Piper*, Gadsby Gallery, Leicester. Limited edition of 450

172. Hughes, Graham. 'Modern medals', article on the exhibition of modern medals at Goldsmiths' Hall, July 1973, incl. medals made for the exhibition by Piper, *Crafts*, No.3, July-August, pp.36–7

173. Mann, William, 'Owen Wingrave: Royal Opera House', *The Times*, 11th May, p.11

174. Rosenthal, Harold, 'Owen Wingrave', 'London Opera diary', *Opera*, July, Vol.24, No.7, pp.643–5

175. Usborne, Karen, 'A profile of John Piper', *Arts Review*, 24th February, Vol.25. No.4, p.95

176. Usborne, Karen, 'John Piper', review of the 1973 one-man exhibition at Marjorie Parr Gallery, *Arts Review*, 10th February, Vol.25, No.3, p.64

177. Wyatt, Leonard, 'John Piper', review of the 1973 one-man exhibition at Playhouse Gallery, Harlow, *Arts Review*, 11th August, Vol.25, No.16, p.550

178. [AU], 'A Piper tapestry for the Rothschild Intercontinental Bank', *Apollo*, December, Vol.98, No.142, p.522

179. [AU], article about the presentation of two tapestries by Piper to the University of the Witwatersrand, *Sunday Express*, Johannesburg, 20th May

1974

180. Arber, N., 'John Piper', review of the 1974 one-man exhibition at the Portland Gallery, Manchester, *Arts Review*, 8th March, Vol.26, No.5, p.115

181. De Maré, Eric, *Photographs of Wales: John Piper*, exh. cat., Welsh Arts Council, Cardiff

182. Rothenstein, Sir John, *Modern English Painters, Vol.3: Wood to Hockney*, Macdonald, London and St Martin's Press, New York, pp.86–99

183. Wright, Barbara, 'John Piper, Phyllis Morgans', review of the 1974 one-man exhibition at Buxton Mill Galleries, *Arts Review*, 19th April, Vol.26, No.8, p.214

184. [AU], *Aspects of Abstract Painting in Britain 1910–1960*, exh. cat., Talbot Rice Art Gallery, Edinburgh

1975

185. Barber, Noël, 'John Piper', review of the 1975 Marlborough Fine Art one-man exhibition, *The Spectator*, 27th September, p.419

186. Learmont, Lavinia, review of the 1975 Marlborough Fine Art one-man exhibition, *Art and Artists*, November, Vol.10, No.8, p.50

187. Mullaly, Terence, 'John Piper, 72, is better than ever', review of the 1975 Marlborough Fine Art one-man exhibition, *The Daily Telegraph*, 14th October

188. Neve, Christopher, 'A passion for places: John Piper's recent work', on the occasion of the 1975 Marlborough Fine Art one-man exhibition, *Country Life*, 25th September, Vol.158, pp.752-3

189. Packer, William, 'John Piper, Marlborough Fine Art', review of the 1975 Marlborough Fine Art one-man exhibition, *Financial Times*, 2nd October

190. Roberts, Keith, 'London', incl. review of the 1975 Marlborough Fine Art one-man exhibition, 'Current and forthcoming exhibitions', *Burlington Magazine*, November, Vol.117, p.751

191. Shone, Richard, 'John Piper', review of the 1975 Marlborough Fine Art one-man exhibition, *Arts Review*, 17th October, Vol.27, No.21, p.592

192. Thuillier, Rosalind, 'John Piper: eye and camera', *Arts Review*, 28th November, Vol.27, No.24, p.694

1976

193. Cobbe, R. A. C., 'Examination of modern paintings: technical information received from artists', *Studies in Conservation*, February, Vol.21, p.27

194. Griffiths, Sarah, 'War painting: a no-man's land between history and reportage', *Leeds Arts Calendar*, Leeds, No.78, pp.24-32. Incl. notes on Piper's 'MOWT vessel in dry dock at Fowey', p.30, and illus. p.26

195. Watson, Francis, 'John Piper', review of the 1976 Marjorie Parr Gallery one-man exhibition, *Arts Review*, 11th June, Vol.28, No.12, p.295

196. Williams, Antonia, 'The pied Pipers', article based on a visit to the Pipers' home, *Vogue*, 15th March, pp.118-21

1977

197. Berthoud, Roger, 'The painter who loves working with craftsmen', *The Times*, 4th November, p.13

198. Bryer, Monte, 'The John Piper Tapestries', *Convocation Commentary*, University of the Witwatersrand, Johannesburg, October, pp.7-8

199. Burr, James, 'A real surrealist in London: Round the galleries', review of the 1977 Marlborough Fine Art one-man exhibition, *Apollo*, November, Vol.106, No.189, p.422

200. Hewison, Robert, *Under siege, literary life in London 1934-45*, Weidenfeld and Nicholson, London

201. Januszczak, Waldemar, 'John Piper, Kendal', review of the 1977 Abbot Hall Gallery one-man exhibition, *The Guardian*, July, p.10

202. Kitchen, Paddy, 'John Piper, Marlborough Fine Art', review of the 1977 Marlborough Fine Art one-man exhibition, *The Times*, 8th November, p.11

203. Loveland, Kenneth, 'Fishguard – Hoddinott's new work: "What the old man does is always right", Fishguard Festival, July 27th', *Opera*, Autumn Festival issue, pp.48-9

204. Quantrill, Malcolm, 'London letter', review of the 1977 Marlborough Fine Art one-man exhibition, *Art International*, December, Vol.21, No.6, pp.61-2

205. Roberts, Keith, 'London' – 'Current and forthcoming exhibitions', *Burlington Magazine*, December, Vol.119, p.877

206. Shone, Richard, *The Century of Change: British Painting Since 1900*, Phaidon Press, Oxford

207. Watson, Francis, 'John Piper', review of the 1977 Marlborough Fine Art one-man exhibition, *Arts Review*, October, Vol.29, No.22, p.649

208. [AU], 'What the old man does is always right', programme, Fishguard Secondary School Theatre, 27th July

1978

209. Anscombe, Isabelle, 'A Matisse to go round your neck', article about Piper among artists designing scarf squares, *The Times*, 16th September, p.10

210. Denvir, Bernard, review of the 1978 Marlborough Fine Art one-man exhibition, 'London', *Art and Artists*, January, Vol.12, No.9, p.41

211. Kendall, Peter, 'John Piper – art on the grand scale', preview of exhibition at Glynn Vivian Art Gallery, Swansea, *South Wales Evening Post*, Swansea, 11th October

212. Mitchell, D. and J. Evans, *Benjamin Britten. Pictures from a life 1913-1976*, Faber and Faber, London

213. Pears, Peter and John Piper, 'John Piper – Early and Recent Pictures', Cardiff Festival of the 20th Century

214. Piper, Myfanwy, 'John Piper's Welsh Connections', Introduction to Swansea Festival exhibition at Glynn Vivian Art Gallery, Swansea, 6th October–4th November

215. Takiguchi, Susumu, article on John Piper's life and work, *Japan Art News*, 1st September, p.8 (in Japanese)

216. Thuillier, Rosalind, 'John Piper', review of the 1978 Bohun Gallery, Henley-on-Thames, one-man exhibition, *Arts Review*, 24th November, Vol.30, No.23, p.649

217. Winder, H. E.,'Show to rival any in world', review, *Rand Daily Mail*, Johannesburg, 10th May

1979

218. Betjeman, Sir John, with Hugh Gordon Porteous, John Hoole and Stewart Mason, *John Piper: 50 Years of Work*, Museum of Modern Art, Oxford

219. Billington, Rachel, 'Painterly pleasures', *Financial Times*, 14th April, p.18

220. Feaver, William, 'Piper's many tunes', article on the Tate Gallery firework display and a review of the 1979 one-man exhibition at Oxford and Colchester, *The Observer*, 10th June, p.15

***221**. Glancey, Jonathan, letter to John Piper, regarding article for *Architectural Review*, 21st June

***222**. Herbert, David, letter inquiring about rights to John Piper's book *Stained Glass*, with a view to reprinting, Herbert Press, London, 22nd November

223. Ingrams, Richard, 'County Counsel', review of the Shell Guides written by John Piper and John Betjeman, *Sunday Telegraph Magazine*, 18th November, pp.17, 21

224. Shaw, C. A., information leaflet about the three Piper tapestries at Hereford Cathedral, Hereford, 15th July

225. Vaizey, Marina, 'John Piper, Oxford Museum of Modern Art', review, *Arts Review*, 22nd June, Vol.31, No.12, pp.330-1

226. West, Anthony, *John Piper*, Martin Secker and Warburg, London. Republished in 1983 by Secker and Warburg

1980

227. Bond, Maurice, 'The King George VI Memorial Chapel' in *Stained Glass at St George's Chapel*, Oxley and Son Ltd, Windsor

228. Strode, Rosamund, 'Britten Memorial Window', explanatory sheet, Aldeburgh Parish Church, Suffolk

229. [AU], 'John Piper', review of the 1980 Regimental Chapel, Manchester Cathedral one-man exhibition, *Arts Review*, 7th November, Vol.32, No.22, p.518

1981

230. Atterbury, Paul, 'John Piper: the Sitwell's Montegufoni', review of the 1981 Maclean Gallery one-man exhibition, 'The arts reviewed, Great Britain', *Connoisseur*, February, Vol.206, No.828, p.86

231. Bland, Alexander, *The Royal Ballet: the first fifty years*, Doubleday, Garden City, New York, pp.71, 82, 93, 119, 212, 213

232. Blyth, Alan, 'Britten's inevitable relationship with the Pipers', *The Times*, 4th June, p.13

233. Blyth, Alan, *Remembering Britten*, Hutchinson, London, pp.28-35

234. Cayzer, Elizabeth, Introduction to *John Piper: The Sitwells' Montegufoni*, Maclean Gallery, London, 28th January–20th February

235. Davey, Peter, 'Robinson College, Cambridge', incl. discussion and illustration of Piper's stained glass for the Chapel, *Architectural Review*, August, Vol.170, pp.83-7

236. Jackson-Stops, Gervase, 'The Sitwells' Tuscan Castle: watercolours by John Piper', written on the occasion of the 1981 Maclean Gallery one-man exhibition, *Country Life*, 29th January, Vol.169, pp.284, 287

237. Medley, Robert, 'The Group Theatre 1932-39', *London Magazine*, January, Vol.20, No.10, pp.47-60

238. Pickering, Felix, 'Selling castles in the air', review of the 1981 Maclean Gallery one-man exhibition, *Times Literary Supplement*, 13th February, p.167

239. [AU], 'John Piper's studios', *Studio International*, Vol.195, No.991/2, pp.92-3

240. [AU], 'The stained glass windows' and 'The ceramic' in *A Guide to Robinson College Chapel*, Cambridge, p.2

1982

241. Archer, Michael, 'A painter and his pots: John Piper's ceramics', *Country Life*, 2nd December, Vol.172, pp.1834-5

242. Bell, Quentin, Foreword to *New Ceramics by John Piper*, Dan Klein Ltd, London, November, pp.3-5

243. Compton, Ann (ed.), *John Piper – Painting in Coloured Light*, incl. Foreword by Jeremy Lewison, Introduction by Martin Harrison, acknowledgements by Ann Compton, and *Stained Glass* and *Art or Anti-Art* by John Piper, Kettle's Yard Gallery, Cambridge

*244. Little, Fiona, letter to John Piper requesting information for publication about his window in Christ's College Chapel, Christchurch, NZ, Christchurch, 27th April

245. Wilson, David (ed.), *Projecting Britain: Ealing Studios film posters* (with an introduction by Bevis Hillier), BFI Publishing, London, posters by Piper for *Pink string and sealing wax* and *Painted Boats* on pp.48-9

246. Wykes-Joyce, Max, review of the 1982 Dan Klein Decorative Arts one-man exhibition, 'Exhibition reviews', *Art and Artists*, November, No.194, p.31

247. [AU], *John Piper and English Neo-Romanticism*, incl. a Foreword by Peter Cannon-Brookes, The 1820 Foundation in association with The National Museum of Wales and the South African National Gallery, Cape Town

1983

248. Barrasford Young, Grahaeme (ed.), *Labrys*, Special Issue on Piper, Vol.9, November 1983. Incl. 'British Romantic Artists' and 'Stained Glass: Art or Anti-art' by Piper, and 'John Piper – a Personal View' by Tony Reichardt, 'A Day with John Piper' by Michael Sellers, 'A Man of Many Parts' by S.John Woods and 'John Piper – Master of All' by John Commander

*248a. Benyon, Catherine, letter to John Piper, regarding article in *House and Garden*, 8th February

249. Charlton, Gill, letter to John Piper, regarding proposed *Telegraph Sunday Magazine* article, 26th September

250. Colvin, Howard, Introduction to exh. cat., *Georgian Arcadia*, Marlborough Fine Art, London, 16th September–16th October

251. Elborn, Geoffrey (ed.), *To John Piper on his Eightieth Birthday – 13 December 1983*, Stourton Press, London, 1983, with Myfanwy Piper, John Betjeman, Henry Moore, Peter Pears, Patrick Reyntiens, and others

252. Fraser Jenkins, David (ed.), *John Piper*, comprehensive catalogue for the retrospective exhibition, Tate Gallery, 30th November 1983–22nd January 1984, Tate Gallery Publications, London, 1983. Incl. essays by John Russell, Rigby Graham, Michael Northen and a biography by Beth Houghton and Hilary Gresty

*253. Glancey, Jonathan, letter to John Piper from *The Architectural Review* suggesting the publication of Piper's collected writings for *AR*, 29th June

254. Harrison, Martin, Introduction to *John Piper – The Romantic Landscape: Photographs 1936-1983*, Olympus Gallery, London

255. Holliday, Clayton S., Introduction to *John Piper – 60 Years of Graphics*, King George VI Art Gallery, Port Elizabeth, 6th March

256. Ingrams, Richard, John Piper, *Piper's Places*, Chatto and Windus, Hogarth Press, London

257. Levinson, Orde, leaflet advertising *John Piper, The Complete Graphic Works. A Catalogue Raisonné 1923-1983*, Faber and Faber, London

258. Merchant, W. Moelwyn, Introduction to *John Piper: Romantic Places*, Marlborough Fine Art, 25th November 1983–14th January 1984

259. Merchant, W. Moelwyn, Introduction to *Piper's Churches*, Lichfield Festival

260. Packer, William, 'The admirable Mr. Piper', *Financial Times*, 6th December

261. Percival, John, *Theatre in my blood*, Herbert Press, London

262. Porter, Henry, 'Lord Gnome's vintage Piper', *The Sunday Times*, 7th August

263. Ross, Alan, *Colours of war: war art 1939-45*, Jonathan Cape, London, pp.50-2

*264. Stamp, Gavin, letter to John Piper requesting interview for *The Tatler*, 29th May

265. Sykes, Bonar and Viscount Eccles, 'Inauguration of New Galleries and John Piper Stained Glass Window, 19 June 1982' (transcript of speeches given at this event), *Wiltshire Archaeological and Natural History Magazine*, Devizes, Vol.77, pp.7-9

*266. Wapshott, Nicholas, letter to John Piper, regarding article for *The Times*, 11th October

267. West, Anthony, *John Piper*, Secker and Warburg, London. Republication of no.226 above

268. [AU], article celebrating John Piper's birthday, *Vogue*

269. [AU], 'Piper and son for Aldeburgh', 'Londoner's Diary', *Evening Standard*, 7th June

270. [AU], exh. programme for the John Piper show at the Tate Gallery 1983-4, Tate Gallery, London 1983. Incl. biography of the artist and commentary on his career, plan of exhibition and reproductions

1984

271. Faulks, Sebastian, 'Romantic vision of a pagan believer', *Daily Telegraph*, 1st July

272. Summerfield, Angela Mary, *John Piper's Book Illustrations 1935-1950* (MA thesis), Courtauld Institute of Art, London, June

273. Piper, Myfanwy, Introduction to *John Piper: Stained Glass*, Brailsford, Baker and Lee Ltd, Ashbourne. A calendar featuring seven windows repr. in colour film transparencies

274. Lang, John, 'Piper's Churches', Foreword, with an Introduction by W. Moelwyn Merchant, Lichfield Cathedral Arts, Lichfield

275. Fraser Jenkins, A. D., *John Piper and Subjects in Wales*, Gee and Son Ltd, Denbigh

*276. [AU], All Saint's Church, Stansfield, Suffolk, letter to John Piper, regarding an article for the church appeal, Suffolk, August

1985

277. Onley, John, 'British artists', review, Kayler Fine Arts Gallery, Exeter

*278. Thain, Alistair, letter detailing proposed book on John Piper, London, 31st July

279. [AU], leaflet about John Piper's collaboration with West Dean Tapestry Studio, West Dean Tapestry Studio, The Edward James Foundation, West Sussex

1987

280. Auty, Giles, 'John Piper: Georgian Arcadia', 'exhibitions', *The Spectator*, 3rd October

281. Cavaliero, Glen, 'And Over Here', 'Book Reviews'. *Country Life*, 5th November

282. Curtis, Anthony, 'Degas to his friends', incl. reviews of *A Painter's Camera* and *John Piper, the complete graphic works …*, 'Books', *Financial Times*, 9th December

283. Fraser Jenkins, David, *A Painter's Camera: Buildings and Landscapes in Britain 1935-1985*, Tate Gallery, London. Incl. a Foreword by Alan Bowness, an Introduction by David Fraser-Jenkins, and a note on equipment by John Piper

284. Hughes, Graham, reviews of 1987 Marlborough Fine Art one-man exhibition and of *John Piper, the complete graphic works …*, *Arts Review*, 9th October

285. Levinson, Orde, *John Piper: The Complete Graphic Works. A Catalogue Raisonné 1923-1983*, Faber and Faber, London. Incl. 'Working with Printers' by John Piper and extracts from his writings. Republished in the present book

286. Lewis, Gloria, 'At The Galleries', review of the 1987 Marlborough Fine Art one-man exhibition, *This Is London*, 9th October

287. McKinley, Nigel, review of the 1987 Marlborough Fine Art one-man exhibition, Autumn

288. Mellor, David (ed.), *A Paradise Lost: The Neo-Romantic Imagination in Britain 1935-1955*, Lund Humphries, London in association with the Barbican Art Gallery, London

289. Mellor, David, 'John Piper', 'Mapping Out British Culture', pp.34-9, see no.288 above

290. Packer, William, 'In praise of older artists in this age of youth', review of the 1987 Marlborough Fine Art one-man exhibition, 'London Galleries', *Financial Times*, 22nd September

291. Russell Taylor, John, 'Romanticism haunting still', 'Galleries', *The Times*, 6th October

292. Weyers, John, 'Talented sister artist of Augustus John'. Incl. review of *John Piper, the complete graphic works …*, 'Art Roundup', *Glasgow Herald*, 5th December

293. White, Roger, 'Genius of the Place', review of the 1987 Marlborough Fine Art one-man exhibition, *House and Garden*, October

294. [AU], Press release about the John Piper tapestries executed at West Dean, West Dean Tapestry Studio, The Edward James Foundation, West Sussex, June

295. [AU], 'A look at Piper's England', preview of the CCA Galleries, Farnham one-man exhibition, *Farnham Herald*, 11th September

296. [AU], 'Piper's England', preview of the CCA Galleries, Farnham one-man exhibition, *Surrey Advertiser*, 11th September

297. [AU], 'Galleries', preview of the Marlborough Fine Art one-man exhibition, 'The Week Ahead', *The Times*, 12th September

1988

298. Edwards, Gregory J., *The Book of the International Film Poster*, Tiger Books International, London

299. Fraser Jenkins, David, 'Flower Paintings by John Piper, 1988', *John Piper*, Waddington Galleries, pp.5-6

300. Fuller, Peter, 'An English Romantic', *Independent Magazine*, 10th December, pp.56-9

301. Fuller, Peter, 'John Piper: Neo-Romanticism in the 1980's', *Modern Painters*, Summer, Vol.1, No.2

***302**. Greig, Geordie, letter to John Piper requesting interview for *The Sunday Times*, 1st November

303. Ingrams, Richard, 'The feel of romantic England', reviews of *A Painter's Camera* and *John Piper, the complete graphic works …*, *The Spectator*, 30th January

***304**. Shott, Sarah, letter to John Piper, regarding use of transparencies in an article for *The Oxford Times*, Waddington Galleries, 9th November

305. S.L.M., review of *John Piper, the complete graphic works …*, *Chronique des arts*, Paris, January-February

306. Summerfield, Angela, review of *John Piper, the complete graphic works …*, *Apollo*, April

307. Yorke, Malcolm, 'John Piper', *The Spirit of Place: Nine Neo-Romantic Artists and Their Times*, Constable, London, pp.70-105

308. [AU], 'Faber and Faber Books on Art and Architecture 1988-1989', (catalogue of new publications), Faber and Faber, London

1989

309. Fraser Jenkins, David, 'Fawley I to X', Introduction to catalogue for the 1989 exhibition at Waddington Galleries, London

310. Ingrams, Richard, 'John Piper', *Modern Painters*, Spring, Vol.2, No.1

311. Peto, Emma, 'Piper calls the tune for church appeal', *Country Times*, February

312. Wilson, Simon, *Tate Gallery: An Illustrated Companion*, Tate Gallery Publications, London

1990

***313**. Freedman, Jacqueline K., letter to John Piper requesting information for research paper, Shaker Heights, Ohio, 10th January

314. Simpson, Ian, *The Challenge of Landscape Painting*, Collins, London

315. Fraser Jenkins, David, *John Piper In Wales* (an Oriel 31 Touring exhibition), Introduction, with an essay 'The Picturesque' by William P. Wilkins

316. [AU], review: 'John Piper at Waddington', *Burlington Magazine*, February

1991

317. Brighton, Trevor, 'The Piper Tapestry' in *Otter Memorial Paper 7*, West Sussex Institute of Higher Education, West Sussex

318. Hicks, Alistair, 'John Hubbard and John Piper', *Modern Painters*, Winter, Vol.4, No.4, pp.92-3

319. Powers, Alan, 'Sub Subversive', review of the 1991 Marlborough Graphics one-man exhibition, *The Architects' Journal*, 13th March

1992

320. Pierrepont, Kate, Introduction to *Piper's Country*, Berkeley Square Gallery, 4th December 1992–23rd January 1993

321. Piper, Myfanwy, 'Virtue' by George Herbert, chosen by Myfanwy Piper, recited by Emily Lewis at the funeral service for John Piper, Fawley Bottom Farm House. See repr. on p.190

322. Winsor, Alan (ed.), 'John Piper' in *Handbook of Modern British Painting 1900-1980*, Scolar Press, Aldershot, Hants, pp.223-4

323. [AU], information leaflet, Bohun Gallery, Henley-on-Thames

324. [AU], Introduction to *The Painter in Glass*, Glynn Vivian Art Gallery, Swansea

1993

325. Collins, Denise, 'John Piper and diversity in his printmaking techniques', leaflet to accompany a talk given at CCA Galleries, Cambridge, 23rd June

326. Fuller, Peter, 'John Piper' in *Modern Artists*, pp.254-63

327. Jones, Kate and David Coke, 'John Piper 1903-1992: A Famous New Start', 'John Piper and The Stage', Pallant House, Chichester, 6th February–3rd April, pp.1-6

1994
328. Coke, David, 'The Chichester Tapestry', leaflet to accompany exhibition of Piper designs for the Chichester tapestry, Pallant House, Chichester, 22nd January-19th February, pp.1-4

329. Garfit, Henry, 'A personal survey of the architectural work of John Piper', a project for Bradfield College's Oxford and Cambridge Board, Art 'A' level examinations

330. Levinson, Orde, *John Piper*, *Iffley Parish Magazine*, Iffley, Oxon, March

331. McCue, Jim, 'The Pick of the Piper collection', *The Times*, 14th December

332. Piper, Myfanwy, letter to Leslie Waddington, December 1993, regarding *John Piper: A Retrospective: Works from the Artist's Studio*, Waddington Galleries, London, 12th January–5th February

333. Wells, Neil, 'Autolithographic Book Illustrations', unpublished

Unknown dates
334. Allsop, Kenneth, 'The mink coats invade Henley', *Evening Standard*, p.16

335. Cheales, Richard and Percy Baneshik, 'Sensational art show', article about Piper exhibition at Pieter Wenning Gallery, Johannesburg

336. Cheales, Richard, 'Piper calls the tune', review of Pieter Wenning Gallery exhibition, Johannesburg

337. Cork, Richard, 'Historic battles to portray the truth', article incl. Piper among commissioned British war artists

338. Merchant, W. Moelwyn, 'Supper At Emmaus: The John Piper Window', article in pamphlet on stained-glass window at Llandaff in *27th Annual Report of the Friends of Llandaff Cathedral*

339. Russell, John, 'Quatre artistes anglais', article which features John Piper as one of four English artists (in French)

340. Stevenson, Jennifer, letter to John Piper regarding article to be published in *Good Housekeeping*

341. Vale, Brian, 'Versatile John Piper'

342. [AU], 'Autumn is cut from the loom', newspaper article plus photograph of one of the *Four Seasons* tapestries at West Dean College

343. [AU], biographical information sheet provided by Christie's, London

344. [AU], 'Patrick Reyntiens describes how he made the Piper window' in *27th Annual Report of the Friends of Llandaff Cathedral*

345. [AU], 'Romantic realist', review of a Piper exhibition in London

346. [AU], 'Tapestry' and 'Ceramics' in *A Landscape Anthology*, p.137

347. [AU], 'The Piper/Reyntiens Windows 1965-66', *An introduction to stained glass in Swansea*, Glynn Vivian Art Gallery, Swansea in association with Swansea City Council

348. [AU], 'The window of joy', article about dedication of a Piper stained-glass window at St Peter's Parish Church, Wolvercote, Oxon

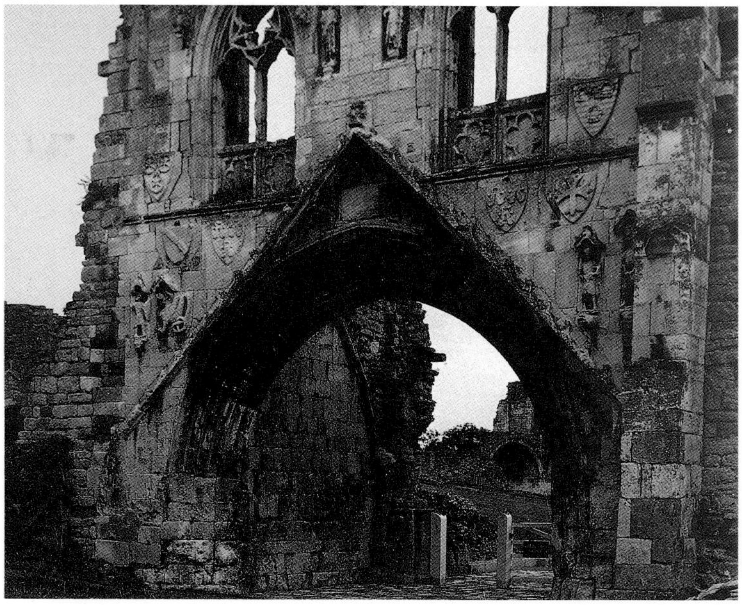

John Piper, *Kirkham Priory, Yorkshire*, *c.*1950

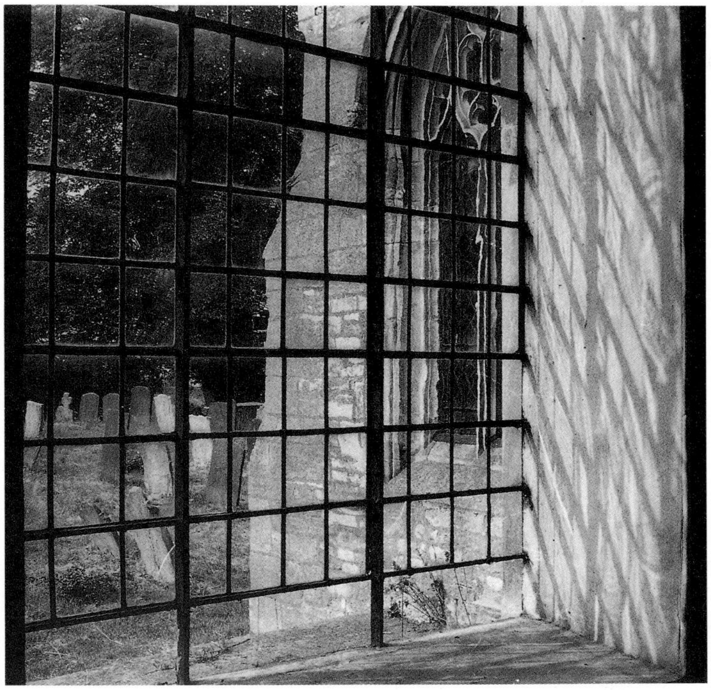

John Piper, *Hougham, Lincolnshire*, date unknown

Sweet day, so cool, so calm, so bright,
The bridal of the earth and sky:
The dew shall weep thy fall tonight,
For thou must die.

Sweet rose, whose hue angry and brave
Bids the rash gazer wipe his eye:
Thy root is ever in its grave,
And thou must die.

Sweet spring, full of sweet days and roses,
A box where sweets compacted lie:
My music shows ye have your closes,
And all must die.

Only a sweet and virtuous soul,
Like seasoned timber never gives;
But though the whole world turn to coal,
Then chiefly lives.

Myfanwy Piper chose a number of items for her grandchildren to read at John Piper's funeral service. 'Virtue' by George Herbert, read by Emily Lewis, was one such item.

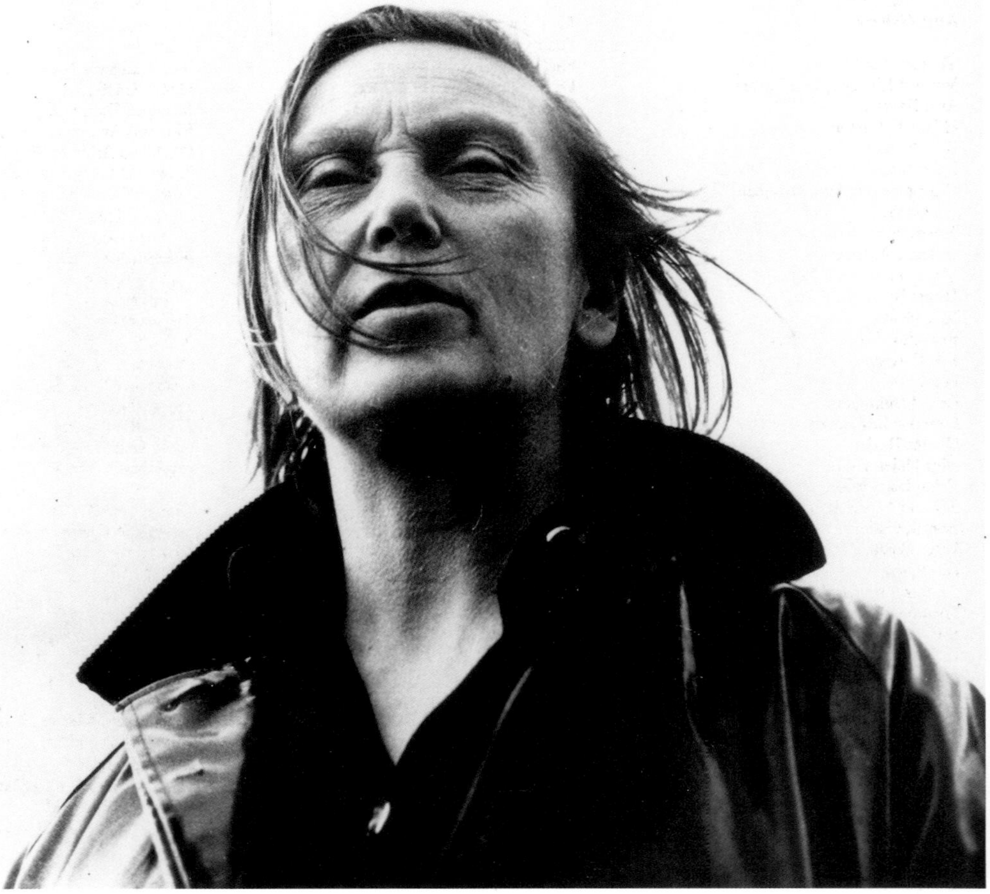

Myfanwy Piper, *c.* 1950. Photograph by John Piper

List of Subscribers

With companies only the corporate name is listed, and unless otherwise specified the subscriber was the Head Office. Where more than one branch of the company exists, a place is also included.

Gwyn Adam and Margaret Heritage
Keith Adams
Garry M. Akers
Mr and Mrs John Aldous
Peter and Celia Amoroso
Tony Ansell
John S. C. K. Anstey
Paul Arnold
The Arts Council of Wales
Timothy Garton Ash
Michael Atkin
Robert Atkin
A. B. Atkinson
Attic Gallery

Terence Banks
Mr and Mrs Stephen Barber
Ann Bardua
Hilary C. Barfor
R. L. Barnett
Revd Simon Barrington-Ward
Bishop Simon and Mrs Jean Barrington-Ward
Norman Barton
Graeme A. Bassett
Mr and Mrs R. E. Benbow
James Bennett
M. J. Bentley
Berkeley Square Gallery
J. A. Bernstein
Peter Berry
David Billingsley
Douglas Billingsley
Bird & Bird
Mrs Helen Birks
Brian Blackwood
Mr and Mrs S. Bliss
Bohun Gallery
Peter Boizot
Bonhams
Arthur Thomas Boulton
Gordon Bowyer
Sir Alan and Lady Bowness
G. R. Boys-Stones
Martin Bradshaw
George and Kay Bragg
Lorna Brazell
John R. B. Brett-Smith
The British Council, London
The British Museum
The Britten-Pears Library
In memory of Mrs G. Broadbent
Lord Broadbridge
Anthony D. Brooks
Ashley Brown
A. and C. Browne
Mr P. Bryan
Mary Budden
William Budden
Brian G. Bull
Paul B. Bull
Grace Burnett
Michael Burrell
Graham and Ludmila Burt
Richard Butt
Professor Peter H. W. Butterworth
Byam Shaw Art School Libary
Dennis and Eileen Byner

Seth Caine
The Lord Camoys
Edward Canham
Sarah Cannon
Sherban Cantacuzino
Philip Carter
Mr J. W. Casper
Roger A. Catley
Peter Catterall
CCA Galleries
The Century Galleries
Dr A. F. Chadwick
John Chambers
Clive Chandler
Paul Channon
Karin Cheftel
Keith G. Cheyney
Andrew J. Chisnall
Derrick Chivers
Revd Canon Methuen Clarke
J. F. Cliffe and P. A. Scott
Peter Coate
Revd Canon Peter G. Cobb
Peter Coe
Paul C. Colbourne
David and José Cole
Raymond E. Coles
Geoffrey A. Collens
Denise Collins
Mr and Mrs Barrie U. Cooke
Trevor Cook
Dr D. Coombe
Pamela Cooper
Terence Cooper
The Hon. Mrs Cotterell
Revd Dr Nicholas Cranfield
Mr Guy H. Crawley
The Rt Hon. Lord Croft
Robert A. Crookbain
David Croom
Philippa Crouch and Stephen Duffy
R. John Cruse
Mihai Cucos
Alan Cudmore

Mr D. R. Dale
John Davies
R. M. Davies
Dr Ian J. Davis
Dr Alan Dawson
Mr and Mrs P. E. Day
Kenneth Dean
Geoff Denman
Gordon A. Dent
The Detroit Institute of Arts
Alan and Maureen Dew
Mark Dicker and Amy Stevens
Ray Dickerson
Mr and Mrs D. E. Dickson
Annette Diester and Stefan Vollmar
The Viscount Downe
Sally Drew
Revd Bruce Driver
Mrs Y. Driver
Stephen Duckworth
Dulwich College Art Department
Professor R. G. Dyson

Pat and Geoffrey Eastop
Edinburgh City Libraries
Richard and Julie Edwards
Mr Ron Else and Sarah Jennings
Eddie Emamooden
James Emes
Epsom College
Eton College
Sue Evans
Tim and Gilean Evans
Clive Eyre
Stephen Eyre

Mr N. Fairhead
Terence Fane-Saunders
Mrs S. J. Faulkner
Luca Fedrizzi
Alistair Ferguson
Francis, Rachel and Harriet Fisher
Nicholas and Pamela Fisher
Jo Flynn
Stephen Foot
A. R. Forrest
John Foulkes
Mr and Mrs H. Fowler-Wright
Frank/Hindley Art Consultants
Julian Freeman
Edward and Sheila Frewin
Miss Haruko Fukuda

Dr Christopher Gabbutt
Frank Gadsby Esq
Mr Frank and Mrs Gee L. Gadsby
The Viscount Gage
The Gallery – Manchester Art House
Henry Garfit
Jean and David Gay
Bim and Arthur Giardelli
Peter and Audrey Gibbs
Lord and Lady Glendevon
Glynn Vivian Art Gallery
Michael Godbee
Robert Goldspink
Mr and Mrs B. K. Gooch
Giles Gordon
Sir John Gorst
Sebastian Gorst
Robert Gower
Rigby Graham
Keith and Dixie Graham
Rigby Graham
Penny R. Granger
Andy Grisdale
Guildhall Library

Mrs J. A. Hadjipateras
Colin and Claire Hailey
Marguerite Hainsworth
David J. Hall
B. R. H. Hall
Sophie Hall
Angela M. Halliday
Revd John Hamblin
Revd N. J. Hancock
W. L. Hannay
Roydon and Marise Harrell
Leo Anthony Harris
Dr S. J. Harrison
Harrow School (Old Speech Room Gallery)
Leslie and Mary Hatt
Mr and Mrs Mark Havelock-Allan
Revd John Hawkins
Louise and Stefan Hayden and Sebastian
The Headcorn Gallery
The Rt Hon. Sir Edward Heath
Helios Gallery
John Henderson
Mr and Mrs J. W. Hepner
Robin Herbert
Hereford Cathedral Library
Hereford City Museum and Art Gallery
A. I. Hett
Mr and Mrs Simon C. W. Hewett
Brian E. Hill
Hillsboro Fine Art
Matthew Hilton
Simon Hilton
John Hind
HMSO Oriel
Alun and Rhiahnon Hoddinott
Mary Holdsworth
Patrick Horsbrugh
Hove Museum and Art Gallery
Diana Howell
Ron Howell Esq
Gilbert Howes
Roderick I. D. Hoyle
R. W. F. Hubank
Mr R. J. P. Hubbard
John Hughes
Mrs J. R. Hughes
Garry Humphreys
Norman and Miriam Hyams
Harry and Anita Hyman

Ibenstein Weavers
Images
Mathew Imms
M. J. Ince

Miss Celia Jackson and Professor Mark Uglow
Nigel Jackson
Richard Jackson
Stephen J. Jackson
M. W. Jacob
Abdul Wahab Jaffer
Mrs S. Mary de Jager
Michael Jenkins
Mrs Margaret Jenks
Jean Jennings
Alexander Philip Johnson
Christopher Johnston
A. D. B. Jones
Christopher D. Jones
Bent Juel-Jensen

Susan and Michael Kay and Charlie
Malcolm Kerr
James Kirkman
Cathy Knapp
Natalie Knight – The Art Source
Mrs Beatrice Knox
John Knox-Crawford
Charles P. Korr

Adrian and Andrea Lack
Revd Stephen C. E. Laird
Cara Lancaster
Robert C. Lancaster
Mark Landless
Mrs Margaret R. Lang
Christopher Langdon
Peter Langley
Toby and Sacha Langton-Gilks
Mrs Jeremy Lansdell
Duncan Large
Peter F. W. Large
Geoffrey Latimer
Debbie Lauterpacht
Michael Lauterpacht
David Lawton
Julian Lax Fine Original Prints
Susan Lea
Jonathan Leathers
Carolyn Leder
David and Val Lermon
Daniel D. Levine
M. D. Lewis
Peter and Jane Lipman
Mr and Mrs Philip Lloyd
Adrian Lloyd-Edwards
Peter Lockyer
John Londei
Julian D. M. Lonergan
D. I. Loose
Michael Lorford
Loughborough College of Art and Design Library

Bruce McDonald
M.J. McLoughlin
Mrs D.J. McMonigall
I.M. McVitie Weston
Dr and Mrs Neil Mackie
Robin and Liz MacLachlan
Magdalen College Library, Oxford
Carol Mahoney
Paul Maine
Revd and Mrs I.G. Mainey
Carole and George Makulski
Pamela Ann Malkin
Malsis School Trust
Mandu
S.J. Mansfield Esq
C.K. Manterfield Esq
Giles de la Mare
Captain J.R. Marigold
His Grace the Duke of Marlborough
Marlborough Graphics, London
D.M. Marlow
Helen Marshall
Mr and Mrs C.B. Martindale
Lisa and Michel Marty
Christine Mason
Nicholas C. Mason
Peter Maynard
Stephen E. Mead
Henry J. Mein
Simon Melhuish-Hancock
Mr W. Mendelsson
Neill Meryl
Mr Alfred Mignano
Raina and Kevin Miles
Mira Godard Gallery
David Montgomery
Grace Moreku
Alan Morrill
Michael Moulder
Jonathan Colin Muirhead
Patrick and Sue Mulcany
Martin Murray
The Museum of Modern Art, Library, New York

Tatsuo Nakamura
National Museums & Galleries of Wales Library
The New Academy Gallery
Antoinette B. Newman
Jennifer Newman
Margaret L. Nicholson
Caroline Nordgreen
Alistair Norris
Nuffield College, Oxford

Patrick O'Donovan
Marian Orchard-Webb
Canon June Osborne
Oundle School
Mr Frank Overton
Peter Russell Owen
Oxford Gallery

Mr and Mrs Eric H. Parker
S.R. Parker
David Parnwell
Mr J.R. and Dr M.D. Parr
S. Pattison
Anna Jennifer Payne
David Pearce
Reg Pengelly
Miss C.E. Perring
Phillips Auctioneers
Dr C.B. Phipps
H.A. Picton
Kenneth Pinder
Dr and Mrs Jack R. Plimmer
Felix Pollak
Brian Porter and Phillip Reilly
D.S. and A.M. Price
Mary Pritchard

Redfern Gallery
Henry J. Rees
John and Sheila Rees
Mr and Mrs D.S. Reid
Nima Reid
Robert E. Reilert
Daphne Renny
Mr Lindsay H. Rich
Dr Aola Richards
Colin Richards
Mr and Mrs Peter Rickenburg
The Rijksmuseum, Amsterdam
Michael Rigelsford
Christopher Robbins
The Robert Gordon University
M.R. Roberts
Owen Roberts
Robinson College, Cambridge
Anne and Richard Rolfe
T.G. Rosenthal
Jeremy Rowe
Royal College of Art
Royal College of Physicians of Edinburgh
Stephen and Elizabeth Runnacles
Lindsay Ann Russell

St Bride Printing Library
St John's College Library, Oxford
Leslie Sacks Fine Art
Keith Salway
Mr and Mrs C.S. Samuel
Sanderson
Mr and Mrs Hugh Sassoon
James M. Sassoon
John M. Sayer
Norman Scarfe
Mr and Mrs R.M. Schofield
Mrs Thelma Seear
Dr N. Seivewright
John and Hilary Seward
Nick Sharpe
Stephen Sharratt
Peter S. Shaw
Mary Sheldon-Williams
Derek Shields
Brian and Norma Shillaker
B.G. Shoosmith
E.Y. Short
Colin M. Simpson
Mr and Mrs Mark Simpson
Kerry-Anne Sinton
Sir Reresby and Lady Sitwell
Judith Skelton
Graham Slater
Ms Rosalind Smallwood
Alan J. Smith
Brian D. Smith
B.J. Smith
Mrs Edyta Smith
Graham P. Smith
Jeremy and Susan Smith
L.P. Smith
Dr Martin Smith
Peter J. Smith
Revd Trevor Southgate
K. Soutter and K. Smurthwaite
Olive Spencer-Smith
Francis Speed
Dr Seymour Spencer
Robert Sterling
A.G. Stimpson
Clive and Di Stirling
Ian and Anne Strover
Royston Summers
Joanne Sumner
Anne Surfling and Pam Wheeler
Frank Tait
Tate Gallery Library
Dr and Mrs J.C. Taylor
P.G. Teare
Rosemary Telford
Jennifer and Wilfred Theakstone
Mr D. Thomas
Mrs E.A. Thomas
Mr and Mrs G. Thomas
Professor M.J. Thomas
Michael G. Thomlin
Jenny and Peter Thompson
Tony and Valerie Thompson
Michael Thomson
Mr Howard J. Thrift
Tidal Wave Gallery
Dr David Tidmarsh
Laurie Todd
Nicholas Trent Esq
Ann and Nick Tricker
Jeremy Trood
John and Jean Turner
William H. Turner
Alan Twyford

University of Ulster Library
Peter Urquhart

Alexandra Vassilikian
Mrs Jean Vickers
Victoria and Albert Museum, London
Albert and Mechtild Vollmar

Geoffrey Walford
Robin Walker
Vee Wallace
Alan Wallis
Jeanne Walter
Tony Watton
Geraint Webb
Miss Susan M. Webb
Mr Neil Weir
Neil and Christine Wells
Bianca Wettstein
Alan White
Revd Derek J. White
David G. Whiting
Dr Anthony S. Wierzbicki
Dr D.G. Wild
Mrs A. Williams
Dr Norma Williams
Rosamund J. Williams
M. Wynn Williams
Jeremy Willoughby
John W. Wilson
Caroline Wiseman
Alistair Woodrow
Nigel and Carol Woolner
Revd Nigel J. Worn
Francis Wright
Paul Wright and Janet Evans-Wright
John Wykes

Boris E. Zerafa

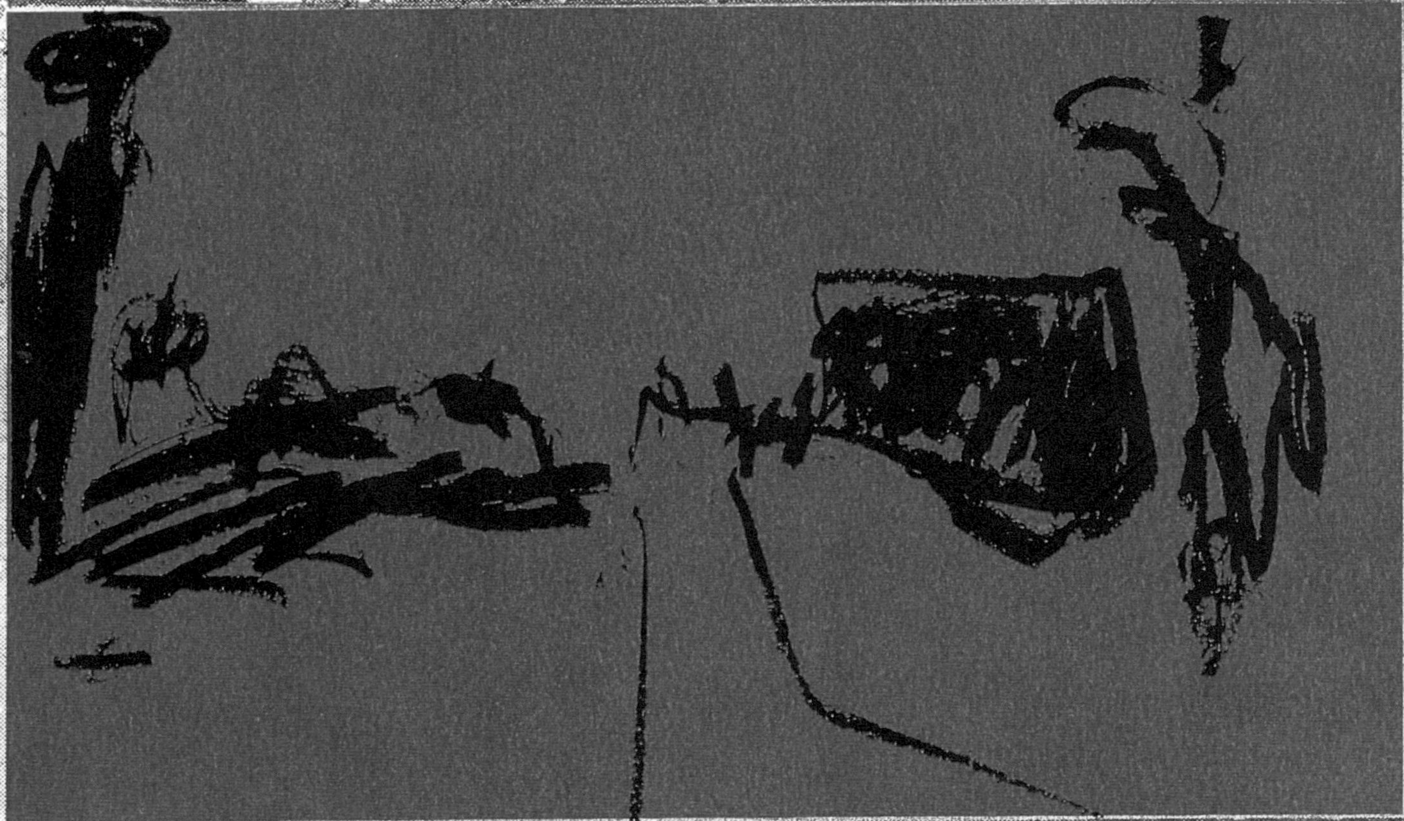

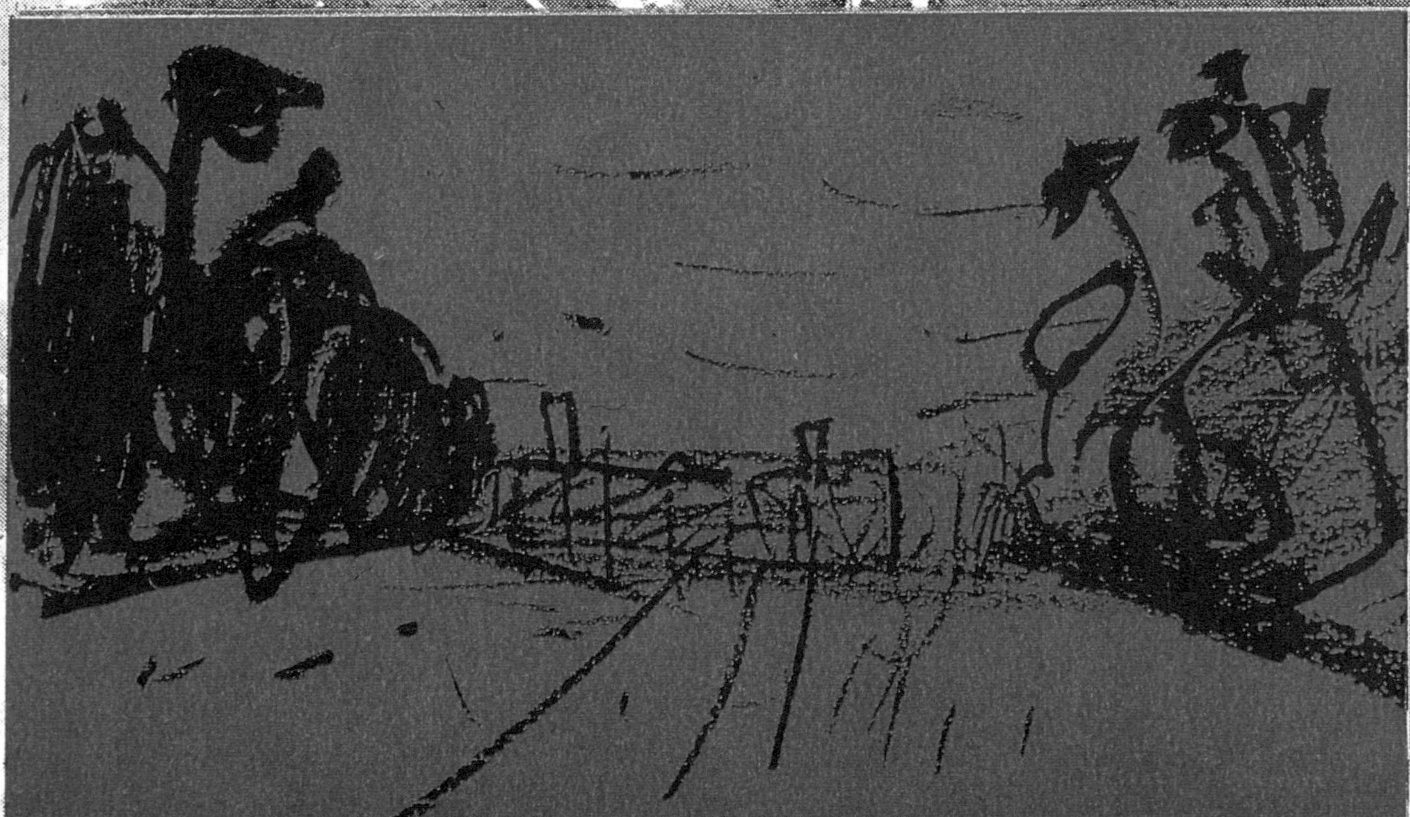